THE FOOD AND COOKING OF
JAPAN & KOREA

THE FOOD AND COOKING OF
JAPAN & KOREA

The very best of two classic Asian cuisines: a guide to ingredients, techniques and 250 recipes shown step by step with 1500 photographs

Features authentic dishes from every region, including sushi and sashimi, miso soup, ramen, tempura, kimchi, barbecued beef and sweet rice cakes

EMI KAZUKO AND YOUNG JIN SONG

southwater

This edition is published by Southwater, an imprint of Anness Publishing Ltd, 108 Great Russell Street, London WC1B 3NA; info@anness.com

www.southwaterbooks.com; www.annesspublishing.com; twitter: @Anness_Books

If you like the images in this book and would like to investigate using them for publishing, promotions or advertising, please visit our website www.practicalpictures.com for more information.

© Anness Publishing Ltd 2015

A CIP catalogue record for this book is available from the British Library.

Publisher: Joanna Lorenz
Editors: Emma Clegg, Margaret Malone and Elizabeth Young
Introduction text: Catherine Best
Japanese Recipes: Yasuko Fukuoka
Designers: Tony Cohen, E-digital Design and Nigel Partridge
Illustrator: Rob Highton
Photographers: Martin Brigdale, Janine Hosegood and Craig Robertson
Stylist: Helen Trent
Production Controller: Ben Worley

PUBLISHER'S NOTE
Although the advice and information in this book are believed to be accurate and true at the time of going to press, neither the authors nor the publisher can accept any legal responsibility or liability for any errors or omissions that may have been made nor for any inaccuracies nor for any loss, harm or injury that comes about from following instructions or advice in this book.

NOTES
Bracketed terms are intended for American readers.

For all recipes, quantities are given in both metric and imperial measures and, where appropriate, in standard cups and spoons. Follow one set of measures, but not a mixture, because they are not interchangeable.

Standard spoon and cup measures are level.
1 tsp = 5ml, 1 tbsp = 15ml, 1 cup = 250ml/8fl oz.

Australian standard tablespoons are 20ml.
Australian readers should use 3 tsp in place of 1 tbsp for measuring small quantities.
American pints are 16fl oz/2 cups.
American readers should use 20fl oz/2.5 cups in place of 1 pint when measuring liquids.

Electric oven temperatures in this book are for conventional ovens.
When using a fan oven, the temperature will probably need to be reduced by about 10–20°C/20–40°F. Since ovens vary, you should check with your manufacturer's instruction book for guidance.

The nutritional analysis given for each recipe is calculated per portion (i.e. serving or item), unless otherwise stated. If the recipe gives a range, such as Serves 4–6, then the nutritional analysis will be for the smaller portion size, i.e. 6 servings. The analysis does not include optional ingredients, such as salt added to taste.

Medium (US large) eggs are used unless otherwise stated.

CONTENTS

INTRODUCTION

In the north-western corner of the vast Pacific Ocean, the three countries of South Korea, North Korea and Japan face each other across the warm, fertile waters of the Sea of Japan. The Korean peninsula, to the west, is only 1,100km (684 miles) miles long, and it perches on the edge of the huge land mass of China, almost completely surrounded by water. To the east of Korea, Japan's intricate island landscape stretches around the Korean peninsula like a protecting arm, with the deep Pacific waters lapping at its eastern coast. The southernmost island of Japan, Kyushu, lies only about 200km (124 miles) from the southern coast of the Korean peninsula across the Korea Strait.

These three countries, with their very different attitudes to life and work, form an area of vibrant contrasts. They embrace light-filled bustling modern cities, natural landscapes seemingly unchanged over centuries, and traditional cultures developed over time. The terrain and seasonal climate fluctuations dictate how to work the land, with farmers growing a mixture of arable crops and rice, and raising cattle for meat and dairy produce. The surrounding waters of the Yellow Sea, the Sea of Japan and the Pacific

Above: The stunning pink cherry blossoms, which are known as sakura, brighten up the city of Fukuoka, Kyushu. In Japan there are over two hundred varieties of sakura.

Below: A cityscape of Jejudo Province, in the Korea Strait.

Ocean are full of delicious fish and shellfish, and these are another very important aspect of the area's economy.

The intriguing diversity of Korea and Japan also unfolds within their eating traditions, with the religious influence of Buddhist, Shintoist and Confucianist rituals, the use of seasonal local ingredients and the delightful culture of sharing multiple dishes between family and friends.

THE LANDSCAPE OF JAPAN AND KOREA

The small Korean peninsula, a spit of land pushing into the sea, is joined to the mainland only on its northern edge, where it touches the land masses of China and Russia. A tiny stretch of the border, only 19km (12 miles) long, skims the southern edges of Siberia just south of Vladivostok. The remainder of the border follows the winding courses of two rivers for 1,416km (880 miles) to separate Korea from the ancient land of Manchuria, now China.

The eastern side of the country is protected from the Pacific Ocean by the curving islands of Japan. The enmity that has persisted between Japan and Korea over many centuries is underlined by the fact that the Koreans now prefer to call the stretch of water that divides them the East Sea, rather than its older name, the Sea of Japan.

Japan is a long archipelago of four main islands and over 3,000 smaller islands, some tiny and uninhabited. The islands of Japan stretch around 2,300km (1,430 miles) from north to south-west but the country's whole crinkled coastline measures an amazing 29,751km (18,486 miles). No wonder the Japanese love to eat fish and shellfish – these fresh ingredients formed the staple diet of most of the population in earlier centuries where they formed their first settlements along the coast, and are still enjoyed today.

MOUNTAINS AND EARTHQUAKES

There are no active volcanoes in Korea, but Japan is a different matter, with 40 active volcanoes at the last count and over a 100 dormant ones. In both countries, a number of hot springs indicate that the earth is quietly rumbling not far below the surface, and small earthquakes are common, with the occasional larger quake such as the one that hit the Japanese city of Kobe in 1995.

Perhaps the most famous sight in Japan is the landscape containing Mount Fuji, an incredibly beautiful conical-shaped extinct volcano which is often capped with snow. Mount Fuji rises majestically from the central part of Honshu, its summit 3,776 metres (12,388 feet) above sea level.

PEOPLE AND POLITICS

Since the division of Korea into North and South in 1953, after the Korean War, the Korean peninsula has been physically divided by a DMZ (De-Militarized Zone) roughly along the 38th parallel, and the North has withdrawn into isolation while the South has embraced the technology and industry of the 21st-century world. Japan, however, has managed to retain its unique culture and politics throughout its scattered islands. All the main cities are in the middle island, Honshu, where the power base of the government in Tokyo controls Japanese life from Hokkaido to Kyushu.

North and South Korea

These two countries are deeply divided between the Communist North and the democratic South. It is difficult for outsiders to obtain much information about daily life in North Korea; but from what we understand about the country, the people live in a relatively restricted fashion, a real contrast to life in bustling, prosperous South Korea. However, longstanding Korean food and farming traditions persist throughout the country, with fresh and natural ingredients grown or gathered locally in what is a productive, industrious land.

Below: A map showing Japan and North and South Korea, and the surrounding countries and seas. The presence of warm and cold currents around the coastlines attracts a variety of fish and shellfish.

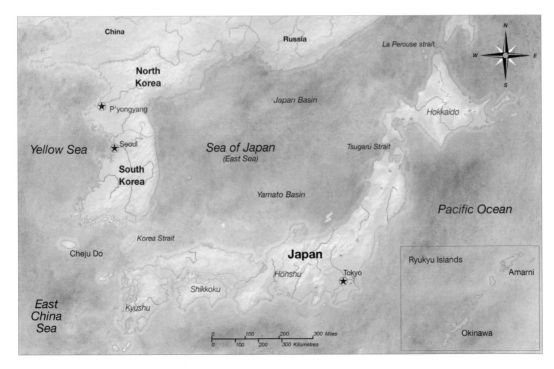

FARMING AND FOOD PRODUCTION

Both countries contain a rich variety of natural fauna and flora, from the native broad-leaved trees of the south, which flourish in the humid tropical climate, to spikier pine trees, larch and juniper in the colder north. Bears, wild boar and deer still roam wild through the forests in North Korea, and vast colonies of breeding birds inhabit the coastal shallows of all three countries.

Much of Japan and Korea is naturally mountainous and unsuited to food production. However, with the high population, especially in Japan, the best possible use must be made of whatever land is available. In the 20th century, inventive techniques of drainage and land reclamation around the coast have made the land area of Japan much greater than its natural boundaries. In previous centuries the Japanese and Koreans were already learning to exploit their beautiful countryside by terracing the lower slopes of the mountains and hills to grow all kinds of crops, particularly rice, which is eaten at almost every meal.

AN EXTREME CLIMATE

In Korea, the terrain is both rugged and beautiful, and the climate comprises harsh extremes: blazing heat in the humid summer and snow in the icy winter. The southern regions have a similar climate to that of Japan, with warm, wet summers

and a regular monsoon season that brings half the year's rainfall in just a few weeks. Further north, where North Korea touches the Chinese/Russian border, it is much drier and colder, with snow on the mountains and freezing temperatures during the winter.

The Japanese climate also varies from north to south, although the north of Japan does not suffer quite so badly from the harsh winter weather experienced by

Below: A Korean farmer ploughs the land by hand in Gyeongju.

Above: Rows of fresh green tea growing in fields in Japan.

North Korea. However, the natural air flow still comes from the cold land mass to the north-west in winter, bringing snow to western Japan, whereas in summer, winds tend to veer round to bring warm, wet air from the south-east. Summer is the rainy season and typhoons quite commonly blow in over the Pacific during August.

Below: A Japanese farmer uses modern rice planting equipment.

Above: A paddy field in Magoksa, South Korea – half of Korea's arable land is given over to the cultivation of rice.

HARVESTS FROM THE SEA

The Korean peninsula and the islands of Japan are set in some of the world's best fishing waters, so it is little wonder that seafood is a major source of protein in the diet of both countries. The intricate coastline and numerous islands, inlets and reefs, and the presence of both a warm and a cold current, attract a wonderful variety of species.

There is a huge tidal flow on the western side of Korea facing China. The Yellow Sea tides rise and fall 5 to 8 metres (17 to 27 feet) every day, keeping the fish moving in shoals all around the coastline. The street markets of Seoul overflow with fish, prawns (shrimp), crabs, oysters and octopus, and this rich harvest is served in every conceivable form – raw, stir-fried, grilled (broiled), stewed, pickled and dried.

Japan is bounded by the warm, relatively shallow waters of the Sea of Japan on its western seaboard and the deeper Pacific to the east. The Pacific coastline south-west of Tokyo is full of natural harbours formed by the warm southern currents, and several of the fishing villages that grew up around these harbours have developed into the vast trading ports of modern Japan. Further north of Tokyo, a cooler current flows down from north to south, bringing plankton and other nutrients for the hungry shoals of fish to feed on. The sea around the coast of central Japan, near Tokyo, where these two currents meet, is one of the most prolific breeding grounds for fish and shellfish of all kinds.

Above: Seafood has always been a major part of the Korean diet and can be easily found on market stalls and stores. The fish and shellfish has been left to dry naturally in order to prolong storing periods.

Above: Tuna fish are being inspected for quality at the Tokyo fishmarket.

COUNTRY LIFE

Both Japan and Korea are small countries that contain enormous variations of landscape, climate and way of life. So many people work in the cities that we think of Japan and South Korea as fast-moving, ultra-modern countries that embrace every modern convenience. And yet, when the traveller leaves the main cities behind and moves out into the rural areas, all this modernity disappears and in the more remote areas the countryside resembles an ancient painting. Cloud-enshrouded mountains dominate the landscape, blanketed by lush meadows and dotted with picturesque villages. Working monasteries open their doors to visitors, and the friendly locals welcome travellers enthusiastically, happy to share their meals and to pass on traditional recipes to interested tourists.

The farmers of Korea and Japan battle against the twin limitations of mountainous terrain and encroaching cities. On every square metre (yard) of level ground you will find either buildings or land used for agriculture. Where there is room for farming, they raise animals for meats – beef, chicken and pork are the most popular – or grow rice, which fills over half the available land wherever there is a small flat space

Above: The magnificent temple of Kiyomizudera in Kyoto, Japan. It takes its name from the waterfall that runs around the temple buildings.

and forms the delicious, glutinous base of every meal. Where other crops are grown, they are usually barley, wheat and corn to mill into flour for tasty pancakes and fritters, or a great variety of delicious vegetables and fruit.

CITY LIFE

Korea and Japan are a fascinating blend of the fiercely traditional and the breathtakingly modern. The lights of the vast capital cities, Tokyo and Seoul, shimmer and sparkle at night, and everywhere there is a vibrant sense of a thriving, prosperous, 21st-century society with a serious work ethic.

Some Japanese and Koreans still shop and cook in the traditional way even in the big cities, although many younger people now embrace a more Western way of life, including adopting a fast-food culture that gives little time for traditional meals. However the family remains an important part of life, and people of all ages generally show great respect for older members of their family as well as in the wider society.

And still, if you look closely in the shadows of the towering buildings, there are traces of the heritage of centuries past. Ancient temples, fortresses and ornate gateways nestle among the high-rise architecture of glass and steel. The furious pace of modern life is tempered by an aged serenity.

Below: The deceptive veneer of Seoul's towering skyline disguises a city of great contrasts, where ancient temples jostle for position with modern skyscrapers.

Above: View of the city of Tokyo and its famous observation tower.

Above: Traditional Korean houses with tiled roofs and the commercial centre of Seoul seen in the distance.

Above: Japan's cities are highly populated. Shibuya is one of Tokyo's busiest railway stations.

Right: A traditional Japanese house in a preserved village in Shizuoka.

Left: A market stand selling a variety of colourful kimchi dishes. Kimchi is a traditional Korean dish made of vegetables with seasonings, the most common is the cabbage variety. Kimchi is very spicy and can also be very sweet. The taste and flavours of kimchi does vary with the cooking styles of the different regions of Korea.

JAPANESE MINIMALISM

Japan and Korea are often seen as exciting and exotic countries, mixing tradition and modernity to striking effect. The food cultures of both countries have many similarities – the emphasis on family meals, multiple dishes and sharing food, for example – but also some differences. In Japan, the attention to detail is paramount in the cuisine as well as in other areas, from painting to microchip production. In Korea, on the other hand, there is more of a sense of nature's abundance, and a glorying in the vivid colours and contrasting tastes of a whole range of ingredients used together.

It is not surprising that in a country like Japan, where the population density is so high in the urban areas because much of the landscape is mountainous and unavailable for housing, people appreciate minimalism in all aspects of their lives. This restraint is seen clearly in the careful simplicity of sushi, its subtle colours glowing, the white rice and orange fish set against green vegetables and dark seaweed wrappings, all presented on a shallow tray. Garnish is all-important to the Japanese, with the most beautiful shapes cut from vegetables and arranged in exquisite patterns to please the eye as much as the taste buds. The

tea ceremony and cha-kaiseki, the meal served with it, is unique to Japanese cuisine and is based on Buddhist principles of harmony and restraint.

KOREAN VIVACITY

In Korea, however, the population in the cities tends to be even denser than in Japan, there is more of an emphasis on contrasting, even clashing colours and flavours. Koreans often make a wide range of dishes for the main meal of the day, based on a large bowl of rice as a solid, nutritious foundation. This exuberant attitude to food and cooking is exemplified by the Korean national dish, kimchi, a vibrant mixture of vegetables and spices, marinated for days, weeks or even months until it becomes a strong-tasting, fermented concoction somewhere between a vegetable side dish and a chutney or pickle. This fierce Korean speciality is added to most savoury recipes or served as a side dish with rice, even for breakfast.

Above: Teppanyaki is a style of Japanese cuisine that uses iron plates to cook food. Teppan means plate, and yaki means grilled or broiled.

Above: A Korean barbecue is a method of cooking some types of meat. Some Korean restaurants have charcoal grills built into the centre of the table.

Above: There is a wide variety of sushi dishes; the same ingredients may even be assembled in different ways to create different dishes.

FRESH FOOD, SIMPLY COOKED

Perhaps one of the defining features of this region of Asia is the relationship that exists between food and nature. In Japan, food is eaten fresh and unadulterated wherever possible. This is considered the best way to experience the true taste of each ingredient and lies at the heart of the Japanese philosophy of eating. The fish and shellfish found so abundantly in the seas off the Japanese coast are often eaten raw, or only very lightly cured with vinegar or salt. Likewise, fresh, seasonal crops from the fields are only lightly cooked to preserve their texture and flavour. Sauces are kept separate and served in little dishes to be dipped into as required. In Korea, however, many dishes are treated to long, slow cooking and flavours are combined in a hearty casserole or a dish of barbecued, marinated meat with vegetables and noodles. In both countries, cooking traditions and recipes are influenced by the season and by what is available locally on the market stalls of every town and city, but techniques of preserving meat, fish and vegetables for the cold months are a particularly strong part of the Korean culture.

Right: Bento is a portioned meal that is common in Japanese cuisine. A bento consists of rice, fish or meat with a side dish of cooked and pickled vegetables.

Above: Yakitori is a popular Japanese dish, made from skewered chicken.

USING THIS BOOK

The book is divided into three main sections. The first section, Culinary Traditions, will detail the developments of Japanese and Korean cuisines, from foreign and historical influences to traditions, festivals and etiquette. The second section, Equipment and Ingredients, introduces the key ingredients from both cultures, and explains all the essential techniques and practices you need to make authentic dishes. No special knowledge is needed. With only a few absolute essentials you will be able to

Above: A variety of grains and seasonings for sale at a market stall.

accommodate Japanese and Korean recipes with minimal fuss.

The final section, The Recipes, is a superb collection featuring the best regional and national cuisine from this corner of Asia, from simple sushi and appetizers to hotpots for all to share.

Japanese and Korean food is a wonderful explosion of tastes and colours, a real feast for the senses. Much of the pleasure lies in the careful selection and preparation of fresh food for these recipes. Use the best ingredients that nature offers and enjoy the delicious results.

CULINARY
TRADITIONS

*This section introduces the cuisines of both Japan
and Korea, from foreign influences and food
etiquette to celebrations and festivals.*

Image: A market in Seoul, South Korea, offering a selection of food and other goods.

FOOD OF JAPAN

Japan is a country filled with stunning natural scenery, traditional temples, and modern and futuristic architecture. One of the great definers of Japanese culture is the food they eat, as well as the way they combine, cook and present the ingredients. Japanese food displays all the great themes of the Japanese lifestyle: simplicity, elegance, attention to detail, an aesthetic sense, and a delight in miniatures.

Left: The bright lights of the Shibuya District, Tokyo; **Above:** Typical Japanese ingredients

THE REGIONS OF JAPAN

Japan is a small country where the land is mountainous and there are numerous bays and peninsulas. There are eight main geographic regions and each region, and even the cities, has their own tastes and specialities, and many dishes are cooked differently. Over recent years, Japanese food has become popular around the world, with dishes such as sushi and tempura being the most well-known.

Hokkaido region

Japan's northern-most and second largest island accounts for one-fifth of the country's total land area. Hokkaido features fertile coastal plains, lakes and beautiful landscapes. The Tsugaru Strait separates Hokkaido from Honshu, although the two islands are connected by the underwater Seikan Tunnel. The largest city on Hokkaido is its capital, Sapporo. Agriculture plays an important role in Hokkaido's economy, as it makes up approximately one fourth of Japan's total arable land. It produces a variety of products, including wheat, soybeans, potatoes, onions, pumpkins, raw milk and beef.

Tohoku region

Located on the north-eastern end of Honshu, Tohoku is a region marked by a mountain that runs roughly down the centre of the region. Tohoku retains a reputation as a remote region, offering breathtaking scenery but with a harsh climate. It is a landscape of rugged coastlines and islands, forested mountains and lakes. The inland location of many of the region's lowlands has led to a concentration of much of the population there.

Kanto region

This is a geographical area of Honshu, the largest island of Japan. The region includes Tokyo, Yokohama, Chiba, Saitama and Kanagawa. Tokyo is not a single city but a municipality containing 23 wards, incorporating many smaller cities, towns and villages within its metropolitan government. The central part of Japan's capital is a thrusting modern landscape with some of the tallest tower blocks in the world. Alongside these are ancient temples and traditional stalls selling tasty street snacks. The Kanto region is highly developed and industrialized.

Chubu region

The Chubu region is the central region of Honshu, Japan's main island. It is located directly between the Kanto region and the Kansai region and includes the major city of Nagoya, beautiful coastlines, extensive mountain resorts, and the famous Mount Fuji.

Kansai region

Also known as the Kinki region, this region lies in the south of Honshu. This region is the cultural heart of Japan, with Osaka and Kyoto forming the core. Osaka is Japan's largest city. It is renowned for its food, as well as selling an array of goods in its shopping districts and centres. Popular regional cuisine in Osaka includes udon noodles, octopus dumplings and pan-fried batter cake. Another major cultural city is Kyoto, which was once the imperial capital of Japan. It is a heritage site, maintaining Japanese traditions in education, religion and cuisine.

Below: Mount Fuji is the highest mountain in Japan. During the summer months, small food huts provide locally produced food for climbers.

Right: Osaka, Japan's largest city, is a paradise for shoppers and food lovers. Osaka is well-known for its food and has many colourful shopping districts and a variety of restaurants.

Chugoko region

This is the westernmost region of Honshu, the largest island in Japan. The Chugoku region consists of Hiroshima, Yamaguchi, Shimane and Tottori. The Chugoku region is characterized by irregular rolling hills and limited plain areas and is divided into two distinct parts by mountains. The city of Hiroshima was rebuilt after it was destroyed by an atomic bomb in 1945 and it is now an industrial metropolis enjoyed by many people.

Shikoku region

This is the smallest of Japan's four main islands, located south of Honshu and east of Kyushu. The land is used extensively, with wheat, barley and rice being farmed, and because of the wheat production, udon noodles have become an important part of the diet. Fruit is also grown, including persimmons, peaches, grapes and citrus fruits. The Yoshino river runs west to east across the boundaries, and it is famous for white-water rafting.

Kyushu region

This is the third largest island of Japan. It is a very rocky and mountainous island. Mount Aso, Japan's most active volcano, is located here, as well as numerous hot springs. The largest city is Fukuoka, which is a major business centre. The major agricultural products from this area are rice, tea, tobacco, soy and sweet potatoes. Fukuoka is home to regional local dishes, such as mentaiko – marinated roe), hakata ramen and motsunabe – a soup hotpot –, and during the night, street stalls, known as yatai, serve ramen.

Right: Japan stretches through 16 degrees of latitude, starting in the north alongside Russia to the warmth of the Pacific in the south, and local produce varies accordingly.

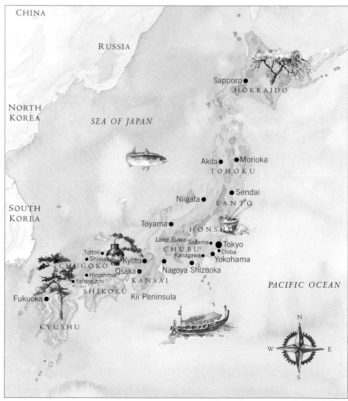

THE DEVELOPMENT OF JAPANESE CUISINE

The first traces of food to be found in Japan were in the remains of prehistoric settlements scattered across southern Japan. An amazing variety of nutritious foods was discovered ranging from wild animals, and all sorts of fish and shellfish to plants, nuts and berries. The various cooking techniques, cutting, crushing, grinding, grilling (broiling) and boiling, were well advanced and the excavated remains from before 200BC suggest that the Japanese had a varied and balanced diet ideal for their needs. This early culinary sophistication in ancient Japan reveals one of the defining features of Japanese cuisine: an ability to use and develop nature's bounty for the community.

Below: This colour woodblock print by Hiroshige (1797–1858) shows the communal nature of rice cultivation.

Above: A 19th-century portrait of Izumi Tadahira (d.1189) with a poem, from 'Famous Generals of Japan'. By the 12th century, feudal warlords had taken over the running of regions, greatly improving rice cultivation.

RICE: A STAPLE FOOD FOR ALL

In Japan, rice is so important that the word for cooked rice, gohan or meshi, also means meal. It not only plays a major part in Japanese cooking, but, since its introduction in the 2nd century BC, rice and its cultivation have been the very foundation of the nation itself.

Rice was probably introduced to Japan from South-east Asia, and the earliest evidence of crop production was found in village settlements dating from around the 2nd century BC to the 2nd century AD. Rice cultivation revolutionized life in the western region of Japan, and from there soon spread further east. The first nation, Yamato, was formed in the west in the 4th century; the first known historical record book mentions 'brewed sake' (an alcoholic drink made from fermented rice) being presented to the *Tenno* (emperor) and a definition of 'refining rice'.

From the 8th to the 12th centuries, when aristocratic culture blossomed, rice became firmly established as a staple food, cooked in various ways for

Above: Coloured woodblock illustration by Hiroshige (1797–1858), showing workers transporting rice.

the upper classes, although the majority of the population was dependent on other lesser-quality grains such as millet. It was the popularity of rice that led to the development of other basic accompaniments, such as seasonings and sauces, and of various cooking techniques. The aristocratic class also contributed to the establishment of eating etiquette, which subsequently influenced cha-kaiseki, the meal served at the tea ceremony, and later Japanese cuisine as a whole.

At the royal court, an increasing number of annual ceremonies and rituals were performed, including Shinto ceremonies (the indigenous religion), and these would be accompanied by food and sake. Sake was, and still is,

regarded as a sacred liquid, cleansing evil spirits. Eating and drinking became an important part of the procedures and cooking itself became a ritual: traces of this can still be seen today in the way top Japanese chefs handle and care for their knives.

By the end of the 12th century the aristocratic society had been replaced by feudal warlords. Techniques of rice production rapidly improved under the feudal system and rice became fully available to the general public on a daily basis during the 13th century.

COMMUNITIES FOUNDED ON RICE

Rice production is a communal process and villages became large 'rice production lines', cultivating the same land, generation after generation, for hundreds of years. The nation was founded on the basis of this village society and even in modern, highly

industrialized Japan, this social cohesion is still evident today. Rice production is very labour-intensive and time-consuming work, and contributed to the Japanese work ethic of industriousness and endurance. Rice also yields more per unit of land than any other crop, which enabled Japan to be among the most densely populated countries for many centuries.

Basic methods of cooking rice, such as boiling, steaming, grilling (broiling) and roasting, as well as early steaming utensils, have long been in evidence in Japan, dating as far back as 200BC. Furthermore, because rice stores well, it was possible for the people to use it for their basic daily food source rather than depend on other, less predictable, crops, animal meats or catches of fish and shellfish. Rice became the staple food and Japanese cuisine developed around it.

THE IMPORTANCE OF SALT

With the development of rice cultivation, salt started to appear and play a great part in the culinary scene. It was extracted from the sea and replaced the former source of salt: animals' intestines. However, due to scarcity and its poor storage qualities, salt was mixed with animal or plant fibres and proteins. The mixture, called hishio, was in effect a nutritious, fermented food as well as a seasoning, and transpired to be one of the most important developments in Japanese culinary history.

The three basic kinds were grain hishio (salt-fermented rice, barley or beans), meat hishio (seafood or animal meat) and grass hishio (plant, berries or seaweed). Hishio later developed into some of the most well-known and important Japanese foods, such as miso and shoyu (grain hishio), shiokara and sushi (meat hishio), and tsukemono pickles (grass hishio).

The idea of fermentation was further developed to produce alcohol using barley, yam and glutinous rice. Although at first this was an alcoholic food, rather than a liquid, it was the origin of Japan's most celebrated drink, sake.

A SACRED LIQUID

During the aristocratic period (the 8th–12th centuries) sake grew in popularity with the upper classes as an important element in ceremonies, rituals and drinks parties and was considered a sacred liquid. There were two kinds: white sake, which was an opaque liquid, and black, which had the added flavour of burnt leaves. The black sake was for presentation to the shrine.

With the influx of Koreans into Japan in the 16th century, new techniques arrived to develop sake further, now using ordinary rice, and over the next few centuries sake improved into the fine, clear drink of today.

SAKE ETIQUETTE

Emerging from the customs of feudal society, Japanese drinking etiquette was established during the 15th–17th centuries. Principal guests initiated the party by drinking three cups of sake each. (This ritual is still seen today at Shinto weddings where the bride and groom drink from three cups in turn, taking three sips from each.) After this initiation ritual, guests moved to a party room and a banquet commenced. Sake played the primary role in the Japanese banquet and indeed dishes of food were mere accompaniments to the appreciation of the drink, the opposite to the development of wine in the West.

Below: Sake is still considered a sacred liquid. The first sake barrels of the year are traditionally dedicated to the parish shrines such as this Tenmangu in Kyoto where the sake barrels are displayed at the entrance to the shrine.

FOREIGN INFLUENCES

From the earliest times, neighbouring China and Korea have exerted great influence over Japan. From AD630 to AD894 more than ten trade missions as well as 500–600 students were sent to the T'ang dynasty of China bringing back cultural influences with them. For example, *Kana*, the Japanese phonetic alphabet, was developed from Chinese characters and the popularity of all things *Chinoiserie* among the upper classes involved all aspects of life, including art, architecture and food. In AD647, a Chinese monk presented milk – sheep's as well as cow's – to the *Tenno* (emperor) and was rewarded with the milking job in the royal household. However, milk never became established as a daily part of the Japanese diet and disappeared completely, as in China, around the 13th century following the arrival of Zen Buddhism.

Right and below: Both Japan's native religion, Shintoism, and Buddhism, introduced from China, have had a large impact on Japanese's culinary culture. Shijyoryu Hochoshiki, *the symbolic cutting of the tofu, is held at Nagano Shinto shrine, right, and the ceremonial dedication to god of the first vegetables from the year's crop is held at a Buddhist temple, below. Some Buddhist temples have restaurants on the premises, serving vegetarian food.*

THE IMPACT OF BUDDHISM

Japanese cooking is largely fish- and vegetable-based and if meat is included it is used very sparingly and often cooked with vegetables. This can be traced back to as early as the 6th century when Buddhism first arrived via China, proclaiming animal slaughter and meat eating to be a sinful act. An Imperial ordinance issued in AD675 banned the eating of beef, horse, dog and chicken. However, the ban seems not to have been fully effective since another official ban had to be issued in AD752 to commemorate the opening of the eyes of the Great Buddha at Todaiji Temple in Nara. As part of that decree, it was forbidden to kill any creature for the whole year, and records show that fishermen were compensated for their loss of earnings with rice. Even with the bans it was not until the period of the 9th–12th centuries that this non-killing philosophy fully spread from Buddhist monks to the upper classes and then to the wider public. Through all, the samurai class continued to enjoy shooting and eating wild boar, deer and birds, in keeping with their lifestyle.

Zen Buddhism and food rituals

At the end of the 12th century, Zen Buddhism, a strict sect of Buddhism, arrived from China and, with it, *shojin ryori*. This was originally simple vegan cooking performed by the monks as part of their severe training. It usually consisted of a bowl of rice, soup and one or two other dishes, but it now refers to a formal vegetarian meal. Many Japanese dishes may appear to be vegetarian but, in fact, vegetables are often cooked in dashi soup: a fish stock. Authentic *shojin ryori* should be purely vegan cooking.

Accompanying the Zen philosophical movement, Chinese foods and cooking techniques (particularly frying) were introduced to Japan. One important arrival was tea, which, although it had been brought back by earlier missions to China, did not become established as a drink among Buddhists and the upper classes until a Zen Buddhist brought back seeds at the end of the 12th century. This led eventually to the development of *cha-kaiseki* (the formal meal served before the tea ceremony), which established the form of Japanese cuisine.

INFLUENCES THROUGH TRADE

Other foreigners, including the Spanish, Portuguese, Dutch and English also greatly influenced Japan as trading with them progressed from the mid 16th century to the closure of the country in the early 17th century. These early foreigners, especially the Portuguese and Spanish, were disparagingly called *Nanban* (southern barbarians), because they arrived in Japan from the south through South-east Asia, and, to Japanese eyes, lacked sensitivity and bodily cleanliness.

The influence their food and cooking methods had upon the Japanese is still evident today. Any dish or sauce with the name *Nanban* derives from this period; nanban-zuke (fried fish or vegetables marinated in a piquant, vinegary sauce) is one such dish. (The name was also used for many other things such as paintings and furniture design.)

With trade, many new vegetables and fruits also arrived: watermelons, sugar cane, chillies, figs, potatoes and the kabocha squash, which derives its name from its parent country, Cambodia. The Portuguese also brought the tomato to Japan although only as a decorative plant.

The most famous foreign import of this period, tempura, was introduced by the Portuguese Jesuits and is now one of the most popular Japanese dishes among Westerners as well as the Japanese themselves. There are several theories as to the root of the word tempura, but one possible explanation is that it derives from the Latin word *tempora*, meaning the Ember Days,

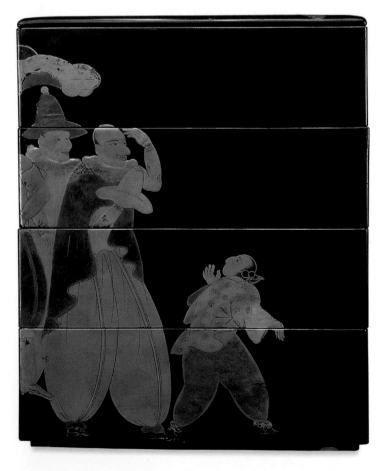

Left: Black lacquer Japanese lunch box with Nanban *figures, from the 17th century. The Japanese called early Europeans, the Spanish and Portuguese in particular,* Nanban, *meaning southern barbarians.*

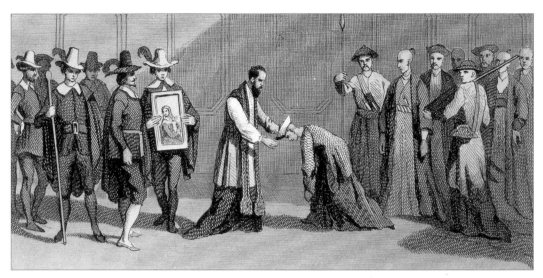

Above: Black and white illustration of the Jesuit Francisco Xavier meeting with Japanese representatives, c. 1551. The Franciscan Xavier first introduced Christianity to Japan in 1549. The Jesuits also engaged in trade with the Japanese, an activity that aroused controversy in Europe and in Japan.

or *Quattuor Tempora*, relating to when Roman Catholics were forbidden to eat meat and ate fish instead. Another theory suggests that it is derived from the Portuguese word *tempero*, meaning seasoning, but no one really knows. One thing is certain however: the first Tokugawa shogun, *Ieyasu*, liked sea-bream tempura so much that he died from overeating it.

Meat-eating was reintroduced by the *Nanban* and became popular among Catholic feudal lords. (There is still a large Catholic community in Nagasaki on the southern island of Kyushu.)

Sweets (candy) and cakes also joined the league of foreign imports and many still bear the names of their foreign

Right: Japanese pottery is renowned for its fine craftsmanship, such as is evident here in this 19th-century Satsuma porcelain vase.

origin: konpeito and aruheito, both little spiky sugar balls, derive from the Portuguese words confeitos and alfeloa; karumera, a fluffy sugar cake, from calamela; and kasutera, wet sponge cake, a speciality of Nagasaki, from *castella*. Drinks such as shochu and red wine also arrived at this time and were regarded as *Nanban* drinks.

CHINAWARE

Another significant influence foreigners had on Japanese culinary history is the substantial development of chinawares produced by the Korean potters brought back to Japan after Japan's assault on Korea in 1592. The Korean potters were extremely ahead of their time in pottery technology and helped to found the basis of Japan's pottery industry. It was the Koreans who first succeeded in making the Japanese porcelain at Arita, now a world-famous name for pottery.

China instead of metal soon became fashionable for serving food and Japan subsequently became one of the greatest china-manufacturing countries in the world, producing such exquisite and diverse chinas as Bizen, Hagi, Imari, Karatsu, Kutani, Mashiko, Mino and Seto, to name but a few. Glassware also made its way to Japan at around the same time.

The variety of good quality chinaware complemented the food that was served on it. This attention to presentation helped to further refine the Japanese food culture and is still an essential part of Japanese cuisine today. Present day Japanese tableware is a very colourful affair, and designs from other countries, such as Wedgwood, are starting to appear.

THE IMPACT OF ISOLATION

The closure of the country to outside contact for 260 years from the early 17th century gave *washoku* (Japanese food) an opportunity to establish its own unique identity. Tokyo became the capital due to the presence of the shogun, but Kyoto remained the cultural centre, where aristocratic and temple *kaiseki* cooking further developed with the introduction of new seasonings such as shoyu (soy sauce) and sugar.

All regions, which were ruled by lords, started to industrialize, and became fiercely competitive, producing and trading their own local specialities. Tokyo, as well as Osaka, near Kyoto, became a centre where all foods and different cooking techniques converged. The regional lords were required to visit Tokyo in turn, bringing their local produce with them. This constant arrival of new ingredients and various cooking methods from all regions contributed to the rich character of Japanese cuisine we see today.

The establishment of restaurants also had an important impact on *washoku*. The first known restaurant in Tokyo opened in the late 17th century, and many more rapidly followed. The restaurants each specialized more or less in a single dish or ingredient such as sushi, soba, kabayaki (grilled eel) or tempura, and this unique feature of the Japanese restaurant scene is still strong to the present day.

Below: Typical street scene in Japan just before the opening of the country to the outside world, c. 1850.

Above: Traditional ways meet modern technology in this illustration of early Japanese train travellers.

RE-OPENING JAPAN

After the country was opened up in the mid 19th century, meat eating was reintroduced. The emperor Meiji Tenno himself ate beef in 1872 and this opened the floodgates to the public's conception that meat-eating was something new and fashionable. Beef-based dishes, such as sukiyaki and shabu shabu, are inventions of this period. French and English breads also flooded in but they were regarded as snacks and cakes.

Integrating newly arrived European cooking methods and ingredients into Japanese cooking, many eclectic dishes, called *yōshoku* (Western food) as opposed to *washoku*, were created. Tonkatsu, pork cutlet, is the most noteworthy, and numerous tonkatsu restaurants opened up all over Japan.

Thus, while the closure of the country may have delayed Japan's modernization for 200 years, it is this period of isolation from the outside world that allowed Japanese cuisine to become established. As a result, instead of being overwhelmed by the introduction of these foreign culinary influences, Japanese food and cooking techniques influenced Western cuisine, and vice versa, in a positive way.

SUSHI: A NATIONAL FAVOURITE

The most famous sushi, called nigiri, are hand-moulded fingers of vinegared rice with slices of raw fish on top. They are only one form of many types of sushi and are a relatively new invention from Tokyo. No one really knows when the word was first used; strictly, the word sushi means to vinegar (originally the rice was thrown away), but as the vinegared rice became the essential ingredient, sushi developed into a term signifying vinegared rice dishes.

LONG-PRESSED SUSHI

The oldest sushi still found in Japan is the funa-zushi of Shiga. This type is a nare-zushi, or long-pressed sushi, made using freshwater fish such as funa, a type of carp, dojo (loach) or namazu (sheatfish). The fish is first salt-cured and then marinated in cooked rice and salt. This is a way to preserve fish; the rice and salt are discarded. The origin of this oldest-surviving sushi can be traced back to hishio, a mixture of raw fish and salt, although some say it goes right back to various other similar fish-preserving methods that existed in China as early as 300BC. Although at one stage the Chinese also developed this method of using rice mixed with salt, the technique had disappeared completely from the Chinese culinary scene by the 17th century.

Above: Chefs working behind the counter in a local sushi restaurant in Miyako, northern Japan.

Below: The outside of a small sushi restaurant in Beppu, Kyushu, Japan. Delivery boys on motorcycles transport freshly made sushi to homes.

MODERN-DAY SUSHI

The process the nare-zushi then took to develop into the present-day sushi is well recorded. First it was simplified; the nare-zushi's long-term pressing, for almost a year, was greatly shortened to about ten days so that the rice could also be eaten before it fully fermented. To hasten the fermentation process and prevent the raw fish from rotting, vinegar was added to the rice. The result is a simple oshi-zushi, meaning pressed sushi, a speciality of Kansai, the region around Osaka. But it was in Tokyo in the 19th century that the process was sped up even more, with the development of nigiri, instant sushi.

Sold from street stalls and stores as a snack, nigiri, also known as edomae, was the fast food of its time. It was and still is the most famous sushi of all.

Today, sushi restaurants abound and sushi chefs are regarded as highly skilled craftsmen who train for a number of years at their craft. Indeed, top sushi restaurants are becoming very expensive places to eat. So, even though sushi remains a snack food, it is undoubtedly a high-quality one.

THE TEA CEREMONY

If it was the English who transformed tea drinking into a lifestyle, it was the Japanese who perfected it as an art form. The tea ceremony is the generally accepted translation for *chadō* or *sadō*, literally meaning 'way of tea'. Also known as *chanoyu*, the ceremonial aspects are just one part of what is a deeply philosophical and profound occasion. It is not exaggerating to say that the tea ceremony is the essence of Japanese culture itself, embracing all divisions of visual art such as scrolled

Right: A 19th-century woodcut showing tea being served at the shogun's palace.

Below: A roadside tea shop on Tokaido, an ancient street running from Tokyo to Osaka. Woodblock print, 1833.

Right: The tea ceremony embodies, for both preparer and receiver, simplicity, mutual respect, harmony and stillness. Tea pavilions and houses surrounded by gardens of natural beauty provide a physical and spiritual haven.

paintings and calligraphy, pottery, flower arranging and even architecture. The tea ceremony expresses the Japanese philosophy for life and etiquette, not just for drinking tea but for entertaining guests and being entertained. It teaches a person where they stand in society and how to behave.

The tea ceremony has now lost much of its connection with Zen Buddhism, but is still very popular among women, particularly young women as part of their bridal training. Learning the way of tea usually takes over ten years, and the learning process can continue throughout a person's life.

EARLY TEA-DRINKING

Tea was first introduced to Japan from China in the 8th century but it was not until the Zen monk, Eisai (1141–1215), brought back tea seeds from China in 1191 that the habit of tea drinking and tea parties began to spread among Buddhists, aristocrats and samurai classes. Early tea drinking consisted of a tea tasting party where the guests bet money on naming the variety of tea they were drinking. This was often followed by a sake drinks party. During the turbulent civil wars of the 15th–16th centuries, the tea party evolved into appreciating tea in tranquillity away from the upheavals of war.

It was another monk, Murata Jukoh (1423–1502), who refined the tea party by placing more emphasis on the Zen philosophy of *wabi* and *sabi* (serenity and simplicity) and establishing *wabi-cha*. He applied to the tea ceremony the famous Zen teaching, *ichigo ichié*, literally meaning 'one life, one meeting', whereby participants should conduct the meeting as if it were a once in a lifetime event, never to be repeated, and thus significantly broadening the meaning and understanding of the way of tea.

THE PRACTICE OF *CHANOYU*

The present day *chanoyu* owes most to Sen-no Rikyu (1522–1591) who put the philosophy of the tea ceremony into practice by laying out every aspect of *chanoyu* in detail. *Chanoyu* became so highly regarded as a social as well as a philosophical activity during his lifetime that he was appointed tea master by two consecutive great shoguns, Nobunaga and Hideyoshi. Sadly, he became too powerful for Hideyoshi to bear and he was eventually forced to commit suicide by the shogun.

Rikyu's teachings of the heart of *chanoyu* can be condensed into four principal characters: *wa* (harmony); *kei* (respect); *sei* (cleanliness); and *jaku* (serenity). In practice, however, he set out seven rules for *chanoyu*: arrange flowers as they appear in nature; burn charcoal only to just simmer the water

in the pot; serve the right amount of tea; make the surroundings cool in summer and warm in winter; prepare for *chanoyu* in good time; be ready for rain, even in fine weather; and respect fellow guests.

Today, three schools of *chanoyu*, *Ura-senké*, *Omote-senké* and *Mushanokoji-senké*, established by Rikyu's three grandsons, follow his teachings. These teachings have spread not only all over Japan but also abroad.

Together with the Zen teaching of *mu* (nothingness), the heart of *chanoyu* was essentially a belief in how one should treat other people in a closely knit society, without thinking of yourself. Sadly, this philosophy seems difficult to apply in the modernized, self-centred era that today at time typifies Japan since its economic expansion and rapid industrialization after World War II.

CHAJI AND CHA-KAISEKI

At about the same time as the tea ceremony was being developed, a form of *shojin ryori* (the Zen Buddhist monk's vegetarian cooking) was also brought back from China. The meal eaten by monks during training is not only vegetarian but modest. *Cha-kaiseki* was developed in line with *shojin ryori*, and early *cha-kaiseki* consisted of bowls of rice and soup and two or, at most, three dishes only.

The tea ceremony accompanied by *cha-kaiseki* is known as *chaji*. The tea ceremony is the main focus, rather than the meal, so *cha-kaiseki* is served first, in order that it does not compete with the appreciation of the tea. Over time, this meal has developed into *kaiseki ryori* (the formal multi-course meal).

The word *kaiseki* comes from 'embraced stone', a warmed stone monks held against their body to help them endure hunger and cold. Present-day *cha-kaiseki* normally consists of rice, soup, an hors d'oeuvre, a grilled (broiled) dish, a simmered dish, a small serving of clear soup, a main dish, a salted vegetable and hot water. Sake is also served. Depending on the occasion, a fish dish, another simmered dish, a

Above: The tea ceremony traditionally played a big part in a young girl's bridal training in Japan and training can continue over a lifetime.

dressed vegetable and a vinegared vegetable will also be added. The dishes and presentation should all reflect the season in which the *chaji* is held.

Formal tea ceremonies

The seven main *chaji* occasions are:
Noon *chaji* The most formal, starting between 11 am and 12 noon
Morning *chaji* Held only in summer, commencing from 6 am
Evening *chaji* Held only in winter, commencing from dusk
Dawn *chaji* Held in midwinter, commencing from 4 am
See-after *chaji* Held for absentees who could not attend the *chaji*
After-meal *chaji* Tea only held after breakfast, lunch or dinner
Ad-lib *chaji* For unexpected guests

The programme for a *chaji* depends on the occasion and will contain various stages. It is a long, formal and very complicated ritualized affair, which for most Westerners will be something both daunting and intriguing.

The rituals of the tea ceremony

Though this cannot describe the sense of the occasion, the following is a brief explanation of the most formal noon *chaji*: first guests enter the room in which the ceremony is to be held via a very small sliding door (often no bigger than the size of an average dog flap), scrolls and flowers are appreciated by the guests before seating, with the main guest at the top, and then descending in order of importance. *Kaiseki* is served on individual trays, and may last up to two hours, followed by the 'first charcoal', involving viewing the incense case. Occasionally incense sniffing is also conducted. Then wagashi (Japanese rice cakes) are served, after which everyone retires to the waiting room.

Upon return, again via the small door, the *koicha* (thick tea) ceremony follows. The host prepares, in front of the guests, matcha (powdered tea) using hot water from the pot. The tea is made into a thick batter-like consistency, hence the name. The bowl is passed around, and everyone sips from the one bowl. The second charcoal is then viewed (to admire how well its burning), followed by the *usucha* (light tea). The tea maker again prepares the tea in front of the guests, this time of a thin consistency, with a bowl for each person. Finally, guests appreciate tea bowls, scrolls and flowers before retiring. Throughout, the conversation is conducted between the main guest and the tea maker (host); the other guests should not speak much.

The above programme differs slightly for the winter half of the year when *kaiseki* is served after the first charcoal.

Different tools, equipment, scrolls, flowers and sweets (candy) are used according to the season and guests wear a kimono of the season as well. The event often lasts for several hours and can be very tiring for young girls who are not used to wearing the kimono and sitting on the floor with legs tightly folded for long periods. However, the ceremony produces a feeling of elation accompanied by an awareness of your whole being and a sense of immersion in an increasingly long-forgotten culture.

TRADITIONS AND FESTIVALS

Japan still maintains many of its old traditions and festivals, from family celebrations on children's days to grand national festivals with processions and people wearing full samurai costumes. These are nearly always accompanied by special celebration food. Today people no longer prepare elaborate food for each festival, as in the past, but nevertheless they still make or buy some special food and drink for each occasion. The following are some of the Japanese annual festivals and the particular foods associated with them.

NEW YEAR'S DAY

January 1st is the most important day in the Japanese calendar and people go to Shinto shrines to pray for happiness and prosperity during the coming year. The celebration food, called o'sechi ryori, consists of various cooked foods such as konbu (kelp seaweed), beans, herring eggs and gomame (dried small fish), and is normally served in square, lacquered containers with tiers, called jubako. Dishes vary but they were traditionally chosen for their particular significance regarding people's hopes

Below: New Year's Festival, by Kunisada (1786–1864), woodcut. Kite flying is traditional on New Year's Day.

for happiness and prosperity. O'sechi is eaten for brunch, perhaps after coming back from the shrine, followed by o'zoni (glutinous rice cake in chicken soup). The celebration lasts for three or seven days, depending on the region, and during this period people visit their friends, families and colleagues. O'sechi and o'zoni are served throughout this time.

SEVEN HERBS RICE GRUEL DAY

Each year on 7 January, nanakusa gayu (rice gruel with seven herbs) is eaten. It is comprised of seri (Japanese parsley), nazuna (shepherd's purse), gogyo (catweed), hakobera (chickweed), hotokenoza (henbit), suzuna (turnip leaf) and suzushiro (radish leaf). These traditional Japanese herbal medicines are eaten in the hope of ensuring good health throughout the year. Nowadays, however, it is not always easy to find these wild herbs, so other herbs are often substituted.

THE COMING-OF-SPRING DAY

Japan has a very hot, humid summer, and a dry, often very cold winter, with a beautifully warm spring and autumn in-between. Each season lasts almost equally for three months. The coming of spring, celebrated on 4 February, is particularly welcomed with a ritual of

throwing beans on the previous night. This ritual, normally using grilled (broiled) soya beans, is to scare devils out of the house, and is accompanied by shouts of 'devils out, happiness in'. Afterwards, everyone eats the same number of beans as their age, and this is said to protect them from any suffering. Holly branches and sardine heads used to be placed at the gate and door of the house to scare away devils, but this is not often practised, particularly in big cities.

THE GIRLS' FESTIVAL

Also known as the Dolls' Festival or the Feast of Peach Blossoms, families with young daughters celebrate their healthy growth on 3 March by displaying an elaborate set of dolls on a red-carpeted tiered altar. The dolls portray the appearance of the aristocracy in the Heian Period (AD794–1185), with the prince and princess on the top tier and their subjects, together with decorations, on the lower tiers (a full set has a total of seven tiers). Tiny rice crackers and small diamond-shape rice cakes in assorted pretty colours are among the decorations displayed, together with a cup of white sake, which is now made from sake pulp diluted with hot water. The families usually have a party for the girls on the day.

Above: An illustration of a regional lantern festival, held at cherry blossom time, c. 1912. Cherry blossom viewing is popular throughout Japan.

THE EQUINOX DAYS

For seven days around the spring equinox (on or around 21 March) and the autumn equinox (on or around 21 September), there are the traditional Buddhist celebrations, when people visit family cemeteries to appease the spirits of their ancestors. The speciality food is o'hagi, which is a rice ball covered with sweet azuki bean paste. Azuki is often used for celebrations, possibly because of its joyous red colour, although the reason for eating o'hagi on this day is not known.

FLOWER VIEWING AND FLOWER FESTIVAL

The Japanese people's love of flowers is renowned and many people make every effort to go to those gardens featuring the flowers of the season. In early April, when cherry blossoms are blooming, there is a slot on all television channels for the nationwide 'cherry blossom forecast' as well as for the weather. Using cherry blossoms as an excuse, families, friends and colleagues get together and have parties under the full bloom, late into the night. No particular food is eaten but many take bento (lunch) boxes, along with sake, beer

and whisky. The flower festival is held at temples on 8 April, the birthday of Shakyamuni Buddha, the founder of Buddhism. Sweet sake is poured over statues of the Buddha and is also drunk.

THE CHILDREN'S DAY

Also known as the Boys' Day, the Japanese celebrate small boys' healthy growth on 5 May just as they do girls on 3 March. Decorations of paper or fabric carp streamers are attached to a tall pole in the garden or rooftop so that they trail in the wind. The sight of these 'live' carps bravely meeting the

Below: The carp has long been a symbol of bravery representing families' wishes for young boys to grow up as brave and strong as the carp.

challenge of swimming up a tumbling waterfall symbolizes the families' wish for their boys to grow up to be as brave as the carps. Kashiwa-mochi (oak-leaf-wrapped glutinous rice cakes stuffed with sweet azuki bean paste) are eaten on this day.

SUMMER FESTIVALS

The Japanese love festivals and many traditional events are held during the summer, starting with the Festival of the Weaver Star on 7 July. The *Gion* Festival of Kyoto, one of the three greatest festivals of Japan, held during 17–24 July, leads various Shinto festivals all over Japan. Sake is always associated with these festivals as it is the sacred liquid dedicated to the gods and goddesses.

Fireworks are enjoyed in summer and the most famous of all displays is held on the Sumida River in Tokyo towards the end of July. Parties on river banks or on boats are very popular at this time of the year.

O'bon, a Buddhist ritual to welcome ancestral spirits to the home shrines on 16 August, brings Japan to a standstill for the whole week as people working away from home travel back to visit the family cemeteries. The *Daimonji-yaki* Festival of Kyoto on 16 August, where a spectacular fire on the mountain in the shape of the Chinese character *dai*, meaning big, can be seen from far away, is said to be related to the tradition of *o'bon*. Regional summer festivals are held around this time with dancing in *yukata* (summer kimono) and evening fairs featuring an array of stalls selling street foods.

THE HARVEST FULL-MOON VIEWING

On the night of the full moon, around 17 September, a tray with dumplings and another food typical of the autumn harvest, such as potatoes, together with some pampas grasses in a vase, is displayed by the window used by the family to view the moon. The next full moon, a month later, is marked with chestnuts in the same way.

CELEBRATIONS FOR CHILDREN

On 15 November the Japanese celebrate children reaching the ages of three, five and seven, and families with children of that age go to the shrine. Red and white sweets (candy), called chitose-amé, symbolize the families' wishes for the children's health and longevity, and are carried and eaten by the children. At home o'sekihan (rice cooked with azuki beans) is usually served.

WINTER SOLSTICE

The winter solstice normally occurs on 23 December and there is an ancient custom of taking a hot bath with yuzu juice (a Japanese citrus fruit), which is believed to help the bather stay healthy throughout the cold winter. It is also traditional to eat kabocha squash on

this day, usually cooked in a thin rice porridge. Yuzu and kabocha sqash are also offered to the gods, expressing the anticipation of spring.

NEW YEAR'S EVE

People traditionally eat soba noodles on New Year's eve while listening to bells ringing 108 times – representing the elimination of 108 sins – starting from midnight at temples throughout Japan.

Above: Decorated boats at the Sanno festival at Tsushima, Owari Province. Woodblock print, 1853 by Hiroshige.

New Year's Eve is a busy day given over to New Year preparations. This was particularly so for merchants in the Edo Period (1603–1867) who had to complete their financial accounts for the year. Soba was an ideal quick meal and it became a nationwide tradition.

SEASONAL AND REGIONAL FOODS

The seasons in Japan last for about three months each, with each new season bringing different produce and a changing catch of fish from the surrounding seas. Geographically, Japan stretches through 16 degrees of latitude, starting in the north alongside Russia to South Korea and the Pacific Ocean at the other extreme, with local produce varying from region to region. Japan is also a country with huge mountain ranges running through the centre from north to south, covering some 75–80 per cent of the land. The produce, as a result, varies not only by season and region but also by altitude.

The clash of warm and cold currents makes the seas around Japan among the world's richest fisheries, with an enormously varied range of fish and shellfish. Japan consumes some three thousand different kinds daily, and that does not include regional varieties.

In Japanese cooking the idea of season persists strongly. There is even a word for seasonal food, *shun*, and this concept is always in the Japanese mind: whenever they cook or eat they look out for something that is in *shun*.

Below: Rows of mezashi (eye-skewered half-dried sardines), a popular daily snack throughout Japan.

SEASONAL FOODS AND DISHES

There is no doubt that the wealth of the seas as well as the variety of fresh local produce contributed to the development of a cuisine rich in regional specialities. The following represent a sample of Japan's fish and vegetables, together with dishes typical of the season.

Spring

Vegetables such as peas, broad (fava) beans and mangetouts (snow peas) are crisp and tender in early spring. One speciality of the season is fresh young bamboo shoots cooked with rice. New ginger shoots are used for making vinegared ginger sticks for grilled fish and ginger slices to accompany sushi. It is also clam-picking time on beaches, and along the rivers anglers are blessed with masu trout. Japanese strawberries are also available in early spring.

Summer

Early in May the season's new katsuo (bonito or skipjack tuna) arrives, and katsuo no tataki (seared and sliced katsuo sashimi with herbs and spices) is cherished at this time of the year. Other fish such as aji (scad or horse mackerel), kajiki (swordfish), suzuki (sea bass) and maguro (big-eye tuna) are all in shun, and best eaten as sashimi (raw fish thinly sliced).

Above: Fresh produce and dried goods at a local market in Tokyo.

New eda-mame (green beans in the pod) are just lightly boiled and served as an accompaniment to chilled beer during the hot summer. Ume (Japanese green apricots) become available from early June, which is the traditional month for *tsukemono* (pickling) in the cook's calendar. Rakkyo (Japanese bulb vegetable), umeboshi (dried and salted ume) and umeshu (ume liqueur) are all prepared for the coming year, or in the case of umeshu for consumption the following summer.

Autumn

In Japan, autumn never passes without either eating grilled (broiled) samma (saury) or at least smelling the aroma released as it is grilled by a neighbour. Salmon, mackerel and sea bream are also all in season; salmon is salted while the others are good for sashimi.

Aubergine (eggplant) is renowned as being so good that mothers-in-law hide it from their daughters-in-law. The king of mushrooms, matsutake, dominates during this season and is either cooked with rice or steamed in clear soup. Autumn is also a fruit season and in particular the beautiful Japanese persimmon, kaki, arrives in abundance.

Winter

The most famous winter fish of all must be fugu. So notoriously poisonous is this fish (just a hint of its liver can prove fatal), that a special license is required to handle it. Fugu-chiri (fugu hotpot) is the dish of the season along with anko-nabe (monkfish hotpot).

Shungiku (garland chrysanthemum), which is in *shun* at this time of the year, is a good accompaniment to hotpot dishes. The two popular Japanese vegetables, hakusai and daikon, are at their best in winter and are pickled in bulk for the coming months. Japanese citrus fruits, such as mikan (satsuma) and yuzu, are abundant and yuzu is even used in baths (chopped in half and added to the hot water – though quite a few are needed). Fishing for wakasagi (Japanese smelt) on ice-covered lakes is a favourite pastime among winter anglers.

REGIONAL FOODS AND DISHES

The regional foods and dishes vary greatly from Hokkaido, the northern island, to Kyushu, the southern island, so 'what's in season?' and 'what's the

Below: The Tokyo fish market deals with the largest volume of fish in the world. The Japanese consume 3,000 kinds of fish and shellfish every day.

Right: A fruit stall in a Tokyo market.

speciality here?' are inevitable questions every Japanese foodie asks wherever he or she goes. Local restaurants are the best places to taste regional variations though all local cuisines are represented in Tokyo and Osaka. The regions are so proud and eager to promote their speciality foods that they even produce their own versions of bento (packed lunch) using local produce, which are sold on the platforms of their mainline stations. These are called ekiben (station bento) and some of the famous ekiben are introduced below as a quick reference to the regional foods.

Hokkaido

Most of the seafood (crabs, oysters, squid, salmon, trout, herring, cod and konbu) come from here. Hokkaido is also the only place in Japan where sheep are reared, so ghengis khan-nabe (lamb barbecue) is a local speciality. Ramen, miso-ramen (ramen noodles in miso soup) in particular, was first developed in Sapporo, the capital of Hokkaido. Regional bento includes kani-meshi (crab rice) at Oshamanbe station, ezo-wappa (assorted Hokkaido specialities with rice) at Asahikawa, and ika-meshi (squid rice) at Mori.

The north of Honshu

From Akita and Niigata through to Toyama facing the Sea of Japan is Japan's treasured rice belt, which consequently produces some of the finest sake. The regional produce also includes various sansai (mountain vegetables) and the maitake mushroom of Akita. A hotpot dish called shottsuru using local fish called hata hata (sailfin sandfish) is Akita's winter speciality while wanko-soba (buckwheat soba served in mouthfuls) is a Morioka speciality. In Sendai there are fish products such as sasa kamaboko (ground fishcake wrapped in bamboo leaves) and nearby Mito is famous for its natto (fermented soya beans) production.

Regional ekiben examples include maitake-wappa (maitake mushroom on Akita komachi rice) at Akita station, sansai-kurimeshi (mountain vegetables and chestnuts with rice) at Morioka, gyu-meshi (beef rice) at Niigata and sake harako-meshi (salmon caviar on rice) at Sendai.

Tokyo and the central region

Japan's capital and the surrounding areas, known as Kanto, may no longer produce much agricultural produce but it is a culinary centre for regional foods and dishes. It has the finest restaurants,

not only of Japanese cuisine but also of other cooking traditions. Tokyo-style cooking tends to use more seasoning and shoyu than Osaka cuisine. Nigiri-zushi (finger sushi with a slice of raw fish on top) is a Tokyo speciality.

Shinshu, the central mountain region, is well known for its soba, wasabi, grapes and wine as well as eels from Lake Suwa, while Shizuoka, the coastal county facing the Pacific Ocean, produces tea and mikan (satsuma). Kama-meshi (nine local ingredients on top of tea rice in a pot) at Yokokawa is the most famous of all ekiben since it started the ekiben phenomenon in Japan some 50 years ago.

Kansai and the west

An area of great importance in culinary matters, Kansai includes both Osaka and Kyoto. The old capital, Kyoto, is considered the birthplace of Japanese cuisine and Osaka is now the culinary heart of Japan. The down-to-earth approach of the Osakans is most evident in their food.

Specialities include udon and udon-suki (shabu shabu, meaning beef and vegetable hotpot, with udon). In Kyoto there are many ryotei (old inn-style restaurants) in the most beautiful, tranquil surroundings, and yuba (dried tofu milk skin) is still produced by hand

Above: Mushrooms grow in abundance across Japan, and are an essential part of everyday cooking.

there. Kansai produces the best wa-gyu (beer-massaged Japanese beef), also known as Kobe or Matsuzaka beef, and other beef dishes such as sukiyaki (beef and vegetables cooked in sweet shoyu), shabu shabu and steak are specialities. In Kansai is a sukiyaki ekiben that has a unique device attached to the box to

automatically warm up the Kobe beef inside. Nagoya, the third largest city after Tokyo and Osaka, produces hatcho-miso (black miso), and kishimen (ribbon noodles) is a famous speciality.

The Kii peninsula, south of Osaka, produces tea and mikan. There are a few good somen eating places around there, while masu-zushi (trout sushi) at Toyama station and mehari-zushi (sushi wrapped in pickled mustard leaf) at Shingu are two of the oldest established ekiben in this region.

Shikoku and Kyushu

Fresh fish and shellfish are abundant all the year round in these two southern islands and Tosa-no tataki, lightly seared katsuo (skipjack tuna) sashimi, is a famous speciality of Shikoku. Various citrus fruits are also produced on these islands, while Kyushu is the largest shiitake producer in Japan. Kashiwa-meshi (chicken rice) at Hakata station, ko-dai sushi (small sea bream sushi) at Tokushima, anago-meshi (conger rice) at Takamatsu and tonkotsu bento (simmered black pork with rice) at Nishi Kagoshima are some of the best ekiben.

Below: A typical bustling, fruit and vegetable market in Ameyokocho Street, in the Ueno district of Tokyo.

COOKING AND EATING

The philosophy of Japanese cooking is to serve food that has retained as much of its natural flavour as possible. It is therefore essential to choose ingredients at their best – they should be very fresh and in their season. If the food needs to be cooked at all this is done for the minimum time possible. The Japanese cook belives that vegetables are best eaten raw or only very lightly cooked, to retain their crunchiness. Otherwise, they may be salted a little to draw out the cold water of the raw ingredient.

PREPARATION AND COOKING METHODS

The most important aspect of Japanese cooking lies in the preparation. As the food is eaten with hashi (chopsticks), it needs to be cut into bitesize pieces. Vegetables of various shapes and textures are cooked to the correct crunchy softness so that they will be appetizing as well as attractive. Fresh fish is almost always filleted and often thinly sliced to eat raw as sashimi. Meats are also thinly sliced most of the time or else minced (ground) meat is used.

If the food, especially vegetables, is to be cooked, it is always very lightly done to retain crispness. Cooking

Below: A diner in Tokyo's Ginza district with decorations of red lanterns.

methods include simmering, grilling (broiling), steaming and frying; roasting is not really part of the Japanese cuisine. Many fish and vegetable dishes involve griddling over a direct heat, but in modern houses this is not done due to the smoke produced, in which case pan-frying may be substituted. Japanese cooking also uses various pickling and marinating methods.

Above: A sumo wrestlers' hotpot restaurant in Tokyo, near the Sumo stadium and wrestlers' accommodation.

TYPICAL MEALS

The traditional Japanese breakfast is a substantial meal. It consists of a bowl of hot, freshly boiled rice, miso soup, thick omelette roll, pickled vegetables and grilled (broiled) small salted fish such as horse mackerel. Today, however, busy people, particularly the young, prefer Western-style ready-made foods such as bread, ham and cheese plus salad and fruits with tea or coffee.

For lunch, Japanese soba (buckwheat noodles), udon (flour noodles) and Chinese-style ramen (egg noodles) are very popular at home as well as in restaurants, while single-dish meals include a tonkatsu rice bowl, a *bento* (lunch) box or curry. Half the population of Japan is said to eat out every single day and lunch is the meal most people eat in restaurants rather than taking a lunch box, which are nowadays mostly made by the mother for her children.

Dinner at home in Japan is a rather casual affair, with each member of the family having a bowl of rice and miso soup probably with an individual main dish of either fish or meat. Two or three

other dishes such as simmered vegetables, marinated fish and pickles will be placed in the centre of the table for everyone to help themselves. Second servings of rice and soup are available, and fruit and green tea are always served to finish the meal.

MENU PLANNING

A formal Japanese banquet will start with hors d'oeuvres, clear soup and sashimi (thinly sliced raw fish) followed in turn by a grilled (broiled) dish, a steamed dish, a simmered dish and finally a deep-fried dish, accompanied by vinegared or dressed salads. The meal finishes with boiled rice, miso soup and pickles. All dishes are served individually on a tray. There are not many desserts in Japanese cuisine possibly because sugar is used in much of the savoury cooking. Also the vast

Left: Families often eat gathered round the kotatsu *(heated table).*

Below: Meal time at ryokan, *a Japanese old style inn. Each diner's food is served on an individual legged tray.*

Etiquette

It is a Japanese custom to hold your cup or glass when someone pours you a drink, and you are expected to return the courtesy.

The same pair of hashi (chopsticks) is used throughout the meal. When not in use, the hashi are left on a hashi rest if there is one. They should be laid close to you, neatly parallel to the edge of the table. Never stick them upright into the rice: the Japanese are rather superstitious and hashi standing vertically in rice reminds them of the incense sticks that stand in ashes at funerals. Never transfer food from one pair of hashi to another; at Japanese funerals, relatives of the deceased pick the human bones from the ashes and transfer them between themselves in this way.

amount of food eaten, over a number of courses, leaves little room for more by the end of the meal. Wagashi (Japanese cakes), which are eaten at tea time with green tea, are too sweet and heavy to eat after a meal, so fresh fruit and green tea usually end the lengthy banquet. Warmed sake is drunk during the meal until the rice is served.

At home a simpler traditional dinner will be served consisting of individual bowls of soup and boiled rice with at least three main dishes, each one cooked differently: for example, sashimi, a grilled dish and a simmered dish. They are placed in the centre of the table for all the family to serve themselves on to individual plates.

For dinner parties at home, a standard menu consists of a plate of hors d'oeuvres to accompany drinks (when a toast may be made) followed by a first course, the main dish and then bowls of rice and soup with some pickles. Sake or ordinary grape wine is not served after the rice has arrived. Fruit and green tea ends the meal.

DRINK

There have been many attempts in the West to find out which wine goes best with Japanese food, and some food and wine experts even claim Champagne best suits the cuisine. However, nothing really matches the mellow, delicate flavour of sake because it does not override the subtle nature of Japanese cuisine. Moreover, while wine may have been developed to complement the food, it was the other way round with sake. It is no exaggeration to claim that Japanese cuisine was developed together with, perhaps even for tasting with, sake.

The Japanese drink lager beer more than any other drink and often start a meal with a glass of ice-cold lager. The lager is usually followed by sake, which is drunk cold in summer and warm in winter, or by shochu (rough sake). A very alcoholic beverage, one of the more popular ways of drinking shochu is to dilute it with hot water and add an umeboshi (dried salted Japanese apricot) to it.

MENU IDEAS

The following are some traditional seasonal menu ideas.

Spring

Oshi-zushi (smoked-salmon pressed sushi
Wakatake-ni (simmered young bamboo shoots in dashi (fish stock))
Beef teriyaki with broccoli
Iridori (simmered assorted vegetables with chicken)
Rice cooked with peas and miso soup with clam and spring onions (scallions)
Assorted fresh fruit and green tea

Summer

Boiled eda-mame (green beans in their pods) with salt
Katsuo no tataki (seared and sliced katsuo sashimi with herbs and spices)
Yuan chicken with fine green beans
Plain boiled rice and miso soup with wakame (seaweed) and tofu
Fruit salad with kanten cubes and chilled mugicha tea

Autumn

Yakitori (grilled chicken)
Grilled aubergine (eggplant) with miso
Tempura
Plain boiled rice and clear soup with matsutake (or cep) mushrooms and somen noodles
Kaki (persimmon) and green tea

Right: Yakitori (grilled chicken)

Left: Saba-zushi (mackerel pressed sushi)

Winter

Shungiku goma-aé (edible chrysanthemum leaves with sesame dressing)
Saba no Tatsuta-agé (fried marinated mackerel fillets)
Sukiyaki (wafer-thin beef slices and assorted vegetables)
Plain boiled rice
Yokan (sweet aduki paste cake) and green tea

Sushi parties

The following are two typical menus for a sushi party, which would be easy and fun to try at home.

Sushi Party 1

Yakitori (grilled chicken)
Salad with Japanese-style dressing
Assorted sushi, such as saba-zushi (mackerel-pressed sushi) and three-colour nori-maki (nori seaweed sushi)
Fruit and green tea

Sushi Party 2

Tsukune (skewered minced (ground) chicken balls)
Salt-steamed kabocha squash
Temaki-zushi (hand-rolled sushi)
Assorted pickles
Fruit and green tea

FOOD OF KOREA

Korea has four distinct seasons and a well-developed agriculture, producing rich rice and diverse grains. Surrounded by sea, Korea is home to plenty of sea and marine products and its cuisine includes a variety of vegetables, chicken and meats as well. Most traditional foods are preserved and fermented for a certain period — producing greater flavours and nutrition.

Left: The magnificent Kyongbokkung Palace, Korea; **Above:** Ingredients used in Korean cooking

THE REGIONS OF KOREA

The remarkably varied terrain of Korea, with its craggy mountains in the east and tidal mud flats in the west, its cold, dry northern hills and humid, fruitful zone in the south, divides itself naturally into provinces along the natural boundaries of mountains and rivers. Until recently, cultural differences between these provinces were very marked and there was little interaction between the people from one side of the mountain peak and those on the other side. Regional variations in language and customs arose and were perpetuated through the ages, giving a subtle difference to the cuisine and food customs of these different parts of the country.

THE PROVINCES OF NORTH KOREA

North Korea is to some extent hidden from the West by the secretive Communist regime which has been in power since Korea was divided after the Second World War, and there have been rumours of great poverty and even food shortages despite its natural resources.

Below: Clusters of city apartment buildings are typical in Korea. Larger complexes have their own food stores.

Pyongan region

In the north-west of North Korea lies the province of Pyongan, which contains the capital city, Pyongyang. Much emphasis has been placed on new building in the capital and the government takes great pride in such massive developments as the gleaming

Above: Pyongyang Grand People's Study House is of monolithic proportions, with 600 rooms housing 30 million books.

metro system, wide new roads that remain largely empty, and the 'Grand People's Study House', a monumental educational establishment that dominates the city from a hilltop.

The Pyongan region is a land of flattish fields and river valleys in the west, with the River Chonchon, a major waterway, flowing right across the centre of the region. Farther east the remote, jagged mountain peaks rise above the plains and the climate is much cooler, with freezing winter temperatures during several weeks of the year.

The western side of the province is the agricultural centre of North Korea, where most of the food is grown in a traditional way handed down from centuries past. Rice is the main crop, but there is a variety of vegetables too, including cabbages, pumpkins, bell peppers and onions. All around the west coast the fishing fleets venture out into the teeming waters to catch carp, mullet and sardines, as well as shellfish such as clams, oysters and crabs.

Farther east the local industries are based on forestry and mining, and food has to be transported to these areas.

Hamgyong region

The Hamgyong province touches the border with Siberia and China at its northern end and descends down the east coast of Korea past the industrial city of Hamhung. This is mountainous country, with the peaks rising to over 2,500m (8,200ft) to the west and forming a natural boundary which would have been very difficult to pass through before modern technologies. Hot springs gush forth from this rocky country, and spas have formed around them to make use of the medicinal qualities of the water.

It is a province of heavy industry based on mining and construction, as well as making plastics and machinery in the many factories on the east coast. Naturally, as the province snakes down the coastline, fishing is the other main occupation, but here the fish are different from those caught in Pyongan province to the west – cod, mackerel and turbot abound in the colder, fresher eastern waters, as well as seafood such as octopus and a regional delicacy, wakame seaweed, which is also popular in Japan just across the sea.

The province also has its own very popular speciality fish, known as myongtae, which is dried and then used in many favourite Korean recipes throughout the country.

Hwanghae region

The Hwanghae province forms the southernmost part of North Korea, located just below Pyongan province, on the western side of the country. This area is one of lush plains with fertile fields growing rice and cereals, as well as vegetables, apples and other fruits; the Hwanghae region is blessed with mild temperatures that are ideal for agriculture. Many types of vegetables, fruits, grains and rice are grown in this region.

Once again fishing forms a major part of the region's industry and therefore its cuisine. Clams and oysters, eel and salmon, laver and kelp form part of the sea's rich harvest, all of which are key ingredients in favourite Korean dishes.

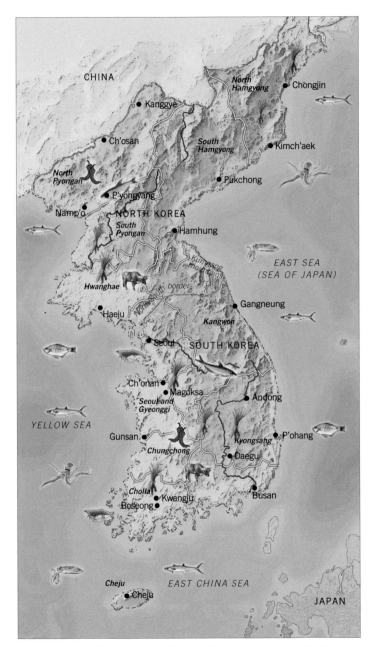

Above: The land of North and South Korea is 30 per cent arable, half of which is rice cultivation; other key crops include herbs, spices and chillies.

THE PROVINCES OF SOUTH KOREA

South Korea is of a similar size geographically to the North, but the similarities end there. The country has embraced Western capitalism with fervour, which means that many of its people now work in manufacturing and service industries rather than as agricultural labourers or fishermen.

Seoul and Gyeonggi region

The capital region of South Korea contains the thriving, ever-growing city of Seoul, where over 10 million people are packed into a small area of flat land encircled by mountains. Smaller cities have sprung up around the capital, making this region the most economically vibrant area of Korea.

Seoul is a city near the west coast, relying for its prosperity on administration and the head-office functions of Korean firms such as Samsung and LG. This means that over 6 million people commute to work in the city daily, causing a problem of traffic congestion and air pollution which the government is working to relieve.

Kangwon region

To the east of Seoul lies the province of Kangwon, which borders the East Sea and faces Japan over the water.

Above: A woman sells laver bread at a market at Yeosu, on the south-western tip of Korea.

Once again, mountains run from north to south through the province, dividing it into eastern and western Kangwon. This is an area that used to rely mainly on mining for its prosperity, but competition from abroad has led to a decline in this industry and the area now suffers from a significant depopulation – the whole province contains less than 2 million people, or under a fifth of the population of Seoul.

Agriculture in this region is mostly concerned with cattle rearing on ranches, and deforestation has been a problem as the land is cleared for this purpose. Beer barley is a favourite crop, and brewing is becoming one of the area's major industries.

A serious food culture
The people of the Seoul and Gyeonggi region are very hardworking and industrious, and this includes their attitude to food – it's a major interest and passion for many people. Not only do they take great care in preparing traditional dishes for the evening meal; the nightlife in Seoul also encourages the consumption of tasty snacks bought from street vendors while strolling through the shopping and entertainment areas after work.

Above: Seoul's street vendors sell a tantalizing array of delicious foods. These tend to be eaten as snacks, rather than full meals.

Chungchong region

This province is located just south of the city of Seoul and benefits hugely, economically speaking, from its proximity to the buzzing, lively capital of Korea. The land is reasonably flat, especially in the south of the region, and as a result farmers are able to grow crops such as rice and corn, as well as raise cattle for both milk and meat. Ginseng, garlic and tobacco are grown too, farther inland on the hilly slopes. Unusually for Korea, a dramatic 75 per cent of the population of this region are involved in farming and food production.

Transportation links are good from the countryside to the city, building an effective infrastructure that means the huge and growing urban population can buy fresh food, which they are unable to grow themselves in densely populated Seoul and other cities. New industries have grown up along the coast, reflecting the rising prosperity of the region, but there is still room for traditional fishing in the warm seas, and the locals are particularly fond of oysters, clams and other seafood.

Cholla region

A long and intricate coastline dominates this province in the south-west of Korea. It includes the far western and southern coasts of Korea, where many tiny inlets and small islands divide the low-lying land from the sea. It is a fertile land, like the Chungchong region, and similar crops are grown here, including rice, sweet potatoes and tobacco, and is now also being reclaimed from the sea for agricultural and industrial use.

Tourism is another major industry in Cholla province, growing fast in recent years. Tourists are attracted to the area to take part in water sports such as diving and fishing, and for the constantly warm temperatures, both on the coast and in inland areas where there are several beautiful lakes and rivers full of fish.

Kyongsang region

Farther round the southern tip of Korea to the east lies Kyongsang province, which is another area of rocky coastline with inland rivers and mountains rising above the coastal plains. Unlike Cholla province, the Kyongsang region contains several bustling major cities which have grown up along the eastern seaboard, including Busan and Daegu, the second and third cities of South Korea. Regional dialects and customs

Above: Persimmons are hung up to dry in South Kyongsang province. Once dried the persimmons, or kkotgam, are a traditional winter delicacy.

have persisted here despite the pace of 21st-century life, as the mountains to the north and west prevented fast, reliable communications until comparatively recently. The Racktong river flows majestically through the centre of the region, leaving flat fertile land in the gentle valleys, with fields of rice as far as the eye can see. Many other crops are grown, including the ubiquitous garlic, tobacco and red chilli peppers. On the southern edge of the Kyongsang province the climate is warm and humid for most of the year, and this provides ideal conditions for growing oranges, watermelons and ginseng.

KOREAN ISLANDS

The seas around the southern and western edges of South Korea are liberally sprinkled with small islands, some of which are inhabited, while others are excellent wild habitats for all kinds of animals and birds. The fishing waters around and between the islands are well stocked with a huge variety of seafood.

Left: Shellfish is prepared at Yongduam (dragon head) rock on Cheju, South Korea's largest island.

Cheju region

Located off the southern coast of Korea, Cheju is the biggest of the thousands of islands in this region. This volcanic rock rises from the sea around South Korea's biggest mountain, Halla-san, some 1,950m (6,400ft) high. The isolation of Cheju island from the mainland has led to many fascinating customs, including the carving of a very impressive 'stone grandfather' (*dol hareubang*) out of lava. The tradition survives that the women of Cheju are the head of the family, and earn a living as free divers for abalone and conch shells.

The generally mild temperatures (a mixture of continental and oceanic climates) and beautiful and dramatic landscape have established Cheju as a popular tourist destination these days, and it offers a variety of sporting activities, ranging from hiking in the mountains to horse riding and swimming. The climate is warm nearly all the year round, an ideal temperature for growing fruit, and oranges, tangerines and pineapples flourish in groves among the volcanic rocks. Fresh fish and shellfish abound in the region and lucky visitors may find them for sale on the beach just minutes after they have been caught.

HISTORICAL INFLUENCES

Korea has always been a crossroads of cultures, absorbing the influences of the surrounding countries while developing a distinct national identity.

From the middle of the 1st century BC Korea began to develop as a recognizable country. This was the beginning of the era of the Three Kingdoms: Koguryo, Paekje and Silla. The kingdoms fought among themselves for dominance until the end of the 7th century, when Silla defeated the other two, with Chinese aid, and unified the peninsula under central rule.

MONGOLIAN AND CHINESE INFLUENCE

The southern migration of Mongolian tribes to Korea in the 1st century BC from Manchuria (now China) brought great changes, in cultural and agricultural terms. The shamanistic beliefs of the Mongols were adopted by the Koreans, as were their cultivation techniques. The Mongols taught the Korean people how to farm the plains, raise cattle and grow crops, and this influenced the country's cuisine, which then started to move away from a predominantly seafood-based diet.

The origins of the Korean tofu and vegetable casserole chungol can be traced back to Mongolia. The Koreans adapted the recipes of migrating Mongol tribes from the north, using local

ingredients to produce regional variations in which the flavours were carefully matched to accompanying dishes.

THE INFLUENCE OF BUDDHISM

At the end of the 7th century Korea entered a long stable period based on Buddhist culture. This had a great effect on the nation's gastronomy, as the slaughtering of animals was prohibited under Buddhist principles.

Diets changed with this dramatic reduction in the consumption of meat, and vegetables took on a much more

Above: The influence of Buddhism in Korea led to the elevated importance of vegetables, over meat, in Korean food.

significant role. Temple meals consisted of soup, rice and vegetable dishes, and omitted strong-smelling ingredients, such as garlic or spring onions (scallions). This influence is still apparent in the namul vegetable dishes of modern Korea, and the technique of marinating in soy sauce, rice vinegar and sesame seeds has barely changed. Interestingly, the simple porridge and vegetable dishes of the Buddhist monks have found a new popularity with today's health-conscious citizens.

CONFUCIANISM

The Buddhist culture flourished into the Koryo dynasty (935–1392). However, although the monks still wielded some influence, the kings of the Koryo dynasty adopted a Chinese governmental approach, which brought the influence of Confucianism to the country and incidentally led to more meat eating.

Towards the end of the Koryo dynasty the Mongols took control of Korea and ruled for around 100 years, before being ousted by General Yi Seong-Gye, who seized political and military power and, in 1392, established the amazingly long-lived Chosun (Yi) dynasty, which ruled for over 500 years until 1910. Confucianism became the

Above: A group of novice Buddhist monks in Seoul, aged between 5 and 7, sheltering from the rain after a head shaving ceremony to celebrate Buddha's birthday.

Above: A Confucian temple in South Korea. Based on the teachings of a Chinese sage, Confucianism is based around the importance of morality, and the cultivation of the civilized individual. The philosophy has had a significant influence on Korea.

state creed, and the Chinese influence steadily took hold, heralding a new era in the national cuisine.

CHINESE INGREDIENTS

Closer ties with China meant that a wide range of spices and seasonings became available, an important driving influence in determining flavour trends. Black pepper and vinegar, molasses and rice wine were now enjoyed by many Koreans.

Tofu was another Chinese ingredient that had a tremendous impact when introduced to Korea. Its ubiquity in Korean cooking, and versatility in different dishes, has meant it is now more popular in Korea than in its native China. Many other dishes from China were introduced after the Korean War, with Chinese restaurants becoming very popular. However, over the past five decades their recipes have been adapted to create popular dishes that are distinctly Korean in their use of local ingredients and spices.

JAPANESE RULE

The Japanese asserted their authority over their neighbours in the 19th and 20th centuries, attempting to impose by the use of force their own religion and education system, and even the adoption of Japanese names by the Koreans. The Koreans fought back with their own independence movement, and after the Second World War, gained freedom from the Japanese.

However, the period of Japanese colonial rule brought many different ingredients to Korea, including the maki roll, sashimi and udon noodles. While the preparation and cooking methods have remained the same as in Japan, the choice of sauces and spices gives a uniquely Korean taste to these dishes, and these adaptations have travelled back to Japan where they are becoming increasingly popular.

THE SEPARATION OF NORTH AND SOUTH

Since the division of Korea into North and South in 1953, after the Korean War, the country has been physically divided by a DMZ (De-Militarized Zone) roughly along the 38th parallel, and the North has withdrawn into isolation from the rest of the world, while the South has enthusiastically embraced the technology and industry of the 21st-century world.

The Korean barbecue

The Chinese had developed sophisticated techniques for seasoning and cooking meat, mostly derived from the Mongolian use of the barbecue. This was hugely influential in Korean cooking and they adopted the principles while retaining their own traditions. Meat was seasoned and cooked on the barbecue, and then wrapped in vegetable leaves to provide complex flavours and help to create meals that were nutritionally balanced. Documents from this era refer to this style of meal: 'In the springtime the wind carries the irresistible scent of wild vegetables over the mountain and the Koryo people enjoy meat with fresh green leaves.' This concept of wrapping meat in green leaves influenced the Chinese in their turn, and seafood wrapped in lettuce leaves remains a popular dish in both China and Korea today.

Above: The traditional ceremonial dress of the Confucianist village of Chunghak-dong, in South Korea.

FESTIVALS AND CELEBRATIONS

As in many other Asian countries, delicious seasonal dishes and beverages are enjoyed during festivals throughout the year. Exciting and elaborate recipes are an integral part of Korean celebrations, from the spicy drinks associated with New Year to the hot chicken stew made to fortify the body against the great heat of the summer.

Religious festivals are now less widely observed in this predominantly secular society, but there are many occasions such as weddings and birthdays when family and friends celebrate together.

SEASONAL FESTIVALS

Korea's agricultural society has always been well aware of the importance of the changing seasons, and this is reflected in time-honoured festivals that celebrate these transitions in nature with food and drink and much merrymaking.

New Year

February is the time the lunar New Year is celebrated, and during this period Koreans enjoy sujunggwa, a spiced punch made with dried persimmons and cinnamon. During this celebration they remember their departed ancestors, and revere their elders with a formal bow.

The traditional meal for this day is a soup called tteokguk, where long strips of rice cake (flavoured with the aromatic herb, wormwood) float in a clear beef broth. It is said that you cannot become another year older without eating a bowl of tteokguk. Another New Year's feast-day dish is the fragrant beef stew, galbi tang.

Above: South Korean Buddhists in traditional costume with lanterns at a parade to celebrate the birthday of Buddha on 15 May.

First Full Moon Day

In springtime Koreans celebrate the First Full Moon Day, which is known as *Jeongwol Daeboreum*. On this day they perform a series of rituals to help prevent bad luck throughout the forthcoming 12 months, waking at dawn to drink rice wine and crack walnuts while praying for good health over the coming year. The two favourite dishes for *Jeongwol Daeboreum* are ogokbap, a recipe of steamed rice mixed with five other grains, and mugeun namul, which is a medley of vegetable dishes such as mushrooms, radish leaves and steamed shoots of young ferns.

Buddha's birthday

The birthday of Buddha on 15 May is a day of celebration and a national holiday. Every temple is decorated with colourful lanterns and holds a special ceremony. In Seoul there is a weeklong festival, the first day with a lantern parade stretching for several kilometers through the heart of Seoul, leading up to the day itself, where religious ceremonies in the morning are followed by a street fair.

Above: The traditional Korean New Year's Day celebration is a formal occasion, which includes ceremonial prayers and food.

Right: October's Silla festival hosts an array of traditional dancing, music, and religious ceremonies as a celebration of Korean history and culture.

The festival of *Sambok*

At the height of summer the three hottest days are celebrated at the Festival of *Sambok*. Called *Chobok*, *Jungbok* and *Malbok*, these days are held in honour of the beginning, middle and end of the lunar calendar's hottest period. The classic dish that is eaten at *Sambok* is samgyetang, which is a soup containing a whole chicken stuffed with rice, ginseng and red dates. These strong-tasting ingredients are believed to boost stamina, and also to give the population the energy to withstand the blazing heat of this time of year.

The festival of *Chuseok*

In the autumn Koreans hold a day of harvest thanksgiving called *Chuseok*. On this day they visit their ancestors' graves to give thanks for a plentiful harvest, and to pray for the well-being of their loved ones. Crescent-shaped rice cakes (songpyeon) are eaten with a taro soup (torantang). The songpyeon are stuffed with beans, nuts and seeds, and then presented at the ancestral memorial service, along with fruit from the harvest.

The festival of *Donji*

The winter solstice of *Donji* towards the end of December is the final festival of the year in Korea. This is the shortest day of the year, and a herald of the bitterly cold weather that will follow for several months. On this day patjuk is eaten, a red bean porridge that contains balls of rice. For Koreans the colour of this dish is of particular significance, as it is an ancient belief that red will drive away evil spirits and ward off bad luck. By eating this porridge on *Donji* a long-held tradition claims that the whole family will then be kept safe from harm throughout the bleak and frosty winter months that follow.

Right: South Korean dancers performing the 'O-go Mu' dance at a festival to celebrate the New Year.

Left: The bride pours wine for the groom, a traditional part of the North Korean wedding banquet.

Wedding sweets

The bride will offer date sweets, made of whole red dates dipped in sugar syrup and rolled in sesame seeds, to her new husband and his family. These are linked in chains and presented on a lacquer platter to her guests, who return the compliment by throwing some of the dates over the couple, just as people in the West throw confetti or rice.

WEDDINGS AND BIRTHDAYS

As well as festivals to mark the passing year, Koreans enjoy many other celebrations that involve some fragrant and unusual dishes. Weddings and birthdays are particular favourites and are a great chance for families and friends to get together and socialize over a celebratory meal.

The wedding feast

On the day of a traditional wedding in Korea, a grand banquet is held to commemorate the event. Ceremonial tables are filled with drinks and laid items that have great significance for the bride and groom. The importance of these two people on this day is reflected in pairs of utensils and foods: for example, two vases filled with bamboo accompany two lit candles, and a brace of chicken is included to symbolize integrity. There are also two bowls filled with rice to ensure wealth, along with red dates, chestnuts and gingko nuts to guarantee their descendants' prosperity. None of these is intended to be eaten by the guests or wedding party; they are part of the complex ritual that surrounds wedding celebrations in Korea.

The wedding banquet itself is usually a plentiful and extravagant affair, with a great number of different small dishes served to the family and guests. Among these the most traditional and popular is a bowl of noodles served in broth, which is imbued with particular significance. In Korea the eating of noodles is associated with a long life. During the centuries of the Koryo and Chosun eras these noodle dishes were reserved for the upper classes. The inclusion of noodles on the tables of festivals and celebrations reflects both the promise of a long and happy life

Above: The bridegroom and his retinue as he travels to the ceremony.

Above: A wedding in Seoul. A traditional marriage used elaborate rituals, including ceremonial bowing and gifts, but most modern-day ceremonies are much simpler.

Right: A festival to celebrate the birthday of North Korea's leader, Kim Jong II.

and the status of enjoying a dish traditionally reserved for the elite. For a wedding this is seen as a signifier of the good health and long lives of the bride and groom, and also of the eternal bond of their marriage.

The thin noodle somyun is also particularly associated with the wedding table, to the extent that the question 'Where can I have somyun noodles?' is often used to imply that the person enquiring is getting married.

The influence of the elaborate style of cuisine favoured by the imperial court can also be seen in gujeolpan, a dish often made for weddings which consists of many different kinds of meat and vegetables with tiny thin pancakes, carefully arranged and served on a special divided plate.

Birthday celebrations: the first year of life

Another occasion surrounded with traditional rituals, a birthday often involves a symbolic celebratory meal. Before a child even reaches their first birthday, a small festival is celebrated on the 100th day after their birth and a simple meal consisting of rice cakes is prepared. This is a tradition that has survived from a much older era when disease took the lives of many children before this date, making it an important milestone for those that survived.

1st birthday rice cakes

A favourite Korean custom involves sharing rice cakes made for a child's first birthday party with 100 people to ensure that the child will live to a venerable age. Rice cakes are even mailed to friends and distant relations who are unable to attend the celebrations in person. The recipients then mail back lengths of thread to the baby, expressing the hope of longevity, and grains of rice, symbolizing future wealth.

While this celebration remains popular, it is now less important than the child's first birthday, called *Dol* in Korea. On this day a ritual meal is prepared, with offerings of rice and soup made to the spirits in gratitude for having kept the mother and child safe from harm. The family and friends then enjoy a glass of rice wine, accompanied by rice cakes and red bean cakes sweetened with honey, to celebrate the child's first birthday. To ensure the continued well-being of the child, and to bring them good luck and joy, red bean cakes are also placed as offerings at the four compass points within the house.

Birthday celebrations: the 60th year

The 60th birthday, which is known as *Hwangop*, is another important festival in Korean culture, as it marks the day when a person has completed the zodiacal cycle. Observed with an extravagant feast, this is a time of great celebration, and reflects the fact that in times gone by comparatively few individuals lived to be 60. This made it all the more important to mark the occasion.

On *Hwangop* the grown-up children traditionally honour their parents with a grand banquet and then propose a toast to their longevity. There is much eating and drinking and merrymaking, although in recent times this has begun to resemble a more Western celebration, with the addition of a birthday cake. However, one dish is still eaten in accordance with the old traditions: a bowl of seaweed soup. This is the same kind of soup that is traditionally given to women just after childbirth, as it is believed that the minerals in the soup help to improve circulation and restore the stamina of new mothers. Eating this dish on one's birthday celebrates birth and also honours the role of the mother.

The few Koreans who made it to their 70th birthday in centuries gone by would have been honoured with another feast on this special day which was known as *Koh-cui*, meaning old and rare. A very similar pattern of celebration with a banquet took place as for *Hwangop*, the 60th birthday. Nowadays many more Koreans reach the milestone of 70 and so enjoy another grand-scale party.

KOREAN CUISINE

The cuisine of Korea is truly the undiscovered gem of Asian cooking: a treasure trove of exotic scents and flavours. Despite the cross-cultural exchanges with China and Japan, and the significant influence they have both had on the evolution of Korean cuisine, it remains quite distinct from either. The cuisines of all the countries share the balance of salty, bitter, hot, sweet and sour – the 'five flavours' – but cooking techniques and ingredients create a marked culinary difference between the three.

THE SPECIALITIES OF KOREA

In Korea, certain key flavours such as garlic, ginger and soy sauce lend themselves to common preparation techniques such as pickling or grilling (broiling). Then there are the signature dishes, such as kimchi (pickled vegetables, often cabbage), bulgogi (barbecued meat or fish) and namul (vegetable side dishes).

One might expect the Koreans to stir-fry in a wok like the Chinese, or eat ingredients raw like the Japanese, as these characteristics would be consistent with their geographical proximity. However, the Koreans have developed their own methods of

cooking, including preservation techniques that give their cuisine a unique array of flavours.

From mild rice dishes and delicate soups, through to pickled vegetables and fiery seafood stews, there is something wonderfully mysterious about the taste of Korean food. Whereas the flavours in Chinese and Thai dishes are easily identifiable, Korean cooking blends fresh and preserved ingredients to create complex tastes. In Korea there is also a

Above: The method of making kimchi varies greatly from region to region, but it always contains fermented vegetables.

generosity of spirit and a desire to share and please, which characterize the experience of eating.

CHARACTERISTIC FLAVOURS

As in Japan, rice, pickles and meat or fish form the basis of the diet. However, the spices and marinades are distinctive

Above: A fish stall in Gonju, in the Gyeonggi region of South Korea.

Above: Korean soups vary from light, highly flavoured broths in summer to substantial stews laden with fish or meat, rice and vegetables in winter months.

to Korea. Food is predominantly
seasoned with the traditional key
flavours of garlic, ginger, soy sauce,
spring onions (scallions) and sesame
oil, plus the careful use of sugar and
rice vinegar. The Koreans are the
greatest consumers of garlic in the
whole of Asia. Delicious spice pastes
are used in many dishes with either the
fermented soya bean paste, doenjang,
or the ubiquitous gochujang, red chilli
paste, providing the foundation of a
multitude of recipes.

Koreans tend to make a
combination of freshly prepared and
preserved foods for each meal, rather
than preparing just one main dish.
The strong taste of Korean food
originates both from their love of
pungent flavours, and from the
preservation techniques that allow
those flavours to develop and intensify.

In addition Koreans make use of
ingredients in different ways to their
neighbours; for example, sesame seeds
are always toasted before being added
to cooking, to emphasize their nutty
flavour. By enhancing certain flavours,
and mixing fresh and pickled tastes,
Korea has found a culinary identity
unlike any other in Asia.

With globalization and the influence
of the Western food industry, Korean
cuisine is evolving at a dramatic rate.
However, despite these multicultural
influences, the basic diet remains the
same as it has for centuries.

SEASONAL CONTRASTS

Like other countries in the temperate
zone, such as Japan, Korea has four
distinct seasons. Spring brings countless

hours of sunshine, gentle breezes and
azure skies. In summer the weather
becomes hot and humid, with heavy
monsoon rains from late June. Autumn is
dry and cloudless, with plenty of sunlight,
followed by the arctic air of winter,
bringing bitterly cold, dry weather and
some snow to the region.

Each of these four seasons provides a
variety of ingredients for the Korean
kitchen, and certain dishes are traditional
at particular times of year. On the hottest
days of summer, for example, Koreans
eat samgyetang, a soup made with

*Above: After rice, garlic is the second-
largest cash crop in Korea, most of
which is grown in the south-west.*

chicken, red dates and ginseng, as it is
said to provide vitality and stamina to
survive the heat. Similarly, kimchi, the
pickled vegetable dish, is a staple food
through the long, harsh winters when
fresh vegetables are scarce. Korean
cuisine embraces the seasonal variety of
its ingredients, and blends the food of the
sea, the field and the mountain, reflecting
a diverse and bountiful terrain.

THE INTRODUCTION OF RICE

Rice proved itself early in the country's history as a staple ingredient for the Korean diet. It grows well in the varying climate, and its inviting taste and the ease with which it could be cooked also had a great effect on the cuisine. Rice became an essential feature of most meals, adopting the same role as bread in the West, and played a major part in establishing the Korean style of eating. It was served as the foundation of the meal, and around this began to grow the idea of cooking a number of small accompanying dishes of soup, meat, vegetables and seafood. Having rice at every meal, and in many dishes, also helped to form the Koreans' sociable way of eating, with each diner partaking freely of any dish on the table.

THE CHILLI PEPPER

Another revolutionary event in Korean culinary history was the introduction of the chilli pepper in the 16th century. In 1592 and 1597 the Japanese invaded Korea, but they were eventually beaten off in 1598 with help from the Chinese.

Below: The heat of chillies is intrinsic to Korean cooking, but their fire is just one element of this multi-layered cuisine.

Catholic priests from Portugal travelled with the Japanese troops and brought the chilli plants and seeds with them from the New World – a long round trip from South America to Asia, via Europe. Prior to this, spiciness had been imparted with the Chinese Sichuan peppercorn, but Korean cooks were wholeheartedly seduced by the flavour and heat of the chilli pepper.

The Koreans adored spicy food, and created gochujang, a red chilli paste that has become a basic ingredient in every Korean kitchen. Countless dishes were built upon its fiery kick, and traditional techniques for preserving

Above: North Korean women harvesting rice at a farm in Uiji county, North Pyongan province.

vegetables were brought to life with its strong, pungent flavour. Koreans believe that red is a colour which offers protection from the devil, and this may also have had a bearing on the all-pervading use of gochujang in their cooking.

HEALTHY EATING

Since the 17th century the Koreans have been increasingly preoccupied with food and health. Various documents were written at that time on

Royal court cuisine

Imperial cuisine is a tradition kept alive by a few restaurants in Korea, mainly in Seoul, where the super-wealthy go to enjoy an expensive meal of meticulously prepared dishes, balancing warm and cold, spicy and mild, soft and crisp, solid and liquid, and a range of colours, all of which may take hours or days to prepare. Even the serving dishes are carefully chosen to reflect the colours or shapes of the food. Although this is not a daily experience for most Koreans, the aim of a careful balance in their food is kept alive through a simpler mixture of the staple dish, rice, and a selection of side dishes (banchan).

*Right: Dried roots, seeds, flowers,
fruit, herbs and fungi on display at
the Herbal Medicine Market, in
Yangnyeong, Seoul.*

the subject of farming and horticulture,
and new ingredients were introduced in
an effort to promote a balanced diet.

Sweet potatoes, for example, were
brought from Japan in the 18th century
to help stave off famine, and quickly
became a common ingredient. These
potatoes were not only eaten as a
vegetable, they were also made into
noodles, known as dangmyun, which
are still found uniquely in Korea.

Modern Korean cuisine is rich in
seafood, vegetables and grains, and
always provides generous amounts of
protein and fibre. Most dishes have a
moderate number of calories and are
low in fat, making for a healthy and
well-balanced diet.

FOOD AS MEDICINE

The Koreans recognize medicinal
qualities in a wide variety of their foods
and beverages, and also use
seasonings and spices as an effective
treatment for certain ailments. A daily
dose of either sea kelp or carrot juice,
for example, is recommended for those
suffering from high blood pressure,
whereas an increased intake of
seaweed or vinegar is considered as an
excellent measure to help prevent a
heart attack. Asthmatics are

recommended Asian pears, apricot
kernels and extracts from the leaves
of gingko trees.

The heavily mountainous region in the
east encourages the growth of culinary
and medicinal herbs and plants. The
country is the world's largest producer of
ginseng, a sweet, liquorice-flavoured root
that has been credited with being
everything from an aphrodisiac to a
restorative. Ginseng is used to make a
renowned Korean tea thought to provide
enhanced stamina, and to help high
blood pressure. Angelica, a peppery
herb with edible leaves and roots, and
wormwood, a bitter, aromatic herb, also
grow abundantly on the high-altitude
slopes, and are used in Korean
temple cooking and for the treatment
of certain illnesses.

THE HARMONY OF OPPOSITES

One of the fundamental principles of
Eastern philosophy is that of the two
universal opposing forces of yin and
yang. This concept has a strong
influence on Koreans' thinking and

*Left: Fermented soya bean cake for sale
at the Herbal Medicine Market in
Yangnyeong, Seoul.*

their approach to cooking, and is
reflected in the ingredients selected
by chefs when preparing dishes with
the intention of achieving harmony in
flavour, colour and presentation.
Traditional Korean cooking – from the
dishes of the royal court to simple
family meals – uses green, red, yellow,
white and black ingredients in equal
amounts, to ensure evenness in the
diet and to reflect the theory of the
five elements from traditional Chinese
philosophy: wood, fire, earth, metal
and water. The dishes will also have
harmonizing yin and yang values: hot
and spicy yang foods stimulate the
body, whereas cool yin foods calm and
nourish the system. Neutral foods are a
balance of yin and yang. The perfect
meal will contain yang dishes to heat
up the body and yin dishes to cool
down the brain.

So Korean cooking is an enticing
fusion of flavours and textures, mixing
dishes from the simple vegetarian fare
of Buddhist monks with those from the
banqueting tables of kings. Various
cultural influences combine ingredients
and techniques in fascinating ways,
creating perhaps unfamiliar, but
delectable meals.

EATING TRADITIONS AND ETIQUETTE

Left: Villagers enjoy a traditional Korean meal which is accompanied by soju, *a distilled grain liquor.*

Left: Villagers enjoy a traditional Korean meal which is accompanied by soju, *a distilled grain liquor.*

(broiled) meat or fish dish is traditionally accompanied by rice, soup and salad, along with a selection of pickled vegetables, or kimchi. The dishes will reflect a range of preparation techniques as well as different ingredients – maybe steamed rice, a simmered casserole of vegetables or fish, and a piece of meat quickly grilled. Sometimes the Koreans eat raw fish dishes, rather like Japanese sushi.

The main dishes are shared between all the diners. Because of this style of eating there is a real spirit of fellowship when dining Korean-style, and this is accentuated by the common practice of cooking food on a gas or charcoal grill at the table, giving mealtimes an inviting, domestic feel.

While the idea of sharing an abundance of small dishes is the same as the Spanish tapas style of dining, the Korean approach requires all the dishes to complement each other. To this end, the recipes of certain dishes will be altered depending on the other dishes being served so that all the elements work in harmony with each other.

All Korean meals are designed to include a harmonious assortment of dishes, and to enjoy the experience of Korean dining fully this is the perfect approach. When you are preparing any of the recipes in this book you should choose a number of dishes – maybe three or four – of contrasting texture and colour, and varying in taste, and serve them together with a dish of rice and a bowl of soup for each person. You will then be sampling a Korean evening meal as it would be eaten in many family homes throughout the peninsula, from a farmhouse in the chilly northern mountains to a high-rise apartment in the bustling cities of the south.

A VARIETY OF TASTES

A typical Korean meal will have a selection of small dishes, rather than a single main dish for each person, and all the food is served together rather than as different courses. A grilled

Traditional Korean dining

Although there is no prescribed order for eating the many dishes served at a traditional meal, many Koreans like to start with a small taste of soup before then sharing the other dishes among themselves. The formation of menus will vary depending on the number of dishes and the occasion, from a mere three or four for an informal family supper to many exotic and glamorous dishes at major celebrations for weddings, special birthdays and festivals.

Right: Koreans taking tea in a tea house. A low table and floor seating is the traditional practice.

Left: Restaurant diners in Seoul. The barbecue hot plate is a standard feature, along with a range of side dishes.

DRINKING

Korean cuisine includes both alcoholic and non-alcoholic drinks, and there are many traditional varieties of both available to drink with meals or snacks or simply as a thirst-quenching brew.

Non-alcoholic drinks

Koreans tend to drink mainly water or boricha, a tea brewed from roasted barley, with their meals. Green tea is also very popular; this is a drink that was introduced with the rise of Buddhism in the 7th century as an indispensable part of temple ceremonies. During the Koryo dynasty (918–1392) tea became popular among the upper classes and nobility, too, even finding a place in the rituals of the royal court.

Alcoholic drinks

Koreans also drink a wide range of alcoholic beverages including the local wine, chungju, a variety of domestically brewed beers, and makgoli, a potent milky-white rice drink. However, the most famous drink in Korea is *soju*, a rough rice wine with a fearsome kick, which was traditionally distilled in Buddhist monasteries. The popularity of soju cannot be overestimated, and no Korean meal is really complete without a glass of this potent liquor.

Drinking etiquette

In the past, Korean drinking was steeped in convention and ceremony, to show respect to drinking companions. Over time these traditions have relaxed, although there are some basic rules by which Koreans still abide. One of these is to allow an older person to sit at the most respected seat at the table, which is the one that is closest to the fireplace or with the best view of the entrance.

Koreans will never pour their own drinks; they believe it is courteous for their companion to pour for them. Both hands are used to receive a drink, and it is more important to accept the drink than actually to drink it; declining the first glass is considered terribly impolite, and it is better to accept the glass and simply touch it against the lips than to refuse it entirely.

The correct amount to drink is a matter of some debate in Korea, and tastes have become more bacchanalian in recent years. However, the traditional wisdom is summed up by an old saying, which translates as 'Don't stop after one glass; three glasses is lacking, five glasses is proper and seven glasses is excessive.'

Below: A traditional Korean tea ceremony in Seoul, South Korea, forming part of a wedding celebration.

TABLE SETTINGS

The classic Korean table setting is one of the most impressive aspects of Korean cuisine and is quite unique, both in its selection of dishes and in its form of presentation. As in other Asian countries, an individual bowl of soup and a dish of rice are provided for every person dining. However, what sets the Korean table distinctively apart from its Asian neighbours is the fact that all the dishes are served simultaneously rather than as one course after another.

The table setting is seen as an important element to enjoying Korean cuisine, and allows dishes to complement one another in terms of flavour while maintaining a nutritional balance. Table settings are normally defined by the main dish, except in the case of ceremonial meals.

THE *BANSANG* TABLE

The most common table setting is based around the serving of a bowl of rice as the main dish, known in Korean as

Right: The Korean bansang *setting consists of a main dish, a rice bowl and sauces with a number of side dishes, or* chups, *ranging from three to 12. This one shows a three-chup setting.*

Above: A table setting for a wedding celebration, with cutlery and glasses provided for each stage of the meal.

bansang or bapsang. Directly translated, ban or bap means cooked rice and *sang* means table, and this form holds true for other table settings. If the main dish served were based on noodles, myun in Korean, then the table setting would be *myunsang*, or 'noodle table'. There are also more elaborate table settings that are defined by an occasion, for instance weddings, birthdays or anniversaries, but these are lavish and have much more sophisticated rules.

Above: Traditionally Korean diners ate their meals at floor height, sitting on cushions. This is still relatively common.

On a traditional *bansang* table setting the main rice dish would be served with soup, a plate of kimchi and a selection of side dishes referred to as chups. The number of side dishes included on the table is reflected in the name given to the setting, with three-, five-, seven-, nine- and twelve-chup settings the most traditional.

Historically this figure was a reflection of social status, with both three- and five-chup meals the staple among the lower classes, and seven- and nine-chup

Eating from the same bowl
Koreans believe that eating food
from the same bowl as their
fellow diners makes for closer
relationships. It is not considered
impolite to ask the host for an
individual bowl or plate, but it is
a rarity among a people whose
Confucian ideals value fellowship
and mutual respect.

meals reserved for the upper classes and
nobility. Twelve-chup meals, or surasang,
were only allowed to be served to the
king, with the expanse of dishes spread
across three separate tables. These more
ostentatious royal menus often took days
to prepare and offered a complex blend
of warm and cold dishes, with mild and
spicy ingredients and a harmony of
textures and colours, all of them served
according to a specific ritual.

Regardless of whether the table has
a three- or a 12-chup setting, the
notion of harmony is still important, and
culinary contrasts are reflected in the
choice of dishes. Hot dishes are served
alongside cold ones, with mild and
spicy ingredients designed to
complement one another while
exhibiting an interesting diversity.
Crunchy vegetables are offset by velvety
stews and porridges, while meat,
seafood, vegetables and rice are
balanced in equal measure.

The Korean dining table
Any formal table setting is based
around a complex historical
design, rich with significance.
The classic Korean table is round,
symbolizing the sun and the yang
virtue, whereas its four legs point
to the ground, signifying the yin
properties of the earth. Korean
dining tables used to be low, and
the diners would sit around them
on floor cushions; these days
tables have become more
Westernized, with chairs rather
than cushions.

LAYING THE TABLE

For each person who is dining, a
covered bowl of rice is set on the left
and a bowl of soup on the right. A
second row of bowls is formed behind
these containing the dipping sauces
and kimchi, while the side dishes are
placed to flank this arrangement.
Hot or cooked dishes always go on
the right, while cold dishes or fresh
vegetables sit on the left. Large
communal dishes, such as stews
and noodle bowls, are always placed
in the very centre of the table to allow
them to be easily shared between all
the diners.

A long-handled, shallow spoon
(*sutgarak*) and a pair of silver or
stainless-steel chopsticks (*jeotgarak*)
are placed next to each soup bowl to
complete the table setting. Unlike
most other Asians, the Koreans prefer
to use a spoon rather than chopsticks
as the main table utensil. Rice, soups
and stews are eaten with the spoon,
whereas chopsticks are used for the
drier side dishes, although the two
are never used simultaneously. This
spoon culture indicates a marked

*Above: This traditional Korean table
arrangement incorporates many small,
tasty side dishes to augment the
obligatory rice dish.*

difference in eating habits to those of
both China and Japan, where bowls are
designed to be small enough to lift
them in order to hold them close
to the mouth when eating with
chopsticks. Korean food is served
in larger, heavier bowls and it is
considered bad manners to pick up
tableware while eating.

The preference for spoons over
chopsticks is due to the softer, more
liquid nature of the dishes that make
up Korean cuisine. The substantial
chige casseroles that are so popular
would be very difficult to eat with
chopsticks, as would the various mixed
rice and porridge dishes.

In the big cities of South Korea, a
meal, especially with traditional dishes,
is still considered to be the highlight of
an evening's entertainment. Even
emigrating families living in Europe or
the USA preserve their traditional ways
of cooking and eating.

FOOD THROUGH THE KOREAN DAY

One of the most intriguing things about the Korean way of life is the different way they organize their mealtimes during the day compared to the way that is usual in the Western world. There is no rigid structure of breakfast, lunch and dinner, with different foods for each one, particularly breakfast. Koreans would consider it strange to eat breakfast cereals or toast, fried eggs and bacon or even muffins only at breakfast time, and at no other time during the day.

BREAKFAST

The Korean family will start the day, as long as there is time before dashing off to work, with a good serving of rice and accompanying dishes, quite similar in character to those eaten during the evening, although the preparation and variety may not be so elaborate. These days many townspeople are too busy to prepare a huge breakfast of the kind needed by farmers working in the fields in past times, so they will eat just soup and rice, or a few side dishes, or rice and kimchi for breakfast.

If there is no time to prepare anything at home for breakfast, busy people still manage to eat before starting work by fitting in a quick visit to a café or street stall serving a traditional Korean breakfast of rice, soup and meat or fish.

Some of the big cities have rows of 'breakfast cafés', with their fronts open to the street, and a row of earthenware pots (*tukbaege*) on the stoves inside containing a simmering porridge-type mixture made of beans, rice or other grains, which are cooked with a lot of water until they are really soft. When you order your breakfast, a raw egg will be broken into the pot and you mix it in yourself when it arrives at the table. There is also a special porridge made of pine nuts, but this would only be eaten on feast days and birthdays, as pine nuts are so expensive.

> **A Korean breakfast feast**
> If you are feeling particularly hungry, you might be tempted to try eating all this for breakfast before a hard day's work.
> - A *tukbaege* containing rice and beansprout porridge, with a raw egg broken on top and mixed in at the table
> - Tofu and vegetable soup
> - Cabbage *kimchi*
> - Grilled (broiled) fish
> - Aubergine (eggplant) salad
> - Steamed shrimps
> - Stir-fried beef strips
> - And finally, a cup of barley tea to aid the digestion

LUNCH

The midday meal is a similar feast, but on a smaller scale than breakfast. This is when most working Koreans will throng the cafes and restaurants for a quick snack, or pick up a pancake or two from a street stall. Children and agricultural workers tend to take their lunch to school or work with them – this will often include easily transported favourites such as kimbap, the Korean rice and seaweed roll.

DINNER

The evening meal is the big event of the Korean day for all families. Most dinners are still cooked by the women in the family, whether or not they work outside the home, and they do not seem to consider it too much of a hardship to spend most of their free time preparing food. Of course, the range of dishes and length of time needed to make them will be defined by the amount of time available. Nevertheless, the evening meal is extremely important in most Korean families, and great care is usually taken to balance the dishes almost without anyone being aware of the time and effort this takes.

Not only will the cook of the family be thinking about the evening meal during the day, she (or sometimes he) will be planning ahead to make sure

Above: Early-rising Korean families enjoy a full and varied breakfast which, though less elaborately prepared than dinner, consists of many of the same staple ingredients such as rice, soup and kimchi.

Right: Hard-working Korean cooks can save time by using dried goods, but these are generally used to prepare the traditional components of a meal, not as ready-made meals.

that there are fresh vegetables in the house, a good stock of rice, and, of course, a pot of kimchi to go with every meal.

READY-MADE FOOD

Nowadays Korean food stores sell all sorts of convenience foods such as ready-made soy sauce, doenjang (fermented soya bean paste) or gochujang (chilli) paste, these all being ingredients that would have been made at home in the days when most women's main job was looking after the house and the family. But now, with more Korean women working outside the home, convenience food starts to establish its place. It is now also possible to buy ready-made kimchi, instant soup and stock mixes, dried fish and herbs, along with a great many other ingredients.

Despite this, the culture of fast food has made very little impact on the big cities of South Korea. The idea of a ready meal would be impossible to contemplate, simply because one dish popped into the microwave and eaten in front of the TV would not constitute a proper dinner to a Korean who had been brought up on a beautifully arranged selection of banchan, rice, soup and stew, with a piece of fish or meat grilled (broiled) at the table. The point of Korean food stores is for convenience, to save the cook a little time by doing some of the pre-cooking preparation. But it is still the case that spending many hours planning meals, buying and combining ingredients, cooking, serving and eating as a social activity are still deeply ingrained within the Korean culture.

Right: Lunch is often eaten on the go. Children tend to take nutritious prepared lunches to schools, and busy workers stop briefly for lunch at local restaurants.

STREET FOOD AND SNACKS

Koreans take their food very seriously, and spend a lot of time preparing it and eating it according to traditional rituals. However, a more relaxed cuisine is available on the street, in the form of tasty little snacks, freshly cooked by street vendors and either munched straight away or, if you can wait, wrapped up to be taken home.

EATING ON THE STREET

The Koreans are sociable people, and love to stroll around their city shopping centres or town markets, or perch on chairs by the roadside, eating mouthfuls of spicy hot dishes in the winter or cold refreshing ones in the summer, and chatting to friends and acquaintances on the street.

Rice rolls (kimbap)

One of the most popular savoury snacks is kimbap, which is a tasty roll rather like Japanese sushi. Kimbap consists of seasoned rice and a medley of little morsels of fried egg, vegetables, meat or fish, all spread on a piece of dried laver, the flat dark-green seaweed, and rolled up. Each bite reveals a whole series of flavours, which are expertly bound together by the spicy rice.

Savoury pancakes (pajeon)

At the next stall you might find a cook expertly frying small pancakes called pajeon. These will always be based on a batter of eggs and flour, and include the ubiquitous spring onions (scallions), green chillies and a selection of other ingredients. It's yet another opportunity to eat kimchi (kimchijeon), this time incorporated into the pancake batter and eaten with a spicy soy sauce dip; or seafood such as oysters (gool pajeon), just a few chopped pieces added to the pancake while the underneath is cooking.

These pancakes are always fried gently so that there is plenty of time for the filling to cook with the batter and for the flavours to mingle. They are served pale beige and soft, not brown and crispy. The simplest version and the cheapest consists of just the batter and spring onions (scallions), and these are very popular all over the country.

More elaborate pancakes are usually the province of restaurants, but you may find some street vendors making them with buckwheat flour or rice flour, or even with cooked rice or ground cooked mung beans mixed into the batter, and a wider range of other ingredients on top including strips of beef or pork, radish, carrot, mussels, clams and anything

Above: Delicious savoury pancakes are served stuffed with spring onions, chillies and meat, seafood or vegetables.

else that comes to hand. A dipping sauce will be a necessary accompaniment to serve alongside these more intricate dishes.

Other savoury snacks

What else can be found to eat in the open air? Other savoury dishes include dumplings (mandu) with a filling of meat, fish or vegetables, or savoury sausages of pork, noodles, vegetables and seasonings packed inside a pig's intestine. To accompany these strong meaty flavours, you may find little slices of liver or lung as well as your small container of spicy dipping sauce. Absolutely nothing is wasted in Korean cooking.

Sweet pancakes (hotteok)

A plain pancake batter is the base of hotteok, but the sweet sauce is folded inside so that all the ingredients, honey, cinnamon, chopped nuts or brown

Left: Shoppers enjoy street food as a delicious and fortifying snack; not a full meal, which is normally eaten at home.

Left: Fishcakes on skewers steaming over potatoes and spring onion broth.

BAR SNACKS

Koreans enjoy a special range of snacks (anju) made to accompany alcoholic drinks, and these are often found in places such as karaoke bars. They tend to be finger foods, such as nuts, small portions of the rice/seaweed roll kimbap, pieces of steamed squid or octopus, and chopped fruit. In fact they are a bitesize version of the side dishes, banchan, which accompany every main meal in Korea.

Street food etiquette

Koreans will often eat snacks while strolling through the streets, window-shopping or chatting to friends. If they are particularly hungry and have bought something quite substantial, such as a seafood pancake with some rice, a sauce and a drink, there may be some chairs and tables provided by the stall so that they can sit down and appreciate the food in comfort.

---

sugar, are incorporated with the batter mixture into a soft cake. These are winter favourites, ideal to warm you up on a freezing day.

Cakes and pastries

Sweet things often come in unusual shapes – for instance:
- bungeoppang (goldfish bread), a small pastry in the shape of fish with a sweetened red bean puree inside
- gukwappang, a similar sweet mixture shaped like a flower
- gyeranppang, shaped like a shell.
Rice cakes are popular at every festival throughout the year, with both sweet and savoury mixtures inside, sometimes both, according to the season.

DRINKS

Korean street stalls sell a wide variety of drinks, both hot and cold, alcoholic and non-alcoholic. A favourite is the grain spirit, soju, a small shot glass of which can be swallowed quickly for winter warmth. Cold punches are favourites during the summer, especially the classic persimmon

Right: Koreans enjoying a picnic, which would typically include pajon (griddle cakes), kimchi and hwajon (rice cakes).

punch, containing spices, fruit and honey to counteract the tart flavour of the persimmon. This punch is considered the most refreshing drink in Korea, and it is one that balances the strong tastes of most Korean food better than a more subtle wine or fruit juice.

EQUIPMENT & INGREDIENTS

This section gives detailed information about all the different utensils and types of food used in Japanese and Korean cuisines, from daily staples to unusual fruits.

Image: Flavourings, fruits and vegetables used in both Japanese and Korean cooking.

THE JAPANESE KITCHEN

The main foods used in Japanese cooking tend to be vegetables and fish, and

the freshness of these ingredients is of utmost importance. The Japanese have

also developed, with characteristic meticulous and delicate care, numerous food

products. The following pages introduce both fresh ingredients and processed

foods, discussing their aroma, taste, texture and appearance, and describing

essential preparation and cooking techniques.

Left: Large prawns, scallops and squid; **Above:** A selection of traditional steamers

EQUIPMENT AND UTENSILS

The most important aspect of Japanese cooking is preparation, cutting in particular, so Japanese kitchens are equipped with a battery of delicate utensils to ensure fresh ingredients will not be spoilt or damaged. Natural materials such as wood, bamboo or earthenware and stoneware are preferred for Japanese cooking to modern stainless steel or plastic versions since they provide a gentle touch on fresh ingredients and absorb extra moisture.

If your kitchen is well equipped with a few basic essential tools, such as a variety of sharp knives and a cutting board, along with a good selection of Western utensils, you really do not need to add anything special to cook Japanese food. Nevertheless, some traditional Japanese utensils, such as the grater, would be useful additions. Many of the utensils shown here are now available at high-quality kitchenware shops, as well as at specialist Japanese shops.

KNIVES

For the Japanese, knives are the cook's heart and soul; professional chefs must have their own and they move with them from job to job. There are well over 20 types of knives used in a professional kitchen, but an ordinary household set is not too different from that of a very good Western one, with the exception of a special sashimi knife, which is about 30cm/12in long with a 2.5cm/1in wide sharp blade.

Many Japanese knives have a single sharp edge on one side of the blade only so they are thinner than most Western equivalents, which makes them better for doing delicate cutting jobs. Top quality knives made in Japan are produced from one piece of carbonized steel in the same way as Japanese swords, with the names of famous blade makers normally inscribed on the shoulder of the blade.

Lesser-quality knives are made from two pieces of steel with only the lower blade made of carbonized steel and the rest of soft steel. Steel is prone to rust, so requires constant care. Stainless steel, ground mixed steel and ceramic knives are also available and are a popular choice for use in ordinary household kitchens.

A standard set of knives consists of a thin blade for vegetables; a cleaver for large fish, meat and poultry; a sashimi knife for slicing fish; and a small knife for peeling and chopping. Look for the maker's name on the blade shoulder as a sign of quality before buying.

Japanese cutting styles
Ingredients need to be cut into sizes and shapes suitable for eating with *hashi* (chopsticks). There are a number of cutting shapes that can be used, and each has its own specific name. Some examples are: *sengiri* (shreds); *wagiri* (rounds); *arare* (dice); *hangetsu* (half-moons); *tanzaku* (oblong and thin); *sainome* (cubes); *sasagaki* (shavings); and *hanagiri* (flowers).

The *hyoshigi* (clapper shape) cut is rectangular and thick, suitable for fairly dense vegetables.

Below: Japanese knives, from front, vegetable knife, sashimi knife, cleaver and all-purpose knife. These knives are all made from one piece of carbonized steel with the maker's name engraved on the blade shoulder.

Shaping vegetables by hand
Practise your decorative cutting techniques with affordable everyday ingredients, such as carrots, where it won't matter too much if you need to start again.

Slice a medium-size carrot into thick chunks then, with a very sharp knife, slice each piece into simple shapes, such as flowers.

SHARPENING STONE

Maintaining well-sharpened knives is an important role of the cook, and Japanese chefs take as great care in selecting grinding stones as in choosing good knives. Natural stone is the best quality and professionals sharpen knives using three stones with varying degrees of density: coarse, medium and dense. However, if you do not carry out the sharpening process properly, you can easily spoil knives, so many people in Japan use professional sharpeners.

CUTTING BOARD

If you cut ingredients properly you are assured of success in Japanese cooking, and the cutting board becomes your stage. The Japanese word for chef, *itamae*, means literally 'before the board', and no Japanese cooking is done without a board. Because of hygiene considerations plastic boards are more popular among housewives, but professionals still prefer wooden

Below: More hygenic than wooden chopping boards, plastic ones are increasingly being used in Japanese homes.

Above: Japanese sharpening stone

boards, since they are gentler to knives, as well as to ingredients.

Boards should be washed thoroughly after use and different ingredients, particularly raw fish and meat, should never be placed on a board at the same time.

SHAPING CUTTERS

Westerners are often amazed how, in Japanese restaurants, everyday vegetables are transformed into beautiful and delicate flowers, leaves or birds. Simple shapes are easily achieved by the use of shaping cutters but many chefs prefer cutting by hand; this forms an important part of their training. Hard and long vegetables, such as carrot and daikon, are first cut into thick pieces with a sharp knife and then sliced. To do properly by hand takes much practice and so shaping cutters may be a more achievable way to add interest and fun to cooking and eating. Simply slice your vegetable and stamp out shapes with the cutters.

Above: Quick and easy to use, shaping cutters come in various sizes.

Left: Porcelain and
aluminium graters

KATSUO-BUSHI SHAVER

A block of dried skipjack
tuna is one of the very
basic foodstuffs found in
Japanese cooking, since its
flakes are the main ingredients
for making dashi stock, and the
sound made by housewives
shaving katsuo-bushi traditionally
greeted families most mornings. Today,
however, flakes in packets are popularly
used. The older generation still use
freshly shaven katsuo-bushi and it is far
superior to ready-made, whether for
dashi or for use as a simple garnish on
top of vegetables.

The shaver comprises a plane on top
of a box and the shaved flakes drop
through into a drawer underneath.

GRATER

If you are going to choose just one
Japanese utensil, the *oroshi-gane* or
daikon-oroshi (fine-toothed daikon
grater) is definitely the one. There are
various types and materials vary,
including aluminium and porcelain,
but they are all basically a flat surface
with numerous fine spikes on it.

The most convenient and cheapest
grater is made of aluminium and has
a small curved base at the end of the
spikes to catch the juice that is exuded
during grating. Japanese cooking uses
a lot of grated daikon and fresh root
ginger, and both the grated flesh and

the juice are used in the recipes. With
ginger, sometimes only the juice is
used, making this feature very useful.

Most graters usually have a small
area with finer spikes for grating dense
spices such as garlic and fresh wasabi.
There is even a grater made
of shark's skin, designed
especially for grating
wasabi, but this is
confined to the
professional kitchen.

Above: A bamboo whisk is used to
prepare the tea during the traditional
tea ceremony.

BAMBOO WHISK

When preparing tea for the
Japanese tea ceremony,
matcha, a high-grade, bright
light green powdered tea, is
whisked with this special
bamboo utensil, rather than
brewed in a pot.

A traditional ceremonial
ritual, the tea is prepared in
front of guests in individual
warmed cups. The tips of the
whisk need to be soaked in hot
water beforehand so that they
aren't stained by the vibrant
green tea. A little water is added
to a small quantity of tea in a bowl,
then vigorously whisked, until frothy.
Do not let the tea stand; rather serve
immediately. Eat wagashi (cakes)
before drinking the tea.

Above: Shaver and block of katsuo-
bushi (dried skipjack tuna)

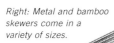

Right: Metal and bamboo skewers come in a variety of sizes.

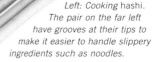

Left: Cooking *hashi. The pair on the far left have grooves at their tips to make it easier to handle slippery ingredients such as noodles.*

GRINDER AND PESTLE

The Japanese *suribachi* and *surikogi* (grinder and wooden pestle) grind to finer granules or paste than their Western counterparts, the mortar and pestle. The *suribachi* is made of clay in the shape of a large pudding bowl, with numerous sharp ridges on the inside surface so that ingredients as diverse as sesame seeds and minced (ground) meat or prawns (shrimp) can be ground into a paste. It then becomes a mixing bowl. A food processor may be easier for grinding larger ingredients, but small items, such as sesame seeds, are best prepared by hand using a *suribachi* and *surikogi*.

COOKING HASHI

Once mastered, *hashi* (chopsticks) will become an indispensable tool in the kitchen as well as on the table. From beating eggs to turning over smaller items of food in a frying pan, a pair of *hashi* is a much more convenient tool than a fork. Cooking *hashi* range in lengths, usually from 25cm/ 10in to over 35cm/14in, and often a pair is tied with a string so that it won't become separated and lost. The longest one for deep-frying keeps your hand away from splashing hot oil. *Hashi* are also very elegant eating utensils. There are many different kinds, including the husband-and-wife pair, children's *hashi* and even *hashi* for a packed lunch. They are often visually attractive too.

WIRE-MESH GRILL

Japanese cooking was developed using wood and charcoal as fuel, so grilling over a fire – wood, charcoal or now, commonly, gas – is the usual cooking method. This simple, round wire mesh, called *yakiami*, is placed over the fire on which fish, meat or vegetables, or even tofu, are cooked. It is a very useful piece of everyday equipment, but the standard metal oven shelf will also serve the purpose.

SKEWERS

Metal and bamboo skewers make grilling easier and prevent food from breaking into bits while cooking. They are also useful for checking how food is cooking without making obvious holes in it. Skewers come in various sizes and the largest metal skewer can be used to pierce a whole fish to create a wavy shape so that it looks alive on the plate once it has been grilled.

When food is served on the skewer, such as yakitori (grilled chicken) or dengaku (grilled tofu), bamboo is used, since it not only looks better but is also easier to handle than hot metal. Small flat bamboo skewers are useful for soft ingredients such as tofu, preventing them from slipping during cooking.

Right: Suribachi *(grinder)* and surikogi *(wooden pestle)*

Grilling with bamboo skewers

Soak bamboo skewers in water for at least 30 minutes before use to prevent the wood from burning while grilling (broiling).

STEAMER

The Japanese use a steamer as often as Westerners use an oven. It is an ideal utensil for gently cooking fresh ingredients in a way that will not diminish their nutritional content or damage their shape. For this reason the steamer is perfect for Japanese cooking.

The traditional Japanese steamer does not look any different from the ones now commonly available in the West except that it comes with a removable base pierced with holes, which is perched in the pan. Choose the widest type that you can find. Although the microwave oven has replaced many utensils, the steamer still rules supreme in Japanese cooking. The microwave oven, however, is extremely handy for heating cooked food, particularly leftover rice.

If you do not have a steamer, it is possible to improvise with a wok and trivet. Place the trivet in the wok, fill the wok one-third full of water and bring to the boil. Place the food in a heatproof bowl on the trivet, cover the wok with the dome-shaped lid and steam the food until it is cooked.

Above: Steamers with pierced base. Japanese steamers usually feature a removable base.

STRAINER

The Japanese mesh strainer, or *zaru*, which is made of bamboo or stainless steel, is another item increasingly making its way into Western kitchens. Extremely effective, it can be used to strain even tiny grains of rice and very fine noodles. Japanese *zaru* come in a number of sizes and shapes, with different uses. Flat *zaru*, for example, are used to cool or air-dry ingredients, in particular vegetables, that are left on them after cooking. Needless to say, all *zaru* must be washed carefully after use and dried out completely before storing.

Right: Bamboo strainers, or zaru, *can be used to strain a whole range of ingredients such as noodles and vegetables, but these large bamboo ones are not really suitable for straining rice as the grains are likely to get caught in the mesh.*

Left: Traditional Japanese pan with a wooden drop-in lid used when cooking delicate ingredients, such as tofu.

Below: The Japanese wooden sieve with its unique mesh will produce a much finer texture than is attainable using a food processor.

PAN AND DROP-IN LID

The traditional Japanese pan, made of aluminium or copper, often has a finely indented surface so that it does not become too hot too quickly and so that the heat spreads evenly over the pan. A one-handled pan, called *yukihira*, will be useful for Japanese as well as other styles of cooking. Drop-in lids are very handy when you are cooking delicate ingredients, such as vegetables or tofu, which you do not want to move about in the pan. The light touch of the wooden lid, placed directly on the food in the pan, keeps it still on the base.

SIEVE

Uragoshi, the Japanese sieve (strainer), consists of a wooden round frame 20cm/8in in diameter and 7.5cm/3in deep, with very fine horsehair, stainless steel or nylon mesh. It is used to sift flours and to strain wet food, by placing it upside down on a plate and pushing the food through the mesh with a wooden spatula. Horsehair is prone to splitting when too dry, so soak the sieve in water before use except when sifting. After use wash carefully, clearing the bits stuck in the mesh, and remove the mesh from the frame and store separately. For stainless steel and nylon mesh, dry thoroughly.

OMELETTE PAN

Tamago-yaki-nabe (the Japanese omelette pan) is reserved for making tamagoyaki (rolled omelette) only. There are many sizes, shapes (rectangular or square) and makes, but the best Japanese one is made of copper, plated inside with tin. Though handy, the straight-sided pan can be replaced by an ordinary frying pan or a small ordinary omelette pan. Trim the edges of the cooked egg to make a rectangular shape.

Above: A Japanese omelette pan used to make rolled omelettes

UTENSILS FOR COOKING WITH RICE

Rice is the staple grain of the whole of Asia, which is well over half the world's population. In Japan, evidence of its production dates as far back as the 2nd century BC. It is not exaggerating to say that rice is at the heart of all Japanese cuisine. Not surprisingly, there are a number of utensils specifically designed for the cooking and use of rice.

RICE COOKER

Traditionally in Japan rice was cooked over a real fire, usually wood, in an *o'kama*, a cast-iron pot with a round base and a tutu-like skirt around the pot that kept the heat to the lower part of the pan. Once cooked, the rice was transferred to an *o'hitsu*, a deep wooden container with a lid, from which the rice was served. This process has now been replaced by the electric cooker, which can keep the rice warm all day. The older generation, however, still yearns for rice cooked over a wood fire, and the ultimate aim of electric rice cooker manufacturers is to re-create the taste of wood-fire cooked rice as closely as possible.

Above: Wooden sushi tub

Right: Lacquered and wooden spatulas

RICE KEEPER

The wooden *o'hitsu* used to be an object every household possessed, but since the introduction of electric rice cookers, which cook and keep rice warm in the one unit, it is more often simply a fashionable addition to modern kitchens or dining rooms. After cooking, rice is transferred to it and, after serving, the remaining rice is kept in it. The wood may not keep the rice warm all day as the electric cooker does, but it does absorb extra moisture and keeps the rice pleasantly moist.

SPATULA

Héra or *shamoji* (the wooden spatula) is probably the most indispensable utensil in a Japanese household. It is often used as a symbol representing the entire household (at such occasions as housewives' protests against rising household costs). There are now many types of Japanese rice spatulas, including bare wood or lacquered ones. The spatula is used for aerating cooked rice and also for pressing wet food through a sieve (strainer) on to a plate.

Left: Electric rice cooker

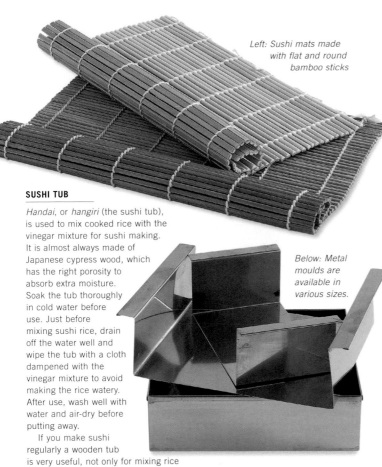

Left: Sushi mats made with flat and round bamboo sticks

SUSHI MAT

Makisu (a bamboo stick mat) is increasingly found in many Western households due to the popularity of sushi. It is a necessary item for making nori-maki (nori-rolled sushi), but is also used for other purposes, such as squeezing water out of cooked salad vegetables before they are dressed. There are basically two types of *makisu*: one, measuring about 22 × 20cm/9 × 8in, and made of bamboo sticks with a pale green, shiny, flat side, is for sushi rolling; the other, a little larger in size, which has triangular or round bamboo sticks threaded together, is for making a pattern of lines on the roll, as when preparing tamagoyaki (thick egg omelette). After use, carefully wash away any food stuck between the sticks, wipe and leave to dry completely before storing.

SUSHI TUB

Handai, or *hangiri* (the sushi tub), is used to mix cooked rice with the vinegar mixture for sushi making. It is almost always made of Japanese cypress wood, which has the right porosity to absorb extra moisture. Soak the tub thoroughly in cold water before use. Just before mixing sushi rice, drain off the water well and wipe the tub with a cloth dampened with the vinegar mixture to avoid making the rice watery. After use, wash well with water and air-dry before putting away.

If you make sushi regularly a wooden tub is very useful, not only for mixing rice but also for serving. An ordinary large mixing bowl may not absorb moisture as a Japanese sushi tub does but it is certainly an acceptable substitute if you make sushi rice only occasionally.

Below: Metal moulds are available in various sizes.

WOODEN MOULD

The rectangular wooden mould is for making oshi-zushi, pressed sushi. This, like the sushi tub, should be soaked well in water before use. Wet the mould before packing with fish and su-meshi. Cover with the lid and press tightly or place a weight such as a book on it. Other moulds are also used to shape cooked rice for party canapés or children's lunch boxes.

METAL MOULD

This double-layered mould is a very useful tool for setting mousse or tofu as well as liquids such as kanten.

Below: Wooden sushi mould for shaping rice into individual canapés, left, and a rectangular wooden sushi mould for making pressed sushi.

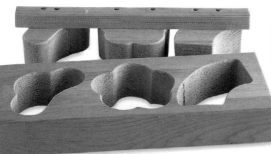

COOKING AT THE TABLE

Always great fun, cooking at the table is very easy to do well and it also enables diners to appreciate fresh food immediately after it's cooked. There is a Japanese utensil designed for every one of the numerous dishes that are cooked at the table, but a portable gas burner and a flameproof earthenware pot are suitable for most dishes. Below are some of the special Japanese pots and pans.

EARTHENWARE POT

Hotpot dishes are Japanese winter favourites; they are used to cook sukiyaki, shabu shabu, oden, yudofu (pot-boiled tofu) and griddles at the table. The Japanese household normally has a table with a gas or electric burner fitted in the centre, the lid to which is removed when they cook at the table. An earthenware pot is ideal for cooking soups, such as shabu shabu, oden and yudofu, as it heats up slowly and retains the heat for some time. It can also be used to cook udon noodles. The pot also looks good on the table. After use, leave it to cool down, then wash it carefully with a sponge and leave to air-dry. Never heat an earthenware pot without water in it.

Right: Earthenware hotpot dish

CAST-IRON POT

Traditionally, the only heating in the house was a *hibachi* (fire urn), or *irori* (floor hearth) for a farmhouse, placed in the centre of the living room. A cast-iron pot was placed on it, or hung from the ceiling, so boiling water was available all day for tea or so that slow-cooking foods could be simmered gently. While the *hibachi* and *irori* are now, unfortunately, rarely used, the cast-iron pot is, not only for its handsome appearance but also for the practicality of cooking and serving hotpot dishes either at home or in restaurants. It is normally black with a wooden lid and a removable handle, which rests on the pot's rim when not in use.

Below: Sukiyaki pan

SUKIYAKI PAN

As its name suggests, this pan is used only for cooking sukiyaki at the table and an ordinary frying pan can be used instead. It is a heavy iron pan with a deep rim, since sukiyaki beef is first pan-fried, then shoyu sauce and other ingredients are added. Diners serve themselves from the pan and add more ingredients as they eat.

YUDOFU POT

Pot-boiled tofu, yudofu, is a favourite Japanese winter dish, traditionally prepared in a yudofu pot, though an ordinary large pan or earthenware pot can be used. The yudofu set usually consists of a pot, a tall metal shoyu dish with flat feet to stand in the pot, a small perforated metal spoon and individual serving bowls. The shoyu dish filled with shoyu is placed in the centre of the pot, which is filled with hot water (so the shoyu also gets warm) surrounded by cubed tofu on a bed of a piece of konbu (dried kelp). Diners mix the sauce with some shoyu from the pot, along with grated fresh root ginger and a herb for flavouring, and serve themselves.

SHABU SHABU POT

This Mongolian-style pot is a popular way of cooking shabu shabu (pot-cooked beef) though an earthenware pot is also suitable. It has a central funnel surrounded by a moat into which hot stock is poured. The pot is placed on a portable gas ring or electric ring on the table and diners cook small pieces of meat and vegetables in the hot stock.

Below: Tray for serving tempura

Above: Tempura fryer

Above: Shabu shabu pot

TEMPURA FRYER

Normally made of heavy iron, the tempura deep-frying pan is two-handled, with a half-circle metal rack perched on the edge for draining. There are several sizes, ranging from those for two people to family-size fryers. A large wok or any deep frying pan can do the job just as well.

Tempura is mostly served on bamboo trays though there are also metal ones, made to the same shape. While not necessary, these trays do make lovely serving tools. When arranging the tempura, first place a piece of *washi* (Japanese paper) on the tray.

The word shabu shabu is onomatopoeic, suggesting something splashing around in water, such as when hand-washing clothes; using *hashi* (chopsticks), diners move thinly sliced beef in a similar motion in the stock to prevent it over-cooking. Once all the meat and vegetables are eaten, rice or noodles are added to the stock and served to finish off the meal. There are a few makes available but the best, and most expensive, ones are made of brass.

ELECTRIC GRIDDLE

This is an essential piece of equipment for the Japanese household and has already started appearing in Western kitchens. It is a round or square non-stick metal griddle with a rim about 5cm/2in deep and an electric heating device underneath. There are many types and makes, but the most popular is the round one, about 40cm/16in in diameter, with a see-through glass lid. The griddle is placed in the centre of the table surrounded by prepared fresh vegetables, meat or fish and shellfish, and diners help themselves. It's an easy family meal, suitable for busy people. Some deeper griddles can be used to roast a whole chicken or other meat.

After all the ingredients have been cooked and eaten, add a little hot water while the griddle is still hot and wipe it clean with kitchen paper. Leave to dry completely before putting away.

PORTABLE GAS STOVE

A very practical piece of equipment, the portable gas stove can be used not only at the table to cook all kinds of hotpot dishes but also outside for mini-barbecues. It has a gas ring and a compartment for the gas cylinder at the side. One cylinder lasts for about two hours, and these are sold either individually or in packets of three. Remove the cylinder after use and store separately.

CROCKERY AND CUTLERY

The appearance and presentation of food is very important to the Japanese, so serving dishes play an important part in Japanese cooking. Japan has been renowned as producers of fine china and porcelain for many centuries and great works of art have been developed around the *kaiseki* tea ceremony and formal banquets.

Japanese tableware is probably the most varied in the world. Even a simple family supper requires individual rice bowls, soup bowls, plates and sauce dishes, as well as serving plates and bowls, and of course sake cups. Lacquer is widely used not only for trays but also for bowls intended for soup or simmered dishes, and for sake vessels. Wooden dishes, as well as utensils, are also popular not only because they are pleasing to look at but also because the natural material complements so well the country's food philosophy.

CHINA DISHES

Japan produces some of the finest china in the world, with such well-known names and styles as Arita, Bizen, Hagi, Imari, Karatsu, Kutani, Mashiko, Mino and Seto.

A household normally possesses sets of rice bowls and soup bowls, various different-size plates, noodle bowls, serving plates and bowls, small dishes for dipping sauces and probably a set of lacquered trays. However, apart from rice bowls and soup bowls, ordinary Western plates can be used for other dishes quite easily.

Below: Hors d'oeuvres tray with sashimi china dish left, bowl for simmered food, at back, and soup bowl, right

Above: Clockwise from left, bowl for steamed or simmered food with lid, noodle bowl and rice bowl.

Right: China soba set: sauce jug, condiment dishes and sauce cups.

China used for a *kaiseki* (banquet):

The *kaiseki* (Japanese banquet) consists of more than a dozen courses, each served separately in plates, bowls or cups of different shapes, sizes and patterns; the materials are chosen with an artist's eye to suit the season and the food being served.

In order of serving, plates, bowls and trays can include an hors d'oeuvres tray, a small sashimi dish, a clear soup bowl and

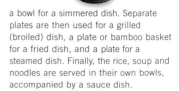

a bowl for a simmered dish. Separate plates are then used for a grilled (broiled) dish, a plate or bamboo basket for a fried dish, and a plate for a steamed dish. Finally, the rice, soup and noodles are served in their own bowls, accompanied by a sauce dish.

Left: Sauce dishes in two sizes, and a rectangular hors d'oeuvres plate.

BENTO BOXES

In the West, bento is known as a dish, as in *makunouchi* bento, but it really means easy meal or take out meal, usually for lunch or a picnic. There are many types of bento box, from lacquer to plastic, and sizes vary from the *makunouchi* bento box, a size similar to a laptop computer, to children's pretty lunch boxes. Elaborate boxes such as *makunouchi* are hardly designed for an 'easy meal', and they are normally made of lacquer with five or six compartments and a sauce corner inside. Some ordinary lunch boxes consist of two boxes, one for fish, meat and vegetables positioned on top of another box for rice.

SERVING TRAYS

At Japanese banquets trays are used in place of table mats. This is because foods for the tea ceremony were traditionally served separately on lacquer trays with legs, which acted as individual tables. Smaller trays, either lacquer, wooden or bamboo, are often used as dishes on which foods are arranged directly or with decoratively folded Japanese paper between the food and the tray.

Above: Square jubako *(lacquered food boxes) with matching* hashi *(chopsticks) and set of bento boxes*

Below: Trays for serving soba noodles can be round with a lid or square.

SOBA TRAYS

Japanese soba noodles, which are dipped in sauce before being eaten, are normally served on a soba tray which is a bamboo mat perched on a bamboo or wooden frame. There are many shapes (square, rectangular or round) and sizes vary greatly. A soba china set normally includes a sauce jug (pitcher) and five sauce cups and condiment dishes.

Below: Flat bamboo tray for serving food

HASHI

In contrast to the numerous items of crockery, the only Japanese cutlery is *hashi*. *Hashi*, or more politely *ohashi*, are shorter and more delicate than Chinese chopsticks and the lower ends are pointed. Traditionally they were made of ivory, but today various woods, lacquer or plastic are popular. They vary in size, and sometimes colour too, depending on who they are meant for. Men's *hashi* are thicker and usually 2.5–4cm/1–1½in longer than women's, and there are various children's *hashi* as well. In a Japanese household each family member usually has his or her own daily pair and another pair kept in a hashi case for use with a lunch box.

Hashi are growing in popularity the world over, and many modern Western-style designs, even using silver, have been introduced to the market. However, Japanese never use metal *hashi* when they eat, since metal ones are used to pick the bones from the ashes of the dead at the crematorium and are therefore not considered a good omen. The Japanese also traditionally serve a bowl of rice with a pair of very thin metal *hashi* every morning to their house temple, which is dedicated to their relatives' and ancestors' souls; metal ones are for the Buddha, as they say.

Above: Simple wooden hashi *in decorative pouches*

Above: Hashi *come in various sizes, colours and materials. Rests are used to avoid placing hashi on the table.*

WARIBASHI

For guests, simple wooden *hashi*, called *waribashi*, can be used. This is a long piece of wood divided in the centre up to the top end where it is broken off for use. Some plain wooden *hashi* are already made into pairs. There are numerous types and shapes, neatly encased in their own paper pouches with various colours, illustrations and inscriptions. Some *waribashi* pouches are designed to use only for celebration meals, so be careful not to use them at a funeral. You would know by the colour of the pouch; if red or similarly bright colour is used, it's for a celebration or a special occasion. If there is a knotted string, or illustration on the pouch, with no loops on the knot, it's particularly used for weddings.

Below: Condiment jar for shoyu with a matching saucer

HASHI REST

During the meal, Japanese place *hashi* crossways on a *hashi* rest or on a dish, and never directly on the table. The *hashi* rest is a boat-shaped piece of porcelain, metal or wood (which may be lacquered), about 5cm/2in long.

CONDIMENT DISH

On the Japanese table a shoyu jar takes the place of a salt and pepper set on the Western table. The size of a short, narrow tumbler, it has a spout and a lid, and normally a matching saucer.

Shichimi (powdered seven-chilli pepper) and sansho (green pepper) are also placed on the table either in the manufacturer's jars or in small, lidded dishes with a tiny spoon in each.

DRINKING VESSELS

Just as the presentation of food is important in Japanese cuisine, attention is also given to how drink is served.

SAKE JUGS

Never serve sake directly from the bottle; instead a *tokkuri* (sake jug) should always be used. It is normally made of china and is heat-resistant so that sake can be warmed in it before serving. The normal *tokkuri* holds 180ml/6fl oz/¾ cup, which relates to the old Japanese measurement of one 'go'.

SAKE CUPS

There are numerous types and makes of sake cup, but basically there are two categories: *choko*, or more politely *ochoko*, and *guinomi*. The *ochoko* are smaller cups, the size of half a golf ball, and the rim is open like a flower; some are so open that the cup itself is almost flat. The *guinomi* are slightly larger cups with a straight rim and are for more casual drinking. There are also larger, flat cups, the size of a small tea saucer. These are more formally called *sakazuki* and are used for occasions such as toasting someone

Right: Sake jugs and cups

or drinking to their future. Traditional Shinto wedding vows are also made by the couple toasting each other in sake, and the wedding *sakazuki* are made of ceremonial red lacquer.

Shochu, distilled alcohol made from various grains and even potato, is drunk in a glass, either straight or diluted.

TEAPOTS

The Japanese teapot looks similar to Western models except for the handle. No Japanese teapot has a fixed hollow handle attached to the side as do Western ones, instead it has either a pan handle or a detachable basket-like looped handle. The smaller pots, called *kyusu*, tend to have a straight pan handle and are used to make better quality teas. These pots have the capacity of only two to three cups.

The terracotta *kyusu* is regarded as particularly good for good-quality teas because of its natural feel. The ones for more casual use, *dobin*, are larger and normally have a looped handle. All Japanese teapots strain tea leaves at the bottom of the spout; a strainer is not needed when you pour the tea out.

Left: Japanese teapots

Above: Japanese tea cups come in various types and sizes, ranging from tiny ones, little larger than eggcups, to larger ones with lids, and his and her sets.

TEACUPS

Japanese teacups and mugs range in size from egg cup to the gigantic mug served at sushi shops, and have no handle as the tea is normally drunk lukewarm. The tall cups usually have a lid and a husband and wife set are also available consisting of a pair of cups, one slightly larger than the other, with lids and saucers. Saucers are wooden, either plain or lacquered.

The tea ceremony is a totally different affair from daily tea drinking. Bowls rather than cups are used and the powdered tea is whisked, using a bamboo brush, in front of the guests.

RICE AND RICE PRODUCTS

Since prehistoric times rice has been grown and eaten in Japan, and because of its rich content of vegetable protein, carbohydrate, vitamins and minerals, it quickly became popular all over the country. By the 7th century it was firmly established as the staple food and has remained so ever since.

Japanese cooking really developed around rice. The plain, yet delicate and subtle flavour of rice made it possible for the Japanese people to develop an appreciation of the exquisite flavours and textures of other natural produce available to them.

As well as a number of types and forms of rice, numerous by-products such as sake, mirin, vinegar and miso have also been derived from rice. Following is a look at the most essential and useful types of rice used in Japanese cooking.

URUCHIMAI

The short grain Japanese variety, *Oryza sativa japonica*, as opposed to the neighbouring South-east Asian countries' long grain, *jawa* and *indica*, was developed over the centuries to suit the climate as well as the taste of the Japanese people. Once cooked, it becomes quite tender and moist but firm enough to retain a little crunchiness. Unlike long grain rice, it becomes slightly sticky, enabling it to be picked up in mouthfuls with a pair of *hashi* (chopsticks). It has a rich, slightly sweet flavour.

There are over 300 different types of short grain rice grown all over Japan in water-filled paddy fields; brand names such as Koshihikari and Sasanisiki are among the most popular. However, most of the Japanese rice sold in the West is produced in California on dry land and some varieties come from Spain. They vary slightly in hardness, but Kahomai (the hardest), Nishiki, Maruyu and Kokuho (all Californian) and Minori (Spanish, the softest) are some of the popular brand names available.

Below: Some popular examples of Japanese short grain rice, clockwise from left, Kahomai, Maruyu, Minori, Kokuho and Nishiki

Cooking Japanese rice

1 Wash the rice thoroughly in cold water, changing the water several times until the water runs clear, then drain the rice in a fine mesh strainer and set aside for 1 hour.

2 Put the rice in a deep pan and add 15 per cent more cold water than rice (for 200g/7oz/1 cup rice you will need about 250ml/8fl oz/ 1 cup water). The water level should not be more than a third from the base of the pan.

3 Cover the pan, place over a high heat and bring to the boil; this may take 5 minutes. Turn the heat to the lowest setting and simmer for 10–13 minutes, or until all the water has been absorbed.

4 Remove the pan from the heat and set aside, still covered, for 10–15 minutes before serving.

COOK'S TIP
To cook genmai (brown rice), wash and drain the rice, then put 2 parts water to 1 part rice into a pan. Bring to the boil, cover, then simmer for 40 minutes.

GENMAI

There are degrees of polishing in rice production, and genmai, brown rice, is the least polished type. It retains its bran and germ and only the husk is removed. It is the most nutritious rice, and is high in fibre, but it takes a lot longer to cook than white rice and is very chewy. Genmai is widely available at health food stores and Asian stores.

MOCHIGOME

This short, opaque grain, also known as glutinous rice, makes a very sticky, dense rice when cooked. It has a high sugar content and is often steamed rather than boiled, then pounded to make mochi (rice cakes) and senbei (rice biscuits). Mochigome is also an important ingredient for making mirin (sweet rice wine).

Culinary uses of rice

As the staple food of Japan, rice is served in one form or another at every meal, including breakfast. It is almost always consumed boiled and served in a bowl together with a bowl of miso

Above: Genmai, brown rice

soup. Other foods are often just mere accompaniments to the rice. Plain boiled rice is also served with other cooked food such as tonkatsu (pork cutlet) and tempura (fried fish and/or fried vegetables) arranged on top as a one-dish meal, usually for lunch. Sometimes seasonal produce, such as young bamboo shoots in spring, green peas in summer and chestnuts or matsutake (wild mushrooms) in autumn, is added while the rice is boiling so an additional typical flavour of the season can be appreciated.

Boiled rice, mixed with vinegar, sugar and salt, also forms the base of all sushi, and top sushi chefs spend at least the first three years of their training perfecting the techniques for cooking rice.

For babies and the elderly as well as the sick, kayu or more politely okayu (rice gruel) can be cooked with three to four times as much water as that used for plain boiled rice. Boiled rice, either hot or cold, can be added to soup to make zosui but it is not suitable for frying.

Mochigome is often used to make celebratory dishes such as sekihan (rice cooked with red beans) for birthdays and other family celebrations and ohagi (steamed mochigome rolled in sweet red bean paste), for the equinox days.

Above: Mochigome

Making sushi rice
Su-meshi (vinegared rice) is the base for all kinds of sushi and it is essential to correctly cook the rice. As a guide, to make hoso-maki (thin nori-rolled sushi), 350g/12oz/1¾ cups short grain rice should make six rolls (about 36 pieces), sufficient to serve four to six people.

1 Cook the rice following the method, opposite. For extra flavour, add a 5cm/2in square of konbu (dried kelp) to the pan of rice and water, removing before the water reaches boiling point.

2 In a measuring cup, mix 45ml/ 3 tbsp Japanese rice vinegar (or white wine vinegar), 37.5ml/ 7½ tsp sugar and 10ml/2 tsp sea salt to the above amount of rice and stir well until dissolved.

3 Transfer the cooked rice to a wet wooden sushi tub or a large mixing bowl, and sprinkle the vinegar mixture evenly over the rice. Using a wooden spatula, fold the vinegar mixture into the rice; do not stir. Leave to cool before using to make sushi.

Preparation and cooking

When cooking Japanese rice it is imperative that it is washed thoroughly first in cold water and then left to drain, ideally for an hour but at least for 30 minutes. This ensures that the rice slowly absorbs the right amount of water left on the surface of the grains without turning it soggy. If time is limited, soak the rice for 10–15 minutes in plenty of water, then drain well. When the rice is well moistened it will turn a soft opaque colour. As a general rule, about 200g/7oz/1 cup rice is needed for two people. It is not advisable to cook less than this

Right: Mochi (rice cakes), made from mochigome rice, are traditional fare for New Year's Day.

Shaping Japanese rice

When making individual su-meshi blocks don't worry if the blocks don't look very neat. To make them perfectly requires at least two years' practice in a sushi restaurant kitchen.

To shape Japanese rice, wet everything – from your hands to the mould, if using – and keep the work surface tidy at all times. Use both hands to squeeze the rice into a densely packed shape.

Using moulds

When making moulded sushi, one option is to use small plastic moulds, which are easily available. Otherwise you can line an eggcup with clear film (plastic wrap), push a topping in, add a dab of wasabi paste, then fill with su-meshi. Seal the end with the clear film and press with your fingers. When ready, remove from the eggcup and unwrap from the clear film.

quantity of rice since the moisture isn't retained satisfactorily in a small amount.

The width, depth and material of the pan used will also make a difference to the end result. One of the best ways to get consistently good results is to use an electric rice-cooker. The microwave oven is not generally used for cooking Japanese rice, but for just one person it may produce a better result than cooking on a stove.

Mochigome (glutinous rice), on the other hand, should be soaked overnight and then steamed, rather than boiled, for 35–40 minutes. A large bamboo steamer is best so that the grains can be spread thinly. If boiling rice, use up to 20 per cent of mochigome in a mixture with ordinary rice.

Genmai should also be soaked for a few hours, ideally overnight; it should then be boiled with twice as much water and cooked for three times as long as ordinary rice.

Storage

Rice tastes best when newly harvested, and then it gradually deteriorates. Although it keeps for a long time, it is best eaten as soon as possible. Transfer raw rice to an earthenware, ceramic or plastic container with a lid and keep it in an airy, cool place away from direct sunlight. Keep rice perfectly dry; if the moisture content creeps up, the rice will soon turn mouldy. Rice available in the West is normally powdered with preservatives, hence its longevity.

RICE PRODUCTS

It is no surprise that the Japanese have developed various products out of rice and that these, in turn, have found a secure place in Japanese cooking.

Mochi

The main product of mochigome (glutinous rice) is mochi (rice cakes), hence the name.

Mochi cakes were traditionally made by hand, an arduous task involving pounding steamed mochigome rice to a very smooth, pliable consistency, then shaping and drying the mass to make a mochi block. The block is normally made into small circular shapes or cut into rectangular pieces, which are eaten, either fried, grilled (broiled) or very lightly boiled, with other accompaniments. Mochi hardens very quickly and is a good preserved food. It is eaten in soup as part of the New Year's celebration meal as mochi is believed to bring long life and wealth. It is also eaten with soy sauce or wasabi.

Mochi can be made at home with an electric mochi-maker, a brilliant recent Japanese invention, but excellent ready-made mochi cakes in packets are easily available at Japanese supermarkets and an unopened packet lasts for months.

Mochi with cheese and nori seaweed

This quick and easy snack is a tasty introduction to mochi.

1 Slice some Cheddar cheese a little smaller than the mochi cakes and about 5mm/¼in thick.

2 Grill (broil) the mochi cakes on each side under a medium heat for 2–3 minutes, turning them frequently to prevent burning. While the grilled mochi are still hot, make a horizontal slit at the side and insert a cheese slice.

3 If you wish, cut an 18 × 20cm/ 7 × 8in nori sheet into four to eight pieces and wrap one piece around each of the cheese stuffed mochi cakes before serving with a little shoyu (Japanese soy sauce).

Right: Nuka (rice bran), is most valued for its strong flavour and is a good base for pickling vegetables.

Shiratama

This flour is comprised mostly of starch taken from mochigome (glutinous rice), which is first soaked in water, then sieved (strained) and dried. It has a subtle flavour and is mostly used in wagashi (Japanese cakes) and sweet dumplings.

Domyoji

Mochigome rice is finely crushed to produce this flour, which is generally used for making wagashi (Japanese traditional cakes) and sometimes for cooking, usually in steamed dishes.

Nuka

This rice bran is traditionally used for pickling vegetables. The rice bran is first lightly roasted to bring out its flavour, then mixed with brine to make a mash, which ferments and makes a unique pickling base. The strong flavour seeps through to the fresh vegetables, making them not only soft with some crunchiness but also adding a very characteristic taste. The smell of rice bran is quite strong; it may not be to everyone's taste but once used to it you will be surprised at how delicious rice bran is. Nuka is now readily available at larger Japanese supermarkets.

Right: Shiratama flour, front, and Domyoji flour

MUGI

Once a substitute for rice whenever production was low, mugi, or barley, is now regarded as a health food by the Japanese; it contains more protein and ten times more fibre than rice. However, it is very difficult to cook and the husk is too deeply ingrained to remove. The Japanese solution to this is to squash or halve it. Oshimugi (squashed barley) and setsudan mugi (cut barley) are cooked with rice, or on their own for a dish called mugi-toro (barley with grated yam). Mugi is usually available from health food stores.

NOODLES

Certainly among the most popular foods in Japan, noodles are one of the oldest, most widely eaten foods in all of Southeast Asia, if not in the world. Noodle stores are dotted along every high street all over Japan and Japanese noodles are also becoming very popular in the West, with soba, udon and ramen all available at larger supermarkets.

SOMEN

These are very fine noodles also made from wheat, but the dough is stretched with the help of vegetable oil to make very thin strips and then air-dried. There are two regions famous for their exceptional somen – Miwa in Nara and Ibo in Himeji – and the somen they produce takes only 1 minute to cook.

SOBA NOODLES

This uniquely Japanese noodle is made of buckwheat flour mixed with ordinary wheat flour. To make buckwheat flour, the black-skinned seeds are first coarsely ground, then the outer skins are removed, and the flour is finely ground. As soba made from just buckwheat flour lacks elasticity and stickiness, wheat flour is usually added to act as a smoothing, binding agent. The colour ranges from dark brownish grey to light beige, depending on how the buckwheat seeds were ground.

Below: Dried somen noodles are available in packet form or in bundles.

Somen with tangy dipping sauce
This is a light, refreshing dish of chilled somen, perfect for lunch on a hot summer's day.

SERVES TWO

INGREDIENTS
200g/7oz somen
ice cubes
watercress, sliced cucumber and tomato, and ice cubes, to garnish
1 spring onion (scallion), finely chopped and grated fresh root ginger, to serve
For the dipping sauce (makes about 200ml/7fl oz/scant 1 cup)
2.5ml/½ tsp dashi
45ml/3 tbsp shoyu
15ml/1 tbsp mirin (or 10ml/ 2 tsp sugar)
120ml/4fl oz/½ cup hot or cold water

3 To make the dipping sauce, add the dashi, shoyu and mirin or sugar to the hot or cold water and stir. Divide the sauce between individual serving cups.

4 Garnish the noodles with some vegetables, such as watercress and sliced cucumber and tomato, and some ice cubes, if you like.

5 Serve the somen noodles in bowls with the chopped spring onion and grated ginger on small individual plates and the dipping sauce also in individual cups. Diners mix the spring onion and ginger in their sauce, then using hashi (chopsticks), dip the somen in the sauce, a few at a time, and eat.

1 Cook the somen in plenty of boiling water for 1–3 minutes following the instructions on the packet. Drain, then wash the outer starch from the somen under cold running water.

2 Place the cooked somen in a large serving bowl and add ice-cold water to cover well.

There is also a green-coloured soba, called chasoba, to which powdered tea has also been added. The finest soba comes from Shinshu, the mountain area of central Japan. Fresh soba is available in Japan and most of the good soba shops make their own every day. It's also common to see a *soba-ya* (noodle store) every 10 yards or so on any high street in Japan, serving fresh soba, and other popular noodles. Cold soba noodles are often eaten in summer and served on a bamboo tray with a dipping sauce. The Japanese love the taste of the noodles themselves; the sauce enhances their flavour. Outside of Japan, prepacked dried soba is sold in bundles of fine strands at larger supermarkets and Asian stores.

Left: Soba noodles from Shinshu, central Japan, are considered to be the finest of all soba noodles produced.

Storage

Dried soba will keep for many months if kept sealed in the original packet, or in airtight containers. Soba, perhaps more so than other Japanese noodle, is considered a health food so makes an ideal store cupboard (pantry) item.

Below: Fine buckwheat soba noodles and green chasoba, which get their distinctive colouring from the addition of powdered tea.

Cooking dried noodles

1 Bring plenty of water to the boil in a pan and add the noodles. For each person use about 115g/4oz dried noodles cooked in at least 600ml/1 pint/2½ cups water.

2 Cook over a medium heat following the instructions on the packet. It normally takes up to 5–6 minutes for soba, 10–13 minutes for udon, 1–3 minutes for somen and hiyamugi, and 5–8 minutes for ramen. Lower the heat if the water starts to boil over.

3 When the noodles are half transparent, they are done. Remove the pan from the heat, drain and wash off the outer starch under running water. Drain again and serve in hot soup or with a dipping sauce.

Left: Usually white, these hiyamugi noodles have occasional brown and pale pink strands.

UDON

This is a thick wheat noodle, which is eaten all over the world and probably has the longest history. To make udon, wheat flour is mixed with salted water to make a dough, then rolled out and thinly sliced. Fresh, raw udon is available in Japan but in the West it is usually either dried or cooked and frozen to be sold in packets.

HIYAMUGI

These thin, white noodles are made in the same way as udon but cut very thinly. They take about 5 minutes to cook and are eaten in hot soup or with a dipping sauce. Dried and bundled hiyamugi is available in packets at Asian supermarkets.

Right: Dried and fresh udon noodles

RAMEN

Literally meaning stretched noodle, ramen originated in China, and is made of wheat flour with added eggs and what the Japanese call kansui, alkali water. The chemical reaction between them makes the wheat dough smooth and stretchable to create very fine noodles. Pure, naturally formed kansui is now hard to obtain and is often substituted with bicarbonate of soda (baking soda). Ramen is eaten with other cooked food with or without soup, and has been meticulously developed in Japan. Almost every county has its own version of the noodles, the soup and the ingredients. It has reached the point of a ramen phenomenon: there is now a museum dedicated to the noodle in Yokohama, south of Tokyo; a ramen village in Hokkaido, the northern island; and appreciation societies everywhere. The popularity has now spread to the West and in recent years many ramen shops have sprung up in big cities, run not only by the Japanese but also by the Chinese largely adopting Japanese-style cooking techniques.

Ramen is available fresh, dried or frozen at large supermarkets and Asian stores. There are also numerous kinds of instant ramen with various flavoured soups in packets. These are very popular as quick, healthy snacks and late-night suppers, especially among the young.

Culinary uses

All Japanese noodles can be cooked in hot dashi-based soup with a few added ingredients, or eaten cold with a dipping sauce. Somen is a useful ingredient because of its white, almost hair-like fineness and is often used in clear soup or as a garnish. Ramen is nearly always cooked in hot meat-based soup (mainly pork) with several added ingredients, or in summer it is eaten cold, topped with a few fresh ingredients.

General preparation and cooking tips

Whether fresh or dried, all noodles need to be boiled, and this should be done carefully to prevent them becoming too soft. Follow the instructions on the packet. Cut a strand in the middle to check the noodles are cooked. If the noodles are to be eaten in hot soup, boil them until they are still a little hard. If they are to be eaten cold, cook thoroughly. Once boiled, wash off the outer starch under cold running water.

All Japanese noodles except ramen are eaten simply, either on their own or with only a few added ingredients and rarely with meat. Ramen, on the other hand, tends to be cooked with an assortment of meat-based ingredients.

Storage

Fresh noodles keep for only a few days in the refrigerator. In dried form, they will keep for a few months if sealed in the packet and stored in a cool place.

Making hand-made udon

MAKES 675G/1½LB

1 Sift 225g/8oz/2 cups plain (all-purpose) flour into a mixing bowl and make a well in the centre. Dissolve 15ml/1 tbsp salt in 150ml/¼ pint/⅔ cup water, pour into the well and gently fold in to make a firm dough.

2 Turn on to a floured work surface and knead until smooth but still firm. Hit hard with a fist at least 100 times to remove any air pockets. Cover with a damp cloth and leave for 2 hours.

3 Roll out on to a lightly floured work surface to make a rectangular sheet, 3mm/⅛in thick. Dust with flour, then fold one long side into the centre.

4 Turn over, dust with flour again and fold the remaining third over the top. (If you look at the end of the folded dough, it will form an S-shape.) Fold the dough in half lengthways.

5 Using a sharp knife, cut the folded dough crossways into 3mm/⅛in thick strips. Separate the strands with your hands. The udon noodles can be frozen at this stage.

6 Bring plenty of water to the boil in a large, deep pan. Add the udon and cook for 25–30 minutes, adding some cold water each time it starts to boil, until the noodles are thoroughly cooked but still slightly firm.

7 Drain and wash well under cold running water to remove the outer starch from the noodles. When ready to eat, reheat in a soup or quickly plunge in boiling water, then drain and serve with dipping sauce.

COOK'S TIP
To check if the noodles are cooked, cut a strip of udon and if the core of the cut face is turning from white to grey, it's done.

VEGETABLES

In recent years an increasing number of exotic vegetables and fruits have been introduced to the West, and many Japanese varieties are now available, which makes Japanese cooking a lot easier. It is interesting to see, too, how Japanese and Western varieties of many ordinary vegetables, such as cucumber and pepper, differ in size, shape and taste.

As Japanese cooking is largely vegetarian oriented, due to Buddhist traditions, the Japanese painstakingly developed the best way to wash, cut and cook each vegetable in order to retain its natural flavour and texture. The following are some of the typical Japanese vegetables.

DAIKON

This long, white, dense vegetable, also known by the Indian name mooli, is a member of the radish family. Used widely in Japanese cooking, it is one of the oldest vegetables and its recorded use dates back to the 8th century. It is also one of the most versatile of vegetables: it can be cooked in soup, chopped for salad, shredded for a sashimi garnish or grated for use as a condiment. It is also made into takuan: bright yellow pickles often used for nori-rolled sushi.

As it is grown all over Japan all year round, there are numerous varieties with different shapes, sizes and hues. The one normally grown in the West (also most commonly available in Japan) is the green neck type, which

has the fading pale-green part at the top of the main body. The most flavoursome ones come on to the market in winter. The leaves are often pickled or cooked in miso soup.

Aroma and flavour

Daikon has an aroma similar to radish and a slightly pungent flavour which is not as bitter as radish. It can be eaten either cooked or uncooked, and is also useful for adding flavour when served as a condiment or in a dipping sauce. The raw texture is crunchy, and, when cooked, daikon becomes fairly soft but does not disintegrate.

Culinary uses

Daikon is used in Japanese cooking for its flavour and texture, and not for its nutrition; it is nearly 95 per cent water. If served raw, it is finely shredded and used as a crystal-white garnish for sashimi and other fish dishes. The shreds mixed with carrot shreds make a good vinegared salad. A subtly pungent dipping sauce is made with shoyu.

Daikon is also used for simmering in dishes with meat or poultry, since it withstands slow cooking, absorbs the flavour and juice of other ingredients, and does not easily disintegrate. Various pickles are made with daikon, too.

Above: Many vegetables that are familiar to Westerners may differ in size, shape or taste. Japanese cucumbers, for example, are smaller and thinner than Western ones.

Preparation and cooking

Select a firm daikon with a shiny, undamaged skin. When cut crossways, the cut surface should be smooth and watery. If the flesh has an opaque, snowflake-like spongy pattern, discard it. Always peel away the outer skin.

Daikon can sometimes be very hard and stringy; in such cases it will be too bitter to eat raw. Instead, cut it into chunks and use in a slow simmering dish, or dice it and put it in soup. Simmering daikon slowly lets it absorb the flavour of the other ingredients.

When cutting daikon into slices or cylinders, shave off the top edges so that they will not cook first.

Storage

Daikon keeps fairly well for a week or two in the refrigerator, but it is best used within three or four days.

Daikon and shoyu dipping sauce

This sauce goes well with grilled (broiled) or pan-fried fish, meat and vegetables or with hotpot dishes, and serves two to four people.

1 Cut about 5cm/2in from the top of a daikon, then trim and peel. Finely grate the daikon, retaining the juice as well. Place in a small serving bowl.

2 Chop a spring onion (scallion) and add to the grated daikon.

3 Serve with lemon wedges for squeezing and a little shoyu in small individual bowls or plates. Each person mixes his or her own sauce using the daikon mixture, lemon juice, shoyu and a drop of chilli oil, if you like.

COOK'S TIP

It's sometimes difficult to find fresh, juicy daikon, though a reputable Caribbean grocer is a good place to try. A fresh daikon is at least 7.5cm/3in in diameter and sounds very dense and heavy when you pat it. Old daikon looks dehydrated and should not be used. Use fresh radishes instead.

Below: Daikon, a member of the radish family, resembles a very large, long, white carrot.

KABU

The turnip, originally grown in the Mediterranean coastal regions and Afghanistan, has been grown in Japan for over 1,300 years. Many types have been crossbred but the most commonly used, kabu, is a small, round-shaped one. This Japanese turnip is far smaller than Western varieties.

The kabu flesh contains sugar, protein, calcium, vitamin C and fibre.

Aroma and flavour

The smell of Japanese kabu is similar to that of a radish. It has a subtle flavour, and, when cooked, develops a slightly bitter-sweet taste.

Culinary uses

Both leaves and root are very good for pickles, and many regions have their own speciality kabu pickles. When kabu is cooked, the central part becomes soft fairly quickly but, just like daikon, it is protected by the hard outer layer so it does not disintegrate. Kabu is good for hotpot dishes as well as for soup.

Preparation and cooking

Although the outer skin is not as hard as daikon, kabu should also be peeled before cooking. However, it is not normally grated and eaten raw, as the flavour is not sufficiently pungent.

Storage

Kabu will keep well for a few days if stored in the refrigerator.

Right: Kabu (turnip)

Shredding daikon

1 Cut about 5cm/2in from the top of a daikon, then trim and peel. Place the daikon, cut side down, on a board. Using a sharp knife, cut off a thin slice. Continue until the daikon is too small to slice.

2 Put all the daikon sheets together, one on top of the other. Using the knife, cut the sheets crossways into thin shreds and place the shreds in ice-cold water. Drain and dry with kitchen paper.

SATOIMO

This small, oval-shaped potato, which originated in India, is one of the oldest vegetables used in Japan and is also very popular in China. Underneath its hairy, striped, dark skin there is a unique slipperiness, which makes the vegetable very easy to peel. It is widely available at Asian food stores. If you can't find it, taro can be substituted.

Aroma and flavour

Satoimo has a faint, potato-like aroma, but the flavour is much richer than ordinary potato and interestingly sweet and bitter at the same time. It also has a dense yet fluffy texture.

Culinary uses

Plain boiled or steamed satoimo, dipped in shoyu, is a popular snack in Japan. It is also excellent in simmered dishes, such as oden (hotpot), and winter soups.

Above: Satoimo, a member of the potato family, has a unique slippery coating under its hairy, striped skin.

Preparation and cooking

To peel, boil whole, then the skin comes off very easily. Wipe off the sliminess with kitchen paper before using.

Storage

Satoimo keeps fairly well, for up to five days, if stored in a cool, airy place away from direct sunlight.

SATSUMA-IMO

Originating in Central America, the sweet potato was introduced to Japan via Spain, the Philippines, China and Okinawa. It first arrived in Satsuma, the southernmost area of Japan, hence its Japanese name, meaning satsuma-potato.

There are numerous types of sweet potato even among the Japanese varieties. The colour of the skin varies from scarlet red to mauve, and the flesh varies from a rich yellow colour to dark mauve. The varieties available in the West are generally tougher and less sweet than Japanese ones.

Aroma and flavour

It has a rich potato aroma and slightly sweet flavour.

Culinary uses

Sweet potato is most often used for simmered, steamed and fried dishes and is good for cooking on a barbecue. It can also be used as an ingredient in savoury cakes and desserts, and plain boiled or steamed satsuma-imo makes a tasty snack.

Above and below: Satsuma-imo (sweet potato) can vary in its size, colour, taste and texture.

Preparation and cooking

As sweet potato contains a high percentage of water, it easily becomes over-soft and soggy. To avoid this, it is best to steam rather than boil sweet potato.

Storage

Sweet potato keeps well for up to one week if stored in a cool, airy place away from direct sunlight.

KABOCHA

This vegetable plays an essential part in Japanese cooking. Originally from Central America, this Japanese squash is the result of various crossbreedings over the last century. It has a dark green and ragged skin and is much smaller than Western squash varieties. The dense flesh is a rich yellow colour and, when boiled, becomes sweet and fluffy. Although it is highly calorific, kabocha is regarded as a health food for its nutritional content, containing both carotene and vitamin A. Along with many other varieties of the squash family, it is now widely available.

Aroma and flavour

Kabocha has a mild chestnut aroma, and the flavour is also similar to, but not as sweet as, the chestnut. The texture is dense, similar to a moist sweet potato.

Culinary uses

To appreciate its delicate flavour, this vegetable is best simply steamed or boiled. It is also used for frying in tempura, as well as for simmering with other vegetables and chicken. The seeds are full of protein, and can be dry-roasted and eaten as a snack on their own or as a tasty accompaniment to drinks.

Salt-steamed kabocha chips

This is a nutritious snack, much healthier than chips (French fries).

1 In a steamer, lightly steam whole kabocha over a high heat for 5–6 minutes until the outer skin becomes soft enough to peel. If using a pan, boil a little water, about 1cm/½in deep, then place the kabocha in it and cook for 3 minutes. Remove from the pan, and cut in half.

2 Using your fingers, take out the seeds from the centre and discard them. (Alternatively, the seeds can be dried, roasted and eaten.)

3 Place the kabocha on a chopping board with the cut-side down and, using a knife, scrape off about a third of the hard skin in strips.

4 Cut into bitesize chunks, and place back into the steamer. Sprinkle over a pinch of coarse salt. Cover and steam over a high heat for about 8–10 minutes until the flesh can be pierced by a cocktail stick.

5 If using a pan, lay the kabocha pieces in the base of a shallow, flat-based pan, then add 45–75ml/ 3–5 tbsp water at the side (not on the kabocha) and sprinkle over a pinch of coarse salt.

6 Cover and cook over a medium heat for about 4 minutes. Reduce the heat to the lowest setting and cook for a further 8–10 minutes.

7 Remove the pan from the heat and leave the kabocha to settle, still covered, for about 5 minutes.

Preparation and cooking

This is a very hard vegetable and not easily cut. It is therefore advisable to lightly steam whole kabocha first in order to soften it slightly before cutting into large chunks. This is most easily done in a steamer, though a large pan will also suffice.

Although the skin is tough, do not remove all of it since the flesh closest to the skin is the tastiest part. Cutting off occasional strips of the skin will create a pretty marbled effect through the contrast of the outer green skin with the inner yellow flesh. This is a moist vegetable that easily disintegrates, so do not cook in too much liquid. An average kabocha will serve four to eight people.

Storage

Choose a heavy, dense kabocha with a dark green, hard, undamaged skin. It is a tough vegetable and keeps well for a week if stored whole in the refrigerator.

Above:
Kabocha has a dark and ragged green skin and the flesh can range from yellow to orange.

NAGA-IMO

This mountain potato, also known as yama-imo, meaning long potato, still grows wild in Japan, as well as being cultivated. The shiny, snowy white flesh is very slippery, and it is for this quality that it is most appreciated. Naga-imo is available in winter from Japanese supermarkets.

Aroma and flavour

Though naga-imo has little aroma, and has a bitter-sweet flavour, it is cherished by the Japanese for its rare, moist sticky texture.

Culinary uses

Among its many uses, the most popular is to grate the flesh to make a slimy thick soup that is eaten with barley rice. Naga-imo can also be shredded for use in vinegared salads, and sliced for frying.

Preparation and cooking

Naga-imo is mostly used uncooked, either grated or shredded. Once peeled, the flesh discolours, so eat immediately or sprinkle with vinegar or lemon juice.

Storage

Like most vegetables of this kind, naga-imo keep fairly well for up to one week in a cool, airy place away from direct sunlight. Once peeled, do not keep, as the white flesh turns an unappealing grey colour.

Left: Naga-imo has an unusual slippery flesh, so rub with a wet cloth after peeling for easy handling.

Below: Vacuum-packed gingko nuts

Right: Shelled and blanched gingko nuts

GINGKO NUT

The Japanese maple tree, *Icho*, bears the exquisite gingko nut, known as ginnan in Japan. It is a favourite delicacy and a traditional accompaniment to sake. The word gingko or ginkgo is a corruption of *ginkyo*, another Japanese name for the maple tree. Ginko nut is available either fresh in its shell, shelled in packets, or shelled and cooked in cans or jars. A dried variety is also available.

Aroma and flavour

Gingko nut has very little aroma but has a fairly prominent milky flavour with a hint of bitterness, which adds vivid freshness to simmered dishes.

Culinary uses

Fried or lightly roasted gingko nuts sprinkled with salt are often served as an hors d'oeuvre. They can also be used for fried and simmered dishes, and in soups.

Preparation and cooking

To break the hard shell, place the nut with the join part vertically on a chopping board and bang on top with a rolling pin. The thin brown membrane should be removed, and the nuts blanched before use in any dish. The best method is to boil the nuts in just enough water to cover them and rub off the thin brown membrane with the back of a ladle. If dried gingko nuts are being used, they need to be soaked in water for several hours before use. Drain before adding to soups and simmered dishes.

Storage

The whole gingko in an undamaged shell keeps for a long time, but once broken, use within a few days. Store unused soaked or canned gingko nuts in fresh water in the refrigerator for up to three days.

KURI

This Japanese variety of chestnut is grown throughout Japan and the southern Korean peninsula, and has a more triangular shape and smoother shell than the Chinese, European or American varieties. Kuri represents autumn and is a useful way to express the season in dishes for *kaiseki* (formal banquet) or tea-ceremony cooking. Apart from fresh kuri, peeled chestnuts are also available in cans, either cooked or uncooked.

Aroma and flavour

The transformation of kuri from its hard whitish raw state to a bright yellow jewel when cooked is quite striking. It is this golden yellow colour that makes it such a valued ingredient, along with its almost sesame-like aroma and subtly sweet, nutty flavour apparent in its cooked form.

Culinary uses

Kuri is one of the most useful and versatile ingredients found in Japanese cooking. It can be eaten just grilled (broiled) or boiled as a snack, or used as a means to express the season on hors d'oeuvres trays. It can also be mashed to make various sizes and shapes of sweet wagashi (Japanese cakes). Kuri gohan (rice cooked with chestnuts) is one

Left: Cooked sweet kuri (Japanese chestnuts)

Chestnut rice

With the golden colour of kuri against the simple white of rice, this is a beautiful, as well as delicious, dish.

SERVES FOUR

INGREDIENTS
    225g/8oz/generous 1 cup
    Japanese short grain rice
    90g/3½oz fresh chestnuts, shelled
    and peeled, or 150g/5oz cooked,
    peeled chestnuts
    5ml/1 tsp sea salt
    25ml/1½ tbsp sake or white wine
    10ml/2 tsp black sesame seeds,
    lightly toasted, to garnish

1 Wash the rice well, changing the water several times, until the water runs clear, then put the rice in a fine mesh strainer, and leave to drain for an hour. Put the rice in a deep pan.

2 If using fresh chestnuts, cut them in half and rinse in cold water. Drain and place on top of the rice.

3 Dissolve the salt in 300ml/½ pint/ 1¼ cups water and add to the pan. Add extra water, if necessary, to fully cover the rice and chestnuts. Pour in the sake or wine.

4 Cover and cook over a high heat for 5–8 minutes until the mixture begins to bubble. Lower the heat and simmer for 10 minutes until the water is absorbed.

5 Leave to stand, still covered, for about 15 minutes, then gently mix the chestnuts into the rice. Try not to break up the chestnuts as you mix them in. Serve in individual rice bowls sprinkled with the black sesame seeds.

of the more popular traditional dishes enjoyed by the Japanese each autumn. Kuri kinton, cooked and mashed kuri with added sugar made into a shiny sweet paste, is a better version of ordinary kinto, which is made with sweet potato, and is one of the dishes at New Year's celebration meals.

Preparation and cooking

Make a slit in the shell before boiling or grilling (broiling) to make peeling easier. When peeling, remove the outer shell and the thin brown membrane attached to the flesh, otherwise it will taste bitter.

Storage

Whole chestnuts keep well for a few weeks. Once peeled, use immediately.

Aroma and flavour

Hakusai has a faint, fresh aroma and a very subtle cabbage flavour. The main quality of this vegetable is neither its aroma nor flavour but its crunchiness and versatility when cooked. As it absorbs the flavour of other ingredients, it is almost always cooked with meat, poultry, fish and other vegetables in a strong sauce.

Culinary uses

Salted hakusai is one of the usual dishes served to accompany plain cooked rice at the Japanese breakfast table. The salt takes the chill off the otherwise hard, iceberg texture of the thick, white core and brings out the colour. It is also used in simmered dishes, hotpots and steamed dishes: when cooked, the green part becomes more vivid and bright, and the white part translucent.

The straight, white trunk becomes flexible when cooked, so it can be rolled either on its own or with spinach, often with minced (ground) meat, poultry or fish stuffed inside, and then simmered. This succulent vegetable is very good for any soup dish: cook with chopped bacon and season with salt, pepper and a drop of shoyu. It's a very easy and delicious dish.

Preparation and cooking

Trim the base, then separate the leaves and wash thoroughly. The white part is very crunchy when raw, but when cooked it quickly becomes soft and stringy and not very easy to chew. So, always cut the leaves crossways against the fibre into bitesize pieces.

Storage

Tightly wrapped, this vegetable will keep well in the refrigerator for quite a long time. So, although it is a relatively large vegetable, a few leaves can be taken out as required over a period of up to two weeks.

KOMATSUNA

Among the numerous kinds of green vegetables, komatsuna is one of the most popular in Japan. It is a member of the radish family and has been crossbred in Japan. Unlike other radishes it does not grow a bulbous tuber. The leaf is smooth and soft, and the stem is thin and delicate. As it is resistant to cold weather, this deep green vegetable used to provide a good supply of winter leaves but today it is grown in the greenhouse all year round. It is not always available in the West but can be substituted by spinach.

Aroma and flavour

Komatsuna has a very subtle aroma and flavour. It is mainly used for its colour as well as for its vitamin content.

Below: Both komatsuna, front, and horenso (spinach), back, should be used on the day of purchase as the leaves wilt quickly.

HAKUSAI

Although its origin can be traced back to the Mediterranean, Chinese cabbage is grown mainly in East Asia around China, the Korean peninsula and Japan. Introduced into Japan from China at the end of the 19th century, and developed to suit the local climate and tastes, it is now one of the most popular ingredients in Japanese cooking.

The Japanese variety, hakusai, meaning white vegetable, is larger and the outer leaves are in fact greener than the Chinese cabbage now widely available in the West. The leaves are also tightly crinkled and inside they are a bright yellow colour with a thick, white core. There are offsprings of this variety such as santo-sai and hiroshima-na, but these are not available in the West.

Hakusai is a winter vegetable and supplies otherwise scarce vitamin C during the cold months.

Culinary uses

Although komatsuna can never take centre stage even in home cooking, it is a very useful green vegetable and commonly used in Japan. Cooked with meat, it provides balance to any fat, and in soup it gives a striking dark green background colour for other ingredients such as white tofu and pink prawns (shrimp). It is also used for pickles.

Preparation and cooking

Wash thoroughly before use and cook very lightly, otherwise the green colour quickly turns an unappetizing grey.

HORENSO

Originating in Western Asia, spinach can be classified into two main types: Eastern and Western. The Eastern variety was brought to Japan from China in the 16th century and commonly has a triangular, zigzag-edged leaf, which is pointed at the top, and a scarlet root. Western varities have a rounder leaf.

Horenso has thin leaves, a delicate texture and a mild, sweet flavour. Recently an East–West crossbreed has been developed, which is also now commonly available in Japan. Spinach is very rich in vitamins A, B1, B2 and C, as well as iron and calcium.

Aroma and flavour

Japanese spinach has a rich grass aroma and a sweet flavour with a hint of bitterness, particularly in the soft lower stem.

Culinary uses

The most popular use for horenso in Japanese cooking is ohitashi (cooked salad with dashi stock). Lightly cooked spinach is also tossed with seed and nut dressings.

Preparation and cooking

Wash thoroughly before use as spinach grows touching the ground and earth gets inside the stems. Always lightly boil first, to get rid of the slight bitterness, except those young spinach leaves that can be used in a salad.

Storage

As is the case with all delicate green vegetables, both komatsuna and spinach are best used on the day of purchase. Even if kept in the coolest part of the refrigerator the leaves will start to wilt almost immediately. There are canned or frozen cooked spinach on the market, but these are rather mushy and their use is limited.

SHUNGIKU

Chrysanthemum leaves are, contrary to what the name suggests, not actually leaves from the chrysanthemum flowers, but from the chrysanthemum vegetable. This vegetable plant has two to three shoots, on which grow several long, narrow zigzag leaves.

Originating in Mediterranean coastal areas, it has only recently become very popular in South-east Asia. It is full of calcium, iron, carotene and vitamin C. There are variations in leaf size and smaller ones can be eaten raw.

Shungiku is cut for eating when the plant reaches about 15–20cm/6–8in high and is brought to market with the stems intact; the stems are also very succulent when cooked.

Aroma and flavour

The leaves have a strong, herbal aroma, and a delicately bitter flavour. The yellowish green leaves turn bright green when cooked, and retain firm texture even if cooked for a long time.

Preparation and cooking

Wash shungiku well, particularly if it is to be eaten raw, and cut off the hard part of the stem. The most cherished quality of this vegetable is its unique aroma, so cook very lightly. To eat the leaves raw, pinch them from the stem.

Culinary uses

Shungiku is indispensable for Japanese hotpot dishes. Its exquisite aroma can also be appreciated in a warm salad, if cooked lightly and tossed in a dressing. It also can be simmered and even fried, as the leaves do not easily disintegrate.

Storage

This relatively tough vegetable keeps fairly well; it will store for up to three days, if kept in the refrigerator.

Left: Shungiku (chrysanthemum leaf); in Japan, medium-size leaves are the most valued, as they are the best for cooking.

Below: In keeping with its size, negi, a giant spring onion, has a robust aroma and flavour.

NEGI

This giant spring onion (scallion), which is 30–50cm/ 12–20in long and 1–2cm/½–¾in in diameter, is a unique Japanese vegetable and, even in Japan, is generally available only in the Tokyo area and eastern Japan. It may look like a slim leek, but the texture is a lot more delicate, rather like that of the spring onion, and it does not have a hard core like the leek. Although the long white part in preference to the green part is mainly used for Japanese cooking, the mineral and vitamin contents are much greater in the green. It is sometimes available at Asian supermarkets.

Aroma and flavour

Negi has a pungent aroma and also a strong onion flavour.

Culinary uses

In Japanese cooking this leek-type vegetable is mainly used finely chopped and added to sauces or soups as a herbal condiment. It gives a fresh, pungent final touch and a decorative look to plain shoyu or hot miso soup.

The white part, finely shredded, is also used to garnish sashimi or any other fish dish; the curled shreds, which resemble silver hair, make an interesting alternative to daikon shreds. It is used for grilling (broiling), in particular with yakitori (skewered grilled chicken) or any other meat. Sukiyaki (pan-cooked beef in sweet shoyu sauce) and shabu shabu (pot-cooked beef in soup) also usually include diagonally chopped negi.

Preparation and cooking

Wash thoroughly and trim the base of the stem. Negi should be cooked very lightly, as when overcooked it has an unpleasant slimy texture. For sauces and soups, it is normally very finely chopped. For hotpots, cut crossways diagonally.

For grilling in recipes such as yakitori, cut straight across into 3–4cm/1¼–1½in pieces, and cut other ingredients in the same way. For decorative curls, see below.

Storage

As with the spring onion, the green part starts to wilt and change colour within about two days even in the refrigerator, but the main white part keeps fairly well for up to three days.

Making spring onion (scallion) curls

1 Choose small, slim spring onions. Trim off most of the green leaves to leave a 7.5cm/3in length.

2 Shred the spring onions lengthways to within about 1cm/½in of the root end. Take care not to cut through the root completely.

3 Place the shredded spring onions in a small bowl of iced water and chill for 15–20 minutes, or until the shredded ends have curled.

RAKKYO

This bulb vegetable originated in the Himalayas and China. It grows in a bunch of six to seven small, thin oval-shaped bulbs, about 7.5cm/3in long. The body is milky white or with a faint purple hue. It is picked young, with each bulb weighing 2–5g/¹⁄₁₆–¹⁄₈oz, but some grow to 10g/¼oz after a year. Rakkyo is available in Japanese markets from late spring to early summer, when many households make rakkyo pickles to last throughout the year. When in season, it is available in Asian stores.

Aroma and flavour

Rakkyo is the Japanese equivalent of garlic; eat just one and the odour will linger on your breath for the rest of the day. It has an intense onion smell with a hint of garlic. Apart from the smell, its flavour is too sharp to eat raw, but once pickled, the brine brings out the high sugar content, which makes it not only more palatable but an ideal addition to hot rice.

Culinary uses

Rakkyo is almost always pickled, either in brine, in sweet vinegar or marinated for a shorter time in shoyu. It is served with rice or Japanese curry.

Preparation and cooking

Trim the root and the top, and wash thoroughly. If the rakkyo is very young, pickle immediately in brine; otherwise blanch quickly and then marinate in shoyu. It will be ready to eat after a week. The longer rakkyo is marinated the milder the taste becomes, but the smell always persists.

Storage

Like onions, the central core of rakkyo starts growing a green shoot after a while, and eventually the whole bulb dries out. It is best to pickle the vegetable immediately after purchase.

Right: Myoga

Above: Pickled rakkyo

MYOGA

This uniquely shaped vegetable is actually the flower bud of the myoga plant, which originated in tropical Asia. The bud grows directly from the root stem in summer in the wild, while cultivated buds are exposed to light twice before picking, to obtain their healthy red colour. Some varieties of the bud grow in autumn, and these usually have a richer flavour than the summer ones.

If the bud is left to grow, it forms a 50–60cm/20–24in long thin stem, which is eaten in winter. Myoga is one of the more unusual Japanese vegetables sometimes available in the West.

Aroma and flavour

Myoga smells and tastes more like a herb than a vegetable, and has a strong, piercing aroma. This crunchy vegetable has a bitter flavour making it unsuitable for eating raw. When pickled in brine for several weeks, the taste becomes milder and sweeter, but, like rakkyo, the sharp aroma remains.

Culinary uses

The most valuable quality of myoga is its unique aroma. It is used for dipping sauces and as a garnish to sashimi or other fish dishes. It is also used for cooked or vinegared vegetables, in soups or for tempura.

Preparation and cooking

Wash off the mud thoroughly. For pickling, use whole or cut in half, then finely slice when ready to eat. For all other purposes, it is better to slice thinly lengthways and use sparingly. Blanch first if using in a salad.

Storage

Myoga is not prone to wilting, but its distinctive aroma will soon fade if stored in the refrigerator. Store myoga at room temperature and use as soon as possible.

GOBO

This thin, brown burdock root was first introduced to ancient Japan from China as a herbal medicine, but it was soon developed by the Japanese into a form suitable for normal consumption. Raw gobo is inedible; when cooked, the grey flesh is quite stringy but it adds a unique texture and flavour to a dish. Its main nutritional content is sugar, but it is also high in fibre and calcium. Fresh gobo is sometimes available at Asian supermarkets, where frozen or canned, cooked gobo is also sold.

Aroma and flavour

Gobo has a unique sesame-like aroma and a slightly bitter flavour when raw. When cooked its sweetness becomes more pronounced.

Culinary uses

The most popular dish that features this root vegetable is kinpira, stir-fried shredded carrot and gobo with chilli and shoyu (soy sauce). It is also used for tempura, simmering dishes and in soups. It makes delicious rice-bran pickles, too.

Preparation and cooking

Scrub the thin outer skin, then shred with a sharp knife as if sharpening a pencil, and soak the root in water for 15 minutes to remove the bitterness. Alternatively, cut gobo into chunks and simmer slowly for a long time.

Storage

Gobo is a tough little root and keeps well even outside the refrigerator for several days.

TAKENOKO

Bamboo shoot is one of the popular vegetables in South-east Asia and is widely available in cans. The Japanese cherish the fresh young shoots, which are inevitably a very seasonal delicacy, only available from late spring to early summer. Most of the content of bamboo shoot is water and it has little nutritional value. Instead, it is appreciated for its pleasant, natural look and crisp texture.

The Japanese make use of the outer, hard brown barks for wrapping sushi or other rice-based lunches. Takenoko is also available pickled as *menma*, and cooked in jars and cans, or also in a dried form at Asian supermarkets.

Below: Takenoko (bamboo shoot) is available in a variety of forms; freshly peeled and cut, back, as a bark for wrapping sushi, left, and as dried strips, front.

Left: Frozen gobo sticks, ready for cooking

Aroma and flavour

Fresh takenoko has a very subtle, earthy aroma and a delicately bitter flavour, which improves with age. Whatever its age, the vegetable is capable of absorbing flavour from the sauce it is cooked with, while retaining its own taste.

Culinary uses

In Japanese cooking, takenoko is almost always slowly simmered, so that its delicate flavour will not be spoiled. Simply cooked fresh bamboo shoots in dashi sauce is one of the most popular dishes at Japanese restaurants. The young, tender shoot is also good for takenoko gohan (rice cooked with bamboo shoots), while the older shoots are best reserved for slow cooking with other vegetables and chicken, or for stir-frying.

Preparation and cooking

The already cleaned young shoot can be sliced or cut into bitesize chunks and cooked immediately, but older ones should be boiled before use. For this, it is advisable to use the milky water in which rice was washed, as the rice bran in the water reduces the bamboo shoot's bitterness. Canned bamboo shoots are ready cooked, so they just need to be rinsed and drained; dried bamboo shoots must be soaked in water for 2–3 hours before use.

Storage

Fresh, uncooked whole bamboo shoot keeps well in the refrigerator for over a week but it will gradually lose its moisture. Most of the fresh ones on the market are usually boiled, and do not last long, so use within two days. Canned, cooked shoots, once opened, should be stored in the refrigerator in fresh water that is changed daily, and used within a week.

Below: Fresh renkon (lotus root) is available in large quantities in winter at Asian supermarkets. Canned or frozen renkon are available all year round, and come peeled, sliced and cooked.

RENKON

Although renkon refers specifically to the lotus root, the lotus plant itself has a long association with Buddhism and has been a regular feature in temple ponds in Japan since ancient times. The first evidence of serving its roots as food was found in a book dating from AD 713.

The root normally has about four sections, and looks like a long, narrow balloon with a few knots, and although the outer skin is light beige, upon peeling it reveals a white, crispy flesh. Renkon has several vertical holes running through to the base, which reveal a flower-like pattern when the root is cut in cross-section, adding a unique look to any dish. Nutritionally, it contains mainly starch with 15 per cent sugar and little else.

Aroma and flavour

Renkon has very little aroma and flavour when raw.

Culinary uses

Renkon's crunchiness as well as its unique pattern is greatly appreciated in Japanese cooking. It is used for simmered dishes, tempura, sushi and for salads with vinegar dressing. It is always dressed or cooked with vinegar, which brings out its sweetness.

Preparation and cooking

Trim the hard part from both ends and peel. Cut into rings and plunge in vinegar and water (see right) to avoid discolouration. Cook in lightly acidulated boiling water. Do not use iron pans.

Storage

Select firm and undamaged renkon. Although the outer skin discolours quickly, the inside keeps fairly fresh for up to five days if stored in the refrigerator.

Right: Canned, cooked renkon slices

Preparing renkon

When sliced and cooked with vinegar, renkon can be used in a salad or marinated in a mixture of rice vinegar, sugar and some salt.

1 Chop the renkon into sections, trim the hard part at the ends of the root and peel.

2 Cut into rings and immediately soak in a mixture of vinegar and water (120ml/4fl oz/½ cup water to 30–45ml/2–3 tbsp vinegar) to prevent discoloration. Allow to soak for about 5 minutes.

3 Boil enough water to cover the renkon, add 15–30ml/1–2 tbsp vinegar and the renkon rings, then cook for about 2 minutes until soft but still crisp. Remove from the heat and drain.

ADUKI BEANS

Also known as azuki (small beans) beans in Japan, aduki are probably the most popular Japanese variety of bean in the West. This bean has very high levels of starch (over 50 per cent), as well as protein and fibre, and some vitamin B$_1$. It is regarded in Japan as a very healthy food.

There are various sizes of aduki, and colours include red, green, yellow and white. Most commonly used is the red variety, mainly for Japanese cakes and desserts. The green bean (mung bean), is used to make harusame (bean vermicelli) and beansprouts are grown from it. Aduki are widely available at supermarkets and health food stores.

Aroma and flavour

Probably due to the high starch content, aduki beans have a faint sweet aroma and a chestnut-like flavour.

Culinary uses

Aduki beans can be simmered in sauce or cooked with rice to make sekihan (red rice) for celebrations, but they are mainly used for making an, a sweet paste, for wagashi (Japanese cakes).

An (sweet bean paste)

There are ready-made bean pastes in cans or they can be bought in powdered form to be reconstituted, but making fresh an from scratch is a far superior and easy option. This recipe makes tsubushi-an (crushed paste) and is used for making o'hagi (sweet, paste-wrapped, glutinous rice balls) and for stuffing mochi cakes. It is also very good spread on toast.

MAKES ABOUT 500G/1¼LB

INGREDIENTS
  200g/7oz/1 cup aduki or
    black beans
  200g/7oz/1 cup sugar
  salt

1 Put the beans in a large pan, add water to cover well and bring to the boil. Drain.

2 Return the drained beans to the pan, add 750ml/1¼ pints/3 cups water and soak the beans for about 24 hours. Discard any beans that remain floating. Place the soaked beans, still in the water in the pan, over a high heat and bring to a rolling boil.

3 Simmer over a very low heat, half-covered, for about 1 hour. Add water from time to time and stir frequently with a wooden spoon until the beans are very soft and the water is almost entirely absorbed.

4 Add the sugar and stir well. Keep stirring until the beans are thoroughly crushed. Add a pinch of salt and, using a large pestle or a rolling pin, mash into a smooth paste.

Left: Green aduki beans, which are used to make bean vermicelli, and red aduki beans, which are used mostly in cakes and desserts.

An also makes a rich addition to Western desserts, such as ice creams, fruit salads, and mousses. Simply arrange an around or on top of the dessert.

Preparation and cooking

Discard any damaged beans. For making sweet bean paste, soak the aduki beans in plenty of water for 24 hours before cooking, and discard those that remain floating. Do not soak if you are making dishes where you wish to retain the shape, colour and aroma of the beans, such as for a decoration for a dessert.

Storage

Aduki beans keep almost indefinitely if stored well away from direct sunlight.

FRESH BEANS

Young beans, such as eda-mame (green beans in the pod), soramame (broad/fava beans), saya-ingen (green beans) and saya-éndo (mangetouts/snow peas), are often used in Japanese cooking. Eda-mame and soramame are also boiled and eaten as a snack.

Boiled eda-mame
This is a good way to appreciate young soya beans in the pod.

1 Separate the pods from the stalks if they are still attached. Trim off the stem end. Sprinkle the pods generously with salt and rub into the bean pods with your hands. Leave for 15 minutes.

2 Boil plenty of water in a large pan, then add the beans and boil over a high heat for 7–10 minutes, or until the beans inside the pods are tender but still crunchy. Drain immediately and refresh briefly under running water.

3 Serve hot or cold in a basket or a bowl with drinks. For extra saltiness, sprinkle with a little salt. To eat, it is acceptable to squeeze the pods with your teeth to push out the beans into your mouth.

EDA-MAME

In Japan, when fresh, young green beans in their hairy pods start appearing in the market, the people know summer has arrived. These beans are called eda-mame meaning branch beans as they are often sold still on the stalks. They are becoming popular outside Japan now, mainly through Japanese restaurants, and are available from summer to early autumn at some Japanese supermarkets.

Fresh young green beans in the pod are delicious boiled and are often served whole as hors d'oeuvres. Keep refrigerated and use within a few days.

Above: Eda-mame (young green beans still in their pods)

Green beans in walnut sauce
This nut-based sauce is a good way to add body and flavour to vegetables.

SERVES FOUR

INGREDIENTS
250g/9oz/1⅔ cups green beans
For the walnut sauce
  65g/2½oz/2 cups shelled walnuts
  15ml/1 tbsp caster
    (superfine) sugar
  15ml/1 tbsp shoyu
  15ml/1 tbsp sake
  30ml/2 tbsp water

1 Trim the beans and then cut them diagonally into 4cm/1½in long nib-shaped pieces. Cook for 2 minutes in boiling water with a generous pinch of salt. Drain.

2 To make the walnut sauce, pound all but 2–4 walnut pieces to a fine paste in a mortar with a pestle.

3 When smooth, add the sugar and shoyu to make a fairly dry paste. Add the sake and water and mix to make a creamy sauce.

4 Put the green beans in a mixing bowl and add the walnut sauce. Stir well to coat the beans evenly.

5 Roughly crush the reserved walnut pieces. Serve the green beans and walnut sauce in individual bowls or on a plate, and sprinkle with the remaining walnut pieces on top. Serve warm.

COOK'S TIP
Other nuts, such as peanuts, or seeds, such as sesame seeds, may also be used to make a tasty dressing for boiled vegetables. For an extra smooth sauce, use a Japanese grinder and wooden pestle, rather than an ordinary Western mortar and pestle.

TOFU AND TOFU PRODUCTS

One of the oldest processed foods of South-east Asia, tofu has become more widely appreciated in recent years due to health-conscious trends around the world. Tofu came to Japan from China in the 8th century and has been one of the most important foods ever since.

As with many other foods, the Japanese developed tofu to a more refined form, as well as producing many new by-products to suit the subtlety and delicacy of Japanese cooking. Tofu is mostly made commercially nowadays, but there are still small tofu-making businesses in many residential areas of Japan, making fresh tofu at dawn every day.

Left: Clockwise from front left, soft or silken tofu, lightly seared tofu and regular, firmer tofu

Pressing tofu

1 Wrap a tofu cake in kitchen paper or, alternatively, place a cake of tofu on a slightly tilting chopping board and place a smaller board on top.

2 If wrapped, place a large plate on top, so that the plate covers the tofu. Put a weight (such as a book) on it and leave it to press for up to 1 hour until all the excess water has been absorbed or has run down the tilted board.

TOFU

Highly nutritious and low in fat and sugar, tofu is made from soya beans, which are first boiled and crushed, then the milk is separated and made into curds with the help of a coagulant. The warm curds are set in moulds for a few hours, then released into a water tank to firm and cool further. A cotton cloth is laid across the base of the moulds to retain the curds while they set and to allow excess water to drain away. Tofu made in this way often has a distinctive cloth mark on its sides and is known as regular tofu. This tofu is called momen-goshi (cotton-sieved tofu), as opposed to the more delicate, softer kinu-goshi (silk-sieved tofu – sold as silken tofu in the West), which is made with thicker milk and without draining the excess water. Both are creamy white in colour.

Japanese tofu, both fresh and in cartons, is available from Asian supermarkets in the West, and is normally of a standard size, 10 × 6 × 4.5cm/4 × 2½ × 1¾in. There is also lightly seared tofu called yaki-dofu, which is available from Japanese shops and is mainly used in hotpot dishes. Other lesser-quality types of tofu are widely available from supermarkets.

The soya bean pulp, after exuding the milk, is not wasted. Called okara, it is used in vegetable cooking, and can occasionally be found at larger Japanese supermarkets.

Aroma and flavour

To the Japanese palate, little of the tofu available outside Japan has the real taste of tofu. Although some fresh tofu has a faint soya bean aroma and milky flavour, many varieties appear to be made of little more than milky water.

Culinary uses

Fresh tofu, silken tofu in particular, is best eaten as it is, cold or hot, with shoyu, chopped spring onion (scallion) and grated ginger, or in soups. The firmer cotton tofu is more suitable for cooking dishes such as agedashi-dofu (fried tofu in dashi sauce) and as tofu steaks. Tofu is also cooked with other vegetables, fish and meat, and used for making a white dressing for salads.

Preparation and cooking

Tofu is very fragile, so handle with care. Silken tofu is normally used as it is, but cotton tofu, if it is going to be fried or mashed to make a dressing, is normally pressed to squeeze out some water to make it a little firmer.

Storage

Fresh tofu should be kept in plenty of water in the refrigerator and can be kept for three days, if the water is changed daily. Follow the use-by dates on cartoned or vacuum-packed tofu.

KOYA-DOFU

Also known as kogori-dofu (frozen tofu), koya-dofu is believed to have been invented by Buddhist monks on the Koya mountain many centuries ago. It is a freeze-dried tofu, and is a quite different substance from regular tofu in texture, colour, flavour and size. It has a spongy texture and rich taste even after it has been soaked in water.

Today, koya-dofu is often available in packets of five pieces together with a powdered soup stock in which to cook it. When purchased this way it simply requires cooking in the soup provided. This modern version is readily available.

Aroma and flavour

Koya-dofu has a much stronger soya bean aroma and richer flavour than cotton or silken tofu. However, it is the unusual, spongy texture that strikes your palate. The beauty of this spongy tofu is that, however long it is cooked, it does not disintegrate.

Culinary uses

Because of its spongy nature, koya-dofu absorbs flavours well, so it is used for simmering with vegetables in a rich soup. It is also used for *shojin ryori*, Buddhist monks' vegetarian cooking.

Left: Koya-dofu (freeze-dried tofu)

Pan-fried koya-dofu in egg batter

The soup-cooked koya-dofu is coated with egg, then fried to make this crisp, delicious appetizer.

SERVES FOUR

INGREDIENTS
  2 cakes of koya-dofu with
    powdered soup
  10ml/2 tsp cornflour (cornstarch)
  2 eggs, beaten
  15ml/1 tbsp finely chopped
    fresh parsley
  oil, for frying
  salt

1 In a large pan, mix the sachets of powdered soup in the volume of water suggested on the packet and bring to the boil. Add the koya-dofu and simmer for 15 minutes. Turn a few times during cooking. Remove the pan from the heat and leave to cool for 10 minutes before lifting out the koya-dofu. Discard the soup.

2 On a board, squeeze out the liquid from the cooked koya-dofu, then slice horizontally into two thin pieces.

Preparation and cooking

If the packet does not contain sachets of powdered soup, koya-dofu needs soaking in hot water for 5 minutes before cooking. Use your hands to squeeze out the milky water a few times until the water becomes clear. However, most koya-dofu is now made so that it can be cooked immediately in the powdered soup provided in the packet.

3 Cut each piece into eight triangles.

4 Add the cornflour and salt to the eggs, stir well until the cornflour has dissolved, then add the parsley. Coat each triangle with the egg batter.

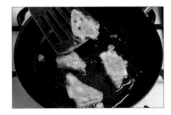

5 Fry the coated triangles in an oiled frying pan for 1–2 minutes on both sides. Drain, then serve.

Dilute the powdered soup in water following the instructions on the packet, lay the koya-dofu on the pan base and cook for the suggested time. Leave to cool, cut into appropriate sizes and eat, or cook again with other vegetables, herbs and flavourings.

Storage

Koya-dofu will keep for a long time stored in its packaging. Follow the use-by date on the packet.

Left: Yuba (dried bean curd skin) is available as flat sheets, rolled and cut, or in thick strips

FRIED TOFU

There are various types of fried tofu commercially produced and commonly used for home cooking in Japan. They are, like tofu, freshly made every day by neighbourhood tofu makers and sold like freshly baked bread. In the West some deep-fried tofu are also freshly made and sold refrigerated at Japanese supermarkets.

YUBA

This is the dried soya bean skin that forms on the surface of the soya bean milk during the tofu-making process. Making yuba is simple, but requires considerable skill: a large pan of soya milk is brought gently to the boil, a thin layer of skin forms on the surface which is skimmed off with a stick in a single swoop, and this is hung up. When it dries, it forms a flat sheet; called yuba. Dried strips are made by rolling up the skin up while still warm, then leaving the strips to dry.

Yuba is a delicacy often used for *shojin ryori* (Buddhist monk's vegetarian cooking). Sold in packets, it comes in various sheet forms, including flat, rolled and cut, or in thick strips, and is increasingly available from many Japanese supermarkets.

Aroma and flavour

Once cooked in soup, yuba gives out a warm soya bean aroma and has a rich, milky flavour with a crunchy texture.

Culinary uses

Yuba is used mainly in clear soups and simmered dishes. It is one of Kyoto's specialities and is often used in their version of the *kaiseki* (formal banquet).

Preparation and cooking

Soften yuba in tepid water for 5 minutes before cooking. Although it does not disintegrate, cook only lightly.

Storage

Yuba will keep for several months if stored in an airtight bag in a cool place.

Below: Clockwise from left, atsu-age (thick deep-fried tofu), in cubes and blocks, abura-age (thin deep-fried tofu sheets), and gammodoki (deep-fried tofu balls with vegetables)

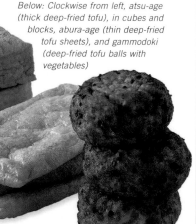

Preparing abura-age

1 Put the abura-age in a sieve and pour boiling water over to wash off any excess oil. Drain and gently pat dry with kitchen paper. If using fresh abura-age, par-boil in rapidly boiling water for 1 minute, then drain and leave to cool. Squeeze out any excess water.

2 Cut each sheet in half and place the pieces on a chopping board. Carefully pull each one open by rubbing the outside with the palm of your hand, in a back and forward motion, to ease apart. Use your fingers to open the bag fully, working your way carefully towards the bottom.

Deep-frying changes the texture and taste of somewhat plain, non-crunchy tofu and not only provides extra protein and oil but also gives the tofu some bite. As it has been fried in vegetable oil, fried tofu is suitable for vegetarians, and is also easier to handle and cook than regular tofu. It can be eaten either heated up or cooked with vegetables and meat.

Abura-age Thin deep-fried tofu is the most commonly used fried tofu in Japanese cooking. It normally comes in a standard size of 12 × 6cm/4½ × 2½in, and 1cm/½in thick, and is often used for cooking with other ingredients, mainly vegetables, and on its own as a source of vegetable protein.

The unusual feature of this fried tofu is that it can be slit open like a pitta bread and stuffed with vegetables or sushi rice. Pour boiling water over before use to reduce the oiliness. It is also used in soups and oden (hotpot) dishes. Abura-age is the only tofu product available in both frozen and fresh forms.

Atsu-age Thick deep-fried tofu is made of a whole coarse tofu and is available in the standard size 10 × 6 × 4.5cm/ 4 × 2½ × 1¾in. Only the outside is golden brown, while the inside remains white. It is sometimes cut into cubes first and then fried. Before use, pour boiling water over it and lightly press in kitchen paper to reduce its oiliness. It can be eaten lightly grilled (broiled) or pan-fried with sauce, as tofu steak. It is also good in soups and hotpot dishes, particularly in oden (hotpot) or in simmered dishes.

Gammodoki Deep-fried tofu with vegetables is another variety that is very popular in home cooking. It is made from chopped vegetables and seeds bound together with crumbled tofu and grated yam. The mixture is then made either into flat discs of about 8cm/3½in diameter or into small balls, and deep-fried. Gammodoki means 'duck look-alike', probably due to its texture more than its look or taste. It is delicious on its own, as well as cooked with other vegetables and meat. It is also used in oden (hotpot dishes).

Home-made gammodoki
Plain soft tofu is transformed into a more substantial dish with added konbu and carrots. Konbu and hijiki can be substituted with shredded green beans.

MAKES ABOUT TWELVE BALLS

INGREDIENTS
  1 standard firm (cotton) tofu
  5 × 2.5cm/2 × 1in piece of konbu
    or 5–10g/⅛–¼oz dried hijiki
  ¼ carrot, peeled
  2 dried shiitake mushrooms,
    softened and stems trimmed
  8 green beans, trimmed
  1 egg
  salt, shoyu and mirin
  15ml/1 tbsp black sesame seeds
  vegetable oil, for deep-frying

1 Wrap a tofu cake in kitchen paper and place on a chopping board. Place a large plate upside down on top. Put a weight on it and leave it to press for about 1 hour until all the excess water has drained out.

2 Meanwhile soak the konbu or hijiki in tepid water for 30 minutes, then drain and chop roughly into 1–2cm/ ½–¾in long shreds.

3 Cut the carrot, shiitake and green beans into 1–2cm/½–¾in shreds.

4 Put the tofu in a *suribachi* (Japanese grinding bowl) or a food processor with the egg, a pinch of salt, and a dash each of shoyu and mirin. Grind or process to a very smooth consistency.

5 Transfer the tofu mixture to a large bowl. Add all the vegetable shreds and sesame seeds and mix well.

6 Heat the oil for frying in a deep frying pan to about 120°C/250°F. Spoon a heaped tablespoonful of the tofu mixture on to your wet palm and mould into a small oval shape about 2cm/¾in thick.

7 Place in the hot oil and deep-fry for 2–3 minutes, or until both sides are a light golden brown; drain on kitchen paper. Repeat this process until all the mixture is used up.

8 When all the tofu balls have been fried, reheat the oil to 170°C/340°F. Fry the balls again to make them crisp. Serve hot as an appetizer or main course, accompanied by some grated daikon with a little shoyu.

GLUTEN PRODUCTS

The gluten from various vegetables, such as potatoes, beans, gourds and wheat, is separated to produce long-lasting food that is quite different in shape, texture and flavour from the original vegetable. Initially developed as a way of preserving vegetables for the winter, gluten products are also appreciated for their unusual shapes and textures, important in Japanese cooking. Gluten products are mostly available in packets and in their dried forms at Japanese supermarkets.

KONNYAKU

An unusual, dense, gelatinous cake derived from the tough root of the konnyaku plant, a kind of yam potato. The thinly sliced root is dried, ground and the chemical compound, mannan, is separated; from this, konnyaku flour is produced. Next the flour is mixed with water, then hardened using lime milk as a coagulant and boiling water, to form cakes. This complicated process is said to have been brought to Japan from China, together with Buddhism, but is now only practised in Japan.

Since konnyaku is mostly water (97 per cent) and the main nutrient, gluco-mannan, cannot

Below: Konnyaku, a gelatinous cake made from flour produced from a yam-like root vegetable

be digested, it is known to be a highly beneficial dietary food. However, due to its unusual appearance (it is also known as devil's tongue) and strange texture, it may need some getting used to before it can be appreciated.

There are many types of konnyaku products made commercially in Japan, such as fresh sashimi (raw konnyaku, thinly sliced), ito-konnyaku (string konnyaku), konnyaku balls and flavoured konnyaku. In the West only ita-konnyaku (standard konnyaku cake) in black (unrefined) or white (refined) and shirataki (fine filament) are

Below: Shirataki (fine white noodles made from the starch of the konnyaku plant) are sold in packets.

normally available from Japanese supermarkets. The standard size of the cake is about 15 × 8 × 4cm/6 × 3½ × 1½in and it is bought packed in water.

Aroma and flavour

Konnyaku has no aroma, nor flavour. It has a slippery, hard jelly-like texture, for which it is most appreciated.

Culinary uses

Fresh konnyaku is eaten raw like sashimi. When cooked, konnyaku is used with other vegetables and meat and also used for soups and hotpots, oden (fish cake hotpot) in particular.

Preparation and cooking

Konnyaku should be parboiled before use. Since it is quite soft, the cake can be torn with the fingers into bitesize pieces, cut into many shapes or made into decorative knots.

Konnyaku does not easily absorb flavours from the sauce or foods it is cooked with, so it is always simmered in a strongly flavoured sauce for as long a time as possible.

Storage

Once the packet is opened, store in plenty of water. Change the water daily, and keep for up to two weeks.

SHIRATAKI

The name shirataki means white waterfall. It is made from the konnyaku plant in the same way as konnyaku but only as a thin white noodle-like filament. Shirataki is sold in an inflated plastic bag filled with water or in cans and is available from Asian supermarkets. It is mainly used for hotpots, especially sukiyaki (table-top cooked beef and vegetables), and for salad dishes. Par-boil and roughly cut the long noodles before use.

Above: Harusame

tied around food, kanpyo is simmered with vegetables and meat. Before use it needs to be softened. Rub with salt and wash vigorously to break down the fibres and increase absorbency. It can then be boiled in water until soft and is normally cooked in a shoyu-based sauce, and used for sushi. Packets of 30–50g/1¼–2oz are available from Asian stores.

KANPYO

These dried gourd ribbons have an unusual role in Japanese cooking; they are used to tie foods together and look more like parcel string than food. The flesh of the calabah gourd, a member of the marrow family, is thinly shaved, then dried to a long ribbon, about 2cm/¾in wide, and whitened by smoking in sulphur. As well as being

FU

These gluten cakes are now used mainly as a decorative garnish. Wheat flour mixed with salt and water in a cloth bag is washed in water until the starch has seeped out and only the gluten is left. This is then steamed until firm to produce fresh fu, which is used instead of meat in Zen Buddhist cooking. Fu originated in China, but the Japanese have developed ultra-light dried fu in many colours, sizes and shapes to garnish soups and hotpots. It is not a pure gluten since wheat, glutinous rice powder and/or baking powder are added to the gluten before drying. Some dried fu is available from Asian stores.

HARUSAME

Meaning spring rain, harusame is a fine, translucent filament made from various starchy roots such as potato and sweet potato, or sometimes green beans. Starch, mixed with boiling water, is made into a gluey mixture, then extruded through fine holes into boiling water. It is then further boiled to harden it, cooled quickly and freeze-dried into crisp, fine filaments. It is available in dried form in packets from Asian supermarkets. Harusame is soaked in tepid water for 5 minutes and used for salads or soups. When the dried harusame is fried it expands to a fluffy white 'bird's nest'. To produce this effect, crush it into pieces, then use as a 'batter' for frying fish and vegetables to make an unusual tempura. Store dried harusame in an airtight packet in a cool, airy place.

Above: Kanpyo (dried gourd ribbons)

Right: Fu (gluten cakes)

MUSHROOMS

The mushroom is a fungus whose developed offshoots grow in or under certain trees. In a relatively warm and wet country in which over 75 per cent of the land is covered by mountains, mushrooms grow in abundance and are used in everyday cooking. Apart from the most popular ones, introduced below, there are the Japanese equivalents of European mushrooms such as hiratake (oyster mushroom family), maitake (hen of the wood), amigasatake (morel), amitake (boletus) and anzutake (chanterelle), as well as numerous regional seasonal varieties available locally.

Most mushrooms consist primarily of water (about 90 per cent) but they are also rich in vitamins D and B$_2$ and vegetable fibre. Some have a distinctive *umami* (rich taste), so are used for making vegetable soup stock.

FRESH SHIITAKE

Meaning *shii* (tree) mushroom, the shiitake is also known, incorrectly, as the Chinese mushroom, though it actually originated in Japan. Shiitake is a fungus that grows in the wild twice a year, in spring and autumn, under trees such as *shii* (*Pasania cuspidata*), oak and chestnut, though today it is also cultivated. It is recognized as a health food for its ability to reduce cholesterol in the blood.

Below: When buying fresh shiitake, look for ones with a dark brown, velvety cap.

There are various types of shiitake, but the ones with a dark brown, velvety cap of approximately 5cm/2in diameter, which are 70–80 per cent open, are regarded as being of the best quality. The variety called donko, meaning winter mushroom, which has a small, thick and dense, dark cap with crevasse-like deep lines on it, is the king of shiitake. It is also known as flower shiitake because of the pattern the lines create on its cap.

Although dried shiitake are widely available, due to increased effort in their cultivation, fresh shiitake are also more available outside of Japan – good news for Japanese cooking.

Aroma and flavour

Fresh shiitake have a distinctive woody aroma and slightly acidic flavour. The mushroom has a soft, slippery texture, which adds an exquisite quality. When dried the flavour intensifies.

Culinary uses

In Japanese cooking, fresh shiitake tend to be used for their subtlety – they absorb rather than override the flavours of the other ingredients. The shiitake is one of the regular ingredients for hotpot dishes containing meat, usually beef, and vegetables, such as shabu shabu or sukiyaki. They can also be simply grilled over a barbecue or battered and fried for tempura.

Grilled fresh shiitake with mustard

1 Wipe off the dirt from fresh shiitake with damp kitchen paper and use a small knife to trim off the hard parts of the stems.

2 Grill (broil) the mushrooms very lightly under a medium heat, or on a barbecue, for 1–2 minutes on both sides. Alternatively, heat a frying pan, add a little oil to just cover the base, and pan-fry the shiitake over a medium heat. Serve with mustard and shoyu.

Preparation and cooking

With a damp piece of kitchen paper wipe, rather than wash, off any earth and dirt, and trim off the hard part of the stem before cooking. When used whole, a decorative cross is often notched into the caps. Fresh shiitake can easily become too soft, so monitor the cooking carefully.

Storage

Choose fresh shiitake with the cap edges curled under. The caps flare out and become floppy within a few days. Store in the vegetable section of the refrigerator.

DRIED SHIITAKE

When shiitake are dried, their aroma and flavour intensify; it is for this enriched fungus flavour, coupled with the convenience of using dried shiitake, that they are most appreciated. The drying process also increases the fibre content to over 40 per cent.

The distinctive taste of shiitake suits Chinese cooking better than Japanese, hence the widely held belief that it is a Chinese mushroom. There are many types and grades of dried shiitake available in packets, but the small, thick donko (winter mushroom) is the most highly rated.

Above: Various dried shiitake; on the far right are dried donko, which are considered the most flavoursome.

Preparing dried shiitake

1 Quickly wash off any dirt under running water and soak in cold water. Dried shiitake must be soaked in tepid water for about 2–3 hours, or overnight. If you are short of time, soak for at least 45 minutes, with a little sugar sprinkled over, before cooking.

2 Remove the shiitake from the soaking water, and gently squeeze out the water. Using your fingers or a knife, trim off the stem and then slice or chop the caps to use in cooking. Use the stems in soups. Don't discard the soaking liquid; rather drain through muslin (cheesecloth), then use in soups or for simmering.

Aroma and flavour

Dried shiitake have a pleasantly strong, roasted aroma and intensified fungus flavour. The increased fibre content gives it more bite than fresh ones.

Culinary uses

In Japanese cooking, dried shiitake are usually cooked in a seasoned liquid, then used for dishes such as simmered vegetables with chicken, mixed sushi and soup noodles.

Storage

Dried shiitake last almost indefinitely if stored in an airtight plastic bag. They can also be frozen, which is a better way of retaining flavour.

ENOKITAKE

Also known as yukinoshita, meaning under the snow, this bundle of tiny berry-cap mushrooms with thin stems grows in the wild on the stumps of *enoki* (hackberry), poplar and persimmon trees in winter. The wild enokitake has brownish orange caps, about 2–8cm/¾–3½in in diameter, but these days is now widely cultivated at a low temperature, without light, to produce bundles of snowy white caps with a maximum diameter of 1cm/½in and long slender stems. Cultivated enokitake is often marketed outside Japan as a new nutritious salad ingredient to be eaten raw.

Aroma and flavour

Enokitake has a very delicate, fresh flavour and a delightfully crisp texture.

Culinary uses

They are one of the regular ingredients for hotpot dishes, such as shabu shabu, and are also delicious in seasonal salads and in soups. Because they do not have an overpowering flavour, they go well with almost anything, and can be wrapped in foil with fish or poultry for cooking on a barbecue. They can also be eaten raw in salads.

Preparation and cooking

Cut off the spongy root, 2.5–5cm/1–2in from the bottom, and wash under cold running water. Use cooked or raw. They cook in no time, so be careful not to overcook. Enokitake are the easiest mushroom to handle, and they give a refreshing, pretty character to dishes.

Storage

Choose shiny white bundles and store in a sealed bag in the refrigerator. Enokitake keep well for up to a week.

Below: Cultivated enokitake

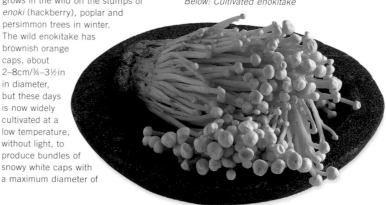

FRUIT

From north to south, Japan covers vast latitudes and so is blessed with a variety of fruits, ranging from apples and pears in the north to various citrus fruits and the Japanese loquat in the south. Mikan, known as satsuma, is probably the most popular Japanese fruit in the West but kaki (persimmon) and nashi (pear) are also making their way into Western supermarkets. The beautiful reddish orange colour of kaki makes it ideal to use in cooking, since it expresses both the fruit season itself and the autumnal colour of the leaves.

Citrus varieties, such as yuzu and sudachi, are all used to add flavour to Japanese cooking.

Left: Yuzu

Below: Sudachi

YUZU

Among the many varieties of citrus fruits used in Japanese cooking, yuzu is the most popular. It is about the size of a clementine with a firm, thick yellow skin and is in season throughout winter. Apart from culinary uses, yuzu is used in the bath in Japan; a hot citrus bath is good for your skin and for warming up your whole body. Yuzu is occasionally available in season from Japanese supermarkets, although lime can be substituted if it cannot be found. A citrus flavouring called *ponzu* is made commercially to resemble the aroma of yuzu and is available in jars.

Aroma and flavour

Yuzu has an unique, sharp and strong, penetrating aroma, which makes it too sharp tasting to eat fresh.

Culinary uses

Yuzu is used almost entirely for its exquisitely aromatic rind. Tiny pieces and slivers from the bright yellow skin are scraped and used to garnish soups, salads, simmered dishes, pickles, relishes and desserts. Although the fruit is not edible, the juice can be used in salad dressings and dipping sauces. The whole outer skin, after the flesh has been removed, is often used as a cup in which to serve hors d'oeuvres.

Preparation and cooking

Using a very sharp knife, cut small pieces just before serving each time the yuzu is used. A few tiny pieces of the rind, up to 5mm/¼in in diameter, will be sufficient to garnish each dish.

SUDACHI

This is another of the many varieties of citrus fruits used in Japanese cooking. Sudachi is a little smaller than yuzu, weighing 30–40g/1¼–1½oz, and has a firm thick green skin and light yellow, moist flesh with relatively large seeds. The juice is not as sharp as that of yuzu, so it is used mainly to garnish sashimi (prepared raw fish), and grilled (broiled) fish and hotpot dishes. The most notable combination, however, is with matsutake (pine mushroom) and the juice is always sprinkled over dishes such as lightly grilled matsutake or steamed matsutake teapot soup. The rind is also finely grated and used as a flavouring for dipping condiments. It has only a short season, appearing in late summer. Sudachi is not normally available outside Japan but lime, or even lemon, make an acceptable substitute.

Right: Kaki, the Japanese persimmon, whose arrival at market heralds the coming of autumn for the Japanese.

KAKI

Also known as Japanese persimmon, the kaki has been grown in Japan for centuries. There are as many as 800–1,000 varieties and those that are available in the West are normally fuyu or jiro. The kaki grows to about 10cm/4in in diameter and has a hard, smooth reddish orange skin and dense but crunchy flesh. It tastes very similar to Sharon fruit, one of the persimmon family. It has a regular, flower-like pattern at the core and can contain eight seeds although it is often seedless, which makes this fruit useful as a decorative garnish.

Kaki fruit in a dish signifies autumn as its reddish colour is suggestive of autumn leaves. It is also used in dressed vegetable dishes and salads. There are some bitter varieties, which are not suitable for eating unprocessed and these are often dried like dates.

MIKAN

Known in the West as satsuma or mandarin, mikan grows in the warmer regions of Japan, particularly on the south and west coasts facing the Pacific Ocean. The English name for mikan, satsuma, comes from the old name for the western coastal region of the southernmost island, Kyushu, from where mikan was first exported.

Mikan is a winter fruit, which is one of the most juicy and sweetest of orange varieties and is also a good source of vitamin C and beta-carotene. Fresh mikan are widely available in the West, and it is also possible to buy canned, peeled whole mikan in syrup.

Aroma and flavour

Mikan has a faint citrus aroma and a sweet, juicy flavour.

Culinary uses

Apart from being eaten raw, mikan is used mainly as a dessert with kanten (agar-agar) or other fruits. After removing the flesh, the intact skin can be used as a cup in which to serve hors d'oeuvres.

Left: Nashi (Japanese pears)

Right: Japanese apples are much larger than Western types – these ones are about 10cm/4in in diameter.

APPLES

Originally from Central Asia, apples are some of the most common fruits grown all over the world: there are said to be more than 10,000 varieties. In Japan up to 1,500 types have existed in the country, though usually only about 20 varieties are commercially grown. Modern varieties of apples are relatively new to Japan; they came from America in 1872. However, Japan has since developed many new varieties and is now exporting its own crossbreeds, such as Fuji, to the West. Japan has also developed varieties that contain what is called honey – a sweet, almost transparent part – found around the core. These types are not normally available outside of Japan.

Fuji is a cross between Kokko and Delicious and is regarded by some as one of the best apples in the world. It is juicy, yet the flesh is dense with a rich aroma and sweet flavour. It keeps well.

NASHI

Simply meaning pear, nashi is a round, russet-coloured Japanese pear now widely available in the West. There are about ten Japanese or crossbreed varieties and popular ones include chojuro and nijusseiki. Since nashi contain 84–89 per cent water, they have a very watery, crunchy texture and are not noticeably sweet. They have an almost transparent flesh and can be used for jam but are mostly eaten raw as hors d'oeuvres or in salads.

UME

Also known as Japanese apricot, ume is one of the oldest fruits grown in Japan. There are about 300 varieties, which are roughly divided into two categories: flowering trees and fruit-bearing trees. Like an apricot, the pale green fruit turns yellow with reddish patterns on it when ripe. It grows to about the size of a golf ball and is harvested from June through to July. Ume is an unusual fruit since you are not supposed to eat it fresh. Not only is it too sharp to eat but the unripe fruit contains prussic acid at its core, which can cause stomach upsets. Instead, it is processed into umeboshi (salted and dried ume), jam, umeshu (ume liqueur) and confectionery.

Below: Unpleasant to eat fresh, the Japanese have developed a number of ways of preparing ume. They can be salted and dried, or made into jams and liqueurs, and even confectionery.

Pickled ume or apricot
This is a simple method for pickling ume (or apricot), which retains the crunchiness of the fruit. A healthy dish, it is good eaten with rice.

MAKES ABOUT 1KG/2¼LB

INGREDIENTS
   1kg/2¼lb unripe ume or young
      small apricots
   15ml/1 tbsp rice vinegar or white
      wine vinegar
   115g/4oz/1 cup salt
   shochu or brandy

1 Wash the ume or apricots and soak in plenty of water for at least 1 hour. Drain and pat dry with kitchen paper.

2 Trim the stem part using a cocktail stick (toothpick) and place the fruit in a freezer bag. Sprinkle the vinegar over the fruits, then add two-thirds of the salt. Holding the bag in one hand, roll the fruit around to distribute the salt.

3 Put half of the remaining salt in a sterilized non-metallic bowl and add the contents of the freezer bag. Sprinkle the rest of the salt on top.

4 Using a cloth dampened with shochu or brandy, wipe the inside of the bowl, then cover the fruits with a shochu- or brandy-sprayed plate and place a clean 1.6kg/3½lb weight on top. Wrap the bowl, plate and weight with clear film (plastic wrap) and cover with a lid.

5 Leave to pickle for a week, during which time unwrap, take the weight off and shake the pan to spread the liquid around the fruits twice daily.

Pickling ume

Properly done, pickled ume will last for several months in the refrigerator and is a healthy stand-by snack or light meal if eaten with boiled rice. When pickling, (see above) it is important to ensure sterile conditions are maintained at all times: once placed in the freezer bag, do not touch the fruit unnecessarily. During the week when it is necessary to shake the pan containing the fruit, again make sure that the prepared fruit and equipment never come into contact with unsterilized items.

   Once the fruit has been allowed to pickle, remove the clear film and transfer the ume or apricots to a sterilized bottle together with the liquid from the bowl, cover and store in the refrigerator. They will mature in about a week and be ready for eating then, though will keep for several months if properly sealed.

Home-made umeboshi
Umeboshi, salted and dried ume, is a unique Japanese pickle, usually eaten with rice for breakfast. It is regarded as having a tonic quality, aiding digestion and keeping the intestinal tract clear. It is often pickled with red shiso leaves for flavour as well as for its bright red colour. The following is a very basic method for salting ume or alternatively young small apricots.

MAKES ABOUT 2.5KG/5½LB

INGREDIENTS
2kg/4½lb ume or young apricots
120ml/4fl oz/½ cup shochu or white wine
360g/12½oz salt

1 Wash the ume or apricots carefully and soak in plenty of water overnight.

COOK'S TIP
After drying in the sun for three days, the fruits are ready to eat, but will mature in one year and their flavour will improve with keeping.

2 Drain and, using a cocktail stick (toothpick), remove the stem part. Pat each fruit dry with a clean cloth, place in a large freezer bag and sprinkle three-quarters of the shochu or white wine evenly over the fruit.

3 Add three-quarters of the salt and roll the fruit around in the bag so the salt is evenly distributed.

4 Put half the remaining salt in a deep non-metallic bowl, then transfer all the ume or apricots to the bowl and evenly sprinkle the fruit with the remaining salt. Thoroughly spray the inside of the bowl with the remaining shochu or white wine.

5 Place a plate over the fruits inside the bowl and put a 4–5kg/9–11lb weight on top. Seal the bowl with clear film (plastic wrap), then cover tightly with a cloth or paper.

6 Leave in a cool place away from direct sunlight for about 10 days or until the liquid rises above the level of the plate.

7 Reduce the weight on top of the fruits by half and leave wrapped for another 10–15 days. Drain.

8 Spread the salted fruits on a flat bamboo strainer and air-dry in the sunlight for three days.

BIWA
The loquat originated in China, though it commonly grows in South-east Asia. Biwa bears yellowish orange, slightly dense fruits, the size of a small egg. and has a faintly acidic, not very sweet flavour and firm texture. The loquat is called biwa, after the guitar-like Asian instrument, which its oval shape resembles. When ripe, biwa peels well to reveal underneath a smooth and shiny surface.

In Japan, the loquat grows along the Pacific coast to Kyushu, the southern island, and is in season in early spring. It is generally consumed fresh, but because of its beautiful yellowish orange colour and small size, biwa is sometimes used decoratively as part of hors d'oeuvres trays to represent the arrival of spring. It is also sometimes used for desserts with jelly or kanten (agar-agar).

ICHIGO
First introduced by the Dutch traders in the middle of the 19th century, the strawberry is a relatively new addition to what is now a huge Japanese fruit industry. Many varieties from the USA, England and France have been cross-bred and Japan now produces various firm, sweet strawberries in differing sizes, such as Toyonoka and Joho. The huge, almost square-shaped Fukuwa Ichigo, formerly the favourite in Japan, is now declining in popularity due to the influx of new varieties.

Ichigo, which are rich in vitamin C, are available all year round in Japan due to the favourable climate and the use of technology in cultivation.

Below: Smaller Western types of ichigo (strawberries) are now more popular in Japan than the traditional large variety.

FISH

There is no doubt that the Japanese are the world's biggest fish eaters. They deal with 3,000 kinds of fish and shellfish daily at the Tokyo fish market, the world's biggest fish market by volume of trade. Choices are far greater in Japan than anywhere else in the world and housewives go shopping for fresh fish every day. The following are some of the essential fish for Japanese cooking.

MAGURO

A member of the mackerel family, maguro or tuna has become widely available in the West. There are several kinds of tuna: blue-fin (black tuna in Japan), big-eye, yellow-fin, long-finned and southern blue-fin. Katsuo, skipjack tuna, although in the same family, is a different group of fish.

The blue-fin is the king of tuna, with deep red meat. It inhabits warm seas around the world reaching the southern coast of Hokkaido, the northernmost island of Japan. In summer it weighs about 350kg/770lb and has a 3m/10ft

Below: Maguro intended for sashimi is classified according to which part of the fish it is from and its oiliness. O-toro, front, is oilier than chu-toro, middle, though both are from the lower part of the fish. Akami, back, is from the upper part of the tuna and is less oily.

long body. The most commonly fished tuna is the big-eye, which grows to 2m/6ft in tropical seas. The lesser-quality long-finned one is usually processed and canned or used as steaks. The southern blue-fin is now becoming as popular as the blue-fin.

Tuna is often sold already skinned and sliced as steaks or in chunks, which can make it sometimes difficult to tell which tuna you are buying.

In Japan, tuna is normally displayed cut into thick rectangular pieces – convenient for sashimi. There are usually two kinds, akami and toro, depending on which part of the fish the flesh comes from. Akami, red meat, is from the main, upper part of the body and toro, oily meat, is from the lower. It is sometimes classified by the degree of oiliness into chu-toro, middle toro, or o-toro, big toro. Akami was more popular than toro before World War II, but now it is generally thought that toro is superior in taste to akami and it is thus priced accordingly.

Aroma and flavour

Maguro has a delicate, sweet flavour and a dense, smooth texture.

Culinary uses

Maguro is most often used for sashimi and sushi, dressed salads, salt grilling (broiling), teriyaki, and simmered dishes. Long-finned tuna is not used raw, but is sold canned as steaks.

Preparation and cooking

Always use fresh fish and avoid any that is discoloured. Trim off any veins.

Storage

Tuna that is to be eaten raw should be used straight away, or stored in the refrigerator for up to two days. It can also be frozen.

Slicing fish for sashimi and sushi
Fish that can be eaten raw include tuna, skipjack tuna, salmon, mackerel, turbot, sea bass and sea bream. Use absolutely fresh fish and avoid ready-cut steaks or filleted fish. Also, do not eat defrosted frozen fish raw.

Slicing tuna, skipjack tuna or salmon
Buy a chunky piece, avoiding the part with veins. Cut the chunk into 2–3cm/¾–1¼in thick, 6–7cm/2½–2¾in wide fillets. To cut for sushi, cut 5mm/¼in thin slices crossways, placing the knife's blade slightly at an angle against the chopping board.

For sashimi, slice 1cm/½in thick pieces, again keeping the blade slightly at an angle.

Slicing smaller or flat fish

Using a sharp knife, fillet and skin the fish carefully, then remove all bones from the fillets. Cut flat fish fillets in half down the centre, then slice very thinly, inserting the blade diagonally.

KATSUO

Skipjack tuna is one of the most important and versatile fish in Japanese cooking, but it is not usually available fresh in the West, since once killed it goes off very quickly. It grows to about 1m/3ft long and weighs up to 20kg/44lb in tropical to subtropical seas, coming up on the warm current in large shoals to the Japanese coasts in spring. Katsuo is a handsome fish, with a deep blue-mauve back and silvery white belly with a few black stripes. In the same katsuo group are frigate mackerel, round frigate mackerel and striped bonito; these are slightly smaller than skipjack tuna.

In Japan, katsuo caught at the beginning of the season – in spring to early summer – is called hatsu-gatsuo (first katsuo), and is regarded as a delicacy. The autumn katsuo are known as modori-gatsuo (returning katsuo) as they are on their way back south. They have a richer flavour and firmer texture.

Aroma and flavour

Katsuo has dark red flesh, much darker than tuna, and a slightly fishy aroma.

Culinary uses

Katsuo is famous for its tataki, seared carpaccio eaten with ginger, garlic and other herbs. It is also dried whole to

Above:
Fresh sake
(salmon), a popular ingredient for
sashimi, and ikura (salmon caviar).

make katsuo-bushi, a hard fish block that is shaved to make the fish flakes used as the base of Japanese dashi stock. Processed and canned skipjack tuna is available outside Japan.

SAKE

While sake refers to salmon only, salmon and trout are categorized in the same group of fish although, rather confusingly, some salmon such as chinook (*Onorhynchus tshawytscha*), cherry (*O. masou masou*) and pink (*O. gorbuscha*) are regarded as trout in Japan. There are also some species such as coho salmon (*O. kisutch*) and blue-back (*O. nerka*) that the Japanese call trout as well as salmon. The king of salmon in Japan is chum salmon (*O. keta*), which has a perfect silvery body. It comes back to the river of its birth for spawning from September to January in Japan and some are caught for artificial insemination to be later released. Ishikari, a region on Hokkaido, the northernmost island, is famous for its salmon fisheries.

Left: Me-kajiki (swordfish) is usually sold in blocks or steaks.

Culinary uses

Salmon is used for sashimi in the West but, due to parasite infestation, not in Japan. For sashimi, ask the fishmonger to cut fresh from a big chunk of salmon rather than use ready-cut steaks.

In Japan, salmon is traditionally often salted and wrapped in an aramaki (straw mat). Fresh salmon is used for grilling (broiling), frying, *saka-mushi* (sake steaming), hotpots and soup dishes. Ishikari-nabe is a salmon hot-pot dish in miso soup. Salmon is also processed to make canned and smoked salmon. Other products from salmon include sujiko (salted whole ovary) and ikura (salmon caviar).

KAJIKI

Also known as kajiki maguro, kajiki is the general term for a group of fish, the two most important examples being ma-kajiki (striped marlin) and me-kajiki (swordfish). They all have a long sword-like beak and a big fin on the back. These fish inhabit subtropical to tropical seas and grow to 3–5m/10–16½ft, some weighing over 500kg/1,100lb.

Aroma and flavour

Kajiki have a taste and firm texture similar to tuna. Ma-kajiki is considered the best and it has a light pink flesh.

Culinary uses

Kajiki is used for processed foods but can also be eaten as sashimi or teriyaki.

Right: Whole and filleted suzuki (sea bass)

SUZUKI

The sea bass grows to about 1m/3ft long and tastes better when over 60cm/24in. It is a handsome fish with big round eyes, a blue-grey back and silvery white belly. The pinkish white flesh, together with the delicate flavour and the chunky texture, adds a pleasant freshness to sashimi and sushi.

If suzuki is to be cooked, it should be done so very lightly with sauce, in soup, steamed or in a hotpot. The flesh is too delicate to be fried.

Sea bass are available all year round, as whole fish or as fillets. They are at their best in spring and early summer, before they spawn. The tastiest specimens are wild, but farmed suzuki are an acceptable alternative.

Below: Red and black tai (sea bream). The flavour and texture of black tai is similar to red, but not as fine.

TAI

In Japanese cooking, sea bream, or tai, has a special place as a celebratory fish simply because the ending of the Japanese word for 'celebration' sounds the same. The largest tai grow to 1m/3ft long but it is the 30–50cm/12–20in fish that is used whole for grilling (broiling). For special occasions, the fish may be shaped before it is grilled with the use of skewers to make it look as if it is still alive and moving to symbolize a vibrant figure bravely swimming through troubled waters. Red tai has a silvery red skin, which becomes redder when grilled, and red is regarded as a cheerful, festive colour in Japan.

The flesh of tai is milky white and flaky when it is cooked so it is used for making soboro (fish flakes). It is also used for sashimi and sushi – such as oshizushi (pressed sushi) – as well as in soups and rice dishes.

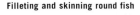

Filleting and skinning round fish

1 Scale and gut the fish, cut off the head and wash under running water. Pat dry with kitchen paper and place the fish flat on a chopping board.

2 Insert a sharp knife as close as possible to the backbone. Cut along the back towards the tail keeping the knife flat to the bone.

3 Turn the fish over and repeat to fillet the other side.

4 Place one fillet at a time skin-side down on the chopping board and insert the blade between the skin and meat at the tail end. Press the skin firmly down with one hand and push the blade along the skin towards the head to remove the skin.

KAREI

There are more than 100 species of the karei family worldwide, including plaice, sole, halibut and flounder, and 20 of these inhabit the seas around Japan. Karei look very similar to hirame (see below) except chiefly for the location of the eyes: karei have eyes on the right-hand side of the body and hirame on the left. Karei also have a smaller mouth. Depending on the species the texture and flesh can vary greatly. Sole is arguably the finest fish of the group, with a firm, delicate flesh and superb flavour. The best halibut has a fine, meaty texture and is usually sold whole, though larger ones may be prepared as steaks or fillets. Flounder has a soft texture and less distinct flavour.

The season for karei varies according to the species, and komochi-garei (pregnant karei) is the most sought after type. Karei are a very versatile fish and are used for sashimi, as well as frying, simmering and grilling (broiling).

HIRAME

A type of flounder, hirame is a flat fish with its eyes on the back. The skin on the back is shiny black; on the belly it is opaque white. It is one of the most commonly used fish in Japanese cooking, being used for sashimi and sushi as well as for frying, simmering and steaming, and in vinegared vegetable dishes and dressed salads. The thin, broad chain-like frill on the edges of the fish, called engawa, is regarded as a delicacy and is used for sashimi, simmered and grilled dishes. You can substitute turbot or lemon sole, if you wish.

Filleting and skinning flat fish

1 Place the fish on a chopping board and, using a sharp knife, make slits in the centre on the bone and both sides just inside the fins.

2 Inserting the blade horizontally between the flesh and the bones, carefully run the top of the blade along the bones separating the meat. Gently pull back the flesh as you proceed, handling the fish with care as you cut.

3 Repeat this procedure to remove the three other fillets, two on either side of the fish.

4 Place a fillet with the skin-side down on the chopping board and insert the blade between the flesh and skin. Start from the tail end of the fillet. Firmly pressing the skin down on the chopping board with the fingers of one hand, run the blade along the skin separating the flesh from the skin. Repeat this with three other fillets.

Above: The fish known in Japan as karei is in fact a family of fish that includes plaice, sole, halibut and flounder.

Left: Whole saba (chub mackerel)

SABA

An attractive streamlined fish, saba (chub mackerel) is a red-meat fish and should be used on the day it is caught, since it goes off very quickly. To check its freshness, make sure the eyes are clear, the skin shiny and that the intestines do not smell. A small saba is better than a large specimen. Saba is a relatively fatty fish, usually with 16 per cent fat, although this increases to over 20 per cent in autumn when it is in season, and 20 per cent protein.

Aroma and flavour

Saba has a succulent flavour but has a fishy smell, which can be moderated through the use of salt. It also goes well with miso and vinegar. In sashimi, eat dipped in a little shoyu with grated fresh root ginger.

Culinary uses

For sashimi, very fresh saba is first salted and then marinated in vinegar. Saba should not be eaten unmarinated due to the risk of parasite infestation. This method of marinating, called *shime-saba*, meaning firming saba, clears parasites. Saba is often fried, though it is not used for tempura as its flavour is quite different from other tempura ingredients and much stronger.

AJI

This is the general term for about 50 species of a group of fish ranging from horse mackerel to scad, which are now often available at good fishmongers in the West. Aji can grow up to 40cm/ 16in, but is normally caught young at 10–20cm/4–8in long. Shima-aji (striped jack), grows to about 1m/3ft. Aji is regarded as a high-quality fish, and is mainly reserved for sashimi. Ordinary aji is a grey, firm fish with a sharp, saw-like line of spiky scales on both sides of its lower body; these should be cut out, otherwise they may hurt you when you handle the fish. The season runs from spring to autumn.

Culinary uses

Very fresh aji is made into tataki, finely chopped flesh eaten with shoyu and grated fresh root ginger. It is also used for grilling (broiling), simmering, and in vinegared dishes. Smaller fish is good for frying whole. Aji is also famous for its dried products such as hiraki-boshi (the whole body is opened and dried) and mirin-boshi (a whole opened body dried with mirin) and kusaya (a strong smelling, opened dried body). Dried aji are available from Asian supermarkets.

Below: Whole aji

Shime-saba (salt and vinegar cured mackerel)

1 Fillet a very fresh mackerel but leave the skin intact. Place the two fillets flesh-side down on a thick bed of salt in a large, flat dish and cover them completely with more salt. Leave for at least 30 minutes, ideally for 3–4 hours.

2 Wash the fillets and pat dry with kitchen paper, then remove all the bones, with tweezers, if you wish.

3 Put about 120ml/4fl oz/½ cup rice vinegar or white wine vinegar in a flat serving dish. Lay the fillets flesh-side down in the dish and sprinkle more vinegar over them. Leave the fillets to marinate for 10 minutes, then drain.

4 Pat dry with kitchen paper and carefully remove the transparent skin with your fingers, working from head to tail, leaving the silver pattern on the flesh intact. For sashimi, cut the fillets crossways into 1–2cm/½–¾in thick slices.

Left: The firm, chunky flesh of ankoh makes this fish ideal for most forms of cooking.

ANKOH

Monkfish or anglerfish, known as ankoh in Japan, is highly symbolic of winter in Japanese culinary terms. Fugu and puffer are similar winter fish.

Culinary uses

A popular fish, ankoh is cooked in a hotpot at the table in restaurants as well as at home. It has a firm, chunky meat, not flaky even when cooked, so it is suitable for simmering, frying or grilling.

All the parts of the ankoh, including the liver, stomach and ovaries, are eaten but the liver is regarded as a particular delicacy and is often compared to foie gras. The liver is normally marinated in a vinegar sauce.

IWASHI

Sardines, iwashi, are the most commonly used fish in Japan, and they account for 25 per cent of the total catch by the sea fisheries. Along with the main species, there are a number of other varities also considered part of the same group, including ma-iwashi (Japanese pilchard), urume-iwashi (big-eye sardine) and a smaller species, katakuchi-iwashi (Japanese anchovy). Ma-iwashi has a blue-green back and silvery white belly with dark dots on both sides of the body. It grows up to 25–30cm/10–12in long. Katakuchi-iwashi grows to about 15cm/6in long. Iwashi is best in winter but is available all year round.

Culinary uses

Fresh iwashi is eaten grilled (broiled), in vinegared dishes, in mixed sushi, fried and minced (ground) into fish balls. However, it is mostly processed to make canned and numerous dried products such as niboshi, which is used for

Below: Beheaded and gutted iwashi (sardines) are packed raw, with their backbones, in oil; the canning process cooks them.

making dashi stock, and mezashi, four to six small half-dried iwashi strung together in a row with a piece of straw. Tiny fries under 3cm/1¼in long are normally dried to make shirasu-boshi (see Fish Products). In the past, export of these fish has been limited due to differing food regulations, but some are now produced in the West and are available from Japanese supermarkets.

SAMMA

Also known as saury, this long, narrow fish has a blue-black back and shiny silver-white belly. It inhabits the seas around North America and Russia, coming down towards Japan in autumn, the best time to eat it since by then it has acquired its maximum fat content of 20 per cent.

Preparation and cooking

In autumn, samma is best grilled (broiled) or pan-fried whole and eaten with a little grated daikon and shoyu to moderate its fishy smell. Dried samma is also very popular. In other seasons when it is less oily, fresh samma is used for making vinegared salads or sushi.

Fresh samma is sold in season at high-quality fishmongers, and cooked samma in cans is often available.

Below: Samma

SHELLFISH

Along with fish, shellfish have always been an indispensable ingredient in Japanese cooking, and Japan probably consumes the widest range of shellfish in the world. Most types are used for sashimi and sushi as well as in other forms of cooking. The following are some of the most popular shellfish used in Japanese cooking that are also widely available outside Japan.

Note: In the US all prawns are called shrimp, then differentiated according to size: small, medium, jumbo. The Japanese, however, use both shrimp and prawn, so US equivalents in brackets will not be provided, to avoid confusion.

EBI

Among the numerous kinds of shellfish used in Japanese cooking, the prawn has the largest market share. If you want to eat prawn sushi, for instance, at a sushi restaurant in Japan, you need to specify which prawn you would like from among at least five kinds likely to be available. Kuruma-ebi (tiger prawn) has a light reddish shell with brown or blue-red stripes and grows to about 20cm/8in long. Ushi-ebi (black tiger prawn) has a dark grey shell with black stripes and, along with kuruma-ebi, supposedly has the best flavour. Both are best eaten raw when very fresh but are also used for grilling (broiling), simmering, frying and in soups.

Below: Ushi-ebi (black tiger prawns) are considered the most flavoursome type of prawn.

Right: Pink shrimps

Korai-egi (Chinese prawn), also known as taisho-ebi, has a light grey shell and is used for tempura and other frying dishes, stir-frying or simmering.

Japanese shrimps, such as shiba-ebi and botan-ebi, are used mainly for cooking, and hokkoku aka-ebi, also known as ama-ebi, is a delicious sushi topping. Tenaga-ebi (freshwater shrimp) has long tentacles and is often used for simmering and frying, while even smaller shrimps, sakura-ebi, are mostly dried. Unfortunately, many of these are not available outside of Japan.

Preparation and cooking

In Japan all prawns and shrimps are available fresh, sometimes still alive, but in the West they generally come on to the market frozen. One advantage of prawns is that they are available all year round. They become bright red or pink when cooked, thus providing colour to a dish. When cooking prawns, leave them in their shells so that they won't lose too much of their flavour.

Ensuring straight prawns

When heated, prawns curl up. For tempura, grills or griddles where you do not wish the prawn to curl, skewer it lengthways with a cocktail stick (toothpick) before cooking and carefully remove it afterwards. If it proves difficult to remove the stick without spoiling the shape of the prawn, for instance when preparing tempura, another option is to hold the unskewered, battered prawn by the tail and lower it into the hot oil very slowly so that it heats section by section. Take care not to touch the hot oil.

Above: Ise-ebi, the Japanese spiny lobster

ISE-EBI

The Japanese spiny lobster, ise-ebi has a brown or reddish purple shell and smaller claws than most American and European lobsters. It grows off the Pacific coast of west Japan to about 35cm/14in, though it also inhabits the seas around the Caribbean, Australia and Africa. Ise-ebi is traditionally used for celebratory meals because the red colour, when cooked, signifies happiness in Japan.

Culinary uses

Lobsters have a uniquely firm, sweet flesh with a delicious flavour. Fresh ones are nearly always eaten as sashimi. At fish restaurants they are often kept in a tank and the chef makes a dish called iki-zukuri (live sashimi) from your choice of lobster in front of you. But beware, the sashimi will be arranged on the dissected shell with the head intact, its sad eyes looking at

you and the tentacles still moving! It is also grilled over charcoal and eaten with citrus shoyu.

KANI

There are about 1,000 different crabs inhabiting the seas around Japan alone. The commonest are tabara-gani (king crab), kegani (horsehair crab) and zuwai-gani (snow crab). As its intestine goes off very quickly, kani is always boiled or steamed, often as soon as it is caught on board the fishing boat, before going to market.

King crabs look like gigantic spiny spiders, but are very good to eat. A mature male king crab can weigh up to 12kg/26½lb and measure almost 1m/39in across. Their triangular bodies are bright red, with a pale cream underside.

Culinary uses

The claw flesh is the main part eaten, most often fresh with citrus shoyu, in salads, in grilled (broiled) and fried dishes, or in hotpots. Crab meat is

Left: Tabara-gani (king crab) claws

also one of the major ingredients for sushi. However, in cooked dishes canned crab meat is more usually used. Be advised that crab sticks or seafood sticks do not usually contain crab meat.

Japanese delicacies

Kani-miso Crab intestine mixture, is considered a delicacy in Japan and is most often served as part of an hors d'oeuvres tray or as an accompaniment to sake. Kani-miso is available canned.

Snow crab The sweet-tasting flesh of this crab is usually sold frozen or canned. The snow crab itself has a roundish pinkish-brown body and long legs. It is also known as the queen of the crabs.

with a hard inside shell and thick flesh. Its season runs from the beginning of autumn to late winter. Kaminari-ika, available at the same time, is a large cuttlefish with tentacles that can grow up to 45cm/18in. Hotaru-ika (firefly squid) is unique. It has a luminous body that grows to a mere 5–7cm/2–2¾in and has an almost transparent skin. It inhabits the seas around Japan and is available from spring to summer. Aka-ika (flying squid) is a large squid with a dark reddish brown skin and a thin, gluey bone inside. It is commonly used for making a range of dried, smoked and marinated squid products.

IKA

Squid is a common shellfish in Japan and several types are used in cooking. Which squid is selected for which dish is determined by taste, texture, colour and seasonal availability.

Surume-ika (Pacific flying squid), also known as Japanese common squid, has a dark, red-brown skin. It grows to about 30cm/12in long with tentacles as much as 20cm/8in long, and is in season throughout summer to autumn. Yari-ika (spear squid) grows to about 40cm/16in with relatively short tentacles and has a faintly reddish body with a pointed head. This squid is most commonly available in the West from winter to late spring.

Above:The flesh of larger cuttlefish, such as kaminari-ika, is delicious finely sliced and used in sashimi.

Kensaki-ika (swordtip squid) is very similar to yari-ika, but with a sharper, pointed head, and it is in season from spring to summer. Aori-ika (board-mantle squid) looks like a big cuttlefish, over 40cm/16in long with 50cm/20in tentacles, but without the calcareous shell and although it is available in summer it is not very common. Koh-ika (cuttlefish) has a round body about 18cm/7in long and 20cm/8in tentacles,

Culinary uses

Fresh squid is used for sashimi only when it is very fresh. Prepared squid can usually be bought in Japanese supermarkets. Always cook very lightly as overcooked squid is unpleasantly tough and chewy. Whole squid is also used for making ika-zushi (ika stuffed with sushi rice).

Preparing squid

1 Rinse the squid thoroughly under cold running water. Put your fingers inside the body, grab the tentacles, together with the soft central bone and intestine, and gently pull out of the cavity.

2 Separate the two flaps from the body so that the white flesh comes away from the skin attached to the flaps. Gently peel off the skin from the flaps and discard.

3 Cut away and discard the intestine. Cut off the tentacles from the head of the squid and rub off the skin.

4 For sashimi, cut the body flesh in half lengthways and then slice each piece crossways into thin strips to reduce its chewy texture. These strips are called ika somen (squid noodles).

5 For geso (tentacle sashimi), divide the ten tentacles into five equal pieces or separate individually, and cut the two long feelers in half.

6 For tempura, pan-frying and grilling (broiling), make criss-cross slits on the skin side of the body and cut into pieces.

COOK'S TIPS
• The tentacles can be tough when fried, so chop the tentacles finely and fry with vegetables.
• To make squid 'flowers', make delicate, diagonal criss-cross slits across the inside of the flesh and cut into small pieces. Use in quick frying dishes.

Right:
Iidako
(baby
octopus)

SQUID PRODUCTS

There are various squid products in Japan, which can increasingly be found at specialist stores in the West.

Surume

This is whole squid opened up and dried, and is one of a number of delicacies served to accompany drinks. It is normally grilled (broiled) whole, torn crossways with the fingers into fine shreds, and eaten sprinkled with a little shoyu. Kensaki-ika (swordtip squid) with its fine, tender flesh, is the best. It is available, whole or shredded in packets, from Japanese supermarkets and the Chinese version is generally available from Asian supermarkets.

Shiokara

This is raw squid, marinated in its own ink and salt. It is served with drinks or rice and is available in jars.

Matsumae-zuke

Another delicacy from the Kansai region, this is made of surume (dried squid), konbu (kelp seaweed) and carrot shreds marinated in mirin and shoyu, It is also served with drinks or rice. Make-your-own packets containing all the ingredients pre-prepared can be bought from Japanese supermarkets.

TAKO

The octopus' contrasting colours of milky white flesh and dark red skin (once heated, octopus skin turns red), together with the unusual round shape of its sliced tentacles, adds interesting character to Japanese cooking. There are over ten types of octopus caught all over the world and their sizes vary from Idako (baby octopuses), which are less than 10cm/4in, to ones over 3m/10ft. The most common octopus are in the *ma-dako* family.

Japanese cooking uses the octopus' eight tentacles, lightly blanched, for sashimi and vinegared salad dishes. Octopus is also used in hotpots, oden in particular, and for making an ink-marinated delicacy to accompany drinks. Prepared tentacles are available from fish counters in Japanese stores.

Preparing octopus for sashimi and sushi

1 Clean an octopus weighing 675g/1½lb, and separate the head and tentacles. Discard the head or reserve for use in another dish.

2 Bring plenty of water to the boil in a large, deep pan, add a halved lemon, 5ml/1 tsp salt and the octopus; bring back to the boil.

3 Cook over a medium heat for 5–6 minutes, taking the octopus out and plunging it back into the boiling water so that all the skin comes into contact with the hot water. Remove from the heat, drain and allow to cool.

4 For sashimi and sushi, use only the cooked tentacles. Separate the tentacles and chill for no more than 15 minutes. Using a sharp knife, slice diagonally into 5mm/¼in thick rings.

Above: Surume,
dried squid, is made
from kensaki-ika
(swordtip squid), and is
ranked first in terms of quality.

Left: Large hamaguri (common hard clams) and asari (Manila clams) are just two of the many clams used in Japanese cooking.

methods of cooking. Hamaguri (hard clam) is the most common and is in season from winter to early spring. It is grilled (broiled), steamed or simmered in soup still in the shell and is also sometimes used shelled for cooking with rice or in hotpots. Clams should be left in salted water to extract the sand in the shell before cooking. They are available fresh, dried, or cooked in cans.

Above: Dried hotate-gai (scallops) are soaked in a little sake and steamed to make them soft and easy to handle. This process also brings out their distinctive flavour.

HAMAGURI

Clams are one of the oldest foods in Japan as is evident from the remains of the shells found in all the prehistoric settlements excavated. They are still a very important ingredient, and many varieties are used for Japanese cooking such as aka-gai (ark shell), asari (Manila clam), tori-gai (cockle), baka-gai or aoyagi (hen clam) and hokki-gai (surf clam). They are all used for sushi and sashimi as well as for all other

Below: Clockwise from top left, fresh cockles, hokki-gai (surf clam), tori-gai (cockle) and aka-gai (ark shell)

HOTATE-GAI

The scallop is a very versatile shellfish because of its size and fish-like texture. There are several members of the scallop family available in Japan, including hotate-gai, the scallop most often sold in the West; itaya-gai

Below: Kaki, pacific oysters

(Japanese scallop), tsukihi-gai (saucer scallop) and hiogi-gai (noble scallop). All varieties are regular, indispensable ingredients for sushi and sashimi. They are used for vinegared salads, or can be salt-grilled, simmered, fried or used in soups. The thin ribbon around the scallop's flesh and the red intestine are not wasted, but are used in soups. Dried scallop is available from most Asian supermarkets and some larger stores.

KAKI

A few Pacific oysters are available in Japan. The most common kaki (giant Pacific oyster) is oblong in shape, about 8cm/3½in long and 5cm/2in wide in contrast to the round European native oyster. It is available all through the year but is at its most flavoursome from November to March.

To eat oyster raw, Japanese-style, dip in a little citrus shoyu. Kaki-fry (fried breaded oyster) is another Japanese speciality. Oysters are also used in clear soups, hotpots and cooked with rice. Kaki are known to cause food poisoning so when eaten raw they should be very fresh. Always buy fresh oysters from a reputable fishmonger.

FISH ROES

The Japanese use all parts of the fish, and its eggs, in particular, are regarded as a delicacy. Since the eggs are normally heavily salted to preserve them, they go well with plain boiled rice. They are also regular ingredients in sushi and are used for making hors d'oeuvres.

TARAKO

Cod ovaries, called tarako, are available at the fish counters of supermarkets in Japan. Sold in pairs, cod ovaries are usually simply grilled (broiled) to eat with boiled rice. Mentaiko is a salted version and karashi mentaiko is a pungent chilli type. Tarako are normally coloured slightly red with vegetable colouring to make them look more attractive. Tarako is used for norimaki (nori-rolled sushi) and also for making hors d'oeuvres.

IKURA

In Russia, all fish eggs are called ikura, but the name is used only for salmon eggs in Japan. Ikura is already salted to preserve it, so it normally keeps for a short time. It is mainly used for sushi, eaten with grated daikon and shoyu, and also for making hors d'oeuvres. It is widely available in jars at supermarkets. Salted whole salmon ovaries called sujiko are available only in Japan.

KAZUNOKO

Salted and dried herring ovaries, kazunoko, were once abundant but are now so scarce that they have become a rare delicacy. Soak in water overnight to soften and remove the salt before use. Kazunoko is usually eaten as it is with a little shoyu and katsuo-bushi, dried skipjack tuna flakes. It is one of the special items that constitute the New Year's day celebration brunch and is also used as a sushi topping. It is rarely available outside Japan, but most sushi restaurants have it on the menu.

UNI

The Japanese sea urchin, or uni, is a dark spiky, round sea creature that varies in size, depending on type, from 3–4cm/1¼–1½in to over 10cm/4in in diameter. Only the ovaries are eaten. Fresh uni is one of the regular items for sushi toppings and is also used for making hors d'oeuvres. It provides an interesting golden coating for some

Above: Kazunoko (salted and dried herring ovaries)

Above: Uni (Japanese sea urchin ovaries)

Left: Ikura (salmon caviar)

seafood, such as squid, that is to be grilled and also an unusual dressing for many shellfish. Salted uni is also available.

Preparation and cooking

Look for urchins with firm spines and a tightly closed mouth (on the underside). To open, wear gloves and use a purpose-made knife, though sharp scissors can also be used. Cut into the soft tissue around the mouth and lift off the top to reveal the coral. Alternatively, slice off the top like a boiled egg. Remove the mouth and innards, which are inedible, but retain the rich juices for use in sauces. Scoop out the bright orange coral.

Below: Tarako (cod ovaries) are usually just slightly red, front, though they turn a brighter red colour when prepared with chilli, back.

FISH PRODUCTS

Numerous fish products are used in Japanese cooking and many are available in the West, fresh or frozen. They are easy to use and very useful as a flavouring in home cooking. The following are some of the items that are increasingly available from larger Japanese supermarkets.

KATSUO-BUSHI

Katsuo, skipjack tuna, is cooked and dried whole to a hard block called katsuo-bushi and then shaved for use. Once it was the housewife's job, first thing in the morning, to shave katsuo-bushi, but today ready-shaved kezuri-bushi or hanagatsuo in various graded packets is widely available. This is one of the main ingredients in dashi stock and it is also used for sprinkling on vegetables or fish as an additional flavouring. Mixed with a little shoyu, it makes a delicious accompaniment to hot boiled rice or stuffing for onigiri (rice balls).

Culinary uses

Kezuri-bushi can be sprinkled on dashi-marinated boiled spinach, or on finely sliced onions; with a little shoyu added, this makes a good accompaniment to drinks. Another option is to mix with shoyu and sprinkle on hot boiled rice or use to stuff rice balls.

Right:
Various sizes and grades of ready-shaved dried fish are now readily available.

Home-made dashi stock
Dashi, fish soup stock, is probably the most frequently used ingredient in Japanese cooking. First dashi stock is used for soups; clear soup in particular. Second dashi stock is for simmering vegetables, meat and fish.

MAKES FOUR BOWLS OF SOUP

INGREDIENTS
  600ml/1 pint/2½ cups water
  10cm/4in standard konbu
  20g/¾oz or 3 × 5g/⅛oz packets
  kezuri-bushi

1 Pour the water into a pan and add the konbu. Leave to soak for 1 hour.

2 Place, uncovered, over a medium heat and bring almost to boiling point. Remove the konbu and reserve it for use in the second dashi stock. Bring the water to the boil.

3 Add about 50ml/2fl oz/¼ cup cold water and immediately add the kezuri-bushi. Bring back to the boil and remove the pan from the heat. Do not stir. Leave the kezuri-bushi to settle to the base of the pan.

4 Strain the mixture through a fine sieve (strainer) and reserve the kezuri-bushi in the sieve to make a second dashi stock. This first dashi stock liquid is now ready for use.

Second dashi stock

MAKES 600ML/1 PINT/2½ CUPS

INGREDIENTS
  reserved konbu and kezuri-bushi
  from first dashi stock
  600ml/1 pint/2½ cups water
  15g/½oz or 3 × 5g/⅛oz packets
  kezuri-bushi

1 Put the reserved konbu and kezuri-bushi from the first dashi into a pan with the water. Bring to the boil, then simmer for about 15 minutes, or until the stock is reduced by a third.

2 Add the kezuri-bushi to the pan and immediately remove the pan from the heat. Skim any scum from the surface and leave to stand for 10 minutes. Strain.

COOK'S TIPS
• Freeze-dried granules called dashi-no-moto can be used to make a quick dashi stock, if preferred.
• Dashi stock can be frozen.

Above: Unagi no kabayaki, grilled eel

NIBOSHI

These hard, dried sardines are used for making a strong-flavoured dashi stock. In contrast to the delicate flavour of kezuri-bushi, niboshi is boiled for about 5 minutes to exude the flavour and make a more robust stock. Hence niboshi stock is used for making rich soups such as miso soup and the soup for soba and udon noodles.

UNAGI NO KABAYAKI

Filleted eel is steamed, then grilled (broiled) with a thick, sweet shoyu sauce. This soft fish does not resemble, or taste, like eel. It is placed on top of hot boiled rice with the accompanying sauce sprinkled with seven-spice chilli powder, or sansho. Unagi no kabayaki is available ready-to-eat in packets, frozen or vacuum-packed.

HIDARA

This dried cod fillet can be grilled, then torn into pieces with the fingers and eaten with rice. It is also used for making snacks to go with drinks, and is available in packets.

SHIRASU-BOSHI

Tiny white fry sardines, shirasu are used to make many dried products. Shirasu-boshi are a soft, plain dried shirasu, which are eaten as they are mixed with other ingredients such as grated daikon and shoyu. They make a good accompaniment for hot boiled rice and are also often used as an hors d'oeuvres and as a stuffing for onigiri (rice balls). Shirasu-boshi are not often easily available outside Japan.

MEZASHI

Meaning eye-pierced, mezashi is made from half-dried whole sardines strung together, four to six at a time, by a piece of straw pierced through the eyes, hence the name. It is just lightly grilled and eaten with hot boiled rice or to accompany sake. The whole sardine including the head, bones, tail and intestines can be eaten, so it is highly nutritional, full of protein and calcium, yet a cheap everyday food. A visually striking dish, and largely new to the Western palate, mezashi is sometimes available at larger Asian food stores.

SHISHAMO

This small, 10–15cm/4–6in long, narrow, pinkish silver fish is unique to the north Pacific and Atlantic oceans. Shishamo is considered one of the best Japanese delicacies to eat with sake, especially komochi-shishamo (shishamo with eggs), and is priced accordingly.

Above:
Shishamo are
considered a delicacy, and are
often dried together on a bamboo straw
for easier handling, then grilled.

TATAMI-IWASHI

Tiny fry sardines are stuck together and dried into a thin sheet shaped like nori (dried seaweed sheet) to make tatami-iwashi. It is then lightly grilled before serving, and makes an excellent accompaniment for drinks as well as for hot boiled rice. Tatami-iwashi is mildly sweet with a rich flavour. It is not normally available outside Japan.

CHIRIMEN-JAKO

A speciality of the Kansai region (Osaka and surrounds), these are another form of dried shirasu (white fry sardines), which have been cooked and often flavoured with shoyu. They are eaten as are and make a good accompaniment for hot rice or in ochazuke (cooked rice in tea). Shoyu-flavoured ones are fairly salty. They are available in packets.

TAZUKURI

Dried small sardines, tazukuri are lightly roasted in a small pan before serving as an accompaniment for drinks or as a snack. They have a distinctive *umami* (rich flavouring). At New Year's time they are coated in sugar and served as part of the savoury celebration hamper. They are not only delicious but also very nutritional as they are full of calcium, which is highly beneficial, especially for growing children. Tazukuri are another fish product available outside Japan.

FISH PASTES

Numerous puréed fish products are used in Japanese cooking, among which the following are the most common. They are normally available frozen from Japanese food stores and are the main ingredients for oden (fish pastes and vegetables cooked in dashi-based soup).

KAMABOKO

Puréed white fish is mixed with a binding agent and made into various shapes and sizes then steamed, boiled or grilled (broiled) to produce kamaboko. The standard product is called ita-kamaboko; a small fish paste cake, about 4–5cm/1½–2in thick and 15cm/6in long, stuck on a wooden board. It can be coloured pink around the outside. Eat finely sliced with shoyu and mustard as an hors d'oeuvre to accompany drinks, or use in soups, hotpots, and with noodles.

SATSUMA-AGE

This is deep-fried kamaboko and is normally shaped into an oval disc measuring about 7.5 × 5cm/3 × 2in. Pour boiling water over the paste to reduce the oil before use. It can be eaten as it is with shoyu, or lightly grilled. It is also used for simmering with vegetables, in soups, hotpots, and in noodle dishes. There are many sizes and colours of

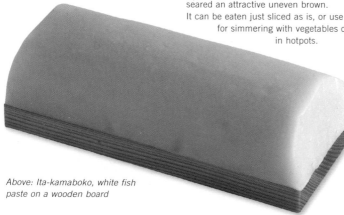

Above: Clockwise from left to right; chikuwa, narutomaki, satsuma-age and hanpen puréed fish products

deep-fried kamaboko and even stuffed and rolled versions as well. Ika-maki is a fried kamaboko roll with squid inside and gobo-maki is stuffed with burdock. Both of these together with ordinary satsuma-age are popular ingredients for oden (fish paste hotpot), and are available, mostly frozen, at Japanese and Asian supermarkets.

CHIKUWA

Puréed fish is moulded around a stick, then steamed and grilled, and the stick removed. Chikuwas normally measure about 15cm/6in long with the hole running this length. The outer skin is seared an attractive uneven brown. It can be eaten just sliced as is, or use for simmering with vegetables or in hotpots.

NARUTOMAKI

This is a kind of kamaboko with a decorative pink swirling pattern inside. It is one of the regular ingredients for ramen, Chinese-style noodles, and is also used in udon noodles and soups.

HANPEN

This puréed shark's flesh is mixed with grated yam and egg whites, shaped into a 7–8cm/3½–3¾in square cake about 1cm/½in thick and then boiled. It has a light, fluffy texture and can be eaten grilled with shoyu and mustard, and is also used for hotpots and soups.

SHINJO

There are many types of ready-made fish balls available in Japan, including yuba-shinjo (shinjo rolled in a sheet of dried soya bean skin). There are also flower-shaped ones in various colours used as garnishes. Some shinjo may be available at Japanese stores.

TSUMIRE

This greyish coloured fish ball is made from red meat fish such as sardines and mackerel and, though firm, has a soft texture. It is a flat disc with a 'crater' in the centre so that it heats quickly and evenly. It is used in soup, oden and hotpot dishes and is available frozen.

Above: Ita-kamaboko, white fish paste on a wooden board

MEAT AND CHICKEN

The eating of meat was banned in Japan for many years, first due to Buddhism and later by the Shogunate for 300 years until 1868. However, game, such as wild boar, hare and mountain birds have always been eaten by some communities. It was only after World War II that meat, mainly beef, pork and chicken, became a part of the general diet. It is still only sparingly used; nearly always thinly sliced or shredded and cooked with vegetables, or minced (ground).

Above: Finely sliced beef for shabu shabu *and* sukiyaki

BEEF

There are four types of wagyu, (Japanese beef): black, reddish brown, hornless and short-horned. Black beef is the most common. Matsuzaka beef, also known as Kobe beef, omi beef and yonezawa beef, are the top-quality meats. They are massaged with beer, which helps to distribute the fat, so making the lean meat more tender, and wagyu meat is pink rather than red. The attention the Japanese give to their beef is highly labour intensive, which accounts for its ferociously high price. Wagyu is not available in the West but you can use sirloin or fillet instead. For sukiyaki and shabu shabu,

Right: Thinly sliced pork

Below: Chicken is used in various ways; minced for making meatballs, skewered for teriyaki, and the thigh for barbecuing.

where almost transparent slices are required, choose a roasting joint without a bone, or fillet. If a joint is used, trim off the fat completely and cut into 4–5cm/1½–2in thick oblong pieces, then freeze for two or three hours. Remove to the refrigerator, leave for

1 hour to half thaw and then slice into paper-thin oblong pieces. Ready-sliced sukiyaki beef is generally available. Trim off any excess fat, if necessary.

PORK

Since ancient times pork has been eaten, even during the period when meat was banned, and it remains popular today. It is thinly sliced, pan-fried and mixed with grated fresh root ginger and shoyu, or else chopped and used as a flavouring in vegetable dishes. Long-simmered pork is delicious with ramen.

CHICKEN

Native regional chickens, called jidori, are popular in Japan, though there are also many mass-produced broiler chickens. Nagoya kochin is one such jidori, with a pinkish golden, firm meat. Minced chicken is often used for making meatballs, sauces or as a flavouring for simmered vegetables. Yakitori is chicken pieces threaded on a bamboo skewer, then grilled (broiled) with sweet taré sauce. Boneless chicken thighs marinated in teriyaki sauce and then grilled are ideal for barbecues. Chicken is also used for hotpots.

SAUCES FOR FLAVOURING AND DIPPING

Shoyu and miso are the two oldest and most important flavouring sauces in Japanese cooking. Although their strong, distinctive flavours means they are used more as condiments for dipping or as flavouring for cooking, rather than as a sauce for coating food. The two also have a preservative quality and are good for marinating raw fish, meat and vegetables.

The Japanese have also developed ready-mixed sauces for certain popular dishes such as sukiyaki and yakiniku (barbecue), as well as Japanese vinegar and mirin, both made from rice.

SHOYU

Japan's ancient seasoning was called hishio, and consisted of a preserve of what was at that time very scarce and precious salt fermented with animal or vegetable protein and fibre. Grain hishio, fermented with grains such

as rice and wheat, and also beans, was developed into miso and its exuded liquid became shoyu. (The present-day sushi is also thought to derive from the ancient fish hishio, raw fish fermented with salt and rice.)

Using new techniques, introduced from China, Japan soon developed its own type of soy sauce, shoyu, made from daizu (soya beans), wheat and salt. First a mixture of soya beans and wheat is made into a culture called koji, helped by active mould; this is then mixed with salt and water, and the mash is left to ferment and brew slowly for one year. After this time it is compressed to exude the liquid, which is then refined. (Mass-produced shoyu does not follow this authentic process but instead uses chemicals to hasten it.)

Shoyu is now widely available from supermarkets, but Japanese shoyu is quite different in aroma and flavour from Chinese varieties.

Aroma and flavour

Shoyu is quite salty, although less salty now than it used to be, due to recent warnings about the role of salty food in heart disease. There are basically two types: usukuchi (light), and koikuchi, (dark). The usukuchi is an all-purpose shoyu, clearer but slightly saltier than koikuchi, which is used for making sauces such as taré for teriyaki. There are also many grades, depending on the grade of soya beans, which are priced accordingly. Tamari is made from soya beans only without wheat, so it is similar to the liquid obtained during the making of miso.

Light shoyu (soy sauce), left, has a lighter colour but saltier flavour than regular shoyu, far left.

Above: Light and dark shoyu. Use light shoyu, left, for flavouring, such as in clear soups, and dark shoyu, above back, in simmered dishes.

Culinary uses

Shoyu is without doubt the single most important ingredient in Japanese cuisine and is used in almost every recipe. When just a drop is added to ingredients, they do not take on the colour of the shoyu; this is called *kakushi-aji* (hidden flavour). It is often used as a dip on its own for sushi, sashimi, pickles and many other dishes. Tamari is a dark shoyu used for making taré sauce and is suitable for those on a wheat-free diet.

Cooking techniques

To avoid the strong colour of shoyu dulling fresh ingredients, add the sauce towards the end of the cooking time, except for long-simmered dishes. For a dip, use shoyu sparingly by pouring only 15–30ml/1–2 tbsp at a time into a small sauce dish. If, for instance, you plunge your sushi into a large bowl of shoyu, it will become too salty or else a lot of shoyu will be left at the end of the meal.

Storage

All manufactured shoyu is pasteurized, with preservatives added. Bottled shoyu, except natural or organic varieties, normally keeps fairly well for a long time. However, the flavour deteriorates gradually, so once opened it is best to use it within three months. Natural, preservative-free shoyu should be kept in the refrigerator. If a thin layer of mould forms on the surface, filter the sauce. Though harmless, do not eat.

MISO

Although lifestyles are rapidly changing, for many Japanese the day still starts with a bowl of miso soup for breakfast. Miso is one of the oldest traditional Japanese ingredients – it was already being made in the 12th century – and its origin can be traced back to the ancient seasoning called hishio, a preserve of salt fermented with grains and beans. Today, boiled daizu (soya beans) is crushed, then mixed with a culture called koji, which is made with wheat and rice, barley or beans. The fermented mixture is allowed to mature for up to three years.

Numerous kinds and brands of miso are available in supermarkets, even outside Japan. They are categorized into three basic grades according to strength of flavour and colour: shiro-miso (white, light and made with rice), aka-miso (red, medium and made with barley), and kuro-miso (black, strong and made with soya beans).

Aroma and flavour

Miso is quite salty and has a strong fermented bean flavour. Shiro-miso is the lightest in saltiness and flavour, aka-miso is of medium flavour, and the strongest is kuro-miso. There are less salty brands for the health conscious.

Culinary uses

Miso is a versatile ingredient and can be simply diluted with dashi stock to make soups, including the soup for miso ramen. It is used as seasoning for simmered dishes or dipping sauces, and also as a marinade for meat and fish. Shiro-miso (white) is a speciality of Kyoto, thus often referred to as Saikyo miso, and is particularly good for soups, dressings and marinades. Shinshu (in central Japan) and Sendai (in the north-east) are also well known for miso production and they produce both light and medium miso. Aka-miso (red) is good for soups and for meat marinades. Hatcho miso, the best kuro-miso (black), is rich and salty, and is good for dipping sauces and soups. It is often used mixed with another lighter miso.

Cooking techniques

If miso is overcooked it loses its subtle aroma, so add the paste towards the end of the cooking time. In soups, use sparingly. Dilute a little with some of the liquid and mix it into the soup. Check the taste and add more if needed.

Storage

In a tightly covered jar, miso will keep for a long time in the refrigerator, but the flavour gradually deteriorates.

Above: Clockwise from top left, aka-miso, shiro-miso, hatcho-miso and kuro-miso

Miso-marinated flat fish or steak
Flat fish such as plaice and turbot are used for this dish, which involves marinating the fish in shiro-miso, a kind of white miso.

1 On a large plate spread a thin layer of shiro-miso (use aka-miso for meat). Cover with kitchen paper and press lightly so that the paper absorbs the miso.

2 Place fish fillets, flesh-side down, or meat on the paper and cover with another piece of paper.

3 Using a knife, press a thin layer of miso on top of the paper so that the paste covers the fish or meat. Marinate fish for about 3 hours; meat can be marinated overnight.

4 Remove the fish or meat from the marinade and grill (broil).

READY-MADE SAUCES

A number of ready-to-use ingredients have been developed in recent years and Japanese cooking is much easier as a result. The following ready-made sauces are available in the West.

MEN-TSUYU

This is a dashi-based condensed sauce for soba and udon noodles. It is made of dashi stock, shoyu, salt, sugar and other ingredients, and is used as a dipping sauce or soup for noodles. The instructions on the packet will state how much water should be added to make a dip for soba and somen, or soup in which to cook udon and soba. It is usual to dilute 1:1 for a dip and 1:8 for soup. Store in the refrigerator.

TONKATSU SAUCE

Tonkatsu (pork cutlet) is one of the most popular dishes in Japan, and this thick brown sauce is the ideal accompaniment, together with shredded cabbage and mustard. It is made of fruits, spices and seasonings. You can easily make your own tonkatsu sauce by mixing a fruit sauce, such as ketchup, and Worcestershire sauce.

TEN-TSUYU

This tasty dipping sauce for tempura is made of dashi stock, shoyu, mirin and a number of seasonings. Ten-tsuyu is normally used undiluted together with a little grated daikon and finely shredded fresh root ginger.

YAKINIKU NO TARE

This Japanese version of barbecue sauce is made of shoyu, spices and various seasonings. It is slightly sweeter than the Western barbecue sauces and is also used for griddled food.

SUKIYAKI SAUCE

This is a sweet shoyu sauce for cooking sukiyaki, made of dashi stock, sugar, sake and seasonings. First thinly sliced beef is pan-fried, then some of this sauce is added, together with vegetables.

Making simple sauces at home

Most Japanese have a number of sauces in their repertoire that can be easily made on the day of use.
Yuan sauce This sauce gives a subtle flavour to rather bland ingredients such as white fish, and enhances the flavours of stronger-flavoured varieties, such as salmon. Mix together 5 parts mirin, 3 parts shoyu to 2 parts sake and 2 parts lime juice. Marinate the fish in the sauce for at least 15 minutes, before frying or cooking over a barbecue.
Tonkatsu sauce Delicious with fried pork, mix together 1 part Worcestershire sauce to 5 parts tomato ketchup. Coat pork slices in flour and beaten egg and deep-fry. Dip into the sauce and eat.

Below: The numerous types of Japanese ready-made sauces include, from left, tonkatsu sauce, sukiyaki sauce, men-tsuyu sauce, ponzu, men-tsuyu sauce for somen and yakiniku no tare.

PONZU

Made of citrus juice, vinegar and seasonings, ponzu is used mixed with shoyu and spices for hotpot dishes.

CURRY ROUX

Japan was first introduced to curry in the middle of the 19th century, not directly from India but via England, where curry powder was concocted and exported. Since then, curry has become one of the most popular daily foods in Japan. The Japanese, as with many introduced ingredients, further developed the powder into an instant curry sauce roux, mixing together all the necessary ingredients such as herbs and spices, fruits, soup stock, sauces and seasonings. It comes in the form of a soft slab, resembling a chocolate bar, in a sectioned plastic tray. All you need to do is boil the fresh ingredients such as meat or shellfish, potato, onion and carrot, and add some of this sauce mix. There are degrees of hotness: mild, medium, hot and very

hot. There are also separate roux for meat and fish. An average packet normally serves 12, but remember that a Japanese portion is very small and it really makes enough for only six to eight adult appetites, particularly if eaten on its own.

Japanese curry is quite sweet, even the very hot type, and usually contains a lot of MSG (monosodium glutamate). If you are unsure of the flavour peculiar to MSG, which can make you a little thirsty afterwards, use this product sparingly.

Left: Many types of curry roux are stocked at Japanese supermarkets. Available in boxed form, they resemble a chocolate bar and are graded by hotness (mild, medium, hot and very hot).

Home-made Japanese curry

Using a ready-mixed roux, a tasty and filling curry can be cooked in less than 30 minutes.

SERVES FOUR

INGREDIENTS
   2 onions, thinly sliced
   30ml/2 tbsp vegetable oil
   500g/1¼lb prawns (shrimp),
     peeled or any meat, cut into
     bitesize pieces
   1 carrot, peeled and chopped
   1–2 potatoes, peeled and
     roughly chopped
   750ml/1¼ pints/3 cups water
   125g/4¼oz (½ packet) curry roux
   15–30ml/1–2 tbsp shoyu or
     Worcestershire sauce,
     to taste (optional)
   rice, to serve

1 In a deep pan, gently stir-fry the onion slices in the vegetable oil until the onions become slightly brown. Add the prawns or meat and continue to stir-fry for 1–2 minutes.

2 Add the carrot and potatoes and stir-fry for another 1–2 minutes. Add the water and bring to the boil. Lower the heat and simmer for 5–10 minutes, more if meat is used, until the prawns and vegetables are cooked.

3 Remove from the heat. Add the roux, broken into small pieces, and stir well until all the roux pieces have melted into the soup. Place the pan back over a medium heat and gently simmer for about 5 minutes, stirring continuously, until the soup thickens.

4 To slightly reduce the sweetness of the curry, add a little shoyu or Worcestershire sauce. Serve with hot boiled rice.

VINEGAR AND MIRIN

Unlike shoyu and miso, Japanese vinegar and mirin (sweet cooking sake) are delicate tasting and good for adding subtle flavours to Japanese cooking. Both are made from rice.

RICE VINEGARS

Unless labelled yonezu (pure rice vinegar), most Japanese vinegars, called su or kokumotsu-su, normally contain other grains besides rice. If less than 40g/1½oz rice was used to make 1 litre/1¾ pint/4 cups of vinegar, it is labelled as kokumotsu-su (grain vinegar). There is also a cheap, mixed product, gohsei-su, which consists of brewed (about 60 per cent) and synthetic vinegar. Rice vinegar and other vinegars and vinegar products can be found at Japanese supermarkets.

Aroma and flavour

Japanese rice vinegar has a mild, sweet aroma and is less sharp than ordinary wine vinegar.

Culinary uses

Vinegar has many qualities. It can be used to refresh and soften saltiness, it acts as an antiseptic, and is a coagulant for proteins. It also prevents food from discolouring, helps to wash off slimy substances from food and to soften small fish bones. It is, therefore, useful from the preparation stage of food to the final seasoning. There are numerous vinegared dishes, such as cucumber and wakame salad, vinegar-cured raw fish, and gari (pickled ginger) to accompany sushi.

Cooking techniques

The slightly mild, subtle, acidic flavour of Japanese vinegar disappears quickly, so add to hot dishes at the last minute.

MIRIN

This amber-coloured, heavily sweetened sake is used only in cooking. It is one of Japan's ancient sake and is made from shochu (distilled sake). Shochu, mixed with steamed glutinous rice and koji (a yeast-like culture made from rice), is brewed and compressed to absorb the liquid, and then filtered. There is a synthetically made, cheap mirin-like liquid available called mirin-fuhmi (mirin flavouring), as opposed to hon-mirin (real mirin). The alcohol content of hon-mirin is 14 per cent and mirin-fuhmi only 1 per cent. These two types of mirin are available in bottles of 300ml/½ pint/1¼ cups or 600ml/1 pint/2½ cup from Asian supermarkets.

Culinary uses

Mirin has a faint sake aroma and syrupy texture, which adds not only a mild sweetness to food but also an attractive shiny glaze and slightly alcoholic flavour. It is used for simmered dishes and in glazing sauces such as taré (for yakitori). Other uses include mirin-boshi (a mirin-coated dried fish), and daikon is pickled in mirin pulp.

Left: Yonezu (rice vinegar) and kokumotsu-su (grain vinegar)

Cooking techniques

Use mirin towards the end of the cooking time to add a subtle sweetness and depth to the flavour of the dish. It is not meant to be used as a sweetener, but if you must, you can use 5ml/1 tsp sugar in place of 15ml/1 tbsp mirin.

Storage

Both vinegar and mirin keep well for a long time if stored in a cool place away from sunlight. The flavour of vinegar will deteriorate gradually, once the bottle is opened, so should be used as soon as possible. Once a bottle of mirin is opened, a white sugary substance will form around the cap, which is the residue after the alcohol evaporates. This is harmless but keep the bottle clean. It is best to use mirin within the *shomi-kikan* (appreciative period), since the flavour deteriorates and after several months it will become mouldy.

Below: When buying rice vinegar, look for hon-mirin, left, rather than mirin-fuhmi, right, which is a cheap imitation.

DRIED FLAVOURINGS

Ever on the look out for tasty accompaniments to rice, the Japanese have developed a number of flavourings, known as tsukudani.

TSUKUDANI

Various foodstuffs, such as konbu (kelp seaweed), shiitake, matsutake, dried herring, clams, beef and even whale meat are made into tsukudani. Konbu is the most popular. It is cut into small pieces and then simmered with shoyu for a long time. It is sometimes cooked with other foods, such as shiitake or matsutake, and fish flakes. Tsukudani is fairly salty and goes well with hot plain boiled rice. An assorted tsukudani set is a popular gift during the traditional gift seasons at the middle and the end of each year. Konbu tsukudani is usually available in packets from Japanese supermarkets all year round.

FURIKAKE

Consisting of various types of granulated fish and vegetable extracts, furikake are popular sprinkled on hot boiled rice. They are also used for making onigiri (rice balls), either mixed with rice or used as a stuffing. Various sprinkles in packets or jars are available from Japanese supermarkets.

Above: Assorted furikake (seafood and vegetable granules)

Above: Ochazuke no moto (flavourings for leftover rice)

Left: Sushi mixes

OCHAZUKE NO MOTO

A favourite Japanese way of enhancing leftover rice is to pour boiling water with added flavouring over it. There are many different flavours of ochazuke no moto available, including salted salmon, cod roe, umeboshi (salted and dried Japanese apricots) and nori, and they are available in individual packets.

SUSHI MIX

This is a packet or jar of pre-prepared ingredients for chirashi-zushi (mixed sushi), made by stirring the packet's contents into the rice. The garnish of shredded nori is also included in the packet. The flavour is sweet and it contains MSG (monosodium glutamate).

PICKLES

For the Japanese, rice and tsukemono (pickled vegetables) have gone hand in hand since ancient times. There are many varieties of tsukemono, also known as oshinko, preserved in all sorts of ways, and different regions have their own speciality. Barrel after barrel of freshly made tsukemono are displayed in the food hall of any department store in Japan and you can sample them before buying. The Japanese do not use vinegar as a pickling agent, instead, rice bran, miso, sake or mirin pulps, mustard, koji (rice malt) or shoyu, together with salt, are used. Salting takes away the coarseness of the hard vegetables and makes them soft and digestible as well as preserving them. It also adds more character and depth to the taste and improves the nutritional content. The following are some of the popular pickles available in packets from Japanese supermarkets.

Above: Naturally pickled daikon, front, and a commercially produced example, back. The latter is darker due to the addition of yellow food colouring.

TAKUAN

Fresh, just harvested daikon are hung for two to three weeks, then salted and pickled in nuka (dry rice bran) and salt. It takes two or three months to mature and the end result is a soft but crunchy, delicious yellow daikon. This tsukemono is said to have been invented by the Buddhist monk Takuan in the 17th century, hence the name. Salty with a hint of sweetness, it is good on its own with hot boiled rice. It is also a regular ingredient for nori maki (nori-rolled sushi) and other rice dishes. Most of the manufactured takuan has bright yellow food colouring added, so for naturally pickled daikon, look for the paler ones and check the label first.

SHIO-ZUKE

This is the general term used for all salted vegetables, and many vegetables, including cucumber, aubergine (eggplant), daikon, hakusai and mustard leaves, are used. Japanese cucumber and aubergine are a lot smaller and more delicate in flavour than Western varieties, so look particularly for those.

NARA-ZUKE

This tsukemono is a speciality of Nara, the ancient capital of Japan. The pulp that mirin is exuded from is used to pickle various vegetables, and nara-zuke (salted daikon pickled in mirin pulp) is one such pickle. It has a sweet flavour with a hint of alcohol. Eat with hot boiled rice.

Above: Shio-zuke (salt-pickled vegetables) can refer to a number of vegetables including, from left, aubergine, radish and cucumber.

Left: Nara-zuke (mirin pulp pickles)

Making a pickled turnip flower

Serve these attractive flowers as an hors d'oeuvre or as an easy garnish for sushi.

1 Trim and peel five small turnips and place, one at a time, between a pair of *hashi* (chopsticks) on a cutting board. Insert a very sharp blade down into the turnip, across the *hashi*, and make parallel cuts until the blade touches the hashi.

2 Turn the turnip 90 degrees, and cut across the first series of cuts.

3 Repeat with the remaining turnips, then place them in a large bowl. Sprinkle with 5ml/1 tsp salt and rub in lightly. Cover with a small plate, place a weight on top and leave for 30 minutes.

4 Mix 250ml/8fl oz/1 cup rice vinegar and 150g/5oz/¾ cup sugar in a deep bowl and stir until the sugar has dissolved. Drain the turnips and pour the vinegar mixture over them. Leave to marinate and soften overnight.

NUKA-ZUKE

This is a traditional method of pickling and each house-hold used to keep a tub of nuka-miso (rice bran mash), which resembles miso and from which it takes its name. Nuka (dry rice bran) is mixed with warm, strong brine into a mash, in which vegetables such as aubergine (eggplant), carrot, cucumber, daikon, hakusai or turnips are buried and left to pickle. It is ready to eat the next day. This makes the vegetables mildly sweet and enriches the flavour, but not without paying the price of its strong odour. The mash must be stirred every day, ideally with bare hands. Although long-serving dutiful wives were once fondly called nuka-miso (smelling wife), today not many wives wish to be appreciated for their smelly hands! Nuka for pickling is available from Japanese stores, although ready-pickled nuka-zuke in packets is more popular.

MISO-ZUKE

The saltiness and strong flavour of miso are the two ideal qualities for making pickles. Red or white miso can be used on its own or often flavoured with mirin and sake to make miso-doko (miso mash). Fish and shellfish, poultry and beef can be marinated before grilling (broiling) and vegetables that have been marinated are then eaten as pickles. All crunchy vegetables are suitable for pickling in miso but gobo (burdock root), is probably better than anything else for pickling in miso. Ready-to-eat gobo miso pickles are usually available in packets at Japanese supermarkets.

RAKKYO

To make rakkyo, spring onions (scallions) are first salted and then pickled in heavily sweetened vinegar. This is traditionally served with curry.

Making rice bran pickles

Nuka-zuke is a traditional pickling method for vegetables such as carrot, daikon and cucumber, and is an old Japanese favourite.

1 Following the instructions on the packet of nuka, mix the water and salt in a pan and bring to the boil. Remove the pan from the heat and leave to cool. The ratio is usually 3 parts nuka to 1 part of salt mixed with 2½ parts of water.

2 Put the rice bran in a large mixing bowl, then add the salted water and mix well. Seal well or transfer the wet nuka to a large container with a tight-fitting lid. Leave to settle for 5 days, stirring well 1–2 times a day.

3 Wash and trim the vegetables (cut big vegetables into smaller sizes), then push them into the bran bed. Softer vegetables are ready within 24 hours and harder ones, such as daikon, within 2 days. Adjust the saltiness by adding more salt or rice bran. Stir the bran well every day even when nothing is being pickled. The bran can be used indefinitely.

BREAD AND BUNS

Bread, called pan in Japan, was first introduced by the Portuguese in the 16th century. However, it wasn't part of the general public's diet until after World War II. In recent years it has become very popular and, although rice still remains the staple food, toast is taking over at the breakfast table in many households. Younger generations now prefer easy-to-make sandwiches to the more elaborate and heavy rice lunch box and the Japanese have developed their own, very fine loaves and unique buns. Today, Japanese bakeries, *yamazaki-ya*, produce many of them abroad. Here are some of the popular ones.

Left: An pan (red bean paste filled bun)

SHOKU PAN

There are two types of Japanese standard loaf: the square loaf and Igirisu-pan (English loaf). Japanese breads are all very soft and wet with a faintly sweet, delicate flavour. They are similar to English milk bread in both

Below: Shoku pan, the Japanese version of a traditional English cottage loaf, can be bought whole or sliced.

taste and texture though the Japanese shoku pan is a little fluffier. Unlike the real English loaf, the Igirisu-pan's cook's hat shape is rather exaggerated and too perfect. All loaves are available in half or whole, and are often ready-cut into six or eight thick slices per half. To keep the softness it should be stored in its cellophane bag and eaten within two to three days, or else refrigerated for up to five days. It can also be frozen.

BUDO PAN

Also known as reizun pan, this raisin bread normally comes as a loaf, weighing about 500g/1¼lb. It is fairly sweet in flavour and has a slightly dense texture but it is not as dense as Western raisin breads. Budo pan should be eaten within two to three days or kept wrapped in the refrigerator for no more than five days. It is available at Japanese supermarkets.

KOPPE PAN

This is an individual-size soft loaf, normally 20–25cm/8–10in long and 7.5–8cm/3–4in wide, and has a faintly sweet flavour. The word, koppe, supposedly comes from a German word, kuppe, meaning the summit. This bread is usually served at school lunch in Japan. It should be eaten within a day or two, or kept in the refrigerator for up to four days. Koppe pan is not often available outside Japan.

AN PAN

A soft round bun about 7–10cm/3–4in in diameter, stuffed in the centre with a sweet aduki paste, called an in Japan. There are two types of aduki paste: a coarse one with the aduki skin mashed in and a smooth one without. An pan stuffed with coarse paste has sesame seeds sprinkled on top to distinguish it from the other one. It is a strange combination of Western

Below: Custard-filled cream pan

Right: Melon pan

bread and Japanese sweet an with a dense texture and tastes more like a cake than a bun. But for young and old alike in Japan it's an all-time favourite snack. It's best eaten as soon as possible but keeps for a few days. It is available at Asian stores.

FRANCE OGURA

This is what Japanese bakers consider French-style an pan, approximately 10cm/4in in diameter and 2cm/1in thick. The bread is slightly drier than ordinary an pan, more like a brioche and has more bite. Ogura is the name of a mountain in Kyoto where the original an (coarse aduki paste with skin mashed in) comes from, but this France ogura has a less sweet flavour than ordinary an pan. It is normally available at Japanese stores along with an pan.

CREAM PAN AND JAM PAN

The cream pan is a triangular or oval-shaped bun stuffed with custard. It has a light and fluffy texture and the flavour is less sweet than an pan. It should be eaten on the day of purchase and it is available at Japanese supermarkets. Jam pan have a slightly rounder shape, to distinguish them from cream pan without having to break it open.

CHOCO KORUNE

This is a spiral-patterned, corn-shaped bun with chocolate cream in the centre. The texture of the bun is firm enough to hold the chocolate cream and it's quite sweet. It should be eaten on the day of purchase. It is not often available outside Japan.

MELON PAN

This is a yellow fluffy bun, with sugar coating on top. It is called melon pan because of the colour and shape, and has nothing to do with the taste. It has a crisp sugary texture outside but light bread inside, and a sweet flavour. It's best eaten while the exterior is still crisp, but keeps for up to three days if kept in the cellophane bag.

CURRY PAN

An oval-shaped, fried bread stuffed with curry; this is the most unusual of all Japanese buns. The curry inside is rather sweet and does not contain many ingredients other than tiny bits of minced (ground) meat, carrot, onion and potato. As it is fried it will keep for up to three days.

AN DOUGHNUT

This popular doughnut has sweet aduki paste inside. As it is fried, the bread is drier than normal Japanese buns and is coated with sugar, so is doubly sweet. It is best eaten as soon as possible.

Above: Curry-filled Japanese buns

CAKES AND SWEETS

Wagashi (Japanese cakes) are an art form in themselves. They are extremely beautiful creations of both ingenuity and observation of nature that only the Japanese could dream up in such a meticulously detailed way. Flowers, petals, foliage and birds are all featured in wagashi from season to season. There are basically three types of wagashi available at Japanese wagashi shops: namagashi (raw, wet cakes) are made of fresh ingredients that do not keep long; han-namagashi (half raw cakes) made of fresh ingredients that are hardened by long cooking, so keep well for a few weeks; and higashi (dry cakes and sweets), which are made from sugar, bean flour or jellies and keep well for a few months. Namagashi and han-namagashi are very dense and sweet, and mostly made of glutinous rice flour, aduki or other bean paste, chestnuts, sweet potatoes and kanten (agar-agar). Higashi are blocks of sugary bean flour and come in many shapes.

The wagashi are eaten not as dessert but as an accompaniment at the tea ceremony as well as at teatime. As they are all freshly made, they harden and go off quickly, particularly namagashi.

The namagashi served at formal tea ceremonies are specifically called omogashi (main, fresh cakes) and are served with koicha (thick matcha tea). With usucha (thin matcha tea), higashi (dry cakes) are normally used.

Wagashi are only available at wagashi shops except for some popular ones consumed daily that can also be frozen. The following are some of the wagashi for daily consumption rather than for the tea ceremony, and are normally available at Japanese wagashi shops or maybe at large supermarkets.

KUSA MOCHI

This is a glutinous rice cake stuffed with aduki paste, but the mochi is mixed with pounded yomogi (mugwort – a wild leaf, which gives it a light green colour. If real yomogi is used, it should contain bits of grass and have a grassy aroma and flavour. However, those normally available at supermarkets are only coloured green, hence have no such aroma and flavour. Unlike daifuku, kusa mochi is a thick mochi cake, which makes it more filling. It is either covered by light flour or wrapped in a leaf to prevent it from sticking. Kusa mochi hardens quickly but, because of its thickness, it keeps for up to three days.

DAIFUKU

This simple cake, made of glutinous rice cake stuffed with sweet aduki paste, is an all time favourite among old and young alike. The glutinous rice flour is steamed, then made into a very smooth dough and stretched to a thin, almost transparent dough that is wrapped around the aduki paste. It's very sticky, so is sold rolled in light flour. It hardens quickly, losing the soft stickiness, so should be eaten within three days. It is available frozen; thaw then eat.

KASHIWA MOCHI

This kashiwa (oak leaf) wrapped glutinous rice cake is a speciality for the Children's Day (Boy's Festival) on 5th of May. There are two kinds: one stuffed with sweet aduki paste and the other containing a sweet miso paste. The latter cake is normally coloured cherry pink to distinguish from the former, and both are wrapped with a fresh oak leaf, which is not supposed to be eaten though edible ones are available.

OHAGI

A mixture of ordinary rice and glutinous rice is pounded to make a rice ball, which is then covered by a thick layer of sweet *an* (aduki paste). This is the most common wagashi eaten at celebrations, and can be made at home.

*Above: Assorted wet and semi-
hard wagashi, left and middle, plus kushi dango,
skewered rice balls coated in sweet aduki paste, right*

Sweet Potato Bean Paste cakes

A mixture of sweet potato and a hint of apple, covered in batter and then seared in a hot pan. Aduki bean paste is also made into cakes by the same method.

MAKES SIX

INGREDIENTS
  about 250g/9oz canned soft
    aduki bean paste (*neri-an*),
    divided into 3 pieces
For the batter
  75g/3oz/⅔ cup plain
    (all-purpose) flour
  pinch of caster (superfine) sugar
  75ml/5 tbsp water
For the stuffing
  150g/5oz sweet potato, peeled
  ¼ red eating apple, cored,
    peeled and chopped
  200ml/8fl oz/1 cup water
  50g/2oz/¼ cup caster
    (superfine) sugar
  ¼ lemon

1 Put all the ingredients for the batter in a bowl and mix well until smooth. Pour the batter into a dish.

2 Dice the sweet potato and soak it in plenty of cold water for 5 minutes to remove any bitterness, then drain the water.

3 Put the chopped apple in a pan. Add the water and sweet potato. Sprinkle in 7.5ml/1½ tsp sugar and cook over a moderate heat until the apple and potato are softened. Add the lemon juice and remove the pan from the heat. Then drain the sweet potato and apple and crush them to a coarse paste with the remaining sugar in a bowl.

4 Using your hands, shape the mixture into three cubes.

5 Heat a non-stick frying pan. Coat a cube of the mixture in batter, then, taking care not to burn your fingers, place the cube on the hot pan and sear each side until the batter has set and cooked.

6 Repeat this procedure with the remaining two cubes and the batter mixture. Arrange each one on a plate and serve hot or cold.

DORA YAKI

Sweet aduki paste sandwiched between two small pancakes is called dora yaki (meaning little 'gong'), and is one of the most popular and longest standing Japanese cakes. The pancakes have a spongy texture and rich egg flavour with a light sweetness through the addition of maple syrup; this combines well with the dense sweetness of the aduki paste. They are sold at Japanese supermarkets as well as cake shops but are also easily made at home.

YOKAN

This hard block of sweet aduki paste is a han-namagashi (half-raw wagashi), so keeps for several months. There are various flavours and textures but two basic types – ogura-yokan (made using coarse paste) and neri-yokan (a smooth paste) – are available at Japanese supermarkets. Yokan normally comes in a rectangular-shaped block about the size of a pencil case. Flavour variations include one with citrus flavouring and another with matcha tea, and there are also yokan mixed with sweet chestnut pieces. Yokan is a very popular sweet to serve with Japanese tea, such as sencha.

SAKURA MOCHI

This is also a kind of glutinous rice cake stuffed with aduki paste, but the dough for this one is made of domyoji (finely cracked glutinous rice), which gives sakura mochi an elegant covering of tiny grains. The domyoji is coloured cherry pink and the cake is wrapped with a cooked edible cherry leaf, which also prevents it from sticking. The sweet leafy aroma and flavour of cherry leaf provides a good balance against the underlying sweetness. This rice cake hardens very quickly, so it's best eaten on the day of purchase.

KUSHI DANGO

Three or four glutinous rice balls, each the size of a quail's egg, are skewered together by a bamboo stick topped with either sweet aduki paste or a thickened clear sauce flavoured with a hint of

shoyu. The rice ball is dense but not as sticky as mochi cakes and is not flavoured. The clear shoyu sauce version has a unique flavour combined with a little sweetness. Dango, meaning rice ball, is always eaten at feasts held during the cherry blossom viewing season in early April.

Right: Rakugan, a type of higashi, or dry cake. Made of a mixture of flour (soya or wheat) and sugar, they are made in moulds of birds, shells and trees.

TEA

Below: Gyokuro (jewel dew) tea, which is made from fresh young tea leaves and is the very best quality tea.

The Japanese have been drinking tea since ancient times, although principally as a herbal remedy until it became popular among the aristocracy and the warrior class during the 13th and 14th centuries. The rise in the popularity of tea-drinking coincided with the spread of Zen Buddhism, out of which developed the rituals of the formal tea ceremony.

The tea that is drunk daily in Japan is green tea, in contrast to the brown or red tea of China and India. Green tea contains more thiamine (vitamin B_1), which gives it its delicious *umami* (rich flavour). Freshly picked tea leaves are immediately steamed to prevent fermentation and blackening, then dried by rolling and crumbling, and finally by hot air. The quality of the tea is judged by the colour and shape of the leaves, and the colour and flavour of the brew. Green tea should not be brewed with boiling water. The better the quality of tea, the less hot the water should be. Several kinds of Japanese tea are available from Asian supermarkets and the following are listed in order of quality.

GYOKURO

Translated as jewel dew, this is the best leaf tea made from young leaves picked in early spring. The dried leaves are very finely rolled and are a shiny, deep green colour. The tea should be brewed in warm water, at about 50°C/122°F, in a small quantity, and drunk on its own or with wagashi (Japanese cakes). It is extremely fragrant and mellow, and the quality is reflected in its price.

SENCHA

Literally meaning infused (steeped) tea, this is the middle-range leaf tea made from good, young leaves. If you visit a Japanese household, this is the tea you will be served, along with wagashi. Each year, shincha (new tea) comes out in the summer. Brew this tea in the same way as gyokuro but in hotter water.

Right:
Sencha tea

Making gyokuro tea
This method will provide enough tea for four people.

1 Fill a kyusu or small teapot with freshly boiled water, then use this water to fill four small teacups and leave to cool for about 5 minutes, until it reaches a temperature of 50–60°C/122–140°F.

2 Empty the teapot and add 20ml/ 4 tsp gyokuro. Pour the warm water in the cups back into the pot and let it brew for 2 minutes.

3 Shake the pot a few times, half-fill the cups, then top them up in turn so that the infusion of the tea is evenly distributed. For second cups, pour slightly hotter water into the pot without changing the leaves or adding more.

Left: Clockwise from left, hojicha, genmaicha and bancha teas

HOJICHA

This is a roasted bancha and brews a slightly bitter brown tea. Freshly roasted hojicha can be made by tossing bancha in a dry frying pan over very high heat for 3 minutes. The roasting infuses (steeps) a smoky aroma and adds character to the basic banch flavour.

GENMAICHA

A mixture of bancha and roasted rice grains, which adds aroma and a mild flavour.

MATCHA

This is a powdered tea, used mainly for the formal tea ceremony. Steamed tea leaves are dried flat and made into a powder that retains the vivid light green colour and fragrant aroma. The tea is made by whisking the powder in hot water in individual cups with a whisk rather than brewing in a pot. Only a tiny amount, 5–10ml/1–2 tsp per 120ml/4fl oz/½ cup water per person, is used.

BANCHA

This coarse tea used for daily consumption is made from larger leaves and stems, and brews a yellowish green tea. It is best drunk with meals and is the tea freely served at Japanese restaurants and offices. There are many grades of bancha and the lower the grade the more stems and twigs are included. Brew bancha just as you would ordinary tea.

Right: Powdered matcha tea – once opened it should be stored in the refrigerator.

MUGICHA

This is not actually tea but whole grains of roasted barley. Mugicha is drunk cold in summer. To make mugicha, boil plenty of water in a large pan and add 120–250ml/4–8fl oz/½–1 cup mugicha to 2 litres/3½ pints/8¾ cups boiling water, depending on how strong you like it. Bring back to the boil, lower the heat and simmer for 5–10 minutes. Strain, discard the barley, then transfer the mugicha to a bottle and chill.

Making matcha

Eat wagashi or something sweet before you drink this tea to best appreciate the flavour of the tea. If you don't have a bamboo whisk use a small fork instead.

1 Warm a large cup (a rice bowl is ideal) with hot water. Soak the tip of a bamboo whisk in the hot water so that the matcha won't stain it. Empty the cup.

2 Put 5–10ml/1–2 tsp matcha, to taste, in the cup and add about 120ml/4fl oz/½ cup hot water.

3 Using the bamboo whisk, first stir, then whisk vigorously until frothy and the powder dissolves.

Above: Mugicha, roasted barley, is now available in tea bags.

ALCOHOLIC DRINKS

Until quite recently sake and its variations had been the sole drinks in Japan. The first available record for a Japanese alcoholic drink was in a Chinese book written around AD 280, wherein the Japanese were said to 'grow rice and hemp', 'drink sake, and dance with music and drink'. However, sake has long been superseded by beer, predominantly lager, as the drink of choice in Japan and may now have given way to whisky or even to wine in popularity. Despite this, sake is still the most respected drink of all. It is increasingly popular outside Japan along with Japanese food and cooking and is readily available.

Beer, whisky and grape wine were all introduced to Japan after the country was forced to open its markets to the world towards the end of the 19th century but only became popular with the general public after World War II. Lager is particularly popular due to the long, warm, humid spring and summer seasons (nothing is more suitable than a glassful of ice-cold lager to combat the climate) and a thriving beer industry has been developed. Many Japanese beers are now exported to the West. On the other hand, grape wine, while very popular, is more difficult to establish as a domestically produced product, so consequently remains a relatively small industry.

SAKE

The Japanese have drunk sake since prehistoric times and it has played a vital role in the development of Japanese cuisine. In the past decade or two, however, the consumption of wine in Japan has increased more than ten-fold, and more and more people now drink wine with their daily meal. Despite this rapid change of habit in Japan, sake remains the drink for Japanese meals such as *kaiseki* (formal banquet) and as such is developing into more of a connoisseur's rather than a daily drink. There are reputedly about 6,000 brands of sake produced by about 2,000 makers in Japan, ranging from mass-produced nationwide brands to smaller regional, exclusive names. Since each brand has a

few different types, there are in total a bewildering 55,000 different kinds of sake sold in Japan. Regional sake, known as jizaké, are seeing a rise in popularity over the often inferior mass-produced ones.

How sake is made

Sake is made from rice, but the rice used for making it is a harder variety than the rice used for eating. The rice is first intensely refined by shaving off the husk made of fat and protein, reducing the grain to just its core. How far it is refined (50, 60 or 70 per cent) determines the quality of the end product. The rice is then soaked in water and steamed at a high temperature. After cooling, it is transferred to a vat and left to turn into koji (rice malt) over a 48-hour period. More steamed rice, a yeast-like agent and water are added and stirred to make a mash, to which steamed rice, koji and water are again added. The mash is finally left in a tank to ferment. It will attain an alcohol content of 18 per cent in about 20 days and the fermented mash is squeezed to exude the liquid. The liquid is then pasteurized at 60°C/140°F and transferred to a brewing tank to mature. Sake-making starts in autumn and the wine is ready in 60 days. To best appreciate it, drink within a year of bottling.

Left: The three kinds of sake: junmai, hon-johzo and ginjo sake

Warming sake

1 Half-fill a small pan with water, bring it to the boil, then lower the heat to minimum.

2 Pour enough sake into a tokkuri (sake jug/pitcher) to bring it to about three-quarters full. Stand it in the water in the pan for about 5 minutes until the sake is warmed to your taste.

3 Check the temperature by lifting the jug and touching the bottom; it is normally indented in the centre. If it feels warm to the touch, it is ready.

Types of sake

The grading system of sake is very complicated but there are basically three kinds: ginjo, junmai and hon-johzo. Ginjo is made from rice refined by 60 per cent. The best, dai-ginjo (big ginjo), is made from rice refined by 50 per cent. Junmai is a pure rice sake while non-junmai sake contains some brewing alcohol and sugar. Hon-johzo is made from rice refined by 70 per cent with an added alcohol content. Ginjo is best drunk when cold, while junmai and hon-johzo are drunk cold or warmed.

There is another category called nama-zake (draught sake). Sake is heated twice during its manufacture but nama-zake is filtered rather than heated before bottling. It is particularly good for drinking chilled on hot summer days.

Most quality sakes are produced on a small scale, often by family run breweries, but have limited distributions even in Japan. Some of the larger sake makers export their quality brands but the majority of sake available overseas is standard factory-made. Some of these sakes are now produced outside Japan too, mainly in the United States, and include Ozeki, Shochikubai, Takara Masamune, Hakusan, Gekkeikan and Hakushika. They are widely available either in bottles or cartons at the food halls of good department stores.

Flavour and keeping qualities

Sake is a clear, fine, colourless wine with a fragrant aroma and subtle flavour. Unlike some wines, it keeps well but, once a bottle is opened, sake should be drunk as soon as possible. Store in a cool, dark place away from direct sunlight.

SHOCHU

Literally meaning fiery spirits, shochu is a distilled spirit made from rice and a mixture of various other grains or even, at times, sweet potatoes. It was initially considered a low-class beverage in Japan but recently shochu has become more fashionable, particularly among the young. The alcohol content is quite high, 20–25 per cent, and some varieties are as high

as 45 per cent, so it is normally drunk diluted with a little hot or cold water, depending on the season.

The most popular way to drink shochu in Japan is as ume-jochu, which is one part shochu diluted with four to five parts hot water. An umeboshi (dried salted Japanese apricot) is added to the glass before drinking. Shochu is also used for making umeshu (Japanese plum liqueur). Both shochu and umeshu are available from Japanese supermarkets.

Left: Shochu is customarily drunk diluted with hot water and accompanied by umeboshi, (dried salted Japanese apricots).

*Right: Super
Nikka 15
Year-Old
whisky*

WHISKY

The Japanese whisky industry started
in the 1920s and the first bottle was
produced by Suntory distillery at
Yamazaki in Kyoto in 1929. Their main
competitor, Nikka, produced their
first one in 1934. The Japanese
market is still dominated by these
two distillers but the giant
Suntory has a staggering 70 per
cent share of all whisky sales
including Scotch imports. The
company was founded in 1899
producing what they called port
wine, now renamed correctly as
sweet wine. Their, as well as
Japan's, first whisky, Suntory
Shirofuda (white label), is still
on the market today but the best
selling blended whisky is by far
the Suntory's Kakubin (square
bottle). There are several other

distillers such as Sanraku Ocean, Kirin
Seagram and Godo Shusei, but their
market shares are very small.

Together with Nikka's Super Nikka
15 Year-Old, Suntory's better varieties
are available at Japanese supermarkets
and at food halls of some upmarket
department stores. Restaurants and
bars in the West that cater for Japanese
abroad also always carry these brands.

BEER

The Japanese beer industry started
towards the end of the 19th century
when the government-owned brewery,
established by the American firm of
Wiegrand and Copeland, was divided
into three regional companies: Asahi in
the west, Sapporo in the east and Kirin
in the centre. It has now grown to over
a £22 billion a year industry, and beer
is the best-selling drink in Japan
making up 55 per cent of the entire
sales of alcoholic drinks. Beer
production is still dominated by the
three giant companies together with
Suntory, which joined them in 1963.
Although Kirin has long enjoyed a
dominant market share of over 60 per
cent, the recent fierce challenge from
Asahi with its hit brand Asahi Super Dry
pushed them into
fighting for
first place,
and both
now have

a market share of around 40 per cent.
Kirin have been exporting their lager
beer to almost every country in the
world for the past 20 years and now,
with their latest success, Ichiban-shibori
(first squeeze), they remain the top
Japanese exporter. Many Japanese
people drink lager as an aperitif and
often change to sake during the meal.

Flavour of Japanese beer

The Japanese cherish nothing more
than a glass of ice-cold lager on hot,
humid summer days, and the vivid and
crisp Japanese lager meets this thirst.
Westerners may find Japanese lager a
little hoppy. There are several types
including canned draught beer, but
Asahi Super Dry, Kirin Ichiban-shibori,
Sapporo Black Label and Suntory Malt
are the most popular brand names.
These are normally available at
Japanese restaurants and
supermarkets, food halls of good
department stores and some larger
supermarkets. An
even hoppier, low-
malt beer has also
been developed in
Japan, but is not
available abroad.

*Below: Kirin,
Sapporo and
Asahi beer*

LIQUEURS

The Japanese do not traditionally have a habit of drinking liqueur at the end of meal, however, drinking liqueurs diluted with soft drinks during the meal is increasingly popular, and the market is now on the increase. The two Japanese-invented ones, umeshu, Japanese apricot liqueur, and the newer Midori, a melon-scented liqueur, have become popular abroad and are available at some food halls of department stores.

Home-made umeshu

A great summer drink, pour over ice or dilute with ice-cold water.

MAKES ABOUT 4 LITRES/
7 PINTS/8½ US PINTS

INGREDIENTS
1kg/2¼lb unripe apricots
675–800g/1½–1¾lb crystallized
  sugar or 500g/1¼lb/scant
  3 cups granulated (white) sugar
1.75 litres/3 pints/7½ cups
  shochu

1 Remove the calyx from the apricots. Wipe each one with kitchen paper or dry dishtowel.

2 Put some of the apricots in a 4 litre/7 pint/8½ US pint screw-top jar, cover with a handful of sugar. Repeat the process until all the apricots and sugar are in the jar.

3 Pour the shochu over the apricots and sugar submerging the fruit. Seal the jar tightly and leave in a dark place, ideally for 1 year but for at least 3 months.

Umeshu

Also known as plum liqueur in the West, this is a white spirit scented with ume (Japanese apricot). Fresh, unripe apricots together with sugar are soaked in white spirit and left for three months. At one time almost every household used to make umeshu with shochu, since shochu was also traditionally made at home. This is less the case today and now there are quite a few drink makers including Choya and Ozeki and even other foodstuff manufacturers such as Kikkoman (shoyu) and Takara (mirin) producing bottled umeshu for export. It has become quite established in Europe, particularly so in Germany and France. Some bottles contain a few whole ume, which can be eaten as well.

Umeshu has a clear golden brown colour and densely sweet flavour with a hint of acidic taste and fruity aroma. It is traditionally a summer drink, poured over ice cubes or diluted with water, but it can also be drunk neat as a liqueur.

Midori

A product of Suntory, Midori is a melon-scented liqueur, invented in 1978. The liqueur base is a grain spirit and the rest of the ingredients are a closely guarded secret. It has a densely sweet, fruity flavour and rich melon aroma. Oddly, Midori is more popular abroad than in Japan, and is sold mostly to America, Australia and Britain. Its clear, elegant green colour and refreshing melon taste make an unusual addition to cocktails, which are its main use. It is also, however, sometimes used in cakes and jellies.

WINE

Japan started growing vines after World War II and now produce good quality grape wines, both red and white, in Kofu, the central mountain area of the mainland, and in Tokachi in Hokkaido, the northernmost island. The output is very small due to the extremely limited land availability. The popularity of wine has grown so enormously in recent times, with a 50 per cent increase each year during the 1990s, that Japanese wines, together with imports from all over the world, are just meeting the domestic demands. Consequently very little Japanese wine is exported abroad.

Below: Midori, melon-scented liqueur, left, and umeshu (plum liqueur), right.

THE KOREAN
KITCHEN

This chapter looks at key equipment and ingredients – from vegetables

and fish to spices, garnishes and fruit – and includes a selection of

basic recipes for preparing the stocks and sauces that characterize

Korean food. Once you're familiar with the ingredients, you'll soon be

enjoying a Korean meal with a steaming pot of rice, fragrant side

dishes, marinated meat, a bowl of soup and a dish of kimchi.

Left: A traditional Korean kitchen; **Above:** A selection of serving bowls.

PREPARING AND SERVING FOOD

Korean cooks know the importance of fresh ingredients, but have also developed ways of storing food for the lean months of the year. When food is fresh and of top quality, it will be cooked quickly in a wok or on a grill; less prime cuts of meat and fish are more likely to be simmered slowly on the stove. A pan of rice steams gently in every Korean kitchen until the grains become really soft and glutinous. Out-of-season food is preserved in pickled or dried forms to be eaten during the freezing winter months. The notable exception is that hardly any dishes are baked; this is because the traditional Korean kitchen had a wood-fired stove, but no oven. The combination of

Below: A wok is found in most Asian kitchens, perfect for preparing quick, delicious food.

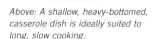

Right: Cast iron griddles have a variety of uses. A flat griddle is perfect for pancakes.

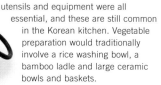

Above: A shallow, heavy-bottomed, casserole dish is ideally suited to long, slow cooking.

cooking techniques leads to the typical adventurous Korean meal, with a variety of tasty dishes to eat with the rice.

COOKING EQUIPMENT

Traditionally, food preparation and preservation was time consuming. Wooden, bamboo, ceramic, stone and metal cooking

utensils and equipment were all essential, and these are still common in the Korean kitchen. Vegetable preparation would traditionally involve a rice washing bowl, a bamboo ladle and large ceramic bowls and baskets.

For the preparation of preserved foods, such as kimchi, condiment mortars, grinding stones and pestles, sieve knives, chopping boards, dough boards and rice cake pattern makers would all have been necessary, as well as oil presses to extract oil from plant seeds such as sesame seeds, beans, rape, red (bell) pepper and castor beans, which are roasted, steamed and then squeezed in an oil press.

For the cooking and heating of food there would have been iron pots, frying pans, steamers and grills. Other implements in the traditional Korean kitchen would be a rice scoop, ladles and a funnel. And for serving dishes on the table, there would have been a

Below: Traditional cooking utensils and serving implements give a dinner party an authentic Korean edge.

Below: A traditional rice sieve. Washing rice until the water runs clear removes excess starch.

charcoal brazier to warm ceramic bowls or casserole pans. This method of warming food on the table remains strong in Korean families today.

While modern appliances such as rice and gas cookers and noodle makers have now taken over the Korean kitchen, cutting down the preparation time and making the cook's life much easier, many of these traditional implements and methods are still integral to food preparation as well as presentation.

COOKING TECHNIQUES

Fresh food is usually cooked quickly in the Korean kitchen, but cooks also use many different techniques, which have evolved over the centuries to extract every last drop of flavour and goodness from other ingredients.

Above: Rice is typically served from a large dish into individual covered bowls.

Barbecuing and grilling

Bulgogi is one of the signature dishes of Korean cuisine. For this, high-quality meat – usually beef – is sliced paper-thin and marinated in a blend of soy sauce, sesame seeds, spring onions (scallions) and ginger. After the flavours have permeated the meat, the beef slices are cooked in a dome-shaped pan placed over a charcoal brazier. The pan has a channel that catches the delicious juices produced during cooking, and they are eaten with rice and vegetables. As the marinade cooks it forms an appetizing glaze over the meat, which is then eaten either with spicy dipping sauce or

wrapped in green leaves with slices of fresh garlic and green bell pepper. Grilling over charcoal is a hugely popular method of cooking, and echoes barbecue techniques introduced by the Mongols. Traditionally a metal brazier, also called a Korean barbecue, is used for making bulgogi on the table. It can also be prepared on a griddle plate and then served at the table. It is often done at the table in restaurants, usually on a gas grill.

Slow cooking

Rice is served with every meal, and is always steamed gently, either in an iron pot or a bamboo steamer, and nowadays often in a rice cooker. Soups and stews are an important part of the Korean diet, and these vary from the simplest mixture of seasonal vegetables and stock to a hearty blend of meat or fish and vegetables. Slow cooking on the stove in an earthenware pot called a *tukbaege* allows the flavours to mingle, and produces fabulous casseroles that are brought to the table still bubbling hot. A flameproof casserole can also be used for such dishes.

Above: Beef being cooked on a table barbecue, from which diners would then help themselves.

Stir-frying

Finally, the Korean cook will make great use of the wok to stir-fry a mixture of ingredients – fish, seafood, vegetables – with a strong-tasting sauce. This healthy cooking process preserves vitamins and minerals, and keeps the delightfully crunchy texture of the food.

Above: A modern rice cooker will cook rice perfectly and free up space on a stove.

PRESERVATION OF FOOD – *KIMCHI*

Ask any Korean which dish he or she cannot live without, and they will answer 'kimchi'. This tasty preparation makes full use of cabbage and other seasonal vegetables, which are preserved by blending them with seasonings and sauces and storing them in large earthenware jars to keep cool and ferment over the long winter months. Kimchi jars were generally stored outside in the courtyard, or buried in the ground; these days refrigerators are a better option, but you will still see rows of kimchi jars on top of the flat roofs of apartment buildings in the big cities.

Kimchi pots vary in size and shape, and contain anything from one to 40 gallons of this delicious preserve. An earthenware lid sits on top and the sealed pots preserve the strong flavours for months. When the jars are opened, the contents will have absorbed all the delicious fiery flavours – a perfect contrast to the chill of the wintry weather.

Koreans will literally eat kimchi on every day of the year and traditionally prepare a large amount during *kimjang* season, which occurs around the time of the autumn harvest. This is an important social event, when kimchi ingredients are blended together in copious quantities. Help is often drafted

Above left and right: Traditional woven dishes and platters are a practical and attractive method for serving up dry and fried foods.

in, and neighbours and friends who have worked hard on kimchi preparation all day are usually rewarded with a meal prepared by the family.

SERVING FOOD

Because the presentation of Korean food still has a strong formal element, considerable emphasis is placed on the nature and presentation of the implements that are used at the table (see also pages 58–9).

Above: Large earthenware jars used for fermenting kimchi. These jars are often placed outside during the colder months so that the kimchi is refrigerated while it matures, a process that can take months.

Above: The unusual combination of using both chopsticks and a spoon to dine with is unique to Korea.

Above: Large ceramic bowls are typically used for holding dishes such as soups and stews, from which all diners serve themselves.

Above: Heavy bowls with thick wooden bases retain heat and protect the often highly laquered table tops.

Above: Korean chopsticks are usually made of silver or brass and can be very highly ornamented at the untapered end.

Serving dishes tend to be of ceramic or stone, and incorporate large bowls for casseroles and soups as well as a selection of smaller dishes for side dishes and kimchi. Wooden, bamboo and metal dishes also feature, bamboo as platters for rice rolls or pancakes. Bamboo containers are also used for preparing vegetables.

Koreans always use a spoon in combination with chopsticks (generally a flat circular spoon with a straight handle), with the spoons being used for rice and soup and chopsticks for everything else. Chopsticks are held between the thumb and fingers of the right hand and are levered to pick up food portions. Traditionally made of brass or silver in Korea, they are now more commonly made of

stainless-steel, in the Korean style of medium length rods that taper to a square blunted end.

When eating with Koreans, avoid picking up the served-up bowls to eat from them, which is considered impolite, and serve the food to your own plate before eating. For anyone who is unused to eating with chopsticks, a knife and fork along with a spoon is quite acceptable. Spoon and chopstick holders can be made of porcelain, wood or silver and are an important feature of the formal table setting.

Porcelain is the preferred material for water glasses. For alcohol, glassware or crystal glassware is preferred, although porcelain can be used for serving rice wine or other alcoholic beverages.

Organizing a Korean meal

It is customary at any Korean meal for several small dishes of different food to be served at the same time. This is organized in the kitchen by having a rice dish in a bamboo steamer over a wok on the stove, while a dish or two of kimchi is ladled out from the pot. An additional recipe involving pancakes or vegetable fritters, for example, can be stir-fried while the rice is cooking, and a pot of soup or a casserole of meat and vegetables can be kept warm in another clay pot until the rest of the meal is ready.

Now the rice is strained through a bamboo or metal strainer and served in individual bowls, with the side dishes (*banchan*) set out in ceramic dishes. The casserole dish (*tukbaege*) is brought to the table straight from the stove. Sometimes a barbecue plate may be used, consisting of an ironware hot plate set into a wooden surround so that the food stays hot and the fingers stay cool.

Left: A ceramic platter with three 'chup' or side dishes for serving at the Korean table.

TRADITIONAL FLAVOURINGS

Seasoning food carefully and plentifully is a must in Korea. Not only was this habitual because spices would preserve food for the months of scarcity during the cold winters, but Korean cooks make sure that the tastes of individual spices blend with each other and the base of vegetables, meat or fish. Furthermore, the influence of Buddhism can be felt in the belief that balanced seasoning leads to good health – the yin and yang of salty and sweet, spicy and mild makes for a general equilibrium in the body.

The traditional technique of seasoning, known in Korea as yangnyum, requires a mixture of spices to be blended with almost medicinal precision. Koreans believe there are five elements – fire, earth, water, wood and metal – that govern everyone's life, and these have their direct counterparts in cooking flavours. The five flavours, salty, sweet, sour, spicy and bitter, balance each other and so should be combined as far as possible at each meal.

The basic seasonings used to create the five different flavours include salt, soy sauce, gochujang chilli paste, doenjang soya bean paste, vinegar and sugar. Aromatic seasonings include ginger, mustard, pepper, sesame oil, sesame seeds, spring onions (scallions), garlic and

Above: Soy sauce is a regular component of Korean meals.

chrysanthemum leaves. Most Korean dishes are cooked with at least half a dozen different ingredients and seasonings, producing a complex and distinctive taste.

THE THREE MAJOR FLAVOURINGS

While any self-respecting Korean cook would insist on using many different ingredients, there are three flavourings that dominate Korean cuisine and without which almost no Korean recipe is complete. These are:
- soy sauce
- soya bean paste, doenjang
- red chilli paste, gochujang

The actual process of making doenjang, gochujang and soy sauce from scratch is a lengthy and complex one. Nowadays few households still make these condiments, relying instead on store-bought alternatives as basic ingredients, which they then combine in traditional and time-honoured recipes for strong marinades, sauces and dips.

Soy sauce

There are a number of types of soy sauce, the by-product of doenjang paste. Light soy sauce is used in soups and to season vegetables, while dark soy sauce is used for roasted, steamed and more hearty dishes.

Soy dip

This dip is widely served with Korean fritters and dumplings, as well as tofu and tempura dishes.

SERVES 4

INGREDIENTS
45ml/3 tbsp dark soy sauce
1 garlic clove, chopped
15ml/1 tbsp cider vinegar
7.5ml/1½ tsp sesame oil
5ml/1 tsp ground sesame seeds

Mix all the ingredients together thoroughly and transfer to a small sauce bowl for dipping.

Doenjang

This paste is made of fermented soya beans. The beans are cooked and dried into blocks, then once the fermentation process has begun with a fine mould appearing on the surface of the blocks, they are added to water and kept in a

Above: Chrysanthemum leaves are used in food, to make tea and as an ingredient in Korean rice wine.

Above: Doenjang paste, made from fermented soya beans, is commonly used to augment soups and stews.

Above: Gochujang is a distinctive dark red chilli paste, its extensive use demonstrates the Korean love of chillies!

warm place to continue fermenting. Once the process is complete, the liquid is drained off to make soy sauce, and the solids are made into doenjang, a salty, tasty paste similar to Japanese miso, ideal for adding a sparkle to stews and soups or for spreading on vegetables such as sticks of celery.

Gochujang

The classic Korean paste called gochujang also uses soya beans as a base, but this time red chillies are added for spice, as well as powdered rice, salt and a little honey or sugar, before the mixture is left to ferment in a warm place. This produces a dark red, rich, concentrated paste which is used to marinate meat and is added to many cooked dishes to give them a spicy tang.

Above: Used in Pork Belly with Sesame Dip (see page 386) this sauce combines gochujang *and* doenjang.

Stir-fried *gochujang* chilli paste

This sauce, called yangnyum gochujang, is often used for the traditional rice dish bibimbap. It is also suited to meat and rice dishes.

SERVES 4

INGREDIENTS
15ml/1 tbsp sesame oil
65g/2½oz beef, finely chopped
2 garlic cloves, crushed
250ml/8fl oz/1 cup gochujang chilli paste
30ml/2 tbsp maple syrup
15ml/1 tbsp sugar

1 Coat a wok or pan with sesame oil and heat over medium heat. Add the beef and garlic, and stir-fry until lightly golden brown.

2 Add the chilli paste and 45ml/ 3 tbsp of water, and stir until it has formed a sticky paste.

3 Add the maple syrup and the sugar, and simmer the mixture in the pan for a further 30 seconds before then transferring to a sauce bowl to serve.

Chilli paste and vinegar sauce

This uncooked sauce, called *cho gochujang*, can be used as either a dip or a dressing with any salad dishes or noodles. Its tart pungency is particularly suited to seafood dishes.

SERVES 4

INGREDIENTS
60ml/4 tbsp gochujang chilli paste
75ml/5 tbsp water
60ml/4 tbsp cider vinegar
15ml/1 tbsp lemon juice
30ml/2 tbsp sugar
2 garlic cloves, crushed
30ml/2 tbsp spring onions (scallions), finely chopped
5ml/1 tsp sesame seeds
15ml/1 tbsp sesame oil

1 Combine all the ingredients in a bowl and mix them together.

2 Transfer the final chilli and vinegar paste to a small sauce bowl before serving it to accompany any Korean salad dish, or with Chinese leaves.

FERMENTING AND PRESERVING

Koreans have developed various ways of preserving food. In the days before refrigeration this enabled them to eat well during the winter when fresh vegetables and salads, fresh meat or seafood were unavailable. The tangy, spicy taste of these foods is now associated with Korean cuisine.

Kimchi

Consisting of pickled vegetables and other foodstuffs preserved in earthenware pots, kimchi is Korea's most famous culinary export. Made for over 2,000 years, it is believed to be a life-giving dish which encourages good health and stamina. Although any pickled and fermented vegetable mixture can be called kimchi, the best-known variety is made with napa cabbage. The vegetables are coated with a mixture that typically includes chilli, ginger, garlic, soy sauce and fish paste, and then sealed in a jar and left to ferment until the flavours have blended. Koreans pickle most vegetables like this, including radishes, cucumber, turnip and aubergine (eggplant), as well as fish, shellfish and fruit. During the fermentation process the vegetables lose much of their flavour, adopting the tastes of the seasonings, but with a greatly enhanced texture.

Kimchi is most often eaten as a side dish at any meal, breakfast, lunch or dinner. However, it also makes a tasty accompaniment to little fried street snacks made of rice and sesame seeds, or may be covered with a thin batter and fried as kimchi fritters (buchimgae).

Kimchi can also be used in a spicy stew with vegetables such as mushrooms and onions, and tofu or seafood for protein. This is simmered on the stove until everything is really hot and all the textures are soft. Koreans would eat the stew with a crunchy vegetable and some glutinous rice for balance.

There are many kimchi variations from the different provinces according to what vegetables or fish are available. For instance, from the province of *Gyeonggi* comes a recipe for turnip

kimchi made with fish sauce, chilli and garlic, onions and salt. A frugal recipe for the winter uses small amounts of cod, which migrates south from the waters around China towards the western coast of the Korean peninsula. The recipe is similar to the one shown here, with the addition of chopped pieces of cod to the soaking brine for a salty, fishy taste. Radish kimchi is another favourite, with a recipe known as 'Young bachelor kimchi' which uses the immature white radish with its fresh green leaves still attached.

Other fermented foods

Jeotgal is a mixture of any seafood, such as fish, shellfish, squid or oysters, including the intestines of the fish so that nothing is wasted, mixed with a salt brine. A colourful dish, it is often bright red with chilli flavouring, and is most often eaten layered with dark green seaweed and pale rice.

Doenjang (soya bean paste) is also fermented and can be preserved for months, taken from the store cupboard whenever needed to brighten a winter stew or vegetable soup.

Below: Traditional cabbage kimchi. The most famous of Korean dishes, and an essential at every meal, the making of kimchi is an ancient and revered art.

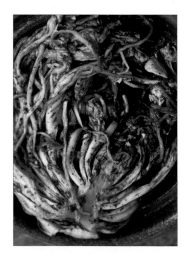

A basic kimchi recipe

INGREDIENTS
1 napa cabbage (Chinese leaf)
15ml/1 tsp salt, plus salt for brine
15ml/1 tsp sugar
15ml/1 tsp chilli pepper flakes
15ml/1 tsp pine nuts
15ml/1 tsp fresh ginger
15ml/1 tsp fresh garlic
15ml/1 tsp anchovy sauce
a handful of watercress
a handful of green onions
a handful of sliced radish

1 Cut the napa cabbage into two.

2 Submerge the cabbage in a couple of handfuls of sea salt and water to cover. Soak for 6 hours, then rinse.

3 Combine the remaining ingredients to form the seasoning.

4 Cut out and discard the hard core of the cabbage halves, and pack the seasoning between each leaf. Wrap one outer leaf tightly around the remaining leaves, and put it all into a sealed ceramic container. Leave for 40 hours and then refrigerate.

SPICES AND OTHER FLAVOURINGS

SPICES

The aromas of doenjang (soya bean paste), gochujang (chilli) paste and soy sauce pervade the Korean kitchen. However, there are many other favourite flavourings. No Korean cook would consider serving a meal that was predominantly flavoured with only one spice; a mixture should be used to make sure that the balance and harmony of the food is just right.

Garlic

This essential aromatic vegetable is used for everything from seasoning soup to creating marinades for meat and fish. It is also used whole as an accompaniment for grilled dishes.

Above: Garlic's pungent flavour makes it a frequent ingredient in Korean cooking.

Chilli

The chilli pepper is the next most important flavouring after garlic. The Korean version varies from mild to fiery, and, combined with garlic, forms the basis of kimchi flavouring.

Above: Chillies only came to Korea in the 16th century, but their fiery heat quickly made them a popular ingredient.

Dried chilli

A single sun-dried red chilli can be used to create a sharp, spicy taste, or used flaked or whole for garnishing and presentation. Sun-dried chillies are often ground into chilli powder, milder than the Indian version, which forms the basis of many Korean recipes.

Ginger

The distinctive sweet piquant taste of ginger is popular all over Asia. Korean cooks, as well as using it in kimchi, like to combine its taste with that of other ingredients, creating a new subtle flavour.

Above: The warmth of ginger adds depth to any dish.

Ginseng

A root best known for its medicinal properties and widely used in Korea to make tea, ginseng is also used in cooking, particularly in the summer chicken soup samgyetang.

Maca

This green herbal root originates in Peru, and is believed to have strong medicinal and energy-giving qualities.

Right: The green powder of the maca root.

Mustard

A favourite accompaniment to fish, the pungency of mustard sauce combines well with the saltiness of the fish. It is made by mixing dried mustard powder with vinegar, water and a little sugar and salt.

Sesame leaves

These leaves are traditionally used as a green vegetable and have a strong nutty aroma. They are also used in salads and as wraps to eat with rice and miso.

Above: Sesame leaves, as well as sesame oil and sesame seeds, are used as flavourings.

HERBS

Green herbs are not generally added to Korean food, and are more likely to be made into tea. Various mixtures of herbs and spices to aid digestion and promote good health have traditionally been concocted to drink after a meal, but the commonest are those made with ginseng, roasted barley or ginger.

DRIED FISH AND SEAFOOD

These are often used to make the stock that forms the basis of soups and stews. Dried anchovies, called myulchi, are used to flavour dishes and these tiny fish are surprisingly versatile. Dried shrimps, known in Korea as barley shrimps, have a nice crunchy texture when stir-fried and blend well with the taste of green chilli.

Above: Dried anchovies have a strong salty taste.

FISH SAUCE

An essential ingredient for making a classic fermented kimchi; any anchovy or fish sauce can be used. It has a multitude of other uses in Korean cooking too.

LIQUID SEASONINGS

Sesame oil

A vital ingredient, sesame oil has a rich nuttiness that imparts flavour to grilled (broiled) and stir-fried dishes.

Bean oil

Widely used in Korean stir-fry dishes, bean oil is colourless and odourless (unlike sesame oil) and using it allows the flavours of the other ingredients in a dish to remain distinct.

Vinegar

Apple and cider vinegar are the most widely used varieties. Persimmon vinegar is a delicious variant, and has an astringent taste that is quite unlike any other seasoning, but this can be difficult to find outside Korea.

Soju

This Korean rice wine is syrupy and sweet when used in cooking. Japanese mirin, although slightly sweeter, is perfectly adequate as a substitute.

NUTS AND SEEDS

Sesame seeds

These are toasted to bring out the distinctive taste, and used as both flavouring and garnish in many recipes. They are also toasted and crushed for sweet or savoury snacks.

Gingko nuts

Used in sweet and savoury dishes, gingko nuts are also served as an alternative to lotus seeds. Grilled and salted, they are a popular snack in both Japan and Korea, and once cooked they turn a delicate shade of green.

OTHER FLAVOURINGS

Salt

Koreans use sea salt, plentiful around this small country. A Korean variation called bamboo salt is made by storing sea salt in bamboo stalks plugged with yellow mud and then roasting it to remove any impurities. This treatment gives the salt a distinctive taste.

Above: The versatility of gingko nuts means that they are used in both sweet and savoury dishes.

Honey and sugar

Both these ingredients are used sparingly as sweeteners in Korean cuisine, as desserts are not the main focus of a meal in Korea. In fact, honey and sugar are more often used in savoury dishes, as part of a recipe for flavourings such as gochujang paste. They can also be added to marinades in order to create a sweet and sour flavour combination.

Above: Sesame oil is often added at the end of cooking to impart flavour, rather than as a cooking aid.

Above: Sesame seeds have a distinctive nutty flavour and also add an element of texture to dishes.

Above: The inordinately popular soju, Korean rice wine, is very strong and best served in small shot glasses.

GARNISHES

Korean cooks pride themselves on the presentation of their food. Every Korean meal is carefully and artistically arranged, and are then eaten at the table with corresponding consideration and dedication.

This attention to detail includes garnishing the food, an art that used to be almost unknown in the food culture of the West, but has always been natural to the Koreans. Restaurants in Europe and the USA now understand the importance of presentation to the diners' appreciation of a meal, and how the eye informs the taste buds – the little dots of balsamic vinegar or sauce around the plate are testament to this.

Garnishes can consist of artfully arranged fresh vegetables, salad leaves, nuts and fruit, or cooked delicacies such as egg strips or tiny portions of minced (ground) meat. Here are just a few ideas for garnishes commonly found in Korean homes and restaurants.

COOKED GARNISHES

Egg strip

Beaten egg is whisked up with a little salt and maybe some sugar, then fried in oil in a small frying pan. A thin omelette will result, which can then be rolled up when cold and cut into shreds to decorate any dish.

Two-colour egg strip

A favourite variation on egg strip, where the beaten egg white and egg yolk are cooked separately and then, when rolled and shredded, form a yellow and white pattern over the dish or around the rim.

Egg roll

This is another variation on the egg strip. This time the cooked, cooled omelette is rolled around a few lightly cooked green beans and bright orange carrots, then thinly sliced to make little circles of yellow, green and orange.

Minced (ground) meat

Small amounts of minced meat can be quickly stir-fried in sesame oil and mixed with chopped chillies, garlic and onions. This tasty mixture is then sprinkled on top of noodle soup.

VEGETABLES AND SALAD LEAVES

Watercress

Koreans love watercress, or minari, for its peppery bite. It can be cooked in stews and stir-fries, or simply arranged a couple of leaves at a time on top of an orange or red dish so as to give an emphatic colour contrast.

Above: Garnishes extend flavour and add visual interest; the finishing touch on this rice dish is fish roe or tobiko.

Shiitake mushrooms

Dried mushrooms are rehydrated or fresh ones gently fried in oil. They can be arranged in overlapping slices on top of a large piece of meat or a bowl of rice, or floated on top of a delicate soup.

Above: This beef noodle dish is garnished with egg strips.

Above: This porridge has a garnish of cress, mushrooms and soy sauce.

Below: Chillies cut into flakes inject colour and piquancy.

Chilli peppers

Red or green chilli peppers are ideal for garnishing as they impart a spicy kick and are a beautiful bright colour.

Dried chilli strips or threads

Sun-dried chillies are made into little flakes, strips or even finer threads. They are often sprinkled on top of a bowl of soup or stew.

Sweet potato crisps

The sweet potato is not an indigenous vegetable; it was brought to Korea by the Japanese in the 18th century. It grows well in Korea, however, and when used as a garnish rather than a main ingredient, it is made into thin crisps, cooked quickly in hot oil.

Spring onions (scallions)

These lend themselves particularly well to fancy garnishing – they can be shredded at one end, sliced into thin diagonal rings or made into little brushes with a ring of chilli in the centre.

Other vegetables

Salad vegetables are sliced finely into little strips and either set on top of a dish or served separately. The vegetables may be served plain or dressed with a little vinegar, sugar, salt and citrus juice. Delicate patterns can be made by cutting cucumber sections or carrots into strips almost to the end, and fanning them out like a flower.

SEEDS, NUTS AND DATES

Sesame seeds

These tiny seeds are usually toasted in a dry pan until they jump and turn brown. They can then be sprinkled on top of soups and stews or served with rice to give a nutty flavour to any dish.

Gingko nuts

Prized for the green colour, that appears when a fresh gingko nut is cooked, these make a good contrast to the predominantly red colour of many Korean dishes.

Pine nuts

These are toasted in a dry pan until they begin to jump around the pan and turn brown. Their taste is brought out by toasting and they blend well with blander dishes such as rice or noodles. Pine nuts can also be sprinkled on top of a stew in the pot before it is brought to the table.

Red dates

Known as jujube in Oriental cooking, these medicinal fruits are oblong in shape and turn a reddish brown when ripe. They have a sweet flavour and a vibrant colour, and are ideal for garnishing sweet or savoury dishes. They are also a common ingredient in cakes and cookies.

Above: The sweetness of red dates, or jujubes, is said to be an aphrodisiac.

Above: This salad with persimmons is dressed with chilli and egg strips.

Above: The garnish on this pumpkin congée is sliced red dates and pine nuts.

Above: This salmon teriyaki is garnished with sesame seeds and whole chives.

RICE AND NOODLES

The rich spiciness of many Korean meat and fish dishes needs a plain, starchy foil, and this contrast is provided by rice and noodles. These two plain ingredients absorb the flavours of any accompanying sauce, and fill the stomach with nourishing warmth.

Above: Short grain rice, the favourite of Korea, has a distinctive stickiness.

RICE

The foundation of all Korean meals, rice dishes are eaten throughout the day. In combination with soup and vegetables it forms an essential part of a nutritious and satisfying Korean meal. In fact rice, or bap as it is known by Koreans, is so essential to every meal that it has become synonymous with the meal itself. 'Did you have bap?' is the common way to ask if an acquaintance has already dined, regardless of the other dishes they had. Koreans believe that their strength comes from the continuing consumption of rice, and that it greatly enhances their stamina. These very hardworking people may have a point.

Rice is traditionally cooked on its own in the Korean kitchen, although sometimes other grains such as millet and barley are included to enhance the flavour, one example being the five-grain rice recipe shown overleaf. Beans and chestnuts are occasionally included with rice dishes, and cooked vegetables, meat or fish are often mixed into the dish before serving. The Koreans, just like the Japanese, eat only the sticky short and medium grain varieties.

Right: Pudding or sweet rice is short and fat with a white kernel. When cooked, it becomes glutinous. It is useful as a binder for gravies, sauces, and fillings, or in sweet dishes.

Short grain rice

This is the staple food of Korea. Called ssal in Korean, this is close in shape and texture to Japanese rice. It becomes soft and sticky when cooked.

Brown rice

This is normally cooked as a mixture with white rice and other grains, and is considered to have better nutritional value than the common short grain variety.

Glutinous or sweet rice

Slightly longer than the common short grain rice, this is only used in rice cakes, cookies and other sweet dishes, where the grains need to bind together.

Mixed grains

Rice grain mixtures are popular in Korea. They vary from region to region, but typically contain combinations of brown rice, sweet rice, wild rice, barley, hulled millet, green peas, yellow peas, black-eyed beans (peas), kidney beans and red

Below: Millet is often used as part of a mixed grain combination.

beans. The Korean dish called Five-grain rice, or Ogokbap combines four other grains (including millet, black beans and sweet beans) with regular rice. Other ingredients can be added, such as soya beansprouts and chestnuts.

> ### Storing rice
> Any leftover cooked rice can be stored in the refrigerator, wrapped with clear film (plastic wrap) in order to help preserve the moisture. Don't keep cooked rice for more than a couple of days.

Left: Brown rice is usually combined with other rice types.

RICE RECIPES

Recipes for two widely eaten Korean rice dishes are given here. The flavours in these rice dishes are understated, and are designed to balance and complement highly spiced meat or fish. Knowing how to cook the basic rice recipes that are shown here is an essential requirement for creating the heart of any Korean meal.

Steamed rice

Koreans cook rice in a steamer, but the same flavour and texture can be created with pan-cooked rice. Short grain Asian rice is the best, although pudding rice can be used. Good quality rice will have a sheen, and the grains should also be free from scratches.

Cooking rice

SERVES 4

INGREDIENTS
400g/14oz/2 cups short grain
  white rice or pudding rice
a drop of sunflower oil

1 Rinse and drain the rice in cold water four or five times. Place in a heavy pan and add water to about 5mm/¼in above the rice. Add a drop of sunflower oil to give the rice a shine, cover with a lid and boil.

2 Lower the heat and leave to steam. Do not remove the lid during cooking.

3 After 12–15 minutes turn off the heat and leave the rice, still covered, to steam for a further 5 minutes.

Mixed grains

Plain steamed rice often has grains, beans and lentils added to create the Korean favourite ogokbap. These extra ingredients give more of a crunch to the dish, and give exotic combinations of flavours. It is believed that sharing ogokbap at the first full moon of the year will bring good luck for the year.

Preparing mixed grains

SERVES 4

INGREDIENTS
40g/1½oz/generous ¼ cup dried
  black beans or sweet beans
50g/2oz/¼ cup barley
50g/2oz/¼ cup millet
50g/2oz/¼ cup brown rice
50g/2oz/¼ cup sorghum or lentils
200g/7oz/1 cup short grain
  white rice
salt

1 Soak the beans, barley, millet, brown rice and sorghum or lentils in cold water for 24 hours. Add the white rice to the soaked grains and beans. Drain and rinse well.

2 Place the rice in a heavy pan and add water (preferably filtered) to about 5mm/¼in above the rice level.

3 Add a pinch of salt, then cover with a lid and bring to the boil.

4 Lower the heat and steam for 12–15 minutes keeping the lid on. Turn off the heat and leave the grains to steam for 5 more minutes.

NOODLES

Korean noodles can be made of different grains and vegetables, the most common being wheat, buckwheat and sweet potato. They are almost as common as rice in Korean cuisine. Noodles should be boiled for a few minutes in lots of water but should never be over-cooked, especially for a stir-fried dish.

Glass noodles

Known as dangmyun, these delicate strands of sweet potato starch are also known as cellophane noodles, Chinese vermicelli, bean threads and bean thread noodles. They are often used as the base for noodle soups or stir-fried dishes, and can also be added to casseroles to provide volume and richness of flavour and texture.

Buckwheat and wheat noodles

Thin and brown in colour, buckwheat noodles are known in Korea as memil. They have a distinctive crunchy texture and are similar in

Above: Originally from Japan, udon noodles are thicker and softer than other types of noodle.

appearance to a softer variety called momil, which are made from wheat flour. These are much better known as the Japanese soba noodle.

Udon noodles

Handmade flat noodles, also called udon noodles or kalguksu, are made from plain wheat flour and are popular for dishes where a more tender texture is suitable.

Somyun

A thin plain flour white noodle, which is often used for noodles served in broth.

Soba noodles

These noodles, which are of Japanese origin, are made of buckwheat flour (soba-ko) and wheat flour (komugi-ko). They are of approximately the same thickness as spaghetti, and are prepared in various hot and cold dishes in Korea. They can be bought dried, but they taste best when handmade.

Below: Soba noodles are made from buckwheat and are similar in length and thickness to Italian spaghetti.

Below: Thick udon noodles in a delicate broth make a quick and tasty lunch.

Above: Thin buckwheat noodles are often bound with wheat flour to prevent them disintegrating while cooking.

Above: Glass, or cellophane, noodles are made of mung bean or sweet potato starch and are almost clear when cooked.

Chilled naengmyun noodles

Noodles are often chilled after cooking for use in salads and other side dishes.

INGREDIENTS
90g/3½oz naengmyun buckwheat noodles

1 Cook the noodles in a large pan of boiling water for 5 minutes. Add a few drops of oil while cooking to help prevent the water from frothing up and boiling over; this also helps to keep the noodles separate when they are drained.

2 Drain the noodles, and then rinse two or three times in cold water until the water runs clear. Chill for 30 minutes.

STOCKS

A good, tasty stock is an essential base for many of the Korean recipes that are introduced here. They will give the depth of flavour that is essential to give an authentic Korean taste to the dish.

STOCK FOR SOUP

A small bowl of soup, steamed rice and some tasty meat, fish and *banchan* (side dishes) is the backbone of a typical Korean meal. Soup is not served as a separate course, but it's often the first thing a Korean diner will taste while the meat is grilling (broiling), keeping hunger pangs at bay with its savoury flavours. At dinner time, soup is usually served in a small dish, one for each person, placed next to the individual rice dish.

One of the most delightful ways to taste this flavoursome brew is while strolling around the town and socializing with friends – it's a common sight to see little cups of piquant soup for sale next to the rice dishes, pancakes and fritters on the stalls of street vendors.

Koreans cook soup, using all sorts of ingredients from meat and vegetables to fish, tofu, seaweed and even tinned food such as hot dogs (the influence of the US troops based here during the Korean War). What they all have in common is a strong, often home-made stock base and

Above: A steaming bowl of hot and spicy beef soup, a delicious and aromatic medley of tastes and textures.

a fiery kick from added chillies, garlic and spices. Korean soup, packed with ingredients, tends to be a heartier dish than many other Asian soups.

HOME-MADE STOCK

There are three basic stock recipes, and these are made whenever they are needed by Korean cooks. These three stocks are based on:

- beef bones, which gives a strong, hearty flavour

- beef without the bones for a more subtle meaty dish
- fish or shellfish, for its distinctive salty tang.

Of course, many other variations exist, using any nutritious food available such as pork spine or ox blood; however, these three recipes highlighted above do form the traditional basis of the vast majority of Korean soups and casseroles.

Beef bone stock

This is a well-known and versatile stock for Korean dishes. Simply add chopped spring onions and a little seasoning for a wholesome, revitalizing soup. It is also great for fortifying the taste of hearty stews or casserole dishes.

MAKES 1 LITRE/1³/₄ PINTS/4 CUPS

INGREDIENTS
1–2 beef bones
90g/3¹/₂oz spring onions
 (scallions)
5 garlic cloves
10g/¹/₄oz fresh root ginger
1 leek, halved
90g/3¹/₂oz Chinese white
 radish
5 peppercorns

1 Soak the beef bones in cold water for approximately 2 hours to drain away any excess blood. Add 1 litre/1³/₄ pints/4 cups water to a large pan, add the bones and bring it to the boil. Immediately drain off the water and rinse the bones.

2 Pour 2.5 litres/4¹/₃ pints/11 cups water into a large pan and add the bones, with the spring onions, garlic cloves, ginger, leek, radish and peppercorns.

3 Bring the stock to the boil, and cook over a high heat until the liquid has reduced by half. Top up the pan with an equivalent amount of water and allow the liquid to reduce again. Repeat one more time until you have just over 1 litre/1³/₄ pints/ 4 cups of stock left in the pan.

4 Strain the stock into a container and refrigerate for future use in soups and casseroles.

Beef flank stock

Stock made from beef flank, a lean cut, is commonly used for a wide range of Korean soups. It has a much cleaner, lighter taste and consistency than bone broth.

MAKES 1 LITRE/1³/₄ PINTS/4 CUPS

INGREDIENTS
600g/1lb 6oz beef flank
5 garlic cloves
1 leek, halved

1 Soak the beef in cold water for 2 hours, then drain.

2 Place the beef, garlic and leek in a large pan, and add 2.5 litres/4³/₄ pints/11 cups water. Bring the pan to the boil, then reduce the heat and simmer for about 2 hours.

3 While the liquid is simmering, skim any fat from the surface of the pan to ensure a more flavourful, leaner stock.

4 Strain the stock into a container for use in soups and casseroles.

Fish stock

A good fish stock is an essential component for fish and shellfish soups or casseroles. Stocks such as this are often boiled for long periods, and the stock can be used several times. This one has a mild seafood flavour and is wonderfully versatile.

MAKES 1 LITRE/1³/₄ PINTS/4 CUPS

INGREDIENTS
1 square of dried kelp seaweed (about 10 x 10cm/4 x 4in)
5 dried anchovies
¹/₃ Chinese white radish, roughly diced

1 Place all the ingredients in a large pan and add 1.5 litres/2¹/₂ pints/6¹/₄ cups water.

2 Place the pan over a high heat and boil for 15 minutes, after which you should discard the anchovies.

3 Boil the stock for an extra 20 minutes, and then strain thoroughly before use.

Dried anchovy stock

This, a variation of the fish stock, uses dried anchovies, and is commonly used in many traditional soups in Japan and China as well as Korea. The result is a pleasantly mild fishy-tasting stock that will blend well with any fish recipe.

MAKES 1 LITRE/1³/₄ PINTS/4 CUPS

INGREDIENTS
10g/¹/₄oz dried anchovies
1 litre/1¾ pints/4 cups water

1 Bring the water to the boil in a large pan or wok and then add the 10g/¹/₄oz dried anchovies to the pan.

2 Boil the stock for 2 minutes and then, using a sieve (strainer), remove and discard the anchovies from the pan.

3 Put the anchovy stock in a container before using in a soup or a casserole. Alternatively, cook and refrigerate the stock for future use.

VEGETABLES, SALADS AND TOFU

The Korean diet is a pretty healthy one. The food is mainly low in fat and high in nutrients, with an emphasis on fresh, seasonal food cooked at home and served to be eaten immediately. When fresh ingredients are not available, there is the spicy concoction kimchi, which preserves both nutrients and flavour by excluding light and heat in a sealed jar.

Vegetables and salads are a vital part of the Korean diet. They balance the solid base of rice and its accompanying protein, and provide essential vitamins and minerals, and a crucial contrast in flavour, colour and texture.

Vegetables can form the basis of a stew, or be added to a piece of meat or fish as a flavourful and pretty garnish. They make up the majority of the side dishes which are set out for diners to share, featuring any number of vegetables such as aubergine (eggplant), radish, sweet potatoes and mushrooms. There may also be a basket of lettuce or chrysanthemum leaves on the table, ready to wrap a piece of meat. Lastly, of course, there

will be a dish or two of kimchi, maybe based on cabbage, radish or turnip.

The high consumption of tofu is linked to Korea's Buddhist roots and to its relatively limited meat resources. Made from sweet soya beans, tofu is still Korea's main source of protein.

KOREAN VEGETABLES

Vegetable and salad dishes vary according to what is in season. The staple vegetables are:

Chinese cabbage

Called baechu or tong baechu in Korea, this is also commonly known as napa cabbage or Chinese leaves, and nowadays can be found in most supermarkets. It has a long white leaf, and looks quite unlike other round cabbage varieties. It is the key ingredient for traditional kimchi.

Chinese white radish

This giant of the radish family can grow to an impressive 30cm/1ft long, and is thick, similar in character to a large parsnip.

Also known by its Japanese name of daikon or its Hindi name of mooli, this vegetable is simply known in Korea as moo. It has an inherent spiciness and sweetness and a pungent flavour.

Leeks

Koreans use daepa, a large variety of the spring onion (scallion) that is sweeter and more flavourful than the small green onion. However, leeks have a similar flavour, and the two are interchangeable.

Spring onions (scallions)

These are the most popular garnish for soups and other dishes, sometimes shredded into elaborate shapes like little brushes. Spring onions crop up everywhere, including in kimchi recipes, stir-fries, soups, stews and flavoured rice. The Korean variant is virtually identical to the Western equivalent.

Garlic

This staple ingredient is added to many dishes, and features as a pickled vegetable in its own right, ready to use

Above: Cabbage is most commonly found in kimchi, widely expounded as one of the world's healthiest foods.

Above: Peppery Chinese radish is usually served cooked, unlike the smaller radishes common to Western kitchens.

Above: Korean food is an amalgamation of carefully constructed flavours; pungent garlic is one of the most popular.

Mung beans

These small round green beans are used in mung bean soufflé and other recipes. The sprouts of the mung bean are also a valuable ingredient, used to make soup or added to stir-fries. Mung beansprouts are favoured over other beansprouts as they have an intense nutty flavour and a pleasing crunchy texture.

Above: Perilla leaves are reminiscent of mint and delicious in salads.

Right: Soft, sweet mung beans are a Korean staple.

during the winter when fresh garlic is not available. It comes into its own in the kimchi pot, where its full flavour complements the spices, salt and spring onions (scallions).

Perilla

Commonly known as wild sesame leaf, perilla is also called kenip. These wonderfully fragrant leaves are used in many ways in the kitchen, and while they look similar to Japanese shiso, the flavour is slightly different. The refreshing properties of this herb bring out a naturally fresh taste in many dishes, and it is also used as a wrap for little parcels of grilled meat.

Korean chives

These are similar to Chinese chives in terms of flavour and texture and in Korea are called buchu. Korean chives are flat green vegetables and are larger than the herb variety more familiar in Western cooking. This delicate vegetable bruises easily so it should be handled and washed with great care.

Minari

This is a small salad leaf with a wonderful aroma, similar in appearance to watercress, and with a long, crunchy stem. It is used in stews and salads, or can be simply blanched and served with a sweet and sour chilli paste dressing. Watercress can be successfully substituted.

Chrysanthemum leaves

Known as sukgot in Korea and cooked in a similar way to spinach, these leaves are strongly aromatic and are often used to suppress the smell of fish or other strong flavours in certain dishes. This herb, with its wonderfully exotic fragrance, can only be found in Korean stores, but the flat-leaf Italian parsley makes a good substitute.

Fern fronds

Also known as 'fiddlehead ferns', fern fronds are rarely used in the Western kitchen. Wild ferns can be poisonous, so use the dried fern fronds, available at any Asian store. Used as a key ingredient in yukgejang soup, these are also seasoned and sautéed for salads.

Above: Korean chives are delicately flavoured and make an attractive and tasty garnish.

Above: Beautifully nutty and full of protein, mung beansprouts are a tasty and nutritious ingredient.

Above: Sweet potatoes are used in sweet and savoury dishes.

Above: Dried kelp imbues soups and stocks with a salty sweetness.

Above: Rice rolls, wrapped in nori, make a delicious lunchtime treat.

Sweet potatoes

This pink or orange-fleshed root vegetable was brought to Korea by the Japanese and quickly became established as a staple food. Sweet potatoes are eaten in both savoury dishes such as stir-fries, where their subtle flavour blends beautifully with mushrooms and garlic, as well as in sweet dishes such as Sweet Potato Jelly (see page 484), where they are cooked until soft.

Mushrooms

There are several varieties which lend their strong, distinctive flavours to many Korean dishes.

- Shiitake mushrooms Called pyogo in Korean, these have a flat round cap, and are dark brown with an

earthy flavour. Bought fresh or dried, if dried, they should be soaked in warm water to reconstitute.
- Enoki mushrooms Also known as enokitake in Japanese, enoki mushrooms have a long, thin stem and tiny cap and an extremely delicate, slightly furry texture. They are generally used for garnishing.
- Oyster mushrooms A delicate pale grey colour and fan-shaped, oyster mushrooms are often used for casseroles and stir-fried dishes, being mild in taste and silky in texture.

SEAWEED

Used in Korean cooking for centuries, seaweed has a high vitamin and protein content. Three kinds of seaweed are:

Dried kelp

This seaweed is known as dashikonbu in Japanese or dahima in Korean, and can be found in Asian stores. It has a rich sea flavour, perfectly suited to making soup stock and salads. Kelp should always be soaked before being used.

Nori

This is the Japanese term for the popular edible flat layer of seaweed known as kim in Korea. It has a colour somewhere between dark blue and black, and is sold dried in small, very thin sheets. It has a crisp texture and a salty flavour with a distinctly toasty aroma, and is used to make the rice rolls so popular as snacks and lunchbox items in Korea.

Above: Shiitake mushrooms, dried and reconstituted with water, are considered to have superior flavour to fresh.

Above: Fresh enoki mushrooms are mild and fruity, with a delicate crunchy texture that is enjoyed cooked and raw.

Above: Oyster mushrooms are firm and meaty and are an ideal way to add flavour and substance to light meals.

Miyuk

An edible seaweed, known as wakame in Japan, miyuk is much softer than dried kelp, and contains a range of vitamins that promote good circulation. A popular Korean soup, which is traditionally served at birthday celebrations, is made from miyuk. This is also given to new mothers as it is believed to improve the circulation and to help them to regain their strength after childbirth.

Above: Nutritious tofu is the perfect meat substitute.

TOFU

This beancurd cake is made from the milky liquid extracted from soya beans, in a method similar to cheesemaking, with sweet soya beans replacing the milk. Tofu is a good vegetarian option that is commonly used as a meat substitute, and has been a principal source of protein for Koreans since the 15th century, and is combined both with vegetables and with meat. It is both delicious and easy to cook, and you'll rarely find a Korean meal that does not include tofu. Traditional tofu dishes include fried tofu (usually mixed with meat), tofu soup (with vegetables, meat, and noodles), tofu cooked in soy sauce, and tofu chige (a spicy soup).

Firm tofu, which is widely available at supermarkets, is pressed from fresh tofu to remove some of the water. It has a much longer product life, but it is not considered as special as fresh tofu.

GRILL ACCOMPANIMENTS – *namul*

Dishes that are grilled (broiled) are frequently accompanied by side orders of fresh mushrooms, garlic, potatoes and other vegetables in Korea. These side dishes are known as *namul*. Side dishes can also include meat and fish, and the whole array of zesty, tasty grill accompaniments is known as *banchan*.

Namul recipes vary considerably. Any type of any available vegetable may be used, and any part of the plant. What is more, these little dishes of radish, cucumber, potato, mushroom, and so on can be served separately or mixed in tasteful combinations to make a powerful range of colours, textures and tastes in one dish.

Namul vegetables are often steamed or stir-fried quickly in order to preserve their vitamins. They can also be served raw and crunchy, or preserved as kimchi.

Above: This namul *combines soya beansprouts, leeks and sesame oil with a garnish of red chilli.*

Shredded spring onion (scallion)

The ubiquitous spring onion (scallion) often appears as an addition to the lettuce leaf wrap – just a pinch of shredded spring onions will give an enhanced zesty flavour. Here is the recipe for this tasty garnish. Serve with grilled meat and seafood dishes.

SERVES 4

INGREDIENTS
¹/₂ leek or 4 spring onions (scallions), thinly shredded
30ml/2 tbsp gochujang Korean chilli powder
30ml/2 tbsp sugar
30ml/2 tbsp cider vinegar
10ml/2 tsp sesame oil

1 Shred the spring onions and leave to soak in cold water for 5 minutes to make them crunchy.

2 Combine the chilli powder, sugar, vinegar and sesame oil in a small bowl, and mix the ingredients together thoroughly.

3 Add the spring onions to the bowl and coat them with the chilli mixture before serving with dishes such as Braised Mackerel with White Radish (see page 318), King Prawns with Ginger and Pine Nut Dressing (see page 341) or Grilled Tiger Prawns (see page 344).

BEEF, PORK AND CHICKEN

Korean cooks, as in many Asian countries, turn first to rice and vegetables to form the bulk of their meals. In past years, protein used to come mainly from fish and shellfish, tofu and other soya bean products, and meat was traditionally a luxury ingredient available only to the rich. Now, however, meat is becoming more popular and affordable in Korea and it features in many a favourite recipe.

COOKING TECHNIQUES

Methods of food preparation have changed with the advent of cheaper prime cuts, with the grill (broiler) or barbecue becoming pretty much indispensable in any Korean household or restaurant. A portable gas or charcoal grill is used to sear the meat, sometimes at the table, so that all its flavour and tenderness is preserved. The meat is then cut into pieces and wrapped in lettuce leaves, often sprinkled with spring onions (scallions), garlic and spicy sauces.

Nothing is wasted, however. The prime cuts are usually grilled quickly, but there are many other parts of the animal that are cooked more slowly in stews or soups, including the spine and other bones, the tail and the tongue. Koreans are also fond of using the less attractive cuts of meat in a typical

Above: Beef, marinated in rice wine, here combined with sesame seeds, is an excellent addition to Korean pancakes.

sausage made of chitterlings (the intestines of the pig) stuffed with rice and flavoured with the animal's blood. Finally, the bones are made into stock to extract every last drop of goodness.

BEEF

Nowadays, beef has become the favourite meat in Korea, and there are many inventive ways of cooking the different cuts to tender perfection.

Above: Griddled beef, or bulgogi, is cooked in a flash and packed with fresh vibrant flavours.

Bulgogi

This classic dish uses thinly sliced beef marinated in soy sauce and oil with spices and garlic, then cooked quickly on a grill at the table. It results in a juicy slice of beef with added flavour.

Skewered beef

The table grill is also used in a series of skewered beef dishes, where alternate chunks of beef steak and vegetables

Meaty snacks
Not only a major part of each meal, meat also features in snacks to be eaten after work, while stopping off by a stall on the way home or strolling through the markets and shops of a big city. If you can wait, these snacks can also be wrapped up to be enjoyed at home. There's a wide choice for the meat-eater: kimbap, with little chunks of meat mixed into the rice filling, or a spicy sausage, or a pancake with tiny strips of pork or beef.

Left: Street food sellers grill or barbecue meat to use in a variety of convenient, tasty and nutritious snacks.

Above: The versatility of beef means that it is enjoyed served in a variety of different ways, cooked and raw.

Above: The finest cuts of raw beef, finely sliced and delicately seasoned, are a Korean delicacy.

Above: Sirloin steak, cut from the lower portion of the ribs, is the next best cut after the fillet or tenderloin.

such as mushrooms and spring onions (scallions) are first marinated in a spicy mix, as for bulgogi, and then threaded on to bamboo skewers to be lightly grilled (broiled).

Bulgalbi

This is a chunkier dish, which consists of a hefty piece of beef rib on the bone, cooked at the table after being marinated in a soy sauce mixture. This cut can also be cooked slowly in a *tukbaege* on the stove, simmered with stock and vegetables until meltingly tender.

Stir-fried dishes

These recipes use beef in finely cut thin strips to add flavour and protein to a predominantly vegetable dish. Cooked in this way, small amounts of best quality beef can be used economically and stretched to feed a whole family – 125g/4¼oz of beef is plenty for four people when it is mixed with a large plateful of shiitake mushrooms and spring onions alongside a good mixture of spices, chilli and garlic.

Raw beef

Koreans are very fond of raw beef in a beef tartare dish, where the best cut of meat is very thinly sliced into ribbons, and is then seasoned with sesame oil and displayed in a round flat dish on a base of lettuce leaves. There will be alternating stripes or concentric circles of meat, strips of the hard, grainy Asian pear and garlic, with toasted pine nuts and an egg broken in the centre. When it is time to serve the dish, it is customary for the cook to break the egg yolk, and each diner then dips his portion of meat into the raw egg.

Ox meat

In the spirit of good husbandry, making use of everything edible from the countryside, Koreans enjoy pressed ox tongue and oxtail broth, simmered until tender. Oxtails can be bought whole or sliced, and are cooked in stock.

Above: Oxtail has a gelatinous quality that makes it an ideal base for soups and broths.

Then the ox meat can either be extracted and mixed back into the soup, or the oxtail can be left whole for the diners to cut and serve themselves. It has a very strong flavour, so the added seasoning should be gentle – ideally a simple combination of garlic, pepper and onions.

Below: Slow cooking leaves large cuts of beef perfectly tender.

Above: Pork is often treated simply, its blandness used to counter and enhance the vibrant flavours of kimchi.

PORK

Commonly eaten in Korea, pork is probably next in popularity to beef these days. Pigs thrive in the colder climate of the north of the country, where there is less room for grazing because of the mountainous landscape, and raising cattle for meat would not be an economical option. Pork is also a good deal cheaper than beef, and with its blander flavour it absorbs spices and garlic beautifully, making a great base for any number of flavourful recipes.

Grilled (broiled) steak and ribs

Boneless pork steaks can be treated in the same way as beef, marinated for several hours in a mixture of soy sauce, garlic, chilli and other spices, and then quickly cooked on a grill (broiler). Ribs are generally cut longer than Chinese spare ribs, with more meat on the bone. Kimchi is the best accompaniment to many a pork dish, as its spicy, tart flavour cuts through the blander, fatty pork.

Samgyupsal

A tasty Korean speciality is known as samgyupsal, or 'three-layer pork'. This is made with a large chunk of pork belly, the 'three layers' consisting of the lean meat, a layer of fat, and finally the thick skin. Koreans do not like to eat the fat and skin layers, but keeping them during the cooking process allows the meat to develop a full tender perfection. The whole chunk of meat is first simmered until tender, and then sliced every $\frac{1}{2}$cm/$\frac{1}{4}$in or so all through the cooked meat part and coated with a seasoning paste made of ginger and toasted pine nuts.

Once the rest of the meal is ready, the piece of meat is steamed gently for a few minutes to heat through, and decorated between the slices with any number of garnishes, ranging from mushrooms, cucumber and chilli threads to sliced egg roll. Each diner pulls off pieces of succulent meat and tasty garnish, leaving the fat and skin below.

CHICKEN

Dishes prepared with chicken are not a favourite of Korean cooks, surprisingly enough. Indeed, despite the fact that chickens are easy to rear and live happily in most climates, they are not a common feature of the Korean countryside and tend to be cooked only on special occasions.

Above: While chicken is not prominent in the Korean diet, it does appear in various recipes.

Samgyetang

Perhaps the best known traditional chicken recipe in Korea is samgyetang. This famous Korean stew consists of a small chicken, not more than 450g/1lb in weight, which is simmered slowly over a low heat in a *tukbaege* (or casserole) along with ginseng root, red dates, garlic and rice. Samgyetang forms a kind of thick, bright red soup which is believed to be particularly beneficial to the health when eaten during the very hottest days of summer.

Stews, soups and stock

Chicken meat is rarely grilled in the style of the beef and pork recipes that we have already mentioned. It will usually be found in a stew or as the basis of noodle soup. Chicken bones and feet make a good stock, particularly when simmered with ginger and onions.

Deep-fried chicken

Fried chicken is a popular evening snack, especially in Korean bars where they are eaten with beer or soju. Korean deep-fried chicken is characterized by a delicate crust, spicy seasoning and deliciously moist meat.

Above: Griddled pork loin should be well done with the exterior seared and slightly blackened.

FISH AND SHELLFISH

The Koreans are fantastically resourceful cooks. They use a multitude of ingredients; they cook their food quickly to preserve its nutritional value; and what they can't eat straight away they preserve for the winter. Above all, they make proper use of the abundant harvest of the sea.

GOOD FOOD FROM THE SEA

This is a country bounded on three sides by water. The landmass of Korea is only about 1,000km (620 miles) long from north to south, but It has a coastline measuring over 8,000km (about 5,000 miles) with over 3,000 islands dotted around the southern and western coasts. So it is no wonder the Korean diet is so rich in fish and shellfish of all kinds.

What is more, the kinds of seafood available vary considerably from one part of the country to another. In the colder waters of the north, cod and other cold-water fish abound, particularly in the winter months when they migrate around the Chinese coast. Farther south in the Yellow Sea, crabs, oysters and other shellfish live in the tidal mudflats; and around the southernmost tip of Korea, into the East Sea facing Japan, there are thousands of squid to be caught and dried in the sun. Busan, South Korea's busy second city and a major port on the south-east coast, has a huge fish market where every kind of seafood is set out for sale every day.

CORNUCOPIA OF SPECIES

There are so many types of fish and shellfish commonly used in Korean cuisine. They are made into stews, soups, stir-fries, grills, street snacks; served with rice, with noodles, with pancakes, as fritters; dried and crushed into paste or sauce or used as a crunchy garnish; even dished up raw, or even live on the plate.

Right: Large prawns are prepared to make the most of their delicious flavour.

Right: Blue crabs live, and are eaten, in abundance around the coasts of South Korea.

Crab

Blue crab is found in the southern part of Korea, in abundance in the muddy tidal estuaries and in the calmer waters between the islands. Crabs are usually cooked live. The cook will plunge them into freezing cold water to stun them before simmering them in boiling stock with lots of vegetables and spices for an excellent casserole. Crab salad is another favourite: the raw crab meat is gently steamed to preserve its flavour, then mixed with crunchy sliced Asian pear and other salad vegetables in a sweet and sour dressing.

Squid

Around the island of Ullung-do, off the east coast of Korea, squid are plentiful. They can be seen drying in the sun all day, draped over washing lines and on roofs. Every bit is eaten, either fresh and cooked or dried as a snack. A local recipe for stuffed squid, fills the seasoned body with a tofu, egg and flour mixture and, after steaming, is then served sliced.

Prawns and shrimps

These are cooked quickly, usually steamed or grilled (broiled). Large prawns (shrimp) or tiger prawns are seasoned and marinated before being threaded on to skewers for grilling. They are usually served with a dipping sauce or just lemon juice to bring out the flavour.

Octopus

The Koreans eat octopus both cooked and raw, although the raw version may seem unnecessarily chewy to the Western taste. Once an octopus is tenderized and gently simmered, it retains a chewy texture, but becomes a delicious delicacy that lends itself to dipping in a spicy sauce, or can then be added to a stir-fried mixture of large spring onions (scallions), ginger, gochujang paste and sesame oil.

Above: Octopus is a choice Korean ingredient, which becomes delightfully tender with cooking.

Abalone

The beautiful abalone shell with its iridescent inner layer lives on the rocks beneath the warm waters around Cheju island off the south coast of Korea. The cleaned shells are a favourite tourist souvenir, and the flesh is eaten chopped up in stews and soups, often mixed with rice in a thick soup garnished with sesame seeds. Canned abalone is available as an acceptable alternative to the fresh variety, which can be difficult to find. It is a source of selenium, magnesium and vitamins B and E.

Above: Oysters are served cooked in pancakes, soups and stews and are said to have health-giving properties.

Above: Abalone is a highly prized ingredient in Korea for its unique flavour and health-giving properties.

Clams, mussels and whelks

These tasty little morsels are often added to a spicy soup. The Koreans like to eat them when they are small, rather than 'the bigger the better' philosophy in the West. Baby clams (chechi) can be simmered with water and a little bundle of Chinese chives to make a subtly flavoured broth which the Koreans claim to be a particularly good hangover remedy. Whelks make popular street snacks, dipped into soy sauce with the usual accompaniments of chilli powder, sesame oil and garlic.

Oysters

In the cold winter months, you can find oysters of the best quality around the Korean coast. They are believed to give strength and good health. One favourite recipe is oyster pancakes, gool pajeon, which are little fritters of egg, rice flour, chilli and oysters, gently fried on both sides until tender.

Anchovies

These little fish are eaten fresh (both raw and cooked) or preserved. They can be simply dried and then reconstituted when needed, or they

Above: Anchovies are a staple of Korean cooking and can be served dried, cooked or raw.

Above: Tasty baby clams are cooked in broth and served as a restorative to those nursing a hangover from too much soju. The small size of these clams in no way diminishes their flavour.

Left: Pollack is undervalued in the Western kitchen, but with its flaky white flesh it is a cheap and environmentally friendly alternative to cod.

Hae san mool jungol

Korean cooks are more than happy to mix fish and meat. Major celebrations such as weddings and birthdays may include the famous buffet-style dish, hae san mool jungol, a stunning assortment of seafood, vegetables and steak, all carefully arranged in a large pan and then gently cooked together in beef broth. The flavours of the meat and fish will be blended beautifully in the savoury broth with a good few spoonfuls of spicy seasoning paste in the centre.

Right: Delicate skate wings are unique for their soft bones and delicious iridescent flesh. In the Korean kitchen the subtle flavours may be enjoyed by poaching the fish and serving in a salad.

can be made into anchovy paste to be added in small quantities whenever a strong fishy taste is required.

Anchovies are very popular, especially around the southern coast of Korea where an Anchovy Festival is held every year in the late spring, with street processions, feasting and fireworks.

Cod

During the winter months, shoals of cod migrate south past the Korean peninsula in search of warmer currents. On the way they are fished, cooked fresh, or dried and salted for cooking later in the year. The cod is a prized and expensive fish, so small amounts are generally made to stretch a long way in a vegetable stew, or seasoned well so that the flavour carries through a large bowl of rice. Pieces of cod can also be preserved with vegetables in a form of kimchi known as seuck bak ji, a preparation method where both the cod and the cabbage are soaked separately overnight in brine before adding spices and sealing them into jars. Pollack is used as a good alternative to cod.

Other salt-water fish

As with their meat dishes, the Koreans use everything edible in the sea, and enjoy flounder, mackerel, sea bass, red snapper, monkfish, herring, bream, skate, pollack and many more. These fish are a great source of low-fat protein, particularly for those near the coast who can buy them fresh from the local market. A piece of fish per person can be simply marinated and grilled (broiled) at the table, or a smaller amount can be divided among many diners by adding vegetables and tofu in a stew or fish soup.

Above: Dried pollack is a classic Korean ingredient. It is eaten as a snack, but is most commonly found in soups and broths.

Below: Large, freshly caught fish, such as bream, are a healthy and nutritious addition to the diet; simply marinated and grilled, or added to a fish soup.

FRUIT, SWEETS AND DRINKS

Sweet recipes are generally associated with special celebrations such as weddings and birthdays, or are eaten between meals as snacks. This is because the Korean diet is based on savoury dishes, and once you have filled up with spicy, savoury delicacies with a bowl of rice, there is little need for a sweet course afterwards.

Above: Astringent persimmons, fresh or dried, are a mainstay of Korean cooking.

FRUIT

Orchards abound in the lush green plains and river valleys of central Korea, although the farmers are now finding it difficult to combat the low price of fruit flooding the country from China, just across the border. Apples are still the most common crop grown in Korea,

followed by mandarin oranges, persimmons (often used in savoury recipes for their astringent quality), peaches, grapes and the grainy Asian pears, which are used as a garnish in a variety of savoury dishes.

SWEETMEATS AND CAKES

The festival of *Chuseok*, in the middle of the autumn season, is the best time to find songpyeon, sweet rice cakes filled with honey or maple syrup or a sweetened red bean, nut and seed mixture. These are part of the offerings made in thanks for a good harvest, and to pray for a good year to follow.

One dish sometimes eaten as a dessert after a meal is tteok, which is a cake-like confection based on rice sweetened with honey and a variety of fillings, such as sesame seeds, sweet pumpkin, dates and pine nuts. The ambivalent attitude of the Koreans to sweet things means that these little cakes are sometimes turned into savouries with beef and vegetables, and served as a light meal at lunchtime.

Other little cakes may be served at any time of day with a cup of barley tea, and are typically made with great care. These delicate confections of

Above: Universally popular, mandarin oranges are one of Korea's most prolific crops and are exported worldwide.

quickly cooked light dough are often coloured with natural ingredients, such as pumpkin (orange) and seaweed (green), and then twisted into attractive shapes.

Above: The Asian pear is grainy in texture and refreshing and light in flavour.

Above: A busy market street in Gonju, South Korea, with fruit and vegetable stalls selling onions, tomatoes, melons, apples and oranges.

Left: Two friends share a pot of green tea and a plate of traditional rice cakes in a tea house in Korea.

brew, either at intervals through the day or in little china cups as an aid to digestion after dinner. It is simply made by dry-roasting barley in a large pan until the grains turn brown. The barley is then cooled, added to a pan of boiling water and simmered until ready, which is when the water has taken on the colour of the roasted barley. The tea can be served at any temperature, depending on the occasion, but it is usually drunk hot in winter and cold in summer.

Koreans do also drink all kinds of other flavoured teas. These can be based on rice, corn, ginger, ginseng, fruit or herbs, and tend to be served hot or cold depending on the season, as with boricha. Fiery ginger tea is for the winter months, and cooling ginseng or fruit tea goes down better on hot summer days.

Above: Tea is served in a variety of flavours and at different temperatures to reflect the seasons.

DRINKS

Koreans enjoy both alcoholic and non-alcoholic drinks. They are as inventive with both as with their food, using local ingredients and combining them in delicious recipes to get just the right balance of sweet and sour, tart and smooth.

Tea

The best-known non-alcoholic drink is roasted barley tea, boricha. Most Korean households will serve this pale

Above: Barley tea is drunk hot or cold and most often consumed between meals to aid digestion.

Punch

There are many recipes for non-alcoholic mixed fruit punch, but the best-loved mixture is persimmon punch, sujeonggwa. The beautiful orange persimmon is quite widely grown in Korea. It is dried and left to soften after harvesting and then steeped in cold water with a large amount of ginger root, cinnamon and sugar. The colour is beautiful – a deep reddish-pink. It is a refreshing cold drink for summer heat and complements a spicy meal.

Soju

The best-known alcoholic drink made in Korea is soju. This colourless drink is rather like vodka, and was originally made from rice or other grains, but it is now often made from sweet potatoes. It is a strong liquor, and a favourite with Koreans.

Wines

Following hard on the heels of soju in terms of popularity comes Korean wine, produced either as a blend of Korean grapes with wines from abroad or based on local fruit supplies. These traditional fruit-flavoured wines are made from locally

available produce, fruits including plum, quince, pomegranate and cherry, and even herbal wines made of ginseng, which are believed to have excellent health benefits. Wines are also produced from flowers such as wild roses, peach blossom, acacia, chrysanthemums and honeysuckle.

Rice wine

Koreans have their own version of rice wine (also called sake), because rice is such a staple food. Both refined (yakju) and unrefined (takju) rice liquor are made. The unrefined is most popular with agricultural and rural workers, who love its thick texture, its milky appearance and its intense alcoholic strength.

Right: Rice wine (sake) is a very popular drink.

THE RECIPES

Some of the world's most exciting dishes come from Japan and Korea. Each country has its own distinct cuisine, but there is a common emphasis on serving the freshest food.

Image: Fried vegetable fritters and boiled dumplings are both popular dishes.

SUSHI & SASHIMI

Rice is the very essence of Japanese and Korean cooking. Almost every dish in these cuisines has been designed to accompany a simple bowl of rice. This chapter includes recipes for simple rolled sushi, hand-moulded sushi, rice balls, and a superb variety of sashimi — all of which are very distinctively Japanese dishes, but there are some Korean versions as well.

Left: Salmon Hoso-Maki; **Above:** Sashimi Moriawase

MARINATED MACKEREL SUSHI

FRESH MACKEREL FILLETS ARE MARINATED, THEN PACKED INTO A MOULD WITH SUSHI RICE TO MAKE SABA-ZUSHI. START PREPARATIONS 8 HOURS IN ADVANCE TO ALLOW THE FISH TO ABSORB THE SALT.

MAKES ABOUT 12

INGREDIENTS
   500g/1¼lb mackerel, filleted
   salt
   rice vinegar
   2cm/¾in fresh root ginger, peeled and
     finely grated, to garnish
   shoyu, to serve
For the su-meshi (vinegared rice)
   200g/7oz/1 cup Japanese short
     grain rice
   40ml/8 tsp rice vinegar
   20ml/4 tsp caster (superfine) sugar
   5ml/1 tsp salt

COOK'S TIP
All future uses, or variations of, su-meshi are based on the basic recipe provided above, hereafter referred to as 1 quantity of su-meshi.

1 Place the fillets skin-side down in a flat dish, cover with a thick layer of salt, and leave them for 3–5 hours.

2 To make the su-meshi, put the rice in a large bowl and wash in plenty of water, until it runs clear. Tip into a sieve and leave to drain for 1 hour.

3 Put the rice into a small, deep pan with 15 per cent more water, i.e. 250ml/8fl oz/1⅛ cups water to 200g/7oz/1 cup rice. Cover and bring to the boil. This takes about 5 minutes.

4 Reduce the heat and simmer for 12 minutes without lifting the lid. You should hear a faint crackling noise. The rice should now have absorbed the water. Remove from the heat and leave for 10 minutes.

5 Transfer the cooked rice to a wet Japanese rice tub or large bowl. In a small bowl, mix the vinegar, sugar and salt until well dissolved. Add to the rice, fluffing the rice with a wet spatula. Do not mash. If you have someone to help you, ask them to fan the rice to cool it quickly. This process makes the su-meshi glossy. Cover the bowl with wet dishtowels and leave to cool.

6 Wipe the salt from the mackerel with kitchen paper. Remove all the remaining bones with tweezers. Lift the skin at the tail end of each fillet and peel towards the head end. Place the skinned fillets in a clean dish, and pour in enough rice vinegar to cover the fish completely. Leave for 20 minutes, then drain and wipe dry with kitchen paper.

7 Line a 25 × 7.5 × 4cm/10 × 3 × 1½in container with some clear film (plastic wrap), twice the size of the container. Lay the fillets in the container, skinned-side down, to cover the base. Cut the remaining mackerel to fill the gaps.

8 Put the su-meshi into the container, and press down firmly with dampened hands. Cover with the clear film and place a weight on top. Leave for at least 3 hours or overnight.

9 Remove the sushi from its container, then slice into 2cm/¾in pieces. After each slice, wipe the knife with kitchen paper dampened with rice vinegar.

10 Arrange on a plate and add a little grated ginger. Serve with shoyu.

Per portion Energy 158kcal/659kJ; Protein 9g; Carbohydrate 15g, of which sugars 1.7g; Fat 6.8g, of which saturates 1.4g; Cholesterol 23mg; Calcium 9mg; Fibre 0g; Sodium 190mg.

HAND-MOULDED SUSHI

ORIGINALLY DEVELOPED IN TOKYO AS STREET FINGER FOOD, NIGIRI-ZUSHI IS PREPARED WITH THE FRESHEST OF FISH AND EATEN WITHIN A MATTER OF A FEW MINUTES OF MAKING.

SERVES FOUR

INGREDIENTS

4 raw king prawns (jumbo shrimp),
   head and shell removed, tails intact
4 scallops, white muscle only
425g/15oz assorted fresh seafood,
   skinned, cleaned and filleted
2 quantities su-meshi
15ml/1 tbsp rice vinegar, for moulding
45ml/3 tbsp wasabi paste from a
   tube, or the same amount of wasabi
   powder mixed with 15ml/1 tbsp water
salt
gari, to garnish
shoyu, to serve

1 Insert a bamboo skewer or cocktail stick (toothpick) into each prawn lengthways. This stops the prawns curling up when cooked. Boil them in lightly salted water for 2 minutes, or until they turn pink. Drain and cool, then pull out the skewers. Cut open from the belly side but do not slice in two. With the point of a sharp knife, scoop up the black vein running down its length. Very gently pull it out, then discard. Open out flat and place on a tray.

2 Slice the scallops horizontally in half, but not quite through. Gently open each scallop at this "hinge" to make a butterfly shape. Place on the tray, cut-side down. Use a sharp knife to cut all the fish fillets into 7.5 × 4cm/3 × 1½in pieces, 5mm/¼in thick. Place all the raw fish and shellfish on the tray, cover with clear film (plastic wrap), then chill.

3 Place the su-meshi in a bowl. Have ready a small bowl filled with 150ml/ ¼ pint/⅔ cup water and the vinegar for moulding. This water is used for your hands while making nigiri-zushi. Take the tray of toppings from the refrigerator.

COOK'S TIP
Don't worry if your su-meshi block doesn't look very neat. Wet your hands with the hand water frequently, and keep the work surface tidy at all times.

4 Wet your hand with the vinegared water and scoop about 25ml/1½ tbsp *su-meshi* into your palm. Gently but firmly grip the *su-meshi* and make a rectangular block. Do not squash the rice, but ensure that the grains stick together. The size of the blocks must be smaller than the toppings.

5 Put the su-meshi block on a damp chopping board. Taking a piece of topping in your palm, rub a little wasabi paste in the middle of it. Put the su-meshi block on top of the fish slice and gently press it. Form your palm into a cup and shape the nigiri-zushi to a smooth-surfaced mound. Place it on a serving tray. Do not overwork, as the warmth of your hands can cause the toppings to lose their freshness.

6 Repeat this process until all of the rice and toppings are used. Serve immediately with a little shoyu dribbled on individual plates. To eat, pick up one nigiri-zushi and dip the tip into the shoyu. Eat a little gari between tasting different sushi to refresh your mouth.

Per portion Energy 392kcal/1636kJ; Protein 29.3g; Carbohydrate 40.5g, of which sugars 0.2g; Fat 12.2g, of which saturates 2.1g; Cholesterol 77mg; Calcium 45mg; Fibre 0.1g; Sodium 86mg.

RICE ROLLS <u>WITH</u> BEEF <u>AND</u> SESAME

SIMILAR TO A MAKI ROLL, THIS KOREAN ALTERNATIVE AVOIDS THE USE OF VINEGAR WHEN COOKING THE RICE, RESULTING IN A DISH THAT IS LESS SOUR THAN ITS JAPANESE COUNTERPART. THE FRESH, CRUNCHY VEGETABLES ARE COMPLEMENTED BY THE SUBTLE FLAVOUR OF THE FISHCAKE.

SERVES FOUR

INGREDIENTS

50g/2oz beef, finely chopped
150g/5oz/3/4 cup short grain rice,
  cooked (400g/14oz/4 cups
  when cooked)
1 Asian fishcake or Japanese surimi,
  thinly sliced
2 eggs, beaten
75g/3oz carrot, cut into strips
25g/1oz spinach
a little soy sauce
a little sesame oil
pinch of sugar
4 sheets dried seaweed paper or
  Japanese nori
75g/3oz pickled Chinese white
  radish, thinly sliced
15ml/1 tbsp sesame seeds
salt and ground black pepper
vegetable oil, for cooking
For the marinade
5ml/1 tsp soy sauce
2.5ml/1/2 tsp sugar
2.5ml/1/2 tsp sesame oil
1 garlic clove, crushed
Seasoning for the rice
2.5ml/1/2 tsp sugar
2.5ml/1/2 tsp rice vinegar
1.25ml/1/4 tsp soy sauce
1.25ml/1/4 tsp sesame oil
1.25ml/1/4 tsp sesame seeds
Seasoning for the fishcake
2.5ml/1/2 tsp soy sauce
2.5ml/1/2 tsp sugar
30ml/2 tbsp sesame oil
15ml/1 tbsp sesame seeds

1 Place the beef in a bowl. Add the marinade ingredients and salt and pepper. Mix and leave for 10 minutes.

2 Mixing the sugar, rice vinegar, soy sauce, sesame oil and sesame seeds. Add the rice and mix well.

3 Mix the soy sauce, sugar, sesame oil and seeds, and black pepper. Cut the fish cake into thin slices and turn them in the seasoning until evenly coated.

4 Place a frying pan over a medium heat and add a little vegetable oil. Pour in the beaten eggs, tilting the pan to make a thin omelette. Slide the omelette out on to a plate and cut into 5mm/1/4in slices.

5 Stir-fry the carrots in the pan, adding oil if necessary, and a pinch of salt. When slightly softened, remove and set aside.

6 Add the fishcake and stir-fry gently for 1 minute, trying not to break up the slices. Remove them and set aside. Add the beef and its marinade to the pan and stir-fry for 2–3 minutes. Remove the beef from the pan and set it aside.

7 Bring about 250ml/8fl oz/1 cup water to the boil in a pan. Add the spinach and bring back to the boil. Drain and rinse the spinach under cold water, then drain again. Place the spinach in a bowl and add a splash of soy sauce, a little sesame oil and a pinch of sugar.

8 Place a sheet of seaweed on a bamboo sushi mat. Spread an even layer of rice over about half the seaweed, keeping the rice about 5mm/1/4in deep.

9 Across the centre of the rice, arrange a few strips of pickled radish (reserve about half for serving) and a quarter each of the carrot, spinach, omelette, fishcake and beef. Drizzle with a little sesame oil and sprinkle with a quarter of the sesame seeds. Dampen the uncovered edge of the seaweed.

10 Using the bamboo mat as a guide, slowly roll up the ingredients from the rice end, rolling the mat over and tucking in the end of the seaweed and rice to start a neat roll. Continue rolling with medium pressure – the wet seaweed should seal the end of the roll. Repeat with the remaining ingredients.

11 Use a sharp knife to slice the seaweed rolls into 2cm/3/4in pieces. Wipe the knife clean after each cut and rinse it under cold water to prevent the mixture from sticking to it.

12 Arrange the slices on a platter and serve with the reserved pickled radish.

Per portion Energy 268kcal/1115kJ; Protein 12.3g; Carbohydrate 33g, of which sugars 2.9g; Fat 9.5g, of which saturates 2g; Cholesterol 127mg; Calcium 79mg; Fibre 1.1g; Sodium 1060mg.

SALMON HOSO-MAKI

THESE SIMPLE LITTLE SUSHI ROLLS ARE VERY GOOD FOR PICNICS AND CANAPÉS, AND THEY MAKE DELIGHTFUL LITTLE TREATS FOR PARTIES. THESE ROLLS SHOULD ALWAYS BE SERVED COLD.

4 Place a sheet of yaki-nori, shiny side down, on a bamboo mat.

5 Divide the rice into 12 portions. Place one portion over the yaki-nori, leaving a ½-inch space at the top and bottom.

6 Spread a little wasabi paste in a line along the middle of the rice and lay one or two sticks of the salmon on this.

MAKES 72 PIECES

INGREDIENTS
    450ml/2 cups sushi rice,
       soaked for 20 minutes in water
       to cover
    45ml/3½ tbsp rice vinegar
    15ml/1 tbsp sugar
    2.5ml/½ tsp salt
    3 sheets yaki-nori seaweed
    400g/14oz salmon in one piece
    wasabi paste
    pickled ginger, for garnish
    Japanese soy sauce, to serve

1 Drain the rice, then put in a pan with 600ml/1 pint/2½ cups of water. Bring to the boil, then lower the heat, cover and simmer for 20 minutes, or until all the liquid has been absorbed.

2 Heat the vinegar, sugar and salt, stir well and cool. Add to the hot rice, then remove the pan from the heat and allow to stand, covered, for 20 minutes.

3 Cut the yaki-nori sheets in half lengthwise. Cut the salmon into 12 × 1cm (½in) sticks, each the same length as the long side of the yaki-nori.

7 Holding the mat and the edge of the yaki-nori, roll up the rice and salmon. Roll the rice tightly so that it encloses the filling firmly. Carefully roll the sushi off the mat. Make 11 more rolls in the same way. Use a wet knife to cut each roll into six slices. Garnish with pickled ginger, and serve with the soy sauce.

Per portion Energy 26kcal/108kJ; Protein 1.3g; Carbohydrate 3.5g, of which sugars 0.2g; Fat 0.7g, of which saturates 0.1g; Cholesterol 3mg; Calcium 2mg; Fibre 0g; Sodium 19mg.

HAND-ROLLED SUSHI

THIS IS A FUN WAY TO ENJOY SUSHI. CALLED TEMAKI-ZUSHI, MEANING HAND-ROLLED, EACH GUEST ROLLS TOGETHER INDIVIDUAL FILLINGS OF FISH AND SHELLFISH, VEGETABLES AND SU-MESHI.

SERVES FOUR TO SIX

INGREDIENTS
   2 quantities su-meshi, made with
      40ml/8 tsp caster (superfine) sugar
   225g/8oz extremely fresh tuna steak
   130g/4½oz smoked salmon
   17cm/6½in Japanese cucumber or
      salad cucumber
   8 raw king prawns (jumbo shrimp)
      or large tiger prawns, peeled and
      heads removed
   1 avocado
   7.5ml/1½ tsp lemon juice
   20 chives, trimmed and chopped into
      6cm/2½in lengths
   1 packet mustard and cress, roots
      cut off
   6–8 shiso leaves, cut in
      half lengthways
To serve
   12 nori sheets, cut into four
   mayonnaise
   shoyu
   45ml/3 tbsp wasabi paste from a
      tube, or the same amount of
      wasabi powder mixed with 15ml/
      1 tbsp water
   gari

1 Put the su-meshi into a large serving bowl and cover with a damp dishtowel.

2 Slice the tuna, with the grain, into 5mm/¼in slices then into 1 × 6cm/ ½ × 2½in strips. Cut the salmon and cucumber into strips the same size as the tuna.

3 Insert bamboo skewers into the prawns, then boil in lightly salted water for 2 minutes. Drain and leave to cool. Remove the skewers and cut in half lengthways. Remove the vein.

4 Halve the avocado and remove the stone (pit). Sprinkle with half the lemon juice and cut into 1cm/½in long strips. Sprinkle on the remaining lemon juice.

5 Arrange the fish, shellfish, avocado and vegetables on a plate. Place the nori sheets on a few plates and put the mayonnaise into a bowl. Put the shoyu in individual bowls, and the wasabi paste in a dish. Heap the gari in a small bowl. Half-fill a glass with water and place four to six rice paddles inside. Arrange everything on the table.

6 Each guest rolls their sushi as follows: take a sheet of nori on your palm, then scoop out 45ml/3 tbsp rice and spread it on the nori sheet. Spread some wasabi in the middle of the rice, then place a few strips of different fillings on top. Roll it up as a cone and dip the end into the shoyu. Have some gari between rolls to refresh your mouth.

Per portion Energy 191kcal/797kJ; Protein 8.2g; Carbohydrate 21.3g, of which sugars 7.7g; Fat 8.2g, of which saturates 1.4g; Cholesterol 19mg; Calcium 26mg; Fibre 0.9g; Sodium 442mg.

ROLLED SUSHI

You will need a makisu (a sushi rolling mat) to make these sushi, called nori maki.
There are two types: hoso-maki (thin-rolled sushi) and futo-maki (thick-rolled sushi).

SERVES SIX TO EIGHT

FUTO-MAKI (THICK-ROLLED SUSHI)
MAKES 16 PIECES

INGREDIENTS
2 nori sheets
1 quantity su-meshi
For the omelette
2 eggs, beaten
25ml/1½ tbsp second dashi stock,
or the same amount of water and
5ml/1 tsp dashi-no-moto
10ml/2 tsp sake
2.5ml/½ tsp salt
vegetable oil, for frying
For the fillings
4 dried shiitake mushrooms, soaked
in a bowl of water overnight
120ml/4fl oz/½ cup second dashi
stock, or the same amount of water
and 1½ tsp dashi-no-moto
15ml/1 tbsp shoyu
7.5ml/1½ tsp caster (superfine) sugar
5ml/1 tsp mirin
6 raw large prawns (shrimp), heads
and shells removed, tails intact
4 asparagus spears, boiled for
1 minute in lightly salted
water, cooled
10 chives, about 23cm/9in long,
ends trimmed

1 To make the omelette, mix the beaten eggs, dashi stock, sake and salt in a bowl. Heat a little oil in a frying pan on a medium-low heat. Pour in just enough egg mixture to thinly cover the base of the pan. As soon as the mixture sets, fold the omelette in half towards you and wipe the space left with a little oil.

2 With the first omelette still in the pan, repeat this process of frying and folding to make more omelettes. Each new one is laid on to the previous omelette, to form one multi-layered omelette. When all the mixture is used, slide the layered omelette on to a chopping board. Cool, then cut into 1cm/½in wide strips.

3 Put the shiitake, dashi stock, shoyu, sugar and mirin in a small pan. Bring to the boil then reduce the heat to low. Cook for 20 minutes until half of the liquid has evaporated. Drain, remove and discard the stalks, and slice the caps thinly. Squeeze out any excess liquid, then dry on kitchen paper.

4 Make three cuts in the belly of the prawns to stop them curling up, and boil in salted water for 1 minute, or until they turn bright pink. Drain and cool, then remove the vein.

5 Place a nori sheet at the front edge of the makisu. Scoop up half of the su-meshi and spread it on the nori as in hoso-maki. Leave a 1cm/½in margin at the side nearest you, and 2cm/¾in at the side furthest from you.

6 Make a shallow depression horizontally across the centre of the rice. Fill this with a row of omelette strips, then put half the asparagus and prawns on top. Place 5 chives alongside, and then put half the shiitake slices on to the chives.

7 Lift the makisu with your thumbs while pressing the fillings with your fingers and roll up gently.

8 When completed, gently roll the makisu on the chopping board to firm it up. Unwrap and set the futo-maki aside. Repeat the process to make another roll.

HOSO-MAKI (THIN-ROLLED SUSHI)
MAKES 24 PIECES

INGREDIENTS
2 nori sheets, cut in half crossways
1 quantity su-meshi
45ml/3 tbsp wasabi paste from a
tube, or the same amount of wasabi
powder mixed with 10ml/2 tsp
water, plus extra for serving
For the fillings
90g/3½oz very fresh tuna steak
10cm/4in cucumber or 17cm/6½in
Japanese cucumber
5ml/1 tsp roasted sesame seeds
6cm/2½in takuan, cut into 1cm/½in
thick long strips

1 For the fillings, cut the tuna with the grain into 1cm/½in wide strips. Cut the cucumber into 1cm/½in thick strips.

2 Place the makisu on the work surface, then place a nori sheet on it horizontally, rough-side up. Spread a quarter of the su-meshi over the nori to cover evenly, leaving a 1cm/½in margin on the side furthest from you. Press firmly to smooth the surface.

3 Spread a little wasabi paste across the rice and arrange some of the tuna strips horizontally in a row across the middle. Cut off the excess.

Futo-maki: Per portion Energy 107kcal/447kJ; Protein 3.8g; Carbohydrate 16.3g, of which sugars 1.3g; Fat 2.9g, of which saturates 0.6g; Cholesterol 52mg; Calcium 17mg; Fibre 0.2g; Sodium 112mg.

4 Hold the makisu with both hands and carefully roll it up, wrapping the tuna in the middle, and rolling away from the side closest to you. Hold the rolled makisu with both hands and squeeze gently to firm the nori-maki.

5 Slowly unwrap the makisu, remove the rolled tuna hoso-maki and set aside. Make another tuna hoso-maki with the remaining ingredients.

6 Repeat the same process using only the cucumber strips with the green skin on. Sprinkle sesame seeds on the cucumber before rolling.

7 Repeat with the takuan strips, but omit the wasabi paste. Keep the sushi on a slightly damp chopping board, covered with clear film (plastic wrap) during preparation. When finished, you should have two hoso-maki of tuna, and one each of cucumber and takuan.

To serve the nori-maki

1 Cut each futo-maki roll into eight pieces, using a very sharp knife. Wipe the knife with a dishtowel dampened with rice vinegar after each cut. Cut each hoso-maki into six pieces in the same way.

2 Line up all the maki on a large tray. Serve with small dishes of wasabi, gari, and shoyu for dipping.

COOK'S TIP
Half-fill a small bowl with water and add 30ml/2 tbsp rice vinegar. Use this to wet your hands to prevent the rice sticking when rolling sushi.

Hoso-maki: Per portion Energy 23kcal/96kJ; Protein 0.5g; Carbohydrate 5g, of which sugars 0g; Fat 0g, of which saturates 0g; Cholesterol 0mg; Calcium 2mg; Fibre 0g; Sodium 0mg.

COMPRESSED SUSHI WITH SMOKED SALMON

THIS SUSHI, KNOWN AS OSHI-ZUSHI, DATES BACK ALMOST A THOUSAND YEARS. OSHI-ZUSHI ARE
SQUARES OF COOKED RICE PRESSED IN A MOULD TOPPED WITH SMOKED OR COOKED FISH.

2 Wet a wooden Japanese sushi mould or line a 25 × 7.5 × 5cm/10 × 3 × 2in plastic container with a large sheet of clear film (plastic wrap), allowing the edges to hang over.

3 Spread half the smoked salmon to evenly cover the bottom of the mould or container. Add a quarter of the cooked rice and firmly press down with your hands dampened with rice vinegar until it is 1cm/½in thick. Add the remainder of the salmon, and press the remaining rice on top.

4 Put the wet wooden lid on the mould, or cover the plastic container with the overhanging clear film. Place a weight, such as a heavy dinner plate, on top. Leave in a cool place overnight, or for at least 3 hours. If you keep it in the refrigerator, choose the least cool part.

5 Remove the compressed sushi from the mould or container and unwrap. Cut into 2cm/¾in slices and serve on a Japanese lacquered tray or a large plate. Quarter the lemon rings.

6 Garnish with two slices of lemon on top of each piece and serve.

COOK'S TIPS
• You can also use smoked haddock instead of smoked salmon, if you like.
• If you don't have a mould or narrow container, use a container about 15cm/6in square. Cut the pressed sushi in half lengthways, then into 2cm/¾in slices. Cut the slices in half to make a nice canapé-type snack for a party.

MAKES ABOUT 12

INGREDIENTS
175g/6oz smoked salmon, thickly sliced
15ml/1 tbsp sake
15ml/1 tbsp water
30ml/2 tbsp shoyu
1 quantity su-meshi
1 lemon, thinly sliced into 6 × 3mm/⅛in rings

VARIATION
Try using other smoked fish for a stronger flavour, such as smoked haddock and smoked mackerel.

1 Lay the smoked salmon on a chopping board and sprinkle with a mixture of the sake, water and shoyu. Leave to marinate for an hour, then wipe dry with kitchen paper.

Per portion Energy 68kcal/286kJ; Protein 4.7g; Carbohydrate 10.2g, of which sugars 0.2g; Fat 0.7g, of which saturates 0.1g; Cholesterol 5mg; Calcium 6mg; Fibre 0g; Sodium 452mg.

JEWEL-BOX SUSHI

CHIRASHI IS THE MOST COMMON FORM OF SUSHI EATEN AT HOME IN JAPAN. A LACQUERED CONTAINER IS FILLED WITH SU-MESHI, AND VARIOUS COLOURFUL TOPPINGS ARE ARRANGED ON TOP.

<u>SERVES FOUR</u>

INGREDIENTS
2 eggs, beaten
vegetable oil, for frying
50g/2oz mangetouts
  (snow peas), trimmed
1 nori sheet
15ml/1 tbsp shoyu
15ml/1 tbsp wasabi paste from a
  tube, or the same amount of wasabi
  powder mixed with 10ml/2 tsp water
1¼ quantity su-meshi made with
  40ml/8 tsp sugar
salt
30–60ml/2–4 tbsp ikura, to garnish
For the fish and shellfish toppings
  115g/4oz very fresh tuna steak,
    skin removed
  90g/3½oz fresh squid, body only,
    cleaned and boned
  4 raw king prawns (jumbo shrimp),
    heads and shells removed,
    tails intact
For the shiitake
  8 dried shiitake mushrooms, soaked
    in 350ml/12fl oz/1½ cups water for
    4 hours
  15ml/1 tbsp caster (superfine) sugar
  60ml/4 tbsp mirin
  45ml/3 tbsp shoyu

1 Slice the tuna across the grain into 7.5 × 4cm/3 × 1½in pieces, 5mm/¼in thick, using a very sharp knife. Slice the squid crossways into 5mm/¼in strips. Place both on a tray, cover with clear film (plastic wrap) and chill.

2 Remove and discard the stalks from the shiitake. Pour the soaking water into a pan, add the shiitake and bring to the boil. Skim the surface and reduce the heat. Cook for 20 minutes, then add the sugar. Reduce the heat further and add the mirin and shoyu. Simmer until almost all the liquid has evaporated. Drain and slice very thinly. Set aside.

3 Insert a bamboo skewer into each prawn lengthways. Boil in salted water for 2 minutes. Drain and leave to cool.

4 Remove the skewers from the prawns. Cut open from the belly side but do not slice in two. Remove the black vein. Open out flat and add to the tray.

5 Beat the eggs in a mixing bowl and add a pinch of salt. Heat a little oil in a frying pan until it smokes. Wipe away the excess oil with kitchen paper. Add enough beaten egg to thinly cover the bottom of the frying pan while tilting the pan. Cook on a medium low heat until the edge is dry and starting to curl. Lift the omelette and turn over.

6 After 30 seconds, transfer to a chopping board. Use the remaining egg mixture to make several omelettes. Pile them up and roll them together into a tube. Slice very thinly to make strands.

7 Par-boil the mangetouts for 2 minutes in lightly salted water, then drain. Cut into 3mm/⅛in diagonal strips. Snip the nori into fine shreds using scissors. Mix with the shoyu and wasabi.

8 Divide half the su-meshi among four large rice bowls. Spread a quarter of the nori mixture over each bowl of su-meshi. Cover with the rest of the su-meshi. Flatten the surface with a wet spatula.

9 Sprinkle over egg strands to cover the surface completely. Arrange the tuna slices in a fan shape with a fan of shiitake on top. Place a prawn next to the tuna and arrange the squid strips in a heap on the other side. Arrange the mangetouts and ikura decoratively on top.

Per portion Energy 384kcal/1609kJ; Protein 23.1g; Carbohydrate 57.3g, of which sugars 7g; Fat 5g, of which saturates 1.3g; Cholesterol 203mg; Calcium 61mg; Fibre 0.4g; Sodium 1191mg.

RICE BALLS <u>WITH</u> FOUR FILLINGS

ONIGIRI, THE JAPANESE NAME FOR THIS DISH, MEANS HAND-MOULDED RICE. JAPANESE RICE IS IDEAL FOR MAKING RICE BALLS, WHICH ARE FILLED HERE WITH SALMON, MACKEREL, UMEBOSHI AND OLIVES. THE NORI COATING MAKES THEM EASY TO PICK UP WITH YOUR FINGERS.

SERVES FOUR

INGREDIENTS

50g/2oz salmon fillet, skinned
3 umeboshi, 50g/2oz in total weight
45ml/3 tbsp sesame seeds
2.5ml/½ tsp mirin
50g/2oz smoked mackerel fillet
2 nori sheets, each cut into
  8 strips
6 pitted black olives, wiped and
  finely chopped
fine salt
Japanese pickles, to serve

For the rice

450g/1lb/2¼ cups Japanese short
  grain rice
550ml/18fl oz/2½ cups water

1 To cook the rice, wash it thoroughly with cold water. Drain and put into a heavy pan. Pour in the water and leave for 30 minutes. Put the lid on tightly and bring the pan to the boil. Reduce the heat and simmer for 12 minutes. When you hear a crackling noise remove from the heat and leave to stand, covered, for about 15 minutes.

2 Stir carefully with a dampened rice paddle or wooden spatula to aerate the rice. Leave to cool for 30 minutes while you prepare the fillings. Thoroughly salt the salmon fillet and leave for at least 30 minutes.

3 Stone (pit) the umeboshi. With the back of a fork, mash them slightly. Mix with 15ml/1 tbsp of the sesame seeds and the mirin to make a rough paste.

4 Wash the salt from the salmon. Grill (broil) the salmon and smoked mackerel under a high heat. Using a fork, remove the skin and divide the fish into loose, chunky flakes. Keep the salmon and mackerel pieces separate.

5 Toast the remaining sesame seeds in a dry frying pan over a low heat until they start to pop.

6 Check the temperature of the rice. It should be still quite warm but not hot. To start moulding, you need a teacup and a bowl of cold water to wet your hands. Put the teacup and tablespoons for measuring into the water. Put fine salt into a small dish. Wipe a chopping board with a very wet dishtowel. Wash your hands thoroughly with unperfumed soap and dry.

7 Remove the teacup from the bowl and shake off excess water. Scoop about 30ml/2 tbsp rice into the teacup. With your fingers, make a well in the centre of the rice and put in a quarter of the salmon flakes. Cover the salmon with another 15ml/1 tbsp rice. Press well.

8 Wet your hands and sprinkle them with a pinch of salt. Rub it all over your palms. Turn the rice in the teacup out into one hand and squeeze the rice shape with both hands to make a densely packed flat ball.

9 Wrap the rice ball with a nori strip. Put on to the chopping board. Make three more balls using the remaining salmon, then make four balls using the smoked mackerel and another four balls using the umeboshi paste.

10 Scoop about 45ml/3 tbsp rice into the teacup. Mix in a quarter of the chopped olives. Press the rice with your fingers. Wet your hands with water and rub with a pinch of salt and a quarter of the toasted sesame seeds. Turn the teacup on to one hand and shape the rice mixture into a ball as above. The sesame seeds should stick to the rice. This time, do not wrap with nori. Repeat, making three more balls.

11 Serve one of each kind of rice ball on individual plates with a small helping of Japanese pickles.

Per portion Energy 548kcal/2288kJ; Protein 15.4g; Carbohydrate 90.8g, of which sugars 1g; Fat 13g, of which saturates 2.1g; Cholesterol 19mg; Calcium 108mg; Fibre 1.3g; Sodium 243mg.

SU-MESHI IN TOFU BAGS

ABURA-AGE (FRIED THIN TOFU) IS DIFFERENT TO OTHER TOFU PRODUCTS. IT CAN BE OPENED UP LIKE A BAG, AND IN THIS RECIPE IT'S SERVED WITH SOY SAUCE-BASED SEASONINGS AND FILLED WITH SU-MESHI.

SERVES FOUR

INGREDIENTS

8 fresh abura-age or 275g/10oz can
  ready-to-use abura-age (contains
  16 halves)
900ml/1½ pints/3¾ cups second
  dashi stock, or the same amount of
  water and 10ml/2 tsp dashi-no-moto
90ml/6 tbsp caster (superfine) sugar
30ml/2 tbsp sake
70ml/4½ tbsp shoyu
generous 1 quantity su-meshi, made
  with 40ml/8 tsp sugar
30ml/2 tbsp toasted white
  sesame seeds
gari, to garnish

1 Par-boil the fresh abura-age in rapidly boiling water for about 1 minute. Drain under running water and leave to cool. Squeeze the excess water out gently. Cut each sheet in half and carefully pull open the cut end to make bags.

2 If you are using canned abura-age, drain the liquid.

3 Lay the abura-age bags in a large pan. Pour in the dashi stock to cover and bring to the boil. Reduce the heat and cover, then simmer for 20 minutes.

4 Add the sugar in three batches during this time, shaking the pan to dissolve it. Simmer for a further 15 minutes.

5 Add the sake. Shake the pan again, and add the shoyu in three batches. Simmer until almost all the liquid has evaporated. Transfer the abura-age to a wide sieve (strainer) and leave to drain.

6 Mix the su-meshi and sesame seeds in a wet mixing bowl. Wet your hands and take a little su-meshi. Shape it into a rectangular block.

7 Open one abura-age bag and insert the block. Press the edges together to close the bag. Once all the bags have been filled, place them on a large serving plate or individual plates with the bottom of the bag on top. Garnish with gari.

COOK'S TIP
To open the abura-age without breaking them, place them on a chopping board and, with the palm of your hand, rub them gently on the board. Then pull apart little by little from the cut end and work towards the bottom. When fully open, put your finger inside to make sure the corners are opened completely.

Per portion Energy 495kcal/2073kJ; Protein 20.5g; Carbohydrate 65.2g, of which sugars 34.5g; Fat 16.7g, of which saturates 0.6g; Cholesterol 0mg; Calcium 1093mg; Fibre 0.6g; Sodium 13mg.

SALMON SASHIMI

THIS JAPANESE SPECIALITY — SLICED RAW FISH — EMPLOYS THE CUTTING TECHNIQUE KNOWN AS HIRA ZUKURI. *THE IS SERVED WITH WASABI — JAPANESE HORSERADISH — AND SOY SAUCE.*

SERVES 4

INGREDIENTS

    2 fresh salmon fillets, skinned and
        any stray bones removed, total
        weight about 400g/14oz
    50g/2oz mooli
    shiso leaves
    Japanese soy sauce and wasabi
        paste, to serve

1 Place the salmon fillets in a freezer for 10 minutes. The salmon fillets will firm up, and be much easier to cut. Remove the fillets from the freezer, then lay them skinned side up with the thick end to your right and away from you.

2 Using a long sharp knife, slice the salmon carefully towards you with the knife slightly tilted to the left. Starting the cut from the point of the knife, then slide the slice away from the fillet, to the right. Always slice from the far side towards you.

3 Finely shred or grate the mooli and place in a bowl of cold water. Leave the mooli to soak in the water for 5 minutes, then drain well.

4 Arrange the salmon in an attractive way on a serving platter, or divide the salmon among four serving plates.

5 Give guests their own plate, together with a little of the shredded mooli and some shiso leaves. The sliced salmon is dipped in soy sauce and wasabi paste, then eaten.

COOK'S TIP
Salmon and tuna are among the most popular choices for sashimi, although almost any type of fish can be used. If you are making sashimi for the first time, choose salmon or tuna and make sure you buy from a reputable fishmonger where you can be sure the fish is absolutely fresh.

Per portion Energy 183kcal/763kJ; Protein 20.4g; Carbohydrate 0.6g, of which sugars 0.5g; Fat 11g, of which saturates 1.9g; Cholesterol 50mg; Calcium 24mg; Fibre 0.1g; Sodium 314mg.

SASHIMI MORIAWASE

THE ARRANGEMENT OF A DISH OF SASHIMI IS AS IMPORTANT AS THE FRESHNESS OF THE FISH. CHOOSE TWO TO FIVE KINDS OF FISH FROM EACH GROUP AND ONLY USE THE FRESHEST CATCH OF THE DAY.

SERVES FOUR

INGREDIENTS
500g/1¼lb total of fish from the
    4 groups
Group A, skinned fillets (cut lengthways
if possible)
    Maguro akami: lean tuna
    Maguro toro: fatty tuna
    Sake: salmon
    Kajiki: swordfish
    Tai: sea bream or red snapper
    Suzuki: sea bass
    Hamachi: yellowtail
    Katsuo: skipjack tuna
Group B, skinned fillets
    Hirame: flounder or sole
    Karei: halibut or turbot
Group C
    Ika: squid body, cleaned, boned
       and skinned
    Tako: cooked octopus tentacles
    Hotate-gai: scallop (the coral, black
       stomach and frill removed)
Group D
    Aka-ebi: sweet prawns (shrimp),
       peeled, heads can be removed,
       tails intact
    Uni: sea urchin
    Ikura: salted salmon roe
To serve
    1 fresh daikon, peeled and cut into
       6cm/2½in lengths
    1 Japanese or salad cucumber
    4 shiso leaves
    2 limes, halved (optional)
    45ml/3 tbsp wasabi paste from a
       tube, or the same amount of
       wasabi powder mixed with
       20ml/4 tsp water
    1 bottle tamari shoyu

1 Make the tsuma (the daikon strands). Slice the daikon pieces very thinly lengthways, then cut the slices into very thin strips lengthways. Rinse thoroughly under running water, drain and put in the refrigerator.

2 Prepare the cucumber. Trim and cut into 3cm/1¼in lengths, then cut each cucumber cylinder in half lengthways.

3 Place the cucumber on a chopping board, flat-side down. Make very fine cuts across each piece, leaving the slices joined together at one side. Then, gently squeeze the cucumber together between your fingers so that the slices fan out sideways. Set them aside and cover with clear film (plastic wrap).

4 Slice the fish. Group A needs *hira giri*, a thick cut: trim the fillet into a long rectangular shape. Skin-side up, cut into 1cm/½in thick slices with the grain.

5 Group B needs *usu zukuri*, very thin slices. Place the fillet horizontally to you on its skinned side. Hold the knife almost horizontally to the fillet, shave it very thinly across the grain.

6 Group C fish each require different cutting styles. Slice the cooked octopus diagonally into 5mm/¼in thick ovals. Slice the scallops in half horizontally. If they are thicker than 4cm/1½in, slice into three.

7 Cut open the squid body and turn to lie on its skinned side, horizontally to you. Score lines 5mm/¼in apart over the surface, then cut into 5mm/¼in strips. Group D is all ready to arrange.

8 Arrange the sashimi creatively. First, take a handful of daikon and heap up on to the serving plate a large mound or several small mounds. Then, base your design on the following basic rules:
Group A and C Put each slice of fish side by side like domino pieces. You can lay them on a shiso leaf.
Group B Use the thin, soft slices to make a rose shape, or overlap the slices slightly, so that the texture of the plate can be seen through them.
Group D Place the prawns by their tails, 2–3 at a time, in a bundle. If the sea urchins come tightly packed in a little box, try to get them out in one piece. The salmon roe can be heaped on thin cucumber slices or scooped into a lime case, made from a half lime, flesh removed. Fill the case with some daikon and place the roe on top.

9 Arrange the cucumber fans, heaped wasabi paste and shiso leaves to perfect your design. Serve immediately. Pour some shoyu into four dishes and mix in the wasabi. As the sauce is quite salty, only dip the edge of the sashimi into it.

Per portion Energy 265kcal/1101kJ; Protein 27g; Carbohydrate 5.7g, of which sugars 5.2g; Fat 15g, of which saturates 2.6g; Cholesterol 64mg; Calcium 61mg; Fibre 1.5g; Sodium 1061mg.

SCALLOPS SASHIMI <u>IN</u> MUSTARD SAUCE

THIS IS A TYPICAL SERVING SIZE FOR LOTS OF JAPANESE DISHES AS A MEAL USUALLY CONSISTS OF AT LEAST THREE DISHES OR MORE. IN TRADITIONAL FORMAL DINING, KAISEKI, MORE THAN A DOZEN SMALL DISHES ARE SERVED ONE AFTER ANOTHER AND THIS ELEGANT DISH CAN BE ONE OF THEM.

2 Put the dried chrysanthemum or the flower petals in a sieve (strainer). Pour hot water all over, and leave to drain for a while. When cool, gently squeeze the excess water out. Set aside and repeat with the watercress.

3 Mix together all the ingredients for the dressing in a small bowl. Add the sliced scallops 5 minutes before serving and mix them well in the dressing without breaking them. Add the flower petals and watercress, then transfer to four small bowls. Serve cold. Add a little more shoyu, if required.

COOK'S TIPS
• Any white fish sashimi can be used in this dish.
• Substitute the watercress with the finely chopped green part of spring onions (scallions).
• Do not attempt to pick chrysanthemums from your garden, as the edible species are different to ornamental ones. Fresh edible chrysanthemums and other edible flowers are now increasingly available at specialist Japanese food stores, or look for dried ones in Asian stores.

SERVES FOUR

INGREDIENTS
8 scallops or 16 queen scallops, cleaned and coral removed
¼ dried sheet chrysanthemum petals (sold as kiku nori) or a handful of edible flower petals such as yellow nasturtium
4 bunches of watercress, leaves only
For the dressing
30ml/2 tbsp shoyu
5ml/1 tsp sake
10ml/2 tsp English (hot) mustard

1 Slice the scallops in three horizontally then cut in half crossways. If you use queen scallops, slice in two horizontally.

Per portion Energy 62kcal/262kJ; Protein 10.5g; Carbohydrate 2.5g, of which sugars 1g; Fat 1g, of which saturates 0.3g; Cholesterol 19mg; Calcium 58mg; Fibre 0.4g; Sodium 852mg.

LEMON SOLE <u>AND</u> FRESH OYSTER SALAD

*OYSTERS, FLAVOURED WITH A RICE-VINEGAR DRESSING, TASTE WONDERFUL WITH LEMON SOLE SASHIMI.
IN JAPAN, MENUS ARE BASED ON WHAT FISH WAS FRESHLY CAUGHT THAT DAY, NOT THE OTHER WAY
AROUND. THIS DISH IS CALLED HIRAME KONBU JIME TO NAMA-GAKI NO SALADA.*

SERVES FOUR

INGREDIENTS
   1 very fresh lemon sole, skinned and
     filleted into 4 pieces
   105ml/7 tbsp rice vinegar
   dashi-konbu, in 4 pieces, big enough
     to cover the fillets
   50g/2oz Japanese cucumber, ends
     trimmed, or ordinary salad
     cucumber with seeds removed
   50g/2oz celery sticks, strings removed
   450g/1lb large broad (fava)
     beans, podded
   1 lime, ½ thinly sliced
   60ml/4 tbsp walnut oil
   seeds from ½ pomegranate
   salt
For the oysters
   15ml/1 tbsp rice vinegar
   30ml/2 tbsp shoyu
   15ml/1 tbsp sake
   12 large fresh oysters, opened
   25g/1oz daikon or radishes, peeled
     and very finely grated
   8 chives

1 Sprinkle salt on the sole fillets. Cover
and cool in the refrigerator for an hour.

2 Mix the rice vinegar and a similar
amount of water in a bowl. Wash the
fish fillets in the mixture, then drain
well. Cut each fillet in half lengthways.

3 Lay one piece of dashi-konbu on a
work surface. Place a pair of sole fillets,
skinned-sides together, on it, then lay
another piece of konbu on top. Cover all
the fillets like this and chill for 3 hours.

4 Halve the cucumber crossways and
slice thinly lengthways. Then slice again
diagonally into 2cm/¾in wide pieces.
Do the same for the celery. Sprinkle the
cucumber with salt and leave to soften
for 30–60 minutes. Gently squeeze to
remove the moisture. Rinse if it tastes
too salty, but drain well.

5 Boil the broad beans in lightly salted
water for 15 minutes, or until soft. Drain
and cool under running water, then peel
off the skins. Sprinkle with salt.

6 Mix the rice vinegar, shoyu and sake
for the oysters in a small bowl.

7 Slice the sole very thinly with a sharp
knife. Remove the slightly chewy dashi-
konbu first, if you prefer.

8 Place some pieces of cucumber and
celery in a small mound in the centre of
four serving plates, then lay lime slices
on top. Garnish with some chopped
chives. Place the oysters to one side of
the cucumber, topped with a few broad
beans, then season with 5ml/1 tsp of
the vinegar mix and 10ml/2 tsp grated
daikon or radishes. Arrange the sole
sashimi on the other side and drizzle
walnut oil and a little lime juice on top.
Add pomegranate seeds and serve.

Per portion Energy 264kcal/1105kJ; Protein 22.7g; Carbohydrate 14.8g, of which sugars 1.9g; Fat 13.1g, of which saturates 1.3g; Cholesterol 56mg; Calcium 143mg; Fibre 7.6g; Sodium 295mg.

SNACKS &
LIGHT BITES

Snacks eaten on the street are commonplace and there are vendors to

satisfy every desire of busy urban dwellers. A popular snack both on

the street and at home in the colder months is the tasty matang, or

Sweet Potato with Almond Syrup. Other tempting traditional snacks

include crispy light and crunchy Tempura, Rolled Omelette,

Pan-fried Kimchi Fritters and Deep-fried Tofu Balls.

Left: Fishcake Kebabs in Seaweed Soup; **Above:** Vegetarian Tempura

SLOW-COOKED DAIKON

Freshly dug daikon is very juicy, and it is praised as the king of winter vegetables in Japan. In this dish, known as Furo Fuki Daikon, the daikon is cooked slowly and served with tangy miso sauce. The rice absorbs the bitter juices, and is then discarded.

SERVES FOUR

INGREDIENTS

- 1kg/2¼lb daikon, cut into 4 × 5cm/ 2in thick discs
- 15ml/1 tbsp rice (any kind except fragrant Thai or basmati)
- 100ml/3fl oz/scant ½ cup hatcho miso
- 60ml/4 tbsp caster (superfine) sugar
- 120ml/4fl oz/½ cup mirin
- 20cm/8in square dried konbu
- rind of ¼ yuzu, shaved with a zester, to serve (optional)

1 Peel the skin from the daikon and shave the top and bottom edge of each section. Plunge into a bowl of cold water. Drain and place flat in a pan.

2 Pour in enough cold water to come 3cm/1¼in above the daikon. Add the rice and put on a high heat. When it comes to the boil, lower the heat and cook for a further 30 minutes.

3 Meanwhile, mix the miso and sugar in a pan and add the mirin, a tablespoonful at a time, to loosen the mixture. Over a medium heat, heat the miso mixture, stirring constantly. When the mixture thickens, turn the heat to very low. Cook, stirring, until the miso sauce is thick enough to stick to a spoon when you lift it from the pan. Remove from the heat and keep warm.

4 When the daikon is cooked (to test, insert a cocktail stick (toothpick): it should go in easily), gently scoop the daikon discs, one by one, on to a flat-bottomed sieve or a plate. Rinse each disc with water, to remove all the bitter juices. Discard the water and rice in the pan and wash the pan thoroughly.

5 Wipe the konbu with a wet cloth, and place in the bottom of the cleaned pan. Replace the daikon and pour in enough water to just cover. Over a very low heat, warm the daikon for 15 minutes to absorb the flavour of the konbu.

6 Place the daikon in individual bowls. Scoop out a little at the top, if you wish, then pour 15–20ml/3–4 tsp of the miso mixture on each piece and serve garnished with yuzu strips, if using. Serve with a spoon and eat it as you would a dessert.

Per portion Energy 147kcal/622kJ; Protein 2.5g; Carbohydrate 34.9g, of which sugars 31.8g; Fat 0.5g, of which saturates 0.3g; Cholesterol 0mg; Calcium 64mg; Fibre 2.3g; Sodium 919mg.

SPINACH WITH TOASTED SESAME SEEDS

O-HITASHI HAS BEEN SERVED AS A SIDE DISH ON JAPANESE DINING TABLES FOR CENTURIES. SEASONAL GREEN VEGETABLES ARE SIMPLY BLANCHED AND COOLED AND FORMED INTO LITTLE TOWERS. WITH A LITTLE HELP FROM SOY SAUCE AND SESAME SEEDS, THEY REVEAL THEIR TRUE FLAVOUR.

SERVES FOUR

INGREDIENTS
    450g/1lb fresh spinach
    30ml/2 tbsp shoyu
    30ml/2 tbsp water
    15ml/1 tbsp sesame seeds
    salt

1 Blanch young spinach leaves in lightly salted boiling water for 15 seconds. For Japanese-type spinach, hold the leafy part and slip the stems into the pan. After 15 seconds, drop in the leaves and cook for 20 seconds.

2 Drain immediately and place the spinach under running water. Squeeze out all the excess water by hand. Now what looked like a large amount of spinach has become a ball, roughly the size of an orange. Mix the shoyu and water, then pour on to the spinach. Mix well and leave to cool.

3 Meanwhile, put the sesame seeds in a dry frying pan and cook on a low heat. Continue to stir or toss the sesame seeds until they start to pop.

COOK'S TIP
Japanese spinach, the long-leaf type with the stalks and pink root intact, is best, but you can use ordinary young spinach leaves, or any soft and deep-green salad vegetables – such as watercress, rocket (arugula), lamb's lettuce – instead of the spinach, if you wish.

4 Once the sesame seeds are golden in colour, remove them from the heat and leave to cool.

5 Drain the cooked spinach and squeeze out the excess sauce with your hands. Line up the spinach in the same direction on a chopping board, then form it into a log shape of about 4cm/1½in in diameter.

6 Squeeze the log shaped spinach again to make it firm. With a sharp knife, cut it across into four cylinders.

7 Place the spinach cylinders on a large plate or individual dishes. Sprinkle with the toasted sesame seeds and a little salt, to taste, and serve.

Per portion Energy 54kcal/222kJ; Protein 4.1g; Carbohydrate 2.5g, of which sugars 2.3g; Fat 3.1g, of which saturates 0.4g; Cholesterol 0mg; Calcium 218mg; Fibre 2.7g; Sodium 692mg.

ROLLED OMELETTE

EASIER TO MAKE THAN IT LOOKS, ALL THAT IS NEEDED TO MAKE THIS LIGHT AND SWEET OMELETTE IS A SUSHI ROLLING MAT, WRAPPED IN CLEAR FILM. USE A ROUND OR RECTANGULAR FRYING PAN.

4 Keeping the rolled omelette in the pan, push back to the farthest side from you. Oil the empty part of the pan again. Pour one-third of the egg mixture in at the empty side. Lift up the first roll with chopsticks, and let the egg mixture run underneath. When it looks half set, roll the omelette around the first roll to make a single roll with many layers.

SERVES FOUR

INGREDIENTS
   45ml/3 tbsp second dashi stock, or
      the same amount of water and a
      pinch of dashi-no-moto
   30ml/2 tbsp mirin
   15ml/1 tbsp caster (superfine) sugar
   5ml/1 tsp shoyu
   5ml/1 tsp salt
   6 large (US extra large) eggs, beaten
   vegetable oil
For the garnish
   2.5cm/1in daikon
   4 shiso leaves (optional)
   shoyu

1 Warm the dashi stock in a small pan. Mix in the mirin, sugar, shoyu and salt. Add to the beaten eggs and stir well.

2 Heat a omelette pan or a rectangular Japanese pan over a medium heat. Soak kitchen paper in a little oil and wipe the pan to grease it.

3 Pour in a quarter of the egg mixture. Tilt the pan to coat it evenly. When the omelette starts to set, roll it up towards you with chopsticks or a spatula.

5 Move the roll gently on to a sushi rolling mat covered with clear film (plastic wrap). Roll the omelette firmly into the roller mat. Leave to stand rolled up for 5 minutes. Repeat the whole process again to make another roll.

6 Grate the daikon with a daikon grater or a very fine grater. Alternatively, use a food processor. Squeeze out the juice with your hand.

7 Cut the rolled omelettes into 2.5cm/1in slices crossways.

8 Lay the shiso leaves, if using, on four small plates and place a few slices of the omelette on top. Put a small heap of grated daikon to one side and add a few drops of shoyu to the top.

Per portion Energy 205kcal/854kJ; Protein 9.5g; Carbohydrate 11.9g, of which sugars 11.9g; Fat 13.8g, of which saturates 3g; Cholesterol 285mg; Calcium 49mg; Fibre 0g; Sodium 686mg.

GRILLED VEGETABLE STICKS

FOR THIS JAPANESE KEBAB-STYLE DISH, MADE WITH TOFU, KONNYAKU AND AUBERGINE, YOU WILL NEED 40 BAMBOO SKEWERS, SOAKED IN WATER OVERNIGHT TO PREVENT THEM BURNING WHEN GRILLED.

SERVES FOUR

INGREDIENTS
1 × 285g/10¼oz packet tofu block
1 × 250g/9oz packet konnyaku
2 small aubergines (eggplants)
25ml/1½ tbsp toasted sesame oil
For the yellow and green sauces
    45ml/3 tbsp shiro miso
    15ml/1 tbsp caster (superfine) sugar
    5 young spinach leaves
    2.5ml/½ tsp sansho
    salt
For the red sauce
    15ml/1 tbsp aka miso
    5ml/1 tsp caster (superfine) sugar
    5ml/1 tsp mirin
To garnish
    pinch of white poppy seeds
    15ml/1 tbsp toasted sesame seeds

1 Drain the liquid from the tofu packet and wrap the tofu in three layers of kitchen paper. Set a chopping board on top to press out the remaining liquid. Leave for 30 minutes until the excess liquid has been absorbed by the kitchen paper. Cut into eight 7.5 × 2 × 1cm/ 3 × ¾ × ½in slices.

2 Drain the liquid from the konnyaku. Cut it in half and put in a small pan with enough water to cover. Bring to the boil and cook for about 5 minutes. Drain and cut it into eight 6 × 2 × 1cm/ 2½ × ¾ × ½in slices.

3 Cut the aubergines into two length-ways, then halve the thickness to make four flat slices. Soak in cold water for 15 minutes. Drain and pat dry.

4 To make the yellow sauce, mix the shiro miso and sugar in a pan, then cook over a low heat, stirring to dissolve the sugar. Remove from the heat. Place half the sauce in a small bowl.

5 Blanch the spinach leaves in rapidly boiling water with a pinch of salt for 30 seconds and drain, then cool under running water. Squeeze out the water and chop finely.

6 Transfer to a mortar and pound to a paste using a pestle. Mix the paste and sansho pepper into the bowl of yellow sauce to make the green sauce.

7 Put all the red sauce ingredients in a small pan and cook over a low heat, stirring constantly, until the sugar has dissolved. Remove from the heat.

8 Pierce the slices of tofu, konnyaku and aubergine with two bamboo skewers each. Heat the grill (broiler) to high. Brush the aubergine slices with sesame oil and grill (broil) for 7–8 minutes each side. Turn several times.

9 Grill the konnyaku and tofu slices for 3–5 minutes each side, or until lightly browned. Remove them from the heat but keep the grill hot.

10 Spread the red miso sauce on the aubergine slices. Spread one side of the tofu slices with green sauce and one side of the konnyaku with the yellow miso sauce from the pan. Grill the slices for 1–2 minutes. Sprinkle the aubergines with poppy seeds. Sprinkle the konnyaku with sesame seeds and serve all together.

Per portion Energy 178kcal/742kJ; Protein 12.9g; Carbohydrate 9.3g, of which sugars 8.6g; Fat 10.2g, of which saturates 1.4g; Cholesterol 0mg; Calcium 761mg; Fibre 1.9g; Sodium 17mg.

VEGETABLE BUCKWHEAT CRÊPE WITH MUSTARD DIP

THIS HISTORIC DISH CELEBRATES THE RANGE OF VEGETABLES NATIVE TO KOREA. THE INGREDIENTS FORM A MEDLEY OF TASTES AND COLOURS, ALL WRAPPED IN A BUCKWHEAT CRÊPE. SLICING THE CRÊPE BEFORE SERVING CREATES BITESIZE PIECES REMINISCENT OF JAPANESE MAKI ROLL.

SERVES FOUR

INGREDIENTS
    50g/2oz minari or watercress
    50g/2oz/½ cup beansprouts
    400g/14oz Chinese white radish,
       finely sliced
    25g/1oz dried shiitake mushrooms
    1 garlic clove, crushed
    5ml/1 tsp spring onion (scallion),
       finely chopped
    5ml/1 tsp soy sauce
    5 red dates, finely chopped
    vegetable oil, for cooking
    1 small carrot
For seasoning
    sesame oil
    sesame seeds
    salt
    sugar
For the buckwheat crêpe
    115g/4oz/1 cup buckwheat flour
    50g/2oz/1 cup wholemeal
       (whole-wheat) flour
    1 egg white, lightly whisked
    5ml/1 tsp salt
For the dip
    15ml/1 tbsp Korean mustard powder
       or German mustard
    15ml/1 tbsp vinegar
    7.5ml/1½ tbsp sugar
    2.5ml/½ tsp soy sauce

1 Bring a pan of water to the boil and add a pinch of salt. Add the watercress and beansprouts, bring back to the boil, then immediately drain them and rinse under cold water. Drain thoroughly, place in a bowl and season with a little sesame oil. Sprinkle lightly with sesame seeds, then set aside.

COOK'S TIPS
• When turning crêpes, slide a knife under the edge to loosen. Then move a spatula as close to the centre as possible and flip to the other side.
• To keep crêpes warm, cover with plastic wrap (clear film) and a thick towel.

2 Prepare another pan of salted boiling water. Add the Chinese radish and boil for about 10 minutes, until cooked and tender. Drain, place the radish in a bowl and season with salt, sesame oil and sesame seeds, then set aside.

3 Soak the shiitake mushrooms in warm water to cover for about 15 minutes, until they have softened.

4 Drain and thinly slice the mushrooms, discarding their stalks. Mix them with the garlic, spring onions and soy sauce. Season with a pinch each of salt and sugar, a little sesame oil and a sprinkling of sesame seeds.

5 Heat a frying pan or wok. Add a little vegetable oil and stir-fry the mushrooms until they are cooked and tender, then remove from the pan and set aside.

6 To make the crêpes, sift the buckwheat and wholemeal flours into a bowl. Add the egg white and a little water, stirring gently.

7 Continue to stir and add more water to make a smooth batter. Leave to rest for 30 minutes before cooking.

8 Heat a pan and pour in a little vegetable oil. Tilt the pan to coat in oil, then pour in a ladleful of batter. Tilt the pan to spread the batter thinly and cook for 30 seconds, until set and browned.

9 Turn the crêpe and cook on the second side. Then remove from the pan and place on a plate. Cover loosely with foil and keep hot in a warm oven. Cook the remaining batter to make additional crêpes.

10 Place a little of each vegetable and some chopped dates in each crêpe and roll up. Slice into bitesize pieces and arrange on a serving platter.

11 To make the mustard dip, mix the mustard powder, vinegar and sugar with the soy sauce and 15ml/1 tbsp water. Transfer to individual dishes and serve with the crêpes.

Per portion Energy 167kcal/699kJ; Protein 6.3g; Carbohydrate 34.9g, of which sugars 2.8g; Fat 1.2g, of which saturates 0.2g; Cholesterol 0mg; Calcium 71mg; Fibre 3g; Sodium 410mg.

SWEET POTATO <u>WITH</u> ALMOND SYRUP

THIS SIMPLE YET INTERESTING KOREAN DISH, CALLED MATANG, IS THOUGHT TO HAVE ITS ORIGINS IN CHINESE COOKING. DEEP-FRIED SWEET POTATO IS COATED IN A SYRUP CONTAINING ALMONDS AND SPRINKLED WITH BLACK SESAME SEEDS, CREATING A DISH THAT IS AT ONCE SAVOURY AND SWEET.

SERVES FOUR

INGREDIENTS

3 sweet potatoes, peeled
115g/4oz/½ cup light muscovado (brown) sugar
2 almonds, crushed
vegetable oil, for deep-frying
black sesame seeds, to garnish

1 Preheat the oven to 200°C/400°F/Gas 6. Cut the sweet potatoes into bitesize slices, then soak them in cold water for 15 minutes to help remove the starch. Drain, and place the potato slices on a baking sheet. Cook in the oven for 20 minutes, or until they have softened slightly. The potato slices should be parboiled rather than cooked through.

2 Put the sugar in a pan with 120ml/4fl oz/½ cup water. Simmer over a medium heat until it has formed a sticky syrup.

3 Remove the pan from the heat and add the crushed almonds.

4 Fill a wok or medium heavy pan one-third full of vegetable oil and heat over a high heat to 170°C/340°F, or when a small piece of bread dropped into the oil browns in 15 seconds.

5 Add the sweet potato. Deep-fry for about 5 minutes, or until golden brown, and then remove from the pan and drain any excess oil on kitchen paper.

6 Combine the potatoes with the syrup, coating each piece evenly. Transfer to a shallow serving dish and garnish with black sesame seeds before serving.

VARIATION
Create a more Western-shape fried potato by cutting the sweet potato into long thin strips, about 2.5cm/¼in thick.

Per portion Energy 667kcal/2819kJ; Protein 5g; Carbohydrate 124.4g, of which sugars 77.4g; Fat 20.2g, of which saturates 2.5g; Cholesterol 0mg; Calcium 115mg; Fibre 7.6g; Sodium 124mg.

SWEET CINNAMON PANCAKES

A CLASSIC KOREAN STREET SNACK, THESE SOFT, SWEET PANCAKE TREATS ARE ADAPTED FROM A CLASSIC CHINESE RECIPE. THEY ARE QUICK AND EASY TO MAKE AND ARE ALWAYS POPULAR WITH CHILDREN. THEY ARE ENJOYED PARTICULARLY DURING THE WINTER, SERVED WARM ON A COLD DAY.

MAKES TEN

INGREDIENTS
    15ml/1 tbsp sugar
    5ml/1 tsp dried yeast
    120ml/4fl oz/½ cup milk
    175g/6oz/1½ cups plain (all-
        purpose) flour
    50g/2oz/½ cup glutinous rice
        flour
    2 tsp salt
For the filling
    30ml/2 tbsp peanuts
    60ml/4 tbsp sugar
    5ml/1 tsp ground cinnamon

1 Pour 120ml/4fl oz/½ cup lukewarm water into a bowl and stir in the sugar. Sprinkle in the yeast and leave to stand, without stirring, for 5 minutes to allow the yeast to begin fermenting.

2 Sift the plain flour and rice flour together into a large mixing bowl. Add the salt, yeast liquid and milk, then mix the ingredients into a firm dough and knead this thoroughly on a lightly floured surface until it becomes smooth and elastic.

3 Replace the dough in the bowl, cover it with a board or a dish towel and leave at room temperature or in a warm place for about 3 hours, until risen and doubled in size.

4 To make the filling, grind the peanuts finely in a food processor and then mix them with the brown and white sugars and the cinnamon.

5 Sprinkle a plate with a little flour. Divide the dough into ten portions. Flatten one piece on your hand, then make a depression in the centre with one finger. Place 30ml/2 tbsp filling on the middle of the dough and wrap the edges around to enclose the filling completely, shaping the dough back into a ball. Place on the plate. Repeat with the remaining dough and filling.

6 Pour a little vegetable oil into a frying pan and heat over a medium heat. Add a ball of dough and press it down with the back of a wooden spoon to flatten it into a round pancake. Prepare three or four at once (depending on the pan size). Fry on both sides until golden, then transfer to a warm plate. Keep hot in a warm oven while cooking the remaining pancakes. Serve warm.

Per portion Energy 119kcal/506kJ; Protein 4.9g; Carbohydrate 20.5g, of which sugars 2.7g; Fat 2.6g, of which saturates 0.9g; Cholesterol 35mg; Calcium 98mg; Fibre 0.7g; Sodium 34mg.

MUNG BEAN SOUFFLÉ PANCAKES

These mung bean pancakes, called bindaetuk in Korean, are deliciously light. Filled with a combination of meat and vegetables, the flavours of rice wine and garlic in the marinade are complemented by the sharpness of the soy and vinegar in the dipping sauce.

SERVES TWO TO THREE

INGREDIENTS

   375g/13oz/2 cups mung beans,
     soaked overnight in cold water
   15ml/1 tbsp pine nuts
   30ml/2 tbsp sweet rice flour
   75g/3oz beef flank, sliced
   200g/7oz prawns (shrimp), peeled
     and finely chopped
   15ml/1 tbsp vegetable oil, plus
     extra for shallow-frying
   1 button (white) mushroom,
     thinly sliced
   ½ onion, thinly sliced
   ½ cucumber, seeded and sliced
   ½ cup cabbage *kimchi* (see page
     65), thinly sliced
   3 spring onions (scallions),
     thinly sliced
   1 red chilli, shredded
   salt and ground black pepper
For the marinade
   5ml/1 tsp mirin or rice wine
   2.5ml/½ tsp grated fresh root ginger
   5ml/1 tsp dark soy sauce
   1 garlic clove, crushed
   2.5ml/½ tsp sesame seeds
   5ml/1 tsp sesame oil
   ground black pepper
For the dipping sauce
   60ml/4 tbsp dark soy sauce
   10ml/2 tsp rice vinegar
   1 spring onion (scallion),
     finely chopped

1 Drain the mung beans and return them to the bowl (without any water). Roll the beans between the palms of your hands to remove the skins. Add plenty of water and the skins will float. Skim off and discard these skins. Rinse the beans thoroughly.

2 Place the peeled beans in a food processor or blender with the pine nuts and pour in 120ml/4fl oz/½ cup water. Blend well until the mixture becomes a thick, coarse milky paste.

3 Transfer the bean paste to a large bowl and then add the rice flour and 5ml/1 tsp salt. Gradually mix the flour and salt into the bean paste until it is thoroughly incorporated.

4 Put the beef into a large bowl. Pour over the mirin or rice wine. Add the ginger, soy sauce, garlic, sesame seeds and oil for the marinade, with black pepper to taste. Mix well to coat all the pieces of beef. Cover, refrigerate and leave to marinate for about 20 minutes, to allow the beef to absorb and develop all the flavours.

5 Season the prawns with salt and pepper and set aside. Combine all the dipping sauce ingredients in a small serving bowl and set aside.

6 Coat a frying pan with vegetable oil and heat over a medium heat. Add the beef, mushroom and onion, and stir-fry until the meat has browned. Next, add the cucumber, cabbage kimchi and spring onions. Toss the ingredients in the pan and remove from the heat.

7 Heat a little oil in a frying pan and add a spoonful of the bean paste, spreading it into a small pancake. Spoon a little of the beef mixture on to the middle of the pancake, with some shredded chilli and a spoonful of chopped prawns. Use a spatula to press the ingredients flat on to the pancake, and fry until golden underneath. Turn and cook until golden on the second side.

8 Make pancakes until the batter and topping mixtures are finished. Arrange the fritters on a large serving platter and serve with the soy dipping sauce.

Per portion Energy 492kcal/2070kJ; Protein 38.2g; Carbohydrate 55.4g, of which sugars 6.9g; Fat 14.2g, of which saturates 2.2g; Cholesterol 108mg; Calcium 175mg; Fibre 11.7g; Sodium 1867mg.

VEGETABLE FRITTERS

THESE LIGHT AND CRUNCHY VEGETABLE FRITTERS ARE EQUALLY GOOD AS AN APPETIZER OR AS A QUICK SNACK ON THE GO. SIMPLE TO PREPARE AND EASY TO COOK, THEY ARE WONDERFULLY APPEALING AS THEY EMERGE GOLDEN BROWN FROM THE FRYING PAN.

SERVES FOUR

INGREDIENTS

    1 potato, thinly sliced
    1 small carrot, thinly sliced
    ½ small white onion, sliced
    ½ courgette (zucchini), thinly sliced
    1 red chilli, seeded and sliced
    salt and ground black pepper
    vegetable oil, for cooking
For the batter
    115g/4oz/1 cup plain
      (all-purpose) flour
    45ml/3 tbsp cornflour (cornstarch)
    1 egg, beaten
    5ml/1 tsp salt
For the dip
    30ml/2 tbsp dark soy sauce
    15ml/1 tbsp fish stock
    15ml/1 tbsp Chinese white
      radish, grated
    5ml/1 tsp vinegar
    5ml/1 tsp sesame seeds

1 To make the batter, sift the flour and cornflour into a bowl. Make a well in the middle and add the beaten egg with 250ml/8fl oz/1 cup water.

2 Blend the egg, water and salt with a wire whisk until smooth. Then gradually work in the flour mixture until it combines in a smooth batter. The batter should be thick enough to hold the vegetables together but it should still pour slowly from a ladle.

3 Place the potato, carrot, onion, courgette and chilli in a bowl. Mix them together well, then pour in the batter and mix it into the vegetables, adding a small amount of seasoning.

4 For the dip, mix the soy sauce, stock, white radish, vinegar and sesame seeds. Then set this aside to allow the flavours to mingle.

5 Heat a little vegetable oil in a frying pan or wok over a medium heat. Ladle three or four small portions of the fritter mixture into the pan (depending on the size of pan) and cook until they are set and golden brown underneath. Turn and cook the fritters on the second side until they are golden.

6 Drain the fritters on kitchen paper and keep hot in a warm oven or grill (broiler) compartment. Cook the remaining mixture in the same way.

7 Divide the dipping sauce among four small individual dishes. Serve the hot fritters on platters with the dishes of dipping sauce.

Per portion Energy 317kcal/1330kJ; Protein 6.7g; Carbohydrate 45.5g, of which sugars 5.3g; Fat 13.3g, of which saturates 1.9g; Cholesterol 48mg; Calcium 77mg; Fibre 2.7g; Sodium 1063mg.

PAN-FRIED KIMCHI FRITTERS

A CLASSIC AND POPULAR KOREAN SNACK, THESE FRITTERS HAVE A CRISP GOLDEN COATING. THE CONTRAST OF THE CRUNCHY EXTERIOR AND SMOOTH FILLING MAKES FOR A DELICIOUS JUXTAPOSITION OF TEXTURES AND THE DISH IS SERVED WITH A ZESTY SOY DIP TO HELP BRING OUT THE FLAVOURS.

SERVES TWO

INGREDIENTS
- 90g/3½oz cabbage kimchi (see page 431), finely chopped
- 1 potato
- a little milk (optional)
- 50g/2oz firm tofu, squeezed to remove excess water
- 25g/1oz/¼ cup plain (all-purpose) flour
- 1 egg, beaten
- 5ml/1 tsp crushed garlic
- 15ml/1 tbsp vegetable oil
- salt and ground black pepper

For the dip
- 45ml/3 tbsp light soy sauce
- 2.5ml/½ tsp sesame oil
- 5ml/1 tsp lemon juice

1 Gently squeeze the kimchi to remove any excess liquid. Boil the potato and mash it, adding a little milk if required.

2 Crumble the tofu into a bowl. Add the kimchi, potato, flour, egg, garlic and seasoning. Mix well and form spoonfuls of mixture into small round patties.

3 Coat a frying pan or wok with the oil and place over a medium heat. Add the patties and fry until golden brown on both sides. Drain on kitchen paper.

4 For the dip, mix the soy sauce, sesame oil and lemon juice, and then serve with the fritters.

Per portion Energy 206kcal/863kJ; Protein 8.4g; Carbohydrate 20.9g, of which sugars 3.8g; Fat 10.5g, of which saturates 1.8g; Cholesterol 105mg; Calcium 188mg; Fibre 1.9g; Sodium 583mg.

DEEP-FRIED TOFU <u>IN</u> DASHI SOUP

A CREAMY TOFU BLOCK IS DEEP-FRIED IN A CRISP THIN BATTER, THEN SOAKED IN HOT BROTH. THIS TASTY AND FILLING JAPANESE DISH IS TYPICAL IN A SHOJIN RYORI *(ZEN VEGETARIAN) MENU.*

SERVES FOUR

INGREDIENTS
  2 × 295g/10¾oz packets
    long-life soft or silken tofu
  vegetable oil, for deep-frying
  30ml/2 tbsp plain
    (all-purpose) flour
For the sauce
  50ml/2fl oz/¼ cup shoyu
  50ml/2fl oz/¼ cup mirin
  pinch of salt
  300ml/½ pint/1¼ cups second
    dashi stock, or the same amount
    of water and 7.5ml/1½ tsp
    dashi-no-moto
For the garnish
  2.5cm/1in fresh root ginger,
    peeled and finely grated
  60ml/4 tbsp finely
    chopped chives

1 Drain the water from the tofu. Carefully open the packet and then wrap the tofu in 2–3 layers of kitchen paper. Set a chopping board, or large plate with a weight, on top to press the tofu, and leave for at least 30 minutes for the excess liquid to be absorbed by the kitchen paper.

2 To make the sauce, place the shoyu, mirin, salt and dashi stock in a small pan over a medium heat. Mix well, cook for 5 minutes, then set aside.

3 Squeeze the grated ginger and make into four small balls. Set aside.

4 Unwrap the tofu and pat dry with another sheet of kitchen paper. Slice one tofu block into four squares each about 2.5 × 6cm/1 × 2½in. Repeat with the other tofu block.

5 Heat the oil to about 190°C/375°F. Dust the tofu with the flour and slide into the oil. Deep-fry until golden brown. Drain well on kitchen paper.

6 Arrange two tofu pieces in each of four small bowls. Reheat the sauce and gently pour from the side of the bowl. Try not to splash over the tofu. Put a ginger ball on the tofu and sprinkle with chives. Serve hot.

Per portion Energy 40kcal/164kJ; Protein 3.9g; Carbohydrate 1.1g, of which sugars 0.9g; Fat 2.2g, of which saturates 0.4g; Cholesterol 24mg; Calcium 187mg; Fibre 0.3g; Sodium 380mg.

STUFFED <u>AND</u> GRILLED THIN TOFU

AGE OR ABURA-AGE, FRIED THIN TOFU, CAN BE USED AS A BAG LIKE A MIDDLE EASTERN PITTA BREAD. HERE, A GENEROUS AMOUNT OF CHOPPED SPRING ONION AND OTHER AROMATIC INGREDIENTS FILL THE BAG. IN JAPAN, SPRING ONIONS ARE THOUGHT TO PREVENT COLDS IN THE WINTER.

SERVES FOUR

INGREDIENTS
  1 packet abura-age (2 abura-age
    per packet)
For the filling
  4 spring onions (scallions),
    trimmed and very finely chopped
  about 15ml/1 tbsp shoyu
  1 garlic clove, grated
    or crushed
  30ml/2 tbsp lightly toasted
    sesame seeds

COOK'S TIP
If opening the abura-age is not easy, use a round-bladed knife and insert the blade gradually to open the bag out.

1 Put the abura-age in a sieve (strainer) and pour hot water from a kettle over to wash off excess oil. Drain and gently dry on kitchen paper.

2 Put one abura-age on a chopping board and roll over several times with a rolling pin.

3 Cut the rolled abura-age in half and carefully open at the cut part to make two bags. Repeat this process with the remaining piece.

4 Put the spring onions, shoyu, garlic and sesame seeds together in a small glass bowl and mix them well. Check the seasoning and add more shoyu, if required.

5 Fill the four bags with the filling. Grill (broil) under a preheated grill (broiler) at high for 3–4 minutes on each side, or until crisp and lightly browned.

6 With a sharp knife, cut each abura-age bag into four triangles and arrange them on four small plates. Serve hot.

Per portion Energy 235kcal/976kJ; Protein 18.4g; Carbohydrate 2.1g, of which sugars 1.2g; Fat 17g, of which saturates 0.6g; Cholesterol 0mg; Calcium 1109mg; Fibre 0.8g; Sodium 278mg.

PAN-FRIED TOFU <u>WITH</u> CARAMELIZED SAUCE

TOFU WAS FIRST INTRODUCED INTO JAPANESE CUISINE BY CHINESE BUDDHIST MONKS. THEY INVENTED MANY DELICIOUS AND FILLING PROTEIN DISHES FROM TOFU AND OTHER SOYA BEAN PRODUCTS.

4 Slice the garlic very thinly to make garlic chips. Heat the vegetable oil in a frying pan and fry the garlic for a few moments until golden. Turn the garlic chips frequently to prevent sticking and burning. Scoop them out on to kitchen paper. Reserve the oil in the pan.

5 Unwrap the tofu block. Slice one block horizontally in half, then cut each half into four pieces. Repeat with the other tofu block. Soak in the marinade for about 15 minutes.

6 Take out the tofu and wipe off the excess marinade with kitchen paper. Reserve the marinade.

7 Reheat the oil in the frying pan and add one piece of butter. When the oil starts sizzling, reduce the heat to medium and add the pieces of tofu one by one. Cook in one layer, if possible.

8 Cover the pan and cook until the edge of the tofu is browned and quite firm, approximately 5–8 minutes on each side. (If the edges burn but the centre is pale, reduce the heat.)

9 Pour the marinade into the pan. Cook for 2 minutes, or until the spring onion becomes very soft. Remove the tofu from the pan and arrange four pieces on each serving plate. Pour the thickened marinade and spring onion mixture over the tofu and top with a piece of butter.

10 Sprinkle with the garlic chips and garnish with the watercress. Serve hot.

SERVES FOUR

INGREDIENTS
    2 × 285g/10¼oz packets tofu blocks
    4 garlic cloves
    10ml/2 tsp vegetable oil
    50g/2oz/¼ cup butter, cut into
     5 equal pieces
    watercress, to garnish
For the marinade
    4 spring onions (scallions)
    60ml/4 tbsp sake
    60ml/4 tbsp shoyu (tamari or sashimi
     soy sauce, if available)
    60ml/4 tbsp mirin

1 Unpack the tofu blocks and discard the liquid, then wrap in three layers of kitchen paper.

COOK'S TIP
Placing a weight on top of the tofu for 30 minutes will make the tofu firmer.

2 Put a large plate or wooden chopping board on top of the tofu block as a weight and leave for 30 minutes to allow time for the excess liquid to be absorbed by the paper.

3 To make the marinade, chop the spring onions finely. Mix with the other marinade ingredients in a ceramic or aluminium tray with sides or a wide, shallow bowl. Leave the mixture to infuse for 15 minutes.

Per portion Energy 271kcal/1127kJ; Protein 12.7g; Carbohydrate 11.5g, of which sugars 10g; Fat 17.9g, of which saturates 7.4g; Cholesterol 27mg; Calcium 742mg; Fibre 0.4g; Sodium 1152mg.

DEEP-FRIED TOFU BALLS

THERE ARE MANY VARIATIONS OF THESE JAPANESE DEEP-FRIED TOFU BALLS CALLED HIRYOZU,
MEANING FLYING DRAGON'S HEAD. THIS IS ONE OF THE EASIEST TO MAKE.

MAKES 16

INGREDIENTS
2 × 285g/10¼oz packets tofu blocks
20g/¾oz carrot, peeled
40g/1½oz/1¼ cups green beans
2 large (US extra large) eggs, beaten
30ml/2 tbsp sake
10ml/2 tsp mirin
5ml/1 tsp salt
10ml/2 tsp shoyu
pinch of caster (superfine) sugar
vegetable oil, for deep-frying
For the lime sauce
45ml/3 tbsp shoyu
juice of ½ lime
5ml/1 tsp rice vinegar
For the garnish
300g/11oz daikon, peeled
2 dried red chillies, halved
and seeded
4 chives, finely snipped

1 Drain the tofu and wrap in a clean
dishtowel or some kitchen paper. Set
a chopping board, or large plate with a
weight, on top and leave for 2 hours, or
until the tofu loses most of its liquid and
its weight is halved.

2 Cut the daikon for the garnish into
about 4cm/1½in thick slices. Make
3–4 holes in each slice with a skewer
or chopstick and insert chilli pieces into
the holes. Leave for 15 minutes, then
grate the daikon and chilli finely.

3 To make the tofu balls, chop the
carrot finely. Trim and cut the beans
into 5mm/¼in lengths. Cook both
vegetables for 1 minute in boiling water.

4 In a food processor, mix the tofu,
eggs, sake, mirin, salt, shoyu and sugar
until smooth. Transfer to a bowl and mix
in the carrot and beans.

5 Fill a wok or pan with oil 4cm/1½in
deep, and heat to 185°C/365°F.

6 Soak a piece of kitchen paper with a
little vegetable oil, and wet your hands
with it. Scoop 40ml/2½ tbsp tofu mixture
in one hand and shape into a ball by
tossing the ball between your hands.

7 Carefully slide into the oil and deep-
fry until crisp and golden brown. Drain
on kitchen paper. Repeat with the
remaining mixture.

8 Arrange the tofu balls on a serving
plate and sprinkle with chives. Put
30ml/2 tbsp grated daikon in each of
four small bowls. Mix the lime sauce
ingredients in a serving bowl. Serve the
balls with the lime sauce to be mixed
with grated daikon by each guest.

Per portion Energy 40kcal/164kJ; Protein 3.9g; Carbohydrate 1.1g, of which sugars 0.9g; Fat 2.2g, of which saturates 0.4g; Cholesterol 24mg; Calcium 187mg; Fibre 0.3g; Sodium 380mg.

VEGETARIAN TEMPURA

IN THE HOT AND HUMID JAPANESE SUMMER, ZEN MONKS EAT DEEP-FRIED VEGETABLES, SHOJIN-AGÉ, TO GET OVER THE FATIGUE OF HARD TRAINING. ALTHOUGH TEMPURA PREPARATION NEEDS A LITTLE EFFORT, TAKE YOUR TIME AND ENJOY THE PROCESS AS AN ARTISTIC ACTIVITY, LIKE THE MONKS DO.

SERVES FOUR

INGREDIENTS
15ml/1 tbsp lemon juice or
  rice vinegar
15cm/6in renkon
½ sweet potato
½ aubergine (eggplant)
vegetable oil and sesame oil, for
  frying (see Cook's Tips)
4 shiso leaves
1 green (bell) pepper, seeded and cut
  lengthways into 2.5cm/1in wide strips
⅛ kabocha squash, cut into 5mm/¼in
  thick half-ring shapes
4 green beans, trimmed
4 fresh shiitake mushrooms
4 okra, trimmed
1 onion, sliced into 5mm/¼in rings
For the batter
200ml/7fl oz/scant 1 cup ice-
  cold water
1 large (US extra large) egg, beaten
90g/3½oz/generous ¾ cup sifted
  plain (all-purpose) flour, plus extra
  for dusting
2–3 ice cubes
For the condiment
450g/1lb daikon
4cm/1½in piece fresh root ginger
For the dipping sauce
400ml/14fl oz/1⅔ cups second dashi
  stock, or the same amount of water
  with 10ml/2 tsp dashi-no-moto
100ml/3fl oz/scant ½ cup shoyu
100ml/3fl oz/scant ½ cup mirin

1 To make the dipping sauce, mix all the ingredients in a pan. Bring to the boil, then remove from the heat. Set aside.

2 Fill a small bowl with cold water and add the lemon juice or rice vinegar. Peel the renkon, then slice it and the sweet potato into 5mm/¼in thick discs. Plunge the pieces into the bowl straightaway to prevent discolouring. Just before frying, drain and pat dry with kitchen paper.

3 Slice the aubergine horizontally into 5mm/¼in thick slices, then halve them lengthways. Soak in cold water until just before frying. Drain and pat dry.

4 To prepare the condiment, peel and grate the daikon and ginger separately, using a daikon-oroshi, or, alternatively, use a food processor. Lightly squeeze out excess liquid from both the daikon and ginger.

5 Line an egg cup with clear film (plastic wrap) and press about 2.5ml/½ tsp grated ginger into the bottom, then put in 30ml/2 tbsp grated daikon. Press again and turn upside-down on to a small plate. Make four of these tiny mounds.

6 To make the batter, pour the ice-cold water into a mixing bowl, add the beaten egg and mix well. Add the flour and very roughly fold in with a pair of chopsticks or a fork. Do not beat. The batter should still be quite lumpy. Add the ice cubes.

7 Pour in enough oil to come halfway up the depth of a wok or deep-fryer. Heat the oil until the temperature reaches about 150°C/300°F.

8 Deep-fry the shiso leaves. Hold the stalk of one leaf in your hand and stroke the leaf across the surface of the batter mix, coating only one side of the leaf. Gently slip it into the oil until it goes crisp and bright green. Leave to drain on kitchen paper. Deep-fry the renkon and sweet potato in the same way; first coating one side in batter then frying until golden.

9 Increase the temperature to 175°C/347°F. Lightly dust the rest of the vegetables with flour, dunk into the batter mix, then shake off the excess. Deep-fry them two to three pieces at a time until crisp. Leave to drain on kitchen paper.

10 Divide the warm dipping sauce among four small bowls. Place with the condiment. Arrange the tempura on a large plate. Serve immediately. Mix the condiment into the sauce, then dip in the tempura as you eat.

COOK'S TIPS
• If you like the strong flavour of sesame oil, mix it with 2 parts vegetable oil. For a lighter flavour, just add a few dashes of toasted sesame oil to the vegetable oil.
• To check the temperature of oil without a thermometer, drop a little batter into the hot oil. At 150°C/300°F it should sink down to the bottom and stay there for about 5 seconds before it floats to the surface. When the temperature reaches 175°C/347°F, a drop of batter sinks to the bottom, but immediately rises to the surface.

Per portion Energy 432kcal/1803kJ; Protein 8.2g; Carbohydrate 47g, of which sugars 24.6g; Fat 24.8g, of which saturates 3.4g; Cholesterol 48mg; Calcium 147mg; Fibre 5.8g; Sodium 1827mg.

BACON-ROLLED ENOKITAKE MUSHROOMS

THE JAPANESE NAME FOR THIS DISH IS OBIMAKI ENOKI: AN OBI (BELT OR SASH) IS MADE FROM BACON AND WRAPPED AROUND ENOKITAKE MUSHROOMS BEFORE GRILLING THEM. THE STRONG, SMOKY FLAVOUR OF THE BACON ACCOMPANIES THE SUBTLE FLAVOUR OF ENOKI VERY WELL.

SERVES FOUR

INGREDIENTS
    450g/1lb fresh enokitake mushrooms
    6 rindless smoked streaky (fatty)
      bacon rashers (strips)
    4 lemon wedges and ground white
      pepper, to serve

1 Cut off the root part of each enokitake cluster 2cm/¾in from the end. Do not separate the stems. Cut the rashers in half lengthways.

2 Divide the enokitake into 12 bunches. Take one bunch, then place the middle of the enokitake near the edge of 1 bacon rasher. You should be able to see 2.5–4cm/1–1½in of enokitake at each end of the bacon.

3 Carefully roll up the bunch of enokitake in the bacon. Tuck any straying short stems into the bacon and slide the bacon slightly upwards at each roll to cover about 4cm/1½in of the enokitake. Secure the end of the bacon roll with a cocktail stick (toothpick). Repeat using the remaining enokitake and bacon to make 11 more rolls.

4 Preheat the grill (broiler) to high. Place the enokitake rolls on an oiled wire rack. Grill (broil) both sides until the bacon is crisp and the enokitake start to burn. This takes about 10–13 minutes.

5 Remove the enokitake rolls and place on a board. Using a fork and knife, chop each roll in half in the middle of the bacon belt. Arrange the top part of the enokitake roll standing upright, the bottom part lying down next to it. Serve with a wedge of lemon and a small heap of ground white pepper.

VARIATION
A bunch of chives can be rolled and cooked in the same way. You can also use young garlic shoots when they are about 12cm/4½in long for this recipe.

Per portion Energy 118kcal/490kJ; Protein 8g; Carbohydrate 0.5g, of which sugars 0.2g; Fat 9.4g, of which saturates 3.2g; Cholesterol 24mg; Calcium 9mg; Fibre 1.3g; Sodium 478mg.

STUFFED AUBERGINE <u>WITH</u> GINGER SAUCE

A POPULAR KOREAN DISH, THE SUCCULENT BEEF FILLING COMPLEMENTS THE CREAMY TEXTURE OF THE BRAISED AUBERGINE BEAUTIFULLY, AND THE WHOLE DISH IS INFUSED WITH THE FLAVOURS OF RICE WINE AND GINGER; AN ADDITIONAL FIERY KICK IS SUPPLIED BY CHILLIES.

SERVES TWO

INGREDIENTS
  2 aubergines (eggplants)
  1 egg
  25ml/1½ tbsp vegetable oil
  1 sheet dried seaweed
  90g/3½oz/scant ½ cup minced
    (ground) beef
  15ml/1 tbsp *mirin* or rice wine
  15ml/1 tbsp dark soy sauce
  1 garlic clove, crushed
  5ml/1 tsp sesame oil
  1 red chilli, seeded
    and shredded
  1 green chilli, seeded
    and shredded
  salt and ground black pepper
  steamed rice, to serve
For the sauce
  30ml/2 tbsp mirin or rice wine
  30ml/2 tbsp dark soy sauce
  5ml/1 tsp fresh root ginger, peeled
    and grated

COOK'S TIP
If you would like to reduce the heat of
the dish, then avoid using the red chilli
and just use the green chilli.

1 Wash and clean the aubergines, and
cut into thick slices of a thickness of
about 2.5cm/1in.

2 Make two cross slits down the length
of each aubergine slice, making sure
that you don't cut all the way through.

3 Sprinkle each aubergine slice with a
little salt and set aside.

4 Beat the egg and season with a
pinch of salt. Coat a frying pan with
10ml/2 tsp vegetable oil and heat over
medium heat.

5 Add the beaten egg and make a
thin omelette, browning gently on
each side. Remove the omelette from
the pan and cut it into thin strips.
Wait until it is cool and then chill in
the refrigerator.

6 Heat the remaining vegetable oil over
high heat. Cut the seaweed into strips
and stir fry with the beef, mirin or rice
wine, soy sauce and garlic. Once cooked,
drizzle the beef with the sesame oil.

7 Place the chillies in a bowl. Add the
egg strips and the beef, and mix
together. Rinse the aubergines and stuff
each slice with a little of the beef mixture.

8 Place all the ingredients for the sauce
into a frying pan, add 200ml/7fl oz/
scant 1 cup of water and salt to taste,
and heat over medium heat. Once the
sauce is blended and bubbling, add the
stuffed aubergine slices. Spoon the
sauce over the aubergines and simmer
for 15 minutes, or until the aubergines
are soft and the skin has become shiny.
Transfer to a shallow dish and serve
with steamed rice.

Per portion Energy 273kcal/1134kJ; Protein 14.3g; Carbohydrate 5.9g, of which sugars 5.3g; Fat 19.9g, of which saturates 5.2g; Cholesterol 122mg; Calcium 42mg; Fibre 4g; Sodium 1145mg.

STEAMED TOFU AND CHIVE DUMPLINGS

THE SLIGHT SPICINESS AND DELICATE TEXTURE OF KOREAN CHIVES MAKE THEM A WONDERFUL INGREDIENT TO ADD TO THESE STUFFED, PAPER-THIN STEAMED DUMPLINGS, CALLED MANDU. HERE THE SUCCULENT FILLING IS MADE WITH TOFU, COMBINED WITH BEEF AND RICE WINE.

SERVES FOUR

INGREDIENTS
    30 dumpling skins
    1 egg, beaten
    spinach leaves to line steamer
For the filling
    3 spring onions (scallions),
       finely chopped
    3 garlic cloves, crushed
    5ml/1 tsp finely grated fresh
       root ginger
    5ml/1 tsp mirin or rice wine
    90g/3½oz/scant ½ cup minced
       (ground) beef
    90g/3½oz firm tofu
    90g/3½oz Korean chives,
       finely chopped
    ½ onion, finely chopped
    30ml/2 tbsp soy sauce
    30ml/2 tbsp sesame oil
    15ml/1 tbsp sugar
    15ml/1 tbsp salt
    10ml/2 tsp ground black pepper
For the dipping sauce
    60ml/4 tbsp dark soy sauce
    30ml/2 tbsp rice vinegar
    5ml/1 tsp Korean chilli powder

1 To make the dipping sauce, mix the soy sauce, rice vinegar and chilli powder in a small serving bowl.

2 For the filling, combine the chopped spring onions, garlic, grated ginger, mirin or rice wine and minced beef into a bowl. Leave to marinate for 15 minutes.

3 Drain off any excess liquid from the tofu then crumble it into a bowl. Add the chopped chives to the seasoned beef, with the tofu and remaining filling ingredients. Mix together thoroughly.

4 Take a dumpling skin and brush with a little beaten egg. Place a spoonful of the stuffing in the middle.

5 Fold into a half-moon shape, crimping the edges firmly to seal. Repeat with the other dumpling skins.

6 Cook over a pan of boiling water in a steamer lined with spinach leaves for 6 minutes. Alternatively, cook them in boiling water for 3 minutes. Arrange on a serving dish and serve with soy dipping sauce.

VARIATIONS
Almost any ingredient can be adapted for mandu fillings: beansprouts, minced (ground) pork, chopped prawns (shrimp), courgettes (zucchini) and cabbage kimchi (see page 431) are favourites.

COOK'S TIPS
• Asian stores often stock dumpling skins and these are quick to use, but they are not difficult to make if you have time. For 8 dumpling skins, sift 115g/4oz/1 cup plain (all-purpose) flour and 30ml/2 tbsp cornflour (cornstarch) together in a bowl and add 2.5ml/½ tsp salt. Pour in 50ml/2fl oz/¼ cup warm water and knead well until a smooth, elastic dough has formed. Cover the bowl with a damp dish towel and leave for 10 minutes. Place on a lightly floured surface and roll out the dough until paper-thin. Use a floured pastry (cookie) cutter or a sharp knife to cut the dough into circles roughly 7.5cm/3in in diameter.
• Dumplings can be cooked in a variety of ways. Steaming is the most popular, but grilling (broiling) and shallow-frying until golden brown also produce delicious results.

Per portion Energy 235kcal/982kJ; Protein 9.9g; Carbohydrate 26.1g, of which sugars 6.5g; Fat 10.8g, of which saturates 2.5g; Cholesterol 14mg; Calcium 208mg; Fibre 2.2g; Sodium 1054mg.

STIR-FRIED RICE CAKE <u>AND</u> VEGETABLES

HEARTY KOREAN RICE CAKE IS A VERSATILE INGREDIENT USED IN MANY DIFFERENT RECIPES. HERE THE
STICKY TEXTURE OF THE RICE CAKE IS COMPLEMENTED BY THE CRUNCH OF VEGETABLES AND A RICH
TASTE OF BEEF. THE REFINED FLAVOURS REFLECT THE SNACK'S ORIGINS AS A ROYAL COURT SNACK.

SERVES FOUR

INGREDIENTS
  1 long Korean rice cake
  5ml/1 tsp sesame oil
  2 dried shiitake mushrooms, soaked
    in warm water for about 30 minutes
    until softened
  50g/2oz carrot
  ¼ cucumber
  50g/2oz beef, thinly sliced
  30ml/2 tbsp vegetable oil
  ¼ onion, finely sliced
For the seasoning
  60ml/4 tbsp dark soy sauce
  15ml/1 tbsp sugar
  2.5ml/½ tsp ground white pepper
  5ml/1 tsp sesame seeds
  15ml/1 tbsp sesame oil
  2 spring onions (scallions),
    finely chopped
  30ml/2 tbsp mirin or rice wine
  2 garlic cloves, crushed

1 Slice the rice cake into 4cm/1½in
lengths and blanch these in salted
boiling water for 2 seconds. Drain and
rinse in cold water, then drain well
again and transfer to a bowl. Coat the
pieces of rice cake with the sesame oil
and set aside.

2 When the soaked shiitake mushrooms
have reconstituted and become soft,
drain and thinly slice them, discarding
the tough stem.

3 Cut the carrot into thin strips. Seed
the cucumber and cut into thin strips.

4 Combine the soy sauce, sugar,
pepper, sesame seeds and oil for the
seasoning in a bowl. Add the beef and
then turn the slices to coat them well
with the seasoning. Cover and set aside
for 15 minutes so that the beef absorbs
the flavours.

5 Combine the spring onions with the
mirin or rice wine and crushed garlic in
a small bowl.

6 Coat a frying pan or wok with the
vegetable oil and place over a medium
heat. When the pan is hot, add the
onion and seasoned beef. Stir-fry until
the beef is browned and the onion
lightly cooked. Then add the
mushrooms, rice cake, carrot and
cucumber to the pan.

7 Continue stir-frying until the
vegetables have softened slightly. Then
pour in the spring onion mixture.
Reduce the heat and cook, stirring
frequently, until the liquid has formed a
sticky glaze to coat the ingredients.
Transfer the mixture to a shallow serving
dish and serve immediately.

VARIATION
A classic and considerably spicier
version of this dish can be achieved by
adding gochujang chilli paste to the
seasoning instead of soy sauce. This
version of the rice cakes traditionally
omits the mushrooms.

Per portion Energy 369kcal/1538kJ; Protein 10.2g; Carbohydrate 35.3g, of which sugars 14.4g; Fat 21.9g, of which saturates 3.6g; Cholesterol 15mg; Calcium 50mg; Fibre 1.5g; Sodium 1806mg.

RICE SEAWEED ROLL <u>WITH</u> SPICY SQUID

THIS KOREAN FAVOURITE, CHUGMU KIMBAP, IS INFLUENCED BY JAPANESE MAKI, ALTHOUGH THE SEAWEED ROLLS ARE SERVED SEPARATELY. THE FLUFFY TEXTURE AND MILD TASTE OF THE RICE ROLL ARE NICELY SET OFF BY THE CRUNCH OF THE RADISH AND THE KICK OF THE CHILLI AND GARLIC.

<u>SERVES TWO</u>

INGREDIENTS
 400g/14oz/4 cups cooked rice
 rice vinegar, for drizzling
 sesame oil, for drizzling
 150g/5oz squid
 90g/3½oz Chinese white radish,
  peeled and diced
 3 large sheets dried seaweed
  or nori
For the squid seasoning
 22.5ml/4½ tsp Korean chilli powder
 7.5ml/1½ tsp sugar
 1 garlic clove, crushed
 5ml/1 tsp sesame oil
 2.5ml/½ tsp sesame seeds
For the radish seasoning
 15ml/1 tbsp sugar
 30ml/2 tbsp rice vinegar
 22.5ml/4½ tsp Korean
  chilli powder
 15ml/1 tbsp Thai fish sauce
 1 garlic clove, crushed
 1 spring onion (scallion),
  finely chopped

1 Put the cooked rice in a bowl and drizzle over some rice vinegar and sesame oil. Mix well, then set aside.

2 Wash the squid carefully, rinsing off any ink that remains. Holding the body firmly, pull away the head and tentacles. If the ink sac is still intact, remove it and discard. Pull out all the innards including the long transparent pen or quill. Peel off and discard the thin purple skin on the body, but keep the two small side fins. Slice the head across just under the eyes, severing the tentacles. Discard the rest of the head.

3 Squeeze the tentacles at the head end to push out the round beak in the centre and discard. Rinse the pouch and tentacles. (The fishmonger will prepare squid if you prefer.) Use a sharp knife to score the squid with a crisscross pattern. Cut into pieces about 5cm/2in long and 1cm/½in wide.

4 Bring a pan of water to the boil over a high heat. Blanch the squid for 3 minutes, stirring constantly, then drain under cold running water.

5 Combine all the squid seasoning ingredients in a bowl, and then coat the squid. Set aside to absorb the flavours.

6 Put the radish in a bowl, then drizzle over some rice vinegar. Leave for 15 minutes. Drain the radish and transfer to a bowl. Add the radish seasoning ingredients, mix well and chill.

7 Place a third of the rice on to one of the sheets of seaweed, roll into a long cylinder and wrap it tightly. Then slice the cylinder into bitesize pieces. Repeat with the remaining seaweed sheets.

8 Arrange the finished rolls on a serving plate and serve with the seasoned squid and the radish.

COOK'S TIP
When cutting rice rolls, use a sharp damp knife and clean it with a damp cloth after each cut.

Per portion Energy 195kcal/830kJ; Protein 8.8g; Carbohydrate 36.2g, of which sugars 4.8g; Fat 2.8g, of which saturates 0.6g; Cholesterol 84mg; Calcium 32mg; Fibre 0.4g; Sodium 312mg.

STUFFED SQUID <u>WITH</u> SOY DIPPING SAUCE

THIS MUCH-LOVED SNACK IS SERVED ON THE STREET CORNERS OF KOREA. THE STEAMED SQUID HAS A SILKEN TEXTURE WHILE THE STUFFING MIXES A VIBRANT RANGE OF FLAVOURS MORE USUALLY FOUND IN DUMPLINGS. THIS DISH IS A DELICIOUS EXAMPLE OF TRADITIONAL MARKET FOOD.

SERVES TWO TO THREE

INGREDIENTS
2 squid
115g/4oz lean frying steak,
    finely chopped
15ml/1 tbsp soy sauce
5ml/1 tsp sugar
5ml/1 tsp sesame oil
½ block firm tofu
50g/2oz/¼ cup beansprouts
1 green chilli, seeded and
    chopped
1 fresh red chilli, seeded
    and chopped
1 spring onion (scallion),
    finely chopped
90g/3½oz/½ cup short grain
    rice, cooked
plain (all-purpose) flour,
    for dusting
For the dipping sauce
1 garlic clove, crushed
45ml/3 tbsp dark soy sauce
5ml/1 tsp sesame oil
salt
ground black pepper

1 To clean the squid, pull out the head and tentacles from the body. Discard the ink sac if it is intact. Then cut off and reserve the tentacles. Discard the head along with the other parts. Discard the long pen or quill from the body and wash the sac, rubbing off the purple skin.

2 Rinse and drain the squid and dry it well on kitchen paper. Then chop the squid tentacles.

3 Place the beef in a bowl and mix in the soy sauce, sugar and sesame oil. Cover and leave to marinate for about 10 minutes.

4 Meanwhile, squeeze the tofu to remove some of the liquid, then crumble it into a bowl. Bring a pan of water to the boil, add the beansprouts, bring the water back to the boil and drain immediately. Finely chop the beansprouts and add to the tofu.

5 Add the chillies and spring onion to the tofu mixture. Add the chopped squid tentacles. Stir in the cooked rice and the beef with its marinade, and mix to thoroughly combine the ingredients.

6 Dust the insides of the squid with flour, then stuff with the tofu mixture. Use bamboo skewers to close the squid and place them in a steamer. Steam over boiling water for about 20 minutes, until the squid is cooked and tender.

7 For the dipping sauce, mix the garlic, soy sauce and sesame oil, adding salt and pepper to taste. Transfer the mixture to a small serving dish.

8 Remove the stuffed squid from the steamer and cut them into slices, then serve with the dipping sauce.

Per portion Energy 335kcal/1414kJ; Protein 39.1g; Carbohydrate 15.9g, of which sugars 3.8g; Fat 11.5g, of which saturates 2.2g; Cholesterol 555mg; Calcium 87mg; Fibre 1.8g; Sodium 432mg.

FISHCAKE KEBABS <u>IN</u> SEAWEED SOUP

FISHCAKES ARE WIDELY EATEN AS STREET SNACKS AS THEY ARE HEARTY, FLAVOURSOME AND EASY TO COOK. THIS JAPANESE-STYLE DISH IS A CLASSIC EXAMPLE, WITH THE TENDER FISHCAKE COOKED ON SKEWERS IN A RICH, SEAWEED-FLAVOURED SOUP. PERFECT FOR A QUICK BITE.

SERVES FOUR

INGREDIENTS
    16 fishcake slices
      or fish balls
    16 wooden skewers
For the soup
    400g/14oz Chinese
      white radish, peeled
    3 sheets dried seaweed
    10ml/2 tsp Thai fish sauce
    10ml/2 tsp light soy sauce
    salt and ground black pepper
For the soy dip
    60ml/4 tbsp dark soy sauce
    5ml/1 tsp sesame seeds
    5ml/1 tsp wasabi
      paste, or to taste

1 Pierce each slice of fishcake or fish ball with a wooden skewer and then set them to one side.

2 To make the dip, mix the dark soy sauce and sesame seeds in a small dish, adding the wasabi paste to taste.

3 To make the soup, put the radish in a pan with the seaweed and 2 litres/3½ pints/8 cups water. Bring to the boil and add the Thai fish sauce and soy sauce.

4 Lay the fishcake kebabs in the liquid and boil for 20 minutes, or until the soup has thickened. Season with salt and pepper.

5 Pour a little soup into each bowl and add four fishcake kebabs. Serve with the spicy soy dip.

COOK'S TIP
You will find fishcake in large pieces or slices and fish balls are available at most Asian food stores.

Per portion Energy 104kcal/435kJ; Protein 6.4g; Carbohydrate 13.1g, of which sugars 3.1g; Fat 3.2g, of which saturates 0.5g; Cholesterol 13mg; Calcium 105mg; Fibre 1g; Sodium 1468mg.

SEAFOOD FRITTERS WITH PEAR AND SOY DIP

Succulent prawns, moist cod fillet and tasty seasoned crab are all battered and lightly sautéed in these Korean bitesize fritters. The crispy prawn fritters have a mushroom and chilli stuffing and all are served with a pear and soy sauce dip.

SERVES FOUR

INGREDIENTS
- 2 eggs, beaten
- vegetable oil, for frying
- salt and ground black pepper

For the prawn fritters
- 5 medium-size prawns (shrimp)
- juice of ½ lemon
- 30ml/2 tbsp white wine
- 2.5ml/½ tsp sesame oil
- 1 dried shiitake mushroom, soaked in warm water for about 30 minutes until softened
- 1 green chilli, finely chopped
- 45ml/3 tbsp plain (all-purpose) flour for dusting

For the crab fritters
- 75g/3oz crab meat
- 3 oyster mushrooms, finely sliced
- ½ green (bell) pepper, finely chopped
- 25g/1oz Korean chives, finely sliced
- 1 garlic clove, thinly sliced
- 2 eggs, beaten
- 45ml/3 tbsp plain (all-purpose) flour
- Extra flour for dusting

For the cod fritters
- 300g/11oz cod fillet
- 7.5ml/1½ tsp dark soy sauce
- 5ml/1 tsp white wine
- 2.5ml/½ tsp sesame oil
- 45ml/3 tbsp plain (all-purpose) flour for dusting

For the dipping sauce
- 45ml/3 tbsp light soy sauce
- 45ml/3 tbsp sugar
- 1 garlic clove, crushed
- 10ml/2 tsp pear juice
- 2.5ml/½ tsp lemon juice
- 1.5ml/¼ tsp Korean chilli powder

1 Combine all the ingredients for the dipping sauce in a small serving bowl.

2 To make the prawn fritters, gently pull off the tail shell. Twist off the head. Peel away the soft body shell and the small claws beneath. Rinse well and season with salt, pepper, lemon juice, white wine and a dash of sesame oil.

3 When the soaked shiitake mushroom has reconstituted and become soft, drain and finely chop it, discarding the tough stem. Mix with the chilli, season with a dash of sesame oil and salt, and dust with a little flour. Set this mushroom stuffing aside. Dust the prawns with flour and then coat them with beaten egg. Set aside.

4 To make the crab fritters, season the crab meat with salt and pepper and place in a bowl. Add the mushrooms, pepper and chives. Then stir in the garlic, eggs and flour, and set the mixture aside.

5 For the cod fritters, cut the fillet into bitesize pieces and season with soy sauce, white wine and sesame oil. Set aside for 20 minutes. Dust with flour, coat in beaten egg and set aside.

6 Coat a large frying pan or wok with vegetable oil and place over a medium heat. Add the prawn and cod fritters, with spoonfuls of the crab mixture.

7 Fry until lightly browned and then add a little of the mushroom mixture to each prawn fritter. When all the fritters are golden on both sides transfer them to a platter. Serve with the dipping sauce.

Per portion Energy 294kcal/1227kJ; Protein 29.3g; Carbohydrate 9.1g, of which sugars 6.1g; Fat 15.3g, of which saturates 2.8g; Cholesterol 287mg; Calcium 103mg; Fibre 1.1g; Sodium 671mg.

DEEP-FRIED LAYERED SHIITAKE AND SCALLOPS

IN THIS JAPANESE DISH, YOU CAN TASTE THREE KINDS OF SOFTNESS: CHEWY SHIITAKE, MASHED NAGA-IMO WITH MISO, AND SUCCULENT SCALLOP. THE MIXTURE CREATES A MOMENT OF HEAVEN IN YOUR MOUTH. IF IT'S DIFFICULT TO EAT WITH CHOPSTICKS, FEEL FREE TO USE A KNIFE AND FORK!

SERVES FOUR

INGREDIENTS

4 scallops
8 large fresh shiitake mushrooms
225g/8oz naga-imo, unpeeled
20ml/4 tsp miso
50g/2oz/1 cup fresh breadcrumbs
cornflour (cornstarch), for dusting
vegetable oil, for deep-frying
2 eggs, beaten
salt
4 lemon wedges, to serve

1 Slice the scallops in two horizontally, then sprinkle with salt. Remove the stalks from the shiitake by cutting them off with a knife. Discard the stalks.

2 Cut shallow slits on the top of the shiitake to form a 'hash' symbol or cut slits to form a white cross. Sprinkle with a little salt.

3 Heat a steamer and steam the naga-imo for 10–15 minutes, or until soft. Test with a skewer. Leave to cool.

4 Wait until the naga-imo is cool enough to handle. Skin, then mash the flesh in a bowl with a masher, getting rid of any lumps. Add the miso and mix well. Take the breadcrumbs into your hands and break them down finely. Mix half into the mashed naga-imo, keeping the rest on a small plate.

5 Fill the underneath of the shiitake caps with a scoop of mashed naga-imo. Smooth down with the flat edge of a knife and dust the mash with cornflour.

6 Add a little mash to a slice of scallop and place on top.

7 Spread another 5ml/1 tsp mashed naga-imo on to the scallop and shape to completely cover. Make sure all the ingredients are clinging together. Repeat to make eight little mounds.

8 Heat the oil to 150°C/300°F. Place the beaten eggs in a shallow container. Dust the shiitake and scallop mounds with cornflour, then dip into the egg. Handle with care as the mash and scallop are quite soft. Coat well with the remaining breadcrumbs and deep-fry in the oil until golden. Drain well on kitchen paper. Serve hot on individual plates with a wedge of lemon.

VARIATION

For a vegetarian option, use 16 shiitake mushrooms. Sandwich the naga-imo mash between two shiitake to make 8 bundles. Deep-fry in the same way as the scallop version.

COOK'S TIPS

• Fresh naga-imo produces a slimy liquid when it's cut. Try not to touch this as some people can react and develop a mild rash. When it's cooked, it is perfectly safe to touch.
• If you can't find naga-imo, use yam or 115g/4oz each of potatoes and peeled Jerusalem artichokes instead. Steam the potatoes and boil the artichokes until both are tender.

Per portion Energy 221kcal/918kJ; Protein 11.2g; Carbohydrate 11.7g, of which sugars 1.5g; Fat 14.6g, of which saturates 2.3g; Cholesterol 107mg; Calcium 50mg; Fibre 1.1g; Sodium 183mg.

SEAFOOD AND SPRING ONION PANCAKE

This Korean pancake makes a great appetizer. Tender squid and scallops are accompanied by the crunch and piquancy of spring onions. Vegetables and seafood stud the crisp surface of the pancake, while the centre is amazingly light and moist.

SERVES FOUR

INGREDIENTS
90g/3½oz squid
2 oysters
5 clams
5 small prawns (shrimp), shelled
3 scallops, removed from
  the shell
15ml/1 tbsp vegetable oil
5 spring onions (scallions), sliced
  into thin strips
½ red chilli, seeded and cut into
  thin strips
½ green chilli, seeded and cut
  into thin strips
50g/2oz enoki mushrooms,
  caps removed
1 garlic clove, thinly sliced
salt and ground black pepper
For the batter
115g/4oz/1 cup plain
  (all-purpose) flour
40g/1½oz/⅓ cup cornflour
  (cornstarch)
5ml/1 tsp salt
5ml/1 tsp sugar
2 eggs, beaten
For the dipping sauce
90ml/6 tbsp light soy sauce
22.5ml/4½ tsp rice vinegar
1 spring onion (scallion),
  finely shredded
1 red chilli, finely shredded
1 garlic clove, crushed
5ml/1 tsp sesame oil
5ml/1 tsp sesame seeds

1 To make the batter, sift the flour and cornflour into a large bowl. Add the salt and sugar. Make a well in the middle. Add the eggs and 200ml/7fl oz/scant 1 cup iced water and whisk lightly, mixing in the flour mixture until smooth.

2 Wash the squid carefully, rinsing off any ink that remains on the body. Holding the body of the squid firmly, pull away the head and tentacles. If the ink sac is still intact, remove it and discard. Pull out all the innards including the long transparent pen. Peel off and discard the thin purple skin on the body, but keep the two small side fins. Slice the head across just under the eyes, severing the tentacles. Discard the rest of the head. Squeeze the tentacles at the head end to push out the round beak in the centre and discard. Rinse the pouch and tentacles well. (Your fishmonger will prepare squid for you, if you prefer.)

3 Chop the cleaned squid into small pieces and place in a bowl.

4 Open the oysters, Cover your hand with a thick folded cloth and take care when using an oyster knife. Hold the flat shell on top. Push the tip of an oyster knife or heavy, short-bladed knife into the hinge of the oyster and twist to prise the shell open. Cut the two muscles inside. Run the blade between the shells to open them. Discard the top shell. Then cut the oyster away from the flat shell. Repeat with the remaining oyster. Add to the squid in the bowl.

5 Open the clam shells and tip each clam into the bowl. Add the prawns and scallops to the bowl. Season the mixture with salt and pepper, and leave to stand for 10 minutes.

6 Make the dipping sauce by combining all the ingredients in a small bowl.

7 Coat a large frying pan with vegetable oil and place over a medium heat. Pour one third of the batter into the pan, ensuring that it is a roughly consistent thickness across the base.

8 Place the spring onions, chillies, mushrooms and garlic on to the pancake and then add the seafood, distributing the ingredients evenly. Pour over the remaining batter and tilt the pan to form an even layer. Cook until the pancake is set and browned underneath, then turn it over and cook briefly to brown the top so that the pancake is golden brown on both sides.

9 Slice the pancake into bitesize pieces and serve it on a plate with the dipping sauce.

Per portion Energy 255kcal/1077kJ; Protein 16.5g; Carbohydrate 33.7g, of which sugars 1.9g; Fat 7.1g, of which saturates 1.4g; Cholesterol 232mg; Calcium 80mg; Fibre 1.4g; Sodium 613mg.

SOUPS &
BROTHS

Soups are a very versatile food. They are enjoyed as snacks, as
accompaniments to main meals or as meals in themselves. Korean soups
are typically light and clear, and are characterized by flavourings such as
seaweed and white radish. Japanese soups often contain noodles, and the
soup stock is made with great care to set off their flavour. Rich broths
using meat or fish are popular during the winter months.

Left: Spicy Potato and Courgette Soup; **Above:** Oxtail Soup

MISO SOUP

Essential to any Japanese meal is a bowl of rice. Next is miso soup, served in a lacquered bowl. Of the many variations, Wakame To Tofu No Miso-shiru definitely comes first.

SERVES FOUR

INGREDIENTS
    5g/⅛oz dried wakame
    ½ × 225–285g/8–10¼oz packet fresh
        soft tofu or long-life silken tofu
    400ml/14fl oz/1⅔ cups second dashi
        stock or the same amount of water
        and 5ml/1 tsp dashi-no-moto
    45ml/3 tbsp miso
    2 spring onions (scallions),
        finely chopped
    shichimi togarashi or sansho
        (optional), to serve

1 Soak the wakame in a large bowl of cold water for 15 minutes. Drain and chop into stamp-size pieces if using the long or broad type.

2 Cut the tofu into 1cm/½in strips, then cut horizontally through the strips. Cut the thin strips into squares.

3 Bring the dashi stock to the boil. Put the miso in a small cup and mix with 60ml/4 tbsp hot stock from the pan. Reduce the heat to low and pour two-thirds of the miso into the pan of stock.

4 Taste the soup and add more miso if required. Add the wakame and the tofu and increase the heat. Just before the soup comes to the boil again, add the spring onions and remove from the heat. Do not boil. Serve sprinkled with shichimi togarashi or sansho, if liked.

COOK'S TIPS
• To make first dashi stock, put a 10cm/4in square piece of dried konbu into a pan. Pour in 600ml/1 pint/2½ cups water and soak for an hour. Heat to near boiling point, then remove from the heat. Remove and reserve the konbu for the second dashi. Add 20g/¾oz kezuri-bushi to the pan and heat on low. Do not stir. Just before it reaches boiling point, turn off the heat. Allow the flakes to settle down to the bottom of the pan. Strain and reserve the kezuri-bushi flakes for the second dashi stock.
• To make second dashi stock, put the reserved konbu and kezuri-bushi from the first dashi into a pan with 600ml/1 pint/2½ cups water. Bring to the boil, then simmer for 15 minutes until the stock is reduced by a third. Add 15g/½oz kezuri-bushi to the pan. Immediately remove from the heat. Skim any scum from the surface. Leave to stand for 10 minutes, then strain.

Per portion Energy 89kcal/371kJ; Protein 12.1g; Carbohydrate 1.9g, of which sugars 1.7g; Fat 3.7g, of which saturates 1g; Cholesterol 32mg; Calcium 21mg; Fibre 0.6g; Sodium 1284mg.

SAVOURY EGG SOUP

THIS JAPANESE CUSTARD-LIKE SOUP IS SOFTER AND RUNNIER THAN A WESTERN CUSTARD PUDDING. IT CONTAINS TASTY SURPRISES, SUCH AS PINK PRAWNS AND JADE-GREEN GINGKO NUTS.

SERVES FOUR

INGREDIENTS

8 gingko nuts in shells (or canned)
4 medium raw tiger prawns (jumbo shrimp), peeled, heads and tails removed
5cm/2in carrot, thinly sliced
4 mitsuba sprigs or 8 chives
75g/3oz chicken breast portion, skinned
5ml/1 tsp sake
5ml/1 tsp shoyu
2 fresh shiitake mushrooms, thinly sliced, stalks discarded
salt
For the custard
3 large (US extra large) eggs, beaten
500ml/17fl oz/2⅓ cups first dashi stock, or the same amount of water and 2.5ml/½ tsp dashi-no-moto
15ml/1 tbsp sake
15ml/1 tbsp shoyu
2.5ml/½ tsp salt

1 Carefully crack the gingko nut shells with a nutcracker and boil the nuts for 5 minutes. Drain. Remove any skin.

2 Insert a cocktail stick (toothpick) into the back of each prawn and remove the vein. Blanch the prawns in hot water until they curl up. Drain and pat dry.

3 Cut the carrot slices into maple-leaf shapes with a sharp knife or a vegetable cutter. Blanch in salted water. Drain.

4 Cut off the mitsuba roots. Cut the stems 2.5cm/1in from the top and keep the leaves. Chop the stems in half and pour hot water over to wilt them. If using chives, chop into 7.5cm/3in lengths and wilt as the mitsuba stems. Put two mitsuba stems or two chives together and tie a knot in the middle.

5 Dice the chicken, then marinate in the sake and shoyu for 15 minutes.

6 To make the custard, put all the ingredients together in a bowl. Mix with chopsticks, and strain into a bowl.

7 Bring a steamer to the boil, then set the heat to very low.

8 Divide the chicken, shiitake, gingko nuts, prawns and carrots among four ramekins. Divide the egg mixture among the ramekins.

9 Put the mitsuba stems or chives on top, and the leaves if you like, and then cover each ramekin with a piece of foil. Carefully place them in the steamer. Steam on low for 15 minutes. Insert a cocktail stick into the egg: if the liquid stays clear, it's set. Serve hot.

VARIATIONS
• For a fish and shellfish variation, use scallops, crab meat, filleted lemon sole and asparagus tips.
• For a vegetarian version, try par-boiled turnips, oyster mushrooms, wakame seaweed and thinly sliced strips of spring onions (scallions).

Per portion Energy 163kcal/681kJ; Protein 16g; Carbohydrate 2.4g, of which sugars 1g; Fat 9.7g, of which saturates 2.3g; Cholesterol 205mg; Calcium 48mg; Fibre 0.5g; Sodium 654mg.

RICE CAKE SOUP

TRADITIONALLY EATEN BY KOREAN FAMILIES ON NEW YEAR'S DAY, THIS CEREMONIAL SOUP IS SIMPLE AND SATISFYING. A TRADITIONAL KOREAN NEW YEAR'S GREETING BETWEEN FRIENDS IS TO ASK IF THE OTHER PERSON HAS EATEN A BOWL OF RICE CAKE SOUP YET.

SERVES FIVE

INGREDIENTS
15g/½oz dried anchovies
200g/7oz beef sirloin,
 thinly sliced
1 garlic clove, crushed
30ml/2 tbsp salt
15ml/1 tbsp light soy sauce
1kg/2¼lb rice cake
½ leek, roughly chopped
2 eggs
vegetable oil, for cooking
dried seaweed paper or
 Japanese nori
ground black pepper

1 Bring 1 litre/1¾ pints/4 cups water to the boil in a wok or pan and add the dried anchovies. Boil over a high heat for 15 minutes. Remove and discard the anchovies. Set the stock aside.

2 Place the beef in a wok or pan over a medium heat. Add the garlic and a little ground pepper and cook gently, turning the slices, for 2 minutes. Add 1 litre/1¾ pints/4 cups water and bring to the boil. Simmer for 10 minutes, then strain the stock into a jug (pitcher) and set the beef aside.

3 Combine the anchovy and beef stocks in a wok or large pan. Add the salt and soy sauce and bring to the boil.

4 Slice the rice cake into bitesize pieces and add these to the boiling stock with the leeks. Bring the stock back to the boil, if necessary, and keep it boiling. Cook the rice cake for about 10 minutes, until tender.

5 Meanwhile, separate the eggs. The yolks are not needed: set them aside for another use. Whisk the whites lightly to break them up. Heat a little oil in a frying pan and add the egg whites, tilting the pan so that they run evenly over the pan. Cook until browned and set into a paper-thin crêpe. Transfer to a plate and leave to cool.

6 Roll up the cooled egg-white omelette and cut into 3cm/1¼in slices. Shake out the slices into strips. Slice the dried seaweed into strips.

7 Season the soup and ladle it into serving bowls. Divide the beef, seaweed and omelette strips among the bowls of soup, piling them up attractively in the middle of each one. Serve immediately.

Per portion Energy 431kcal/1817kJ; Protein 18.3g; Carbohydrate 63.2g, of which sugars 1.1g; Fat 13.4g, of which saturates 3.3g; Cholesterol 101mg; Calcium 68mg; Fibre 1.1g; Sodium 374mg.

SOYA BEANSPROUT SOUP

THIS GENTLE KOREAN BROTH, KONGNAMUL, IS EASY TO MAKE AND EASY ON THE PALATE, WITH JUST A HINT OF SPICINESS AND A REFRESHING NUTTY FLAVOUR. IT IS REPUTED TO BE THE PERFECT SOLUTION FOR CALMING THE STOMACH AFTER A HEAVY DRINKING SESSION.

SERVES FOUR

INGREDIENTS
    200g/7oz/generous 2 cups
       soya beansprouts
    1 red or green chilli
    15 dried anchovies
    1 spring onion (scallion),
       finely sliced
    3 garlic cloves, chopped
    salt

1 Wash the soya beansprouts, and trim off the tail ends.

2 Seed the chilli and cut it diagonally into thin slices.

3 Boil 750ml/1¼ pints/3 cups water in a wok or pan and add the dried anchovies. After boiling for 15 minutes remove the anchovies and discard.

4 Add the soya beansprouts and boil for 5 minutes, ensuring the lid is kept tightly on. Add the spring onion, chilli and garlic, and boil for a further 3 minutes. Finally, add salt to taste, ladle the soup into bowls and serve.

COOK'S TIPS
• Soya beansprouts and dried anchovies are available at some Asian stores. If you are unable to find dried anchovies, then 5ml/1 tsp Thai fish sauce can be used as a substitute.
• The soup can be made using sprouted mung beans, but they should not be boiled for as long as the soya beansprouts – allow about 2 minutes to heat them and retain their texture.

VARIATION
To make a spicier version of this soup simply add 5ml/1 tsp of chilli powder to each bowl. The result is hotter and said to be great for curing a cold.

Per portion Energy 41kcal/173kJ; Protein 4.6g; Carbohydrate 2.7g, of which sugars 1.2g; Fat 1.4g, of which saturates 0.2g; Cholesterol 7mg; Calcium 46mg; Fibre 1g; Sodium 445mg.

WHEAT NOODLES IN SOYA BEAN SOUP

STRANDS OF THIN WHEAT NOODLES TASTE GREAT IN A MILD AND DELICIOUSLY NUTTY CHILLED SOUP, MAKING AN IDEAL DISH DURING A HOT KOREAN SUMMER. THE ICED BROTH IS TOPPED WITH SUCCULENT STRIPS OF CUCUMBER AND WEDGES OF FRESHLY CUT TOMATO WEDGES.

SERVES FOUR

INGREDIENTS
  185g/6½oz/1 cup soya beans
  30ml/2 tbsp sesame seeds
  300g/11oz thin wheat noodles
  salt
  1 cucumber, cut into thin strips
    and 1 tomato, cut into wedges,
    to garnish

VARIATION
For a quick and easy version of this dish use 250ml/8fl oz/1 cup unsweetened soya milk rather than the soaked soya beans. Simply add the ground sesame seeds to the soya milk and chill to make the soup.

COOK'S TIP
To separate the skins and rubbed beans, place them in a bowl of cold water: the skins will float and can be skimmed off.

1 Soak the soya beans overnight. Rinse in cold water and remove the skins.

2 Gently toast the sesame seeds in a dry pan until they have lightly browned. Place the peeled soya beans and the sesame seeds in a food processor. Add 1 litre/1¾ pints/4 cups water and process until fine. Strain through muslin (cheesecloth), collecting the liquid in a jug (pitcher). Chill the soya and sesame milk in the refrigerator.

3 Bring a pan of water to the boil and cook the noodles, making sure they are well covered. When they are cooked, drain them and rinse them well in cold water.

4 Place a portion of the wheat noodles in each soup bowl, and pour over the chilled soya and sesame liquid. Garnish the bowls with strips of cucumber and tomato wedges, then season with salt and serve.

Per portion Energy 268kcal/1121kJ; Protein 20.1g; Carbohydrate 17.9g, of which sugars 3.4g; Fat 13.3g, of which saturates 1.7g; Cholesterol 0mg; Calcium 174mg; Fibre 8.7g; Sodium 6mg.

NOODLE SOUP <u>WITH</u> OYSTER MUSHROOMS

COLLOQUIALLY KNOWN AS 'MARKETPLACE NOODLES', THIS KOREAN DISH HAS LONG BEEN ENJOYED AS A QUICK AND SIMPLE LUNCH. THE OYSTER MUSHROOMS GIVE THE MILD BROTH AN APPETIZING RICHNESS. SERVE WITH AN ACCOMPANIMENT OF RADISH KIMCHI AND A BOWL OF STEAMED RICE.

SERVES TWO

INGREDIENTS
    75g/3oz beef
    30ml/2 tbsp light soy sauce
    2 eggs, beaten
    45ml/3 tbsp vegetable oil
    4 oyster mushrooms
    75g/3oz courgette (zucchini)
    sesame oil, for drizzling
    115g/4oz plain noodles
    1 spring onion (scallion),
      finely chopped
    1 dried red chilli, thinly sliced
    2 garlic cloves, crushed
    salt and ground white pepper
    sesame seeds, to garnish

1 Pour 500ml/17fl oz/2¼ cups water into a pan and bring to the boil. Add the beef and cook until tender, about 20 minutes. Remove the meat and slice into thin strips.

2 Strain the cooking liquid through a sieve (strainer) into a jug (pitcher). Then add the light soy sauce to the stock and set to one side.

3 Season the beaten eggs with a pinch of salt. Coat a frying pan with 10ml/2 tsp vegetable oil and heat over a medium heat. Add the beaten eggs, swirling the pan to coat it evenly, and make a thin omelette. Cook until set and lightly browned on each side.

4 Slide the omelette from the pan on to a board and roll it up, then slice it thinly and shake out the slices into thin strips.

5 Cut the oyster mushrooms and courgette into thin strips. Sprinkle both with a little salt. Pat dry with kitchen paper after 5 minutes.

6 Heat the remaining vegetable oil in a wok over a medium heat. Quickly stir-fry the mushrooms and drizzle with sesame oil before setting them aside. Add and lightly fry the courgette until it softens, then remove. Finally, stir-fry the beef until lightly browned, and set aside.

7 Bring a pan of water to the boil. Add the plain noodles and bring back to the boil. Cook for 3–5 minutes, or according to the packet instructions, until just tender. Drain the noodles and rinse in cold water. Leave to drain again. Quickly reheat the reserved beef stock.

8 Place the noodles at the base of a soup dish or divide between two individual bowls. Cover with the mushrooms, courgette and sliced beef. Top with the spring onion, chilli and garlic, then pour over the beef stock until roughly one third of the ingredients are covered. Finally, sprinkle with sesame seeds before serving.

COOK'S TIP
Spare egg yolks can be used for mayonnaise. To freeze, lightly whisk them with sugar, noting the weight of sugar and number of yolks on the label.

Per portion Energy 492kcal/2059kJ; Protein 23.1g; Carbohydrate 40.4g, of which sugars 3.3g; Fat 27.7g, of which saturates 4.9g; Cholesterol 213mg; Calcium 60mg; Fibre 2.3g; Sodium 1167mg.

DUMPLING SOUP

THERE ARE MANY VARIETIES OF READY-TO-EAT DUMPLINGS, FROM PORK AND PRAWN TO CHICKEN AND SPINACH, AND AS THEY ARE WIDELY AVAILABLE, THIS DISH IS SIMPLE TO MAKE AND A DELIGHT TO EAT.

SERVES TWO

INGREDIENTS
    750ml/1¼ pints/3 cups beef stock
    16 frozen dumplings
    1 spring onion (scallion), sliced
    ¼ green chilli, sliced
    1 garlic clove, crushed
    15ml/1 tbsp light soy sauce
    salt and ground black pepper

1 Place the stock in a pan and bring to the boil. Add the frozen dumplings, cover, and boil for 6 minutes.

2 Add the sliced spring onions, chilli, garlic and soy sauce to the pan, and boil for 2 minutes.

3 Season with salt and black pepper before serving.

Per portion Energy 106kcal/445kJ; Protein 2g; Carbohydrate 12.6g, of which sugars 0.6g; Fat 6.1g, of which saturates 3.4g; Cholesterol 5mg; Calcium 30mg; Fibre 0.5g; Sodium 842mg.

COLD SUMMER CUCUMBER SOUP

NATURALLY COOL AND REFRESHING CUCUMBER IS SHARPENED WITH CIDER VINEGAR IN THIS CHILLED SOUP, WHICH IS PERFECT FOR COOLING EVERYONE DOWN AT LUNCH ON A HOT SUMMER DAY. IT MAKES A GREAT APPETIZER FOR ANY HOT NOODLE OR BARBECUE DISH.

SERVES FOUR

INGREDIENTS
    2 cucumbers, peeled, halved and seeded
    1 garlic clove, crushed
    50g/2oz spring onions (scallions), sliced
    30ml/2 tbsp cider vinegar
    30ml/2 tbsp sugar syrup (see Winter
      Kimchi Soup, page 260)
    salt

1 Slice the cucumbers into long, thin strips, sprinkly with salt and leave for 10 minutes.

2 Combine 500ml/17fl oz/2 generous cups water with the crushed garlic, spring onions, vinegar and sugar syrup.

3 Add the sliced cucumber before ladling the soup into bowls.

Per portion Energy 40kcal/166kJ; Protein 0.8g; Carbohydrate 9.2g, of which sugars 9.1g; Fat 0.2g, of which saturates 0g; Cholesterol 0mg; Calcium 20mg; Fibre 0.6g; Sodium 30mg.

COLD RADISH KIMCHI SOUP

THIS ICE-COLD SOUP IS NORMALLY SERVED AS AN ACCOMPANIMENT TO A HOT DISH, SUCH AS GRILLED OR BARBEQUED MEAT. THE SPICY SEASONING CONTRASTS DELICIOUSLY WITH THE CHILLED BROTH.

SERVES EIGHT

INGREDIENTS
    1 Chinese leaves (Chinese
       cabbage)
    150g/5oz Chinese white radish,
       peeled and diced
    50g/2oz/¼ cup salt
    50g/2oz Korean chilli flakes
    1 Asian pear, peeled and diced
    2 cucumbers, finely sliced
    75g/3oz watercress
    75g/3oz spring onions (scallions),
       roughly sliced
    10 garlic cloves, crushed
    25g/1oz fresh root ginger,
       finely sliced
    25g/1oz/3 tbsp pine nuts,
       to garnish

1 Slice the cabbage and cut the radish into cubes measuring about 3cm/1¼in. Place the vegetables in a large bowl. Add 250ml/8fl oz/1 cup water and the salt, and leave to stand for 1 hour.

2 Pour 2 litres/3½ pints/8¾ cups water into a very large large bowl. Tie the chilli flakes in a muslin (cheesecloth) bag, and then put it in the water.

3 Cover the bowl and set it aside until the water has taken on the colour and flavour of the chilli. Then remove the bag and skim out any flakes that may have escaped from the bag and are left in the water.

4 Drain the cabbage and radish and add them to the chilli water. Leave to stand for 30 minutes.

5 Add a further 2 litres/3½ pints/8¾ cups water. Stir in the Asian pear, cucumbers, watercress, spring onions, garlic and ginger. Set the soup aside for 30 minutes to allow the flavours to develop and mingle.

6 Season the soup with a little salt, if required, then serve garnished with the pine nuts.

Per portion Energy 92kcal/382kJ; Protein 3.4g; Carbohydrate 8g, of which sugars 5.7g; Fat 5.4g, of which saturates 0.5g; Cholesterol 0mg; Calcium 67mg; Fibre 2.2g; Sodium 15mg.

WINTER KIMCHI SOUP

The spicy flavours of chilli and ginger in this chilled soup are uniquely warming on a cold winter's night. Traditionally, the soup was served with sweet potatoes, which would have been baked in the embers of the household fire.

SERVES FOUR

INGREDIENTS

3 Chinese white radishes, peeled
115g/4oz/½ cup salt
4 spring onions (scallions), shredded
1 garlic clove, sliced
115g/4oz fresh root ginger, sliced
2 red chillies, seeded and sliced
3 green chillies, seeded and sliced
1 Asian pear, peeled and diced
sugar syrup, to taste
10g/¼oz/1 tbsp pine nuts, to garnish

COOK'S TIP
To make a light sugar syrup, dissolve 225g/8oz/1 cup sugar in 600ml/ 1 pint/2½ cups water in a pan over a medium heat, stirring occasionally. Bring to the boil and boil for 2–3 minutes, until the syrup has reduced slightly. Take care not to allow the sugar to burn. Leave the syrup to cool. Store the syrup in an airtight jar in the refrigerator, where it will keep for up to 2 weeks. Alternatively, freeze the syrup in 50ml/2fl oz/¼ cup containers.

1 Place the Chinese white radishes in a bowl. Pour in 3.5 litres/6 pints/15 cups water and the salt, and leave them to soak overnight.

2 The next day, add the spring onions to the radishes in salt water and leave them to stand for 30 minutes.

3 Tie the garlic and ginger in a muslin (cheesecloth) bag and add to the radishes and spring onion with the red and green chillies. Cover and leave to stand for another day in the refrigerator.

4 Remove the radishes from the mixture, cut them into bitesize dice and then return the pieces to the soup. Remove and discard the garlic and ginger.

5 Add the pear to the soup, adding a little sugar syrup if it is too salty. Serve garnished with pine nuts.

COOK'S TIP
Peeled radishes are milder than unpeeled ones. To prepare a radish, slice off the roots and leaves, wash under cold running water and drain.

Per portion Energy 48kcal/198kJ; Protein 1.7g; Carbohydrate 5.9g, of which sugars 5.8g; Fat 2.1g, of which saturates 0.2g; Cholesterol 0mg; Calcium 37mg; Fibre 2g; Sodium 28mg.

SPICY POTATO AND COURGETTE SOUP

THIS KOREAN TAKE ON A TYPICAL WESTERN SOUP IS SEASONED WITH SPICES FOR A LIVELY KICK. THE GOCHUJANG CHILLI PASTE HELPS TO THICKEN THE SOUP AND GIVE IT A SILKY TEXTURE. THE ADDITION OF POTATOES AND BEEF MAKE IT A REALLY HEARTY AND FILLING MEAL IN A BOWL.

SERVES TWO

INGREDIENTS
    5ml/1 tsp salt
    400g/14oz baby new
      potatoes, peeled
    5ml/1 tsp sesame oil
    15ml/1 tbsp Korean chilli powder
    5ml/1 tsp gochujang chilli paste
    1 garlic clove, crushed
    115g/4oz minced (ground) beef,
      finely chopped
    1 small courgette (zucchini), halved
      and sliced
    1 red chilli, seeded and thinly sliced
    ½ small leek, thinly sliced
    5ml/1 tsp sake
    1 spring onion (scallion), shredded,
      to garnish

1 Bring 750ml/1¼ pints/3 cups water to the boil in a large pan. Add the salt and the potatoes.

2 Mix the sesame oil, chilli powder, gochujang paste and garlic with the beef until well combined. Add the seasoned beef mixture to the pan and boil for 5 minutes.

3 Add the courgette and boil for a further 3 minutes. Then add the chilli, leek and sake and boil for 2 minutes. Garnish with the spring onion.

COOK'S TIP
Chopping minced (ground) beef breaks it down into very fine pieces. Shape the meat in a neat block and chop it in both directions using a large knife.

Per portion Energy 371kcal/1552kJ; Protein 18.6g; Carbohydrate 38.2g, of which sugars 5.6g; Fat 17.1g, of which saturates 5.3g; Cholesterol 35mg; Calcium 70mg; Fibre 4.1g; Sodium 73mg.

SPICY SOFT TOFU STEW

THE UNDERLYING FIERY SPICINESS OF THIS KOREAN DISH, CALLED SUNDUBU CHIGE, REALLY HELPS TO EMPHASIZE ITS SEAFOOD FLAVOURS. CLAMS AND PRAWNS ARE SERVED IN A PIQUANT SOUP WITH A MEDLEY OF VEGETABLES, WITH CREAMY TOFU MELTING INTO THE RICH SAUCE.

SERVES TWO TO THREE

INGREDIENTS
1 block soft tofu
15ml/1 tbsp light soy sauce
6 prawns (shrimp)
6 clams
25g/1oz enoki mushrooms
15ml/1 tbsp vegetable oil
50g/2oz beef, finely chopped
7.5ml/1½ tsp Korean chilli powder
5ml/1 tsp crushed garlic
500ml/17fl oz/generous 2 cups water
  or beef stock
⅓ leek, sliced
½ red chilli, sliced
½ green chilli, sliced
2.5ml/½ tsp dark soy sauce
1.5ml/¼ tsp Thai fish sauce
salt

1 Break the block of tofu into small pieces with your hands, place them in a bowl and marinate with the light soy sauce and a pinch of salt for about 1 hour.

2 Scrub the clams in cold running water. Discard the caps from the enoki mushrooms.

3 To shell the prawns, gently pull off the tail shell. Twist off the head. Peel away the soft body shell and the small claws beneath. Rinse well.

4 In a flameproof casserole dish or heavy pan, heat the vegetable oil over a high heat. Add the chopped beef and stir-fry until the meat has browned.

5 Add the chilli powder, garlic and a splash of water to the pan. Stir-fry, coating the meat with the spices. Add the water or stock and bring to the boil.

6 Add the clams, prawns and tofu, and boil for a further 4 minutes.

7 Reduce the heat slightly and add the leek, chillies and mushrooms. Continue to cook until the leek has softened. Then stir in the dark soy sauce and Thai fish sauce. Season with salt if necessary, and serve.

VARIATION
To give the dish a spicy tang, add 50g/2oz chopped *kimchi* while you are stir-frying the beef.

Per portion Energy 170kcal/709kJ; Protein 21.4g; Carbohydrate 2.1g, of which sugars 1.5g; Fat 8.4g, of which saturates 1.5g; Cholesterol 140mg; Calcium 378mg; Fibre 0.8g; Sodium 734mg.

SOYA BEAN PASTE STEW

This rich Korean stew, doenjang chige, is a really thick and hearty casserole. The slow cooking imparts a deep, flavour full of spiciness. It is a satisfyingly warm dish, ideal for cold evenings, and goes particularly well with the flavour of flame-grilled meat.

SERVES TWO

INGREDIENTS
½ courgette (zucchini)
25g/1oz enoki mushrooms
15ml/1 tbsp sesame oil, plus extra
  for drizzling
50g/2oz beef, finely chopped
30ml/2 tbsp doenjang soya
  bean paste
½ onion, finely chopped
10ml/2 tsp finely chopped garlic
550ml/18fl oz/2½ cups fish stock
1 red chilli, seeded and
  sliced diagonally
½ block firm tofu, diced
1 spring onion (scallion), sliced,
  to garnish

1 Thickly slice the courgette, and then cut the slices into quarters. Discard the caps from the enoki mushrooms.

2 In a casserole dish or heavy pan, heat the sesame oil over a high heat. Add the beef and soya bean paste to the pan, and cook until golden brown. Then add the onion and garlic to the pan and sauté gently. Add the fish stock and bring to the boil.

3 Next add the chilli and courgette slices and boil for 5 minutes. Add the tofu and mushrooms and boil for a further 2 minutes. Reduce the heat and simmer the stew gently for 15 minutes.

4 Garnish with sliced spring onion and a drizzle of sesame oil, and serve.

COOK'S TIPS
• When making fish stock, you can use stock (bouillon) cubes for convenience, but to make an authentic fish stock from scratch, simply simmer a handful of dried anchovies in 1 litre/1¾ pints/ 4 cups water for 30 minutes, and then strain the stock into a jug (pitcher).
• This dish is traditionally cooked in a heavy stone pot known as a *tukbaege*, although a heavy pan or casserole will work as well. Serve the dish in the heavy cooking pot so it remains warm and continues to cook once it is on the table.
• Enoki mushrooms are sometimes found in supermarkets under the name of snow puff mushrooms.

Per portion Energy 166kcal/690kJ; Protein 13g; Carbohydrate 4.8g, of which sugars 3.2g; Fat 10.7g, of which saturates 2.2g; Cholesterol 15mg; Calcium 169mg; Fibre 3.1g; Sodium 25mg.

CLEAR SOUP <u>WITH</u> SEAFOOD STICKS

THIS DELICATE JAPANESE SOUP, O-SUMASHI, WHICH IS OFTEN EATEN WITH SUSHI, IS VERY QUICK TO MAKE IF YOU PREPARE THE FIRST DASHI BEFOREHAND OR IF YOU USE FREEZE-DRIED DASHI-NO-MOTO.

<u>SERVES FOUR</u>

INGREDIENTS
    4 mitsuba sprigs or 4 chives and a
        few sprigs of mustard and cress
    4 seafood sticks
    400ml/14fl oz/1⅔ cups first dashi
        stock, or the same amount of water
        and 5ml/1 tsp dashi-no-moto
    15ml/1 tbsp shoyu
    7.5ml/1½ tsp salt
    grated rind of yuzu (optional),
        to garnish

1 Mitsuba leaves are normally sold with the stems and roots on to retain freshness. Cut off the root, then cut 5cm/2in from the top, retaining both the long straw-like stem and the leaf.

2 Blanch the stems in hot water from the kettle. If you use chives, choose them at least 10cm/4in in length and blanch them, too.

3 Take a seafood stick and carefully tie around the middle with a mitsuba stem or chive, holding it in place with a knot. Do not pull too tightly, as the bow will easily break. Repeat the process to make four tied seafood sticks.

4 Hold one seafood stick in your hand. With your finger, carefully loosen both ends to make it look like a tassel.

5 Place one seafood stick in each soup bowl, then put the four mitsuba leaves or mustard and cress on top.

6 Heat the stock in a pan and bring to the boil. Add shoyu and salt to taste. Pour the stock gently over the mitsuba and seafood stick. Sprinkle with grated yuzu rind, if using.

VARIATION
You can use small prawns (shrimp) instead of seafood sticks. Blanch 12 raw prawns in boiling water until they curl up and form a full circle. Drain. Tie mitsuba stems to make four bows. Arrange three prawns side by side in each bowl and put the mitsuba bows and leaves on top.

Per portion 30kcal/125kJ; Protein 5.4g; Carbohydrate 1g, of which sugars 0.9g; Fat 0.5g, of which saturates 0.1g; Cholesterol 23mg; Calcium 36mg; Fibre 0.2g; Sodium 877mg.

CLEAR COD SOUP

THIS QUICK SOUP IS A POPULAR DAILY DISH IN KOREA, OFTEN MADE AS A FAMILY EVENING MEAL. IT PACKED WITH DELICIOUS INGREDIENTS. A GLASS OF SOJU IS THE PERFECT ACCOMPANIMENT.

SERVES FOUR

INGREDIENTS
  25g/1oz dried anchovies
  600g/1lb 6oz cod fillet, skinned and
    cut into wide strips
  225g/8oz Chinese white radish,
    peeled and diced
  2 garlic cloves, crushed
  2 spring onions (scallions),
    roughly sliced
  ½ leek, finely sliced
  ½ block firm tofu, cubed
  ½ hot red chilli, seeded
    and sliced
  50g/2oz enoki mushrooms
  50g/2oz watercress
  salt and ground black pepper

1 Bring 1.5 litres/2½ pints/6¼ cups water to the boil in large pan and add the dried anchovies. Boil for 10 minutes over a high heat. At the end of this time use a slotted spoon to remove the anchovies. Discard the anchovies and retain the stock.

2 Add the cod and radish. Simmer the soup for about 4 minutes, until the fish is opaque and just cooked.

3 Stir in the garlic, spring onions and leek. Add the tofu and let the soup simmer for a further 10 minutes, but do not stir or the tofu will break up.

COOK'S TIPS
• For an especially spicy soup, increase the quantity of hot chilli and use one or more chillies to taste.
• Spicy soups are suitable in the hottest months, when perspiration has a cooling effect, or to combat the cold of winter.
• For a milder version, use a plump, mild variety with one seeded and sliced chilli.

4 Add the enoki mushrooms, watercress, chilli and salt. Increase the heat and boil for 2 minutes. Add pepper and serve.

Per portion 164kcal/687kJ; Protein 32.3g; Carbohydrate 1.7g, of which sugars 1.5g; Fat 3.1g, of which saturates 0.5g; Cholesterol 73mg; Calcium 196mg; Fibre 1g; Sodium 350mg.

HOT AND SPICY FISH SOUP

THIS KOREAN SOUP HAS A DELICIOUS SPICY KICK. THE WHITE FISH FLAKES HAVE THE BITE OF RED CHILLI, AND THE WATERCRESS AND SPRING ONIONS ADD A REFRESHING ZESTY QUALITY.

SERVES THREE TO FOUR

INGREDIENTS
    1 cod, filleted and skinned,
      head separate
    225g/8oz Chinese white radish,
      peeled and cut into 2cm/¾in cubes
    ½ onion, chopped
    2 garlic cloves, crushed
    22.5ml/4½ tsp Korean
      chilli powder
    5ml/1 tsp gochujang
      chilli paste
    2 spring onions (scallions),
      roughly sliced
    1 block firm tofu, cubed
    90g/3½oz watercress or
      rocket (arugula)
    salt and ground black pepper

1 Slice the cod fillets into three or four large pieces and set the head aside.

2 Bring 750ml/1¼ pints/3 cups water to the boil and add the fish head, radish, onion, crushed garlic, a pinch of salt. the chilli powder and gochujang chilli paste. Boil for 5 minutes more.

3 Remove the fish head and add the sliced fillet to the pan. Simmer until the fish is tender, about 4 minutes.

4 Add the spring onions, tofu, and watercress or rocket. Simmer the soup without stirring for 2 minutes more. Season with salt and pepper and serve.

Per portion Energy 132kcal/554kJ; Protein 23.4g; Carbohydrate 2.8g, of which sugars 2.3g; Fat 3g, of which saturates 0.5g; Cholesterol 46mg; Calcium 300mg; Fibre 1.1g; Sodium 80mg.

SEARED SALMON RAMEN

RAMEN IS A JAPANESE NOODLE SOUP FOR WHICH A GOOD STOCK IS ESSENTIAL. HERE, THE LIGHTLY SPICED BROTH IS ENHANCED BY SLICES OF FRESH SALMON AND CRISP VEGETABLES.

SERVES 4

INGREDIENTS

  1.5 litres/2½ pints/6¼ cups good
    vegetable stock
  2.5cm/1in piece fresh root ginger,
    finely sliced
  2 garlic cloves, crushed
  6 spring onions (scallions), sliced
  45ml/3 tbsp soy sauce
  45ml/3 tbsp sake
  450g/1lb salmon fillet, skinned
    and boned
  5ml/1 tsp groundnut (peanut) oil
  350g/12oz ramen or udon noodles
  4 small heads pak choi
  1 red chilli, seeded and sliced
  50g/2oz/¼ cup beansprouts
  salt and ground black pepper

1 Pour the stock into a large pan and add the ginger, garlic, and a third of the spring onions. Add the soy sauce and sake. Bring to the boil, then reduce the heat and simmer for 30 minutes.

2 Meanwhile, remove any pin bones from the salmon using tweezers, then cut the salmon on the slant into 12 slices, using a very sharp knife.

3 Brush a ridged griddle or frying pan with the oil and heat until very hot. Sear the salmon slices for 1–2 minutes on each side until tender and marked by the ridges of the pan. Set aside.

4 Cook the ramen or udon noodles in boiling water for 4–5 minutes or according to the packet instructions.

5 Once the noodles are cooked, drain them well and place under cold running water. Drain again and set aside.

6 Strain the broth into a clean pan and season to taste, then bring to the boil. Break the pak choi into leaves and add to the pan. Using a fork, twist the noodles into four nests and put these into bowls. Add three slices of salmon to each bowl. Divide the remaining spring onions, the chilli and beansprouts among the bowls, then ladle the broth around the ingredients.

Per portion Energy 572kcal/2406kJ; Protein 34..1g; Carbohydrate 65.2g, of which sugars 3.1g; Fat 21.2g, of which safurates 4.6g; Cholesterol 83mg; Calcium 150mg; Fibre 4g; Sodium 826mg.

SPICY POLLACK SOUP

THIS KOREAN SOUP HAS A WONDERFUL REFRESHING SPICINESS AND IS OFTEN ENJOYED AS AN AUTUMNAL DISH. THE MINARI CONTRIBUTES A PEPPERY FLAVOUR THAT COMPLEMENTS THE DELICATE FLAVOUR OF THE POLLACK BUT WATERCRESS MAKES AN EQUALLY GOOD ALTERNATIVE.

SERVES FOUR

INGREDIENTS

- 600g/1lb 6oz pollack fillet
- 15ml/1 tbsp sake
- 5ml/1 tsp sesame oil
- 15ml/1 tbsp Korean chilli powder
- 5ml/1 tsp gochujang chilli paste
- 2 garlic cloves, crushed
- 115g/4oz Chinese white lradish, peeled
- 10g/¼oz dried anchovies
- 5ml/1 tsp dark soy sauce
- 5ml/1 tsp light soy sauce
- ¼ block firm tofu, cubed
- 10g/¼oz leek, thinly sliced
- 1 red chilli, seeded and thinly sliced
- 10g/¼oz enoki mushrooms
- 20g/¾oz chrysanthemum leaves
- 20g/¾oz watercress or Korean minari
- salt and ground black pepper

1 Remove any bones from the pollack fillet and cut it diagonally into strips. Place the fish in a bowl with the sake, sesame oil and a pinch of salt, and toss the strips to coat them in seasoning. Place in the refrigerator for 1 hour.

2 Drain off the liquid, leaving the fish in the bowl. Add the chilli powder, gochujang paste and garlic and toss gently, coating the fish with the mixture. Leave to stand for 10 minutes.

3 Cut the radish into 3cm/1¼in cubes. Bring 1 litre/1¾ pints/4 cups water to the boil in a large pan and add the dried anchovies. Boil for 2 minutes, then remove and discard the anchovies.

4 Add the radish, dark and light soy sauces, and boil for a further 2 minutes.

5 Add the pollack and simmer the soup gently for 3 minutes, until the fish is just cooked.

6 Finally, add the tofu, leek, red chilli, enoki mushrooms, chrysanthemum leaves and watercress. Stir the ingredients into the soup gently to avoid breaking them up. Simmer the soup for a further 3 minutes.

7 Add seasoning, if required, then ladle into bowls and serve immediately.

VARIATIONS

- Any thick-filleted white fish can be used in this soup as a substitute for the pollack. For example, cod, haddock, hake or hoki are all suitable. Thin fish fillets will disintegrate.
- The soup can also be made with a mixture of seafood, such as prepared squid, prawns and mussels instead of the white fish.
- Alternatively, use half white fish and half seafood.

Per portion Energy 175kcal/733kJ; Protein 31.1g; Carbohydrate 2.3g, of which sugars 0.8g; Fat 3.7g, of which saturates 0.5g; Cholesterol 71mg; Calcium 162mg; Fibre 0.4g; Sodium 372mg.

SPINACH AND CLAM SOUP

THE LEAFY FLAVOUR OF THE FRESH SPINACH MARRIES PERFECTLY WITH THE NUTTY TASTE OF THE DOENJANG SOYA BEAN PASTE TO MAKE THIS MOUTHWATERING KOREAN SOUP WITH CLAMS.

SERVES THREE

INGREDIENTS
9 clams
90g/3½oz spinach
2 spring onions (scallions)
40g/1½oz/scant ¼ cup minced
  (ground) beef
15ml/1 tbsp doenjang soya bean paste
15ml/1 tbsp crushed garlic
salt

1 Scrub the clams in cold water, and rinse the spinach. Cut the spring onions lengthways and then into 5cm/2in strips.

2 Stir the beef and soya bean paste over a medium heat until they are cooked.

3 Pour in 750ml/1¼ pints/3 cups water and boil. Add the clams and spinach and simmer for 5 minutes.

4 When the clams have opened, add the spring onions and garlic. Discard any closed clams. Season and serve.

Per portion Energy 90kcal/377kJ; Protein 11.1g; Carbohydrate 4.7g, of which sugars 3.8g; Fat 3.1g, of which saturates 1.1g; Cholesterol 30mg; Calcium 119mg; Fibre 2.2g; Sodium 1471mg.

POLLACK AND EGG SOUP

POPULAR AS A RESTORATIVE AFTER A NIGHT OUT, THIS KOREAN DISH IS MOST COMMONLY SERVED FOR BREAKFAST. MADE WITH DRIED FISH AND FRESH EGG AND SERVED WITH A BOWL OF RICE AND A DISH OF KIMCHI, IT ALSO MAKES A PERFECT LUNCH OR LIGHT SUPPER.

SERVES SIX

INGREDIENTS
115g/4oz dried pollack
25g/1oz/¼ cup plain (all-purpose) flour
7.5ml/1½ tsp sesame oil
200g/7oz Chinese white radish,
  peeled and diced
1 garlic clove, crushed
7.5ml/1½ tsp salt
1 spring onion (scallion), shredded
1 egg

1 Shred the pollack and rinse, drain and toss in the flour. Heat the sesame oil, add the fish, radish and garlic, then stir-fry.

2 Add 2 litres/3½ pints/8¾ cups water and bring to the boil. Reduce the heat, cover and simmer for 15 minutes. Skim off the surface film. Stir in the salt and spring onion. Crack the egg in the pan and stir until set. Serve.

Per portion Energy 107kcal/450kJ; Protein 18g; Carbohydrate 3.9g, of which sugars 0.8g; Fat 2.3g, of which saturates 0.5g; Cholesterol 61mg; Calcium 29mg; Fibre 0.5g; Sodium 216mg.

SPICY SEAFOOD NOODLE SOUP

JAMPONG IS A SPICY, GARLIC-INFUSED SEAFOOD STEW. THICK JAPANESE UDON NOODLES ARE ADDED TO THE RICH BROTH, WHICH IS FLAVOURED WITH CHARACTERISTICALLY KOREAN SEASONINGS, TO CREATE AN ENTICING FUSION DISH. ADD A BOWL OF STEAMED RICE FOR THE PERFECT QUICK LUNCH.

SERVES TWO

INGREDIENTS
50g/2oz pork loin
50g/2oz mussels
50g/2oz prawns (shrimp)
90g/3½oz squid
15ml/1 tbsp vegetable oil
1 dried chilli, sliced
½ leek, sliced
2 garlic cloves, finely sliced
5ml/1 tsp grated fresh
   root ginger
30ml/2 tbsp Korean
   chilli powder
5ml/1 tsp mirin or rice wine
50g/2oz bamboo shoots, sliced
½ onion, roughly chopped
50g/2oz carrot, roughly chopped
2 Chinese leaves (Chinese cabbage),
   roughly chopped
750ml/1¼ pints/3 cups
   beef stock
light soy sauce, to taste
300g/11oz udon or flat
   wheat noodles
salt

1 Slice the pork thinly, put it on a plate and set aside.

2 Prepare the seafood. Scrub the mussels with a stiff brush and rinse them under cold running water. Discard any that remain closed after being sharply tapped. Scrape off any barnacles from the shells and remove the 'beards' with a small knife. Rinse well. Hold each prawn between two fingers and gently pull off the tail shell. Twist off the head. Peel away the soft body shell and the small claws beneath. Rinse well.

3 Wash the squid. Holding the body, pull away the head and tentacles. Remove and discard the ink sac, if intact. Pull out the innards including the long transparent pen. Discard the thin purple skin, but keep the two small side fins. Slice off the head just under the eyes (discard it), severing the tentacles.

4 Squeeze the tentacles at the head end to push out the round beak in the centre and discard. Rinse the pouch and tentacles. Score the flesh of the body sac in a crisscross pattern, and slice into 2cm/¾in pieces.

5 Coat a pan with the vegetable oil and place over high heat. When hot, add the chilli, leek, garlic and ginger. Stir-fry until the garlic has lightly browned and add the sliced pork. Stir-fry quickly. Then add the chilli powder and mirin or rice wine, and stir to coat the ingredients thoroughly.

6 Add the bamboo shoots, onion and carrot, and stir-fry until soft.

7 Add the seafood and cabbage and cook over a high heat for 30 seconds. Pour in the beef stock and bring to the boil. Reduce the heat. Season with salt and soy sauce, then cover and simmer for 3 minutes. Discard any closed mussels.

8 Cook the udon or wheat noodles in a pan of boiling water until soft, then drain and rinse with cold water. Place a portion of noodles in each soup bowl, ladle over the soup and serve.

Per portion Energy 778kcal/3288kJ; Protein 39.5g; Carbohydrate 122.8g, of which sugars 9.4g; Fat 17.7g, of which saturates 1.4g; Cholesterol 176mg; Calcium 104mg; Fibre 6.9g; Sodium 734mg.

OCTOPUS AND WATERCRESS SOUP

THIS RICH AND REFRESHING SEAFOOD SOUP HAS A WONDERFULLY RESTORATIVE QUALITY. DELICIOUS OCTOPUS IS COOKED IN A RICH VEGETABLE BROTH, WITH WHITE RADISH, CHILLI AND WATERCRESS ADDING A DISTINCTIVE FLAVOUR THAT IS QUINTESSENTIALLY KOREAN.

SERVES TWO TO THREE

INGREDIENTS

1 large octopus, cleaned
150g/5oz Chinese white
   radish, peeled
1/2 leek, sliced
20g/3/4oz kelp or spinach leaves
3 garlic cloves, crushed
1 red chilli, seeded and sliced
15ml/1 tbsp light soy sauce
75g/3oz watercress or
   rocket (arugula)
salt and ground black pepper

VARIATION
For a spicier version of this soup try adding a teaspoon of Korean chilli powder. This gives the dish a really tangy kick.

COOK'S TIP
The sweet root of white radish is not the only part which is eaten. The radish leaves, rich in iron, calcium and vitamin C, can be sautéed or eaten raw in salad.

1 Rinse the octopus in salted water and cut into pieces about 2.5cm/1in long.

2 Then prepare the peeled white radish by dicing it finely.

3 Pour 750ml/1¼ pints/3 cups water into a large pan and bring to the boil. Reduce the heat and then add the radish, leek, kelp or spinach, and crushed garlic.

COOK'S TIP
It is possible to cook Chinese white radish for a long time without it losing its taste and texture. It can also be grated and is a crisp and juicy addition to a salad.

4 Simmer the contents of the pan over a medium heat until the radish softens and becomes clear. Discard the kelp and leek and then add the sliced chilli.

5 Add the prepared pieces of octopus, increase the heat and boil for 5 minutes. Season with soy sauce, salt and pepper, and then add the watercress or rocket.

6 Remove the pan from the heat, cover and leave to stand for 1 minute while the leaves wilt into the liquid. Ladle into bowls and serve.

Per portion Energy 106kcal/449kJ; Protein 19.9g; Carbohydrate 2.6g, of which sugars 2.3g; Fat 1.9g, of which saturates 0.5g; Cholesterol 48mg; Calcium 108mg; Fibre 1.7g; Sodium 386mg.

RICE & NOODLES

Rice and noodles form the backbone of every meal in Japan and Korea.
Sticky short and medium grain rice varieties are preferred and are
traditionally cooked on their own, although additions such as beans,
chestnuts and soya beansprouts are also popular. Hot and cold noodle
dishes are favourites — ranging from hearty noodle dishes such as Tokyo-style
Ramen Noodles in Soup to chilled Spicy Buckwheat Noodles.

Left: Oyster Rice; **Above:** Stir-fried Udon Noodles

SOYA BEANSPROUT RICE

BLENDED THROUGH THE RICE, SOYA BEANSPROUTS IMPART A PLEASING CRUNCHINESS AND REFRESHING FLAVOUR, WHICH IS ENHANCED BY GARLIC, CHILLIES AND SPRING ONION. THIS KOREAN DISH HAS THE REPUTATION OF BEING IRRESISTIBLE — IT IS IMPOSSIBLE TO REFUSE A SECOND HELPING.

SERVES FIVE

INGREDIENTS
200g/7oz/1 cup short grain rice
450g/1lb/2 cups soya
  beansprouts
1 garlic clove, crushed
5ml/1 tsp light soy sauce
15ml/1 tbsp sesame oil
salt
For the sauce
1 garlic clove, crushed
2.5ml/½ tsp grated fresh
  root ginger
7.5ml/1½ tsp seeded and sliced
  jalapeño pepper
15ml/1 tbsp seeded and sliced
  red chilli
2.5ml/½ tsp sugar
45ml/3 tbsp light soy sauce
30ml/2 tbsp sesame seeds
1 spring onion (scallion),
  finely chopped
7.5ml/1½ tsp Korean chilli
  powder
45ml/3 tbsp finely chopped
  button (white) mushrooms

1 Soak the rice in cold water for 30 minutes, drain in a sieve (strainer) and then rinse it well.

2 Bring 750ml/1¼ pints/3 cups water to the boil in a pan and then add a pinch of salt.

3 Add the soya beansprouts to the pan and boil for 3 minutes. Drain the sprouts, reserving the cooking liquid and rinse.

4 Place the soya beansprouts in a bowl. Add the garlic, soy sauce, sesame oil and a pinch of salt. Mix and set aside.

5 Place the rice in a pan and pour in enough of the reserved cooking liquid to cover the rice by about 1cm/½in. Bring to the boil and cook for 5 minutes.

6 Add the soya beansprouts, reduce the heat and cook for a further 12 minutes, until all the water has evaporated.

7 Using a small dish, thoroughly combine the garlic, ginger, jalapeño pepper, chilli, sugar, soy sauce, sesame seeds, spring onion, chilli powder and button mushrooms.

8 To serve, divide the rice among serving bowls and top with the ginger and sesame seed sauce.

COOK'S TIP
Beans are easily sprouted at home. Mung beans are particularly simple and quick, as are soya beans and chickpeas. You simply need to soak them in water overnight, and then drain them and place in a jar. Cover with a cloth and keep in a shaded place at room temperature. Rinse twice a day to keep the beans moist and fresh.

Per portion Energy 233kcal/974kJ; Protein 7.2g; Carbohydrate 36.6g, of which sugars 3g; Fat 6.4g, of which saturates 0.9g; Cholesterol 0mg; Calcium 70mg; Fibre 1.9g; Sodium 860mg.

GINSENG <u>AND</u> RED DATE RICE

THE MIXTURE OF RICE AND GRAINS IN THIS DISH CREATES A PLEASING APPEARANCE AND DELICIOUSLY COMPLEX FLAVOUR. THE MEDICINAL PROPERTIES OF GINSENG HAVE LONG BEEN VALUED IN KOREA AND THIS TRADITIONAL CEREMONIAL DISH IS RENOWNED FOR INCREASING STAMINA AND VITALITY.

<u>SERVES FOUR</u>

INGREDIENTS
   115g/4oz/²⁄₃ cup mixed grains
   50g/2oz/¼ cup short grain rice or
     pudding rice
   50g/2oz/¼ cup glutinous, sticky or
     pearl rice
   50g/2oz/¼ cup brown rice
   10 aduki or red beans
   5 red dates
   10 chestnuts, cooked and peeled
   fresh ginseng root
   salt

VARIATION
For a different combination, use short grain rice with the mixed grain selection.

1 Combine the grains, the three types of rice and the aduki or red beans in a bowl. Pour in cold water to cover and leave to soak for 2 hours. Drain the rice mixture through a sieve (strainer) and rinse thoroughly under cold water. Transfer the rice and beans to a large pan.

2 Discard the seeds from the dates and slice the dates into small pieces. Halve the chestnuts and slice the ginseng root into two pieces (do not slice the ginseng if it is a small piece).

3 Add the dates, chestnuts and ginseng to the rice and mix together thoroughly. Pour in water to cover the ingredients by about 1cm/½in. Add a pinch of salt. Bring to the boil and cook for five minutes, then reduce the heat and simmer for a further 15 minutes or until all the water has evaporated. Stir thoroughly and serve.

COOK'S TIPS
• Mixed grain rice is made from a mixture of brown rice, sweet rice, wild rice, barley, hulled millet, green peas, yellow peas, black-eyed beans (peas), kidney beans and red beans. It is available from Korean or Japanese food stores.
• Glutinous rice is a sticky rice. There are many types of short grain rice, including Western pudding and risotto rice. Pearl rice sometimes refers to short, or round, grain rice. Asian and wholefood stores stock many varieties.

Per portion Energy 383kcal/1609kJ; Protein 8.3g; Carbohydrate 84.4g, of which sugars 2.1g; Fat 1.5g, of which saturates 0.2g; Cholesterol 0mg; Calcium 33mg; Fibre 2.1g; Sodium 4mg.

TOBIKO AND VEGETABLE RICE

THE SHIMMERING, TRANSLUCENT YELLOW GLOBES OF FLYING FISH ROE MAKE A DAZZLING ADDITION TO THIS KOREAN RICE DISH AND A MIXTURE OF VEGETABLES PROVIDE CRISP TEXTURE AND A FRESH TASTE. IT IS POPULAR DURING THE SUMMER EITHER FOR LUNCH OR AS A LIGHT SUPPER.

SERVES FOUR

INGREDIENTS
400g/14oz/2 cups sticky rice,
    freshly cooked
2 leaves from a round (butterhead)
    lettuce, finely sliced
2 red cabbage leaves, finely sliced
½ cucumber, deseeded and finely
    sliced lengthways
25g/1oz carrot, finely
    sliced lengthways
25g/1oz Chinese white radish, peeled
    and finely sliced lengthways
60ml/4 tbsp sushi ginger or Japanese
    gari, finely sliced
50g/2oz/4 tbsp flying fish roe or
    Japanese *tobiko*
30ml/2 tbsp sesame oil
For the garnish
20g/¾oz cress
30ml/2 tbsp sesame seeds
For the vinegar dressing
45ml/3 tbsp cider vinegar
60ml/4 tbsp sugar
salt

1 For the dressing, heat a small pan over a low heat and add the vinegar, sugar and a pinch of salt. Once the mixture has started to bubble, remove the pan from the heat and set it aside for a few minutes to allow the vinegar to evaporate.

COOK'S TIP
To add a finishing touch, drizzle the rice, vegetables and fish roe with a little sesame oil. Garnish with cress and sesame seeds before serving.

2 Combine the dressing with the cooked rice in a large bowl, mixing thoroughly. A flat wooden spatula or special rice paddle is ideal for turning the rice, mixing it without damaging the grains.

3 Mix the lettuce, red cabbage, cucumber, carrot and white radish. Spoon the rice into four bowls and top with the vegetables. Add the ginger and finish with fish roe or *tobiko* on top.

Per portion Energy 341kcal/1432kJ; Protein 8.8g; Carbohydrate 53g, of which sugars 21.9g; Fat 11.7g, of which saturates 1.8g; Cholesterol 41mg; Calcium 148mg; Fibre 3.4g; Sodium 31mg.

STIR-FRIED KIMCHI AND RICE

UBIQUITOUS KOREAN KIMCHI IS NORMALLY ENJOYED AS AN APPETIZER OR ACCOMPANIMENT BUT THIS DISH TURNS IT INTO A MAIN COURSE. STIR-FRYING THE KIMCHI BRINGS OUT ITS NATURAL SWEETNESS, WHILE THE INCLUSION OF RICE BALANCES SOME OF THE CHILLI SPICINESS.

2 Add the cooked rice and mix it with the kimchi before adding the green pepper and sesame oil. Stir-fry for a further 5 minutes.

3 Divide the rice between two bowls and garnish with the chopped chives and a sprinkle of sesame seeds.

COOK'S TIP
Use scissors to chop chives and spring onions instead of a knife. Hold them in a bunch over a bowl and snip tiny slices.

SERVES TWO

INGREDIENTS
45ml/3 tbsp vegetable oil
5ml/1 tsp Korean chilli powder
500g/1¼lb kimchi, cut into bitesize pieces
200g/7oz/1 cup sticky rice, cooked
½ small green (bell) pepper, seeded and finely chopped
15ml/1 tbsp sesame oil
For the garnish
30ml/2 tbsp chopped chives
15ml/1 tbsp sesame seeds

1 Heat a wok over a medium heat. Add the vegetable oil, chilli powder and kimchi. Stir-fry until lightly browned.

Per portion Energy 697kcal/2900kJ; Protein 13.2g; Carbohydrate 98g, of which sugars 17.6g; Fat 27.7g, of which saturates 3.5g; Cholesterol 0mg; Calcium 200mg; Fibre 7.3g; Sodium 23mg.

SASHIMI RICE

WHILE JAPANESE SASHIMI RICE IS ACCOMPANIED EXCLUSIVELY BY WASABI AND SOY SAUCE, THIS KOREAN VARIATION INCLUDES VEGETABLES AND IS SERVED WITH A SPICY, SOUR SAUCE. ACCOMPANIED BY A BOWL OF MISO SOUP, THIS IS WIDELY POPULAR AS A QUICK, YET SATISFYING, LUNCH DISH.

SERVES FOUR

INGREDIENTS

    115g/4oz Chinese white
      radish, peeled
    115g/4oz sangchi green
      leaves, shredded
    50g/2oz perilla or shiso leaves,
      thinly sliced
    ½ cucumber, thinly sliced
    4 garlic cloves, crushed
    4 green chillies, seeded and
      sliced
    45ml/3 tbsp sesame oil
    250g/9oz tuna steak
    400g/14oz/2 cups sticky rice,
      freshly cooked
For the sauce
    115g/4oz gochujang chilli paste
    100ml/3½fl oz/scant ½ cup
      cider vinegar
    45ml/3 tbsp sugar
    3 garlic cloves, crushed
    30ml/2 tbsp sesame seeds
    30ml/2 tbsp sake
    30ml/2 tbsp sesame oil

1 Prepare the sauce: mix the gochujang chilli paste, cider vinegar, sugar, garlic, sesame seeds, sake and sesame oil in a bowl. Mix well, then set aside to allow the flavours to mingle.

2 Cut the radish into short lengths, then finely slice these and cut the slices into short fine strips.

3 Soak the radish strips in cold water for 15 minutes, then drain them and place in a bowl.

4 Add the sangchi green leaves, perilla or shiso, cucumber, garlic and chillies to the radish. Pour in 1 tablespoon of the sesame oil and toss the ingredients.

5 Slice the tuna into bitesize pieces, about 1 x 2cm/½ x ¾in.

6 Place the tuna in a bowl. Add 1 tablespoon of the sesame oil and mix gently to coat the fish.

7 Mix the remaining sesame oil with the rice and divide it among four bowls.

8 Place the vegetables on top of the rice and then lay the tuna mixture over the vegetables. Pour the sauce into side dishes and serve with the rice.

COOK'S TIP
Make a point of buying tuna from a good fishmonger for this dish. As it is served raw you should be sure that it is extremely fresh and that it has not previously been frozen.

Per portion Energy 457kcal/1915kJ; Protein 21.1g; Carbohydrate 44.7g, of which sugars 13.7g; Fat 22.8g, of which saturates 3.7g; Cholesterol 18mg; Calcium 158mg; Fibre 1.9g; Sodium 80mg.

RED RICE WRAPPED ᴵᴺ OAK LEAVES

THIS JAPANESE RICE DISH, SEKIHAN, IS COOKED FOR SPECIAL OCCASIONS AND TAKES EIGHT HOURS TO PREPARE. EDIBLE KASHIWA (OAK) LEAVES ARE USED WHEN PREPARED FOR A BOY-CHILD'S FESTIVAL.

SERVES FOUR

INGREDIENTS
    65g/2½oz/⅓ cup dried aduki beans
    5ml/1 tsp salt
    300g/11oz/1½ cups mochigome
    50g/2oz/¼ cup Japanese
        short grain rice
    12 kashiwa leaves (optional)
For the goma-shio
    45ml/3 tbsp sesame seeds (black
        sesame, if available)
    5ml/1 tsp ground sea salt

1 Put the aduki beans in a heavy pan and pour in 400ml/14fl oz/1⅔ cups plus 20ml/4 tsp water.

2 Bring to the boil, reduce the heat and simmer, covered, for 20–30 minutes, or until the beans look swollen but are still firm. Remove from the heat and drain. Reserve the liquid in a bowl and add the salt. Return the beans to the pan.

3 Wash the two rices together. Drain in a sieve and leave for 30 minutes.

4 Bring another 400ml/14fl oz/1⅔ cups plus 20ml/4 tsp water to the boil. Add to the beans and boil, then simmer for 30 minutes. The beans' skins should start to crack. Drain and add the liquid to the bowl with the reserved liquid. Cover the beans and leave to cool.

5 Add the rice to the bean liquid. Leave to soak for 4–5 hours. Drain the rice and reserve the liquid. Mix the beans into the rice.

6 Bring a steamer of water to the boil. Turn off the heat. Place a tall glass upside down in the centre of the steaming compartment. Pour the rice and beans into the steamer and gently pull the glass out. The hole in the middle will allow even distribution of the steam. Steam on high for 10 minutes.

7 Using your fingers, sprinkle the rice mixture with the reserved liquid from the bowl. Cover again and repeat the process twice more at 10 minute intervals, then leave to steam for 15 minutes more. Remove from the heat. Leave to stand for 10 minutes.

8 Make the goma-shio. Roast the sesame seeds and salt in a dry frying pan until the seeds start to pop. Leave to cool, then put in a small dish.

9 Wipe each kashiwa leaf with a wet dishtowel. Scoop 120ml/4fl oz/½ cup of the rice mixture into a wet tea cup and press with wet fingers. Turn the cup upside down and shape the moulded rice with your hands into a flat ball. Insert into a leaf folded in two. Repeat this process until all the leaves are used. Alternatively, transfer the red rice to a large bowl wiped with a wet towel.

10 Serve the red rice with a sprinkle of goma-shio. The kashiwa leaves (except for fresh ones) are edible.

Per portion Energy 432kcal/1807kJ; Protein 12.4g; Carbohydrate 78.7g, of which sugars 0.5g; Fat 7.2g, of which saturates 1g; Cholesterol 0mg; Calcium 105mg; Fibre 2.2g; Sodium 496mg.

FIVE INGREDIENTS RICE

CHICKEN AND VEGETABLES ARE COOKED WITH SHORT GRAIN RICE MAKING A HEALTHY JAPANESE LUNCH DISH CALLED KAYAKU-GOHAN. SERVE WITH A SIMPLE, CLEAR SOUP AND TANGY PICKLES.

SERVES FOUR

INGREDIENTS

275g/10oz/1⅓ cups Japanese short
  grain rice
90g/3½oz carrot, peeled
2.5ml/½ tsp lemon juice
90g/3½oz gobo or canned
  bamboo shoots
225g/8oz oyster mushrooms
8 mitsuba sprigs, root part removed
350ml/12fl oz/1½ cups second
  dashi stock, or the same amount
  of water and 7.5ml/1½ tsp dashi-
  no-moto
150g/5oz chicken breast portion,
  skinned, boned and cut into
  2cm/¾in dice
30ml/2 tbsp shoyu
30ml/2 tbsp sake
25ml/1½ tbsp mirin
pinch of salt

1 Put the rice in a bowl and wash with cold water. Change the water until it is clear. Tip the rice into a sieve (strainer) and leave to drain for 30 minutes.

2 Using a sharp knife, cut the carrot into 5mm/¼in rounds, then cut the discs into flowers.

COOK'S TIP
Although gobo or burdock is recognized as a poisonous plant in the West, the Japanese have long been eating it, but it must be cooked. It contains iron and other acidic elements that are harmful if eaten raw, but after soaking in alkaline water and cooking for a short time, gobo is no longer poisonous.

3 Fill a small bowl with cold water and add the lemon juice. Peel the gobo and then slice with a knife as if you were sharpening a pencil into the bowl. Leave for 15 minutes, then drain. If using canned bamboo shoots, slice into thin matchsticks.

4 Tear the oyster mushrooms into thin strips. Chop the mitsuba sprigs into 2cm/¾in long pieces. Put them in a sieve and pour over hot water from the kettle to wilt them. Allow to drain and then set aside.

5 Heat the dashi stock in a large pan and add the carrots and gobo or bamboo shoots. Bring to the boil and add the chicken. Remove any scum from the surface, and add the shoyu, sake, mirin and salt.

6 Add the rice and mushrooms and cover with a tight-fitting lid. Bring back to the boil, wait 5 minutes, then reduce the heat and simmer for 10 minutes. Remove from the heat without lifting the lid and leave to stand for 15 minutes. Add the mitsuba and serve.

Per portion Energy 331kcal/1386kJ; Protein 16.2g; Carbohydrate 61.1g, of which sugars 5.6g; Fat 1.2g, of which saturates 0.2g; Cholesterol 26mg; Calcium 32mg; Fibre 1.5g; Sodium 567mg.

CHICKEN AND EGG ON RICE

*THIS DISH IS CALLED OYAKO DON WHICH MEANS A PARENT (THE CHICKEN) AND A CHILD (THE EGG).
IT IS TRADITIONALLY COOKED IN A DON-BURI, WHICH IS A DEEP, ROUND CERAMIC BOWL WITH A LID,
AND IS ESSENTIAL TABLEWARE IN JAPAN; RESTAURANTS OFTEN USE THEM IN LUNCHTIME MENUS.*

SERVES FOUR

INGREDIENTS

250g/9oz chicken thighs, skinned
and boned
4 mitsuba sprigs or a handful of
mustard and cress
300ml/½ pint/1¼ cups second dashi
stock, or the same amount of water
and 25ml/1½ tbsp dashi-no-moto
30ml/2 tbsp caster (superfine) sugar
60ml/4 tbsp mirin
60ml/4 tbsp shoyu
2 small onions, sliced
thinly lengthways
4 large (US extra large) eggs, beaten
275g/10oz/scant 1½ cups Japanese
short grain rice cooked with 375ml/
13fl oz/scant 1⅔ cups water
shichimi togarashi, to serve (optional)

1 Cut the chicken thighs into 2cm/¾in square bitesize chunks. Remove the root part from the mitsuba, and chop into 2.5cm/1in lengths.

2 Pour the dashi stock, sugar, mirin and shoyu into a clean frying pan with a lid and bring to the boil. Add the onion slices and lay the chicken pieces on top. Cook over a high heat for 5 minutes, shaking the pan frequently.

3 When the chicken is cooked, sprinkle with the mitsuba or mustard and cress, and pour the beaten eggs over to cover the chicken. Cover and wait for 30 seconds. Do not stir.

4 Remove from the heat and leave to stand for 1 minute. The egg should be just cooked but still soft, rather than set. Do not leave it so that the egg becomes a firm omelette.

5 Scoop the warm rice on to individual plates, then pour the soft eggs and chicken on to the rice. Serve immediately with a little shichimi-togarashi, if a spicy taste is desired.

COOK'S TIP

Ideally, this dish should be cooked in individual shallow pans with lids. A small omelette pan can work perfectly well.

Per portion Energy 455kcal/1910kJ; Protein 25g; Carbohydrate 71.9g, of which sugars 16.9g; Fat 7.7g, of which saturates 2.1g; Cholesterol 256mg; Calcium 56mg; Fibre 0.1g; Sodium 1196mg.

OYSTER RICE

THIS DISH IS A KOREAN CLASSIC. THE DISTINCTIVE FLAVOUR OF OYSTERS INFUSES THIS RECIPE AND IS COMPLEMENTED BY A SUBTLE HINT OF GINGER. SAKE ADDS AN ALMOST IMPERCEPTIBLE SWEETNESS, WHILE FLAKES OF DRIED SEAWEED COMPLETE THE SEAFOOD SEASONING.

SERVES FOUR

INGREDIENTS

300g/11oz/1½ cups short grain rice
3cm/1¼in fresh root ginger, peeled
  and finely sliced
10 oysters, shucked, rinsed
  and drained
15ml/1 tbsp light soy sauce
30ml/2 tbsp sake
salt
dried seaweed paper or Japanese
  nori, shredded, to garnish

COOK'S TIP
Use a short, blunt but tough, oyster knife
for opening oysters (see page 249).

3 Place the rice in a pan and pour in enough oyster stock to cover the rice by about 1cm/½in. Bring to the boil and cook for 5 minutes. Add the oysters and ginger, reduce the heat and cook for 15 minutes, until the water has evaporated.

4 Mix thoroughly and serve garnished with shredded seaweed.

1 Soak the rice for 30 minutes, then drain in a sieve (strainer) and rinse well. Soak the ginger in cold water for 10 minutes to remove some of its heat, then drain.

2 Bring 500ml/17fl oz/generous 2 cups water to the boil in a pan. Add the oysters, soy sauce, sake and a pinch of salt. Boil for 3 minutes, then drain the oysters and ginger, reserving the cooking liquid.

Per portion Energy 320kcal/1338kJ; Protein 11g; Carbohydrate 61.4g, of which sugars 0.2g; Fat 1g, of which saturates 0.1g; Cholesterol 29mg; Calcium 85mg; Fibre 0g; Sodium 433mg.

BROWN RICE AND MUSHROOMS IN CLEAR SOUP

THIS IS A GOOD AND QUICK WAY OF USING UP LEFTOVER RICE. IN THIS HEARTY DISH, KNOWN AS GENMAI ZOUSUI, BROWN RICE IS USED FOR ITS NUTTY FLAVOUR. SHORT GRAIN JAPANESE OR ITALIAN BROWN RICE, WHICH CAN BE FOUND IN HEALTH FOOD STORES, ARE BEST FOR THIS RECIPE.

SERVES FOUR

INGREDIENTS
1 litre/1¾ pints/4 cups second dashi stock, or the same amount of water and 20ml/4 tsp dashi-no-moto
60ml/4 tbsp sake
5ml/1 tsp salt
60ml/4 tbsp shoyu
115g/4oz fresh shiitake mushrooms, thinly sliced
600g/1lb 5oz cooked brown rice (see Cook's Tip)
2 large (US extra large) eggs, beaten
30ml/2 tbsp chopped fresh chives
For the garnish
15ml/1 tbsp sesame seeds
shichimi togarashi (optional)

1 Mix the dashi stock, sake, salt and shoyu in a large pan. Bring to the boil, then add the sliced shiitake. Cook for 5 minutes over a medium heat.

2 Add the cooked brown rice to the pan and stir gently over a medium heat with a wooden spoon. Break up any large chunks, and thoroughly warm the rice through.

3 Pour the beaten eggs into the pan as if drawing a whirlpool. Lower the heat and cover. Do not stir.

4 Remove the pan from the heat after about 3 minutes, and allow to stand for 3 minutes more. The egg should be just cooked. Sprinkle the chopped chives into the pan.

5 Serve the dish in individual bowls. Garnish with sesame seeds and shichimi togarashi, if you like.

COOK'S TIP
To cook brown rice, wash and drain, then put 2 parts water to 1 part rice into a pan. Bring to the boil, cover, then simmer for 40 minutes, or until the water has been absorbed. Leave to stand, covered, for 5 minutes.

Per portion Energy 280kcal/1180kJ; Protein 8.4g; Carbohydrate 50g, of which sugars 2.4g; Fat 4.7g, of which saturates 1.3g; Cholesterol 95mg; Calcium 48mg; Fibre 2.1g; Sodium 1111mg.

RICE IN GREEN TEA WITH SALMON

A FAST FOOD, OCHA-ZUKE IS A COMMON JAPANESE SNACK TO HAVE AFTER DRINKS AND NIBBLES. IN THE KYOTO REGION, OFFERING THIS DISH TO GUESTS USED TO BE A POLITE WAY OF SAYING THE PARTY WAS OVER. THE GUESTS WERE EXPECTED TO DECLINE THE OFFER AND LEAVE IMMEDIATELY!

SERVES FOUR

INGREDIENTS
150g/5oz salmon fillet
¼ nori sheet
250g/9oz/1¼ cups Japanese short grain rice cooked using 350ml/ 12fl oz/1½ cups water
15ml/1 tbsp sencha leaves
5ml/1 tsp wasabi paste from a tube, or 5ml/1 tsp wasabi powder mixed with 1.5ml/¼ tsp water (optional)
20ml/4 tsp shoyu
salt

1 Thoroughly salt the salmon fillet and leave for 30 minutes. If the salmon fillet is thicker than 2.5cm/1in, slice it in half and salt both halves.

2 Wipe the salt off the salmon with kitchen paper and grill (broil) the fish under a grill (broiler) for about 5 minutes until cooked through. Remove the skin and any bones, then roughly flake the salmon with a fork.

3 Using scissors, cut the nori into short, narrow strips about 20 x 5mm/¾ x ¼in long, or leave as long narrow strips, if you prefer.

4 If the cooked rice is warm, put equal amounts into individual rice bowls or soup bowls. If the rice is cold, put in a sieve (strainer) and pour hot water from a kettle over it to warm it up. Drain and pour into the bowls. Place the salmon pieces on top of the rice.

5 Put the sencha leaves in a teapot. Bring 600ml/1 pint/2½ cups water to the boil, remove from the heat and allow to cool slightly. Pour into the teapot and wait for 45 seconds. Strain the tea gently over the top of the rice and salmon. Add some nori and wasabi, Trickle shoyu over if using, and serve.

Per portion Energy 296kcal/1238kJ; Protein 12.5g; Carbohydrate 50.7g, of which sugars 0.7g; Fat 4.5g, of which saturates 0.7g; Cholesterol 19mg; Calcium 22mg; Fibre 0g; Sodium 729mg.

ABALONE PORRIDGE

THE UNIQUE FLAVOUR OF ABALONE MAKES IT A PRIZED INGREDIENT IN KOREAN COOKING AND THE PREPARATION TIME IS WELL WORTH THE EFFORT. AS PART OF TRADITIONAL KOREAN MEALS, WHICH OFTEN INCLUDE NINE COURSES, THIS DISH IS CONSIDERED A SOPHISTICATED APPETIZER.

5 Thinly slice the abalone and pound each slice to tenderize it. Mix the abalone slices with the sesame oil, sake, soy sauce and salt and pepper.

6 Heat a wok or frying pan over a high heat. Add the abalone and seasoning, and cook the slices for 30 seconds on each side, then remove from the heat.

SERVES TWO

INGREDIENTS
  115g/4oz/⅔ cups short grain rice or
    pudding rice
  300g/11oz fresh abalone, shelled
  ½ small leek, chopped
  ½ small onion, chopped
  1 oyster mushroom
  15ml/1 tbsp sesame oil
  5ml/1 tsp sake
  5ml/1 tsp light soy sauce
  salt and ground white pepper
For the garnish
  a little vegetable oil
  10g/¼oz enoki mushrooms
  20g/¾oz cress
  soy sauce

1 Soak the rice in cold water for 30 minutes. Drain in a sieve (strainer) and rinse really well, then grind coarsely in a food processor.

2 Trim the black skin from around the outside of the abalone and set aside the flesh from the centre. Place the black skin in a pan.

3 Add the leek, onion, oyster mushroom and 120ml/4fl oz/½ cup water to the pan. Bring to the boil and simmer for 10 minutes.

4 Strain the stock through a sieve, then pour it into a jug (pitcher) and discard the flavouring ingredients.

7 Bring the rice and stock to the boil. Reduce the heat to low, add the abalone and its cooking juices, and simmer until smooth and creamy. Heat a little oil in the wok. Add the enoki mushrooms and cook for a few seconds. Spoon the porridge into bowls and garnish with mushrooms, cress and soy sauce.

Per portion Energy 407kcal/1702kJ; Protein 25.5g; Carbohydrate 54.7g, of which sugars 3.9g; Fat 9.4g, of which saturates 1.6g; Cholesterol 62mg; Calcium 108mg; Fibre 3.6g; Sodium 974mg.

VEGETABLE PORRIDGE

WITH A TEXTURE SIMILAR TO RISOTTO, THIS KOREAN DISH MAKES A POPULAR, FORTIFYING BREAKFAST. BECAUSE IT USES SESAME OIL RATHER THAN BUTTER, IT IS LIGHTER THAT ITS ITALIAN EQUIVALENT AND IS WIDELY REGARDED AS A NUTRITIOUS OPTION BY HEALTH-CONSCIOUS KOREANS.

SERVES TWO

INGREDIENTS
   115g/4oz/⅔ cup short grain rice
      or pudding rice
   1 dried shiitake mushroom
   15ml/1 tbsp sesame oil
   1 spring onion (scallion),
      finely chopped
   1 small carrot, finely chopped
   750ml/1¼ pints/3 cups vegetable
      or fish stock
   salt and ground black pepper
For the garnish
   2 quail's egg yolks
   sesame seeds

1 Soak the rice in cold water for 30 minutes, then drain and rinse well.

2 Soak the shiitake mushroom in warm water for about 15 minutes, or until soft, then chop finely, discarding the stalk.

3 Coat a pan with the sesame oil and place on medium heat. Add the spring onion, carrot, mushroom and a pinch of salt and stir-fry briefly. Add the rice and stir-fry for 1 minute to coat the grains.

4 Pour in the stock. Reduce the heat when the stock simmers. Simmer the mixture, stirring gently, until the porridge has thickened to a smooth consistency. Season with salt and pepper.

5 Spoon the porridge into bowls. Garnish each portion with a quail's egg yolk and a sprinkling of sesame seeds.

COOK'S TIP
Instead of the quail's egg yolk, finish the porridge with a halved boiled egg, if preferred. The result is different – stirring in the uncooked yolk enriches the porridge as the yolk lightly cooks in the hot mixture – but it still tastes good.

VARIATION
For a more meat-based variation of vegetable porridge, use chicken stock instead of vegetable and fish stock.

Per portion Energy 310kcal/1292kJ; Protein 6.1g; Carbohydrate 57.8g, of which sugars 8.4g; Fat 6.1g, of which saturates 0.8g; Cholesterol 0mg; Calcium 49mg; Fibre 2.1g; Sodium 5mg.

PUMPKIN CONGEE

THE NATURAL SWEETNESS OF PUMPKIN IS EXCELLENT IN THIS POPULAR AUTUMNAL SNACK, WHICH IS SUITABLE BOTH AS AN ACCOMPANIMENT TO SAVOURY DISHES AND AS A DESSERT. DESPITE ITS HUMBLE ORIGINS AS A FARMER'S STAPLE, THIS CONGEE IS ENJOYED THROUGHOUT KOREAN SOCIETY.

SERVES TWO TO THREE

INGREDIENTS
   600g/1lb 6oz pumpkin, seeded,
     peeled and cut into chunks
   75g/3oz/⅔ cup sweet or glutinous
     rice flour
   30g/1¼oz/2 tbsp sugar
   5 chestnuts, cooked, peeled
     and crushed
   salt
For the garnish
   1 red date, seeded and finely sliced
   6 pine nuts

COOK'S TIP
Canned pumpkin pieces or purée can be used in this recipe. Cooked, puréed pumpkin freezes very well and is ideal for making dishes such as this one.

1 Place the pumpkin in a large pan and add just enough water to cover the pieces. Bring to the boil and simmer until the pumpkin is soft, then drain, reserving the cooking liquid. Cool the pumpkin slightly before blending it to a smooth paste in a food processor, adding a little of the reserved cooking water if it is very thick. Set aside.

2 Place the rice flour in a pan and stir in 200ml/7fl oz/scant 1 cup water. Cook over medium heat, stirring, until boiling and thickened.

3 Gradually stir in the pumpkin and sugar with a pinch of salt. Add the chestnuts. Simmer the congee briefly, stirring until it is smooth and creamy.

4 Ladle the congee into glass dishes or bowls and serve decorated with sliced red date and pine nuts.

Per portion Energy 185kcal/781kJ; Protein 3.4g; Carbohydrate 41g, of which sugars 15g; Fat 1g, of which saturates 0.3g; Cholesterol 0mg; Calcium 77mg; Fibre 3.2g; Sodium 4mg.

MIUM CONGEE

ORIGINATING IN CHINA, THIS RICE PORRIDGE IS POPULAR ALL OVER ASIA. AS A MEDICINAL DISH, SERVED TO RESTORE STAMINA, MIUM IS TRADITIONALLY MADE USING ONLY RICE; HOWEVER, THE OTHER INGREDIENTS BRING AN UNFORGETTABLE FLAVOUR, ESPECIALLY WHEN FINISHED WITH A SWIRL OF SOY SAUCE.

<u>SERVES ONE</u>

INGREDIENTS
   50g/2oz/¼ cup short grain rice or
     pudding rice
   1 small piece ginseng root, halved
   25g/1oz dried seaweed
   1 dried shiitake mushroom
   2 red dates
   3 chestnuts, cooked and peeled
   30g/1¼oz leeks

1 Soak the rice in cold water for 30 minutes, then drain and rinse. Place the rice in a pan and add the ginseng, seaweed, shiitake mushroom, dates, chestnuts and leeks.

2 Pour in 1 litre/1¾ pints/4 cups water. Bring to the boil, reduce the heat and cover the pan.

3 Simmer for 20–30 minutes, stirring occasionally, until the rice has broken down and the congee is smooth and milky in consistency.

4 To serve, pour the mixture through a sieve (strainer) into a bowl and discard the flavouring ingredients.

COOK'S TIP
Try kelp or wakame seaweed – dahima or miyuk in Korean – in this dish. A dash of soy sauce makes a finishing touch.

Per portion Energy 238kcal/997kJ; Protein 4.9g; Carbohydrate 51.8g, of which sugars 2.8g; Fat 1.2g, of which saturates 0.2g; Cholesterol 0mg; Calcium 31mg; Fibre 1.9g; Sodium 4mg.

PINE NUT CONGEE

RICH AND NUTRITIOUS, PINE NUTS ARE VALUED IN KOREAN COOKING FOR THEIR DISTINCTIVE, SLIGHTLY FRAGRANT FLAVOUR. IN THIS DELICIOUS DISH THE PINE NUTS GIVE THE RICE A WOODY TASTE AND SUBTLE SWEETNESS AS WELL AS A PLEASING TEXTURE.

<u>SERVES ONE</u>

INGREDIENTS
   115g/4oz/⅔ cup short grain rice or
     pudding rice
   50g/2oz/⅓ cup pine nuts, ground,
     plus 6 pine nuts
   1 red date, seeded and thinly
     sliced, to garnish

1 Soak the rice in plenty of cold water for 30 minutes.

2 Drain the rice in a sieve (strainer) and rinse it well. Shake it thoroughly to get rid of excess water, then grind it to a powder in a food processor.

3 Place the ground pine nuts in a food processor. Pour in 200ml/7fl oz/ scant 1 cup water and process to a fine paste.

4 Place the ground rice in a pan with 750ml/1¼ pints/3 cups water and bring to the boil.

5 Reduce the heat, cover the pan and simmer for 20 minutes. The grains will break down and produce a milky congee.

6 Remove the pan from the heat and stir in the pine nuts. Serve garnished with the whole pine nuts and red date.

Per portion Energy 806kcal/3359kJ; Protein 16.1g; Carbohydrate 106.3g, of which sugars 14.5g; Fat 34.9g, of which saturates 2.3g; Cholesterol 0mg; Calcium 37mg; Fibre 1.7g; Sodium 3mg.

LUNCH-BOX RICE <u>WITH</u> THREE TOPPINGS

SAN-SHOKU BENTO IS A TYPICAL BENTO (LUNCH BOX) MENU FOR JAPANESE CHILDREN. COLOURFUL TOPPINGS AND A VARIETY OF TASTES HOLD THEIR ATTENTION SO THEY DON'T GET BORED.

MAKES FOUR LUNCH BOXES

INGREDIENTS
275g/10oz/scant 1½ cups Japanese
   short grain rice cooked using
   375ml/13fl oz/scant 1⅔ cups
   water, cooled
45ml/3 tbsp sesame seeds, toasted
salt
3 mangetouts (snow peas), to garnish
For the iri-tamago (yellow topping)
   30ml/2 tbsp caster (superfine) sugar
   5ml/1 tsp salt
   3 large (US extra large) eggs, beaten
For the denbu (pink topping)
   115g/4oz cod fillet, skinned
     and boned
   20ml/4 tsp caster (superfine) sugar
   5ml/1 tsp salt
   5ml/1 tsp sake
   2 drops of red vegetable colouring,
     diluted with a few drops of water

COOK'S TIP
Try using a few different vegetable
colourings for the denbu.

For the tori-soboro (beige topping)
   200g/7oz minced (ground)
     raw chicken
45ml/3 tbsp sake
15ml/1 tbsp caster (superfine) sugar
15ml/1 tbsp shoyu
15ml/1 tbsp water

1 To make the iri-tamago, add the sugar and salt to the eggs in a pan. Cook over a medium heat, stirring with a whisk or fork as you would to scramble an egg. When it is almost set, remove from the heat and stir until the egg becomes fine and slightly dry.

2 To make the denbu, cook the cod fillet for 2 minutes in a large pan of boiling water. Drain and dry well with kitchen paper. Skin and remove all the fish bones.

3 Put the cod and sugar into a pan, add the salt and sake, and cook over a low heat for 1 minute, stirring with a fork to flake the cod. Reduce the heat to low and sprinkle on the colouring. Continue to stir for 15–20 minutes, or until the cod flakes become very fluffy and fibrous. Transfer the denbu to a plate.

4 To make the tori-soboro, put the minced chicken, sake, sugar, shoyu and water into a small pan. Cook over a medium heat for about 3 minutes, then reduce the heat to medium-low and stir with a fork or whisk until the liquid has almost evaporated.

5 Blanch the mangetouts for about 3 minutes in lightly salted boiling water, drain and carefully slice into fine 3mm/⅛in sticks.

6 Mix the rice with the sesame seeds in a bowl. With a wet spoon, divide the rice among four 17 × 12cm/6½ × 4½in lunch boxes. Flatten the surface using the back of a wooden spoon.

7 Spoon a quarter of the egg into each box to cover a third of the rice. Cover the next third with a quarter of the denbu, and the last section with a quarter of the chicken topping. Use the lid to divide the boxes, if you like. Garnish with the mangetout sticks.

Per portion Energy 515kcal/2160kJ; Protein 29.3g; Carbohydrate 72.3g, of which sugars 17.4g; Fat 11.8g, of which saturates 2.3g; Cholesterol 191mg; Calcium 125mg; Fibre 0.9g; Sodium 863mg.

COLD SOMEN NOODLES

*AT THE HEIGHT OF SUMMER, HIYA SOMEN — COLD SOMEN NOODLES SERVED IMMERSED IN COLD
WATER WITH ICE CUBES AND ACCOMPANIED BY SAUCES AND RELISHES — ARE A REFRESHING MEAL.*

SERVES FOUR

INGREDIENTS
300g/11oz dried somen noodles
For the dipping sauce
   105ml/7 tbsp mirin
   2.5ml/½ tsp salt
   105ml/7 tbsp shoyu
   20g/¾oz kezuri-bushi
   400ml/14fl oz/1⅔ cups water
For the relishes
   2 spring onions (scallions), trimmed
     and finely chopped
   2.5cm/1in fresh root ginger, peeled
     and finely grated
   2 shiso leaves, finely chopped
     (optional)
   30ml/2 tbsp toasted sesame seeds
For the garnishes
   10cm/4in cucumber (a small salad
     cucumber is the best)
   5ml/1 tsp salt
   ice cubes or a block of ice
   ice-cold water
   115g/4oz cooked, peeled small
     prawns (shrimp)
   orchid flowers or nasturtium flowers
     and leaves

1 To make the dipping sauce, put the mirin in a medium pan and bring to the boil to evaporate the alcohol. Add the salt and shoyu and shake the pan gently to mix. Add the kezuri-bushi and mix with the liquid. Add the water and bring to the boil. Cook over vigorous heat for 3 minutes without stirring. Remove from the heat and strain through muslin or a jelly bag. Leave to cool, then chill in the refrigerator for at least an hour before serving.

2 Prepare the cucumber garnish. If the cucumber is bigger than 4cm/1½in in diameter, cut in half and scoop out the seeds, then slice thinly. For a smaller cucumber, first cut into 5cm/2in lengths, then use a vegetable peeler to remove the seeds and make a hole in the centre. Slice thinly. Sprinkle with the salt and leave in a sieve for 20 minutes, then rinse in cold water and drain.

3 Bring at least 1.5 litres/2½ pints/6¼ cups water to the boil in a large pan. Meanwhile, untie the bundle of somen. Have 75ml/2½fl oz/⅓ cup cold water to hand. Somen only take 2 minutes to cook. Put the somen in the rapidly boiling water. When it foams again, pour the glass of water in. When the water boils again, the somen are ready. Drain into a colander under cold running water, and rub the somen with your hands to remove the starch. Drain well.

4 Put some ice cubes or a block of ice in the centre of a chilled, large glass bowl, and add the somen. Gently pour on enough ice-cold water to cover the somen, then arrange cucumber slices, prawns and flowers on top.

5 Prepare all the relishes separately in small dishes or small sake cups.

6 Divide approximately one-third of the dipping sauce among four small cups. Put the remaining sauce in a jug (pitcher) or gravy boat.

7 Serve the noodles cold with the relishes. The guests are invited to put any combination of relishes into their dipping-sauce cup. Hold the cup over the somen bowl, pick up a mouthful of somen, then dip them into the sauce and eat. Add more dipping sauce from the jug and more relishes as required.

Per portion Energy 445kcal/1885kJ; Protein 29.3g; Carbohydrate 16.3g, of which sugars 23.7g; Fat 9.2g, of which saturates 0.7g; Cholesterol 56mg; Calcium 109mg; Fibre 2.9g; Sodium 2420mg.

BUCKWHEAT NOODLES WITH DIPPING SAUCE

COLD SOBA NOODLES ARE OFTEN EATEN IN SUMMER AND SERVED ON A BAMBOO TRAY WITH A DIPPING SAUCE. THE JAPANESE LOVE THE TASTE OF THE NOODLES; THE SAUCE ENHANCES THEIR FLAVOUR.

SERVES FOUR

INGREDIENTS
    4 spring onions (scallions),
        finely chopped
    ½ nori sheet, about 10cm/4in square
    400g/14oz dried soba noodles
    5ml/1 tsp wasabi paste from a tube,
        or 5ml/1 tsp wasabi powder mixed
        with 2.5ml/½ tsp water
For the dipping sauce
    30g/1¼oz kezuri-bushi
    200ml/7fl oz/scant 1 cup shoyu
    200ml/7fl oz/scant 1 cup mirin
    750ml/1¼ pints/3 cups water

1 To make the dipping sauce, mix all the ingredients in a small pan. Bring to the boil, and cook for 2 minutes. Reduce the heat to medium, and cook for a further 2 minutes. Strain through muslin (cheesecloth). Cool, then chill.

2 Soak the spring onions in ice-cold water in a bowl for 5 minutes. Drain and squeeze out the excess water.

3 Toast the nori over a medium flame until dry and crisp, then cut it into short strips, 3mm/⅛in wide, with scissors.

4 Heat 2 litres/3½ pints/9 cups water in a large pan. The water should not fill more than two-thirds of the pan's depth.

5 Bring to the boil, then add the soba. Distribute the noodles evenly in the pan, and stir to prevent them sticking. When the water is bubbling, pour in about 50ml/2fl oz/¼ cup cold water to lower the temperature.

6 Repeat this process and cook for the length of time stated on the packet, or about 5 minutes. To test if the noodles are ready, pick one out and cut it with your finger. It should be just tender to the touch.

7 Put a large sieve (strainer) under cold running water. Pour the cooked soba into the sieve, and wash thoroughly with your hands. Rub the soba well to remove the starch; the soba should feel slightly elastic. Drain again.

8 Pour the cold dipping sauce into four cups. Put the wasabi and spring onions into individual dishes for each guest. Divide the soba among four plates or baskets. Sprinkle with nori strips and serve cold, with the sauce, wasabi and spring onions.

9 Instruct each guest to mix the wasabi and onions into the dipping sauce. To eat, hold the dipping-sauce cup in one hand. Pick up a mouthful of soba from the basket or plate using chopsticks and dip the end into the dipping sauce, then slurp the noodles in with your lips.

COOK'S TIP
Other condiment ideas include yuzu or lime rind, finely grated radish, thinly sliced garlic or grated fresh root ginger.

Per portion Energy 449kcal/1905kJ; Protein 12.1g; Carbohydrate 91.7g, of which sugars 17.9g; Fat 6.3g, of which saturates 0g; Cholesterol 0mg; Calcium 35mg; Fibre 3.1g; Sodium 360mg.

STIR-FRIED UDON NOODLES

UDON NOODLES ORIGINATED IN JAPAN BUT QUICKLY BECAME POPULAR IN KOREA. THE MEDLEY OF
SEAFOOD, MEAT AND VEGETABLES IN THIS STIR-FRY IS ENHANCED BY THE SWEET, SALTY SAUCE.

SERVES FOUR

INGREDIENTS
    200g/7oz squid, cleaned
      and skinned
    350g/12oz udon noodles
    8 tiger prawns (shrimp), shelled
    4 mussels, shucked
    30ml/2 tbsp vegetable oil
    115g/4oz beef sirloin, cut
      into strips
    ½ onion, finely sliced
    1 green (bell) pepper, seeded
      and finely sliced
    1 carrot, finely sliced
    50g/2oz oyster mushrooms, sliced
    ½ lettuce, shredded
    15ml/1 tbsp chilli oil
    salt and ground black pepper
For the sauce
    15ml/1 tbsp oyster sauce
    10ml/2 tsp sugar
    30ml/2 tbsp sake
    45ml/3 tbsp dark soy sauce

1 Score diagonal cuts across the
squid flesh with a sharp knife, taking
great care not to cut right through,
and then cut the sacs into strips of
about 2cm/¾in.

2 Bring a pan of water to the boil and
add the udon noodles. Boil them for
3 minutes and then drain the noodles.
Rinse the cooked noodles under cold
water and set aside.

VARIATIONS
• For a quick dish, use prepared mixed
seafood that is already blanched.
• Replace the udon noodles with ramen.

3 Bring 1 litre/1¾ pints/4 cups water
to the boil in a large pan and add a
pinch of salt. Add the squid, prawns
and mussels to the pan, bring the
water back to the boil, and then drain
and set aside.

4 For the sauce, mix the oyster sauce,
sugar, sake and soy sauce in a bowl.
Set the sauce aside to allow the flavours
to mingle.

5 Heat the vegetable oil in a wok over a
high heat and add the beef, then stir-fry
for 3 minutes. Continue stir-frying, add
the onion, pepper, carrot, mushrooms and
lettuce, and stir-fry for 2 more minutes.

6 Add the blanched seafood. Add the
noodles and sauce, and stir-fry until the
seafood is reheated and cooked and all
the ingredients are coated. Season with
chilli oil and black pepper, and serve.

Per portion Energy 594kcal/2502kJ; Protein 36g; Carbohydrate 76g, of which sugars 10.1g; Fat 18.1g, of which saturates 2.4g; Cholesterol 232mg; Calcium 85mg; Fibre 3.8g; Sodium 1072mg.

PO JANG MA CHA STREET NOODLES

Sold by mobile vendors on bustling street corners in Korea, these noodles are a popular, filling snack. The fishcake and seaweed perfectly complement each other and create a light, nourishing dish, which is also quick and easy to prepare at home.

SERVES THREE

INGREDIENTS

300g/11oz somyun thin
   wheat noodles
150g/5oz fishcake, sliced, or fish balls
2 sheets dried tofu or Japanese
   yuba, sliced
dried seaweed paper or Japanese
   nori, shredded
2 spring onions (scallions), shredded
5ml/1 tsp sesame seeds
5ml/1 tsp Korean chilli powder
For the stock
   dried seaweed paper or japanese nori
   50g/2oz Chinese white radish
   10g/¼oz dried anchovies
   1 leek, sliced
   3 garlic cloves, peeled
   ½ white onion, sliced
   30ml/2 tbsp dark soy sauce
   salt and ground black pepper

1 First make the stock. Bring 2 litres/3½ pints/8¾ cups water to the boil in a large pan. Add the dried seaweed paper, radish, dried anchovies, leek, garlic, onion and soy sauce.

2 Bring back to the boil, reduce the heat slightly and boil the stock steadily for 15 minutes. Strain the stock, discarding the flavouring ingredients. Sample the stock and season to taste.

3 Bring a pan of water to the boil and add the somyun noodles. Simmer for about 1 minute, then drain. Place a portion of noodles into each of three soup bowls.

4 Bring the stock to the boil. Add the fishcake or fish balls and dried tofu or yuba. Boil for 10 minutes, until the tofu is tender.

5 Pour the soup over the noodles in the bowls. Garnish with the seaweed, spring onions and sesame seeds and sprinkle with chilli powder before serving.

VARIATION
Fresh tofu can be used as an alternative to dried tofu, but it should not be boiled for 10 minutes. At step 4, add the fishcake or fish balls and simmer for 5 minutes, then add the fresh tofu in one piece and simmer for a further 5 minutes. Use a large spatula or flat draining spoon to lift the tofu carefully from the soup. Slice it and divide it among the bowls, adding it to the noodles. Then pour in the soup. This way the tofu will not disintegrate.

Per portion Energy 505kcal/2133kJ; Protein 16.2g; Carbohydrate 82.2g, of which sugars 3.7g; Fat 14.7g, of which saturates 1.2g; Cholesterol 25mg; Calcium 77mg; Fibre 3.7g; Sodium 767mg.

SPICY BUCKWHEAT NOODLES

THIS CHILLED KOREAN SALAD, CALLED BIBIM NAENGMYUN, IS IDEAL FOR A SUMMER LUNCH DISH AND IS NOT TIME-CONSUMING TO MAKE. THE COOL TEMPERATURE OF THE BUCKWHEAT NOODLES CONTRASTS WITH THE SPICINESS OF THE DRESSING, AND ASIAN PEAR ADDS A DELICIOUS SWEETNESS.

SERVES TWO

INGREDIENTS
90g/3½oz naengmyun buckwheat
noodles
1 hard-boiled egg
½ cucumber
½ Asian pear
ice cubes, to serve
For the sauce
30ml/2 tbsp gochujang chilli paste
5ml/1 tsp Korean chilli powder
30ml/2 tbsp sugar
10ml/2 tsp sesame oil
1 garlic clove, finely chopped
2.5ml/½ tsp soy sauce
5ml/1 tsp sesame seeds

1 Cook the noodles in a large pan of boiling water for 5 minutes. Drain them, and then rinse two or three times in cold water until the water runs clear. Chill for 30 minutes.

2 Slice the hard-boiled egg in half. Seed the cucumber and slice it into long, thin matchstick strips. Peel and core the Asian pear and slice it into fine matchstick strips.

COOK'S TIP
Be sure to use a large pan with plenty of water when cooking naengmyun noodles, as they contain a lot of starch so will stick to the pan and each other easily. Add a few drops of oil while cooking to help prevent the water from frothing up and boiling over; this also helps to keep the noodles separate when they are first drained.

3 In a large bowl combine all the ingredients for the sauce and blend them together well. Arrange the noodles in the centre of a large serving platter. Pour over the sauce and then sprinkle with the pear and cucumber strips. Place the egg on the top and add ice cubes to the plate before serving.

Per portion Energy 337kcal/1421kJ; Protein 9.4g; Carbohydrate 58.3g, of which sugars 25.1g; Fat 9g, of which saturates 1.3g; Cholesterol 105mg; Calcium 52mg; Fibre 3.3g; Sodium 133mg.

POT-COOKED UDON IN MISO SOUP

UDON IS A WHITE WHEAT NOODLE, WHICH IS POPULAR IN JAPAN. HERE, IN THIS DISH KNOWN AS MISO NIKOMI UDON, THE NOODLES ARE COOKED IN A CLAY POT WITH A RICH MISO SOUP.

SERVES FOUR

INGREDIENTS

200g/7oz chicken breast portion,
   boned and skinned
10ml/2 tsp sake
2 abura-age
900ml/1½ pints/3¾ cups second
   dashi stock, or the same amount
   of water and 7.5ml/1½ tsp
   dashi-no-moto
6 large fresh shiitake mushrooms,
   stalks removed, quartered
4 spring onions (scallions), trimmed
   and chopped into 3mm/⅛in lengths
30ml/2 tbsp mirin
about 90g/3½oz aka miso or
   hatcho miso
300g/11oz dried udon noodles
4 eggs

1 Cut the chicken into bitesize pieces. Sprinkle with sake and leave to marinate for 15 minutes.

2 Put the abura-age in a sieve (strainer) and thoroughly rinse with hot water from the kettle to wash off the oil. Drain on kitchen paper and cut each abura-age into four squares.

3 To make the soup, heat the second dashi stock in a large pan and bring to the boil. Add the chicken pieces, shiitake mushrooms and abura-age and cook for 5 minutes. Remove from the heat and add the spring onions.

4 Put the mirin and miso paste into a small bowl. Scoop 30ml/2 tbsp soup from the pan and mix this in well.

5 To cook the udon, boil at least 2 litres/3½ pints/9 cups water in a large pan. The water should not come higher than two-thirds the depth of the pan. Cook the udon for 6 minutes and drain.

6 Put the udon in one large flameproof clay pot or casserole (or divide among four small pots). Mix the miso paste into the soup and check the taste. Add more miso if required. Ladle in enough soup to cover the udon, and arrange the soup ingredients on top of the udon.

7 Put the soup on a medium heat and break an egg on top. When the soup bubbles, wait for 1 minute, then cover and remove from the heat. Leave to stand for 2 minutes.

Per portion Energy 439kcal/1855kJ; Protein 28.8g; Carbohydrate 59.5g, of which sugars 3.9g; Fat 11.1g, of which saturates 1.8g; Cholesterol 225mg; Calcium 59mg; Fibre 2.9g; Sodium 1907mg.

SOBA NOODLES IN HOT SOUP WITH TEMPURA

WHEN YOU COOK JAPANESE NOODLE DISHES, EVERYONE SHOULD BE READY AT THE DINNER TABLE,
BECAUSE COOKED NOODLES START TO SOFTEN AND LOSE THEIR TASTE AND TEXTURE QUITE QUICKLY.

SERVES FOUR

INGREDIENTS

400g/14oz dried soba noodles
1 spring onion (scallion), sliced
shichimi togarashi (optional)

For the tempura

16 medium raw tiger or king prawns
  (jumbo shrimp), heads and shell
  removed, tails intact
400ml/14fl oz/1⅔ cups ice-cold water
1 large (US extra large) egg, beaten
200g/7oz/scant 2 cups plain
  (all-purpose) flour
vegetable oil, for deep-frying

For the soup

150ml/¼ pint/⅔ cup mirin
150ml/¼ pint/⅔ cup shoyu
900ml/1½ pints/3¾ cups water
25g/1oz kezuri-bushi or 2 × 15g/
  ½oz packets
15ml/1 tbsp caster (superfine) sugar
5ml/1 tsp salt
900ml/1½ pints/3¾ cups first dashi
  stock or the same amount of water
  and 12.5ml/2½ tsp dashi-no-moto

1 To make the soup, put the mirin in a large pan. Bring to the boil, then add the rest of the soup ingredients apart from the dashi stock. Bring back to the boil, then reduce the heat to low. Skim off the scum and cook for 2 minutes. Strain the soup and put back into a clean pan with the dashi stock.

2 Remove the vein from the prawns, then make 5 shallow cuts into each prawn's belly. Clip the tip of the tail with scissors and squeeze out any moisture from the tail.

3 To make the batter, pour the ice-cold water into a bowl and mix in the beaten egg. Sift in the flour and stir briefly; it should remain fairly lumpy.

4 Heat the oil in a wok or deep-fryer to 180°C/350°F. Hold the tail of a prawn, dunk it in the batter, then plunge it into the hot oil. Deep-fry 2 prawns at a time until crisp and golden. Drain on kitchen paper and keep warm.

5 Put the noodles in a large pan with at least 2 litres/3½ pints/9 cups rapidly boiling water, and stir frequently to stop them sticking.

6 When the water foams, pour in about 50ml/2fl oz/¼ cup cold water to lower the temperature. Repeat when the water foams once again. The noodles should be slightly softer than *al dente* pasta. Tip the noodles into a sieve and wash under cold water with your hands to rinse off any oil.

7 Heat the soup. Warm the noodles with hot water, and divide among individual serving bowls. Place the prawns attractively on the noodles and add the soup. Sprinkle with sliced spring onion and some shichimi togarashi, if you like. Serve immediately.

Per portion Energy 794kcal/3356kJ; Protein 28g; Carbohydrate 135g, of which sugars 22.9g; Fat 19.5g, of which saturates 1.8g; Cholesterol 145mg; Calcium 155mg; Fibre 4.5g; Sodium 3278mg.

UDON NOODLES WITH EGG BROTH AND GINGER

IN THIS JAPANESE DISH, CALLED ANKAKE UDON, THE SOUP FOR THE UDON IS THICKENED WITH
CORNFLOUR AND RETAINS ITS HEAT FOR A LONG TIME. A PERFECT LUNCH FOR A FREEZING COLD DAY.

2 Heat at least 2 litres/3½ pints/9 cups water in a large pan, and cook the udon for 8 minutes or according to the packet instructions. Drain under cold running water and wash off the starch with your hands. Leave the udon in the sieve.

3 Pour the soup into a large pan and bring to the boil. Blend the cornflour with 60ml/4 tbsp water. Reduce the heat to medium and gradually add the cornflour mixture to the hot soup. Stir constantly. The soup will thicken after a few minutes. Reduce the heat to low.

4 Mix the egg, mustard and cress, and spring onions in a small bowl. Stir the soup once again to create a whirlpool. Pour the eggs slowly into the soup pan.

5 Reheat the udon with hot water from a kettle. Divide among four bowls and pour the soup over the top. Garnish with the ginger and serve hot.

COOK'S TIP
You can use ready-made noodle soup, available from Japanese food stores. Follow the instructions to dilute with water or use straight from the bottle.

SERVES FOUR

INGREDIENTS
400g/14oz dried udon noodles
30ml/2 tbsp cornflour (cornstarch)
4 eggs, beaten
50g/2oz mustard and cress
2 spring onions (scallions),
   finely chopped
2.5cm/1in fresh root ginger, peeled
   and finely grated, to garnish
For the soup
1 litre/1¾ pints/4 cups water
40g/1½oz kezuri-bushi
25ml/1½ tbsp mirin
25ml/1½ tbsp shoyu
7.5ml/1½ tsp salt

1 To make the soup, place the water and the soup ingredients in a pan and bring to the boil on a medium heat. Remove from the heat when it starts boiling. Stand for 1 minute, then strain through muslin (cheesecloth). Check the taste and add more salt if required.

Per portion Energy 517kcal/2187kJ; Protein 19.5g; Carbohydrate 87.7g, of which sugars 7g; Fat 12.4g, of which saturates 1.7g; Cholesterol 190mg; Calcium 130mg; Fibre 3.2g; Sodium 1019mg.

SAPPORO-STYLE RAMEN NOODLES <u>IN</u> SOUP

THIS IS A RICH AND TANGY SOUP FROM SAPPORO, THE CAPITAL OF HOKKAIDO, WHICH IS JAPAN'S MOST NORTHERLY ISLAND. RAW GRATED GARLIC AND CHILLI OIL ARE ADDED TO WARM THE BODY.

SERVES FOUR

INGREDIENTS
  250g/9oz dried ramen noodles
For the soup stock
  4 spring onions (scallions)
  6cm/2½in fresh root ginger, quartered
  raw bones from 2 chickens, washed
  1 large onion, quartered
  4 garlic cloves
  1 large carrot, roughly chopped
  1 egg shell
  120ml/4fl oz/½ cup sake
  90ml/6 tbsp miso (any colour)
  30ml/2 tbsp shoyu
For the toppings
  115g/4oz pork belly
  5cm/2in carrot
  12 mangetouts (snow peas)
  8 baby corn
  15ml/1 tbsp sesame oil
  1 dried red chilli, seeded
    and crushed
  225g/8oz/1 cup beansprouts
  2 spring onions (scallions), chopped
  2 garlic cloves, finely grated
  chilli oil
  salt

1 To make the soup stock, bruise the spring onions and ginger by hitting with a rolling pin. Boil 1.5 litres/2½ pints/6¼ cups water in a heavy pan, add the bones, and cook until the meat changes colour. Discard the water and wash the bones under running water.

2 Wash the pan and boil 2 litres/3½ pints/9 cups water, then add the bones and other stock ingredients except for the miso and shoyu. Reduce the heat to low, and simmer for 2 hours, skimming any scum off. Strain into a bowl through a muslin- (cheesecloth-) lined sieve (strainer), this will take about 1–2 hours. Do not squeeze the muslin.

3 Cut the pork into 5mm/¼in slices. Peel and halve the carrot lengthways then cut into 3mm/⅛in thick, 5cm/2in long slices. Boil the carrot, mangetouts and corn for 3 minutes in water. Drain.

4 Heat the sesame oil in a wok and fry the pork slices and chilli. When the colour of the meat has changed, add the beansprouts. Reduce the heat to medium and add 1 litre/1¾ pints/4 cups soup stock. Cook for 5 minutes.

5 Scoop 60ml/4 tbsp soup stock from the wok and mix well with the miso and shoyu in a bowl. Stir back into the soup. Reduce the heat to low.

6 Bring 2 litres/3½ pints/9 cups water to the boil. Cook the noodles until just soft, following the instructions on the packet. Stir constantly. If the water bubbles up, pour in 50ml/2fl oz/¼ cup cold water. Drain well and divide among four bowls.

7 Pour the hot soup on to the noodles and heap the beansprouts and pork on top. Add the carrot, mangetouts and corn. Sprinkle with spring onions and serve with garlic and chilli oil.

Per portion Energy 449kcal/1886kJ; Protein 16.2g; Carbohydrate 60.5g, of which sugars 11.2g; Fat 17.5g, of which saturates 4.3g; Cholesterol 21mg; Calcium 68mg; Fibre 4.9g; Sodium 1956mg.

TOKYO-STYLE RAMEN NOODLES IN SOUP

RAMEN IS A HYBRID CHINESE NOODLE DISH PRESENTED IN A JAPANESE WAY, AND THERE ARE MANY REGIONAL VARIATIONS FEATURING LOCAL SPECIALITIES. THIS IS A LEGENDARY TOKYO VERSION.

SERVES FOUR

INGREDIENTS
250g/9oz dried ramen noodles
For the soup stock
   4 spring onions (scallions)
   7.5cm/3in fresh root ginger, quartered
   raw bones from 2 chickens, washed
   1 large onion, quartered
   4 garlic cloves, peeled
   1 large carrot, roughly chopped
   1 egg shell
   120ml/4fl oz/½ cup sake
   about 60ml/4 tbsp shoyu
   2.5ml/½ tsp salt
For the cha-shu (pot-roast pork)
   500g/1¼lb pork shoulder, boned
   30ml/2 tbsp vegetable oil
   2 spring onions (scallions), chopped
   2.5cm/1in fresh root ginger, peeled
     and sliced
   15ml/1 tbsp sake
   45ml/3 tbsp shoyu
   15ml/1 tbsp caster (superfine) sugar
For the toppings
   2 hard-boiled (hard-cooked) eggs
   150g/5oz menma, soaked for
     30 minutes and drained
   ½ nori sheet, broken into pieces
   2 spring onions (scallions), chopped
   ground white pepper
   sesame oil or chilli oil

1 To make the soup stock, bruise the spring onions and ginger by hitting with the side of a large knife or a rolling pin. Pour 1.5 litres/2½ pints/6¼ cups water into a wok and bring to the boil. Add the chicken bones and boil until the colour of the meat changes. Discard the water and wash the bones under water.

2 Wash the wok, bring another 2 litres/3½ pints/9 cups water to the boil and add the bones and the other soup stock ingredients, except for the shoyu and salt. Reduce the heat to low, and simmer until the water has reduced by half, skimming off any scum. Strain into a bowl through a muslin- (cheesecloth-) lined sieve (strainer). This will take 1–2 hours.

3 Make the *cha-shu*. Roll the meat up tightly, 8cm/3½in in diameter, and tie it with kitchen string.

4 Wash the wok and dry over a high heat. Heat the oil to smoking point in the wok and add the chopped spring onions and ginger. Cook briefly, then add the meat. Turn often to brown the outside evenly.

5 Sprinkle with sake and add 400ml/14fl oz/1⅔ cups water, the shoyu and sugar. Boil, then reduce the heat to low and cover. Cook for 25–30 minutes, turning every 5 minutes. Remove from the heat.

6 Slice the pork into 12 fine slices. Use any leftover pork for another recipe.

7 Shell and halve the boiled eggs, and sprinkle some salt on to the yolks.

8 Pour 1 litre/1¾ pints/4 cups soup stock from the bowl into a large pan. Boil and add the shoyu and salt. Check the seasoning; add more shoyu if required.

9 Wash the wok again and bring 2 litres/3½ pints/9 cups water to the boil.

10 Cook the ramen noodles according to the packet instructions until just soft. Stir constantly to prevent sticking. If the water bubbles up, pour in 50ml/2fl oz/¼ cup cold water. Drain well and divide among four bowls.

11 Pour the soup over the noodles to cover. Arrange half a boiled egg, pork slices, menma and nori on top, and sprinkle with spring onions.

12 Serve with pepper and sesame or chilli oil. Season to taste with a little salt, if you like.

Per portion Energy 359kcal/1503kJ; Protein 36.1g; Carbohydrate 19.8g, of which sugars 9.8g; Fat 15.4g, of which saturates 3.4g; Cholesterol 174mg; Calcium 248mg; Fibre 1.8g; Sodium 930mg.

FISH

There are numerous tasty and healthy fish dishes in the Japanese and Korean

culinary tradition. Many employ a wide variety of cooking methods, ranging

from 'cooking' the fresh fish in vinegar, to flavouring it with seaweed, or

lightly deep-frying in tempura. Recipes range from chilled seafood salads,

such as Skate Salad with Mustard, Garlic and Soy Dressing to slow-cooked

casseroles such as Monkfish with Soya Beansprouts.

Left: Griddled Sea Bream with Orange Dipping Sauce; **Above:** Salmon Teriyaki

SKATE SALAD <u>WITH</u> MUSTARD, GARLIC <u>AND</u> SOY DRESSING

THE SHARPNESS OF THE MUSTARD AND PUNGENCY OF THE GARLIC OFFSET THE FLAVOUR OF THE SKATE PERFECTLY IN THIS DISH. IN KOREA, IT IS POPULAR AS AN APPETIZER, OR AS A LIGHT LUNCH IN THE SUMMER, THIS RECIPE BLENDS AN ARRAY OF GREEN LEAVES TO PROVIDE A REFRESHING SALAD.

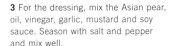

2 Remove the skate flesh from the cartilage of the wing. Shred the flesh and set it aside.

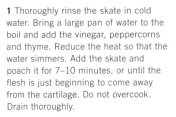

3 For the dressing, mix the Asian pear, oil, vinegar, garlic, mustard and soy sauce. Season with salt and pepper and mix well.

4 Place the rocket, watercress, mixed leaves and diced tomatoes in a large serving bowl. Add the shredded skate and toss the ingredients together.

5 Pour the dressing over the salad, toss lightly and garnish with orange zest.

SERVES FOUR

INGREDIENTS
800g/1¾lb skate
15ml/1 tbsp white wine vinegar
15 peppercorns
1 thyme sprig
115g/4oz rocket (arugula)
115g/4oz watercress
200g/7oz mixed salad leaves
2 tomatoes, seeded and diced
finely pared orange zest, to garnish
For the dressing
30ml/2 tbsp grated Asian pear
30ml/2 tbsp virgin olive oil
30ml/2 tbsp white wine vinegar
30ml/2 tbsp crushed garlic
10ml/2 tsp English (hot) mustard
5ml/1 tsp dark soy sauce
salt and ground black pepper

1 Thoroughly rinse the skate in cold water. Bring a large pan of water to the boil and add the vinegar, peppercorns and thyme. Reduce the heat so that the water simmers. Add the skate and poach it for 7–10 minutes, or until the flesh is just beginning to come away from the cartilage. Do not overcook. Drain thoroughly.

Per portion Energy 219kcal/919kJ; Protein 33.6g; Carbohydrate 4.4g, of which sugars 4.2g; Fat 7.5g, of which saturates 1g; Cholesterol 0mg; Calcium 257mg; Fibre 2.8g; Sodium 637mg.

GRIDDLED SEA BREAM <u>WITH</u> ORANGE DIPPING SAUCE

This typical Korean recipe showcases the delicacy of this wonderful fish by keeping the seasoning to a minimum and grilling it to give a subtle smoky taste. The sweet sharpness and fresh quality of the orange dipping sauce unlock a mouthwatering flavour.

SERVES TWO

INGREDIENTS
  1 large sea bream, gutted
    and cleaned
  30ml/2 tbsp white wine
  5ml/1 tsp sesame seeds, ground
  1 red chilli, seeded and sliced
  1 garlic clove, crushed
  5ml/1 tsp finely chopped fresh
    root ginger
  5ml/1 tsp sesame oil
  15ml/1 tbsp plain (all-purpose) flour
  30ml/2 tbsp vegetable oil
  salt
  2 spring onions (scallions), finely
    sliced, to garnish
For the dipping sauce
  15ml/1 tbsp sugar
  20ml/4 tsp orange juice
  45ml/3 tbsp dark soy sauce
  1 garlic clove, crushed
  5ml/1 tsp grated fresh root ginger
  60ml/4 tbsp vegetable or kelp stock
  7.5ml/1½ tsp rice vinegar

1 Make diagonal slashes on both sides of the sea bream, then place it in a dish and pour over the white wine. Leave to stand for 10 minutes.

2 Mix the ground sesame seeds with the chilli, garlic, ginger and sesame oil. Add a pinch of salt and mix well. Drain the wine off the fish and rub the sesame mixture into the slashes in the bream and also into the fish cavity. Leave to marinate for 30 minutes.

3 Meanwhile make the dipping sauce. Simmer the sugar and orange juice in a small pan over a low heat until reduced to a concentrated syrup.

4 Add the soy sauce, garlic, ginger and stock and simmer for 3 minutes, then strain the liquid into a jug (pitcher). Add the vinegar and stir well, then set aside.

5 Heat a griddle pan or frying pan over a medium heat and add the oil. Dust the bream with flour and wrap the tail in foil. Cook for 10 minutes, turning once, until the skin turns crisp and brown and the flesh is springy to the touch.

6 Place the fish on a warmed serving dish. Garnish with the spring onions and serve with the dipping sauce.

Per portion Energy 436kcal/1828kJ; Protein 45.7g; Carbohydrate 16.4g, of which sugars 10.5g; Fat 21.3g, of which saturates 1.8g; Cholesterol 95mg; Calcium 136mg; Fibre 0.5g; Sodium 1879mg.

MONKFISH WITH SOYA BEANSPROUTS

This dish blends the fragrant taste and delicate texture of monkfish with the crunchy, nutty qualities of soya beansprouts. Coated with a fierce chilli sauce, the heat gives way to a delicious combination of distinctively Korean flavours.

SERVES TWO TO THREE

INGREDIENTS
    600g/1lb 6oz monkfish fillets
    1 sheet dried kelp
    30ml/2 tbsp vegetable oil
    300g/11oz soya beansprouts
    50g/2oz/7 tbsp cornflour
        (corn starch)
    115g/4oz watercress or Korean
        minari, chopped
    ½ leek, sliced
    1 green chilli, seeded
        and sliced
    1 red chilli, seeded and sliced
    15ml/1 tbsp sesame oil
    salt and ground black pepper
    7.5ml/1½ tsp sesame seeds,
        to garnish
For the sauce
    90ml/6 tbsp Korean chilli powder
    2 garlic cloves, crushed
    5ml/1 tsp grated fresh
        root ginger
    30ml/2 tbsp sugar
    15ml/1 tbsp sake or mirin
    15ml/1 tbsp rice vinegar
    5ml/1 tsp cider vinegar

1 Cut the monkfish into 5cm/2in strips. Sprinkle with a little salt and leave to stand for 2 hours.

2 For the sauce, mix the chilli powder, crushed garlic, grated ginger, sugar, sake or mirin, rice vinegar and cider vinegar in a jug (pitcher). Add a little salt and pepper and mix the ingredients well. Set aside to allow the flavours to mingle.

3 Bring 300ml/½ pint/1¼ cups water to the boil in a pan and add the dried kelp. Reduce the heat a little and cook for 10 minutes. Then you need to strain and reserve the stock, discarding the kelp.

4 Heat a pan over high heat and add the vegetable oil. Stir-fry the monkfish for 2 minutes and add the kelp stock. Simmer for 3 minutes. Add the soya beansprouts and cover. Simmer for 3 more minutes.

5 Mix the cornflour to a smooth paste with 50ml/2 fl oz/¼ cup warm water. Stir the sauce into the fish mixture. Reduce the heat before adding the watercress, leeks, chillies and cornflour paste. Simmer the mixture gently, stirring, until the sauce is thickened.

6 Spoon the monkfish and sauce on to plates, drizzle with sesame oil and garnish with sesame seeds before serving.

COOK'S TIP
Fresh monkfish should be kept cool at all times and should not be left unrefrigerated for long. As soon as you get the fish home, rinse it in cold water, and pat dry with kitchen paper. The best way to store it is on a cake rack in a shallow pan filled with crushed ice. Cover with cling wrap or foil and keep in the coldest part of the refrigerator. You can do this for up to two days.

Per portion Energy 421kcal/1775kJ; Protein 38.3g; Carbohydrate 36.4g, of which sugars 13.3g; Fat 15g, of which saturates 2.1g; Cholesterol 28mg; Calcium 136mg; Fibre 2.5g; Sodium 73mg.

MARINATED AND GRILLED SWORDFISH

IN MEDIEVAL TIMES, SAIKYO (THE WESTERN CAPITAL OF ANCIENT JAPAN) HAD A VERY SOPHISTICATED CULTURE. ARISTOCRATS COMPETED WITH EACH OTHER AS TO THEIR CHEF'S SKILLS, AND MANY OF THE CLASSIC RECIPES OF TODAY ARE FROM THIS PERIOD. KAJIKI SAIKYO YAKI IS ONE SUCH EXAMPLE.

SERVES FOUR

INGREDIENTS
    4 × 175g/6oz fresh
        swordfish steaks
    2.5ml/½ tsp salt
    300g/11oz saikyo or shiro miso
    45ml/3 tbsp sake
For the asparagus
    25ml/1½ tbsp shoyu
    25ml/1½ tbsp sake
    8 asparagus spears, with the hard
        ends discarded, and each spear
        cut into three pieces

1 Place the swordfish in a shallow container. Sprinkle with the salt on both sides and leave for 2 hours. Drain and wipe the fish with kitchen paper.

2 Mix the miso and sake, then spread half across the bottom of the cleaned container. Cover with a sheet of muslin (cheesecloth) the size of a dishtowel, folded in half, then open the fold. Place the swordfish, side by side, on top, and cover with the muslin. Spread the rest of the miso mixture on the muslin. Make sure the muslin is touching the fish. Marinate for 2 days in the coolest part of the refrigerator.

3 Preheat the grill (broiler) to medium. Oil the wire rack and grill (broil) the fish slowly for about 8 minutes on each side, turning every 2 minutes. If the steaks are thin, check every time you turn the fish to see if they are ready.

4 Mix the shoyu and sake in a bowl. Grill the asparagus for 2 minutes on each side, then dip into the bowl. Return to the grill for 2 minutes more on each side. Dip into the sauce again and set aside.

5 Serve the steak hot on four individual serving plates. Garnish with the drained, grilled asparagus.

Per portion Energy 213kcal/893kJ; Protein 32.7g; Carbohydrate 2.5g, of which sugars 2.2g; Fat 7.3g, of which saturates 1.6g; Cholesterol 72mg; Calcium 16mg; Fibre 0.3g; Sodium 2008mg.

SEARED SWORDFISH WITH CITRUS DRESSING

KAJIKI NO TATAKI SALAD IS A GOOD EXAMPLE OF HOW THE JAPANESE TRY OUT NEW DISHES FROM ALL OVER THE WORLD AND SOON START TO ARRANGE THEM IN A JAPANESE WAY. FRESH FISH IS SLICED THINLY AND SEARED OR MARINATED, THEN SERVED WITH SALAD LEAVES AND VEGETABLES.

SERVES FOUR

INGREDIENTS
  75g/3oz daikon, peeled
  50g/2oz carrot, peeled
  1 Japanese or salad cucumber
  10ml/2 tsp vegetable oil
  300g/11oz skinned fresh swordfish
    steak, cut against the grain
  2 cartons mustard and cress
  15ml/1 tbsp toasted
    sesame seeds
For the dressing
  105ml/7 tbsp shoyu
  105ml/7 tbsp second dashi stock,
    or the same amount of water and
    5ml/1 tsp dashi-no-moto
  30ml/2 tbsp toasted sesame oil
  juice of ½ lime
  rind of ½ lime, shredded into
    thin strips

1 Make the vegetable garnishes first. Use a very sharp knife, mandolin or vegetable slicer with a julienne blade to make very thin (about 4cm/1½in long) strands of daikon, carrot and cucumber. Soak the daikon and carrot in ice-cold water for 5 minutes, then drain well and keep in the refrigerator.

2 Mix together all the ingredients for the dressing and stir well, then chill.

3 Heat the oil in a small frying pan until smoking hot. Sear the fish for 30 seconds on all sides. Plunge it into cold water in a bowl to stop the cooking. Dry on kitchen paper and wipe off as much oil as possible.

4 Cut the swordfish steak in half lengthways before slicing it into 5mm/¼in thick pieces in the other direction, against the grain.

5 Arrange the fish slices into a ring on individual plates. Mix the vegetable strands, mustard and cress and sesame seeds. Fluff up with your hands, then shape them into a sphere. Gently place it in the centre of the plate, on the swordfish. Pour the dressing around the plate's edge and serve immediately.

COOK'S TIP
This dish is traditionally made with fillet cut with the grain. To prepare, cut it in half lengthways, then slice against the grain by holding a knife horizontally to the chopping board.

Per portion Energy 223kcal/925kJ; Protein 15.4g; Carbohydrate 3.6g, of which sugars 3.3g; Fat 16.4g, of which saturates 2.5g; Cholesterol 31mg; Calcium 46mg; Fibre 0.9g; Sodium 1975mg.

VEGETABLES AND SALMON IN A PARCEL

IN THIS JAPANESE RECIPE, THE VEGETABLES AND SALMON ARE WRAPPED AND STEAMED WITH SAKE IN THEIR OWN MOISTURE. WHEN MAKING SAKA-MUSHI, ARRANGING THE FISH AND ALL THE VEGETABLES CAN BE TRICKY, BUT WHEN YOU OPEN THE PARCEL, YOU'LL FIND A COLOURFUL GARDEN INSIDE.

3 Slice the carrot very thinly, then with a Japanese vegetable cutter or sharp knife, cut out 8–12 maple-leaf or flower shapes. Carefully slice the spring onions in half lengthways with a sharp knife. Trim the mangetouts.

4 Cut four sheets of foil, each about 29 × 21cm/11½ × 8½in wide. Place the long side of one sheet facing towards you. Arrange the salmon and shimeji mushrooms in the centre, then place a spring onion diagonally across them. Put 2 shiitake on top, 3–4 mangetouts in a fan shape and then sprinkle with a few carrot leaves.

5 Sprinkle the marinade and a good pinch of salt over the top. Fold the two longer sides of the foil together, then fold the shorter sides to seal. Repeat to make four parcels.

6 Place the parcels on a baking sheet and bake for 15–20 minutes in the middle of the preheated oven. When the foil has expanded into a balloon, the dish is ready to serve. Serve unopened with a little extra shoyu, if required.

SERVES FOUR

INGREDIENTS
600g/1lb 5oz salmon
  fillet, skinned
30ml/2 tbsp sake
15ml/1 tbsp shoyu, plus extra
  to serve (optional)
about 250g/9oz fresh shimeji
  mushrooms
8 fresh shiitake mushrooms
2.5cm/1in carrot
2 spring onions (scallions)
115g/4oz mangetouts
  (snow peas)
salt

1 Preheat the oven to 190°C/375°F/ Gas 5. Cut the salmon into bitesize pieces. Marinate in the sake and shoyu for about 15 minutes. Drain and reserve the marinade.

2 Clean the shimeji mushrooms and chop off the hard root. Remove and discard the stalks from the shiitake. Carve a shallow slit on the top of each shiitake with a sharp knife inserted at a slant. Repeat from the other side to cut out a notch about 4cm/1½in long, then rotate the shiitake 90° and carefully carve another notch to make a small white cross in the brown top.

Per portion Energy 303kcal/1263kJ; Protein 33.2g; Carbohydrate 2.2g, of which sugars 1.8g; Fat 17g, of which saturates 3g; Cholesterol 75mg; Calcium 54mg; Fibre 1.7g; Sodium 341mg.

SALMON WITH BLACK-EYED BEANS

TRADITIONALLY, THIS JAPANESE DISH WAS SERVED IN THE COLDEST TIME OF THE YEAR USING ONLY PRESERVED FOOD SUCH AS SALTED SALMON AND DRIED VEGETABLES. HERE, FRESH SALMON AND VEGETABLES ARE USED INSTEAD. IT KEEPS FOR 4–5 DAYS IN A COOL PLACE.

SERVES FOUR

INGREDIENTS

150g/5oz salmon fillet, boned
 and skinned
400g/14oz can black-eyed beans
 (peas) in brine
50g/2oz fresh shiitake mushrooms,
 stalks removed
50g/2oz carrot, peeled
50g/2oz daikon, peeled
5g/⅛oz dashi-konbu about 10cm/
 4in square
60ml/4 tbsp water
5ml/1 tsp caster (superfine) sugar
15ml/1 tbsp shoyu
7.5ml/1½ tsp mirin
salt
2.5cm/1in fresh root ginger, peeled
 and thinly sliced or grated,
 to garnish

1 Slice the salmon into 1cm/½in thick pieces. Thoroughly salt the fillet and leave for 1 hour, then wash away the salt and cut it into 1cm/½in cubes. Par-boil in rapidly boiling water in a small pan for 30 seconds, then drain. Gently wash under running water.

2 Slice the fresh ginger thinly lengthways, then stack the slices and cut into thin threads. Soak in cold water for 30 minutes, then drain well.

3 Drain the can of beans and tip the liquid into a medium pan. Set the beans and liquid aside.

4 Chop all the vegetables into 1cm/½in cubes. Wipe the dried konbu with a damp dishtowel or kitchen paper, then snip with scissors.

5 Add the salmon, vegetables and konbu to the bean liquid with the beans, water, sugar and 1.5ml/¼ tsp salt. Bring to the boil. Reduce the heat to low and cook for 6 minutes or until the carrot is cooked. Add the shoyu and cook for 4 minutes. Add the mirin, then remove the pan from the heat, mix well and check the seasoning. Leave for an hour. Serve garnished with the ginger.

Per portion Energy 198kcal/834kJ; Protein 16.9g; Carbohydrate 22.8g, of which sugars 3.9g; Fat 5g, of which saturates 1g; Cholesterol 19mg; Calcium 37mg; Fibre 4.1g; Sodium 294mg.

SALMON TERIYAKI

Japanese dishes are very popular in Korea, and the taste of this traditional teriyaki sauce echoes the flavour of the hugely popular Korean dish bulgogi. The marinade is rich and complex, combining the sweetness of maple syrup with the saltiness of soy sauce.

2 Mix the sugar, sake or mirin, maple syrup and light soy sauce in a small jug (pitcher) until thoroughly combined.

3 Heat a frying pan or wok over a medium heat. Add the oil and then add the salmon, reserving the marinade. Cook the salmon, turning as necessary, until it is lightly browned on both sides.

4 Reduce the heat and pour over any reserved marinade and the sake mixture. Turn the salmon to ensure the pieces are evenly coated. Cook gently for a few minutes, until the juices form a sticky glaze on the fish.

5 Transfer the salmon to plates, garnish with sesame seeds and whole chives and serve.

COOK'S TIPS
• Dried ground ginger should not be substituted for fresh ginger.
• When buying fresh ginger, look for firm ginger with smooth skin (skin that is wrinkled means that the root is dry and will have less flavour).

SERVES FOUR

INGREDIENTS
  1 garlic clove, crushed
  5ml/1 tsp grated fresh root ginger
  30ml/2 tbsp dark soy sauce
  15ml/1 tbsp rice vinegar
  400g/14oz salmon fillet, cut into
    4 portions
  10ml/2 tsp sugar
  15ml/1 tbsp sake or mirin
  5ml/1 tsp maple syrup
  30ml/2 tbsp light soy sauce
  60ml/4 tbsp olive oil
For the garnish
  5ml/1 tsp sesame seeds
  whole chives

1 Combine the garlic, ginger, dark soy sauce and rice vinegar in a shallow dish large enough to hold the salmon. Mix well, then add the salmon portions and coat them with the marinade. Cover and leave to marinate for 1 hour.

Per portion Energy 239kcal/995kJ; Protein 24.8g; Carbohydrate 2.1g, of which sugars 1.7g; Fat 13.3g, of which saturates 2.3g; Cholesterol 58mg; Calcium 93mg; Fibre 0.3g; Sodium 323mg.

TERIYAKI SEA BASS

You can use whole fish or thick fillets for this Japanese-style recipe, which is also excellent made with bream, porgy, snapper, pomfret and trevally. Serve the fish with fried rice and stir-fried green vegetables, such as pak choi, if you like.

SERVES FOUR

INGREDIENTS

1 sea bass, about 1.4–1.5kg/
   3–3½lb, scaled and cleaned
8 spring onions (scallions)
60ml/4 tbsp teriyaki marinade or
   dark soy sauce
30ml/2 tbsp cornflour (cornstarch)
juice of 1 lemon
30ml/2 tbsp rice wine vinegar
5ml/1 tsp ground ginger
60ml/4 tbsp groundnut (peanut) oil
2 leeks, shredded
2.5cm/1in piece fresh root ginger,
   peeled and grated
105ml/7 tbsp chicken or fish stock
30ml/2 tbsp rice wine or dry sherry
5ml/1 tsp caster (superfine) sugar
salt and ground black pepper

1 Make several diagonal slashes on either side of the sea bass so it can absorb the flavours, then season the fish inside and out with salt and ground black pepper. Place the fish in a shallow dish.

2 Trim the spring onions and cut them in half lengthways, then slice them diagonally into 2cm/¾in lengths. Put half of the sliced spring onions in the cavity of the fish and reserve the rest for later use.

3 In a shallow dish, mix together the teriyaki marinade or dark soy sauce, the cornflour, lemon juice, rice wine vinegar and ground ginger to make a smooth, runny paste.

4 Pour the marinade on to the fish, working it into the slashes, and turning the fish so it is covered thoroughly. Then leave the fish to marinate for 20–30 minutes, turning it several times.

5 Heat a wok or frying pan that is large enough to hold the sea bass comfortably. Add the oil, then the leeks and grated ginger.

6 Cook the fish gently for about 5 minutes, until the leeks are tender. Then remove the leeks and ginger with a slotted spoon and leave to drain on kitchen paper, leaving the oil in the wok or pan.

7 Lift the sea bass out of the marinade and lower it carefully into the hot oil. Cook over a medium heat for 2–3 minutes on each side.

8 Stir the stock, rice wine or sherry and sugar into the marinade, with salt and pepper to taste.

9 Pour the mixture over the fish. Return the leeks and ginger to the wok, together with the reserved spring onions. Cover and simmer for about 15 minutes, until the fish is cooked through. Serve with the remaining spring onions.

Per portion Energy 300kcal/1253kJ; Protein 31.1g; Carbohydrate 7.5g, of which sugars 6.7g; Fat 15.4g, of which saturates 2g; Cholesterol 120mg; Calcium 229mg; Fibre 2.6g; Sodium 271mg.

FISH CAKES <u>and</u> VEGETABLES

ODEN IS A SATISFYING AND EASY JAPANESE DISH TO MAKE AT HOME AS YOU CAN BUY A VARIETY OF
ASSORTED READY-MADE FISH BALLS AND FISH CAKES FROM ASIAN FOOD STORES.

SERVES FOUR

INGREDIENTS
   30 × 7.5cm/12 × 3in dashi-konbu
   675g/1½lb daikon, peeled and cut
     into 4cm/1½in lengths
   12–20 ready-made fish balls and
     cakes (4 of each kind)
   1 konnyaku
   1 atsu-age
   8 small shiitake mushrooms,
     stalks removed
   4 medium potatoes, unpeeled,
     soaked in a bowl of water
   4 hard-boiled eggs, unshelled
   285g/10¼oz packet tofu block, cut
     into 8 cubes
   English (hot) mustard, to serve
For the soup stock
   1.5 litres/2½ pints/6¼ cups
     second dashi stock, or the same
     amount of water and 10ml/2 tsp
     dashi-no-moto
   75ml/5 tbsp sake
   15ml/1 tbsp salt
   40ml/8 tsp shoyu

1 Wrap the dashi-konbu in a wet, clean dish towel for 5 minutes, or until soft enough to bend easily by hand without breaking. Snip the wet dish towel in half crossways, then cut each into four ribbons lengthways. Tie the centre of each 'ribbon'.

2 Slightly shave the edges of each of the daikon cylinders.

3 Place all the fish balls and cakes, konnyaku and atsu-age in a large pan. Add enough hot water to cover all the ingredients, then drain.

4 Cut the konnyaku in quarters, then cut each quarter in half diagonally to make eight triangles. Cut large fish cakes in half. Put two shiitake mushrooms on to each of four bamboo skewers.

5 Mix all the ingredients for the soup stock, but only fill the pot or casserole by two-thirds. Add the daikon and potatoes and bring to the boil. Add the hard-boiled eggs. Reduce the heat to low and simmer for an hour, uncovered, skimming occasionally.

6 Increase the heat to medium and add the other ingredients. Cook, covered, for 30 minutes, then bring to the table cooker and keep warm on the lowest heat. Serve with mustard. Top up the pot with stock when it has reduced to half.

VARIATIONS
Deep-fry fish-ball mixtures in hot oil at 180°C/350°F until golden.
Fish Balls with Chives Process 150g/5oz chopped skinned cod fillet, 50g/2oz queen scallops, 1 egg white, 10ml/2 tsp grated ginger juice, 15ml/1 tbsp cornflour (cornstarch), 15ml/1 tbsp salt and 5ml/ 1 tsp sake in a food processor. Mix with 15ml/1 tbsp chopped chives.
Prawn Balls Combine 200g/7oz raw peeled small prawns (shrimp), 50g/2oz pork fat, 15ml/1 tbsp grated ginger juice, 1 egg white, 15ml/1 tbsp salt and 15ml/1 tbsp cornflour in a processor.
Squid and Ginger Balls Blend 200g/7oz chopped squid, 1 egg white, 15ml/ 1 tbsp cornflour, 10ml/2 tsp ginger juice and 15ml/1 tbsp salt in a food processor. Mix with 10ml/2 tsp chopped ginger.

Per portion Energy 370kcal/1555kJ; Protein 37.1g; Carbohydrate 28.8g, of which sugars 5.8g; Fat 10.4g, of which saturates 2.4g; Cholesterol 236mg; Calcium 327mg; Fibre 3.1g; Sodium 1926mg.

FISH AND VEGETABLE HOTPOT

THIS JAPANESE DISH, CALLED YOSE NABE, IS COOKED AND EATEN AT THE TABLE, TRADITIONALLY USING A CLAY POT. YOU WILL NEED A FLAMEPROOF CASSEROLE AND A PORTABLE TABLE-TOP STOVE.

SERVES FOUR

INGREDIENTS
    225g/8oz salmon, scaled and cut into
        5cm/2in thick steaks with bones
    225g/8oz white fish, cleaned and
        scaled then chopped into 4 chunks
    300g/11oz chicken thighs, cut into
        large bitesize chunks with bones
    4 hakusai leaves, base part trimmed
    115g/4oz spinach
    1 large carrot, cut into 5mm/¼in
        thick rounds or flower shapes
    8 fresh shiitake mushrooms, stalks
        removed, or 150g/5oz oyster
        mushrooms, base trimmed
    2 thin leeks, washed and cut
        diagonally into 5cm/2in lengths
    285g/10¼oz packet tofu block,
        drained and cut into 16 cubes
    salt
For the hot-pot liquid
    12 × 6cm/4½ × 2½in dashi-konbu
    1.2 litres/2 pints/5 cups water
    120ml/4fl oz/½ cup sake
For the condiments
    90g/3½oz daikon, peeled
    1 dried chilli, halved and seeded
    1 lemon, cut into 16 wedges
    4 spring onions (scallions), chopped
    2 × 5g/⅛oz packets kezuri-bushi
    1 bottle shoyu

1 Arrange the various prepared fish and chicken on a large serving platter.

2 Boil plenty of water in a large pan and cook the hakusai for 3 minutes. Drain and leave to cool. Add a pinch of salt to the water and boil the spinach for 1 minute, then drain under running water.

3 Squeeze the spinach and lay on a sushi rolling mat, then roll it up firmly. Leave to rest, then unwrap and take the cylinder out. Lay the hakusai leaves next to each other on the mat. Put the cylinder in the middle and roll again firmly. Leave for 5 minutes, then unroll and cut into 5cm/2in long cylinders.

4 Transfer the hakusai cylinders to the platter along with all the remaining vegetables and the tofu.

5 Lay the dashi-konbu on the bottom of the clay pot or flameproof casserole. Mix the water and sake in a small bowl.

6 Insert a skewer into the the daikon two to three times, and insert the chilli pieces. Leave for about 5 minutes, then grate finely. Drain in a sieve (strainer) and squeeze the liquid out. Shape into a mound and put in a bowl. Put all the other condiments into small bowls.

7 Fill the pot or casserole with two-thirds of the water and sake mixture. Bring to the boil, then reduce the heat. Put the carrot, shiitake, chicken and salmon into the pot. When the colour of the meat and fish changes, add the rest of the ingredients in batches, and eat once cooked.

Per portion Energy 317kcal/1325kJ; Protein 45.9g; Carbohydrate 5.9g, of which sugars 5.1g; Fat 12.3g, of which saturates 2.2g; Cholesterol 133mg; Calcium 455mg; Fibre 2g; Sodium 1961mg.

SHELLFISH

*Japan and Korea are surrounded by sea, and because of this shellfish
are strongly evident in the diets. Spices and chilli paste make frequent
appearances, usually complemented by milder ingredients such as
watercress. Recipes range from salads, such as Spicy Whelk Salad
and Prawn Tempura to a stir-fried squid and a jalapeño
flavoured Fiery Octopus.*

Left: Crab Meat Salad with Garlic Dressing; **Above:** Clams and Spring Onions with Miso and Mustard Sauce

SQUID AND SEAWEED WITH CHILLI DRESSING

THIS KOREAN CHILLED SEAFOOD SALAD MAKES A GREAT APPETIZER AND REALLY DOES STIMULATE THE APPETITE. THE FLAVOURS OF CHILLI AND RICE VINEGAR ARE BALANCED BY SWEET MAPLE SYRUP, WITH THE KELP PROVIDING AN UNUSUAL AND TANTALIZING AROMA AND TASTE.

SERVES TWO

INGREDIENTS
    400g/14oz squid
    200g/7oz dried kelp,
      roughly chopped
    2 cucumbers, thinly sliced
    10ml/2 tsp sesame seeds
    6 spring onions (scallions),
      finely chopped
    2 dried red chillies, finely chopped
    salt
For the dressing
    30ml/2 tbsp rice vinegar
    2 garlic cloves, crushed
    60ml/4 tbsp gochujang
      chilli paste
    60ml/4 tbsp maple syrup
    15ml/1 tsp grated fresh
      root ginger

COOK'S TIP
If you can't find kelp, try spinach with a squeeze of lemon juice.

1 Wash the squid carefully, rinsing off any ink. Holding the body firmly, pull away the head and tentacles. If the ink sac is intact, remove it and discard. Pull out all the innards including the long transparent pen. Peel off and discard the thin purple skin on the body, but keep the two small side fins. Slice the head across just under the eyes, severing the tentacles. Discard the rest of the head. Squeeze the tentacles at the head end to push out the round beak in the centre and discard. Rinse the pouch and tentacles well. (Your fishmonger will prepare squid for you if you prefer.) Use a sharp knife to score the squid with a crisscross pattern, and slice into generous pieces about 4cm/1½in long.

2 Soak the kelp in cold water for 20 minutes and blanch in boiling water for 1 minute, draining it almost immediately to retain its texture and colour.

3 Squeeze any excess water from the leaves by hand. Roughly chop the kelp into bitesize pieces.

4 Put the cucumber in a colander and sprinkle with salt. Leave for 10 minutes, and pour away any excess liquid. Put the dressing ingredients in a large bowl.

5 Bring a pan of water to the boil. Blanch the squid for 3 minutes, stirring, then drain under cold running water.

6 Place the squid, cucumber and kelp on a platter and pour the dressing over the dish. Chill in the refrigerator and sprinkle with the sesame seeds, spring onions and chillies before serving.

Per portion Energy 321kcal/1354kJ; Protein 35.6g; Carbohydrate 30g, of which sugars 27.3g; Fat 7.3g, of which saturates 1.3g; Cholesterol 450mg; Calcium 247mg; Fibre 3.3g; Sodium 433mg.

SPICY STIR-FRY SQUID

THE SECRET TO THIS DISH IS TO STIR-FRY THE SQUID VERY BRIEFLY, RETAINING ITS CREAMY TEXTURE AND DISTINCTIVE FLAVOUR. THE SAUCE IS THICKENED WITH KOREAN CHILLI PASTE, WHILE THE SAKE AND MAPLE SYRUP ADD A SUBTLE SWEETNESS WHICH OFFSETS THE FIERY DRESSING.

SERVES TWO TO THREE

INGREDIENTS
  1 squid, cleaned and skinned
  30ml/2 tbsp vegetable oil
  65g/2½oz carrot, cut into
    fine strips
  1 red chilli, seeded and sliced
  1 green chilli, seeded and sliced
  1 white onion, roughly chopped
  2 cabbage leaves, roughly chopped
  7.5ml/1½ tsp Korean chilli powder
  1 garlic clove, crushed
  30ml/2 tbsp sake
  15ml/1 tbsp gochujang chilli paste
  7.5ml/1½ tsp maple syrup
  5ml/1 tsp sesame oil
  5ml/1 tsp sesame seeds,
    to garnish

1 Score diagonal cuts across the squid flesh, taking care not to cut right through, and then cut the sacs into 2cm/¾in strips.

2 Heat a large pan or wok over a medium heat. Add the vegetable oil, carrot, red and green chillies, onion and cabbage and gently coat them in the oil.

3 Add the squid and the chilli powder, and toss the ingredients together until the squid has taken on the colour of the chilli powder.

4 Stir in the garlic, sake, chilli paste, maple syrup and sesame oil. Increase the heat and stir-fry until the squid is cooked and tender. Sprinkle with the sesame seeds, to garnish, and serve.

COOK'S TIP
Squid is widely available throughout the year, either fresh or frozen. The freezing and thawing process actually breaks down some of the tough muscle fibres so that the squid becomes more tender. Frozen squid is sold as tubes (bodies) and as tentacles. It has a long freezer life.

Per portion Energy 134kcal/562kJ; Protein 15.1g; Carbohydrate 4.8g, of which sugars 3.5g; Fat 6.2g, of which saturates 0.9g; Cholesterol 202mg; Calcium 23mg; Fibre 0.9g; Sodium 956mg.

FIERY OCTOPUS

Here octopus is stir-fried to give it a rich meaty texture, then smothered in a fiery chilli sauce, so the dish is an appealing medley of octopus absorbed with gochujang spiciness and the zing of jalapeño chillies. Serve with steamed rice and a bowl of soup.

SERVES TWO

INGREDIENTS

2 small octopuses, cleaned
  and gutted
15ml/1 tbsp vegetable oil
½ onion, sliced 5mm/¼in thick
½ carrot, thinly sliced
½ leek, thinly sliced
75g/3oz jalapeño chillies, washed
  and trimmed
2 garlic cloves, crushed
10ml/2 tsp Korean chilli powder
5ml/1 tsp dark soy sauce
45ml/3 tbsp gochujang
  chilli paste
30ml/2 tbsp mirin or rice wine
15ml/1 tbsp maple syrup
sesame oil and sesame seeds,
  to garnish

COOK'S TIP
To make the octopus more tender, knead it with a handful of plain (all-purpose) flour and rinse in salted water.

1 Blanch the octopuses in boiling water to soften slightly, but do not leave them in too long. Drain them well, and cut into pieces that are approximately 5cm/2in long.

2 Heat the oil in a frying pan over a medium-high heat and add the onion, carrot, leek and jalapeño chillies. Stir-fry for 3 minutes.

3 Add the octopus and garlic and sprinkle over the chilli powder. Stir-fry for 3–4 minutes, or until the octopus is tender. Add the soy sauce, gochujang paste, mirin or rice wine, and maple syrup. Mix well and stir-fry for 1 minute more.

4 Transfer to a serving platter and garnish with a drizzle of sesame oil and a sprinkling of sesame seeds.

COOK'S TIPS
• If the taste is too fiery, mix some softened vermicelli noodles in with the stir-fry to dilute the chilli paste.
• Rice wine, also called Shaoxing rice wine, is used both for drinking and cooking, but when used for cooking it has a lower alcohol content. It is widely available in supermarkets as well as specialist Asian stores.

WAKAME WITH PRAWNS AND CUCUMBER IN VINEGAR DRESSING

THIS JAPANESE SALAD DISH, CALLED SUNO-MONO, USES WAKAME SEAWEED, WHICH IS NOT ONLY RICH IN MINERALS AND B COMPLEX VITAMINS AND VITAMIN C, BUT ALSO MAKES YOUR HAIR LOOK SHINY.

2 Peel the prawns, including the tails. Insert a cocktail stick (toothpick) into the back of each prawn and gently scoop up the thin black vein running down its length. Pull it out, then discard.

3 Boil the prawns in lightly salted water until they curl up completely to make full circles. Drain and cool.

4 Halve the cucumber lengthways. Peel away half of the green skin with a zester or vegetable peeler to create green and white stripes. Scoop out the centre with a tablespoon. Slice very thinly with a sharp knife or a mandolin. Sprinkle with 5ml/1 tsp salt, and leave for 15 minutes in a sieve (strainer).

5 Blanch the wakame very briefly in boiling water. Drain and cool under cold running water. Add to the cucumber in the sieve. Press the cucumber and wakame to remove the excess liquid. Repeat this two to three times.

6 Mix the dressing ingredients in a mixing bowl. Stir well until the sugar has dissolved. Add the wakame and cucumber to the dressing and mix.

7 Pile up in four small bowls. Lean the prawns against the heap. Garnish with ginger.

SERVES FOUR

INGREDIENTS
 10g/¼oz dried wakame
 12 medium raw tiger prawns
  (jumbo shrimp), heads removed
  but tails intact
 ½ cucumber
 salt
For the dressing
 60ml/4 tbsp rice vinegar
 15ml/1 tbsp shoyu
 7.5ml/1½ tsp caster (superfine) sugar
 2.5cm/1in fresh root ginger, peeled
  and cut into thin strips, to garnish

1 Soak the wakame in a pan or bowl of cold water for 15 minutes until fully open. The wakame expands by three to five times its original size. Drain.

VARIATION
For a vegetarian version, omit the shellfish and add a handful of toasted pine nuts.

Per portion Energy 39kcal/164kJ; Protein 6.8g; Carbohydrate 2.5g, of which sugars 2.4g; Fat 0.3g, of which saturates 0g; Cholesterol 73mg; Calcium 34mg; Fibre 0.1g; Sodium 339mg.

KING PRAWNS <u>WITH</u> GINGER <u>AND</u> PINE NUT DRESSING

THIS KOREAN DISH HAS BEEN PASSED DOWN FROM THE ROYAL BANQUETING TABLES OF A BYGONE AGE. SUCCULENT STEAMED PRAWNS ARE MIXED WITH SHREDDED BEEF AND COATED WITH A RICH DRESSING.

SERVES TWO

INGREDIENTS
   6 large king prawns (jumbo shrimp)
   20g/¾oz fresh root ginger, peeled
     and sliced
   15ml/1 tbsp mirin or rice wine
   ½ cucumber
   75g/3oz bamboo shoots, sliced
   90g/3½oz beef flank
   15ml/1 tbsp vegetable oil
   salt and ground white pepper
For the dressing
   60ml/4 tbsp pine nuts
   10ml/2 tsp sesame oil
   salt and ground black pepper

1 Prepare a steamer over a large pan of boiling water, with a small bowl in place under the steamer to catch any liquid. Place the prawns in the steamer with the ginger, and pour over the mirin or rice wine. Steam for 8 minutes.

2 Seed the cucumber and slice it lengthways into thin strips. Sprinkle with salt, and then leave to stand for 5 minutes. Squeeze the cucumber gently to remove any liquid.

3 Remove the prawns from the steamer, discarding the ginger. Remove the bowl of liquid from beneath the steamer and set it aside.

4 Blanch the bamboo shoots in boiling water for 30 seconds. Remove, slice and sprinkle with salt. Add the beef to the boiling water and cook until tender. Drain and leave to cool.

5 Make a shallow cut down the centre of the back of each prawn. Pull out the black vein and then rinse the prawn thoroughly. Slice them into 2cm/½in pieces. Transfer to the refrigerator.

6 Slice the beef thinly, cut into bitesize pieces and chill in the refrigerator. Coat a frying pan or wok with the vegetable oil and quickly stir-fry the cucumber and bamboo shoots, then chill them.

7 To make the dressing, roughly grind the pine nuts in a mortar and pestle and then transfer to a bowl. Add 45ml/ 3 tbsp of the prawn liquid from the bowl and add the sesame oil with a pinch of salt and pepper. Mix well.

8 Set all the chilled ingredients on a platter and pour over the dressing before serving.

Per portion Energy 416kcal/1724kJ; Protein 24.7g; Carbohydrate 3.5g, of which sugars 2.7g; Fat 33.8g, of which saturates 4.3g; Cholesterol 124mg; Calcium 62mg; Fibre 1.5g; Sodium 619mg.

PRAWN TEMPURA

KNOWN AS TUIGUIM IN KOREA, THIS DISH IS ALSO A JAPANESE FAVOURITE. THE TRICK TO GREAT TEMPURA IS TO KEEP THE BATTER AS LIGHT AND CRISP AS POSSIBLE BY NOT STIRRING IT TOO VIGOROUSLY. BATTER MIXTURE IS AVAILABLE FROM ALL ASIAN GROCERS.

SERVES FOUR

INGREDIENTS

15 raw tiger prawns (shrimp)
5ml/1 tsp sesame oil
5ml/1 tsp sake
150g/5oz/1½ cups batter mix
50g/2oz/7 tbsp cornflour
    (cornstarch)
ground black pepper
For the dipping sauce
    5ml/1 tsp fish bouillon powder
        or Japanese hondashi
    50g/2oz Chinese white radish,
        peeled and grated
    5ml/1 tsp finely chopped fresh
        root ginger
    1 spring onion (scallion),
        finely chopped
    15ml/1 tbsp maple syrup
    15ml/1 tbsp sugar
    30ml/2 tbsp light soy sauce
    30ml/2 tbsp lemon juice

1 Chill 250ml/8fl oz/1 cup water ready for the batter. Remove the heads and the shells from the prawns, leaving the tail intact.

2 With a sharp knife make a slit down the centre of the curved back of each prawn and remove the black vein with the point of the knife. Rinse under cold water and dry gently with kitchen paper.

3 Combine the sesame oil, sake and a little ground pepper in a bowl. Add the prawns and coat them in the mixture. Cover and place in the refrigerator for 15 minutes.

4 Meanwhile prepare the dipping sauce. Mix the bouillon powder with 100ml/3½fl oz/scant ½ cup warm water until it has fully dissolved.

5 Add the Chinese radish, ginger and spring onion. Thoroughly mix in the maple syrup, sugar, light soy sauce and lemon juice, then divide among four small dishes and chill.

6 Place the batter in a bowl and add the chilled water. Mix the batter gently without stirring too vigorously, as this will add air to the mixture and reduce the crispness.

7 Heat vegetable oil in a wok to 180°C/350°F or until a cube of day-old bread browns in 30–60 seconds. Meanwhile, place the cornflour in a bowl. Drain the prawns and coat them in the cornflour.

COOK'S TIP
To make a good fish batter yourself, combine 150g/5oz/1¼ cups yellow corn meal, ¼ tbsp black pepper, ¼ tbsp salt, ¼ tbsp paprika, ½ tbsp garlic powder and ½ tbsp garlic salt.

8 One at a time, shake the prawns lightly to remove any excess cornflour and dip them into the batter mix.

9 Deep-fry the prawns in the oil for 2 minutes, until crisp and golden. Drain on kitchen paper and serve immediately, with the dipping sauce.

Per portion Energy 221kcal/923kJ; Protein 14.1g; Carbohydrate 14.3g, of which sugars 3.5g; Fat 12.3g, of which saturates 1.5g; Cholesterol 146mg; Calcium 72mg; Fibre 0.3g; Sodium 688mg.

GRILLED TIGER PRAWNS

THIS KOREAN DISH IS OFTEN ENJOYED DURING THE SUMMER. THE MARINADE ENHANCES THE FLAVOUR OF THE PRAWNS AND THE STIR-FRIED VEGETABLES ADD A BEAUTIFUL TOUCH TO THE PRESENTATION.

SERVES TWO

INGREDIENTS

6 raw tiger prawns (shrimp)
10ml/2 tsp white wine
15ml/1 tbsp sake
2.5ml/½ tsp chilli oil
7.5ml/1½ tsp sesame oil
1 garlic clove, finely sliced
½ green chilli, seeded and sliced
½ red chilli, seeded and sliced
½ shiitake mushroom, finely sliced
30ml/2 tbsp dark soy sauce
a little lemon juice
salt and ground black pepper
finely pared lemon zest, to garnish

COOK'S TIPS

• If using wooden skewers, soak them in cold water for 15 minutes to prevent them from burning during cooking.
• This dish is well suited to the barbecue. Drizzle with marinade as the prawns cook.

1 Prepare six small skewers for the prawns. Remove the head and shell from the prawns, leaving the tail intact. Make a small slit with a sharp knife down the centre of the curved back of each prawn and remove the black vein with the point of the knife. Rinse in cold water and dry gently with kitchen paper.

2 Thread each prawn on to a skewer, piercing first through the tail and then through the head.

3 Score the skewered prawns on both sides and then place them in a bowl.

4 Add the wine, sake and chilli oil to the bowl. Season with salt and pepper, then toss the prawns to coat them evenly in the marinade and set aside for 15 minutes.

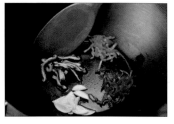

5 Meanwhile, heat a wok over medium heat and add the sesame oil. One ingredient at a time, stir-fry the garlic, chillies and shiitake mushrooms, keeping them separate. Season with a pinch of salt and set aside.

6 Heat a griddle pan or frying pan over medium heat and cook the prawns, brushing them with soy sauce as they cook to help prevent them from burning.

7 Grill (broil) the prawns for about 5 minutes, turning once, or until their flesh is opaque.

8 Remove the prawns from the skewers and arrange three on each plate. Add a little of the stir-fried vegetables and a squeeze of lemon juice. Garnish with a little lemon zest and serve.

Per portion Energy 142kcal/593kJ; Protein 13.4g; Carbohydrate 9g, of which sugars 8.7g; Fat 6g, of which saturates 0.7g; Cholesterol 146mg; Calcium 67mg; Fibre 0.2g; Sodium 144mg.

DEEP-FRIED SMALL PRAWNS ᴬᴺᴰ CORN

This Japanese dish is called Kakiagé, an inexpensive style of tempura. This is only one of many versions and it is a good way of using up small quantities of vegetables.

SERVES FOUR

INGREDIENTS
    200g/7oz small cooked, peeled
      prawns (shrimp)
    4–5 button (white) mushrooms
    4 spring onions (scallions)
    75g/3oz/½ cup canned, drained
      or frozen corn, thawed
    30ml/2 tbsp frozen peas, thawed
    vegetable oil, for deep-frying
    chives, to garnish
For the tempura batter
    300ml/½ pint/1¼ cups very cold
      ice water
    2 eggs, beaten
    150g/5oz/1¼ cups plain
      (all-purpose) flour
    1.5ml/¼ tsp baking powder
For the dipping sauce
    400ml/14fl oz/1⅔ cups second
      dashi stock, or the same
      amount of water and 5ml/1
      tsp dashi-no-moto
    100ml/3fl oz/scant ½ cup shoyu
    100ml/3fl oz/scant ½ cup mirin
    15ml/1 tbsp chopped chives

1 Roughly chop half the prawns. Cut the mushrooms into small cubes. Slice the white part from the spring onions and chop this roughly.

2 To make the tempura batter, in a medium mixing bowl, mix the cold water and eggs. Add the flour and baking powder, and very roughly fold in with a pair of chopsticks or a fork. Do not beat. The batter should still be quite lumpy. Heat plenty of oil in a wok or a deep-fryer to 170°C/338°F.

3 Mix the prawns and vegetables into the batter. Pour a quarter of the batter into a small bowl, then drop gently into the oil. Using wooden spoons, carefully gather the scattered batter to form a fist-size ball. Deep-fry until golden. Drain on kitchen paper.

4 In a small pan, mix all the liquid dipping-sauce ingredients together and bring to the boil, then immediately turn off the heat. Sprinkle with chives.

5 Garnish the kakiage with chives, and serve with the dipping sauce.

Per portion Energy 370kcal/1558kJ; Protein 17.8g; Carbohydrate 50.4g, of which sugars 17.7g; Fat 12.3g, of which saturates 2g; Cholesterol 193mg; Calcium 124mg; Fibre 2.1g; Sodium 1964mg.

FRIED PRAWN BALLS

In Japan, these round fried balls, Shinjyo, along with tiny rice dumplings and sweet chestnuts, are made as an offering to the moon to celebrated the arrival of autumn.

MAKES ABOUT 14

INGREDIENTS
  150g/5oz raw prawns
    (shrimp), peeled
  75ml/5 tbsp second dashi stock
    or the same amount of water and
    2.5ml/½ tsp dashi-no-moto
  1 large (US extra large) egg white,
    well beaten
  30ml/2 tbsp sake
  15ml/1 tbsp cornflour (cornstarch)
  1.5ml/¼ tsp salt
  vegetable oil, for deep-frying
To serve
  25ml/1½ tbsp ground sea salt
  2.5ml/½ tsp sansho
  ½ lemon, cut into 4 wedges

1 Mix the prawns, dashi stock, beaten egg white, sake, cornflour and salt in a food processor or blender, and process until smooth.

2 Scrape from the sides and transfer to a small mixing bowl.

3 In a wok or small pan, heat the vegetable oil to 175°C/347°F.

4 Take two dessertspoons and wet them with a little vegetable oil. Scoop about 30ml/2 tbsp prawn-ball paste into the spoons and form a small ball.

5 Carefully plunge the ball into the hot oil and deep-fry until lightly browned. Drain on a wire rack. Repeat this process, one at a time, until all the prawn-ball paste is used.

6 Mix the salt and sansho together on a small plate. Serve the fried prawn balls on a large serving platter or on four individual serving plates.

7 Garnish with lemon wedges and serve hot with the sansho salt.

COOK'S TIP
Serve the salt and sansho in separate mounds on each plate, if you like.

Per portion Energy 41kcal/170kJ; Protein 2.1g; Carbohydrate 1g, of which sugars 0g; Fat 3.2g, of which saturates 0.4g; Cholesterol 21mg; Calcium 9mg; Fibre 0g; Sodium 446mg.

SEAFOOD SALAD WITH FRUITY DRESSING

IN THIS JAPANESE DISH, WHITE FISH IS SEARED, THEN SERVED WITH PRAWNS AND SALAD IN AN APRICOT AND APPLE DRESSING. THE FRUIT FLAVOURS MAKE A DELICATE ACCOMPANIMENT TO THE FISH.

SERVES FOUR

INGREDIENTS
  1 baby onion, sliced lengthways
  lemon juice
  400g/14oz very fresh sea bream or
    sea bass, filleted
  30ml/2 tbsp sake
  4 large king prawns (jumbo shrimp),
    heads and shells removed
  about 400g/14oz mixed salad leaves
For the fruity dressing
  2 ripe apricots, skinned and
    stoned (pitted)
  ¼ apple, peeled and cored
  60ml/4 tbsp second dashi stock or
    the same amount of water and
    5ml/1 tsp dashi-no-moto
  10ml/2 tsp shoyu
  salt and ground white pepper

1 Soak the onion slices in ice-cold water for 30 minutes. Drain well.

2 Bring a pan half-full of water to the boil. Add a dash of lemon juice and plunge the fish fillet into it. Remove after 30 seconds and cool immediately under cold running water for 30 seconds to stop the cooking. Cut into 8mm/⅓in thick slices crossways.

3 Pour the sake into a small pan, bring to the boil, then add the prawns. Cook for 1 minute, or until their colour has completely changed to pink.

4 Cool immediately under cold running water for 30 seconds to again stop the cooking. Cut the prawns into 1cm/½in thick slices crossways.

5 Slice one apricot very thinly, then set aside. Purée the remaining dressing ingredients in a food processor. Add salt, if required, and pepper. Chill.

6 Lay a small amount of mixed leaves on four plates. Mix the fish, prawn, apricot and onion slices in a bowl. Add the remaining leaves, then pour on the dressing and toss well. Heap up on the plates and serve immediately.

COOK'S TIP
You can use a knife and fork to eat these salads, of course; however, marinated fish definitely tastes better with wooden rather than metal cutlery.

Per portion Energy 157kcal/662kJ; Protein 25g; Carbohydrate 5.3g, of which sugars 4.9g; Fat 3.2g, of which saturates 0.5g; Cholesterol 129mg; Calcium 186mg; Fibre 1.6g; Sodium 299mg.

SEAFOOD SALAD IN MUSTARD DRESSING

THE CLASSIC KOREAN INGREDIENTS OF SEAFOOD, CHESTNUTS AND SALAD VEGETABLES ARE GIVEN A NEW TWIST HERE WITH THE ADDITION OF ENGLISH MUSTARD, GIVING THE DISH A PLEASANT HEAT. SIMPLE TO PREPARE, THIS IS A PERFECT QUICK SNACK OR APPETIZER.

SERVES TWO

INGREDIENTS
50g/2oz squid
50g/2oz king prawns
(jumbo shrimp)
50g/2oz jellyfish (optional)
50g/2oz cooked whelks
90g/3½oz Asian pear
⅓ carrot
½ medium cucumber
25g/1oz Chinese leaves (Chinese cabbage), shredded
25g/1oz chestnuts, sliced
25g/1oz crab meat or
seafood stick
For the dressing
15ml/1 tbsp ready-made English (hot) mustard
30ml/2 tbsp sugar
15ml/1 tbsp milk
45ml/3 tbsp cider vinegar
5ml/1 tsp chilli oil
2.5ml/½ tsp dark soy sauce
5ml/1 tsp salt

1 Wash the squid carefully, rinsing off any ink. Holding the body firmly, pull away the head and tentacles. If the ink sac is intact, remove it and discard. Pull out all the innards including the long transparent pen. Peel off and discard the thin purple skin on the body, but keep the two small side fins. Slice the head across just under the eyes, severing the tentacles. Discard the rest of the head.

2 Squeeze the tentacles at the head end to push out the round beak in the centre and discard. Rinse the pouch and tentacles well. (Your fishmonger will prepare squid for you if you prefer.) Score the squid with a crisscross pattern, and slice into strips about 2cm/½in wide.

3 Hold each prawn between two fingers and pull off the tail shell. Twist off the head. Peel away the soft body shell and the small claws. Make a shallow cut down the centre of the curved back of the prawn. Pull out the black vein with a cocktail stick (toothpick). Rinse well. Slice the prawns and jellyfish, if using, into similar sized pieces.

4 Bring a pan of lightly salted water to the boil and blanch the squid, prawns and jellyfish for 3 minutes, then drain. Thinly slice the whelks.

5 Peel the Asian pear. Cut the pear into thin strips and do the same with the carrot. Seed the cucumber and cut into thin strips.

6 Combine all the dressing ingredients in a bowl until they are well blended. Take a large serving platter and arrange the vegetable strips, Chinese leaves and chestnuts in rows, or fan them out around the centre of the plate.

7 Arrange the seafood on the platter, including the crab meat or seafood stick. Pour over the dressing and chill well in the refrigerator before serving.

COOK'S TIP
Although jellyfish makes an exotic component of this dish, it can be very difficult to find outside China, Japan and Korea. Selected specialist Asian stores may stock it, but outside the Far East it tends to be a rare delicacy.

Per portion Energy 206kcal/872kJ; Protein 18g; Carbohydrate 29.8g, of which sugars 23.9g; Fat 2.4g, of which saturates 0.6g; Cholesterol 230mg; Calcium 62mg; Fibre 2.4g; Sodium 1282mg.

BLUE CRAB CASSEROLE

THE PERFECT CENTREPIECE FOR ANY MEAL, THIS RICH AND HEARTY SOUP IS TRADITIONALLY SHARED BETWEEN THE WHOLE FAMILY. ALTHOUGH LIVE BLUE CRABS ARE NOT ALWAYS READILY AVAILABLE AND CAN BE SUBSTITUTED WITH EUROPEAN CRAB, THEY DO GIVE THIS CASSEROLE UNSURPASSED FLAVOUR.

SERVES FOUR

INGREDIENTS

2 live blue crabs
7.5ml/1½ tsp sesame oil
15ml/1 tbsp Korean chilli powder
2 garlic cloves, crushed
300g/11oz Chinese white radish,
    peeled and diced
300g/11oz courgette (zucchini),
    thinly sliced
50g/2oz green chilli, seeded
    and sliced
20g/¾oz red chilli, seeded
    and sliced
5ml/1 tsp light soy sauce
5ml/1 tsp dark soy sauce
5ml/1 tsp salt
5ml/1 tsp sugar
275g/10oz leeks, roughly sliced
50g/2oz chrysanthemum leaves
50g/2oz watercress or Korean minari
15ml/1 tbsp doenjang soya bean paste
15ml/1 tbsp sake

1 Put the crabs in iced water for at least 5 minutes to stun them. Remove their top shells and small legs (set these aside). Remove the entrails, gills and mouth parts. Slit the crabs down the middle on a heavy board, using a heavy knife and a meat mallet or rolling pin to give four pieces. See also cook's tips below.

2 Place the crab shells and legs in a large pan. Pour in 1.5 litres/2½ pints/6¼ cups water and bring to the boil. Reduce the heat and simmer for 1 hour, skimming occasionally to remove any scum, if necessary. Strain the stock, discarding the shells and legs.

3 Heat a large pan over a low heat and add 50ml/2fl oz/¼ cup of the crab stock. Stir in the sesame oil, half the chilli powder and the garlic. Bring to the boil, then reduce the heat and simmer the mixture briefly.

4 Pour in the rest of the stock, stirring to mix it with the chilli-flavoured stock and add the radish. Bring the stock back to the boil, then reduce the heat and simmer for 10 minutes.

5 Add the crabs, courgette and green and red chillies, and boil for a further 10 minutes, until the crab turns bright orange. Add the remaining chilli powder, the light and dark soy sauces, salt and sugar. Bring the soup back to the boil.

6 The final stage is to add the leeks, chrysanthemum leaves, watercress or minari, doenjang soya bean paste and sake. Remove the pan from the heat and cover it, then leave the soup to stand for 2 minutes. To serve, ladle the soup into bowls, including a piece of the crab in each.

COOK'S TIPS
• Blue crab is a popular American species providing mainly body meat. If it is not readily available, the common or European crab can be used. These crabs have meaty legs, which should be used rather than discarded.
• An alternative way of preparing a live crab is to place it in a freezer, pre-set at the fast-freeze setting, for a few hours. This is a more humane way of killing the crab before cutting it up.

Per portion Energy 168kcal/700kJ; Protein 20.5g; Carbohydrate 7g, of which sugars 6.3g; Fat 6.4g, of which saturates 0.9g; Cholesterol 63mg; Calcium 57mg; Fibre 3.4g; Sodium 1055mg.

SPICY SCALLOPS WITH ENOKI MUSHROOMS

FRAGRANT STEAMED SCALLOPS ARE HERE GIVEN A SPICY TWIST WITH SHREDS OF CHILLI PEPPER IN THIS KOREAN DISH. ENOKI MUSHROOMS AND SAUTÉED OMELETTE MATCH THE ELEGANT FLAVOURS OF THE SEAFOOD, AND SHREDDED SEAWEED AND LEMON ZEST MAKE AN ATTRACTIVE GARNISH.

SERVES TWO

INGREDIENTS

5 scallops, with shells
30ml/2 tbsp vegetable oil
10ml/2 tsp sesame oil
2 egg yolks, beaten
1 sheet dried seaweed
1 red chilli, seeded and
    finely sliced
½ green (bell) pepper,
    finely sliced
65g/2½oz enoki mushrooms
salt and ground white
    pepper
grated rind of 1 lemon,
    to garnish

1 First of all scrub the scallop shells. Then cut the hinge muscles at the scallop's base with a sharp knife and lift off the rounded shell.

2 Scrape away the beard-like fringe, which is next to the white scallop with its orange coral, and remove the intestinal thread. Then you can ease the scallop and the coral right away from the shell.

3 Heat 15ml/1 tbsp vegetable oil in a wok and stir-fry the scallops until browned. Season with sesame oil, salt and pepper.

4 Place the scallop shells into a pan of boiling water and then drain. Add 10ml/2 tsp oil to the wok and heat it over a low heat.

5 Pour in the beaten egg yolks and add a pinch of salt. Cook to form a thin omelette. Once set, remove from the pan and slice into strips.

6 Cut the seaweed into thin strips. Add the chilli and the pepper to the pan, adding oil if required, and stir-fry with a pinch of salt.

7 Place the scallop shells in a steamer, and set one scallop on each shell. Place the pepper mixture, some omelette strips and some mushrooms on each shell, and steam for 4 minutes.

8 Garnish with the seaweed strips and a sprinkle of lemon rind.

COOK'S TIP
Enoki mushrooms have a mild flavour and a crunchy texture. They should be refrigerated in paper bags and can be stored for up to 14 days.

Per portion Energy 325kcal/1356kJ; Protein 27.2g; Carbohydrate 6.8g, of which sugars 3.1g; Fat 21.3g, of which saturates 3.8g; Cholesterol 249mg; Calcium 59mg; Fibre 1.2g; Sodium 193mg.

POULTRY

Poultry marries well with sweet and spicy flavours and appears in many
Japanese and Korean dishes. Despite the growing popularity of deep-
fried chicken, the traditional methods of griddling and stewing are still
firm favourites, and chicken or duck is often used to give a rich flavour
to vegetables and rice. Spicy chicken dishes, such as the fiery sweet
Gochujang Chicken Stew, are a welcome warming treat on cold nights.

Left: Sweet and Spicy Chicken; **Above:** Pot-cooked Duck and Green Vegetables

GRILLED SKEWERED CHICKEN

The Japanese always accompany drink with nibbles. The nibbles are generally called tsumami, and grilled skewered chicken dipped in yakitori sauce is one of the most popular. There are thousands of dedicated yakitori bars in Japan.

SERVES FOUR

INGREDIENTS
  8 chicken thighs with skin, boned
  8 large, thick spring onions
    (scallions), trimmed
For the yakitori sauce
  60ml/4 tbsp sake
  75ml/5 tbsp shoyu
  15ml/1 tbsp mirin
  15ml/1 tbsp caster (superfine) sugar
To serve
  shichimi togarashi, sansho or
    lemon wedges

1 First, make the yakitori sauce. Mix all the ingredients together in a small pan. Bring to the boil, then reduce the heat and simmer for 10 minutes, or until the sauce has thickened.

2 Cut the chicken into 2.5cm/1in cubes. Cut the spring onions into 2.5cm/1in long sticks.

3 To grill (broil), preheat the grill (broiler) to high. Oil the wire rack and spread out the chicken cubes on it. Grill both sides of the chicken until the juices drip, then dip the pieces in the sauce and put back on the rack. Grill for 30 seconds on each side, repeating the dipping process twice more.

4 Set aside and keep warm. Gently grill the spring onions until soft and slightly brown outside. Do not dip. Thread about four pieces of chicken and three spring onion pieces on to each of eight bamboo skewers.

5 Alternatively, to cook on a barbecue, soak eight bamboo skewers overnight in water. This prevents the skewers from burning. Prepare the barbecue. Thread the chicken and spring onion pieces on to skewers, as above. Place the sauce in a small bowl with a brush.

6 Cook the skewered chicken on the barbecue. Keep the skewer handles away from the fire, turning them frequently until the juices start to drip. Brush the chicken with sauce. Return to the coals and repeat this process twice more until the chicken is well cooked.

7 Arrange the skewers on a platter and serve sprinkled with shichimi togarashi or sansho, or accompanied by lemon wedges.

Per portion Energy 165kcal/695kJ; Protein 22g; Carbohydrate 9g, of which sugars 8.8g; Fat 2.9g, of which saturates 0.8g; Cholesterol 105mg; Calcium 24mg; Fibre 0.4g; Sodium 1429mg.

GRILLED CHICKEN SKEWERS

THESE JAPANESE CHICKEN BALLS, KNOWN AS TSUKUNE, ARE ANOTHER YAKITORI BAR REGULAR AS WELL AS A FAVOURITE FAMILY DISH, AS IT IS EASY FOR CHILDREN TO EAT DIRECTLY FROM THE SKEWER. YOU CAN MAKE THE BALLS IN ADVANCE UP TO THE END OF STEP 2, AND THEY FREEZE VERY WELL.

SERVES FOUR

INGREDIENTS
300g/11oz skinless chicken,
  minced (ground)
2 eggs
2.5ml/½ tsp salt
10ml/2 tsp plain (all-purpose) flour
10ml/2 tsp cornflour (cornstarch)
90ml/6 tbsp dried breadcrumbs
2.5cm/1in piece fresh root
  ginger, grated
For the 'tare' yakitori sauce
60ml/4 tbsp sake
75ml/5 tbsp shoyu
15ml/1 tbsp mirin
15ml/1 tbsp caster (superfine) sugar
2.5ml/½ tsp cornflour (cornstarch)
  blended with 5ml/1 tsp water
To serve
shichimi togarashi or
  sansho (optional)

1 Soak eight bamboo skewers overnight in water. Put all the ingredients for the chicken balls, except the ginger, in a food processor and blend well.

2 Wet your hands and scoop about a tablespoonful of the mixture into your palm. Shape it into a small ball about half the size of a golf ball. Make a further 30–32 balls in the same way.

3 Squeeze the juice from the grated ginger into a small mixing bowl. Discard the pulp.

4 Fill a pan with water and bring to the boil, then add the ginger juice.

5 Add the chicken balls to the boiling water and boil for about 7 minutes, or until the colour of the meat changes and the balls float to the surface. Scoop out the cooked balls using a slotted spoon and drain on a plate covered with kitchen paper.

6 In a small pan, mix all the ingredients for the yakitori sauce, except for the cornflour liquid. Bring to the boil, then reduce the heat and simmer for about 10 minutes, or until the sauce has slightly reduced. Add the cornflour liquid and stir until the sauce is thick. Transfer to a small bowl.

7 Thread 3–4 balls on to each skewer. Cook under a medium grill (broiler) or on a barbecue, keeping the skewer handles away from the fire. Turn them frequently for a few minutes, or until the balls start to brown. Brush with sauce and return to the heat. Repeat the process twice. Serve, sprinkled with shichimi togarashi or sansho, if you like.

Per portion Energy 332kcal/1397kJ; Protein 30.3g; Carbohydrate 29g, of which sugars 7.4g; Fat 9.7g, of which saturates 2.6g; Cholesterol 339mg; Calcium 84mg; Fibre 0.6g; Sodium 325mg.

GOCHUJANG CHICKEN STEW

THIS WARMING AUTUMN STEW IS FILLED WITH VEGETABLES AND SPICES TO WARD OFF THE COLD.
CHILLIES AND KOREAN GOCHUJANG CHILLI PASTE SUPPLY A VIVID RED COLOUR AND GIVE THE
CHICKEN A FIERY QUALITY, AND A DELICIOUS HINT OF SWEETNESS OFFSETS THE PIQUANCY.

SERVES FOUR

INGREDIENTS
  3 potatoes
  1 carrot
  2 onions
  1 chicken, about 800g/1¾lb
  30ml/2 tbsp vegetable oil
  2 garlic cloves, crushed
  3 green chillies, seeded and
    finely sliced
  1 red chilli, seeded and
    finely sliced
  15ml/1 tbsp sesame oil
  salt and ground black pepper
  2 spring onions (scallions), finely
    chopped, to garnish
For the marinade
  30ml/2 tbsp mirin or rice wine
  salt and ground black pepper
For the seasoning
  15ml/1 tbsp sesame seeds
  10ml/2 tsp light soy sauce
  30ml/2 tbsp gochujang
    chilli paste
  45ml/3 tbsp Korean
    chilli powder

1 Peel the potatoes and cut into
bitesize pieces. Soak them in cold
water for approximately 15–20 minutes
and then drain.

2 Peel the carrot and onions and cut
into medium-size pieces.

3 Divide up the whole of the chicken,
including the skin and bone. Then
cut it into bitesize pieces and place
in a dish.

4 Combine the marinade ingredients
and pour over the chicken. Stir to coat
thoroughly and leave for 10 minutes.

5 Heat 15ml/1 tbsp vegetable oil in a
frying pan or wok and quickly stir-fry
the crushed garlic. Add the chicken and
stir-fry, draining off any fat that comes
from the meat during cooking. When
lightly browned, place the chicken on
kitchen paper to remove any excess oil.

6 To make the seasoning, grind the
sesame seeds in a mortar and pestle.
Combine the soy sauce, gochujang
paste, chilli powder and the ground
sesame seeds in a bowl and mix
together thoroughly.

7 In a pan heat the remaining
vegetable oil and add the potatoes,
carrot and onions. Briefly cook over
a medium heat, stirring, then add
the chicken.

8 Pour over enough water so that
two-thirds of the meat and vegetables
are immersed in the water, and bring
the pan to the boil. Then add the
chilli seasoning and reduce the heat.
Stir the seasoning into the water and
simmer until the volume of liquid has
reduced by about one-third. Add the
sliced chillies.

9 Simmer for a little longer until the
liquid has thickened slightly.

10 Add the sesame oil, transfer the
contents to deep serving bowls and
garnish with the chopped spring onion
before serving.

COOK'S TIP
When selecting a chicken, always make
a point of using a good quality, or
preferably an organic, one as the results
are far tastier.

Per portion Energy 470kcal/1955kJ; Protein 27.4g; Carbohydrate 20.4g, of which sugars 4.7g; Fat 31.5g, of which saturates 7.5g; Cholesterol 128mg; Calcium 56mg; Fibre 2.3g; Sodium 296mg.

FIERY SOY CHICKEN <u>WITH</u> NOODLES

THIS DISH IS A FAVOURITE FROM ANDONG, A PROVINCE IN THE SOUTH OF THE KOREAN PENINSULA WHICH IS FAMOUS FOR ITS FOOD AND DRINK. BRAISING MAKES THE CHICKEN WONDERFULLY TENDER, WHILE ALLOWING THE SOY SAUCE TO RELEASE ITS NUTTY FLAVOUR AND LOSE ITS SALTINESS.

SERVES FOUR

INGREDIENTS
   1 chicken, about 800g/1¾lb
   22.5ml/4½ tsp grated fresh
     root ginger
   45ml/3 tbsp white wine
   75g/3oz glass noodles
   30ml/2 tbsp vegetable oil
   2 dried red chillies, sliced
   2 small green chillies, seeded
     and sliced
   1 carrot, diced
   150g/5oz potato, diced
   ½ cucumber, roughly chopped
   ½ cabbage
   ½ white onion, diced
   1 leek, roughly chopped
For the sauce
   100ml/3½fl oz/scant ½ cup soy sauce
   75ml/5 tbsp brown sugar
   45ml/3 tbsp maple syrup
   75ml/5 tbsp sake or mirin
   30ml/2 tbsp crushed garlic
   7.5ml/1½ tsp grated fresh
     root ginger
   15ml/1 tbsp sesame oil
   5ml/1 tsp caramel
   7.5ml/1½ tsp sesame seeds
   ground black pepper

1 Cut the chicken, with skin and bone, into pieces about 4cm/1½in wide. Bring a pan of water to the boil. Add the chicken and boil for 3 minutes, then drain and place in a bowl.

2 Add the ginger and white wine to the chicken and mix thoroughly. Leave to stand for about 30 minutes.

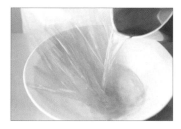

3 Meanwhile place the noodles in a bowl and pour in warm water to cover, then set aside to soak for 10 minutes.

4 For the sauce, mix the soy sauce, sugar, maple syrup, sake or mirin, garlic, ginger, sesame oil, caramel and sesame seeds in a bowl. Mix well, adding pepper to taste.

5 Heat a wok or pan over a medium heat. Add the vegetable oil and briefly stir-fry the chillies. Add the chicken and stir-fry briefly, then pour in the sauce.

6 Stir-fry for a further 2 minutes. Pour in enough water to cover the chicken and increase the heat to bring the sauce to the boil.

7 Once the mixture is boiling add the carrot and potatoes. Boil until the liquid has reduced by half. Add the cucumber, cabbage and onion.

8 Reduce the heat and part-cover the pan, then simmer until most of the liquid has evaporated and the chicken and vegetables are cooked but not overcooked. Stir occasionally during cooking to ensure that the ingredients do not burn.

9 Add the leek and glass noodles to the pan and mix the ingredients thoroughly. Serve the chicken with a side dish of *kimchi* or vegetable *namul*.

COOK'S TIP
Glass noodles are also known as transparent cellophane noodles, bean threads, Chinese vermicelli and bai fun. Made from the starch of mung beans they offer a good wheat-free ingredient.

Per portion Energy 538kcal/2254kJ; Protein 28.5g; Carbohydrate 51.5g, of which sugars 31.9g; Fat 25.5g, of which saturates 6.6g; Cholesterol 128mg; Calcium 64mg; Fibre 1.8g; Sodium 1961mg.

CHICKEN <u>WITH</u> SOY DRESSING

THIS DISH, A FAVOURITE OF THE KOREAN ROYAL COURT, SMOTHERS TENDER CHICKEN IN A RICH MUSHROOM SAUCE. STRIPS OF POULTRY ARE COATED WITH A STICKY GLAZE THAT BLENDS WOODLAND FLAVOURS WITH SOY SAUCE AND GINGER. SERVE WITH RICE, SOUP AND KIMCHI.

SERVES TWO

INGREDIENTS
    1 leek, roughly sliced
    10ml/2 tsp chopped fresh
      root ginger
    300g/11oz chicken breast fillet
    10ml/2 tsp sesame oil, plus extra
      for drizzling
    salt and ground black pepper
For the sauce
    6 dried shiitake mushrooms,
      soaked in warm water for about
      30 minutes
    30ml/2 tbsp vegetable oil
    1 garlic clove, finely chopped
    10 oyster mushrooms, sliced
    30ml/2 tbsp dark soy sauce
    60ml/4 tbsp maple syrup
    30ml/2 tbsp plain
      (all-purpose) flour
    2 eggs, beaten
    salt and ground black pepper

1 Place the leek, root ginger and chicken in a pan, cover with water and bring to the boil. After 5 minutes remove the chicken from the water with a slotted spoon. Strain the liquid into a measuring jug (cup).

2 When the soaked shiitake mushrooms have reconstituted and become soft, drain and slice them, discarding the tough stems.

3 Tear the cooked chicken into strips and add salt, pepper and sesame oil.

4 Stir-fry the garlic in the vegetable oil and add the mushrooms and soy sauce. Sauté for a few minutes.

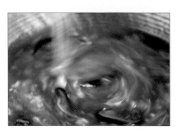

5 Pour in 300ml/½ pint/1¼ cups of stock. Add the maple syrup and stir. Bring the sauce to the boil, add the flour and simmer, stirring until the sauce thickens. Add the beaten egg, gently poaching it.

6 Place the strips of chicken on a serving platter, pour over the mushroom sauce and drizzle with sesame oil.

COOK'S TIP
Oyster mushrooms are available in colours that range from soft brown to grey. Their delicate, mild flavour and velvety texture are hard to match, but they can be substituted with cooked white mushrooms. Keep them refrigerated in paper bags and they will be fresh for up to 7 days.

Per portion Energy 567kcal/2381kJ; Protein 47.2g; Carbohydrate 39.7g, of which sugars 27.3g; Fat 25.6g, of which saturates 4.5g; Cholesterol 314mg; Calcium 95mg; Fibre 3.2g; Sodium 1321mg.

CHICKEN MARINATED ᴵᴺ CHILLI PASTE

Hot, spicy, garlicky and a little sweet, this is a tasty Korean dish. Griddled for a version that is quick to prepare, it has the same delicious scorched flavour as the slow-smoked variety. Stuffed cucumber kimchi makes a refreshing accompaniment.

SERVES FOUR

INGREDIENTS
   900g/2lb chicken breast fillet or
      boneless thighs
   2 round (butterhead) lettuces
   vegetable oil
   4 spring onions (scallions), shredded
For the marinade
   60ml/4 tbsp gochujang red
      chilli paste
   45ml/3 tbsp mirin or rice wine
   15ml/1 tbsp dark soy sauce
   4 garlic cloves, crushed
   25ml/1½ tsp sesame oil
   15ml/1 tbsp grated fresh
      root ginger
   2 spring onions (scallions),
      finely chopped
   10ml/2 tsp ground black pepper
   15ml/1 tbsp lemonade

3 Coat the chicken with the prepared marinade, making sure that all the pieces are covered with the marinade.

4 Marinate the chicken in the refrigerator for about 3 hours.

5 Remove the outer leaves from the heads of lettuce, keeping them whole. Rinse well and place in a serving dish.

6 Lightly coat a heavy griddle pan or frying pan with vegetable oil and place it over a medium heat (the griddle can be used over charcoal).

1 To make the marinade, put all the gochujang marinade ingredients in a bowl and combine until they are mixed well, then leave to one side.

2 Cut the chicken portions into small bitesize pieces.

7 Griddle the chicken for 15 minutes, or until the meat is cooked and has turned a deep brown. Increase the heat briefly to scorch the chicken and give it a smoky flavour.

VARIATION
Butterhead lettuces are perfect to use as wraps because the leaves are so soft and tender, but you can choose to substitute them with red leaf lettuce, iceberg lettuce, romaine lettuce or the slightly bitter escarole.

8 Serve by wrapping the chicken pieces in lettuce leaves with a few shredded spring onions.

COOK'S TIPS
• In restaurants, lettuce wraps are usually offered as an appetizer, but they can also be a very successful main course. Children enjoy them as they can eat them with their hands.
• Chicken skin is unpopular today because of its high calorie and high fat content. However, in this dish the thick layer of yellow fat under the skin is removed before cooking, thus greatly reducing the fat content.

Per portion Energy 279kcal/1178kJ; Protein 55g; Carbohydrate 2g, of which sugars 2g; Fat 5.7g, of which saturates 1.1g; Cholesterol 158mg; Calcium 39mg; Fibre 0.9g; Sodium 405mg.

SUMO WRESTLER'S HOTPOT

THIS FILLING HOT-POT, CALLED CHANKO NABE, IS PROBABLY RESPONSIBLE FOR THE VAST SIZE OF SUMO WRESTLERS, AS IT IS THEIR FIRST MEAL OF THE DAY AFTER 4–6 HOURS OF MORNING EXERCISE. YOU NEED A JAPANESE CLAY POT OR HEAVY PAN AND A PORTABLE TABLE STOVE OR A PLATE WARMER.

SERVES FOUR TO SIX

INGREDIENTS
    2 abura-age
    1 bunch of shungiku or pak choi (bok
        choy), 200g/7oz, root part trimmed
    1 large leek, trimmed
    1 daikon, thickly peeled
    ½ hakusai
    1 dashi-konbu, 4 × 10cm/1½ × 4in
    350g/12oz chicken or duck, boned
        and cut into large bitesize pieces
    12 shiitake mushrooms, stalks
        removed, a cross cut into each cap
    285g/10¼oz packet tofu block,
        drained and cut into 8 cubes
For the fish balls
    6 sardines, about 350g/12oz,
        cleaned and filleted
    2.5cm/1in fresh root ginger, chopped
    1 large (US extra large) egg
    25ml/1½ tbsp miso (any except
        hatcho or aka)
    20 chives, roughly chopped
    30ml/2 tbsp plain (all-purpose) flour
For the soup stock
    550ml/18fl oz/2½ cups sake
    550ml/18fl oz/2½ cups water
    60ml/4 tbsp shoyu
For the citrus pepper (optional)
    grated rind of 1 lime
    10–12 white peppercorns

1 Make the fish balls by chopping all the ingredients on a chopping board, or use a mortar and pestle to grind them. Alternatively, use a food processor. Pulse briefly so the texture is rough, not fine. Transfer to a container, cover with clear film (plastic wrap) until needed.

2 Blanch the abura-age in rapidly boiling water for 30 seconds. Drain under cold running water and squeeze out the water by hand. Cut each abura-age in half lengthways, and then quarter crossways to make eight rectangles. Cut each rectangle in half diagonally to make two triangles. You should have 32 triangles.

3 Cut the shungiku or pak-choi into 6cm/2½in lengths. Cut the leek diagonally in 2.5cm/1in thick oval shapes. Cut the daikon into 5mm/¼in rounds. Cut the hakusai leaves into strips crossways, keeping the leaves and stalks separate.

4 Grind the citrus pepper ingredients, if using, in a mortar using a pestle and set aside in a small bowl.

COOK'S TIP
At the end of the meal there is a tasty, rich soup left in the pot. Add 200g/7oz cooked udon noodles into the remaining soup and bring to the boil again. After 2 minutes, serve the noodles in bowls with plenty of soup and sprinkle the chopped chives on top.

5 Lay the dashi-konbu on the base of the pan. Pour in the ingredients for the soup stock to fill half the pan, and bring to the boil on a high heat.

6 To cook the fish balls, reduce the heat to medium. Scoop up the fish-ball paste with a spoon and shape roughly like a rugby ball using a palette knife (metal spatula). Drop into the boiling stock. Repeat until all the paste is used. Skim the surface of the stock frequently. Cook for 3 minutes.

7 Carefully add the chicken pieces, daikon rounds, the stalks of the hakusai, the shiitake and leek, then the tofu and abura-age. Simmer for about 12 minutes, or until the chicken is cooked. Add the soft parts of the hakusai and the shungiku and wait for 3 minutes. Remove from the heat.

8 Put the pan on the portable stove on the table, set at the lowest heat, or on a plate warmer. Serve small amounts of the ingredients in individual bowls. Guests help themselves from the pot. Sprinkle on citrus pepper, if you like.

Per portion Energy 311kcal/1301kJ; Protein 38.4g; Carbohydrate 5.4g, of which sugars 4.2g; Fat 13.5g, of which saturates 1.4g; Cholesterol 73mg; Calcium 1099mg; Fibre 3g; Sodium 853mg.

CUBED CHICKEN AND VEGETABLES

A POPULAR JAPANESE COOKING STYLE SIMMERS VEGETABLES OF DIFFERENT TEXTURES WITH A SMALL AMOUNT OF MEAT TOGETHER IN DASHI STOCK. THIS CHICKEN VERSION IS KNOWN AS IRIDORI.

SERVES FOUR

INGREDIENTS

   2 chicken thighs, about 200g/7oz,
     boned, with skin remaining
   1 large carrot, trimmed
   1 konnyaku
   300g/11oz satoimo or small potatoes
   500g/1¼lb canned take-no-ko,
     drained
   30ml/2 tbsp vegetable oil
   300ml/½ pint/1¼ cups second
     dashi stock, or the same amount
     of water and 7.5ml/1½ tsp
     dashi-no-moto
   salt
For the simmering seasonings
   75ml/5 tbsp shoyu
   30ml/2 tbsp sake
   30ml/2 tbsp caster (superfine) sugar
   30ml/2 tbsp mirin

1 Cut the chicken into bitesize pieces. Chop the carrot into 2cm/¾in triangular chunks, the ran-giri shape. To do this, cut the carrot slightly diagonally and turn it 90° each time you cut.

COOK'S TIP
When you cut satoimo, it produces a sticky juice. Rinsing with salt and water is the best way of washing it off.

2 Boil the konnyaku in rapidly boiling water for 1 minute and drain under running water. Cool, slice it crossways into 5mm/¼in thick rectangular strips.

3 Cut a 4cm/1½in slit down the centre of a strip without cutting the ends. Carefully push the top of the strip through the slit to make a decorative tie. Repeat with all the konnyaku.

4 Peel and halve the satoimo. Put the pieces in a colander and sprinkle with a generous amount of salt. Rub well and wash under running water. Drain. If using small potatoes, peel and cut the potatoes in half, and leave aside.

5 Halve the canned take-no-ko, then cut into the same shape as the carrot.

6 In a medium pan, heat the vegetable oil and stir-fry the chicken pieces until the surface of the meat turns white. Add the carrot, konnyaku ties, satoimo or potatoes and take-no-ko. Remember to stir the mixture well each time you add a new ingredient.

7 Add the dashi stock and bring to the boil. Cook on a high heat for 3 minutes then reduce to medium-low. Add the simmering seasonings, cover the pan then simmer for 15 minutes, until most of the liquid has evaporated, shaking the pan from time to time.

8 When the satoimo is soft, remove the pan from heat and transfer the chicken and vegetables to a large serving bowl. Serve immediately.

Per portion Energy 302kcal/1266kJ; Protein 20g; Carbohydrate 27.8g, of which sugars 16g; Fat 12.1g, of which saturates 1.7g; Cholesterol 39mg; Calcium 659mg; Fibre 1.2g; Sodium 1388mg.

POT-COOKED DUCK <u>AND</u> GREEN VEGETABLES

PREPARE THE INGREDIENTS FOR THIS JAPANESE DISH, KAMO NABE, BEFOREHAND, SO THAT THE COOKING CAN BE DONE AT THE TABLE. USE A HEAVY PAN OR CASSEROLE WITH A PORTABLE STOVE.

SERVES FOUR

INGREDIENTS

4 duck breast fillets, about 800g/
 1¾lb total weight
8 large shiitake mushrooms, stalks
 removed, a cross cut into each cap
2 leeks, trimmed and cut diagonally
 into 6cm/2½in lengths
½ hakusai, stalk part removed and
 cut into 5cm/2in squares
500g/1¼lb shungiku or mizuna, root
 part removed, cut in half crossways
For the stock
 raw bones from 1 chicken, washed
 1 egg shell
 200g/7oz/scant 1 cup short grain
 rice, washed and drained
 120ml/4fl oz/½ cup sake
 about 10ml/2 tsp coarse sea salt
For the sauce
 75ml/5 tbsp shoyu
 30ml/2 tbsp sake
 juice of 1 lime
 8 white peppercorns, roughly crushed
For the soup
 130g/4½oz Chinese egg noodles,
 cooked and loosened
 1 egg, beaten
 1 bunch of chives
 freshly ground white pepper

1 To make the stock, put the chicken bones into a pan three-quarters full of water. Bring to the boil and drain when it reaches boiling point. Wash the pan and the bones again, then return to the pan with the same amount of water. Add the egg shell and then bring to the boil. Simmer, uncovered, for 1 hour, skimming frequently. Remove the bones and egg shell. Add the rice, sake and salt, then simmer for 30 minutes. Remove from the heat and set aside.

2 Heat a heavy frying pan until just smoking. Remove from the heat for 1 minute, then add the duck breasts, skin-side down. Return to a medium heat and sear for 3–4 minutes, or until crisp. Turn over and sear the other side for 1 minute. Remove from the heat.

3 When cool, wipe the duck fat with kitchen paper and cut the breast and skin into 5mm/¼in thick slices. Arrange on a large serving plate with all the prepared vegetables.

4 Heat through all the ingredients for the sauce in a small pan and transfer to a small jug (pitcher) or bowl.

5 Prepare four dipping bowls, four serving bowls and chopsticks. At the table, bring the pan of soup stock to the boil, then reduce to medium-low.

6 Add half of the shiitake and leeks. Wait for 5 minutes and put in half of the stalk part of the hakusai. Add half of the duck and cook for 1–2 minutes for rare or 5–8 minutes for well-done meat.

7 Each person prepares some duck and vegetables in a serving bowl and drizzles over a little sauce. Add the soft hakusai leaves, shungiku and mizuna to the stock as you eat, adjusting the heat as you go. When the stock is less than a quarter of the pot's volume, top up with 3 parts water to 1 part sake.

8 When the duck has been eaten, bring the reduced stock to the boil. Skim the oil from the surface, and reduce the heat to medium. Add the noodles, cook for 1–2 minutes and check the seasoning. Add more salt if required. Pour in the beaten egg and swirl in the stock. Cover, turn off the heat, then leave to stand for 1 minute. Decorate with the chopped chives and serve with ground pepper.

Per portion Energy 626kcal/2633kJ; Protein 52.3g; Carbohydrate 69.4g, of which sugars 6g; Fat 18.6g, of which saturates 18.6g; Cholesterol 277mg; Calcium 110mg; Fibre 4.3g; Sodium 1640mg.

PORK

Pork is widely eaten throughout Japan and Korea, as it is easily available and cheap to buy. The recipes in this section include classic dishes such as the crisp and spicy Pork Belly with Sesame Dip, and the succulent Griddled Doenjang Pork which has a lovely roast chestnut flavour. Chilli paste is often added to set the tastebuds alight.

Left: Grilled Green Tea Pork with Soya Dip; **Above:** Sweet and Sour Pork

POACHED PORK WRAPPED IN CHINESE LEAVES

MELTINGLY TENDER PORK, IMBUED WITH THE KOREAN FLAVOURS OF DOENJANG SOYA BEAN PASTE AND GARLIC, IS COMBINED WITH A ZESTY RADISH STUFFING AND WRAPPED IN PARCELS OF CHINESE LEAVES. THIS DISH, CALLED BOSSAM, IS PERFECT AS AN APPETIZER OR AS A NIBBLE WITH DRINKS.

5 Prepare the poaching liquid by putting the garlic, onion and leek in a large pan. Mix in the *doenjang* soya bean paste and sake or rice wine, and then add the pork. Add enough water to cover the pork and heat to bring the liquid to the boil.

6 Cook the pork for 30–40 minutes, until tender. To test if the meat is ready, push a skewer into the meat – it should pass through cleanly.

7 Drain the Chinese leaves and tear off the leaves, keeping them whole, and place them on a serving plate.

8 Transfer the stuffing mixture to a serving dish. Once the pork is cooked, remove it from the liquid and slice it into thin bitesize pieces. Serve the pork with the stuffing and Chinese leaves.

9 To eat, take a slice of the pork and place it on a Chinese leaf. Then spoon a little of the stuffing on to the meat and wrap it into a parcel before eating it.

SERVES THREE TO FOUR

INGREDIENTS
  1 head Chinese leaves
    (Chinese cabbage)
  5 garlic cloves, roughly chopped
  ½ onion, roughly chopped
  1 leek, roughly chopped
  15ml/1 tbsp doenjang soya
    bean paste
  120ml/4fl oz/½ cup sake or rice wine
  675g/1½lb pork neck
  salt
  sugar
For the stuffing
  500g/1¼lb Chinese white radish,
    peeled and thinly sliced
  3 chestnuts, sliced
  ½ Asian pear, sliced
  65g/2½oz minari, watercress,
    or rocket (arugula), chopped
  45ml/3 tbsp Korean chilli powder
  5ml/1 tsp Thai fish sauce
  2 garlic cloves, crushed
  2.5ml/½ tsp grated fresh root ginger
  5ml/1 tsp honey
  5ml/1 tsp sesame seeds

1 Soak the whole head of Chinese leaves in salty water (using 50g/2oz of salt) for about 1 hour, or until the leaves have softened.

2 To make the stuffing, put the white radish into a colander and sprinkle with salt. Leave to stand for 10 minutes, then rinse and transfer to a large bowl.

3 Add the chestnuts, pear and chopped minari, watercress or rocket to the bowl and mix together well.

4 Add the other stuffing ingredients, with salt to taste, and stir thoroughly.

Per portion Energy 332kcal/1391kJ; Protein 40.2g; Carbohydrate 18.7g, of which sugars 14.9g; Fat 7.9g, of which saturates 2.6g; Cholesterol 106mg; Calcium 136mg; Fibre 5.9g; Sodium 507mg.

ROASTED <u>AND</u> MARINATED PORK

YUAN, A JAPANESE SAUCE MADE FROM SAKE, SHOYU, MIRIN AND CITRUS FRUIT, IS OFTEN USED TO
MARINATE INGREDIENTS EITHER BEFORE OR AFTER COOKING. IN THIS RECIPE, THE SAUCE GIVES A
DELICATE FLAVOUR TO PORK. IF POSSIBLE, LEAVE THE MEAT TO MARINATE OVERNIGHT.

SERVES FOUR

INGREDIENTS
    600g/1lb 5oz pork fillet
    1 garlic clove, crushed
    generous pinch of salt
    4 spring onions (scallions),
        trimmed, white part only
    10g/¼oz dried wakame,
        soaked
        in water for 20 minutes
        and drained
    10cm/4in celery stick,
        trimmed and cut in half
        crossways
    1 carton mustard and cress
For the yuan sauce
    105ml/7 tbsp shoyu
    45ml/3 tbsp sake
    60ml/4 tbsp mirin
    1 lime, sliced into
        thin rings

4 Cut the white part of the spring
onions in half crossways, then in half
lengthways. Remove the round cores,
then lay the spring onion quarters flat
on a chopping board. Slice them very
thinly lengthways to make fine shreds.

5 Soak the shreds in a bowl of ice-cold
water. Repeat with the remaining parts
of the spring onions. When the shreds
curl up, drain and gather them into a
loose ball.

6 Cut the drained wakame into 2.5cm/
1in squares or narrow strips. Slice the
celery very thinly lengthways. Soak in
cold water, then drain and gather
together as before.

7 Remove the pork from the marinade
and wipe with kitchen paper. Slice it
very thinly. Strain the marinade and
keep it in a gravy boat or jug (pitcher).
Arrange the sliced pork on a large
serving plate with the vegetables around
it. Serve cold with the yuan sauce.

1 Preheat the oven to 200°C/400°F/
Gas 6. Rub the pork with crushed garlic
and salt, and leave for 15 minutes.

2 Roast the pork for 20 minutes, then
turn the meat over and reduce the oven
temperature to 180°C/350°F/Gas 4.
Cook for a further 20 minutes, or until
the pork is cooked and there are no
pink juices.

3 Meanwhile, mix the yuan sauce
ingredients in a container that is big
enough to hold the pork. When the
meat is cooked, immediately put it in
the sauce, and leave it to marinate for
at least 2 hours, or overnight.

Per portion Energy 241kcal/1015kJ; Protein 33.4g; Carbohydrate 10.6g, of which sugars 10.3g; Fat 6.2g, of which saturates 2.1g; Cholesterol 95mg; Calcium 33mg; Fibre 0.4g; Sodium 1983mg.

PAN-FRIED PORK WITH GINGER SAUCE

REPUTEDLY CREATED BY A CANTEEN DINNER LADY AT A TOKYO UNIVERSITY DURING THE 1970S, THIS DISH, KNOWN AS BUTA-NIKU SHOGA YAKI, IS PARTICULARLY POPULAR WITH YOUNGSTERS.

SERVES FOUR

INGREDIENTS
450g/1lb pork chops, boned and trimmed
1 small onion, thinly sliced lengthways
50g/2oz/¼ cup beansprouts
50g/2oz mangetouts (snow peas), trimmed
15ml/1 tbsp vegetable oil
salt
For the marinade
15ml/1 tbsp shoyu
15ml/1 tbsp sake
15ml/1 tbsp mirin
4cm/1½in piece fresh root ginger, very finely grated, plus juice

1 Wrap the pork chops in clear film (plastic wrap) and freeze for 2 hours. Cut into 3mm/⅛in slices, then into 4cm/1½in wide strips.

2 To make the marinade, mix all the ingredients in a plastic container. Add the pork and marinate for 15 minutes. Meanwhile, heat the oil in a heavy frying pan on a medium-high heat. Add the onion and fry for 3 minutes.

3 Take half of the pork slices out from the marinade and add to the frying pan. Transfer the meat to a plate when its colour changes; this will only take about 2–3 minutes. Repeat the process with the rest of the meat and reserve the marinade. Transfer all the cooked pork slices and onions to the plate.

4 Pour the reserved marinade into the pan and simmer until it has reduced by one-third. Add the beansprouts and mangetouts, then the pork and increase the heat to medium-high for 2 minutes. Heap the beansprouts on individual serving plates and lean the meat, onions and mangetouts against them. Serve immediately.

Per portion Energy 176kcal/738kJ; Protein 25.2g; Carbohydrate 2.4g, of which sugars 1.7g; Fat 7.4g, of which saturates 1.9g; Cholesterol 71mg; Calcium 20mg; Fibre 0.7g; Sodium 258mg.

DEEP-FRIED PORK FILLET

KNOWN AS TON-KATSU, SOME JAPANESE RESTAURANTS SERVE JUST THIS ONE INVIGORATING DISH. THE PORK IS ALWAYS GARNISHED WITH JUST A HEAP OF VERY FINELY SHREDDED WHITE CABBAGE.

SERVES FOUR

INGREDIENTS
1 white cabbage
4 pork loin chops or cutlets, boned
plain (all-purpose) flour, to dust
vegetable oil, for deep-frying
2 eggs, beaten
50g/2oz/1 cup dried white breadcrumbs
salt and ready-ground mixed pepper
prepared English (hot) mustard, to garnish
Japanese pickles, to serve
For the ton-katsu sauce
60ml/4 tbsp Worcestershire sauce
30ml/2 tbsp good-quality tomato ketchup
5ml/1 tsp shoyu

1 Quarter the cabbage and remove the central core. Slice the wedges very finely with a vegetable slicer or a sharp knife.

2 Make a few deep cuts horizontally across the fat of the meat. This prevents the meat curling up while cooking. Rub a little salt and pepper into the meat and dust with the flour, then shake off any excess.

3 Heat the oil in a deep-fryer or a large pan to 180°C/350°F.

4 Dip the meat in the beaten eggs, then coat with breadcrumbs. Deep-fry two pieces at a time for 8–10 minutes, or until golden brown. Drain on a wire rack or on kitchen paper. Repeat until all the pieces of pork are deep-fried.

5 Heap the cabbage on four individual serving plates. Cut the pork crossways into 2cm/¾in thick strips and arrange them to your liking on the cabbage.

6 To make the ton-katsu sauce, mix the Worcestershire sauce, ketchup and shoyu in a jug (pitcher) or gravy boat. Serve the pork and cabbage immediately, with the sauce, mustard and Japanese pickles. Pickles can also be served in separate dishes, if you like.

Per portion Energy 385kcal/1607kJ; Protein 40.2g; Carbohydrate 30.9g, of which sugars 9.6g; Fat 21g, of which saturates 4.2g; Cholesterol 253mg; Calcium 131mg; Fibre 2.5g; Sodium 633mg.

PORK GOCHUJANG STEW

*THIS DELICIOUS KOREAN STEW OF TENDER PORK LOIN IS VIBRANTLY COLOURED WITH RED CHILLI
AND HAS A FIERY TASTE TO MATCH. THE SUCCULENT PORK IS COOKED WITH AN ARRAY OF
VEGETABLES IN AN AROMATIC, THICK SOUP WITH AN UPLIFTING KICK OF GINGER.*

SERVES FOUR

INGREDIENTS

250g/9oz pork loin
30ml/2 tbsp vegetable oil
1 garlic clove, crushed
30ml/2 tbsp gochujang chilli paste
5ml/1 tsp Korean chilli powder
90g/3½oz potato, cubed
20g/¾oz fresh root ginger, peeled
1 green chilli, sliced
½ leek, sliced
1 courgette (zucchini), sliced
5ml/1 tsp sesame oil
50g/2oz minari, watercress or rocket
  (arugula), roughly chopped
5ml/1 tsp sesame seeds, to garnish

COOK'S TIP
To make this dish spicier increase the
quantity of gochujang chilli paste.

1 Trim any excess fat from the pork
and roughly cut the meat into bitesize
cubes. Place a heavy pan over a high
heat and add the vegetable oil. Add the
garlic and pork and stir until the meat
is lightly browned on all sides. Then
add the gochujang chilli paste and
chilli powder, and briefly sauté the
ingredients, evenly coating the meat
with the spices.

2 Add the potato, fresh root ginger and
chilli and then pour in enough water to
cover all the ingredients. Bring the pan
to the boil and add the leek, courgette
and sesame oil. Stir the mixture well and
cover the pan. Cook over a high heat for
3 minutes, then reduce the heat and
simmer for a further 5 minutes. Skim off
any excess fat from the surface as the
dish stews.

3 Remove from the heat and stir in the
minari, watercress or rocket. Discard
the root ginger and ladle the stew into
bowls. Garnish with the sesame seeds
before serving.

Per portion Energy 220kcal/918kJ; Protein 17.2g; Carbohydrate 15.2g, of which sugars 2.2g; Fat 10.6g, of which saturates 2g; Cholesterol 39mg; Calcium 45mg; Fibre 1.6g; Sodium 55mg.

SPICY PORK STIR-FRY

THIS SIMPLE DISH, CALLED CHEYUK BOKUM, IS QUICK TO PREPARE AND MAKES THE THINLY SLICED PORK FABULOUSLY SPICY. THE POTENT FLAVOUR OF KOREAN CHILLI PASTE THAT PREDOMINATES IN THE SEASONING FOR THE PORK WILL SET THE TASTEBUDS AFLAME. SERVE WITH A BOWL OF RICE.

SERVES TWO

INGREDIENTS
    400g/14oz pork shoulder
    1 onion
    ½ carrot
    2 spring onions (scallions)
    15ml/1 tbsp vegetable oil
    ½ red chilli, finely sliced
    ½ green chilli, finely sliced
    steamed rice and miso soup, to serve
For the seasoning
    30ml/2 tbsp dark soy sauce
    30ml/2 tbsp gochujang chilli paste
    30ml/2 tbsp mirin or rice wine
    15ml/1 tbsp Korean chilli powder
    1 garlic clove, finely chopped
    1 spring onion (scallion),
      finely chopped
    15ml/1 tbsp grated fresh root ginger
    15ml/1 tbsp sesame oil
    30ml/2 tbsp sugar
    ground black pepper

COOK'S TIP
This dish also works well with chicken. Replace the pork shoulder with 400g/14oz chicken thighs and omit the ginger from the seasoning.

1 Freeze the pork shoulder for 30 minutes and then slice it thinly, to about 5mm/¼in thick. Cut the onion and carrot into thin strips and roughly slice the spring onions lengthways.

2 To make the seasoning, combine the seasoning ingredients in a large bowl, mixing together thoroughly to form a paste. Add a splash of water if needed.

3 Heat a wok or large frying pan, and add the vegetable oil.

4 Once the oil is smoking, add the pork, onion, carrot, spring onions and chillies, in that order. Stir-fry, keeping the ingredients moving all the time.

5 Once the pork has lightly browned add the seasoning and thoroughly coat the meat and vegetables. Stir-fry for 2 minutes more, or until the pork is cooked through. Serve immediately with rice and a bowl of miso soup to help neutralize the spicy flavours of the dish.

Per portion Energy 430kcal/1799kJ; Protein 44.1g; Carbohydrate 21.3g, of which sugars 20.4g; Fat 19.2g, of which saturates 4.3g; Cholesterol 126mg; Calcium 44mg; Fibre 1.2g; Sodium 1216mg.

PORK BELLY ᵂᴵᵀᴴ SESAME DIP

SAMGYUPSAL IS A HUGELY POPULAR DISH IN KOREA, AND IS OFTEN ENJOYED AS AN EVENING SNACK WITH A GLASS OF SOJU. THINLY SLICED PORK BELLY IS GRIDDLED UNTIL THE OUTSIDE IS CRISP, LEAVING A SMOOTH TEXTURED CENTRE. THE MEAT IS THEN IMMERSED IN A SALTY SESAME DIP, BEFORE BEING WRAPPED IN LETTUCE LEAVES WITH A SPOONFUL OF RED CHILLI SAUCE.

SERVES THREE

INGREDIENTS
    675g/1½lb pork belly
    2 round (butterhead) lettuces
For the dip
    45ml/3 tbsp sesame oil
    10ml/2 tsp salt
    ground black pepper
For the sauce
    45ml/3 tbsp gochujang chilli paste
    75ml/5 tbsp doenjang soya
      bean paste
    2 garlic cloves, crushed
    1 spring onion (scallion), finely
      chopped
    5ml/1 tsp sesame oil

1 Freeze the pork belly for 30 minutes and then slice it very thinly, to about 3mm/⅛in thick. (You could ask the butcher to do this, or buy the meat pre-sliced at an Asian store.)

2 To make the dip, combine the sesame oil, salt and pepper in a small serving bowl.

3 To make the sauce, blend the chilli paste, *doenjang* soya bean paste, garlic, spring onion and sesame oil in a bowl, mixing the oil thoroughly into the paste. Transfer to a serving bowl.

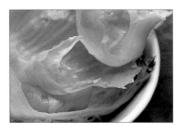

4 Remove the outer leaves from the heads of the lettuce, keeping them whole. Rinse well and place in a serving dish.

5 Heat a griddle pan or frying pan over a high heat (the griddle can be used over charcoal).Then add the sliced pork to the pan and cook until the surface of the pork is crisp and golden brown.

6 Serve the pork with the accompanying dishes of lettuce, sesame dip and chilli sauce. To eat, take a strip of pork and dip it into the sesame dip. Then place the meat in a lettuce leaf and add a small spoonful of the chilli sauce. Wrap the lettuce leaf into a parcel and enjoy.

COOK'S TIP
Any soft green leaf lettuce can be used; for example, Little Gem (Bibb) or any kind of crisphead lettuce such as iceberg. Rinse well before eating.

VARIATION
You can add other ingredients to the lettuce parcel, if you like. Some popular additions include shredded spring onion, sliced kimchi or sliced raw garlic.

Per portion Energy 991kcal/4093kJ; Protein 37g; Carbohydrate 1.1g, of which sugars 0.6g; Fat 93.1g, of which saturates 31.4g; Cholesterol 162mg; Calcium 37mg; Fibre 1.2g; Sodium 1475mg.

GRIDDLED DOENJANG PORK

DOENJANG SOYA BEAN PASTE GIVES A LOVELY ROAST-CHESTNUT FLAVOUR TO THE PORK IN THIS CLASSIC KOREAN RECIPE, MARRYING WELL WITH THE GRIDDLED TASTE OF THE MEAT. THE MARINADE IS MILD AND GIVES THE PORK A RICH AND SUCCULENT BARBECUE TEXTURE.

SERVES THREE

INGREDIENTS
   675g/1½lb pork loin
   2 round (butterhead) lettuces
   4 spring onions (scallions),
    shredded
For the marinade
   30ml/2 tbsp doenjang soya
    bean paste
   15ml/1 tbsp Thai fish sauce
   22.5ml/4½ tsp sugar
   1 spring onion (scallion),
    finely chopped
   5ml/1 tsp grated fresh root ginger
   1 onion, finely chopped
   5ml/1 tsp cornflour (cornstarch)
   1 garlic clove, crushed
   15ml/1 tbsp mirin or rice wine
   15ml/1 tbsp milk
   salt and ground black pepper

COOK'S TIP
You can store fresh root ginger in an airtight container in the refrigerator for up to a month. It is also possible to freeze whole ginger pieces, or grated ginger, and it will thaw quickly. When buying ginger, look for sections that are plump, and avoid wrinkled skin.

1 Trim off any excess fat and roughly cut the pork into bitesize pieces.

2 To make the marinade, put the doenjang paste, Thai fish sauce, sugar, spring onion and ginger in a large bowl and then mix the ingredients together thoroughly.

3 Add the onion, cornflour and garlic, and pour in the mirin or rice wine and milk. Season with salt and pepper and mix well.

4 Add the pork to the bowl and coat it well with the marinade. Leave the mixture in the bowl for approximately 30 minutes.

5 Remove the outer leaves from the heads of lettuce, keeping them whole. Rinse them well and place them in a serving dish.

6 Place a heavy griddle pan or frying pan over a high heat and once hot reduce to a medium heat (the griddle can be used over charcoal). Add the marinated pork and cook well, turning as required. The meat should be well done, with the exterior seared and slightly blackened and no pinkness inside.

7 Serve by wrapping the meat in a lettuce leaf with pieces of shredded spring onions.

Per portion Energy 355kcal/1493kJ; Protein 50g; Carbohydrate 17.4g, of which sugars 12.4g; Fat 9.9g, of which saturates 3.4g; Cholesterol 142mg; Calcium 74mg; Fibre 1.7g; Sodium 168mg.

BARBECUED PORK RIB <u>IN</u> CHILLI SAUCE

POPULAR AS A SNACK TO ACCOMPANY A GLASS OF SOJU, THESE KOREAN PORK RIBS ARE SERVED WITH GREEN LEAVES TO WRAP THE MEAT BEFORE EATING. THE PORK IS GLAZED WITH A SWEET AND SPICY SAUCE AND HAS A WONDERFULLY CHARRED, SMOKY TASTE WITH A LOVELY CHEWY TEXTURE.

SERVES FOUR

INGREDIENTS
1kg/2¼lb pork ribs
60ml/4 tbsp gochujang chilli paste
45ml/3 tbsp Korean chilli powder
30ml/2 tbsp sake or mirin
60ml/4 tbsp sugar
30ml/2 tbsp soy sauce
½ white onion, grated
4 garlic cloves, crushed
7.5ml/1½ tsp grated fresh
   root ginger
45ml/3 tbsp maple syrup
30ml/2 tbsp sesame oil
salt and ground black pepper
sesame seeds, to garnish

COOK'S TIP
The barbecued pork is best served with an accompaniment of green leaves, in which the meat can be wrapped before eating with fingers.

1 Place the pork ribs in a large bowl and pour in enough cold water to cover them, then leave them to soak for about 20 minutes. Drain the ribs and pat dry with kitchen paper.

2 Remove the bones from the ribs and trim off any excess fat. Slice the meat into 5cm/2in pieces.

3 Make the marinade. Mix the chilli paste and powder, sake or mirin, sugar, soy sauce, onion, garlic, ginger, maple syrup, sesame oil, salt and pepper in a bowl. Mix well. Add the meat and coat thoroughly with the mixture. Place in the refrigerator and leave it to marinate for at least 3 hours.

4 Heat a griddle or frying pan over a medium heat and add the pork with the marinade. Cook, turning the pieces once or twice, for 25–30 minutes, until the pork is properly cooked and the sauce has formed a glaze.

5 Arrange the pork on a serving plate. Sprinkle with sesame seeds to garnish and serve.

Per portion Energy 638kcal/2663kJ; Protein 49.9g; Carbohydrate 20g, of which sugars 13.8g; Fat 40.8g, of which saturates 14.1g; Cholesterol 165mg; Calcium 83mg; Fibre 1.1g; Sodium 994mg.

BEEF

Beef is a popular meat with the Japanese and Koreans, who enjoy
its rich flavours and textures. It is often barbecued, fried, seared
on the griddle, charcoal grilled or flame grilled. Beef is usually seasoned
before cooking, to allow it to soak up the flavourings. Favourite meals
enjoyed in the Summer are chilled ribbons of beef such as Ribbon Beef
Tartare, and a lightly seared Beef and Asian Pear Salad.

Left: Grilled Beef in Sweet Soy Marinade; **Above:** Beef Rissoles

SLICED SEARED BEEF

JAPANESE CHEFS USE A COOKING TECHNIQUE CALLED TATAKI TO COOK RARE STEAK. THEY NORMALLY USE A COAL FIRE AND SEAR A CHUNK OF BEEF ON LONG SKEWERS, THEN PLUNGE IT INTO COLD WATER TO STOP IT COOKING FURTHER. USE A WIRE MESH GRILL OVER THE HEAT SOURCE TO COOK THIS WAY.

SERVES FOUR

INGREDIENTS

500g/1¼lb chunk of beef thigh
  (a long, thin chunk looks better
  than a thick, round chunk)
generous pinch of salt
10ml/2 tsp vegetable oil

For the marinade
200ml/7fl oz/scant 1 cup
  rice vinegar
70ml/4½ tbsp sake
135ml/4½fl oz/scant ⅔ cup shoyu
15ml/1 tbsp caster
  (superfine) sugar
1 garlic clove, thinly sliced
1 small onion, thinly sliced
sansho

For the garnish
6 shiso leaves and shiso flowers
  (if available)
about 15cm/6in Japanese or ordinary
  salad cucumber
½ lemon, thinly sliced
1 garlic clove, finely grated (optional)

1 Mix the marinade ingredients in a small pan and warm through until the sugar has dissolved. Remove from the heat and leave to cool.

COOK'S TIPS
• If you don't have a mesh grill or griddle, heat 15ml/1 tbsp vegetable oil in a hot frying pan to sear the beef. Wash all the oil from the meat and wipe off any excess with a kitchen paper.
• If preparing this dish ahead of time, spear the beef rolls with a cocktail stick (toothpick) to secure.

2 Generously sprinkle the beef with the salt and rub well into the meat. Leave for 2–3 minutes, then rub the oil in evenly with your fingers.

3 Fill a large mixing bowl with plenty of cold water. Put a mesh grill tray over the heat on the top of the stove, or heat a griddle to a high temperature. Sear the beef, turning frequently until about 5mm/¼in of the flesh in from the surface is cooked. Try not to burn grid marks on the meat. Immediately plunge the meat into the bowl of cold water for a few seconds to stop it from cooking further.

4 Wipe the meat with kitchen paper or a dish towel and immerse fully in the marinade for 1 day.

5 Next day, prepare the garnish. Chop the shiso leaves in half lengthways, then cut into very thin strips crossways. Slice the cucumber diagonally into 5mm/¼in thick oval shapes, then cut each oval into 5mm/¼in matchsticks. Scoop out the watery seed part first if using an ordinary salad cucumber.

6 Remove the meat from the marinade. Strain the remaining marinade through a sieve (strainer), reserving both the liquid and the marinated onion and garlic.

7 Using a sharp knife, cut the beef thinly into slices of about 5mm/¼in thick.

8 Heap the cucumber sticks on a large serving plate and put the marinated onion and garlic on top. Arrange the beef slices as you would sashimi, leaning alongside or on the bed of cucumber and other vegetables. You can also either make a fan shape with the beef slices, or, if the slices are large enough, you could roll them.

9 Fluff the shiso strips and put on top of the beef. Decorate with some shiso flowers, if using. Lightly sprinkle with the lemon rings, and serve with the reserved marinade in individual bowls.

10 To eat, take a few beef slices on to individual plates. Roll a slice with your choice of garnish, then dip it into the marinade. Add a little grated garlic, if you like.

Per portion Energy 258kcal/1079kJ; Protein 28.7g; Carbohydrate 9.8g, of which sugars 9.8g; Fat 11.7g, of which saturates 4.8g; Cholesterol 73mg; Calcium 20mg; Fibre 0.3g; Sodium 82mg.

BEEF <u>AND</u> ASIAN PEAR SALAD

PAN-FRIED BEEF AND ASIAN PEAR COMBINE WITH PINE NUTS AND CHESTNUTS IN THIS DISH, TO CREATE A SALAD THAT PROVIDES THE QUINTESSENTIAL LIGHT SUMMER SUPPER IN KOREA.

SERVES FOUR

INGREDIENTS
300g/11oz fillet steak,
 thinly sliced
15ml/1 tbsp dark soy sauce
1 garlic clove, crushed
10ml/2 tsp sesame oil
1 Asian pear
15ml/1 tbsp sugar
15ml/1 tbsp rice vinegar
30ml/2 tbsp pine nuts
5 cooked chestnuts, finely chopped
salt and ground black pepper
vegetable oil, for cooking

1 Mix the steak with the soy sauce, garlic, sesame oil and a little salt and pepper and marinate for 20 minutes.

2 Meanwhile, peel, core and slice the pear, then cut the slices into fine strips. Place in a small bowl and pour in cold water to cover.

3 Stir the sugar and rice vinegar into the bowl. Leave to stand for 5 minutes. Then drain and set aside.

4 Heat a frying pan over a high heat and add a little vegetable oil. Add the beef with its marinade and sauté briefly, then reduce the heat and fry gently until the meat is well cooked.

5 Transfer the beef to a serving dish. Add the pear, pine nuts and chestnuts, toss the ingredients together and serve immediately.

Per portion Energy 234kcal/976kJ; Protein 18.6g; Carbohydrate 8.9g, of which sugars 5.2g; Fat 14g, of which saturates 3.5g; Cholesterol 44mg; Calcium 15mg; Fibre 1.5g; Sodium 300mg.

PAPER-THIN SLICED BEEF COOKED IN STOCK

THE JAPANESE NAME FOR THIS DISH, SHABU SHABU, REFERS TO 'WASHING' THE WAFER-THIN SLICES OF BEEF IN HOT STOCK. YOU WILL NEED A PORTABLE STOVE TO COOK THIS MEAL AT THE TABLE.

SERVES FOUR

INGREDIENTS
600g/1lb 5oz boneless beef sirloin
2 leeks, trimmed and cut into strips
4 spring onions (scallions), quartered
8 shiitake mushrooms, less stalks
175g/6oz oyster mushrooms, base
   part removed, torn into small pieces
½ hakusai, base part removed and
   cut into 5cm/2in squares
300g/11oz shungiku, halved
275g/10oz tofu, halved then cut in
   2cm/¾in thick slices crossways
10 × 6cm/4 × 2½in dashi-konbu
   wiped with a damp cloth
For the ponzu (citrus sauce)
juice of 1 lime made up to 120ml/
   4fl oz/½ cup with lemon juice
50ml/2fl oz/¼ cup rice vinegar
120ml/4fl oz/½ cup shoyu
20ml/4 tsp mirin
4 × 6cm/1½ × 2½in dashi-konbu
5g/⅙oz kezuri-bushi
For the goma-dare (sesame sauce)
75g/3oz white sesame seeds
10ml/2 tsp caster (superfine) sugar
45ml/3 tbsp shoyu
15ml/1 tbsp sake
15ml/1 tbsp mirin
90ml/6 tbsp second dashi stock, or
   the same amount of water and
   5ml/1 tsp dashi-no-moto
For the condiments
5–6cm/2–2½in daikon, peeled
2 dried chillies, seeded and sliced
20 chives, finely snipped

1 Mix all the ponzu ingredients in a glass jar and leave overnight. Strain and keep the liquid in the jar.

2 Make the goma-dare. Gently roast the sesame seeds in a dry frying pan on a low heat until the seeds pop. Grind the sesame seeds to form a smooth paste. Add the sugar and grind, then add the other ingredients, mixing well. Pour 30ml/2 tbsp of the mixture into each of four small bowls, and put the rest in a jug (pitcher) or bowl.

3 Prepare the condiments. Pierce the cut ends of the daikon deeply several times with a skewer, then insert pieces of chilli. Leave for 20 minutes, then grate the daikon into a sieve (strainer). Divide the pink daikon among four small bowls. Put the chives in another bowl.

4 Cut the meat into 1–2mm/¹⁄₁₆in thick slices, and place on a large serving plate. Arrange the vegetables and tofu on another large plate.

5 Fill a flameproof casserole three-quarters full of water and add the dashi-konbu. Bring everything to the table and heat the casserole.

6 Pour 45ml/3 tbsp ponzu into the grated daikon in each bowl, and add the chives to the bowls of goma-dare.

7 When the water comes to the boil, remove the konbu and reduce the heat to medium-low. Add a handful of each ingredient except the beef to the casserole.

8 Each guest picks up a slice of raw beef using chopsticks and holds it in the stock for 3–10 seconds. Dip the beef into one of the sauces and eat. Remove the vegetables and other ingredients when they are cooked, and eat with the dipping sauces. Skim the surface occasionally.

Per portion Energy 492kcal/2050kJ; Protein 46.7g; Carbohydrate 12.8g, of which sugars 11.6g; Fat 28.4g, of which saturates 7.8g; Cholesterol 87mg; Calcium 517mg; Fibre 3.7g; Sodium 3047mg.

SIMMERED SHORT RIBS <u>IN</u> NOODLE SOUP

THIS SLOW-COOKED KOREAN DISH, CALLED GALBITANG, CONTAINS SHORT RIBS AND CUBES OF ASIAN RADISH IN AN EXQUISITELY RICH SOUP, WITH FINE DANGMYUN NOODLES HIDING JUST BELOW THE SURFACE. A PIQUANT CHILLI SEASONING IS ADDED JUST BEFORE SERVING.

2 Cut the radish into 2cm/½in cubes. Place the seasoning ingredients in a bowl and mix thoroughly.

3 Place the ribs in a large heavy pan and cover with 1 litre/1¾ pints/4 cups water. Cook over a high heat for 20 minutes and add the radish and salt. Reduce the heat and cook for 7 minutes, then add the noodles and cook for 3 minutes more.

4 Ladle the soup into bowls and add a generous spoonful of the seasoning just before serving.

COOK'S TIP
Made from sweet potatoes, dangmyun noodles are available at Asian stores.

SERVES FOUR

INGREDIENTS
　900g/2lb beef short ribs, cut into
　　5cm/2in squares
　350g/12oz Chinese white
　　radish, peeled
　5ml/1 tsp salt
　90g/3½oz dangmyun noodles
For the seasoning
　45ml/3 tbsp soy sauce
　15ml/1 tbsp chilli powder
　50g/2oz spring onions (scallions),
　　roughly chopped
　5ml/1 tsp sesame oil
　1 chilli, finely sliced
　ground black pepper

1 Soak the ribs in a bowl of cold water for 10 hours to drain the blood, changing the water halfway. Drain the ribs and place in a large pan, cover with water and place over a high heat. Once the water has boiled remove the ribs, rinse them in cold water and set aside.

Per portion Energy 437kcal/1830kJ; Protein 52.1g; Carbohydrate 19.8g, of which sugars 3.1g; Fat 17g, of which saturates 6.7g; Cholesterol 126mg; Calcium 40mg; Fibre 1.6g; Sodium 1174mg.

BARBECUED BEEF SHORT RIBS

THE SECRET TO THIS DISH, CALLED GALBI, IS TO MARINATE THE BEEF OVERNIGHT TO ALLOW THE FLAVOURS TO INFUSE. THE NATURAL FRUIT ACIDITY IN THE PEAR HELPS TO TENDERIZE THE MEAT, AND THE SAKE ADDS A SLIGHTLY SWEET EDGE. STUFFED CUCUMBER KIMCHI MAKES A PERFECT SIDE DISH.

SERVES FOUR

INGREDIENTS
  900g/2lb beef short ribs, cut
    into 5cm/2in squares
  shredded spring onions (scallions),
    seasoned with Korean chilli powder
    and rice vinegar, to serve
For the marinade
  4 spring onions (scallions), finely sliced
  ½ onion, finely chopped
  1 Asian pear
  60ml/4 tbsp dark soy sauce
  60ml/4 tbsp sugar
  30ml/2 tbsp sesame oil
  15ml/1 tbsp sake or rice wine
  10ml/2 tsp ground
    black pepper
  5ml/1 tsp sesame seeds
  2 garlic cloves, crushed
  5ml/1 tsp grated fresh
    root ginger

1 To make the marinade, place the spring onions and onion in a large bowl. Core and chop the Asian pear, being careful to save the juices, and add to the bowl. Add the remaining marinade ingredients and mix together thoroughly.

COOK'S TIP
Butchers should be happy to prepare short ribs for you; ask for pieces approximately 5cm/2in square.

2 Add the short ribs to the marinade, stirring to coat them. Leave to stand for at least 2 hours to allow the flavours to permeate and the meat to soften.

3 Heat a heavy griddle pan or frying pan and add the ribs. Keep turning them to cook the meat evenly. When they become crisp and dark brown, serve immediately with a bowl of seasoned shredded spring onions.

Per portion Energy 373kcal/1563kJ; Protein 49.5g; Carbohydrate 9.4g, of which sugars 9.3g; Fat 15.5g, of which saturates 6.7g; Cholesterol 126mg; Calcium 35mg; Fibre 0.5g; Sodium 852mg.

BRAISED BEEF STRIPS WITH SOY AND GINGER

FINE STRIPS OF BRAISED BEEF ARE ENHANCED BY A RICH, DARK SOY AND GARLIC SAUCE, WITH A PIQUANT KICK OF ROOT GINGER AND JALAPEÑO CHILLIES. MUSCOVADO SUGAR ADDS AN IMPERCEPTIBLE SWEETNESS. THIS IS AN EXCELLENT SIDE SERVING TO ACCOMPANY A LARGER STEW OR NOODLE DISH.

SERVES TWO TO THREE

INGREDIENTS

450g/1lb beef flank
25g/1oz piece fresh root
   ginger, peeled
100ml/3½fl oz/scant ½ cup
   dark soy sauce
75g/3oz light muscovado (brown)
   sugar
12 garlic cloves, peeled
6 jalapeño chillies

COOK'S TIP

With a beef cut other than the flank, the meat should be cut into thin strips to ensure it is tender when cooked.

1 Bring a large pan of water to the boil and add the beef. Cook for around 40 minutes until tender. Drain the meat and rinse it in warm water. Leave the beef to cool, then roughly slice it into strips about 5cm/2in long.

2 Place the peeled root ginger in a large pan with the beef and add 300ml/½ pint/1¼ cups water. Bring to the boil, cover and then reduce the heat and simmer for 30 minutes. Skim the fat from the surface of the liquid as the meat cooks. The liquid should have reduced to half its initial volume.

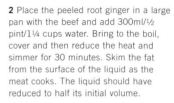

3 Add the soy sauce, muscovado sugar and garlic, and simmer for a further 20 minutes. Then add the jalapeño chillies, and cook for a further 5 minutes.

4 Discard the root ginger, and serve in bowls with generous quantities of the garlic and chillies.

Per portion Energy 408kcal/1713kJ; Protein 37.8g; Carbohydrate 34.3g, of which sugars 29.1g; Fat 14.2g, of which saturates 5.7g; Cholesterol 87mg; Calcium 33mg; Fibre 1.4g; Sodium 2472mg.

BRAISED SHORT RIBS STEW

THIS SLOW COOKED, RICHLY COLOURED STEW IS A POPULAR DISH AT A KOREAN FEAST, WHICH IS TRADITIONALLY EATEN ON NEW YEAR'S DAY. NAMUL VEGETABLES MAKE AN IDEAL ACCOMPANIMENT, SERVED ALONGSIDE RADISH KIMCHI AND A BOWL OF STEAMED RICE.

SERVES FOUR

INGREDIENTS
 900g/2lb short ribs, cut into 5cm/
  2in squares
 3 dried shiitake mushrooms, soaked
  in warm water for about 30 minutes
  until softened
 ½ onion, roughly cubed
 ½ carrot, roughly cubed
 ½ potato, roughly cubed
 75g/3oz Chinese white radish, peeled
  and roughly diced
 2 spring onions (scallions),
  finely sliced
 4 chestnuts
 2 red dates
 30ml/2 tbsp mirin or rice wine
 4 ginkgo nuts, to garnish
For the seasoning
 ½ Asian pear or kiwi fruit
 60ml/4 tbsp light soy sauce
 20ml/4 tsp sugar
 2 garlic cloves, crushed
 5ml/1 tsp finely grated fresh
  root ginger
 15ml/1 tbsp sesame seeds
 20ml/4 tsp sesame oil
 ground black pepper

1 Soak the short ribs in a large bowl of cold water for approximately 3 hours to help drain the blood from the meat. Change the water halfway through, once it has discoloured.Then drain the ribs thoroughly.

2 Place the ribs in a large pan, cover with water and put over a high heat. Bring to the boil and then remove the ribs and rinse them in cold water. Strain the cooking liquid into a jug (pitcher), and set aside.

3 When the soaked shiitake mushrooms have reconstituted and become soft, drain and slice them, discarding the stems.

4 To make the seasoning, peel and core the Asian pear or kiwi fruit, and grate into a large bowl to catch the juice.

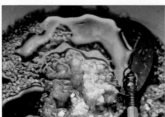

5 Add the other seasoning ingredients to the bowl and mix them together.

6 Use a knife to make deep cuts in the ribs and place them in the bowl of seasoning. Coat the meat, working the mixture well into the slits, and leave it to absorb the flavours for 20 minutes.

7 Transfer the ribs and seasoning mixture to a large pan. Add the sliced mushrooms and the chunks of onion, carrot, potato, radish and spring onions.

8 Then add the whole chestnuts and red dates. Pour 200ml/7fl oz/scant 1 cup water over the ingredients and set the pan over high heat.

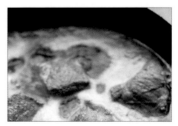

9 Once the liquid begins to boil add the mirin or rice wine and cover the pan. Reduce the heat and simmer for 1 hour, or until the meat has become very tender. If necessary, top up the level of liquid from the jug so that there is enough to cover all of the ingredients. Serve with a garnish of ginkgo nuts.

Per portion Energy 533kcal/2223kJ; Protein 49.6g; Carbohydrate 16.7g, of which sugars 10.3g; Fat 30.1g, of which saturates 9g; Cholesterol 126mg; Calcium 35mg; Fibre 1.5g; Sodium 147mg.

SIMMERED BEEF SLICES <u>AND</u> VEGETABLES

*THIS SIMPLE AND EASY TO COOK JAPANESE DISH, NIKU JYAGA, IS A TYPICAL HOME-COOKED MEAL
AND IS ONE OF THE TRADITIONAL DISHES REFERRED TO AS 'MOTHER'S SPECIALITY'.*

SERVES FOUR

INGREDIENTS
    250g/9oz beef fillet (or any cut),
        very thinly sliced
    1 large onion
    15ml/1 tbsp vegetable oil
    450g/1lb small potatoes, halved
        then soaked in water
    1 carrot, cut into 5mm/¼in rounds
    45ml/3 tbsp frozen peas, defrosted
        and blanched for 1 minute
For the seasonings
    30ml/2 tbsp caster (superfine) sugar
    75ml/5 tbsp shoyu
    15ml/1 tbsp mirin
    15ml/1 tbsp sake

1 Cut the thinly sliced beef slices into 2cm/¾in wide strips, and slice the onion lengthways into 5mm/¼in pieces.

2 Heat the vegetable oil in a pan and lightly fry the beef and onion slices. When the colour of the meat changes, drain the potatoes and add to the pan.

3 Once the potatoes are coated with the oil in the pan, add the carrot. Pour in just enough water to cover, then bring to the boil, skimming a few times.

4 Boil vigorously for 2 minutes, then move the potatoes to the bottom of the pan and gather all the other ingredients to sit on top of the potatoes. Reduce the heat to medium-low and add all the seasonings. Simmer for 20 minutes, partially covered, or until most of the liquid has evaporated.

5 Check if the potatoes are cooked. Add the peas and cook to heat through, then remove the pan from the heat. Serve the beef and vegetables immediately in four small serving bowls.

Per portion Energy 276kcal/1160kJ; Protein 17.8g; Carbohydrate 31.5g, of which sugars 13.2g; Fat 9.2g, of which saturates 2.9g; Cholesterol 36mg; Calcium 28mg; Fibre 2.3g; Sodium 1394mg.

SUKIYAKI

FOR THIS CLASSIC JAPANESE DISH, YOU WILL NEED A SUKIYAKI PAN OR A SHALLOW CAST-IRON PAN,
AND A PORTABLE TABLE STOVE TO COOK THIS TRADITIONAL DISH OF BEEF AND VEGETABLES.

SERVES FOUR

INGREDIENTS

600g/1lb 5oz well-marbled beef
   sirloin, without bone, sliced into
   3mm/⅛in slices
15ml/1 tbsp sake
1 packet shirataki noodles, about
   200g/7oz, drained
2 large onions, cut into 8 slices
   lengthways
450g/1lb enokitake mushrooms,
   root part removed
12 shiitake mushrooms,
   stalks removed
10 spring onions (scallions), trimmed
   and quartered diagonally lengthways
300g/11oz shungiku, cut in half
   lengthways, or watercress
250–275g/9–10oz tofu, drained and
   cut into 8–12 large bitesize cubes
4–8 very fresh eggs, at room
   temperature
about 20g/¾oz beef fat
For the wari-shita sauce
75ml/5 tbsp second dashi stock, or
   the same amount of water and
   5ml/1 tsp dashi-no-moto
75ml/5 tbsp shoyu
120ml/4fl oz/½ cup mirin
15ml/1 tbsp sake
15ml/1 tbsp caster (superfine) sugar

1 Arrange the beef slices on a large serving plate. Sprinkle with the sake and leave to settle.

2 Par-boil the shirataki in rapidly boiling water for 2 minutes, then drain. Wash under cold running water and cut into 5cm/2in lengths. Drain well.

3 Mix all the ingredients for the wari-shita sauce in a small pan and place over a medium heat until the sugar has dissolved. Pour into a jug (pitcher) or bowl.

4 On a tray, arrange all the vegetables, shirataki and tofu. Break one egg into each of four small serving bowls. Take everything to the table.

5 Start cooking when the guests are seated at the table. Heat the pan on a table cooker until very hot, then reduce the heat to medium, and add some beef fat. When it has melted, add the spring onions and onion slices, then increase the heat. Stir-fry for 2 minutes, or until the onions become soft. The guests should now start to beat the egg in their bowls.

6 Add a quarter of the *wari-shita* sauce to the pan. When it starts to bubble, add about a quarter of the vegetables, tofu and shirataki. Place them side by side but do not mix them. Keep some space clear for the beef.

7 Cook one beef slice per guest at a time. Put four slices in the space you kept in the pan. As they change colour, remove them immediately from the pan and dip them into the beaten egg. Eat straight away. Cook the vegetables and other ingredients in the same way; they might take 10–15 minutes to cook. Add the remaining ingredients as you eat. Add more wari-shita sauce when it is reduced in the pan. Add another egg to the dipping bowls if required.

Per portion Energy 868kcal/3633kJ; Protein 71.5g; Carbohydrate 51.7g, of which sugars 11.1g; Fat 43.2g, of which saturates 13.1g; Cholesterol 662mg; Calcium 605mg; Fibre 6.5g; Sodium 1695mg.

GRIDDLED BEEF WITH SESAME AND SOY

BULGOGI IS ONE OF KOREA'S MOST POPULAR DISHES. THIN STRIPS OF SIRLOIN ARE MARINATED IN SESAME OIL AND SOY SAUCE, THEN GRILLED OVER A CHARCOAL BRAZIER. THE MEAT WITH ITS DELICIOUS GLAZE IS OFTEN ENJOYED WITH A PIQUANT DIPPING SAUCE OR WITH FRESH GREEN LEAVES.

2 Shred one of the spring onions and set aside for a garnish. Finely slice the remaining spring onions, the onion and pear. Combine all the marinade ingredients in a large bowl to form a paste, adding a little water if necessary.

3 Mix the beef in with the marinade, making sure that it is well coated. Leave in the refrigerator for at least 30 minutes or up to 2 hours (if left longer the meat will become too salty).

SERVES FOUR

INGREDIENTS
    800g/1¾lb sirloin steak
For the marinade
    4 spring onions (scallions)
    ½ onion
    1 Asian pear
    60ml/4 tbsp dark soy sauce
    60ml/4 tbsp sugar
    30ml/2 tbsp sesame oil
    10ml/2 tsp ground black pepper
    5ml/1 tsp sesame seeds
    2 garlic cloves, crushed
    15ml/1 tbsp lemonade

1 Finely slice the steak, and tenderize by bashing with a meat mallet or rolling pin for a few minutes. Then cut into bitesize strips.

4 Heat a griddle pan gently. Add the meat and cook over a medium heat. Once the meat is cooked through, transfer it to a large serving dish, garnish with the spring onion and serve.

Per portion Energy 330kcal/1382kJ; Protein 47.3g; Carbohydrate 8.2g, of which sugars 8.1g; Fat 12.1g, of which saturates 4.5g; Cholesterol 102mg; Calcium 22mg; Fibre 0.2g; Sodium 141mg.

GRILLED BEEF <u>IN</u> SWEET SOY MARINADE

DARK SOY SAUCE HAS A CHARACTERISTIC TASTE COMPLEMENTED BY THE REFINED SWEETNESS OF THE HONEY. MARINATING THE BEEF MAKES THE MEAT TENDER, AND ALSO CREATES A CRISPY COATING WHEN IT IS PAN-FRIED. THIS DISH CAN BE ACCOMPANIED BY RICE, FRESH VEGETABLES OR A CRISP SALAD.

SERVES TWO TO THREE

INGREDIENTS

200g/7oz sirloin or fillet steak

For the marinade

75ml/5 tbsp dark soy sauce

30ml/2 tbsp sesame oil

2 garlic cloves, crushed

15ml/1 tbsp honey

15ml/1 tbsp sesame seeds

vegetable oil, for cooking

1 spring onion (scallion), finely
   shredded, to garnish

1 Beat the steak gently on a board with a steak mallet or the bottom of a heavy pan until it is about 1cm/½in thick.

2 Combine the soy sauce, sesame oil, garlic and honey in a shallow bowl and stir in the sesame seeds until all the ingredients are thoroughly mixed.

3 Add the steak to the bowl with the soy and sesame mixture and turn it several times to ensure that it is well coated with the marinade and the sesame seeds. Cover and leave to marinate for an hour.

4 Heat a griddle pan or frying pan over a high heat, then add a little vegetable oil. Remove the beef from the marinade, allowing the excess to drip off, and lay it in the pan. Cook for 2–3 minutes on each side, until it is browned and only just cooked.

5 Transfer the steak to a serving dish, garnish with the spring onions and serve immediately.

Per portion Energy 264kcal/1095kJ; Protein 15.4g; Carbohydrate 2.1g, of which sugars 2g; Fat 21.6g, of which saturates 4.2g; Cholesterol 41mg; Calcium 39mg; Fibre 0.4g; Sodium 743mg.

BEEF AND MUSHROOM CASSEROLE

IN THIS PERFECT EXAMPLE OF A KOREAN CASSEROLE DISH, CALLED BEOSEOT CHUNGOL, A MEDLEY OF MUSHROOMS ARE SLOW COOKED WITH BEEF IN A SAUCE SEASONED WITH GARLIC AND SESAME. IDEAL AS A WINTER DISH, ITS EARTHY MUSHROOM FLAVOUR IS ENLIVENED WITH SPRING ONIONS AND CHILLIES.

SERVES TWO

INGREDIENTS
150g/5oz beef
2 dried shiitake mushrooms,
   soaked in warm water for
   about 30 minutes until softened
25g/1oz enoki mushrooms
1 onion, sliced
400ml/14fl oz/1⅔ cups water
   or beef stock
25g/1oz oyster mushrooms,
   thinly sliced
6 pine mushrooms, cut into
   thin strips
10 spring onions (scallions), sliced
2 chrysanthemum leaves
   or spinach, and ½ red and
   ½ green chilli, seeded
   and shredded, to garnish
steamed rice, to serve
For the seasoning
30ml/2 tbsp dark soy sauce
3 spring onions (scallions), sliced
2 garlic cloves, crushed
10ml/2 tsp sesame seeds
10ml/2 tsp sesame oil

VARIATION
You can choose to omit the beef
and add a selection of vegetables to
suit your taste to create a good
vegetarian alternative.

1 Slice the beef into thin strips and
place in a bowl. Add the seasoning
ingredients to the beef and mix together
well, making sure that you coat the beef
evenly. Leave to absorb the flavours for
20 minutes.

2 When the soaked shiitake
mushrooms have fully reconstituted
and become soft, drain and thinly slice
them, discarding the stems in the
process. Discard the caps from the
enoki mushrooms.

3 Place the seasoned beef and the
onion in a heavy pan or flameproof
casserole and then add the water or
beef stock.

4 Add all the mushrooms and the
spring onions to the beef mixture in
the pan, and then bring the mixture
to the boil.

5 Once the pan is bubbling reduce
the heat and simmer the mixture for a
further 20 minutes.

6 Transfer the contents of the pan to a
serving dish, or alternatively you can
serve the dish directly from the
casserole. Garnish the dish with the
chrysanthemum leaves or spinach, and
the shredded chilli, and then serve the
dish at the table accompanied by
steamed rice.

COOK'S TIPS
• Pine mushrooms can be difficult
to find; in this case other wild
mushrooms will also work well.
• Chrysanthemum leaves have a
distinctive flavour and a bright green
colour. The cooked greens have a dark
colour, a thick texture and a fragrant and
addictive texture.
• When preparing steamed rice, always
rinse the rice before cooking to get rid
of any impurities. You should also soak
the rice immediately after rinsing. If any
rice floats on the water, then discard
these grains.

VARIATIONS
• Although this recipe is designed to be
simmered to achieve a more delicate
taste, for a more traditional chungol
dish, serve the casserole as soon as it
has boiled to maintain the freshness of
the ingredients.
• If you can't find chrysanthemum
leaves, spinach leaves can be used as a
good substitute. The leaves are usually
blanched briefly to soften them, but
young leaves can be served raw.

Per portion Energy 227kcal/945kJ; Protein 21.1g; Carbohydrate 5.5g, of which sugars 4.4g; Fat 13.6g, of which saturates 3.9g; Cholesterol 44mg; Calcium 72mg; Fibre 2.4g; Sodium 1125mg.

BEEF RISSOLES

By combining the beef with a selection of distinctively Korean ingredients this recipe is full of rich and complex flavours. While the meat in the middle of the rissole remains succulent, pan-frying gives this hearty dish a lovely crisp coating.

3 Add the beef, leek, garlic, mushrooms, rice flakes, sesame oil, maple syrup and soy sauce to the onion. Knead the ingredients together by hand until they are thoroughly combined. Add as much stock as required to moisten and bind the ingredients, ensuring that the mixture remains firm and sticky.

4 Once the ingredients are combined, shape small handfuls of the mixture into small round patties.

5 Heat a frying pan over a medium heat and add a little vegetable oil. Add the patties and fry them, turning once, until they are golden brown on both sides and cooked through.

6 Drain the patties on kitchen paper and serve hot, garnished with the ground pine nuts.

COOK'S TIP
Glutinous rice flakes are available at Asian supermarkets but can be hard to track down. Roughly ground sticky rice makes a suitable alternative.

SERVES TWO TO THREE

INGREDIENTS
a little vegetable oil
½ small white onion, finely chopped
300g/11oz beef sirloin or rib, minced (ground)
1 thick slice leek, finely chopped
2 garlic cloves, crushed
40g/1½oz button (white) mushrooms, finely chopped
90ml/6 tbsp glutinous rice flakes
15ml/1 tbsp sesame oil
15ml/1 tbsp maple syrup
90ml/6 tbsp soy sauce
about 105ml/7 tbsp beef stock
15ml/1 tbsp pine nuts, to garnish

1 Grind the pine nuts with a mortar and pestle in preparation for the garnish.

2 Heat the vegetable oil in a pan or wok and cook the chopped onion gently until it browns. Transfer to a bowl.

Per portion Energy 419kcal/1743kJ; Protein 23.7g; Carbohydrate 32g, of which sugars 7.7g; Fat 22g, of which saturates 7.7g; Cholesterol 60mg; Calcium 41mg; Fibre 1.9g; Sodium 1164mg.

KNEADED SIRLOIN STEAK

THIS KOREAN RECIPE RELIES ON THE FLAVOUR OF HIGH-QUALITY SIRLOIN STEAK. KNEADING THE MEAT WITH SALT MAKES IT DELICIOUSLY TENDER. ACCOMPANIED BY A BOWL OF SOUP, THE SMOKY AROMA AND GRILLED TASTE OF THIS DISH ARE WITHOUT EQUAL.

SERVES FOUR

INGREDIENTS
 450g/1lb beef sirloin
 2 round (butterhead) lettuces
For the marinade
 8 garlic cloves, chopped
 75g/3oz oyster mushrooms, sliced
 3 spring onions (scallions),
  finely chopped
 20ml/4 tsp mirin or rice wine
 10ml/2 tsp salt
 salt and ground black pepper
For the spring onion mixture
 8 shredded spring onions
  (scallions)
 20ml/4 tsp rice vinegar
 20ml/4 tsp Korean chilli powder
 2 tsp sugar
 10ml/2 tsp sesame oil

1 Slice the beef into bitesize strips and place in a bowl. Add the garlic, mushrooms and spring onions. Pour in the mirin or rice wine and add the salt and several twists of black pepper.

2 Mix the marinade together, evenly coating the beef. Knead the meat well to tenderize. Chill, and leave for 2 hours.

3 Mix the spring onion mixture ingredients together. Remove the outer leaves from the lettuce and rinse well.

4 Place a griddle pan over a medium heat and add the beef. Cook until the meat has darkened. Wrap the meat in a lettuce leaf with a pinch of the spring onion mixture and serve.

Per portion Energy 188kcal/786kJ; Protein 27.6g; Carbohydrate 4g, of which sugars 3.9g; Fat 6.9g, of which saturates 2.6g; Cholesterol 57mg; Calcium 26mg; Fibre 0.9g; Sodium 83mg.

BEEF VEGETABLE RICE WITH QUAIL'S EGGS

In this Korean dish, called bibimbap, vegetables garnish a bed of pearly steamed rice, which is then seasoned with sesame and soy sauce. Lightly browned beef is added and the dish is topped with a fried quail's egg and a scoop of gochujang chilli paste.

SERVES FOUR

INGREDIENTS
    400g/14oz/2 cups short grain
        rice or pudding rice, rinsed
    a drop of sunflower oil
    1 sheet dried seaweed
    4 quail's eggs
    vegetable oil, for shallow-frying
    sesame seeds, to garnish
For the marinade
    30ml/2 tbsp dark soy sauce
    15ml/1 tbsp garlic, crushed
    15ml/1 tbsp sliced spring
        onions (scallions)
    5ml/1 tsp sesame oil
    5ml/1 tsp rice wine
    200g/7oz beef, shredded
    10ml/2 tsp vegetable oil
    salt and ground black pepper
For the namul vegetables
    150g/5oz white radish, peeled
    1 courgette (zucchini)
    2 carrots
    150g/5oz/generous ½ cup soya
        beansprouts, trimmed
    150g/5oz fern fronds (optional)
    6 dried shiitake mushrooms,
        soaked in warm water for about
        30 minutes until softened
    ½ cucumber
For the namul seasoning
    10ml/2 tsp sugar
    17.5ml/3½ tsp salt
    35ml/2½ tbsp sesame oil
    7.5ml/1½ tsp crushed garlic
    a splash of dark soy sauce
    1.5ml/¼ tsp chilli powder
    5ml/1 tsp sesame seeds
    vegetable oil, for stir-frying
For the gochujang sauce
    45ml/3 tbsp gochujang chilli paste
    7.5ml/1½ tsp sugar or honey
    10ml/2 tsp sesame oil

1 Place the rice in a pan and add water to 5mm/¼in above the rice. Add the sunflower oil, cover and bring to the boil. Lower the heat and simmer. Do not remove the lid. After 12–15 minutes turn off the heat and steam for 5 minutes.

2 For the marinade, blend the soy sauce, garlic, spring onions, sesame oil, rice wine, and salt and pepper. Add the beef, mix and marinate for 1 hour. Roll up the seaweed and slice into thin strips.

3 Mix the ingredients for the gochujang sauce and place them in a serving bowl. Cut the white radish, courgette and carrots into thin strips.

4 Blend 5ml/1 tsp sugar, 5ml/1 tsp salt and 5ml/1 tsp sesame oil, with 2.5ml/½ tsp crushed garlic, and coat the radish strips. Flash fry. Repeat with the carrots.

5 Blend 5ml/1 tsp salt and 5ml/1 tsp sesame oil with 2.5ml/½ tsp crushed garlic and a little water. Coat the courgette.

6 Heat 5ml/1 tsp vegetable oil in a wok and flash fry the courgette until soft.

7 Briefly cook the soya beansprouts in boiling water. Mix 15ml/1 tbsp sesame oil with 2.5ml/½ tsp salt, 1.5ml/¼ tsp chilli powder and 2.5ml/½ tsp sesame seeds. Sweeten with a pinch of sugar and use to coat the soya beansprouts.

8 Drain and slice the shiitake mushrooms, discarding the stems. Quickly stir-fry in 5ml/1 tsp vegetable oil and season with a pinch of salt. Transfer to the plate.

9 Seed the cucumber, cut into thin strips and transfer to the plate.

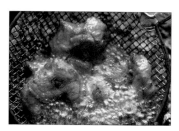

10 Heat 10ml/2 tsp vegetable oil in the wok and stir-fry the beef until tender and golden brown.

11 Divide the rice among four bowls and arrange the namul vegetables and beef on top. Fry the quail's eggs, and place one in the centre of each bowl. Garnish with a sprinkling of sesame seeds and ribbons of dried seaweed. Serve with the gochujang sauce.

Per portion Energy 645kcal/2688kJ; Protein 23.7g; Carbohydrate 88.5g, of which sugars 7.7g; Fat 21.4g, of which saturates 4.4g; Cholesterol 86mg; Calcium 73mg; Fibre 2.3g; Sodium 1781mg.

SALADS, TOFU & KIMCHI

Salads, both with and without meat, are made of ingredients that include green leaves, white cabbage, seaweed and spinach, and tofu is a versatile soya beancurd used mainly for a variety of classic pan-fried, stewed or blanched dishes. Of course, no Korean meal is complete without the national dish of kimchi — a dish of notable flavour with the fiery kick of red chilli.

Left: Pak Choi Kimchi; **Above:** Stuffed Pan-fried Tofu

BAMBOO SHOOT SALAD <u>WITH</u> PERSIMMON

CRUNCHY BAMBOO COMBINES PERFECTLY WITH SEASONED BEEF AND PERSIMMON AND ADDS AN APPETIZING SWEETNESS TO THIS POPULAR KOREAN DISH. THE COMBINATION OF THE FRESH, PEPPERY WATERCRESS AND CRISP BEANSPROUTS MAKE THIS INTO AN UNMISSABLE SALAD.

3 Heat 15ml/1 tbsp of the vegetable oil in a frying pan over a medium heat. Stir-fry the beef and mushrooms until cooked, then remove from the pan and chill.

4 Trim the beansprouts and blanch gently in boiling water for 3 minutes. Drain. Blanch the bamboo shoots for about 3 minutes. Drain.

5 In a bowl combine all the dressing ingredients and mix well. Set aside.

6 Beat the egg and coat a frying pan with the remaining vegetable oil over a medium heat. Add the beaten egg and make a thin omelette, browning each side. Remove and cut into thin strips.

7 Serve the beef with the bamboo shoots, watercress and beansprouts, garnished with chilli and egg strips.

SERVES ONE TO TWO

INGREDIENTS
200g/7oz bamboo shoots
2 dried shiitake mushrooms, soaked
  in warm water for about 30 minutes
  until softened
50g/2oz beef flank, thinly sliced
25ml/1½ tbsp vegetable oil
90g/3½oz/scant ½ cup
  beansprouts
1 egg
90g/3½oz watercress or
  rocket (arugula)
salt
½ red chilli, seeded and thinly
  sliced, to garnish

For the seasoning
  7.5ml/1½ tsp dark soy sauce
  10g/¼oz red persimmon, finely
    chopped
  ½ spring onion (scallion), finely
    chopped
  1 garlic clove, crushed
  5ml/1 tsp sesame seeds
  2.5ml/½ tsp sesame oil
  ground white pepper
For the dressing
  60ml/4 tbsp dark soy sauce
  60ml/4 tbsp water
  30ml/2 tbsp rice vinegar
  40g/1½oz red persimmon, finely
    chopped
  5ml/1 tsp sesame seeds

1 Thinly slice the bamboo shoots and cut into bitesize pieces. When the soaked shiitake mushrooms have become soft, drain and thinly slice them, discarding the tough stems.

2 Put the beef slices in a bowl. Add the seasoning ingredients and the drained shiitake mushrooms, and mix together well, so that the meat is thoroughly coated in the seasoning.

Per portion Energy 268kcal/1115kJ; Protein 17g; Carbohydrate 9.1g, of which sugars 6.1g; Fat 18.6g, of which saturates 3.6g; Cholesterol 119mg; Calcium 164mg; Fibre 3.5g; Sodium 2489mg.

ASSORTED SEAWEED SALAD

KAISOU SALADA IS A FINE EXAMPLE OF THE TRADITIONAL JAPANESE IDEA OF EATING: LOOK AFTER YOUR APPETITE AND YOUR HEALTH AT THE SAME TIME. SEAWEED IS A NUTRITIOUS, ALKALINE FOOD AND RICH IN FIBRE. MOREOVER, IT HAS VIRTUALLY NO CALORIES!

SERVES FOUR

INGREDIENTS
5g/⅛oz each dried wakame, dried
arame and dried hijiki seaweeds
about 130g/4½oz enokitake
mushrooms
2 spring onions (scallions)
a few ice cubes
½ cucumber, cut lengthways
250g/9oz mixed salad leaves
For the marinade
15ml/1 tbsp rice vinegar
6.5ml/1¼ tsp salt
For the dressing
60ml/4 tbsp rice vinegar
7.5ml/1½ tsp toasted sesame oil
15ml/1 tbsp shoyu
15ml/1 tbsp second dashi stock, or
the same amount of water with a
pinch of dashi-no-moto
2.5cm/1in piece fresh root ginger,
finely grated

1 Soak the wakame for 10 minutes in one bowl of water and, in a separate bowl of water, soak the arame and hijiki for 30 minutes together.

2 Trim the hard end of the enokitake stalks, then cut the bunch in half and separate the stems.

3 Cut the spring onions into thin, 4cm/1½in long strips, then soak the strips in cold water with a few ice cubes to make them curl up. Drain. Slice the cucumber into thin, half-moon shapes.

4 Cook the wakame and enokitake in boiling water for 2 minutes, then add the arame and hijiki for a few seconds. Immediately remove from the heat. Drain and sprinkle over the vinegar and salt while still warm. Chill.

5 Mix the dressing ingredients in a bowl. Arrange the mixed salad leaves in a large bowl with the cucumber on top, then add the seaweed and enokitake mixture. Decorate with spring onion strips and serve with the dressing.

Per portion Energy 36kcal/149kJ; Protein 2.2g; Carbohydrate 2.4g, of which sugars 2.3g; Fat 2g, of which saturates 0.3g; Cholesterol 0mg; Calcium 69mg; Fibre 1.7g; Sodium 307mg.

SPINACH KIMCHI SALAD

This appetising summer salad is simple to make and is a perfect accompaniment for any noodle dish. While the ingredients for the dressing are the same as for traditional kimchi, this is not preserved and so the taste is lighter.

2 Place the rice in a medium pan. Add 50ml/2fl oz/¼ cup water and bring to the boil over a high heat. Reduce the heat, part cover the pan and simmer for about 20 minutes, until the liquid turns milky. Add the chilli powder, spring onions, anchovy sauce and green and red chillies. Mix thoroughly and remove from the heat. Then add the garlic and the ginger.

3 Toss the leek and onions with the spinach in a large serving dish. Pour over the dressing and toss the salad. Serve immediately.

SERVES TWO TO THREE

INGREDIENTS
    500g/1¼lb spinach
    1 leek, finely sliced
    2 mild onions, finely sliced
For the dressing
    15ml/1 tbsp glutinous rice
    90ml/6 tbsp Korean chilli powder
      (40g/1½oz in weight)
    8 spring onions, finely sliced
    30ml/2 tbsp anchovy sauce
    1 green chilli, seeded and
      finely chopped
    1 red chilli, seeded and finely chopped
    3 garlic cloves, crushed
    5ml/1 tsp grated fresh root ginger

1 Trim off any tough stems from the spinach with a sharp knife and then slice the leaves into large pieces. Rinse the spinach leaves under cold running water. Drain them well and then set aside.

Per portion Energy 112kcal/468kJ; Protein 10.8g; Carbohydrate 9.7g, of which sugars 5g; Fat 3.4g, of which saturates 0.5g; Cholesterol 8mg; Calcium 405mg; Fibre 5.9g; Sodium 807mg.

WHITE CABBAGE SALAD <u>IN</u> KIMCHI DRESSING

THE WHITE CABBAGE USED HERE HAS A NATURAL SWEETNESS AND DELICIOUS CRISP TEXTURE WHICH IS COMPLEMENTED BY THE SPICINESS OF A TRADITIONAL KIMCHI DRESSING. THIS SALAD IS A QUICK, REVITALIZING DISH TO ENJOY YEAR ROUND AS A SIDE SERVING OR LIGHT LUNCH.

SERVES FOUR

INGREDIENTS
1 Chinese leaves (Chinese
  cabbage)
25g/1oz/2 tbsp salt
10g/¼oz/2½ tsp short grain rice
  or pudding rice
2 leeks, finely sliced
1 white onion, finely sliced
115g/4oz spring onions (scallions),
  roughly chopped
15ml/1 tbsp sesame seeds
For the dressing
50g/2oz Korean chilli powder
½ white onion, finely grated
15ml/1 tbsp fermented shrimps,
  finely chopped
30ml/2 tbsp anchovy sauce
2 garlic cloves, crushed
7.5ml/1½ tsp grated fresh
  root ginger

COOK'S TIP
The kimchi dressing adds a spicy heat to
a cool salad, making this a perfect
summer dish.

VARIATION
Adapt the kimchi dressing by serving it
with chunky noodles that have been
cooked lightly in butter, spiked with
salty fish and blanketed with the
fiery dressing.

1 Cut the Chinese leaves lengthways
into quarters. Place in a bowl and
sprinkle with the salt. Leave to stand for
30 minutes and then drain off any
liquid that has collected in the bowl.

2 Place the rice in a small pan with
50ml/2fl oz/¼ cup water and simmer
over a low heat, stirring gently, until the
grains break down to give a smooth,
milky mixture.

3 For the dressing, mix the chilli
powder, onion, shrimps, anchovy sauce,
garlic and ginger in a bowl, then add
the milky cooked rice. Stir gently to
combine the flavours.

4 Slice off the core from the Chinese
leaves and separate the leaves. Place
the leaves in a large bowl.

5 Add the leeks, white onion and
spring onions to the bowl, and pour
over the dressing. Mix thoroughly so
that the leaves are well coated with
the dressing. Garnish with sesame
seeds and serve.

Per portion Energy 90kcal/377kJ; Protein 5.8g; Carbohydrate 9.2g, of which sugars 5.2g; Fat 3.5g, of which saturates 0.6g; Cholesterol 19mg; Calcium 134mg; Fibre 3.8g; Sodium 169mg.

GREEN LEAF SALAD IN CHILLI DRESSING

SERVED AS AN ACCOMPANIMENT TO GRILLED SEAFOOD, THE KOREAN SANGCHI IN THIS RECIPE ADDS A HINT OF BITTERNESS WHILE THE SPICINESS OF THE DRESSING GIVES A REFRESHING EDGE. A VARIETY OF GREEN SALAD LEAVES CAN BE USED IN THIS RECIPE, HOWEVER, DEPENDING ON WHAT IS IN SEASON.

SERVES TWO TO THREE

INGREDIENTS
    250g/9oz green salad leaves or
      Korean sangchi
    115g/4oz leeks, finely sliced
    1 white onion, finely sliced
    2 green chillies, seeded and
      finely sliced
    1 red chilli, seeded and finely sliced
    15ml/1 tbsp sesame seeds,
      to garnish
For the dressing
    5ml/1 tsp pine nuts, ground
    15ml/1 tbsp Korean chilli powder
    5ml/1 tsp sesame oil
    1 garlic clove, crushed
    30ml/2 tbsp light soy sauce
    30ml/2 tbsp fish stock or water

1 Tear the leaves or sangchi into bitesize pieces. Mix the leeks, onion and green and red chillies.

2 For the salad dressing, mix the pine nuts with the chilli powder, sesame oil, garlic, soy sauce and stock or water in a bowl.

3 Stir the dressing gently, allowing the flavours to mingle, and then add the chillies, onion and leeks.

4 Place the green leaves or *sangchi* in a salad bowl and pour over the dressing. Toss the salad, garnish with sesame seeds and serve.

Per portion Energy 54kcal/224kJ; Protein 2.5g; Carbohydrate 4.1g, of which sugars 4g; Fat 3.2g, of which saturates 0.4g; Cholesterol 0mg; Calcium 58mg; Fibre 1.7g; Sodium 719mg.

CHINESE CHIVE AND ONION SALAD

THIS LIVELY KOREAN SALAD IS A COMBINATION OF CRUNCHY SALAD LEAVES AND CABBAGE WITH A CHILLI POWDER AND SOY DRESSING. IT IS DELICIOUS SERVED ON ITS OWN AS A VEGETABLE DISH OR AS A REFRESHING ACCOMPANIMENT TO GRILLED MEAT OR SEAFOOD.

SERVES TWO TO THREE

INGREDIENTS
   50g/2oz Chinese chives
   1 thin wedge Chinese leaves (Chinese
      cabbage), finely sliced
   1 thin slice red cabbage, finely sliced
   ¼ white onion, finely sliced
For the dressing
   15ml/1 tbsp soy sauce
   7.5ml/1½ tbsp Korean chilli powder
   7.5ml/1½ tbsp sesame seeds
   7.5ml/1½ tbsp sesame oil
   5ml/1 tsp cider vinegar
   5ml/1 tsp lemon juice
   5ml/1 tsp sugar
   1 garlic clove, crushed

1 Trim both ends off the Chinese chives and cut them into 5cm/2in long pieces.

2 Soak the onion, and the red cabbage and Chinese leaves, separately in two bowls of iced water for about 5 minutes, to soften the flavour of the cabbage.

3 Drain the onion and cabbage, then combine them with the chives in a serving dish and mix thoroughly.

4 For the dressing, combine the soy sauce, chilli powder, sesame seeds and oil, vinegar, lemon juice, sugar and garlic in a bowl. Mix the ingredients.

5 Drizzle the dressing over the chive mixture and serve.

Per portion Energy 47kcal/197kJ; Protein 1.7g; Carbohydrate 6.2g, of which sugars 5.7g; Fat 1.9g, of which saturates 0.3g; Cholesterol 0mg; Calcium 53mg; Fibre 1.8g; Sodium 362mg.

BLANCHED TOFU ^{WITH} SOY DRESSING

THE SILKY CONSISTENCY OF THE TOFU ABSORBS THE DARK SMOKY TASTE OF THE SOY DRESSING IN THIS RICH AND FLAVOURFUL KOREAN DISH. TOFU HAS A NUTTY QUALITY THAT BLENDS AGREEABLY WITH THE SALTY SWEETNESS OF THE SOY SAUCE AND THE HINTS OF GARLIC AND SPRING ONION.

SERVES TWO

INGREDIENTS
    2 blocks firm tofu
    salt
For the dressing
    10ml/2 tsp finely sliced spring
      onion (scallion)
    5ml/1 tsp finely chopped
      garlic
    60ml/4 tbsp dark soy sauce
    10ml/2 tsp chilli powder
    5ml/1 tsp sugar
    10ml/2 tsp sesame seeds

1 Mix the spring onion and garlic with the soy sauce, chilli powder, sugar and sesame seeds. Leave to stand for a few minutes.

2 Meanwhile, bring a large pan of water to the boil, and add a pinch of salt. Place the whole blocks of tofu in the water, being careful not to let them break apart.

3 Blanch the tofu for 3 minutes. Remove and place on kitchen paper to remove any excess water.

4 Transfer the tofu to a plate, and cover with the dressing. Serve, slicing the tofu as desired.

COOK'S TIP
Koreans traditionally eat this dish without slicing the tofu, preferring instead to either eat it directly with a spoon or pick it apart with chopsticks. It may be easier, however, to slice it in advance if you are serving it as an accompanying dish.

Per portion Energy 160kcal/669kJ; Protein 16.1g; Carbohydrate 6.7g, of which sugars 5.6g; Fat 7.8g, of which saturates 0.9g; Cholesterol 0mg; Calcium 954mg; Fibre 0.1g; Sodium 2144mg.

STUFFED PAN-FRIED TOFU

AN EASY ACCOMPANIMENT FOR A MAIN COURSE, OR A GREAT APPETIZER. SQUARES OF FRIED TOFU STUFFED WITH A BLEND OF CHILLI AND CHESTNUT GIVE A PIQUANT JOLT TO THE DELICATE FLAVOUR. THE TOFU HAS A CRISPY COATING, SURROUNDING A CREAMY TEXTURE, WITH A CRUNCHY FILLING.

SERVES TWO

INGREDIENTS
    2 blocks firm tofu
    30ml/2 tbsp Thai fish sauce
    5ml/1 tsp sesame oil
    2 eggs
    7.5ml/1½ tsp cornflour
      (cornstarch)
    vegetable oil, for shallow-frying
For the filling
    2 green chillies, finely chopped
    2 chestnuts, finely chopped
    6 garlic cloves, crushed
    10ml/2 tsp sesame seeds

1 Cut the two blocks of tofu into 2cm/¾in slices and then cut each slice in half. Place the tofu slices on pieces of kitchen paper to blot and absorb any excess water.

2 Mix together the Thai fish sauce and sesame oil. Transfer the tofu slices to a plate and coat them with the fish sauce mixture. Leave to marinate for 20 minutes. Meanwhile, put all the filling ingredients into a bowl and combine them thoroughly. Set aside.

3 Beat the eggs in a shallow dish. Add the cornflour and whisk until well combined. Take the slices of tofu and dip them into the beaten egg mixture, ensuring an even coating on all sides.

VARIATION
Alternatively, you can serve the tofu with a light soy dip instead of the spicy filling.

4 Place a frying pan or wok over a medium heat and add the vegetable oil. Add the tofu slices to the pan and sauté, turning over once, until they are golden brown.

5 Once cooked, make a slit down the middle of each slice with a sharp knife, without cutting all the way through. Gently stuff a large pinch of the filling into each slice, and serve.

Per portion Energy 291kcal/1213kJ; Protein 23g; Carbohydrate 7.8g, of which sugars 1.3g; Fat 19.1g, of which saturates 3.4g; Cholesterol 209mg; Calcium 1014mg; Fibre 0.8g; Sodium 88mg.

VEGETABLE <u>AND</u> TOFU CAKE <u>WITH</u> MUSTARD DIP

This Korean dish is filled with a mouthwatering blend of tastes and textures, yet is remarkably simple to prepare. The contrast between the delicate texture of the tofu and the crunchiness of the mangetouts is delightful, and the sesame seeds add a hint of nuttiness. Eaten with the mustard dip, it is perfect as a snack or as a side dish.

SERVES TWO

INGREDIENTS
1 block firm tofu
1 carrot, finely chopped
115g/4oz mangetouts (snow peas), sliced
3 eggs
5ml/1 tsp sake or mirin
10ml/2 tsp salt
5ml/1 tsp grated fresh root ginger
5ml/1 tsp sesame oil
5ml/1 tsp sesame seeds
ground black pepper
vegetable oil, for greasing mould
For the mustard dip
45ml/3 tbsp Dijon mustard
15ml/1 tbsp sugar syrup (see below)
7.5ml/1½ tsp soy sauce
30ml/2 tbsp rice vinegar
salt
To make sugar syrup
1 part white sugar to 2 parts water (see cook's tip)

1 Bring a large pan of salted water to the boil. Add the block of tofu and then bring it back to the boil.

2 Use a large fish slice, metal spatula, or sieve (strainer) to remove and drain the tofu from the pan.

3 Crumble the block of tofu on to a piece of muslin (cheesecloth), and then squeeze it to drain off any excess water.

4 Bring a fresh batch of water to the boil and blanch the carrot for 1 minute.

5 Add the mangetouts, bring back to the boil and then drain the vegetables. The vegetables should be slightly cooked but retain their crunchy texture.

6 Beat the eggs and sake or mirin together briefly, then add them to the crumbled tofu.

7 Mix in the mangetouts and carrots, ginger, sesame oil and sesame seeds. Season with a little black pepper and mix well.

8 Grease a 18cm/7in mould with a little oil. Pour the mixture into the mould and place in a steamer. Lay a piece of foil over the top of the mould, to keep steam out and steam over boiling water for 20 minutes, until the mixture is set and firm.

9 Meanwhile, for the dip, mix the mustard, syrup, soy sauce and vinegar. Season with a little salt. Mix thoroughly and pour into two small serving bowls.

10 Slide a metal spatula or palette knife between the tofu and the mould. Cover with a serving plate and then invert mould and plate. Remove the mould and serve the tofu sliced, with the dipping sauce.

COOK'S TIP
To make sugar syrup, dissolve 1 part white sugar in 2 parts water over a low heat.

Stir until the sugar has dissolved, then bring to the boil for 1 minute. Remove from the heat and leave to cool. Store the syrup in a screw-top jar in the refrigerator for up to 2 weeks. You can also freeze it in ice cube trays.

Per portion Energy 320kcal/1334kJ; Protein 23g; Carbohydrate 16.4g, of which sugars 14.9g; Fat 18.7g, of which saturates 3.7g; Cholesterol 285mg; Calcium 662mg; Fibre 3.8g; Sodium 657mg.

SIMMERED TOFU <u>WITH</u> VEGETABLES

A TYPICAL JAPANESE DINNER AT HOME CONSISTS OF A SOUP, THREE DIFFERENT DISHES AND A BOWL OF RICE. ONE OF THE THREE DISHES IS ALWAYS A SIMMERED ONE LIKE THIS.

SERVES FOUR

INGREDIENTS

4 dried shiitake mushrooms
450g/1lb daikon
2 atsu-age, about 200g/7oz each
115g/4oz/¾ cup green beans,
  trimmed and cut in half
5ml/1 tsp rice (any except for
  fragrant Thai or white basmati)
115g/4oz carrot, peeled and cut into
  1cm/½in thick slices
300g/11oz baby potatoes, unpeeled
750ml/1¼ pints/3 cups second dashi
  stock, or the same amount of water
  and 7.5ml/1½ tsp dashi-no-moto
30ml/2 tbsp caster (superfine) sugar
75ml/5 tbsp shoyu
45ml/3 tbsp sake
15ml/1 tbsp mirin

1 Soak the dried shiitake in 250ml/ 8fl oz/1 cup water for 2 hours. Drain and discard the liquid. Remove and discard the stalks.

2 Peel the daikon and slice into 1cm/½in discs. Shave the edge of the daikon discs to ensure they are evenly cooked. Plunge into cold water.

3 Put the atsu-age in a sieve (strainer), and wash off the excess oil with hot water from the kettle. Drain and cut into pieces of about 2.5 × 5cm/1 × 2in.

4 Boil the green beans for 2 minutes and then drain them, cooling them under running water.

5 Cover the daikon with water in a pan and add the rice. Bring to the boil then reduce the heat to medium-low. Cook for 15 minutes, then drain. Discard the rice.

6 Put the atsu-age and the mushrooms, carrot and potatoes into the pan with the daikon. Add the dashi stock, bring to the boil, then reduce the heat to low. Regularly skim off any scum that comes to the surface. Add the sugar, shoyu and sake, gently shaking the pan to mix the ingredients thoroughly.

7 Cut baking parchment into a circle 1cm/½in smaller than the pan lid. Place the paper inside the pan to seal the ingredients. Cover with the lid and simmer for 30 minutes, or until the sauce has reduced by at least a half. Add the green beans for 2 minutes so that they just warm through.

8 Remove the paper and add the mirin. Taste the sauce and adjust with shoyu if required. Remove from the heat.

9 Arrange the ingredients attractively in groups on a large serving plate. Pour over a little sauce, and serve warm or cold.

Per portion Energy 142kcal/597kJ; Protein 4.2g; Carbohydrate 27.6g, of which sugars 15.1g; Fat 0.9g, of which saturates 0.3g; Cholesterol 0mg; Calcium 92mg; Fibre 3.3g; Sodium 1406mg.

BRAISED TOFU

THE INGREDIENTS IN THE SAUCE PROVIDE A RANGE OF TASTES: SWEET, SALTY, NUTTY AND SPICY, AND REDUCING THE SAUCE DURING COOKING FORMS A IRRESISTIBLE STICKY GLAZE FOR THE CUBED TOFU.

SERVES TWO TO THREE

INGREDIENTS

   1 block firm tofu, diced
   250ml/8fl oz/1 cup anchovy
     or seafood stock
   45ml/3 tbsp soy sauce
   1 sheet dried kelp, chopped
   15ml/1 tbsp honey
   1 garlic clove, crushed
   ½ white onion, finely chopped
   1 green chilli, seeded
     and sliced
   1 red chilli, seeded and sliced
   15ml/1 tbsp Korean chilli powder
   5ml/1 tsp sesame seeds, to
     garnish

1 Cut the tofu into 1cm/½in cubes and place in a pan. Add 250ml/8fl oz/1 cup cold water, the anchovy or seafood stock, soy sauce and kelp.

2 Stir in the honey and garlic, then bring to the boil. Cover and boil for 5 minutes.

3 Add the onion, chillies and chilli powder. Reduce the heat and simmer, uncovered, for a further 10 minutes, until the liquid has reduced to a small amount of sauce.

4 Transfer to a serving dish and garnish with sesame seeds.

Per portion Energy 118kcal/490kJ; Protein 8.2g; Carbohydrate 14g, of which sugars 8.8g; Fat 3.7g, of which saturates 0.4g; Cholesterol 0mg; Calcium 385mg; Fibre 1.9g; Sodium 1076mg.

CLASSIC CABBAGE KIMCHI

MADE WITH CHINESE LEAVES, THIS IS THE CLASSIC VARIETY OF KIMCHI AND THE ONE MOST LIKELY TO BE FOUND AT ANY MEAL. THE SPICINESS OF THE CHILLI CONTRASTS WITH THE FISH SAUCE AND A HINT OF TANGY SPRING ONION. THIS DISH TAKES A MINIMUM OF TWO DAYS TO PREPARE.

SERVES TEN

INGREDIENTS
1 head Chinese leaves (Chinese cabbage), about 2kg/4¹/₂lb
salt
For the marinade
50g/2oz/¹/₄ cup coarse sea salt
75ml/5 tbsp water
30ml/2 tbsp table salt
For the seasoning
2 oysters (optional)
¹/₂ Chinese white radish, about 500g/1¹/₄lb, peeled and thinly sliced
25g/1oz Korean chives
25g/1oz minari, watercress or rocket (arugula)
5 garlic cloves
15g/¹/₂oz fresh root ginger, peeled
¹/₂ onion
¹/₂ Asian pear, or ¹/₂ kiwi fruit
1 chestnut, sliced
3 spring onions (scallions), sliced
50g/2oz/¹/₄ cup Korean chilli powder
120ml/4fl oz/¹/₂ cup Thai fish sauce
5ml/1 tsp sugar
1 red chilli, sliced

1 Make a deep cut across the base of the head of Chinese leaves and split it in two. Repeat this with the two halves, splitting them into quarters. Then place the quartered head in a bowl and cover it with water, adding 30ml/2 tbsp salt. Leave the quarters to soak for around 2 hours.

2 Drain the cabbage and sprinkle with the sea salt for the marinade, making sure to coat between the leaves. Leave to stand for 4 hours.

3 Hold an oyster with the rounded shell up. Push the tip of a short-bladed knife into the hinge and twist to prise the shell open.

4 Cut the muscles of the oyster inside. Run the blade between the shells to open them. Cut the oyster away from the flat shell. Repeat with the other oyster. Season with a pinch of salt.

5 Cut the radish slices into fine strips. Cut the chives and minari, watercress or rocket into 5cm/2in lengths. Finely chop the garlic, ginger, onion and Asian pear or kiwi fruit. Combine the seasoning ingredients with 120ml/4fl oz/¹/₂ cup water.

6 Rinse the softened quarters of Chinese leaves in cold running water. Place in a large bowl and coat with the seasoning mixture, ensuring that the mixture gets between the leaves and that no leaf is left uncovered.

7 The outermost leaf of each quarter of cabbage will have softened. This can be wrapped tightly around the other leaves to help the seasoning permeate throughout the whole.

8 Place the Chinese leaves in an airtight container. Leave to stand at room temperature for 5 hours, then leave in the refrigerator for 24 hours.

COOK'S TIP
Kimchi can be stored for up to 5 months in the refrigerator. The flavour may, by then, be too pungent for the vegetable pickle to be eaten raw, but at this stage it can be used to flavour cooked dishes. If the kimchi is to be stored for a long period, use a covered container and wash it well with sterilizing fluid.

Per portion Energy 73kcal/303kJ; Protein 3.6g; Carbohydrate 13.5g, of which sugars 12.9g; Fat 0.6g, of which saturates 0.1g; Cholesterol 0mg; Calcium 121mg; Fibre 5.1g; Sodium 383mg.

WHITE KIMCHI

This stuffed cabbage version may be more time-consuming and ambitious to prepare than most kimchi, but it is nevertheless a firm favourite. With an elegant appearance and a subtle refined flavour, this dish is regarded as a luxurious accompaniment to any meal.

3 For the stuffing, mix the red and green chillies, radish, spring onions, ginger, red dates and watercress in a bowl. Add the fermented shrimps, sugar and garlic. Then mix all the ingredients until they are thoroughly combined.

4 Rinse the cabbage and drain the leaves. Push the stuffing mixture in between the leaves, then place the stuffed halves into a bowl and pour over the kelp stock. Leave the cabbage to soak for a day at room temperature.

5 Remove the cabbage from the stock and slice each piece lengthways into quarters. Transfer to a bowl, cover and chill lightly. Garnish with pine nuts before serving.

SERVES FOUR

INGREDIENTS
1 white cabbage (Chinese cabbage)
100g/3³/₄oz salt
1 sheet dried kelp
¹/₂ white onion, finely grated or puréed
1 apple, thinly sliced
1 Asian pear, thinly sliced
1 red date, thinly sliced
20g/³/₄oz/2 tbsp pine nuts, ground
For the stuffing
  2 red chillies, seeded and sliced
  2 green chillies, seeded and sliced
  200g/7oz Chinese white radish,
    peeled and finely sliced
  50g/2oz spring onions (scallions),
    roughly chopped
  15ml/1 tbsp grated fresh root ginger
  2 red dates, seeded and sliced
  40g/1¹/₂oz watercress or Korean
    minari, roughly chopped
  15ml/1 tbsp fermented shrimps,
    finely chopped
  scant 5ml/1 tsp sugar
  5 garlic cloves, crushed

1 Cut the cabbage in half lengthways and place on a large dish. Sprinkle the salt over the cut surface. Spray the cabbage with water, then leave for 5 hours until the leaves have softened and lost their crispness.

2 Meanwhile bring 2.5 litres/4 pints/ 10 cups water to the boil in a pan and add the kelp. Reduce the heat slightly and simmer for 10 minutes, then strain the stock into a bowl and set it aside. Stir the onion, apple, Asian pear, red date and a pinch of salt into the kelp stock.

Per portion Energy 107kcal/446kJ; Protein 4.3g; Carbohydrate 13.8g, of which sugars 13.1g; Fat 4g, of which saturates 0.3g; Cholesterol 0mg; Calcium 122mg; Fibre 5.2g; Sodium 384mg.

DICED WHITE RADISH KIMCHI

WHITE RADISH KIMCHI IS TRADITIONALLY EATEN AS THE AUTUMN EVENINGS START TO DRAW IN, AS IT HAS A SPICINESS THAT FORTIFIES AGAINST THE COLD. THE PUNGENT AROMAS AND TANGY FLAVOURS MAKE THIS ONE OF THE MOST POPULAR VARIETIES OF KIMCHI.

SERVES FOUR

INGREDIENTS
  1.5kg/3¹/₂lb Chinese white
    radish, peeled
  225g/8oz/2 cups coarse
    sea salt
For the seasoning
  5ml/1 tsp sugar
  75ml/5 tbsp Korean chilli powder
  1 garlic clove, crushed
  ¹/₂ onion, finely chopped
  3 spring onions (scallions),
    finely sliced
  15ml/1 tbsp sea salt
  5ml/1 tsp Thai fish sauce
  5ml/1 tsp fresh root ginger, peeled
    and finely chopped
  22.5ml/4¹/₂ tsp light muscovado
    (brown) sugar

COOK'S TIP
Adjusting the seasoning makes a big difference to this dish. For extra kick, add a finely chopped red chilli to the seasoning, but be warned, this will make the dish extremely hot. Alternatively, blend half an onion in a food processor and add it to the seasoning to achieve a a tangier taste and a subtle sweetness.

1 Cut the radish into 2cm/³/₄in cubes. Place in a bowl and coat with the sea salt. Leave for 2 hours, draining off any water that collects at the bottom of the bowl. Drain well at the end of salting.

2 Combine all the ingredients for the seasoning and mix well with the salted radish. Place the radish in an airtight container and seal. Leave at room temperature for 24 hours and chill.

Per portion Energy 73kcal/302kJ; Protein 3.1g; Carbohydrate 14g, of which sugars 13.6g; Fat 0.8g, of which saturates 0.4g; Cholesterol 0mg; Calcium 81mg; Fibre 3.7g; Sodium 1203mg.

SPRING ONION KIMCHI

ALTHOUGH THIS KIMCHI DOES NOT HAVE THE SAME SPICINESS AS OTHER VARIETIES, THE SPRING ONIONS PROVIDE A UNIQUE PUNGENCY AND FLAVOUR. THE RICE MARRIES THE SPICY FLAVOURS AND SPRING ONIONS TOGETHER, WHILE THE SUGAR GIVES AN UNDERLYING HINT OF SWEETNESS.

SERVES SIX

INGREDIENTS
  200g/7oz Chinese white
    radish, peeled
  400g/14oz spring onions
    (scallions), trimmed
  200ml/7fl oz/scant 1 cup dried
    anchovy stock
  50g/2oz/⅓ cup sticky or pearl rice
  115g/4oz Korean chilli powder
  15ml/1 tbsp fermented shrimps,
    finely chopped
  2 garlic cloves, crushed
  120ml/4fl oz/½ cup anchovy
    sauce
  7.5ml/1½ tsp sugar
  5ml/1 tsp grated fresh root ginger

1 Cut the Chinese radish into bitesize pieces and place in a bowl with the spring onions. Pour over the anchovy stock and shuffle the vegetables down into it as far as possible. Cover and leave to soak in a cool place for 1 hour, then drain well.

2 Place the rice in a pan and pour in 200ml/7fl oz/scant 1 cup water. Bring to the boil, reduce the heat and cover. Cook over a very low heat for 15 minutes, until the rice is cooked.

3 In a large bowl, mix the chilli powder, fermented shrimps, garlic, anchovy sauce, sugar and ginger in a bowl.

4 Mix the cooked sticky rice and chilli mixture in a large bowl until well combined. Add the spring onions and turn them with the mixture by hand until thoroughly mixed. (Wear rubber gloves to protect your hands from the chilli powder.) Alternatively, use a spoon and fork to turn the spring onions carefully, taking care to avoid bruising or breaking them.

5 Take a bunch of 4–5 spring onions and use another spring onion to tie them in a bundle. Tie all the spring onions into bundles, keeping the sticky rice and seasoning coating on them. Replace the bundles in the bowl, cover and leave them to stand for a day at room temperature. Chill before serving.

Per portion Energy 77kcal/321kJ; Protein 7.4g; Carbohydrate 10.6g, of which sugars 3.8g; Fat 4.7g, of which saturates 0.3g; Cholesterol 7mg; Calcium 121mg; Fibre 1.3g; Sodium 652mg.

STUFFED CUCUMBER KIMCHI

A CLASSIC SUMMER VARIETY OF KIMCHI. THE REFRESHING NATURAL SUCCULENCE OF CUCUMBER IS PERFECT ON A HOT, HUMID DAY. THE SPICINESS OF THE CHILLI IS NEUTRALIZED BY THE MOISTNESS OF THE CUCUMBER AND THE COMBINED FLAVOURS INVIGORATE THE PALATE.

SERVES 4

INGREDIENTS
    15 small pickling cucumbers
    30ml/2 tbsp sea salt
    1 bunch Chinese chives
For the seasoning
    1 onion
    4 spring onions (scallions),
        thinly sliced
    75ml/5 tbsp Korean chilli powder
    15ml/1 tbsp Thai fish sauce
    10ml/2 tsp salt
    1 garlic clove, crushed
    7.5ml/1¹/₂ tsp grated fresh root ginger
    5ml/1 tsp sugar
    5ml/1 tsp sesame seeds

1 If the cucumbers are long, cut them in half widthways. Make two slits in a cross down the length of each cucumber or cucumber half, making sure not to cut all the way to the end. Coat thoroughly with salt and leave for 1 hour.

2 Cut the Chinese chives into 2.5cm/1in lengths, discarding the bulb.

3 Combine the onion and spring onions with the Chinese chives in a bowl. Add 45ml/3 tbsp of the chilli powder and add the Thai fish sauce, salt, garlic, ginger, sugar and sesame seeds. Mix the ingredients thoroughly by hand, using plastic gloves to prevent the chilli powder from staining your skin. Alternatively, use a spoon and fork to fold the ingredients together.

4 Lightly rinse the cucumbers to remove the salt crystals. Coat with the remaining chilli powder and press the seasoning into the slits. Put the cucumber into an airtight container and leave at room temperature for 12 hours before serving.

COOK'S TIPS
• Cucumber kimchi can be stored in the refrigerator, although it is best eaten within two days.
• Traditional British cucumbers are not the best choice for this recipe – large smooth-skinned gherkins or ridge cucumbers are better. They have a firmer texture, with less watery flesh and are used for all types of pickles in European recipes. They are delicious with the spicy kimchi seasoning and they retain a refreshingly crisp texture.

Per portion Energy 32kcal/131kJ; Protein 2.5g; Carbohydrate 3.9g, of which sugars 3.4g; Fat 2.1g, of which saturates 0.2g; Cholesterol 0mg; Calcium 88mg; Fibre 1.4g; Sodium 2067mg.

STUFFED GREEN CHILLI KIMCHI

THIS CRUNCHY, REFRESHING KIMCHI IS A POPULAR SIDE DISH. IT IS NOT AS SPICY AS CLASSIC CABBAGE KIMCHI AND IT IS OFTEN SERVED AS A MILDER ACCOMPANIMENT TO GRILLED MEAT OR SEAFOOD. ITS HEAT CAN BE ADJUSTED BY THE USE OF MILD OR MORE POWERFUL CHILLIES.

SERVES FOUR

INGREDIENTS
- 30ml/2 tbsp salt, plus extra for seasoning
- 20 mild green chillies
- 45ml/3 tbsp chilli flakes
- 500ml/17fl oz/generous 2 cups dried anchovy stock
- 15ml/1 tbsp fermented shrimps, finely chopped
- 1/2 white onion, finely grated or puréed

For the stuffing
- 2 onions, finely chopped
- 1/2 Chinese white radish, peeled and finely sliced
- 5 red chillies, seeded and sliced
- 5 garlic cloves, crushed
- 15g/1/2oz fresh root ginger, peeled and grated

COOK'S TIPS
The dried chilli flakes in the stock and the red chillies used in the stuffing bring heat to the dish. For a milder dish, use less pungent chillies.

1 Pour 1 litre/1³/₄ pints/4 cups water into a bowl and then add the salt. Slice the tops off the green chillies and remove the seeds, while leaving the pods whole.

2 Add the green chillies to the salt water and leave them to soak for 30 minutes, drain thoroughly and set aside.

3 Tie the chilli flakes in a muslin (cheesecloth) bag, place this in a bowl and pour in 500ml/17fl oz/generous 2 cups water.

4 Set aside the bowl until the water has taken on the colour and flavour of the chillies, then remove the bag and skim out any of the flakes that have escaped.

5 Mix the anchovy stock with the chilli water and add the fermented shrimps. Add the grated or puréed onion.

6 Mix the onions, white radish, red chillies, garlic and ginger for the stuffing. Season with a pinch of salt and blend thoroughly.

7 Stuff the mild green chillies with this garlic and ginger mixture, packing it in firmly but also taking care not to break the chilli.

8 Place the stuffed chillies in the bowl with the anchovy and chilli stock and leave them to soak for a day at room temperature.

9 Remove the chillies from the stock and place them in a serving dish. Drizzle over a little of the stock and chill them well in the refrigerator before serving at the table.

PAK CHOI KIMCHI

The pak choi green leaves that originated in China have been adopted all over Asia. In Korea they are used widely in making kimchi. This version is easy to prepare, with pumpkin adding sweetness and helping to marry the other flavours.

SERVES FOUR

INGREDIENTS
    8 small, white-stemmed pak choi
        (bok choi)
    15ml/1 tbsp sesame seeds, to garnish
For the stuffing
    250g/9oz pumpkin, peeled
        and seeded
    115g/4oz leeks, finely chopped
    1 garlic clove, crushed
    30ml/2 tbsp light soy sauce
    5ml/1 tsp grated fresh root ginger
    30ml/2 tbsp Korean chilli powder
    5ml/1 tsp sesame oil
    7.5ml/1½ tsp pine nuts, ground

1 Make sure the pak choi is fresh, crisp and bright. Reject any limp, bruised or broken pieces. Slice the pak choi in half lengthways. Rinse the pieces under running water, then drain and set aside.

2 Finely grate the pumpkin and place it in a bowl with the leeks and garlic.

3 Add the soy sauce, ginger, chilli powder, sesame oil, pine nuts and a pinch of salt. Mix thoroughly.

4 Place the pieces of pak choi in a serving bowl. Stuff the pumpkin mixture in between the leaves. Sprinkle any remaining stuffing over the top of the pak choi. Garnish with sesame seeds and serve.

COOK'S TIPS
• If pumpkin is not available, butternut squash can be used for this dish. To prepare the pumpkin or squash, discard the seeds, fibres and pith from the middle and cut off the thick peel. Then cut the flesh into chunks.
• A food processor can be used for speeding up preparation. Start by grinding the pine nuts as they are dry (a small bowl is ideal for this). Then chop the leeks, garlic and ginger together. Finally use the grating blade for the pumpkin – or cheat and chop the vegetable finely instead.

Per portion Energy 77kcal/317kJ; Protein 6.1g; Carbohydrate 4.6g, of which sugars 3.9g; Fat 5.5g, of which saturates 0.6g; Cholesterol 0mg; Calcium 284mg; Fibre 4.2g; Sodium 519mg.

SPICY KIMCHI STEW

THIS HEARTY PORK AND KIMCHI DISH, KIMCHI CHIGE, IS A RICH STEW BUBBLING WITH FLAVOUR AND PIQUANCY AND IS TRADITIONALLY COOKED IN A HEAVY CLAY BOWL CALLED A TUKBAEGE. THE SLOW COOKING ALLOWS THE FLAVOURS TO MINGLE, CREATING COMPLEX, ENTICING TASTE COMBINATIONS.

SERVES FOUR

INGREDIENTS

    4 dried shiitake mushrooms, soaked
      in warm water for about 30 minutes
    150g/5oz firm tofu
    200g/7oz boneless pork chop
    300g/11oz cabbage kimchi (see
      page 431)
    45ml/3 tbsp vegetable oil
    1 garlic clove, crushed
    15ml/1 tbsp Korean chilli powder
    750ml/1¼ pints/3 cups vegetable
      stock or water
    2 spring onions (scallions),
      finely sliced
    salt

1 When the shiitake mushrooms have reconstituted and become soft, drain and slice them, discarding the stems.

2 Dice the tofu into cubes approximately 2cm/³/₄in square.

3 Dice the pork into bitesize cubes with a sharp knife and then slice the kimchi into similar sized pieces. Squeeze out any excess liquid from the kimchi until it ceases to drip.

4 Pour the vegetable oil into a pan or wok and place over a medium heat. Add the pork and garlic and sauté until it is crisp and brown.

5 Once the pork has turned dark brown add the kimchi and chilli powder, and stir-fry for another 60 seconds, tossing the ingredients together.

6 Add the vegetable stock or water and bring to the boil. Add the tofu, mushrooms and spring onions, cover and simmer for 10–15 minutes. Season with salt and serve the mixture hot and bubbling from the pan.

VARIATIONS
• Create a lighter dish by substituting drained canned tuna for the pork.
• Alternatively, fresh tuna steak can be used and cut up in the same way as the pork chop. Use fish stock to emphasize the flavour.

COOK'S TIP
This recipe is better suited to firm tofu, rather than soft tofu, because it is less likely to break up during cooking. The majority of supermarkets sell firm tofu in long-life packs (usually as well as the fresh varieties in the chiller cabinets). The long-life packs provide a good kitchen standby.

Per portion Energy 185kcal/770kJ; Protein 15.1g; Carbohydrate 4.2g, of which sugars 4g; Fat 12.1g, of which saturates 1.9g; Cholesterol 32mg; Calcium 234mg; Fibre 1.8g; Sodium 534mg.

STIR-FRIED KIMCHI

ALTHOUGH KIMCHI IS CHARACTERISTICALLY A COLD DISH, THIS STIR-FRIED VERSION GIVES THE VEGETABLES A LIGHT QUALITY AND SUBTLE FLAVOUR. THE PUNGENCY OF THE RAW KIMCHI IS KNOCKED BACK DURING THE COOKING PROCESS, AND IS REPLACED BY A DELICIOUS NUTTY SWEETNESS.

1 Slice the cabbage kimchi into 2cm/3/4in lengths and roughly chop the pork into similar sized pieces.

2 Coat a pan with the vegetable oil and stir-fry the garlic until lightly browned. Add the pork and stir-fry until it is golden. Add the kimchi and stir-fry.

3 Continue to stir-fry until the kimchi has darkened. Add the spring onion, soy sauce, sesame seeds, sesame oil and sugar, and quickly stir-fry. Ensure that all the ingredients are completely mixed.

4 Serve immediately with an accompaniment of steamed rice or a dish of noodles in broth.

VARIATIONS
• Peeled raw prawns (shrimp) can be used in place of the pork.
• Prepared squid rings (the tender body sac) are also delicious cooked in this recipe instead of the pork.
• For a vegetarian kimchi, leave out the meat. Firm tofu can be added to make a more substantial version.

SERVES FOUR

INGREDIENTS
  150g/5oz cabbage kimchi (see page 431)
  50g/2oz pork
  15ml/1 tbsp vegetable oil
  2 garlic cloves, finely chopped
  1 spring onion (scallion), sliced
  5ml/1 tsp dark soy sauce
  2.5ml/1/2 tsp sesame seeds
  5ml/1 tsp sesame oil
  2.5ml/1/2 tsp sugar
  steamed rice or noodles in broth,
    to serve

Per portion Energy 84kcal/348kJ; Protein 4.7g; Carbohydrate 2.9g, of which sugars 2.9g; Fat 6g, of which saturates 0.9g; Cholesterol 11mg; Calcium 36mg; Fibre 1.3g; Sodium 135mg.

TOFU AND STIR-FRIED KIMCHI

THE MILD FLAVOURS OF STIR-FRIED CABBAGE KIMCHI ARE A PERFECT COMPLEMENT TO THE DELICATE TASTE OF BLANCHED TOFU. THE HINT OF SWEETNESS AND UNDERLYING SPICINESS IN THE KIMCHI CONTRASTS WITH THE SMOOTH, CREAMY TEXTURE AND SOYA BEAN NUTTINESS OF THE TOFU.

SERVES THREE TO FOUR

INGREDIENTS

90g/3¹/₂oz cabbage kimchi (see page 431)
50g/2oz pork
15ml/1 tbsp vegetable oil
1 garlic clove, thinly sliced
5ml/1 tsp salt
5ml/1 tsp sugar
5ml/1 tsp sesame seeds
5ml/1 tsp sesame oil
1 block firm tofu

1 Slice the kimchi into 2cm/³/₄in lengths, and roughly chop the pork into similar sized pieces.

2 Coat a pan or wok with the vegetable oil and stir-fry the pork and garlic until crisp and golden. Season to taste with the salt.

3 Stir in the kimchi and quickly stir-fry the mixture over a high heat until it has become dark brown.

4 Add the sugar, sesame seeds and sesame oil to the stir-fried kimchi. Combine well and continue to stir-fry for a further 30 seconds. Then remove the pan from the heat and cover it with a lid while slicing the tofu.

5 Meanwhile, place the whole block of tofu into a pan of boiling water, ensuring that it is covered. Boil for 3–4 minutes, making sure that the water is not bubbling too rapidly, and then remove. Drain the tofu, and blot any excess water with kitchen paper.

6 Cut the tofu into slices about 1cm/¹/₃in thick. Arrange the warm tofu slices on a large plate or on individual dishes and place the pork and kimchi mixture in the middle. Serve warm.

COOK'S TIP
A pasta pan, with an integral strainer, is good for lowering delicate tofu into hot water and for draining it at the end of the cooking process.

Per portion Energy 98kcal/407kJ; Protein 7g; Carbohydrate 2.5g, of which sugars 2.3g; Fat 6.7g, of which saturates 1g; Cholesterol 8mg; Calcium 257mg; Fibre 0.6g; Sodium 504mg.

VEGETABLE
ACCOMPANIMENTS

The mountainous slopes of Japan and Korea provide an array of wild vegetables as well as other produce, all of which are the inspiration for many classic dishes, such as Cabbage 'Noodle' Pancake and Spinach Namul. There are also distinctive combinations of vegetables, mushrooms and seaweed, as well as delicious condiments for grilled dishes, such as Black Beans with Sweet Soy and Pickled Garlic.

Left: Pan-Fried Chilli Parsnip and Shiitake; **Above:** Cabbage 'Noodle' Pancake

ACORN JELLY <u>AND</u> SEAWEED <u>IN</u> SOY DRESSING

ACORN JELLY IS A DELICACY RARELY FOUND OUTSIDE OF KOREA. THE JELLY HAS A SUBTLE BITTERNESS, BUT THE SEAWEED BRINGS OUT ITS DISTINCTIVE NUTTY FLAVOUR, WHILE THE SOY DRESSING ADDS OVERTONES OF SWEETNESS AND SALTINESS. BEST SERVED WITH NOODLES AS A LIGHT SUMMER DISH.

2 Pour the acorn mixture into a pan and stir until the liquid boils, then simmer for 2–3 minutes. Add the salt and 1 teaspoon of the sesame oil, and simmer for 5 minutes, until the liquid reduces and becomes sticky.

3 Pour the liquid into a mould and leave it to cool and set.

4 Mix the sesame seeds with the soy sauce and add the remaining sesame oil.

5 Cut the seaweed paper into a manageable size. Turn out the jelly, cut into slices and arrange on a plate. Crumble the seaweed over, then drizzle with the dressing before serving.

SERVES FOUR

INGREDIENTS
  50g/2oz/½ cup acorn powder
  5ml/1 tsp salt
  15ml/1 tsp sesame oil
  5ml/1 tsp sesame seeds
  30ml/2 tbsp dark soy sauce
  dried seaweed paper or
    Japanese nori

COOK'S TIP
Acorn powder is available at most Asian supermarkets.

1 Stir 750ml/1¼ pints/3 cups water into the acorn powder. Stir until the powder and water are well mixed together.

Per portion Energy 57kcal/236kJ; Protein 0.7g; Carbohydrate 5.2g, of which sugars 1.4g; Fat 3.8g, of which saturates 0.6g; Cholesterol 0mg; Calcium 16mg; Fibre 0.6g; Sodium 1027mg.

SWEET LOTUS ROOT

THE ROOT OF THE LOTUS FLOWER HAS A UNIQUE FLAVOUR AND CLEAN, CRISP TASTE AND IS A GREATLY OVERLOOKED INGREDIENT IN THE WESTERN KITCHEN. HISTORICALLY, THIS KOREAN SPECIALITY WAS EATEN BY THE KING AS A DESSERT, BRAISED WITH SUGAR RATHER THAN SOY, AS HERE.

SERVES TWO TO THREE

INGREDIENTS
    15ml/1 tbsp cider vinegar
    300g/11oz lotus root, peeled
    60ml/4 tbsp soy sauce
    30ml/2 tbsp sugar
    45ml/3 tbsp maple syrup
    10ml/2 tsp sesame oil
    sesame seeds, to garnish

3 Return the slices to the rinsed-out pan and add just enough water to cover them. Add the soy sauce. Bring to the boil and cook for 20 minutes, by which time the lotus root should have taken on the colour of the soy sauce.

4 Add the sugar and maple syrup, then reduce the heat and simmer for about 30 minutes. Mix in the sesame oil, coating the lotus root slices carefully. Transfer to a serving dish and garnish with a sprinkle of sesame seeds.

1 Pour 750ml/1¼ pints/3 cups water into a bowl and add the vinegar. Cut the lotus root into slices about 1cm/½in thick and place them in the vinegar water. Leave to soak for about 30 minutes, then drain. Be careful not to leave the lotus root in the water for too long or it will begin to turn black.

2 Bring 750ml/1¼ pints/3 cups water to the boil in a pan and add the lotus root. Boil for 2 minutes and then drain the lotus root and rinse the slices thoroughly under cold water.

COOK'S TIPS
• Once peeled fresh lotus root will discolour very quickly. Treat it in the same way you would an apple, ensuring that it is soaked in the acidulated water as soon as it is peeled will slow down this process.
• If possible use a mature lotus root for this recipe, as the starchy quality of the larger roots will be ideal for absorbing the flavours during the cooking process. Smaller lotus roots are often eaten raw and are delicious in salads.

Per portion Energy 131kcal/555kJ; Protein 1.2g; Carbohydrate 28.3g, of which sugars 28.1g; Fat 2.2g, of which saturates 0.3g; Cholesterol 0mg; Calcium 54mg; Fibre 1.1g; Sodium 1525mg.

BLACK BEANS <u>WITH</u> SWEET SOY

*Simple to make, and popular as an accompaniment, this is among the oldest of
traditional dishes and is a staple of the customary Korean table. The black beans
have a sweet, nutty taste that is well matched by the salty tang of soy sauce.*

SERVES TWO TO THREE

INGREDIENTS

   300g/11oz/2 cups canned
     black beans, drained
   120ml/4fl oz/½ cup
     maple syrup
   30ml/2 tbsp sugar
   100ml/3½fl oz/scant ½ cup
     light soy sauce
   5ml/1 tsp sesame seeds,
     to garnish

1 Rinse the beans, then drain them.

2 Bring 750ml/1½pints/3 cups water to
the boil in a pan and add the beans.
Boil the beans for 5 minutes, by which
time any odour from them should have
disappeared. Drain the beans and rinse
out the pan.

3 Bring 450ml/¾ pint/scant 2 cups
water to the boil in the pan. Add the
beans and maple syrup.

4 Boil for 3 minutes, then add the sugar
and soy sauce.

5 Reduce the heat under the pan
and simmer over low heat, until the
liquid has reduced to form a thick,
rich sauce.

6 Remove from the heat and leave to
cool. Transfer the cooled beans to a
dish and garnish with sesame seeds
before serving.

VARIATION
If you liquidize this tasty recipe, it
makes a delicious accompaniment to
fish, such as grilled sea bass or red
snapper fillets.

Per portion Energy 275kcal/1166kJ; Protein 7.8g; Carbohydrate 61.1g, of which sugars 47.8g; Fat 1.5g, of which saturates 0.2g; Cholesterol 0mg; Calcium 94mg; Fibre 5.8g; Sodium 2840mg.

PICKLED GARLIC

ALTHOUGH THE PREPARATION INVOLVED IN THIS DISH TAKES SOME WORK, ONCE THE GARLIC IS PRESERVED IT WILL LAST FOR MONTHS. SERVED WITH GRILLED DISHES OR AS PART OF A TABLE SETTING WITH RICE, SOUP AND KIMCHI, THIS IS A UBIQUITOUS PART OF THE KOREAN DINING EXPERIENCE.

SERVES EIGHT

INGREDIENTS
25 garlic bulbs
350ml/12fl oz/1½ cups
cider vinegar
450ml/¾ pint/scant 2 cups
soy sauce
200g/7oz/1 cup sugar

1 Peel off the outer layers of the garlic, taking care to keep the bulbs intact. Rinse the garlic bulbs, then drain them well.

2 Take a large heatproof jar with an airtight lid. It must be big enough to hold the garlic and 1.2 litres/2 pints/5 cups liquid. Pour in 750ml/1¼ pints/3 cups water and the vinegar. Then add the bulbs of garlic and cover the jar. Leave at room temperature for 3 days.

3 Drain off the vinegar solution from the jar, leaving the garlic in place. Heat 350ml/12fl oz/1½ cups water in a pan and add the soy sauce and sugar. Simmer for 5 minutes, then pour the liquid over the garlic in the jar.

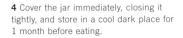

4 Cover the jar immediately, closing it tightly, and store in a cool dark place for 1 month before eating.

Per portion Energy 171kcal/723kJ; Protein 5.8g; Carbohydrate 38.4g, of which sugars 29g; Fat 0.4g, of which saturates 0.1g; Cholesterol 0mg; Calcium 29mg; Fibre 2.6g; Sodium 1784mg.

CARROT <u>IN</u> SWEET VINEGAR

IN THIS JAPANESE SIDE DISH, CALLED SAN BAI ZU, FINE CARROT STRIPS ARE MARINATED IN RICE VINEGAR, SHOYU AND MIRIN. IT MAKES A GOOD ACCOMPANIMENT FOR OILY FOODS SUCH AS TERIYAKI.

SERVES FOUR

INGREDIENTS
    2 large carrots, peeled
    5ml/1 tsp salt
    30ml/2 tbsp sesame seeds
For the sweet vinegar marinade
    75ml/5 tbsp rice vinegar
    30ml/2 tbsp shoyu (use the pale
        awakuchi soy sauce if available)
    45ml/3 tbsp mirin

COOK'S TIP
This marinade is called san bai zu, and is one of the essential basic sauces in Japanese cooking. Dilute the marinade with 15ml/1 tbsp second dashi stock, then add sesame seeds and a few dashes of sesame oil for a very tasty and healthy salad dressing.

1 Cut the carrots into thin matchsticks, 5cm/2in long. Put the carrots and salt into a mixing bowl, and mix well with your hands. After 25 minutes, rinse the wilted carrot in cold water, then drain.

2 In another bowl, mix together the marinade ingredients. Add the carrots, and leave to marinate for 3 hours.

3 Put a small pan on a high heat, add the sesame seeds and toss constantly until the seeds start to pop. Remove from the heat and cool.

4 Chop the sesame seeds with a large, sharp knife on a large chopping board. Place the carrots in a bowl, sprinkle with the sesame seeds and serve cold.

Per portion Energy 110kcal/461kJ; Protein 2g; Carbohydrate 16.4g, of which sugars 16g; Fat 4.5g, of which saturates 0.7g; Cholesterol 0mg; Calcium 70mg; Fibre 1.8g; Sodium 1040mg.

FRIED AUBERGINE <u>WITH</u> MISO SAUCE

IN NASU-MISO, STIR-FRIED AUBERGINE IS COATED IN A RICH MISO SAUCE. MAKE SURE THE OIL IS SMOKING HOT WHEN ADDING THE AUBERGINE PIECES, SO THAT THEY DO NOT ABSORB TOO MUCH OIL.

SERVES FOUR

INGREDIENTS
    2 large aubergines (eggplant)
    1–2 dried red chillies
    45ml/3 tbsp sake
    45ml/3 tbsp mirin
    45ml/3 tbsp caster (superfine) sugar
    30ml/2 tbsp shoyu
    45ml/3 tbsp red miso (use either the
        dark red aka miso or even darker
        hatcho miso)
    90ml/6 tbsp sesame oil
    salt

VARIATION
Sweet (bell) peppers could also be used for this dish instead of the aubergine. Take 1 red, 1 yellow and 2 green peppers. Remove the seeds and chop them into 1cm/½in strips, then follow the rest of the recipe.

1 Cut the aubergines into bitesize pieces and place in a large colander, sprinkle with some salt and leave for 30 minutes to remove the bitter juices. Squeeze the aubergine pieces by hand. Remove the seeds from the chillies and chop the chillies into thin rings. Mix the sake, mirin, sugar and shoyu in a cup. In a separate bowl, mix the red miso with 45ml/3 tbsp water to make a loose paste.

2 Heat the oil in a large pan and add the chilli. When you see pale smoke rising from the oil, add the aubergine, and, using cooking hashi, stir-fry for about 8 minutes, or until tender. Lower the heat to medium. Add the sake mixture to the pan, and stir for 2–3 minutes. If the sauce starts to burn, lower the heat. Add the miso paste to the pan and cook, stirring, for another 2 minutes. Serve hot.

Per portion Energy 221kcal/916kJ; Protein 1.4g; Carbohydrate 13.7g, of which sugars 13.4g; Fat 16.9g, of which saturates 2.5g; Cholesterol 0mg; Calcium 20mg; Fibre 2g; Sodium 805mg.

WHITE RADISH SANGCHAE

THE RED CHILLI AND SESAME OIL DRESSING ADDS AN UNDERSTATED SPICINESS AND NUTTY AFTERTASTE TO THIS HEALTHY KOREAN DISH. THE WHITE RADISH, ALSO KNOWN AS DAIKON, IS A COMMONLY USED INGREDIENT IN ASIAN COOKING AND IS VALUED FOR ITS MEDICINAL PROPERTIES.

SERVES TWO

INGREDIENTS
    225g/8oz Chinese white radish, peeled
    ½ red chilli, shredded, and 1.5ml/
        ¼ tsp sesame seeds, to garnish
For the marinade
    5ml/1 tsp cider vinegar
    2.5ml/½ tsp sugar
    1.5ml/¼ tsp salt
    7.5ml/1½ tsp lemon juice
    2.5ml/½ tsp Korean chilli powder

VARIATIONS
• The radish takes on the red colour of
the chilli powder, but for an interesting
alternative replace the chilli powder with
2.5ml/½ tsp wasabi. This will give the
radish a green tint and a sharper taste.
• Make an alternative sesame oil
marinade with 2.5ml/½ tsp sesame oil
2.5ml/½ tsp vegetable oil, 120ml/
4fl oz/½ cup white wine vinegar,
50g/2oz/¼ cup sugar, 1.5ml/¼ tsp
salt and a pinch of pepper.

1 Cut the radish into thin strips
approximately 5cm/2in long.

2 To make the marinade, mix the
vinegar, sugar, salt, lemon juice and
chilli powder together in a small bowl,
and ensure that the ingredients are
thoroughly blended.

3 Place the radish in a bowl, and add
the marinade. Leave to marinate for 20
minutes, then place in the refrigerator
until the dish has chilled thoroughly.

4 Mix well again, then garnish with the
shredded red chilli pepper and the
sesame seeds before serving.

Per portion Energy 22kcal/91kJ; Protein 1g; Carbohydrate 3.2g, of which sugars 3.2g; Fat 0.7g, of which saturates 0.2g; Cholesterol 0mg; Calcium 27mg; Fibre 1.1g; Sodium 209mg.

CUCUMBER SANGCHAE

THE REFRESHING, SUCCULENT TASTE OF THIS KOREAN SALAD MAKES A PERFECT ACCOMPANIMENT FOR A MAIN MEAL ON A HOT SUMMER'S NIGHT. SMALL PICKLING CUCUMBERS ARE THE BEST FOR THIS DISH; THEY ARE NOT AS WATERY AS THE LARGER SPECIMENS AND THEY DO NOT REQUIRE PEELING.

SERVES FOUR

INGREDIENTS
    400g/14oz pickling or
      salad cucumber
    30ml/2 tbsp salt
For the dressing
    2 spring onions (scallions),
      finely chopped
    2 garlic cloves, crushed
    5ml/1 tsp cider vinegar
    5ml/1 tsp salt
    2.5ml/½ tsp Korean chilli powder
    10ml/2 tsp toasted sesame seeds
    10ml/2 tsp sesame oil
    5ml/1 tsp gochujang chilli paste
    10ml/2 tsp sugar

1 Cut the cucumber lengthways into thin slices and put into a colander. Sprinkle with the salt, mix well and leave for 30 minutes.

2 Place the cucumber slices in a damp dish towel and gently squeeze out as much of the water as possible.

3 Place the spring onions in a large bowl. Add the crushed garlic, vinegar, salt and chilli powder, and combine until well mixed. Sprinkle in the sesame seeds and mix in the sesame oil, chilli paste and sugar.

4 Blend the cucumber with the dressing. Chill before serving.

Per portion Energy 105kcal/432kJ; Protein 3.3g; Carbohydrate 9.2g, of which sugars 7.4g; Fat 6.2g, of which saturates 0.9g; Cholesterol 0mg; Calcium 78mg; Fibre 2.2g; Sodium 1973mg.

KOREAN CHIVE SANGCHAE

THE KOREAN CHIVE HAS A GARLIC NUANCE IN BOTH TASTE AND AROMA, AND THE LEAVES HAVE A SOFT, GRASSLIKE TEXTURE. THIS DISH IS THE PERFECT ACCOMPANIMENT TO ANY GRILLED MEAT, AND IS A TASTY ALTERNATIVE TO THE CLASSIC SHREDDED SPRING ONION SALAD.

SERVES TWO

INGREDIENTS
    200g/7oz fresh Korean or
      Chinese chives
    1 green chilli, seeded and
      finely sliced
    10ml/2 tsp sesame seeds,
      to garnish
For the seasoning
    30ml/2 tbsp dark soy sauce
    2 garlic cloves, crushed
    10ml/2 tsp Korean chilli powder
    10ml/2 tsp sesame oil
    10ml/2 tsp sugar

COOK'S TIP
Korean chives are available in most Asian markets in 225g/½lb or 450g/1lb bundles. When shopping for these chives, try to select those that are bright green with a crisp texture.

1 Clean the chives, then trim off the bulbs and discard. Slice roughly into 4cm/1½in lengths. Combine with the chilli in a bowl.

2 To make the seasoning, mix the soy sauce, garlic, chilli powder, sesame oil and sugar together, and then add it to the bowl with the chives and chilli. Mix until well coated, then chill.

3 Garnish with sesame seeds and serve. The chives can be attractively arranged in alternating layers laid at right angles.

VARIATION
For a traditional alternative use 150g/5oz shredded spring onion (scallion) in place of the chives, and add 15ml/1 tbsp cider vinegar and 15ml/1 tbsp soy sauce to the seasoning.

Per portion Energy 105kcal/434kJ; Protein 4.3g; Carbohydrate 7g, of which sugars 6.7g; Fat 6.7g, of which saturates 0.9g; Cholesterol 0mg; Calcium 196mg; Fibre 2.3g; Sodium 1196mg.

DAIKON AND CARROT

This refreshing dish, called Namasu in Japan, is an essential part of the New Year's celebration meal. The bright colour combination of white daikon and red carrot is particularly favoured by many Japanese as it is regarded as a symbol of happiness. Start preparations for this recipe the day before it is to be eaten.

SERVES FOUR

INGREDIENTS
   20cm/8in daikon
   2 carrots, peeled and cut into
      5cm/2in pieces
   5ml/1 tsp salt
   45ml/3 tbsp caster (superfine) sugar
   70ml/4½ tbsp rice vinegar
   15ml/1 tbsp sesame seeds

COOK'S TIP
This dish can be served with halved hard-boiled eggs, the yolk seasoned with a little mayonnaise and shoyu, and accompanied by sticks of cucumber rolled in smoked salmon. Offer a tiny cup of warm sake to drink with it.

1 Cut the daikon into three pieces, then thickly peel the skin. Slice both vegetables very thinly lengthways then crossways to make very thin matchsticks. Alternatively, shred them with a grater or use a mandolin to achieve a similar effect.

2 Place the daikon and carrot in a mixing bowl. Sprinkle with the salt and mix well with your hands. Leave for about 30 minutes. Drain the vegetables in a sieve and gently squeeze out the excess liquid, then transfer them to another mixing bowl.

3 Mix the sugar and rice vinegar together in a bowl. Stir well until the sugar has completely dissolved in the vinegar. Pour over the daikon and carrot, and leave for at least a day, mixing at least two to three times. To serve, mix the two vegetables evenly and heap in the middle of a small bowl or a plate. Sprinkle with sesame seeds and serve.

Per portion Energy 89kcal/373kJ; Protein 1.5g; Carbohydrate 16.2g, of which sugars 16g; Fat 2.5g, of which saturates 0.4g; Cholesterol 0mg; Calcium 55mg; Fibre 1.9g; Sodium 510mg.

SPINACH WITH PEANUT SAUCE

Traditional Japanese cooking rarely uses fat or oil, and nuts have long been an important source of essential nutritional oils in the Japanese diet. In this recipe, called Horenso Peanuts Aé, peanuts are transformed into a creamy sauce and mixed with spinach.

SERVES FOUR

INGREDIENTS
   450g/1lb spinach
For the peanut sauce
   50g/2oz/⅓ cup unsalted
      shelled peanuts
   30ml/2 tbsp shoyu
   7.5ml/1½ tsp caster (superfine) sugar
   25ml/1½ tbsp second dashi
      stock, or the same amount
      of warm water with a pinch
      of dashi-no-moto

VARIATIONS
• You can use walnuts or sesame seeds to make different types of sauce.
• Young nettle leaves and coriander (cilantro), blanched and mixed with the peanut sauce, make an interesting 'not quite Japanese' dish.

1 First, make the peanut sauce. Grind the shelled peanuts in a suribachi or a mortar and pestle. Alternatively, use an electric grinder.

2 Transfer the crushed nuts to a small mixing bowl and stir in the shoyu, sugar and dashi stock. When thoroughly mixed, the sauce will look like runny peanut butter.

3 Blanch the spinach for 30 seconds in rapidly boiling water until the leaves are wilted. Drain and cool under running water for 30 seconds.

4 Drain again and lightly squeeze out the excess water. Add the peanut sauce to the spinach in a bowl and mix gently but thoroughly. Serve on individual plates or small bowls.

Per portion Energy 111kcal/460kJ; Protein 6.7g; Carbohydrate 6.3g, of which sugars 5.3g; Fat 6.7g, of which saturates 1.2g; Cholesterol 0mg; Calcium 202mg; Fibre 3.1g; Sodium 959mg.

BRAISED TURNIP <u>WITH</u> PRAWN <u>AND</u> MANGETOUT

TAKI-AWASE IS AN ELEGANT DISH IN WHICH THREE COLOURS — THE PINK OF THE PRAWNS, THE WHITE OF THE TURNIPS AND THE GREEN OF THE MANGETOUTS — RESEMBLE A LADY'S SPRING KIMONO.

SERVES FOUR

INGREDIENTS

8 small turnips, peeled
600ml/1 pint/2½ cups second dashi
stock, or the same amount of water
and 7.5ml/1½ tsp dashi-no-moto
10ml/2 tsp shoyu (use the Japanese
pale awakuchi soy sauce
if available)
60ml/4 tbsp mirin
30ml/2 tbsp sake
16 medium raw tiger prawns (jumbo
shrimp), heads and shells removed
with tails intact
dash of rice vinegar
90g/3½oz mangetouts (snow peas)
5ml/1 tsp cornflour (cornstarch)
salt

1 Par-boil the turnips in boiling water for 3 minutes. Drain, then place them side by side in a deep pan. Add the dashi stock and cover with a saucer to submerge the turnips. Bring to the boil, then add the shoyu, 5ml/1 tsp salt, the mirin and sake. Reduce the heat to very low, cover and simmer for 30 minutes.

2 Insert a cocktail stick (toothpick) into the back of each prawn, and gently scoop up the thin black vein running down its length. Very carefully pull the vein out, then discard.

3 Blanch the prawns in boiling water with the vinegar until the colour just changes. Drain. Cook the mangetouts in lightly salted water for 3 minutes. Drain well, then set aside.

4 Remove the saucer from the turnips and add the cooked prawns to the stock for about 4 minutes to warm through. Scoop out the turnips, drain and place in individual bowls. Transfer the prawns to a small plate.

5 Mix the cornflour with 15ml/1 tbsp water and add to the pan that held the turnips. Increase the heat a little bit and shake the pan gently until the liquid thickens slightly.

6 Place the mangetouts on the turnips and arrange the prawns on top, then pour about 30ml/2 tbsp of the hot liquid from the pan into each bowl. Serve immediately.

Per portion Energy 83kcal/351kJ; Protein 6.4g; Carbohydrate 12g, of which sugars 10.4g; Fat 0.6g, of which saturates 0g; Cholesterol 49mg; Calcium 92mg; Fibre 3.5g; Sodium 68mg.

KABOCHA SQUASH WITH CHICKEN SAUCE

IN THIS JAPANESE DISH, KNOWN AS KABOCHA TORI-SOBORO KAKE, THE MILD SWEETNESS OF KABOCHA, SIMILAR TO THAT OF SWEET POTATO, GOES VERY WELL WITH THE RICH MEAT SAUCE.

SERVES FOUR

INGREDIENTS
    1 kabocha squash, about 500g/1¼lb
    ½ yuzu or lime
    20g/¾oz mangetouts (snow peas)
    salt
For the chicken sauce
    100ml/3fl oz/scant ½ cup water
    30ml/2 tbsp sake
    300g/11oz lean chicken,
      minced (ground)
    60ml/4 tbsp caster (superfine) sugar
    60ml/4 tbsp shoyu
    60ml/4 tbsp mirin

1 Halve the kabocha, then remove the seeds and fibre around the seeds. Halve again to make four wedges. Trim the stalky end of the kabocha wedge.

2 Remove strips of the peel on each of the wedges, cutting off strips lengthways of about 1–2.5cm/½–1in wide. The kabocha wedges will now have green (skin) and yellow (flesh) stripes. This will help preserve the kabocha's most tasty part just beneath the skin, and also allows it to be cooked until soft as well as being decorative.

3 Chop each wedge into large bitesize pieces. Place them side by side in a pan. Pour in enough water to cover, then sprinkle with some salt. Cover and cook for 5 minutes over a medium heat, then lower the heat and simmer for 15 minutes until tender. Test the kabocha by pricking with a skewer. When soft enough, remove from heat, cover and leave for 5 minutes.

4 Slice the yuzu or lime into thin discs, then hollow out the inside of the skin to make rings of peel. Cover with a sheet of clear film (plastic wrap) until needed. Blanch the mangetouts in lightly salted water. Drain and set aside.

5 To make the chicken sauce, bring the water and sake to the boil in a pan. Add the minced chicken, and when the colour of the meat has changed, add the sugar, shoyu and mirin. Stir continuously with a hand whisk until the liquid has almost all evaporated.

6 Pile up the kabocha on a large plate, then pour the hot meat sauce on top. Add the mangetouts and serve, garnished with yuzu or lime rings.

COOK'S TIP
Use tofu for a vegetarian sauce. Wrap in kitchen paper and leave for 30 minutes. Mash with a fork, then add in step 5.

Per portion Energy 172kcal/728kJ; Protein 19.6g; Carbohydrate 20g, of which sugars 19.2g; Fat 1.1g, of which saturates 0.4g; Cholesterol 53mg; Calcium 53mg; Fibre 1.4g; Sodium 1115mg.

DAIKON LAYERED <u>WITH</u> SMOKED SALMON

THE TRADITIONAL JAPANESE RECIPE CALLS FOR LAYERED, SALTED SALMON AND DAIKON, PICKLED IN A
WOODEN BARREL FOR A LONG TIME. THIS MODERN VERSION IS LESS SALTY AND FAR EASIER TO MAKE.

<u>SERVES FOUR</u>

INGREDIENTS
   10cm/4in daikon, about 6cm/2½in
     in diameter, peeled
   10ml/2 tsp salt
   5ml/1 tsp rice vinegar
   5cm/2in square dashi-konbu,
     chopped into 1cm/½in strips
   50g/2oz smoked salmon,
     thinly sliced
   2.5ml/½ tsp white poppy seeds

COOK'S TIPS
• You can use a mandolin, a food cutter
or a vegetable slicer to make paper-thin
slices of daikon.
• If unsure, taste the daikon after salting
and squeezing to check whether it needs
to be rinsed. The degree of saltiness will
depend on the original water content of
the daikon.

1 Slice the daikon very thinly into
rounds. Put in a shallow container,
sprinkle with salt and vinegar, and add
the snipped dashi-konbu. Mix and rub
gently with the hands. Cover and leave
in the refrigerator for 1 hour.

2 Drain in a sieve (strainer) and squeeze
out the excess liquid. If necessary, rinse
with running water for 30 seconds, then
drain and squeeze out again.

3 Cut the smoked salmon slices into 4cm/
1½in squares. Take 1 slice of daikon,
top with a salmon slice, then cover with
another daikon slice. Repeat until all
the salmon is used. Place in a shallow
container, cover, then leave to pickle at
room temperature for up to 1 day.

4 Arrange the daikon rounds on a
serving plate and put a pinch of poppy
seeds in the centre.

Per portion Energy 29kcal/122kJ; Protein 2.8g; Carbohydrate 0.5g, of which sugars 0.5g; Fat 1.8g, of which saturates 0.3g; Cholesterol 6mg; Calcium 12mg; Fibre 0.3g; Sodium 500mg.

BROCCOLI <u>AND</u> CUCUMBER PICKLED <u>IN</u> MISO

THE STEM OF THE BROCCOLI IS USUALLY WASTED BECAUSE OF THE FIBROUS TEXTURE, BUT YOU WILL
BE SURPRISED HOW TASTY IT IS WHEN MARINATED OR PICKLED.

<u>SERVES FOUR</u>

INGREDIENTS
   3 broccoli stems (use the florets in
     another dish, if you wish)
   2 Japanese or salad cucumbers,
     ends trimmed
   200ml/7fl oz/scant 1 cup miso
     (any kind)
   15ml/1 tbsp sake
   1 garlic clove, crushed

1 Peel the broccoli stems and quarter
them lengthways.

2 With a vegetable peeler, peel the
cucumber every 5mm/¼in to make
green-and-white stripes. Cut in half
lengthways. Scoop out the centre with a
teaspoon. Cut into 7.5cm/3in lengths.

3 Mix the miso, sake and crushed garlic
in a deep plastic or metal container with
a lid. Remove half the miso mix.

4 Lay some of the broccoli stems and
cucumber flat in the container and
push into the miso mix. Spread a little
of the reserved miso over the top of the
broccoli and cucumber as well.

5 Repeat this process to make a few
layers of vegetables and miso, filling up
the container. Cover with the lid and
leave in the refrigerator for 1–5 days.

6 Take out the vegetables, wash off the
miso under running water, then wipe
with kitchen paper.

7 Cut the broccoli stem pieces in half,
then slice into thin strips lengthways.

8 Cut the cucumber into 5mm/¼in thick
half-moon slices. Serve cold.

VARIATION
Carrot, turnip, kohlrabi, celery, radish or
thinly sliced cabbage stems can be used
in this way. The garlic can be replaced
by ginger, chilli or lime rind.

Per portion Energy 54kcal/227kJ; Protein 5.6g; Carbohydrate 4.9g, of which sugars 3.8g; Fat 1g, of which saturates 0.2g; Cholesterol 0mg; Calcium 66mg; Fibre 2.9g; Sodium 1789mg.

BROAD BEANS, DAIKON AND SALMON ROE

SORA-MAME NO AE-MONO IS A TYPICAL TSUMAMI BAR SNACK EATEN THROUGHOUT JAPAN. THIS UNUSUAL COMBINATION OF COLOURS, FLAVOURS AND TEXTURES MAKES A VERY REFRESHING DISH.

3 Tear the nori with your hands into small flakes about 1cm/½in square.

4 In a small pan, cook the broad beans in their shells in plenty of rapidly boiling salted water for about 4 minutes.

5 Once the beans are cooked, drain in a sieve and then immediately cool the beans under some cold running water. Once they are cooled, remove the skins.

6 Mix the wasabi paste with the shoyu in a small mixing bowl. Add the nori flakes, toasted if you wish, and skinned beans, and mix well.

7 Divide the beans among four individual small bowls, heap on the finely grated daikon, then spoon the ikura on top. Serve the beans cold. Ask your guests to mix everything well just before eating.

COOK'S TIP
Toasting the nori sheet gives it a crisp texture and enhances its flavour. Before tearing into small pieces, wave the edge of the nori over a medium gas flame very quickly a few times.

SERVES FOUR

INGREDIENTS
   200g/7oz daikon, peeled
   1 nori sheet
   1kg/2¼lb broad (fava) beans in their pods, shelled
   1.5ml/¼ tsp wasabi paste from tube or 2.5ml/½ tsp wasabi powder mixed with 1.5ml/¼ tsp water
   20ml/4 tsp shoyu
   60ml/4 tbsp ikura
   salt

1 Grate the daikon finely with a daikon grater, or use a food processor to chop it into fine shreds.

2 Place the grated daikon in a sieve (strainer) and let the juices drain.

Per portion Energy 79kcal/335kJ; Protein 7.4g; Carbohydrate 11.6g, of which sugars 2.5g; Fat 0.6g, of which saturates 0.2g; Cholesterol 0mg; Calcium 59mg; Fibre 6.2g; Sodium 369mg.

CABBAGE 'NOODLE' PANCAKE

THE ORIGIN OF THIS JAPANESE PANCAKE IS SAID TO GO BACK TO THE DAYS OF RATIONING AFTER WORLD WAR II, WHEN FLOUR MADE UP FOR THE LACK OF RICE, AND CABBAGE WAS USED FOR BULK.

MAKES EIGHT

INGREDIENTS
    400g/14oz/3½ cups plain
       (all-purpose) flour
    200ml/7fl oz/scant 1 cup water
    2 large (US extra large) eggs, beaten
    pinch of salt
    4 spring onions (scallions),
       roughly chopped
    400g/14oz white cabbage, very
       finely sliced
    vegetable oil, for frying
    Japanese o-konomi yaki sauce or
       Worcestershire sauce
    English (hot) mustard
    mayonnaise
    kezuri-bushi
    ao nori
    beni-shoga
For the toppings
    225g/8oz pork chops, boned
    225g/8oz raw prawns (shrimp),
       heads and shells removed
    115g/4oz queen scallops

1 To prepare the pork topping, put the pork chops in the freezer for 1–2 hours, then wait until they're half defrosted, then slice very thinly by pressing the meat on to the chopping board with your palm and cutting horizontally with a sharp knife. Set the slices aside.

2 To make the pancakes, put the flour into a large mixing bowl and mix well with the water. Add the beaten eggs and salt and blend together. Add the spring onions and one-third of the sliced cabbage, then mix well. Repeat until all of the cabbage is evenly mixed.

3 Put a heavy frying pan on high heat. When hot, oil the base with kitchen paper soaked in oil. Remove from the heat when the oil starts to smoke and wait for 10–15 seconds until the smoke dies down. Reduce the heat to medium and return the frying pan back to the heat.

4 With a ladle, pour some of the mixture into the centre of the pan. Make a circle of about 2.5cm/1in thick and 10cm/4in in diameter.

5 Sprinkle the surface of the pancake with one-eighth of the prawns and queen scallops. Lay some pork slices on top. Gently press the toppings down using a tablespoon.

6 When the edge of the pancake is cooked and the surface has started to dry, turn it over by sliding it to the far end of the pan, then sliding in two spatulas, turning it over towards you. Gently press the pancake to the base of the pan with a spatula, then stretch it out to 15cm/6in in diameter, and half the thickness.

7 After 2–3 minutes, turn over again. If the surface is still wet, turn over and cook for another few minutes. While the pancake is still in the frying pan, with the topping-side up, add the sauces and seasonings. First, spread on some o-konomi yaki sauce or Worcestershire sauce. Then add a little mustard and mayonnaise. Sprinkle with kezuri-bushi and ao nori.

8 Put the pancake on to a plate and keep warm while you make seven more pancakes in the same way. Serve hot with a sprinkle of beni-shoga on top.

COOK'S TIP
This recipe is ideal for cooking at the table on a hot-plate with guests. Eat the pancakes as you cook.

Per portion Energy 313kcal/1322kJ; Protein 31.4g; Carbohydrate 42g, of which sugars 3.3g; Fat 7.8g, of which saturates 1.5g; Cholesterol 127mg; Calcium 132mg; Fibre 2.7g; Sodium 122mg.

COURGETTE NAMUL

THE FRESH TASTE OF THE COURGETTE IN THIS KOREAN NAMUL DISH MINGLES WITH THE FLAVOURS OF SESAME OIL AND A HINT OF SEAFOOD. THE DRIED SHRIMP GIVES A PLEASING CRUNCHINESS, WHICH CONTRASTS NICELY WITH THE SOFTER TEXTURE OF THE COURGETTE.

<u>SERVES TWO</u>

INGREDIENTS

2 courgettes (zucchini), finely sliced
10ml/2 tsp sesame oil
30ml/2 tbsp vegetable oil
2 garlic cloves, crushed
40g/1½oz dried shrimp
finely chopped spring onion (scallion)
  and sesame seeds, to garnish
salt

1 Place the courgettes in a colander, lightly sprinkle them with salt and leave to stand for 20 minutes. Drain off any excess liquid and transfer to a bowl.

2 Add the sesame oil to the courgette slices and mix together to coat.

3 Coat a frying pan or wok with the vegetable oil and heat over a high heat. Add the seasoned courgettes and crushed garlic, and stir-fry briefly. Add the dried shrimp and stir-fry quickly until they become crispy, but the courgettes should retain their bright green colour.

4 Remove from the heat, and transfer to a shallow dish. Garnish with the spring onion, and sprinkle over the sesame seeds before serving.

COOK'S TIP
You will find dried shrimp at most specialist Asian stores.

VARIATION
Chopped fresh prawns (shrimp) can be substituted as an alternative to dried shrimp; they will provide a similar flavour, although won't have the same crunchy texture.

Per portion Energy 213kcal/883kJ; Protein 15g; Carbohydrate 3.9g, of which sugars 3.7g; Fat 15.3g, of which saturates 2g; Cholesterol 101mg; Calcium 294mg; Fibre 2g; Sodium 869mg.

SHIITAKE MUSHROOM NAMUL

IN THIS TEMPTING KOREAN NAMUL DISH THE DISTINCTIVE TASTE OF SESAME OIL EMPHASIZES THE RICH AND MEATY FLAVOUR OF THE SHIITAKE MUSHROOMS. THE LATTER ARE QUICKLY SAUTÉED TO SOFTEN THEM AND TO ACCENTUATE THEIR CHARACTERISTIC EARTHY TASTE.

SERVES TWO

INGREDIENTS

   12 dried shiitake mushrooms,
      soaked in warm water for about
      30 minutes until softened
   10ml/2 tsp sesame seeds
   2 garlic cloves, crushed
   30ml/2 tbsp vegetable oil
   ½ spring onion (scallion),
      finely chopped
   10ml/2 tsp sesame oil
   salt

1 When the soaked shiitake mushrooms have reconstituted and become soft, drain and slice them, discarding the stems, and then place them in a bowl. Add the sesame seeds, crushed garlic and a pinch of salt, and blend the ingredients together.

2 Coat a frying pan or wok with the vegetable oil and place over high heat. Add the seasoned mushroom slices and quickly stir-fry them, so that they soften slightly but do not lose their firmness.

3 Remove from the heat and stir in the spring onion and sesame oil. Transfer to a shallow dish and serve.

COOK'S TIP
It is important that the shiitake mushrooms are drained thoroughly to ensure that their dark colour does not overwhelm the dish. Having drained them, then squeeze the mushrooms gently to remove all the excess liquid, and finally pat them dry with kitchen paper.

Per portion Energy 167kcal/689kJ; Protein 2.2g; Carbohydrate 1.1g, of which sugars 0.2g; Fat 17.2g, of which saturates 2.2g; Cholesterol 0mg; Calcium 38mg; Fibre 1.2g; Sodium 4mg.

WHITE RADISH NAMUL

THIS SUBTLE DISH BLENDS THE SWEETNESS OF WHITE RADISH WITH A DELICIOUS NUTTY AFTERTASTE.
BLANCHING THE WHITE RADISH SOFTENS IT, LEAVING IT WITH A SILKY TEXTURE.

SERVES TWO

INGREDIENTS
 400g/14oz Chinese white
  radish, peeled
 50g/2oz leek, finely sliced
 20ml/4 tsp sesame oil, plus
  extra for drizzling
 5ml/1 tsp salt
 60ml/4 tbsp vegetable oil
 ½ red chilli, seeded and finely
  shredded, to garnish

1 Slice the radish into 5cm/2in
matchstick lengths. Blanch in a pan of
boiling water for 30 seconds.

2 Drain, and squeeze to remove any
excess water. Pat dry with kitchen paper.

3 Mix the leek with the sesame oil and
salt in a large bowl.

4 Sauté the radish in the vegetable oil
for 1 minute. Add the leeks and sauté
for a further 2 minutes. Garnish with the
chilli and a drizzle of sesame oil.

Per portion Energy 137kcal/565kJ; Protein 1.8g; Carbohydrate 4.5g, of which sugars 4.3g; Fat 12.5g, of which saturates 1.8g; Cholesterol 0mg; Calcium 45mg; Fibre 2.4g; Sodium 1005mg.

SPINACH NAMUL

USING THE STEMS AS WELL AS THE LEAVES OF THE SPINACH GIVES A SUBTLE CRUNCH TO THIS DISH.
THE HINT OF BITTERNESS IN THE SPINACH IS BALANCED BY THE SALTY SOY SAUCE.

SERVES TWO

INGREDIENTS
 500g/1¼lb spinach
 60ml/4 tbsp dark soy sauce
 2 small garlic cloves, crushed
 20ml/4 tsp sesame oil
 2.5ml/½ tsp rice wine
 20ml/4 tsp sesame seeds
 30ml/2 tbsp vegetable oil
 salt

1 Trim the ends of the spinach stalks.
Cut the leaves and stalks into
10cm/4in lengths. Blanch the spinach
in a pan of lightly salted water for
approximately 30 seconds. Drain the
spinach, and rinse well under cold
running water.

2 Mix the soy sauce, garlic, sesame
oil and rice wine together in a
large bowl. Add the spinach and
thoroughly coat the leaves and stems
with the seasoning mixture. In a dry
pan lightly toast the sesame seeds
until they are golden brown, then
set aside.

3 Heat the vegetable oil in a frying
pan or wok, and sauté the spinach
over a high heat for 20 seconds.
Transfer to a serving dish and
garnish with the toasted sesame
seeds before serving.

Per portion Energy 293kcal/1208kJ; Protein 10.1g; Carbohydrate 7.4g, of which sugars 6.1g; Fat 24.8g, of which saturates 3.2g; Cholesterol 0mg; Calcium 499mg; Fibre 6.2g; Sodium 2488mg.

CUCUMBER NAMUL

THIS SAUTÉED DISH RETAINS THE NATURAL SUCCULENCE OF THE CUCUMBER, WHILE ALSO INFUSING THE RECIPE WITH A PLEASANTLY REFRESHING HINT OF GARLIC AND CHILLI.

SERVES TWO

INGREDIENTS
200g/7oz cucumber
15ml/1 tbsp vegetable oil
5ml/1 tsp spring onion (scallion),
 finely chopped
1 garlic clove, crushed
5ml/1 tsp sesame oil
sesame seeds, and seeded and
 shredded red chilli, to garnish
salt

COOK'S TIP
You can adapt this dish and tone down the hot chilli garnish by substituting the red chilli for a milder green chilli.

1 Thinly slice the cucumber and place the slices in a colander. Sprinkle with salt, then leave to stand for about 10 minutes. Then drain off any excess liquid and transfer the cucumber to a clean bowl.

2 Coat a frying pan or wok with the vegetable oil, and heat it over a medium heat. Once hot, add the spring onion, garlic and cucumber, and quickly stir-fry together.

3 Remove from the heat, add the sesame oil and toss lightly to blend the ingredients. Place in a shallow serving dish and garnish with the sesame seeds and shredded chilli before serving.

Per portion Energy 74kcal/304kJ; Protein 0.8g; Carbohydrate 1.7g, of which sugars 1.6g; Fat 7.1g, of which saturates 0.9g; Cholesterol 0mg; Calcium 20mg; Fibre 0.7g; Sodium 4mg.

SOYA BEANSPROUT NAMUL

THE DELICATE SPICINESS OF THE RED CHILLI AND NUTTY FLAVOUR OF THE SESAME OIL CREATE A TANTALIZING DISH. CRISPY SOYA BEANSPROUTS CAN BE REPLACED WITH MUNG BEANSPROUTS.

SERVES TWO

INGREDIENTS
300g/11oz/generous 1 cup
 soya beansprouts
60ml/4 tbsp vegetable oil
⅔ red chilli, seeded
 and sliced
1 baby leek, finely sliced
10ml/2 tsp sesame oil
salt

VARIATION
Try this with different beansprouts.

1 Wash the soya beansprouts, and trim the tail ends. Cover them with a light sprinkling of salt, and leave them to stand for 10 minutes.

2 Bring a pan of water to the boil, and add the beansprouts. Cover and boil for 3 minutes, then drain.

3 Place a frying pan or wok over medium heat and add the vegetable oil.

4 Add the soya beansprouts, and sauté gently for 30 seconds. Add the chilli and leek, and stir-fry together so that the ingredients are thoroughly blended.

5 Transfer to a shallow dish and then drizzle with a little sesame oil before serving the namul.

Per portion Energy 282kcal/1167kJ; Protein 5.2g; Carbohydrate 7.5g, of which sugars 4.4g; Fat 26g, of which saturates 3.2g; Cholesterol 0mg; Calcium 42mg; Fibre 3.4g; Sodium 9mg.

PAN-FRIED CHILLI PARSNIP ~AND~ SHIITAKE

THIS DISH HAS ITS ROOTS IN THE TEMPLES OF KOREA, ALTHOUGH THIS CONTEMPORARY VERSION ADDS MORE SPICES AND SEASONING THAN THE ORIGINALS. THE NATURAL SWEETNESS OF THE PARSNIPS IS PERFECTLY BALANCED BY THE SPICINESS OF THE DRESSING.

3 Heat a frying pan and add a little vegetable oil. Sauté the finely sliced parsnips until they are softened and lightly browned.

4 Transfer the parsnips to a bowl and add enough of the chilli sauce mixture to coat the parsnips well.

5 Discard the stalks from the shiitake mushrooms and spoon the remaining chilli sauce mixture into the caps.

6 Return the sautéed parsnips to the pan, with the chilli sauce, and then add the shiitake mushrooms.

SERVES FOUR

INGREDIENTS
  150g/5oz parsnips, finely sliced
  a little vegetable oil
  115g/4oz fresh shiitake mushrooms
  salt
  15ml/1 tbsp pine nuts, ground,
    to garnish
  sesame oil, to season
For the sauce
  45ml/3 tbsp gochujang
    chilli paste
  5ml/1 tsp Korean chilli powder
  15ml/1 tbsp maple syrup
  5ml/1 tsp sugar
  5ml/1 tsp soy sauce
  5ml/1 tsp sesame oil

1 Place the parsnips in a bowl and add a little sesame oil and salt. Coat the slices evenly. Set aside for 10 minutes.

2 For the sauce, mix the chilli paste and powder, maple syrup, sugar, soy sauce and sesame oil with a little water.

7 Cook the parsnip and mushroom mixture over low heat, allowing the chilli mixture to fully infuse the vegetables and form a sticky glaze. Then add more of the gochujang chilli sauce if necessary.

8 When the vegetables are cooked and the liquid has reduced, transfer them to a serving dish. Season the mixture with sesame oil and sprinkle with ground pine nuts, then serve.

Per portion Energy 86kcal/362kJ; Protein 2.3g; Carbohydrate 10.4g, of which sugars 6.4g; Fat 4.4g, of which saturates 0.5g; Cholesterol 0mg; Calcium 26mg; Fibre 2.1g; Sodium 106mg.

SLOW-COOKED SHIITAKE WITH SHOYU

SHIITAKE COOKED SLOWLY ARE SO RICH AND FILLING, THAT SOME PEOPLE CALL THEM 'VEGETARIAN STEAK'. THIS JAPANESE DISH, KNOWN AS FUKUMÉ-NI, CAN LAST A FEW WEEKS IN THE REFRIGERATOR, AND IS A USEFUL AND FLAVOURFUL ADDITION TO OTHER DISHES.

SERVES FOUR

INGREDIENTS
20 dried shiitake mushrooms
45ml/3 tbsp vegetable oil
30ml/2 tbsp shoyu
25ml/1½ tbsp caster
   (superfine) sugar
15ml/1 tbsp toasted sesame oil

VARIATION
To make shiitake rice, cut the slow-cooked shiitake into thin strips. Mix with 600g/1lb 5oz/5¼ cups cooked rice and 15ml/1 tbsp finely chopped chives. Serve in individual rice bowls and sprinkle with toasted sesame seeds.

1 Start soaking the dried shiitake the day before. Put them in a large bowl almost full of water. Cover the shiitake with a plate or lid to stop them floating to the surface of the water. Leave to soak overnight.

2 Measure 120ml/4fl oz/½ cup liquid from the bowl. Drain the shiitake into a sieve. Remove and discard the stalks.

3 Heat the oil in a wok or a large pan. Stir-fry the shiitake over a high heat for 5 minutes, stirring continuously.

4 Reduce the heat to the lowest setting, then add the measured liquid, the shoyu and sugar. Cook until there is almost no moisture left, stirring frequently. Add the sesame oil and remove from the heat.

5 Leave to cool, then slice and arrange the shiitake on a large plate.

Per portion Energy 133kcal/553kJ; Protein 1.2g; Carbohydrate 7.4g, of which sugars 7.2g; Fat 11.2g, of which saturates 1.4g; Cholesterol 0mg; Calcium 8mg; Fibre 0.6g; Sodium 537mg.

BRAISED SHIITAKE MUSHROOM <u>AND</u> ONION

IN THIS DISH, THE EARTHY FLAVOURS OF THE MUSHROOMS ARE BALANCED BY THE NATURAL SWEETNESS OF THE ONION AND GARLIC. A KOREAN STAPLE AND AN IDEAL ACCOMPANIMENT FOR FISH AND SEAFOOD.

SERVES TWO TO THREE

INGREDIENTS
  10 fresh shiitake mushrooms
  ½ white onion, finely diced
  5 garlic cloves, crushed
  1 spring onion (scallion),
    shredded
  5ml/1 tsp sesame seeds
For the sauce
  60ml/4 tbsp dark soy sauce
  15ml/1 tbsp sesame oil
  10ml/2 tsp maple syrup

1 Discard the stalks from the shiitake mushrooms and cut each cap in half.

2 Boil 350ml/12fl oz/1½ cups water. Add the soy sauce, sesame oil, maple syrup, mushrooms, onion and garlic.

3 Reduce the heat under the pan and simmer until the mushrooms are tender and the cooking liquid has reduced to form a rich sauce.

4 Transfer to a dish and serve sprinkled with spring onion and sesame seeds.

COOK'S TIP
Substitute the shiitake mushrooms with field (portobello), cremini or button (white) mushrooms.

Per portion Energy 117kcal/489kJ; Protein 3.5g; Carbohydrate 14.9g, of which sugars 13g; Fat 5.3g, of which saturates 0.8g; Cholesterol 0mg; Calcium 40mg; Fibre 2.2g; Sodium 1103mg.

SHREDDED LEEK WITH SESAME

THIS SIMPLE VEGETABLE DISH IS A KOREAN CLASSIC AND SOMETIMES INDISPENSABLE ACCOMPANIMENT TO BARBECUED OR GRILLED MEAT DISHES, ESPECIALLY PORK-BASED ONES.

SERVES THREE TO FOUR

INGREDIENTS

    250g/9oz leeks or spring onions
      (scallions)
    15ml/1 tbsp Korean chilli powder
    10ml/2 tsp sesame oil
    1 garlic clove, crushed
    5ml/1 tsp cider vinegar
    5ml/1 tsp sugar
    10ml/2 tsp sesame seeds
    salt

1 Finely shred the leeks or spring onions diagonally with a sharp knife and place in a large bowl. Pour in cold water and add a quantity of ice, then leave the leeks to soak for about 5 minutes.

2 Meanwhile, to make a dressing, put the chilli powder, sesame oil, garlic and vinegar in a bowl and mix together well.

3 Add the sugar and stir until it dissolves into the mixture.

4 Add the sesame seeds and season to taste with a little salt.

5 Drain the leeks and place them in a serving bowl.

6 Pour the dressing over the leeks and toss well before serving.

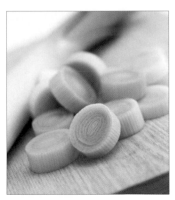

Per portion Energy 58kcal/242kJ; Protein 2g; Carbohydrate 4.5g, of which sugars 2.7g; Fat 3.8g, of which saturates 0.6g; Cholesterol 0mg; Calcium 39mg; Fibre 1.6g; Sodium 3mg.

NEW POTATOES COOKED <u>IN</u> DASHI STOCK

NIKKOROGASHI IS A SIMPLE YET SCRUMPTIOUS JAPANESE DISH. AS THE STOCK EVAPORATES, THE ONION BECOMES SOFT AND CARAMELIZED, MAKING A WONDERFUL SAUCE THAT COATS THE POTATOES.

SERVES FOUR

INGREDIENTS

15ml/1 tbsp toasted sesame oil
1 small onion, thinly sliced
1kg/2¼lb baby new potatoes, unpeeled
200ml/7fl oz/scant 1 cup second
  dashi stock, or the same amount
  of water with 5ml/1 tsp
  dashi-no-moto
45ml/3 tbsp shoyu

1 Heat the sesame oil in a wok or large pan. Add the thinly sliced onion and stir-fry for about 30 seconds. Add the new potatoes.

2 Stir constantly, using cooking hashi for ease, until all the potatoes are well coated in sesame oil.

COOK'S TIP
Japanese chefs use toasted sesame oil for its distinctive strong aroma. If the smell is too strong, use a mixture of half sesame and half vegetable oil.

3 Pour on the dashi stock and shoyu and reduce the heat to the lowest setting. Cover and cook for 15 minutes, turning the potatoes every 5 minutes so that they are evenly cooked.

4 Uncover the wok or pan for a further 5 minutes to reduce the liquid. If there is already very little liquid remaining, remove the wok or pan from the heat, cover and leave to stand for 5 minutes.

5 Transfer to a deep serving bowl. Pour the sauce over the top and serve.

Per portion Energy 210kcal/890kJ; Protein 4.8g; Carbohydrate 42.4g, of which sugars 4.9g; Fat 3.5g, of which saturates 0.7g; Cholesterol 0mg; Calcium 21mg; Fibre 2.7g; Sodium 829mg.

STEAMED AUBERGINE <u>WITH</u> SESAME SAUCE

THIS JAPANESE AUTUMN RECIPE, NASU RIKYU-NI, REPRESENTS A TYPICAL ZEN TEMPLE COOKING STYLE.
SEASONAL VEGETABLES ARE CHOSEN AND COOKED WITH CARE. THIS DISH IS DELICIOUS COLD.

<u>SERVES FOUR</u>

INGREDIENTS
  2 large aubergines (eggplants)
  400ml/14fl oz/1⅔ cups second dashi
    stock, or the same amount of water
    with 5ml/1 tsp dashi-no-moto
  25ml/1½ tbsp caster (superfine)
    sugar
  15ml/1 tbsp shoyu
  15ml/1 tbsp sesame seeds, finely
    ground in a suribachi or mortar
    and pestle
  15ml/1 tbsp sake
  15ml/1 tbsp cornflour (cornstarch)
  salt
For the accompanying vegetables
  130g/4½oz shimeji mushrooms
  115g/4oz/¾ cup fine green beans
  100ml/3fl oz/scant ½ cup second
    dashi stock, or the same amount of
    water with 5ml/1 tsp dashi-no-moto
  25ml/1½ tbsp caster
    (superfine) sugar
  15ml/1 tbsp sake
  1.5ml/¼ tsp salt
  dash of shoyu

1 Peel the aubergines and cut in
quarters lengthways. Prick all over with
a skewer, then plunge into salted water
for 30 minutes.

2 Drain the salted water. Place the
drained aubergines in a steamer, or in a
hot wok with a bamboo basket inside.
Then steam them for 20 minutes, or
until the aubergines are soft. If the
aubergine quarters are too big and
long to fit in the steamer, cut them
in half to fit.

3 Mix the dashi stock, sugar, shoyu and
1.5ml/¼ tsp salt together in a large pan.
Gently transfer the aubergines to this
pan, then cover and cook over a low
heat for a further 15 minutes. Take a
few tablespoonfuls of stock from the
pan and mix with the ground sesame
seeds. Add this mixture to the pan.

4 Thoroughly mix the sake with the
cornflour, add to the pan with the
aubergines and stock and shake the pan
gently, but quickly. When the sauce
becomes quite thick, remove the pan
from the heat.

5 While the aubergines are cooking,
prepare and cook the accompanying
vegetables. Wash the mushrooms and
cut off the hard base part. Separate the
large block into smaller chunks with
your fingers. Trim the green beans and
cut in half.

6 Mix the stock with the sugar, sake,
salt and shoyu in a shallow pan. Add
the green beans and mushrooms and
cook for 7 minutes until just tender.
Serve the aubergines and their sauce in
individual bowls with the accompanying
vegetables over the top.

Per portion Energy 79kcal/333kJ; Protein 2.9g; Carbohydrate 10.2g, of which sugars 9.6g; Fat 2.9g, of which saturates 0.5g; Cholesterol 0mg; Calcium 52mg; Fibre 3.3g; Sodium 272mg.

SWEET SNACKS
& DRINKS

It is not customary to have a dessert after a meal in Japan and Korea, so dishes such as Sweet Rice Balls and Three-colour Ribbon Cookies, tend to be eaten as an accompaniment to tea. Sweet drinks appear in many varieties, and green teas and grain teas are available everywhere, with common favourites being the soothing Green Tea Latte and refreshing Barley Tea.

Left: Persimmon Sorbet in Ginger Punch; **Above:** Sweet Rice with Red Dates

POACHED PEAR <u>WITH</u> PEPPERCORNS

FOR THIS KOREAN DISH, CALLED BAESUK, ASIAN PEARS ARE GENTLY POACHED UNTIL TENDER IN LIQUID SWIMMING WITH BLACK PEPPERCORNS AND SLICED GINGER. IT IS SWEET, BUT HAS A DELICATE SPICINESS WHICH MAKES FOR A CLEANSING AND REFRESHING END TO A MEAL.

<u>SERVES FOUR</u>

INGREDIENTS
  2 Asian pears
  20 black peppercorns
  10g/¼oz fresh root ginger, peeled
    and sliced
  25g/1oz/2 tbsp sugar
  pine nuts, to decorate

1 Peel and core the Asian pears with a sharp knife. Then cut each one into six pieces.

COOK'S TIP
When choosing Asian pears at your supermarket, pick those that look the most even in shape, firm and free of any soft spots.

2 Press two or three peppercorns into the smooth outer surface of each piece.

3 Place 750ml/1¼ pints/3 cups water in a large pan and add the ginger. Bring to the boil and cook for 10 minutes, or until the flavour of the ginger has suffused the water. Add the sugar and then the pears. Reduce the heat, and simmer for 5 minutes, or until the pears have softened.

4 Transfer the fruit and liquid to a bowl. Cool, remove the sliced ginger and place the bowl in the refrigerator to chill for a while.

5 Place three pieces of pear in a bowl for each person. Pour over the poaching liquid and decorate with pine nuts.

VARIATION
Asian pears are crisp and mild, whereas European pears tend have a more aromatic and buttery flavour. If you cannot find Asian pears, then Conference pears can be used in their place. They should be cored and used whole – one per person – rather than sliced.

Per portion Energy 60kcal/253kJ; Protein 0.3g; Carbohydrate 15.4g, of which sugars 15.4g; Fat 0.1g, of which saturates 0g; Cholesterol 0mg; Calcium 12mg; Fibre 1.7g; Sodium 3mg.

SWEET BEANS ᴼᴺ ICE FLAKES

FOR THIS REFRESHING, CHILLED DESSERT, UNIQUE TO KOREA, CRUNCHY ICE FLAKES ARE COATED WITH A PURÉE OF RED BEANS AND MAPLE SYRUP AND THEN TOPPED WITH FRESH FRUIT. THIS IS UNQUESTIONABLY THE MOST POPULAR CHOICE FOR A HOT SUMMER'S DAY IN KOREA.

SERVES TWO

INGREDIENTS
75g/3oz/½ cup red kidney beans,
    soaked overnight
115g/4oz/generous ½ cup sugar
5ml/1 tsp salt
30ml/2 tbsp maple syrup
ice cubes
30ml/2 tbsp condensed milk
90ml/6 tbsp milk
1 kiwi fruit, sliced
2 strawberries

1 Place the red kidney beans in a pan, cover with water and bring to the boil. Boil fast for 10 minutes, then simmer until the beans have softened. Drain and leave to cool, then roll them between the palms of your hands to remove the skins.

2 Put the peeled beans, sugar, salt and maple syrup into a food processor or blender and purée together to a fine paste. Put the puréed beans into a pan and simmer them until the paste has reduced to the consistency of a custard. Cool, then chill.

3 Use an ice crusher, food processor or blender to crush the ice into flakes (you will need 2 litres/3½ pints/8 cups of ice flakes) and transfer to a serving bowl.

4 Mix the condensed milk and milk in a jug (pitcher) and pour over the ice flakes in the bowl. Pour the bean paste over the top and decorate with the kiwi fruit and strawberries before serving.

VARIATION
A variety of fruits can be used depending on what is available or in season. Blueberries and raspberries both make delicious alternatives.

Per portion Energy 462kcal/1968kJ; Protein 11.4g; Carbohydrate 105.1g, of which sugars 88.4g; Fat 2.5g, of which saturates 1.2g; Cholesterol 6mg; Calcium 145mg; Fibre 7g; Sodium 1063mg.

SWEET ADUKI BEAN PASTE JELLY

IN THIS CLASSIC JAPANESE DESSERT A DARK RED KANTEN AND SWEET BEAN CUBE IS CAPTURED IN A CLEAR KANTEN JELLY, AND LOOKS LIKE A SMALL STONE TRAPPED IN A BLOCK OF MOUNTAIN ICE.

SERVES 12

INGREDIENTS

200g/7oz can aduki beans
40g/1½oz/3 tbsp caster
  (superfine) sugar
For the kanten jelly
2 × 5g/⅛oz sachets powdered kanten
100g/3¾oz/½ cup caster sugar
rind of ¼ orange in one piece

1 Drain the beans, then tip into a pan over a medium heat. When steam begins to rise, reduce the heat to low.

2 Add the sugar one-third at a time, stirring constantly until the sugar has dissolved and the moisture evaporated. Remove from the heat.

3 Pour 450ml/¾ pint/scant 2 cups water into a pan, and mix with one kanten sachet. Stir until dissolved, then add 40g/1½oz of the sugar and the orange rind. Bring to the boil and cook for about 2 minutes, stirring constantly until the sugar has all dissolved. Remove from the heat and discard the orange rind.

4 Transfer 250ml/8fl oz/1 cup of the hot liquid into a 15 × 10cm/6 × 4in container so that it fills only 1cm/½in. Leave at room temperature to set.

5 Add the bean paste to the kanten liquid in the pan, and mix well. Move the pan on to a wet dishtowel and keep stirring for 8 minutes.

6 Pour the bean and kanten liquid into an 18 × 7.5 × 2cm/7 × 3 × ¾in container and leave to set for 1 hour at room temperature, then 1 hour in the refrigerator. Turn upside down on to a chopping board covered with kitchen paper. Leave for 1 minute, then cut into 12 rectangular pieces.

7 Line 12 ramekins with clear film (plastic wrap). With a fork, cut the set kanten block into 12 squares. Put one square in each ramekin, then place a bean and kanten cube on top of each.

8 Pour 450ml/¾ pint/scant 2 cups water into a pan and mix with the remaining kanten sachet. Bring to the boil, add the remaining sugar, then stir constantly until dissolved. Boil for a further 2 minutes, and remove from the heat. Place the pan on a wet dishtowel to cool quickly and stir for 5 minutes, or until the liquid starts to thicken.

9 Ladle the liquid into the ramekins to cover the cubes. Twist the clear film at the top. Leave to set in the refrigerator for at least 1 hour. Carefully remove the ramekins and clear film and serve cold on serving plates.

Per portion Energy 65kcal/278kJ; Protein 1.5g; Carbohydrate 15.5g, of which sugars 12.4g; Fat 0.1g, of which saturates 0g; Cholesterol 0mg; Calcium 10mg; Fibre 0.6g; Sodium 2mg.

SWEET PANCAKE

In this sweet Japanese dish, the pancakes resemble a little gong, hence its name Dora Yaki; 'dora' meaning a gong. The pancakes can be folded to make a half gong.

MAKES SIX–EIGHT DORA YAKI PANCAKES

INGREDIENTS
  65g/2½oz/5 tbsp caster
    (superfine) sugar
  3 large (US extra large)
    eggs, beaten
  15ml/1 tbsp maple syrup or
    golden (light corn) syrup
  185g/6½oz/1⅔ cups plain (all-
    purpose) flour, sifted
  5ml/1 tsp bicarbonate of soda
    (baking soda)
  150ml/¼ pint/⅔ cup water
  vegetable oil, for frying
For the sweet bean paste
  250g/9oz canned aduki beans
  40g/1½oz/3 tbsp caster sugar
  pinch of salt

1 To make the sweet bean paste, put the canned aduki beans and their liquid into a pan, then heat over a medium heat. Add the sugar gradually and stir the pan vigorously.

2 Continue to cook over a low heat until the liquid has almost evaporated and the beans have become mushy. Add the salt and remove from the heat. Stir for 1 minute, then leave to cool.

3 Mix the sugar, eggs and syrup in a mixing bowl. Blend well until the sugar has dissolved, then add the flour to make a smooth batter. Cover and leave for 20 minutes.

4 Mix together the bicarbonate of soda and water in a cup and then mix into the batter.

5 Heat a little oil in a small frying pan until very hot. Remove from the heat and wipe with kitchen paper. Return to a medium heat and ladle some batter into the centre. Make a small pancake about 13cm/5in in diameter and 5mm/¼in thick.

6 Cook for about 2–3 minutes on each side until both sides are golden brown. Reduce the heat if the outside burns before the inside is cooked. Make a further 11–15 pancakes.

COOK'S TIP
You can make a half 'gong' by folding a pancake in the middle and filling the inside with a little of the bean paste.

7 Take one pancake and spread about 30ml/2 tbsp of the sweet bean paste in the middle leaving about 2.5cm/1in around the edge. Cover with another pancake. Place on a tray and repeat until all the pancakes are used. Serve the filled pancakes warm or cold.

Per portion Energy 222kcal/941kJ; Protein 7.2g; Carbohydrate 38.9g, of which sugars 15.8g; Fat 5.3g, of which saturates 1g; Cholesterol 71mg; Calcium 106mg; Fibre 1.8g; Sodium 117mg.

SWEET RICE BALLS

Fluffy rice balls are filled with a delicious sweet bean paste to create a light, succulent dessert. The sweets are coated with red dates, chestnuts and sesame seeds, which give them an unusual texture. The fruit and nuts contrast with the meltingly tender rice.

3 Sift the flour and salt into a bowl and add 300ml/½ pint/1¼ cups warm water. Mix well and knead for 10 minutes. Take a small piece of dough, make an indent with your finger and add a little bean paste. Wrap the dough over and form into a ball.

4 Bring a large pan of water to the boil and add the rice balls. Cook for 7 minutes, then drain and rinse well in cold water.

5 Separate the rice balls into three groups. Roll one third in the chopped dates, another third in the chestnuts and the last in the toasted sesame seeds. Arrange on a serving platter.

SERVES FOUR

INGREDIENTS
  375g/13oz/2 cups red kidney
    beans, soaked overnight
  200g/7oz/1 cup sugar
  30ml/2 tbsp black sesame seeds
  20 red dates, stoned (pitted) and
    finely chopped
  20 chestnuts, finely chopped
  400g/13oz/3½ cups sweet
    rice flour
  5ml/1 tsp salt

1 Place the beans in a pan, cover with water and bring to the boil. Boil fast for 20 minutes, then drain and leave to cool. Roll them between the palms of your hands to remove the skins. Purée the peeled beans and sugar to a fine paste. Simmer the purée in a pan until the paste resembles a custard consistency.

2 Toast the sesame seeds in a dry pan. Place the dates, chestnuts and sesame seeds in three separate shallow dishes.

Per portion Energy 973kcal/4111kJ; Protein 30.1g; Carbohydrate 199.9g, of which sugars 66g; Fat 7.9g, of which saturates 1.1g; Cholesterol 0mg; Calcium 224mg; Fibre 19.8g; Sodium 34mg.

SWEET RICE <u>WITH</u> RED DATES

*TRADITIONALLY USED FOR ANCESTRAL MEMORIAL SERVICES, BIRTHDAYS AND WEDDINGS, THIS KOREAN
SWEET CAKE IS NOW ENJOYED TO CELEBRATE ANY OCCASION. THE RED DATES HAVE A RICH FRUITY
FLAVOUR THAT PERMEATES THE RICE, CREATING A SWEET, APPETIZING DESSERT.*

SERVES FOUR

INGREDIENTS
  400g/14oz/2 cups glutinous rice
  115g/4oz/½ cup brown sugar
  8 cooked chestnuts,
    finely chopped
  8 dried red dates, seeded
    and chopped
  15ml/1 tbsp sesame oil
  30ml/2 tbsp raisins
  5ml/1 tsp ground cinnamon
  pine nuts
  salt

1 Soak the rice in plenty of cold water
for 20 minutes. Drain the rice and place
it in a heavy pan or a rice cooker.

2 Add the brown sugar and 200ml/
7fl oz/scant 1 cup water to the pan.
Stir all the ingredients well.

COOK'S TIPS
• If you are cooking on the type of
electric cooker that retains heat, when
the water boils, transfer it to another
ring on the lowest setting to prevent
the rice from cooking too quickly and
sticking to the bottom of the pan.
• Rice cookers are relatively
inexpensive to buy, and are particularly
useful for cooking Korean recipes which
always include rice. The cookers are
thermostatically controlled and very
useful for preventing burning. To use a
rice cooker for this recipe, follow the
manufacturer's instructions and cook
until the rice is fully cooked and the
liquid has been fully absorbed.

3 Add the chestnuts, dates, sesame oil
and raisins to the rice. Add a little of the
cinnamon and a pinch of salt. Add water
until it covers the rice by about 2cm/¾in.

4 Bring to the boil, reduce the heat to
the lowest setting and stir the rice once.
Cover the pan tightly and cook as gently
as possible for 20 minutes.

5 Remove the pan from the heat and
leave to stand, without uncovering the
pan, for 15 minutes.

6 Arrange a portion of rice on each
plate. Mould it neatly in a small ring
or ramekin dish, if liked. Decorate the
dish with the pine nuts and a dusting
of cinnamon.

Per portion Energy 582kcal/2450kJ; Protein 9.5g; Carbohydrate 125.3g, of which sugars 44.5g; Fat 4.9g, of which saturates 0.5g; Cholesterol 0mg; Calcium 50mg; Fibre 1.4g; Sodium 13mg.

THREE-COLOUR RIBBON COOKIES

THESE KOREAN RIBBON COOKIES, CALLED MAEJAKGWA, TASTE AS GOOD AS THEY LOOK. THE CRISP TWISTS OF WAFER-THIN DOUGH ARE TINTED IN PASTEL SHADES OF GREEN, YELLOW AND PINK, AND HAVE A HINT OF GINGER. THEY ARE PERFECT SERVED WITH A SWEET DRINK OR A CUP OF GREEN TEA.

SERVES FOUR

INGREDIENTS
    30ml/2 tbsp pine nuts, finely ground
    vegetable oil, for deep-frying
For the green cookies
    115g/4oz/1 cup plain
        (all-purpose) flour
    2.5ml/½ tsp salt
    10g/¼oz grated fresh root ginger
    30ml/2 tbsp seaweed, finely ground
For the yellow cookies
    115g/4oz/1 cup plain
        (all-purpose) flour
    2.5ml/½ tsp salt
    10g/¼oz grated fresh root ginger
    50g/2oz sweet pumpkin, finely
        minced (ground)
For the pink cookies
    115g/4oz/1 cup plain
        (all-purpose) flour
    2.5ml/½ tsp salt
    10g/¼oz grated fresh root ginger
    50g/2oz apricot flesh, finely
        minced (ground)
For the syrup
    250ml/8fl oz/1 cup water
    200g/7oz/1 cup sugar
    30ml/2 tbsp honey
    2.5ml/½ tsp cinnamon
    salt

1 To make the green cookies, sift the flour and salt into a large bowl and mix in the grated ginger, ground seaweed and a splash of water. Knead gently into a smooth, elastic dough.

2 Place on a lightly floured surface and roll out the dough to about 3mm/⅛in thick. Cut the dough into strips 2cm/¾in wide and 5cm/2in long.

3 To make the yellow cookies, sift the flour and salt into a large bowl and mix in the grated ginger, minced pumpkin and a splash of water. Continue as for the green cookies, kneading the dough, rolling out and cutting into strips 2cm/¾in wide and 5cm/2in long.

4 To make the pink cookies, sift the flour and salt into a large bowl and mix in the grated ginger, minced apricot and a splash of water. Continue as for the green cookies.

5 Score three cuts lengthways into each cookie, and bring one end of the strip back through the centre slit to form a loose knot.

6 To make the cinnamon syrup, put the water, sugar and honey in a pan, and add a pinch of salt. Bring to the boil without stirring, then add the cinnamon and continue to boil, stirring until the syrup becomes sticky. Pour into a bowl.

7 Pour a generous amount of vegetable oil into a heavy pan, and heat over a medium heat to 150°C/300°F, or when a small piece of bread browns in about 20 seconds. Add the cookies and deep-fry until golden brown.

8 Drain the cookies on kitchen paper, then dip into the cinnamon syrup. Arrange on a serving plate and dust the cookies with the ground pine nuts before serving.

COOK'S TIPS
• Although getting the cookies to form the right shape can seem difficult at first, it will become much easier with practice. Don't lose heart.
• As an alternative to ingredients that colour the dough, you can use edible food colourings to introduce other colours and make them more appealing for children.

Per portion Energy 669kcal/2827kJ; Protein 9.7g; Carbohydrate 126.5g, of which sugars 60.7g; Fat 17.3g, of which saturates 1.8g; Cholesterol 0mg; Calcium 154mg; Fibre 3.2g; Sodium 498mg.

SAKE AND GINGER COOKIES

YAKWA ARE AMONG THE BEST KNOWN AND MOST TRADITIONAL SWEETS IN KOREA. LIGHT AND CRISP,
THESE COOKIES HAVE A UNIQUE TASTE CREATED BY A COMBINATION OF MAPLE SYRUP AND SAKE,
COMPLEMENTED BY A DELICIOUS HINT OF GINGER. PERFECT SERVED WITH A CUP OF GREEN TEA.

SERVES TWO

INGREDIENTS
   350g/12oz/3 cups plain
     (all-purpose) flour
   45ml/3 tbsp sesame oil
   25g/1oz fresh root ginger, peeled
     and grated
   90ml/6 tbsp sake or rice wine
   90ml/6 tbsp golden (light corn)
     syrup or maple syrup
   2.5ml/½ tsp white pepper
   30ml/2 tbsp pine nuts
   vegetable oil, for deep-frying
For the syrup
   250ml/8fl oz/1 cup water
   200g/7oz/1 cup sugar
   30ml/2 tbsp honey
   5ml/1 tsp cinnamon
   salt

1 Sift the flour and add the sesame oil. Mix in the grated ginger, sake or rice wine, syrup, pepper and a splash of water. Knead into an elastic dough.

2 Roll the dough out on a floured surface to about 1cm/½in thick. Use a biscuit (cookie) cutter to cut the cookie shapes out of the dough.

3 Place the water, sugar and honey in a pan, and add a pinch of salt. Bring to the boil without stirring, then add the cinnamon and cook, stirring, until the syrup thickens and becomes sticky. Pour into a bowl and set aside.

4 Grind the pine nuts to a fine powder in a mortar and pestle.

5 Place a generous amount of vegetable oil in a pan, and heat over a medium heat until a small piece of bread browns in about 20 seconds. Add the cookies and deep-fry until golden brown.

6 Remove any excess oil by blotting the cookies on kitchen paper and then dip them into the syrup. Arrange on a serving plate and dust the cookies with ground pine nuts.

Per portion Energy 719kcal/3027kJ; Protein 6.7g; Carbohydrate 119.8g, of which sugars 76.9g; Fat 25.1g, of which saturates 3g; Cholesterol 0mg; Calcium 111mg; Fibre 1.9g; Sodium 67mg.

FLOWER PETAL RICE CAKES <u>IN</u> HONEY

THIS GORGEOUS KOREAN DISH, CALLED HWACHUN, USES EDIBLE FLOWER PETALS TO FLAVOUR RICE CAKES, WHICH ARE THEN DRIZZLED WITH HONEY. ITS SOPHISTICATED APPEARANCE IS MATCHED BY ITS REFINED, EXQUISITE TASTE. SERVE WITH A CUP OF GREEN TEA.

SERVES FOUR

INGREDIENTS
20 edible flower petals
225g/8oz/2 cups sweet
 rice flour
2.5ml/½ tsp salt
vegetable oil, for shallow-frying
honey, for drizzling

1 Rinse the flower petals, and gently pat them dry with kitchen paper.

2 Sift the flour and salt into a bowl and add 300ml/½ pint/1¼ cups of warm water. Mix well and knead for 10 minutes. Place on a lightly floured surface and roll out the dough to 1cm/½in thick. Use a floured 5cm/2in biscuit (cookie) cutter to cut the dough into rounds.

3 Heat the oil in a frying pan over a low flame. Add the rice cakes and fry for 2 minutes, or until lightly browned. Flip over and cook on the other side, and then remove from the pan. Place on kitchen paper to blot the excess oil, then arrange on a serving platter.

4 Sprinkle the petals over the rice cakes, and then drizzle with honey.

COOK'S TIPS
• A number of different flowers have edible petals, including roses, azaleas, apple blossom, carnations and chrysanthemums, and they can sometimes be found at supermarkets or grocery stores.
• If you have food or pollen allergies, check with your doctor before consuming flower petals to avoid any adverse reaction.
• Do not eat petals from flowers that have been sprayed with pesticides, so either grow your own, or check the growing conditions with the supplier.

Per portion Energy 255kcal/1065kJ; Protein 3.6g; Carbohydrate 45.1g, of which sugars 0g; Fat 6g, of which saturates 0.7g; Cholesterol 0mg; Calcium 14mg; Fibre 1.1g; Sodium 249mg.

PERSIMMON SORBET <u>in</u> GINGER PUNCH

THE SWEET, AUTUMNAL FLAVOUR OF RIPE PERSIMMON GIVES THIS KOREAN DESSERT A WONDERFULLY MELLOW TASTE. THE RICH, CREAMY SORBET SITS IN A BOWL OF PUNCH WHERE THE AROMATIC QUALITY OF THE FRUIT IS OFFSET BY THE INVIGORATING PEPPERY TASTE OF THE GINGER.

SERVES FOUR

INGREDIENTS
 300g/11oz persimmon purée
 75g/3oz dextrose or glucose
 10ml/2 tsp caster (superfine) sugar
 30ml/2 tbsp lemon juice
 Persimmon and walnut punch, to
  serve (see page 493)

COOK'S TIPS
• Dextrose is another name for glucose. This is available in powder form from health food shops or among speciality sweeteners and sugars.
• The sorbet can also be made in an ice cream maker, following the manufacturer's instructions.

1 Heat the persimmon purée in a pan over a low heat. Add the dextrose and use a whisk to stir it into the purée.

2 Add the sugar and bring to the boil. Once the mixture begins to bubble pour into a bowl, and leave to cool.

3 Stir in the lemon juice and chill the mixture thoroughly in the refrigerator, for about 10 hours.

4 Turn the freezer to the fast freeze setting, following the manufacturer's instructions. Transfer the mixture to a shallow freezer container.

5 Freeze the mixture, removing the container and stirring every 30 minutes or so to break up ice crystals as they form. The sorbet should be smooth and creamy.

6 To serve, place a scoop of sorbet in each bowl and pour over the ginger and persimmon punch.

Per portion Energy 109kcal/461kJ; Protein 0.3g; Carbohydrate 28.3g, of which sugars 28.3g; Fat 0.1g, of which saturates 0g; Cholesterol 0mg; Calcium 14mg; Fibre 1.1g; Sodium 4mg.

GREEN TEA ICE CREAM

IN JAPAN AND KOREA IT IS UNUSUAL TO EAT A DESSERT, BUT FRESH FRUIT AND PUNCH ARE POPULAR CHOICES TO CONCLUDE A MEAL. THIS EASTERN TAKE ON A TRADITIONAL WESTERN DESSERT CREATES A LOVELY MIX OF FLAVOURS, WITH THE ENERGIZING PROPERTIES OF GREEN TEA.

SERVES FOUR

INGREDIENTS
  2 egg yolks
  200ml/7fl oz/scant 1 cup
    whole milk
  30ml/2 tbsp caster (superfine) sugar
  30ml/2 tbsp green tea powder
    or *maca*
  120ml/4fl oz/½ cup hot water
  200ml/7fl oz/scant 1 cup double
    (heavy) cream

1 Turn the freezer to the fast freeze setting, or in step 6 if time allows for chilling the mixture before freezing.

2 Whisk the egg yolks in a large heatproof bowl. Add the milk and sugar and stir until the sugar has dissolved.

3 Place the bowl over a pan of barely simmering water over a low heat. Stir until this custard mixture thickens slightly, to coat the back of a mixing spoon thinly. Remove from the heat.

4 Add the green tea powder or maca to the hot water and stir until dissolved.

5 Cool the green tea mixture a bit before adding to the custard.

6 Stand the bowl containing the custard and green tea inside a larger one. Add ice and water to the outer bowl to cool the custard quickly. Stir during cooling.

7 Whip the double cream until thick and light, but not stiff, then fold it into the custard. Transfer it to a shallow freezer container. If possible. Chill the mixture for 6–12 hours before freezing, as this helps to prevent ice crystals from forming and makes the mixture smoother. Place in the freezer. For best results, stir the mixture every 30 minutes or so, until it is thick and smooth and creamy.

COOK'S TIP
If using an ice-cream making machine, follow the manufacturer's instructions. The double cream will not have to be whisked before it is added to the custard and frozen.

Per portion Energy 308kcal/1273kJ; Protein 2.3g; Carbohydrate 8.7g, of which sugars 8.7g; Fat 29.6g, of which saturates 17.5g; Cholesterol 169mg; Calcium 40mg; Fibre 0g; Sodium 16mg.

SWEET POTATO JELLY

WHILE DESSERTS ARE UNCOMMON IN KOREA, THIS DELICATELY SWEET JELLY IS SOMETIMES SERVED AFTER A MEAL. IT IS ALSO POPULAR AS A SNACK OR AS A LIGHT ACCOMPANIMENT TO AFTERNOON TEA. THE MAPLE SYRUP GIVES IT A RICH AND DISTINCTIVE UNDERTONE.

2 Drain and mash the potatoes until completely smooth, then mix in the maple syrup and sesame seeds. Bring 200ml/7fl oz/scant 1 cup water to simmering point over a medium heat. Add the gelatine and stir until dissolved.

3 Add the sweet potato to the pan and stir well. Simmer for 5 minutes, stirring frequently, and remove from the heat.

4 Grease a mould with a little oil. Pour in the potato mixture and cool. Then chill until the jelly has set.

5 Cover the mould with a board and invert. Lift the mould off the jelly. Slice and arrange on a shallow dish to serve.

SERVES TWO

INGREDIENTS

    2 small sweet potatoes
    60ml/4 tbsp maple syrup
    30ml/2 tbsp black sesame seeds
    15ml/1 tbsp powdered gelatine
    vegetable oil, for greasing mould

1 Peel the sweet potatoes and cut them into chunks, then place them in a pan. Add enough water to cover and then bring to the boil over a high heat. Reduce the heat slightly and simmer the potatoes for approximately 15 minutes, until they are tender.

Per portion Energy 310kcal/1309kJ; Protein 4.6g; Carbohydrate 55.8g, of which sugars 32.3g; Fat 9.2g, of which saturates 1.4g; Cholesterol 0mg; Calcium 142mg; Fibre 4.8g; Sodium 144mg.

CITRON AND POMEGRANATE PUNCH

DUE TO THE SCARCITY OF POMEGRANATES IN KOREA THIS PUNCH WAS HISTORICALLY ONLY ENJOYED BY THE ARISTOCRACY. WITH A BLEND OF SHARPNESS AND SWEETNESS, THIS PUNCH IS WONDERFULLY THIRST QUENCHING AND A GREAT WAY TO FINISH A MEAL IN THE SUMMERTIME.

SERVES THREE

INGREDIENTS
   200g/7oz sugar
   1 citron
   ½ Asian pear
   45ml/3 tbsp pomegranate seeds
   15ml/1 tbsp pine nuts

1 Place 1.2 litres/2 pints/5 cups water in a bowl and add the sugar. Stir until the sugar has dissolved completely, then chill well.

2 Pare off the outer surface of the rind from the citron in fine shreds with a zester. Alternatively, use a fairly coarse grater, and set aside, then halve the fruit and squeeze out the juice. Add a pinch of sugar to the citron juice and set it aside.

3 Scrape the remainder of the squeezed flesh from the rind along with soft pith. Cut the pieces of rind in half.

4 Use a sharp knife to cut the inner white layer from the yellow outer layer of rind. Finely slice the white rind.

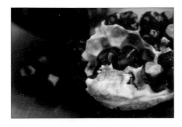

5 Finely slice the Asian pear and divide the slices among three glasses.

6 Add a little of the sliced white citron rind to each glass and divide the citron juice among them.

7 Top up with the sugar water and sprinkle with citron zest. Cover and chill for 20 minutes to allow the citron flavour to infuse the punch.

8 Add a tablespoon of pomegranate seeds to each glass and decorate with the pine nuts before serving.

COOK'S TIPS
• Citron fruit will be available in many Asian grocery stores. If it is not available, instead use the juice and zest of one large lemon, without using the rind.
• Use lime and orange slices, or pomegranate seeds and pineapple chunks, for a colourful garnish.
• To remove the seed sacs from a pomegranate, score the pomegranate and put in a bowl of water. Break the fruit open underwater so that the seeds sink to the bottom and the white membrane floats to the top. Then strain the membrane out and remove the seed sacs. You can refrigerate or freeze them for later use.

Per portion Energy 311kcal/1323kJ; Protein 1.2g; Carbohydrate 73.4g, of which sugars 73.4g; Fat 3.5g, of which saturates 0.2g; Cholesterol 0mg; Calcium 48mg; Fibre 1.2g; Sodium 5mg.

STEAMED CAKE <u>WITH</u> SWEET POTATOES

THIS JAPANESE STEAMED CAKE, KNOWN AS MUSHI-KASUTERA, IS NOT TOO SWEET, AND CAN BE EATEN LIKE BREAD. THE SECRET IS A LITTLE MISO, WHICH ADDS A SUBTLE SALTINESS TO THE CAKE.

SERVES FOUR

INGREDIENTS
200g/7oz/scant 2 cups plain
  (all-purpose) flour
140g/4¾oz/scant ¾ cup caster
  (superfine) sugar
45ml/3 tbsp sweetened
  condensed milk
4 eggs, beaten
40g/1½oz shiro miso
150g/5oz sweet potatoes
10ml/2 tsp cream of tartar
2.5ml/½ tsp bicarbonate of soda
  (baking soda)
30ml/2 tbsp melted butter

1 Sift the flour and the sugar together into a large mixing bowl. In a separate bowl, beat the condensed milk, eggs and shiro miso together to make a smooth cream. Add to the flour and mix together well. Cover the bowl with clear film (plastic wrap) and leave to rest for 1 hour.

2 Trim the hard end of the sweet potatoes and thinly peel, then cut into 2cm/¾in dice. Cover with water. Drain just before using. Preheat the steamer, and line with muslin (cheesecloth).

3 Mix the cream of tartar and bicarbonate of soda with 15ml/1 tbsp water. Add to the cake mixture with the melted butter and two-thirds of the diced sweet potato. Pour the cake mixture into the steamer, then push the rest of the sweet potato on to the surface of the cake.

4 Steam the cake for 30 minutes, or until risen to a dome shape. Remove from the heat and cool a little. Serve warm or cold, cut into wedges.

Per portion Energy 512Kcal/2165kJ; Protein 12.9g; Carbohydrate 90.5g, of which sugars 46.5g; Fat 13.6g, of which saturates 6.3g; Cholesterol 210mg; Calcium 162mg; Fibre 2.5g; Sodium 862mg.

STICKY RICE CAKE WRAPPED <u>IN</u> SWEET ADUKI BEAN PASTE

THIS TEA-TIME SNACK, OHAGI, IS AN ABSOLUTE FAVOURITE AMONG ALL AGES IN JAPAN. IT IS ALSO MADE ON OCCASIONS SUCH AS BIRTHDAYS AND FESTIVALS. DECORATE WITH CAMELLIA LEAVES.

MAKES TWELVE

INGREDIENTS
150g/5oz glutinous rice
50g/2oz Japanese short grain rice
410g/14¼oz can aduki beans
  (canned in water, with sugar
  and salt)
90g/3½oz/6½ tbsp caster
  (superfine) sugar
pinch of salt

1 Put the two kinds of rice into a sieve, wash well under running water, then drain. Leave for 1 hour to dry.

2 Tip the rice into a heavy cast-iron pan or flameproof casserole with a lid, and add 200ml/7fl oz/scant 1 cup water.

3 Cover and bring to the boil, then reduce the heat to low and simmer for 15 minutes, or until a slight crackling noise is heard from the pan. Remove from the heat and leave to stand for 5 minutes. Remove the lid, cover with a dishtowel and leave to cool.

4 Pour the contents of the aduki bean can into a pan and cook over a medium heat. Add the sugar a third at a time, mixing well after each addition. Reduce the heat to low and mash the beans using a potato masher. Add the salt and remove from the heat. The consistency should be of mashed potatoes. Heat it over a low heat to remove any excess liquid. Leave to cool.

5 Wet your hands. Shape the sticky rice into 12 golf-ball-size balls.

6 Dampen some muslin (cheesecloth) and place on the work surface. Scoop 30ml/2 tbsp of aduki bean paste and spread in the centre of the muslin about 5mm/¼in thick. Put a rice ball in the middle, then wrap the ball up in the paste using the muslin. Open the cloth and gently remove the ball. Repeat the process until all the rice balls are used up. Serve at room temperature.

Per portion Energy 128kcal/541kJ; Protein 4.3g; Carbohydrate 27.2g, of which sugars 8.2g; Fat 0.5g, of which saturates 0.1g; Cholesterol 0mg; Calcium 14mg; Fibre 1.2g; Sodium 3mg.

SWEET KABOCHA SQUASH CAKE<u>WITH</u> NASHI

YOKAN (CAKE) IS A VERY SWEET JAPANESE DESSERT OFTEN MADE WITH AZUKI BEANS. IN THIS VERSION, KABOCHA SQUASH IS USED INSTEAD OF AZUKI AND THE CAKE IS SERVED WITH FRUITS.

SERVES FOUR

INGREDIENTS

1 × 350g/12oz kabocha squash
30ml/2 tbsp plain
  (all-purpose) flour
15ml/1 tbsp cornflour (cornstarch)
10ml/2 tsp caster (superfine) sugar
1.5ml/¼ tsp salt
1.5ml/¼ tsp ground cinnamon
25ml/1½ tbsp water
2 egg yolks, beaten

To serve
  ½ nashi

1 Cut the kabocha into three or four wedges. Scoop out the seeds with a spoon. Cut into chunks.

2 Steam the kabocha in a covered steamer for about 15 minutes over a medium heat. Check if a chopstick can be pushed into the centre easily. Remove and leave, covered, for 5 minutes.

3 Remove the skin from the kabocha. Mash the flesh and push it through a sieve using a wooden spoon.

4 Transfer the flesh to a mixing bowl, add the rest of the cake ingredients, and mix well.

5 Roll out the sushi mat as you would if making a sushi roll. Wet some muslin or a dish towel slightly with water and lay it on the mat. Spread the kabocha mixture evenly and roll up the mat. Close both outer ends by rolling up or folding the muslin over.

6 Put the rolled kabocha in the makisu back into the steamer for 5 minutes. Remove from the heat and leave to set for 5 minutes. Peel and slice the nashi

7 When cooled, cut the cake into 2.5cm/ 1in thick slices and serve on four small plates with the sliced nashi.

Per portion Energy 91kcal/382kJ; Protein 2.8g; Carbohydrate 13.8g, of which sugars 4.2g; Fat 3.1g, of which saturates 0.9g; Cholesterol 101mg; Calcium 50mg; Fibre 1.1g; Sodium 7mg.

GREEN AND YELLOW LAYERED CAKES

THIS DESSERT IS MADE BY MOULDING CONTRASTING MIXTURES IN A SMALL POUCH. ITS JAPANESE NAME, CHAKIN-SHIBORI, MEANS A POUCH SHAPE AND SHIBORI MEANS A MOULDING ACTION.

MAKES SIX

INGREDIENTS
For the yolk mixture (kimi-an)
    6 small hard-boiled eggs
    50g/2oz/¼ cup sugar
For the pea mixture (endo-an)
    200g/7oz/1¾ cups frozen peas
    40g/1½oz/3 tbsp sugar

1 Make the yolk mixture. Shell the eggs, cut them in half and scoop the yolks into a sieve placed over a bowl. Press the yolks through the sieve. Add the sugar and mix well.

2 To make the pea mixture, cook the peas in lightly salted boiling water for about 3–4 minutes, until softened. Drain and place in a mortar, then crush with a pestle. Transfer the paste to a pan. Add the sugar and cook over a low heat until thick. Stir constantly so that the mixture does not burn.

COOK'S TIP
Use a food processor instead of a mortar and pestle, if you prefer. Process the mixture for a few seconds to make the coarse paste.

3 Spread out the pea paste in a shallow dish so that it can cool as quickly as possible. Then divide both mixtures into six portions.

4 Wet a piece of muslin (cheesecloth) or thin cotton and wring it out well. Place a portion of the pea mixture on the middle of the cloth and put a similar amount of the yolk mixture on top.

5 Wrap the pea and egg mixture up in the cloth and twist the top of the cloth to join the mixtures together and mark a spiral pattern on the top. Unwrap and place on a plate. Make five more cakes in the same way. Serve cold.

Per portion Energy 160kcal/673kJ; Protein 8.6g; Carbohydrate 19.5g, of which sugars 16.4g; Fat 6.1g, of which saturates 1.7g; Cholesterol 190mg; Calcium 44mg; Fibre 1.6g; Sodium 71mg.

ADUKI BEAN SOUP WITH MOCHI RICE CAKE

*THESE BEANS ARE COMMONLY USED IN TRADITIONAL JAPANESE DESSERTS. THIS SWEET SOUP FOR
WINTER IS EATEN BETWEEN MEALS AS A SNACK, BUT NEVER AFTER THE MEAL AS IT IS QUITE FILLING.*

SERVES FOUR

INGREDIENTS
    130g/4½oz/⅔ cup dried aduki beans
    pinch of baking powder
    130g/4½oz/scant ¾ cup caster
        (superfine) sugar
    1.5ml/¼ tsp salt
    4 mochi

1 Soak the aduki beans overnight in
1 litre/1¾ pints/4 cups water.

2 Pour the beans and the soaking water
into a heavy large pan, then bring to the
boil. Reduce the heat to medium-low
and add the baking powder. Cover the
pan and cook for about 30 minutes.
Add a further 1 litre/1¾ pints/4 cups
water and bring back to the boil.
Reduce the heat to low and cook for
a further 30 minutes.

3 To test that the beans are ready, pick
out and press one bean between the
fingers. It should crush without any
effort. If it is still hard, cook for another
15–20 minutes, then check again.

4 Divide the sugar into two equal heaps.
Add one heap to the pan containing the
beans and stir gently. Cook for about
3 minutes, then add the rest and wait
for another 3 minutes.

5 Add the salt and cook for another
3 minutes. The soup is now ready to
eat. Reduce the heat and keep warm.

6 Cut the mochi in half. Grill (broil)
under a moderate heat until light golden
brown and puffy. Turn several times.

7 Put two pieces of mochi into small
soup bowls and pour the soup around
them. Serve hot, and eat with a ceramic
or wooden spoon.

COOK'S TIP
This is an easy method to cook aduki for
people with little time. Soak the beans in
a pan overnight. Next morning, empty
the beans and liquid into a pan and
bring to the boil. Transfer the beans and
liquid to a vacuum flask. Seal and leave
until the evening, ready for adding the
sugar in step 4.

Per portion Energy 270kcal/1148kJ; Protein 12.4g; Carbohydrate 52g, of which sugars 35.1g; Fat 2.9g, of which saturates 0.5g; Cholesterol 0mg; Calcium 331mg; Fibre 2.7g; Sodium 10mg.

SWEET MUNG BEAN SOUP

THIS SWEET SOUP CAN BE MADE WITH A VARIETY OF DIFFERENT SORTS OF BEANS, RICE, TAPIOCA, BANANAS OR EVEN LOTUS SEEDS AND ROOT VEGETABLES SUCH AS TARO.

<u>SERVES FOUR TO SIX</u>

INGREDIENTS

225g/8oz/1 cup skinned split
  mung beans, soaked in water
  for 3 hours and drained
500ml/17fl oz/2¼ cups
  coconut milk
50g/2oz/¼ cup caster
  (superfine) sugar
toasted coconut shavings
  (optional), to serve

COOK'S TIP
Be sure to buy the bright yellow, peeled, split mung beans for this soup rather than the whole green ones. If you can't find split mung beans in your local food store, they are widely available in specialist Asian stores.

1 Put the mung beans in a pan and pour in 500ml/17fl oz/2¼ cups water. Bring the water to the boil, stirring constantly, then reduce the heat and simmer gently for 15–20 minutes until all the water has been absorbed and the mung beans are soft enough to purée. Press the beans through a sieve (strainer), or purée them in a blender.

2 In a large heavy pan, heat the coconut milk with the caster sugar, stirring until the sugar has dissolved. Gently stir in the puréed mung beans, making sure the soup is thoroughly mixed and heated through. Serve hot in individual warmed bowls sprinkled with toasted coconut shavings, if you like.

Per portion Energy 240kcal/1025kJ; Protein 15g; Carbohydrate 45g, of which sugars 20g; Fat 1g, of which saturates 0g; Cholesterol 0mg; Calcium 57mg; Fibre 0g; Sodium 100mg

SWEET RICE PUNCH

A THIRST-QUENCHING RICE AND MALT PUNCH, SHIKHAE *HAS A LOVELY SWEET TASTE WITH A HINT OF SPICE. IT IS THE MOST WIDELY ENJOYED OF KOREAN DRINKS, PARTICULARLY ON A HOT DAY WHEN NOTHING BEATS A BOWL OF THE FRAGRANT CHILLED LIQUID WITH ICE CUBES FLOATING ON TOP.*

SERVES FOUR

INGREDIENTS
450g/1lb/4 cups malt
30ml/2 tbsp caster
  (superfine) sugar
350g/12oz/3 cups cooked rice
10g/¼oz fresh root ginger,
  peeled and sliced
1 cinnamon stick
1 red date, thinly sliced, pine nuts,
  and ice cubes, to serve

COOK'S TIP
The sorbet can be made in an ice cream maker, following the manufacturer's instructions.

1 Roughly blend the malt in a food processor, then place in a large bowl. Add 1.5 litres/2½ pints/6¼ cups water and leave for 1 hour. Drain the liquid through muslin (cheesecloth) into a bowl, reserving the malt in the cloth. Repeat this process again, pouring the liquid repeatedly through the malt-lined cloth. After three or four times the liquid should thicken and become opaque. Discard the malt.

2 Add the sugar and increase the heat. Bring the mixture to the boil, removing the pan from the heat as soon as the mixture begins to bubble. Then pour the mixture into a bowl, and leave to cool.

3 Put the cooked rice into a large pan and add the malt liquid. Heat gently to 40°C/104°F or hand hot and keep at that temperature for about 5 hours. Once the rice grains begin to float on the surface, remove the rice from the liquid, cool it down and place in a bowl in the refrigerator to chill.

4 Turn the heat under the malt liquid to high. Once it is boiling, add the sliced ginger and the cinnamon stick, then simmer for a few minutes. Discard the ginger and cinnamon, and transfer the liquid to a jug (pitcher). Cool and chill in the refrigerator.

5 In a small bowl combine the chilled rice and malt liquid. Add a sprinkling of sliced red date, a handful of pine nuts and some ice cubes before serving.

Per portion Energy 186kcal/791kJ; Protein 3.5g; Carbohydrate 42.5g, of which sugars 8.4g; Fat 1.4g, of which saturates 0.3g; Cholesterol 0mg; Calcium 26mg; Fibre 1.8g; Sodium 2mg.

PERSIMMON AND WALNUT PUNCH

THIS NON-ALCOHOLIC PUNCH IS A POPULAR DESSERT IN KOREA. THE SWEETNESS OF THE DRIED PERSIMMONS IS MATCHED BY THE SHARPNESS OF THE CINNAMON, AND THE DISH HAS A REFRESHING FRUITY KICK THAT EFFECTIVELY BALANCES OUT A SPICY MAIN MEAL.

SERVES FOUR

INGREDIENTS
12 dried persimmons
12 walnuts
150g/5oz fresh root ginger, peeled
   and thinly sliced
1 cinnamon stick/½ tsp ground
   cinnamon
450g/1lb/2 cups light muscovado
   (brown) sugar
30ml/2 tbsp maple syrup or golden
   (light corn) syrup
30 pine nuts

1 Seed the dried persimmons and soak them in cold water until they have softened. Then make an incision into the centre of each, and stuff each one with a walnut. Set aside.

2 Pour 1 litre/1¾ pints/4 cups water into a pan and add the ginger and cinnamon stick or powder. Place over a low heat and simmer gently for 15 minutes, or until the water has taken on the flavour of the ginger and cinnamon.

3 When the liquid has reduced by about a fifth to a quarter, strain it through muslin (cheesecloth) into a large jug (pitcher).

4 Pour the liquid back into the pan, add the sugar and maple or golden syrup and then bring the contents to the boil again.

5 Remove the pan from the heat and pour the punch into a jug. Cool, then chill in the refrigerator.

6 Place three persimmons in a small serving bowl for each person, and then pour over the chilled liquid. Decorate each bowl with a sprinkling of pine nuts, and serve.

Per portion Energy 379kcal/1589kJ; Protein 4.9g; Carbohydrate 48.4g, of which sugars 48.3g; Fat 19.8g, of which saturates 1.6g; Cholesterol 0mg; Calcium 47mg; Fibre 1.6g; Sodium 31mg.

SWEET SOYA MILK

*THIS DELICIOUS SWEET DRINK IS OFTEN INFUSED WITH PANDANUS LEAVES OR FRESH GINGER,
AND SERVED HOT OR CHILLED. IT IS A NOURISHING DRINK, ENJOYED BY CHILDREN AND ADULTS.
IF YOU CAN'T FIND PANDANUS LEAVES, SUBSTITUTE THEM WITH A VANILLA POD.*

MAKES 1.2 LITRES/2 PINTS/5 CUPS

INGREDIENTS
  225g/8oz/1¼ cups soya beans,
    soaked overnight and drained
  1.5 litres/2½ pints/6¼ cups water
  2 pandanus leaves, slightly bruised
  15ml/2 tbsp sugar

VARIATION
To make ginger-flavoured soya milk, stir
in 25g/1oz grated ginger with the sugar.
Bring the liquid to the boil and simmer
for 10 minutes, then turn off the heat
and leave to infuse for 20 minutes more.

1 Put a third of the soya beans into a
blender with a third of the water. Blend
until thick and smooth. Pour the purée
into a bowl and repeat with the rest of
the beans. Strain the purée through a
fine sieve (strainer) to extract the milk.
Discard the solids. Line the sieve with a
piece of muslin (cheesecloth), then
strain the milk again.

2 Pour the milk into a pan and bring it
to the boil. Stir in the pandanus leaves
with the sugar, until it has dissolved.
Return the milk to the boil, reduce the
heat and simmer for 10 minutes.

3 Remove the pandanus leaves, then
ladle the hot milk into cups and serve,
You can also leave it to cool, then chill
in the refrigerator.

Per portion Energy 384kcal/1584kJ; Protein 35g; Carbohydrate 9.g, of which sugars 9g; Fat 19g, of which saturates 4g; Cholesterol 0mg; Calcium 156mg; Fibre 0g; Sodium 384mg

ICED ADUKI AND MUNG BEAN DRINK

THIRST-QUENCHING AND APPETIZING AT THE SAME TIME, THIS SWEET ICED DRINK IS A DELIGHTFUL TREAT. TWO KINDS OF SWEETENED BEANS ARE COLOURFULLY LAYERED WITH CRUSHED ICE, DRENCHED IN COCONUT MILK AND TOPPED WITH JELLIED AGAR AGAR.

SERVES FOUR

INGREDIENTS
   50g/2oz dried split mung beans,
      soaked for 4 hours and drained
   50g/2oz red aduki beans, soaked
      for 4 hours and drained
   25g/1oz/2 tbsp sugar
For the syrup
   300ml/½ pint/1¼ cups
      coconut milk
   50g/2oz/¼ cup sugar
   25g/1oz tapioca pearls
   crushed ice, to serve
   15g/½oz jellied agar agar, soaked
      in warm water for 30 minutes
      and shredded into long strands,
      to decorate

2 In a heavy pan, bring the coconut milk to the boil. Reduce the heat and stir in the sugar, until it dissolves. Add the tapioca pearls and simmer for about 10 minutes, until they become transparent. Leave to cool and chill in the refrigerator.

3 Divide the beans among four tall glasses, add a layer of crushed ice, then the aduki beans and more ice. Pour the coconut syrup over the top and decorate with strands of agar agar. Serve immediately with straws and long spoons.

1 Put the mung beans and aduki beans into two separate pans with 15g/l/½oz/ 1 tbsp sugar each. Pour in enough water to cover and, stirring all the time, bring it to the boil. Reduce the heat and leave both pans to simmer for about 15 minutes, stirring from time to time, until the beans are tender but not mushy – you may have to add more water. Drain the beans, leave to cool and chill separately in the refrigerator.

COOK'S TIP
Many variations of rainbow drinks are served throughout South-east Asia, some combining ingredients such as lotus seeds, taro, sweet potato, and tapioca pearls with exotic fruits. Served in tall, clear glasses in the markets, restaurants and bars they are popular in both Vietnam and Cambodia.

Per portion Energy 188kcal/800kJ; Protein 6g; Carbohydrate 42g, of which sugars 25g; Fat 0.5g, of which saturates 0.2g; Cholesterol 0mg; Calcium 55mg; Fibre 2.5g; Sodium 87mg

GREEN TEA LATTE

This Asian twist on an Italian classic is a delightful, sweet beverage. The green tea has a refreshing quality and imbues the hot milk with its distinctive flavour, a little like that of green tea ice cream. Use water instead of milk to enhance the green tea flavour.

SERVES FOUR

INGREDIENTS

1 litre/1¾ pints/4 cups milk
60ml/4 tbsp green tea powder
    or maacha
30ml/2 tbsp sugar
120ml/4fl oz/½ cup
    whipping cream
10ml/2 tsp caster (superfine) sugar

VARIATION
You can replace the caster suger with the same amount of honey.

1 Heat the milk in a pan over a low heat until it simmers gently. Add the green tea powder and sugar and stir well.

2 Remove from the heat and pour the tea into a bowl or jug (pitcher). Leave to cool before chilling.

3 When ready to serve the tea, whisk the cream until it begins to thicken. Then add the caster sugar and continue to whisk until the cream is light and fluffy.

4 Pour the chilled green tea into tall glasses and top with whipped cream. Dust each glass with a little green tea powder and serve.

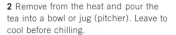

Per portion Energy 269kcal/1126kJ; Protein 9.2g; Carbohydrate 23g, of which sugars 23g; Fat 16.4g, of which saturates 10.3g; Cholesterol 46mg; Calcium 323mg; Fibre 0g; Sodium 116mg.

GRAIN TEAS

THESE SIMPLE TEAS ARE A HEALTHY CHOICE AND PERFECT FOR THOSE WHO PREFER TO AVOID CAFFEINE. UBIQUITOUS IN KOREAN HOUSEHOLDS, THEY USE BARLEY, CORN AND BROWN RICE, ALL NATIVE TO THE COUNTRY, AND THE ROASTED GRAINS CREATE A SUBTLE SMOKY TASTE.

VERSION 1: BARLEY TEA
   75ml/5 tbsp barley

VERSION 2: CORN TEA
   75ml/5 tbsp dried corn

VERSION 3: BROWN RICE TEA
   75ml/5 tbsp husked brown rice

BARLEY TEA

1 Heat a heavy pan over a medium heat and add the barley.

2 Toast the barley in the dry pan, shaking it all the time, until lightly browned. Take care not to burn the grains. Remove from the heat and transfer to a dish.

3 Bring 500ml/17fl oz/generous 2 cups water to the boil and add the barley.

4 Remove the pan from the heat and leave to infuse for about 5 minutes, until the water has taken on the colour of the barley.

5 Strain and serve the tea in cups or heatproof glasses.

CORN TEA

1 To make the corn tea, bring 500ml/17fl oz/generous 2 cups water to the boil in a pan and then add the dried corn to the pan.

2 Bring the pan back to the boil, reduce the heat and cover the pan. Simmer for 20 minutes.

3 Strain the tea through a fine sieve (strainer) in order to remove the grain. To serve the tea, pour the liquid into cups or heatproof glasses.

BROWN RICE TEA

1 Rinse the rice under running water in a sieve. Drain and then dry thoroughly on a dish towel.

2 Toast the rice as for the barley (see above), until it is golden brown. Bring 500ml/17fl oz/generous 2 cups water to the boil and add the toasted rice.

3 Reduce the heat, cover the pan and simmer for 30–40 minutes. Strain to remove the rice and serve the tea in cups or in heatproof glasses.

Per portion Energy 8kcal/32kJ; Protein 0.8g; Carbohydrate 1.2g, of which sugars 0g; Fat 0g, of which saturates 0g; Cholesterol 0mg; Calcium 12mg; Fibre 0g; Sodium 0mg.

GLOSSARY

A

abura-age fried thin rectangular blocks of tofu that are commonly used in Japan. The only tofu product that is available both frozen and fresh

aka miso a type of Japanese misu that is medium-strength flavoured and made with dark red soybean paste

ao nori green seaweed flakes

arame a type of seaweed that is brownish in colour

atsu-age thick, deep-fried tofu. These are usually bought in pieces: 1 atsu-age = 1 piece

awakuchi shoyu pale Japanese soy sauce

azuki beans small beans that are often used in sweet recipes, also known as aduki beans. They are available in red, green yellow and white, but the most common variety is red.

B

baechu Korean word for Chinese cabbage

banchan Korean side dishes

bap the Korean term for cooked rice

bapsang a Korean table setting

beni-shoga a type of Japanese pickle, a salt-pickled finely shredded root ginger

bibimbap popular Korean dish, which means mixed meal. The dish consists of rice and meat dish and can be eaten hot or cold.

boricha Japanese term for roasted barley tea, known in Korean as mugicha

buchimgae fried pancake dish typical of Korean cuisine made from meats, seafood or vegetables and mixed in a batter, then pan-fried

buchu Korean chives

bulgalbi type of Korean beef stew, which can also be made with pork

bulgogi Korean dish that consists of marinated grilled (broiled) or barbecued beef

bungeoppang Korean name for the Japanese fish-shaped sweet pastry taiyaki

Busan city in South Korea

C

cha-shu Japanese pot-roast pork that is usually cooked at a low temperature and seasoned with honey and soy

chapssal Korean term for glutinous short-grain rice

chechi Korean term for baby clams

Cheju island of South Korea

chige Korean casserole

cho gochujan chilli paste and vinegar sauce

Chobok one of the three hottest days in the Korean summer

Cholla province in South Korea

Chonchon river in North Korea

Chosun Korean dynasty 1392–1910

Chungchong province in South Korea

chungju Korean wine

chungol a type of tofu casserole that is common in Korean food

chup Korean side dish

Chuseok major Korean autumn harvest festival and three-day holiday

D

Daegu fourth largest city in South Korea

daepa Korean term for a large spring onion (scallion)

dahima Korean term for dried kelp

daikon a long, milk-flavoured white vegetable of the radish family, known as mu in Korea. Also known as Chinese radish or mooli

daikon-oroshi a fine-toothed grater used in Japanese cuisine that is especially intended for daikon

dangmyun sweet potato noodles, glass noodles

dashi-konbu dried kelp seaweed

dashi-no-moto freeze-dried stock granules for making a quick stock with water

dashi stock a stock for soups and hotpots using kezuri-bushi and konbu. It is possible to make your own dashi stock but stock granules (dashi-no-moto) are also available.

doenjang a traditional Korean soya bean paste, which is translated as 'thick paste'

Dol Korean 1st birthday

dol hareubang large stone grandfather statues found on Jeju Island off the southern tip of Korea

Donji winter solstice festival in Korea

E

eda-mame Japanese name for a dish of fresh young green beans that are boiled in water together with condiments such as salt and served whole

enokitake small delicately flavoured mushrooms with slender stalks, used in Asian cuisines, particularly those of China, Japan and Korea

G

galbi tang a type of beef stew that is common in Korea

gammodoki a Japanese dish of deep-fried tofu balls with vegetables

gari a Japanese condiment consisting of thinly sliced and pickled ginger

ginnan gingko nuts

gobo (burdock root) a long, stick-like root vegetable

gochugaru Korean chilli powder
gochujang chilli paste used in Korean cooking
gool pajeon oyster pancakes
gujeolpan elaborate dish for wedding feasts consisting of nine different foods on a wooden plate with nine divided sections in an octagon shape
gukwappang flower-shaped sweet Korean pastry
Gyeonggi the most populous province in South Korea
gyeranppang shell-shaped sweet Korean pastry

H

hae san mool jungol Korean mixed meat and fish dish
hakusai (Chinese cabbage) a vegetable with white stem and green leaves
Halla-san mountain on Cheju island in Korea
Hamgyong province in North Korea, which was one of the eight provinces of Korea during the Joseon Dynasty
Hamhung second largest city in North Korea
Hangul Korean phonetic script
harusame Japanese term for thin cellophane noodles made from aduki beans or starchy roots
hashi Japanese term for chopsticks, also known as otemoto
hatcho Japanese miso dark brown soybean paste
hijiki twiggy, black marine algae (seaweed) available dried. Recent studies have shown that hijiki contains potentially toxic quantities of inorganic arsenic, and some food safety agencies have advised against its consumption.
hotteok a variety of filled sweet pancakes, a popular street food in South Korea

Hwanghae province in North Korea, was one of the eight provinces of Korea during the Joseon Dynasty
Hwangop Korean 60th birthday

I

ikura large invidual spheres of salted orange-red salmon roe. Used raw in Japanese cuisine to make sushi

J

jakju Korean rice liquor
Jeongwol Daeboreum First Full Moon Day in Korea
jeotgal a salted fermented preserved seafood in Korean cuisine
jeotgarak Korean term for chopsticks
jujube red dates
Jungbok one of the three hottest summer days in Korea

K

kabocha a Japanese variety of winter squash with dark green skin, yellow flesh and a nutty flavour
kaki Japanese persimmon, also known as Sharon fruit
kalguksu a Korean dish consisting of hand-made, knife-cut flat noodles
Kangwon South Korean province
kanten (agar-agar) a gelling agent made from seaweed that is used as an ingredient to make Japanese desserts
kashiwa salted Japanese oak leaves
katsuo-bushi Japanese name for preparation of whole cooked and dried block of katsuo (skipjack tuna), ready for shaving
kenip wild sesame leaf
kezuri-bushi ready shaved, dried katsuo (skipjack tuna) flakes for use in the making of dashi fish stock

kiku nori Japanese term for dried crysanthemum petals in a sheet
kim Korean term for flat dark seaweed
kimbap Korean rice and meat snack roll
kimchi traditional Korean dish consisting of pickled and fermented vegetables
kimchi pajeon a Korean pancake with kimchi
kimjang seasoning used for preparing the Korean dish kimchi
kinako yellow soya bean flour commonly used in Japanese cuisine, similar to the flavour of peanut butter, which is commonly used in Japanese cooking
Koguro one of the Three Kingdoms of Korea, the other two being Paekje and Silla
Koh-cui Korean 70th birthday
konbu giant kelp seaweed, sold dried as dashi-konbu, which is widely-eaten in Japan
konnyaku a Japanese dense, gelatinous cake made from the konnyaku, a yam-like plant
Koryo Korean Buddhist dynasty
koya-dofu Japanese frozen tofu
Kyongsang one of the eight provinces of Korea during the Joseon Dynasty, located in the south-east of Korea

M

makgoli alcoholic rice drink native to Korea
maki sushi dish from Japan
makisu a rolling mat made of bamboo that is used for making sushi used in Japanese food preparation
Malbok one of the three hottest days during a Korean summer
mandu a type of filled savoury dumpling used in Korean cuisine

matcha a type of Japanese powdered green tea

memil Korean term for buckwheat noodles, similar to Japanese soba noodles

menma a Japanese condiment made from pickled or dried bamboo shoots. It is a common topping for noodle soup.

minari a type of Korean salad leaf

mirin a Japanese sweet rice wine used for cooking rather than drinking

miso a traditional Japanese seasoning consisting of a mixture of fermented soybeans and grains that mature into a paste of different strengths

mitsuba a Japanese aromatic herb used mostly for soups. Member of the parsley family

miyuk a type of seaweed used in Korean cooking

mizuna Japanese greens with a mild peppery flavour

mochi Japanese rice cakes made from mochigome rice and moulded into a variety of shapes

mochigome the Japanese term for glutinous rice

momil Korean wheat noodles

mooli a white radish used in Japanese cooking, also known as daikon

mugeun namul a medley of Korean vegetable dishes

mung bean small green beans, used in the cuisines of South-east Asia

myongtae Korean term for dried fish

myulchi Korean term for dried anchovies

myun Korean cooked noodles

myunsang Korean table setting

N

naga-imo (or yama-imo) a Japanese mountain potato similar to a yam

namul Korean vegetable side dishes, which can be made from all types of vegetables

nashi Japanese pear

natto Japanese fermented soya beans

nori Japanese name for dried, paper-thin edible seaweed products

O

ogokbap Korean mixed grain rice

P

Paekje One of the Three Kingdoms of Korea. The other two were Koguro and Silla.

pajeon a Korean pancake dish made of eggs and flour

pak choi (bok choy) a Chinese loose-leafed brassica with white stems

patjuk Korean red bean soup or porridge, eaten as a dessert. It is known as shiruko in Japan.

perilla wild sesame leaf

pyogo Korean term for shiitake mushrooms

Pyongan North Korean province

Pyongyang capital city of North Korea

R

Racktong river in South Korea

ramen a Japanese noodle dish served in a broth with meat or vegetable toppings

renkon a Japanese root from the lotus plant

S

saikyo Japanese miso pale yellow soybean paste, and lightly flavoured

sake a Japanese traditional rice wine used for drinking and cooking, sometimes known as o-sake

Sambok Korean summer festival

samgyetang type of Korean soup, made from chicken and gingseng

samgyupsal a Korean dish consisting of thick layers of pork belly

sang Korean table

sashimi Japanese delicacy of raw fish and shellfish that is sliced into thin pieces and arranged decoratively, and served with a dipping sauce

sansho ground Japanese pepper with a minty aroma

satoimo Japanese term for taro plant

second dashi stock stock made from reserved liquid from first dashi stock

sencha Japanese green tea

Seoul capital city of South Korea

seuck bak ji cod kimchi

shichimi togarashi a common Japanese seven-spice powder containing chilli, sesame, poppy, hemp, shiso, sansho and nori

shiitaki a variety of fungus, which originated in Japan, with a brown cap and white stem, available dried as well as fresh

shimeji a meaty-textured mushroom that is popular in Japan

shiratake translucent Japanese noodles made from konnyaku

shiro miso Japanese pale yellow soybean paste, lightly flavoured

shiso Japanese basil-flavoured leaves used as a herb garnish

shoga Japanese fresh ginger

shoyu Japanese soy sauce

shungiku Japanese term for the edible leaves from the vegetable chrysanthemum (not the garden plant)

Silla one of the Three Kingdoms of Korea, the other two being Paekje and Koguro

soba a type of thin Japanese noodles made from buckwheat flour

soba tsuyu Japanese instant soya soup base

soju Korean alcoholic beverage that can be made from rice, potato, wheat, barley or sweet potato

somen very fine Japanese noodles made from wheat flour. Usually served cold with a dipping sauce

somyun noodles eaten at the Korean wedding feast

songpyeon Korean cakes made from glutinous rice

sora mame Japanese broad (fava) beans

sujunggwa a Korean traditional fruit punch, usually made from persimmons spiced with cinnamon and ginger and served cold

sukgot Korean term for chrysanthemum leaves

sukiyaki raw wafer-thin meat, tofu and vegetables slowly cooked at the table

su-meshi vinegared rice, the essential basis for all sushi

surasang a style of cooker in Korean cuisine meaning that twelve dishes should be served as accompaniments to the rice and soup

suribachi and **surikogi** a Japanese mortar and pestle. The ceramic bowl **(suribachi)** is used with a wooden pestle **(surikogi)**.

sushi small rolls of su-meshi (vinegar rice) topped with ingredients such as fish

sutgarak Korean spoon

T

takanotsume a very hot, fresh red chilli pepper from Japan

takenoko edible fresh, young bamboo shoots, used in numerous Japanese dishes and broths and available fresh and canned

takju a Korean milky, sweet alcoholic rice liquor

takuan a popular Japanese pickle. It is usually made from a daikon radish. It is known as danmuji in Korea

tamari shoyu a Japanese naturally fermented dark soy sauce

taro a root vegetable. Known as satoimo in Japan, and toran in Korea.

tempura a popular Japanese dish of deep-fried battered vegetables, seafood or meats. The lumpy batter is made with ice-cold water.

tofu a nutritious, coagulated soya bean protein. There are many different varieties, including fresh tofu and processed tofu. It has very little flavour or smell and it can be used either in savoury or sweet dishes.

tong baechu kimchi is the most common kimchi. It is made with Chinese cabbage leaves.

tsukemono Japanese pickled vegetables, such as daikon, turnip, cucumber, which is served as a side dish with rice or drinks

tsuma a daikon cut very thinly into strands, for decorative purposes

tsumami dishes to accompany drinks

tteok steamed Korean rice cakes made with glutinous rice flour

tteokguk a traditional Korean soup with rice dish eaten during the New Year celebrations

tukbaege a Korean unglazed earthenware casserole dish used to serve soup, stews and other boiled dishes

U

udon thick wheat-flour noodles from Japan. They are usually served hot as a noodle soup in a mild flavoured broth.

Ullung-do a South Korean island famed for cuttlefish.

umeboshi salted pickled ume, a fruit similar to apricot. The fruits are very sour and salty in taste and are usually served as a side dish to rice.

usukuchi shoyu reduced salt Japanese soy sauce

usu zukuri a Japanese term meaning 'thinly sliced'. It is used in reference to very thin slices of white fish.

W

wakame a curly seaweed, available in a dried form

wasabi a Japanese pungent root, known as 'Japanese horseradish'. Wasabi is a member of the Brassicaceae family, which includes cabbages, mustard and horseradish. The root is used as a spice and is available as a paste or in powder form. It has an extremely strong flavour.

Y

yakitori a Japanese dish of skewered grilled (broiled) chicken. It is made of several small pieces of meat, skewered on to a bamboo skewer and cooked over charcoal

yangnyum Korean seasoning

yangnyum gochujang a Korean type of chilli paste that is stir-fried

Yi Syeong-Gye founder of the Chosun dynasty

yukgejang Korean soup with fern fronds

yuzu a popular citrus fruit used in Japanese cooking. It looks like a very small grapefruit and can be either yellow or green depending on how ripe it is.

SHOPPING INFORMATION

AUSTRALIA
Asian Food 4U
45 Plaza Parade
Maroochydore QLD 4558
Tel: (07) 5443 8109
www.buyasianfood.com.au
Online Asian supermarket

Asian Supermarket Pty Ltd
3/116 Charters Towers Rd
Hermit Park QLD 4812
Tel: (07) 4772 3997
Fax: (07) 4771 3919
Asian supermarket

David Jones
86–108 Castlereagh Street
Sydney NSW 2000
Tel: (02) 9266 5544
www.davidjones.com.au
Shopping centre

Ettason
2A Birmingham Avenue
Villawood NSW 2163
Tel: (02) 9728 2288
www.ettason.com
Exotic Asian grocer

Exotic Asian Groceries
16 Surfers Avenue
Mermaid Beach QLD 4218
Tel: (07) 5572 0750
www.exoticgroceries.com.au
Exotic Asian grocer

Hoya's Mixed Business
365 Anzac Parade
Kingsford NSW 2032
Tel: (02) 9313 8074
General grocer

Welcome Fresh Food
Shop 91, Sunnybank Plaza
Cnr Mains Rd &
McCullough Street
Sunnybank
Brisbane QLD 4109
Tel: (07) 3345 7688
www.welcomefreshfood.com.au
Asian supermarket

NEW ZEALAND
Tokyo Food
www.tokyofood.co.nz
*Large chain of Japanese
food stores*

CANADA
T & T Supermarkets
www.tnt-supermarket.com
Chain of Asian supermarkets
(refer to website for store
locations)

FRANCE
Ace Mart
63, rue Saint-Anne
75002 Paris
Tel: 01 42 97 56 80
Korean grocery store

Kioko
46, rue des Petits Champs
75002 Paris
Tel: 01 42 61 33 65
www.kioko.fr
Japanese supermarket

Kimchï Lyon
21, avenue Félix Faure
69003 Lyon
Tel: 04 78 62 75 30
www.kimchilyon.com
Korean supermarket

UK
Arigato
48–50 Brewer Street
London W1F 9TG
Tel: 020 7287 1722
Japanese supermarket

Atari-Ya Foods
595 High Road, Finchley
London N12 0DY
Tel: 020 8446 6669
www.atariya.co.uk
Japanese supermarket

Centre Point Food Store
20–21 St Giles High Street
London WC2H 8LN
Tel: 020 7836 9860
www.cpfs.co.uk
Korean supermarket

H-Mart
Unit 1, Leigh Close
New Malden
Surrey KT3 3NW
Tel: 020 3274 2020
www.hmart.co.uk
Korean groceries

Hoo Hing
Bond Road, off Western Road
Mitcham, Surrey CR4 3FL
Tel: 020 8687 2633
www.hoohing.com
Japanese supermarket chain

Japan Centre
19 Shaftesbury Avenue
London W1D 7ED
Tel: 020 3405 1246
www.japancentre.com
Japanese supermarket

Kingston Korean Festival
The Fairfield
Kingston Town Centre
Kingston-upon-Thames
www.kingston.gov.uk
Summer festival

Korea Foods
Unit 4
Wyvern Industrial Estate
Beverley Way, New Malden
Surrey KT3 4PH
Tel: 020 8949 2238
www.koreafoods.co.uk
Importer of Korean food

Nak Won
89 Kingston Road
New Malden KT3 3PA
Tel: 020 8949 6474
Korean cake shop

Seoul Mate
29 Museum Street
London WC1A 1LH
Tel: 020 7636 4787
www.bibimbabcafe.com
Korean supermarket

SeeWoo
The Point, 29 Saracen Street
Hamilton Hill
Glasgow G22 5HT
Tel: 0845 078 8818
www.seewoo.com

Tazaki Foods
www.tazakifoods.com
Specialist Korean ingredients

T.K. Trading Japanese foods
Unit 6-7 The Chase Centre
Chase Road, Park Royal
London NW10 6QD
Tel: 020 8453 1743
www.japan-foods.co.uk
Japanese supermarket

Wing Tai Supermarket
Unit 11a The Aylesham
Centre, Rye Lane
London SE15 5EW
Tel: 020 7635 0714
www.wingtai.co.uk
Asian supermarket

USA
99 Ranch Market
Tel: 1-800-600-8292
www.99ranch.com
Chain of Asian markets

Asian Food Market
1011 Route 22 West
North Plainfield, NJ 07060
Tel: (908) 668-8382
www.asianfoodmarkets.com
Specialist Asian food store

H-Mart
300 Chubb Avenue
Lyndhurst NJ 07071
www.hmart.com
Online Asian superstore

Japanese Style
Route 1, Box 301-B
New Prague, MN 56071
Tel: (877) 226 4387
www.japanesestyle.com
Specialist Japanese products

Daido Market
522 Mamaroneck Avenue
White Plains, NY 10605
Tel: (914) 683-6735
daidomarket.com
Japanese grocer

Franchia
12 Park Avenue
New York, NY 10016
Tel: (212) 213-1001
www.franchia.com
Korean teahouse and shop

Japan Super
www.japansuper.com
Online Japanese grocer

Katagiri
224 East 59th Street
New York, NY 10022
Tel: (212) 755-3566
katagiri.com
Japanese supermarket

Koamart
3692 Grayburn Road
Pasadena, CA 91107
www.koamart.com
Online Korean superstore

Marukai Market
12121 W Pico Blvd.
Los Angeles, CA 90064
Tel: (310) 806-4120
www.marukai-market.com
Japanese grocer

Minamoto Kitchoan
509 Madison Avenue
New York, NY 10022
Tel: (212) 489-3747
www.kitchoan.com
(Also in San Francisco)
Japanese bakery

Mitsuwa Marketplace
100 E. Algonquin Road
Arlington Heights, IL 60005
Tel: (847) 956-6699
www.mitsuwa.com
*Japanese foodstore chain,
also in CA and NJ*

Pacific Mercantile Co.
1925 Lawrence Street
Denver, CO 80202
Tel: (303) 295-0293
www.pacificeastwest.com
Fine Asian food and gifts

Posharp Inc.
219 Quincy Ave
Quincy, MA 02169
www.posharpstore.com
Korean grocer

Sunrise Asian Food Market
70 West 29th Avenue
Eugene, Oregon 97405
Tel: (541) 343-3295
see.org/sunrise
www.sunriseasianfood.com
Fresh Asian food and spices

Tanto
839 White Plains Road
Scarsdale, NY 10583
Tel: (914) 725-9100
www.nytanto.com
Japanese restaurant

SOUTH AFRICA
Korean Market
451 Premier Centre
Main Road, Observatory
Cape Town
Western Cape 7925
Tel: 021 448 3420
Korean grocer

Yat Sang Chinese
Supermarket
Penge St
Pretoria 0081
Tel: 012 991 3020
www.yatsang.co.za
*Supermarket with
Korean food*

INDEX

ACKNOWLEDGEMENTS

Authors' acknowledgements
Emi Kazuko: I am indebted to many of my Japanese friends, who readily responded to my many questions with their expert knowledge gained through cooking for their respective families for over 30 years. I am particularly grateful to my bosom friend Katsuko Hirose, without whose support, especially in research, I could not have written this book. I also thank Yasuko Fukuoka, who wrote the recipe section of this book so well; a wonderful result for her first professional work in English.

Yasuko Fukuoka: Love and thanks for help, encouragement and patience to: Nayo and Hiroji Fukuoka; Susan Fleming; Atsuko Console and her friends; Yoko Ono and my mentor, Kazuko-san, but most of all to Paul Ellis, who had to try all the recipes day after day for months, then had to feed me for many days while I was writing.

With grateful thanks to Ran Restaurant at 58–59 Great Marlborough Street, London for their help with photographing equipment.

Also to Veronica Birley of Tropix Photo Library for her trip to Korea with our project in mind.

The publishers would like to thank the following for permission to reproduce their images: t = top; b = bottom; r = right; l = left

AKG London: p28t; Alamy: p43t Eye Ubiquitous/Alamy, p50br LOOK Die Bildagentur der Fotografen GmbH/Alamy, p57b Horizon International Images Limited/Alamy, p191tl Peter Jordan/Alamy; The Art Archive: p20bl, p24, p29, p30; Bridgeman Art Library: Irises at Horikin, No.56 in the series '100 Views of Edo', (Meisho Edo hyakkei) pub. 1857, (colour woodblock print) by Ando or Utagawa Hiroshige (1797–1858) Fitzwilliam Museum, Uni. of Cambridge, UK, p20tr, Otsu, illustration from 'Fifty Three Stations of the Tokaido Road', pub. by Takenouchi Magohachi, c. 1831–4 (coloured woodblock) by Ando or Utagawa Hiroshige (1797–1858) Victoria & Albert Museum, London, UK p21, Satsuma oviform vase decorated with woman playing the samisen, 19th century (porcelain), Private Collection/Bonhams p25b, The Teahouse at Mariko, from the series '53 Stations on the Eastern Coast Road', 1833 (woodblock print) by Ando or Utagawa Hiroshige (1797–1858) Fitzwilliam Museum, Uni. of Cambridge, UK p28b, New Year's Festival, (woodcut) by Utagawa Hiroshige (1797–1864) Victoria & Albert Museum, London, UK p31, A Carp Swimming among Waterweeds, c.1832 (ink) by Katsushika II Taito (Hokusen) (fl.1820–50) Chester Beatty Library, Dublin p32b, Decorated Boats at the Sanno Festival at Tsushima, Owari Province from 'Famous Places of the Sixty Provinces', 1853 (colour woodblock print by Ando or Utagawa Hiroshige (1797–1858) Blackburn Museum and Art Gallery, Lancashire, UK p33; Cephas Picture Library: p22, p23t & b, p27t & b, p35t, p36b, p37t & b, p38t; Corbis: p14–15, p42t KCNA/epa/ Corbis, p42b Alain Nogues/Corbis, p43b Alain Nogues/Corbis, p44t Catherine Karnow/Corbis, p44b Neil Beer/Corbis, p45t STF/epa/Corbis, p45b Catherine Karnow/Corbis, p46t Christophe Boisvieux/ Corbis, p46b Kim Kyung-Hoon/Reuters/Corbis, p47b Michel Setboun/Corbis, p48t Kim Kyung-Hoon/Reuters/ Corbis, p48b Nathan Benn/Corbis, p49t Atlantide Phototravel/Corbis, 49b Cha Young-Jin/epa/Corbis; 50t Earl and Nazima Kowall/Corbis; p50bl Michel Setboun/Corbis, p51 KCNA/epa/ Corbis, p52t Michael Freeman/Corbis, p52br Bob Krist/Corbis, p54t Gerald Bourke/Reuters/ Corbis, p56 Michael Setboun/Corbis, p59t Studio Eye/Corbis, p60 Nathan Benn/Corbis, p62t Michel Setboun/Corbis, p64 Michael Freeman/Corbis; iStockphoto: p2, 4bl & tr, 5br, p6t, p8, p9tr & b, p10–13, p46t, p166bl; Japanese Information and Cultural Centre, Embassy of Japan, London: p34tr, p35b, p36t, p38b; Mary Evans Picture Library: p25t, p26t & b, p32t; Tropix Photo Library: p53 , p56b, p57t,p58tl, 58tr,; p61t, p61b, p62b, p63b, p190bl;Dr. Steven Turnbull: p34bl.

All other photographs © Anness Publishing.